CASS   LIBRARY   OF   AFRICAN   STUDIES

MISSIONARY RESEARCHES AND TRAVELS
No. 19

General Editor: ROBERT I. ROTBERG

*Associate Professor, Department of Political Science,
Massachusetts Institute of Technology*

ON THE

THRESHOLD OF CENTRAL AFRICA

MISSIONARY RESEARCHES AND TRAVELS

No. 10.   Frederick Stanley Arnot
Garenganze; Or, Seven Years' Pioneer Mission Work in Central Africa (1889)
With a new introduction by Professor Robert I. Rotberg.
New Edition.

No. 11.   Hope Masterton Waddell
Twenty-Nine Years in the West Indies and Central Africa. A Review of Missionary Work and Adventure 1829-1858 (1863)
With a new introduction by G. I. Jones.
Second Edition.

No. 12.   W. A. Elmslie
Among the Wild Ngoni (1899; 1901)
With a new introductory note by Ian Nance.
Third Edition.

No. 13.   Robert Pickering Ashe
Two Kings of Uganda. Or, Life by the Shores of Victoria Nyanza. Being an Account of a Residence of Six Years in Eastern Equatorial Africa (1889)
With a new introduction by Professor John Rowe.
Second Edition.

No. 14.   A. M. Mackay
A. M. Mackay, Pioneer Missionary of the Church Missionary Society to Uganda (1890). By his sister (J. W. H.).
With a new introductory note by Professor D. A. Low.
New Edition.

No. 15.   Samuel Crowther
Journal of an Expedition up the Niger and Tshadda Rivers undertaken by Macgregor Laird, Esq., in connection with the British Government in 1854 (1855)
With a new introduction by Professor J. F. A. Ajayi.
Second Edition.

No. 16.   Charles New
Life, Wanderings, and Labours in Eastern Africa. With an Account of the First Successful Ascent of the Equatorial Snow Mountain, Kilima Njaro. And Remarks upon East African Slavery (1873; 1874)
With a new introduction by Alison Smith.
Third Edition.

No. 17.   Ruth Fisher
Twilight Tales of the Black Baganda. The Traditional History of Bunyoro-Kitara, a Former Uganda Kingdom (1911)
With a new introduction by Professor Merrick Posnansky.
Second Edition.

No. 18.   James Frederick Schön and Samuel Crowther
Journals of the Rev. James Frederick Schön and Mr. Samuel Crowther, who, with her Majesty's Government, accompanied the Expedition of the Niger in 1841, on behalf of the Church Missionary Society (1842)
With a new introduction by Professor J. F. A. Ajayi.
Second Edition.

ON THE THRESHOLD OF CENTRAL AFRICA

A Record of Twenty Years' Pioneering Among
The Barotsi of the Upper Zambesi

BY

FRANÇOIS COILLARD

THIRD EDITION

WITH A NEW INTRODUCTION BY

MAX GLUCKMAN
Professor of Social Anthropology,
University of Manchester

FRANK CASS & CO. LTD.

1971

Published by
FRANK CASS AND COMPANY LIMITED
67 Great Russell Street, London WC1B 3BT

New introduction Copyright © 1971 Max Gluckman

First edition	1897
Second edition	1902
Third edition	1971

ISBN 0 7146 1865 9

Printed in Great Britain by Clarke, Doble & Brendon Ltd.
Plymouth and London

INTRODUCTION TO
THE THIRD EDITION

I

Recently, when on a State visit to Paris, Dr. Kenneth Kaunda, the President of Zambia, insisted on altering the arrangements made by the French Government, so that he could visit the headquarters of the Paris Evangelical Mission Society. When a French official pointed out the difficulties that would be created, President Kaunda said there need be none, he would go himself alone on foot. But the French insisted that he had to go with an escort of motorcycle police, and with television cameras. Thus the President of Zambia proclaimed his appreciation of the work of the French-speaking missionaries, from France itself and Switzerland and the Italian Piedmont, of Sotho (Basuto) evangelists, and of their British artisans and supporters, all of whom had done so much to bring education and technical skills, besides the Gospel, to Barotseland (since 1969 the Western Province of Zambia).[1]

This book contains an account of a most important contribution to the history of social developments in Zambia, as well as an account of a most important African people and their first contacts with a settled Christian mission. The leader of that mission to the Lozi (Barotse) was the Rev. François Coillard. On two expeditions, the first from 1877 to 1878, he was accompanied by his wife and niece, by a young French missionary, by a number of Sotho evangelists and their families, and by Sotho wagon-drivers and other attendants. On the second expedition (1880), there were also an English and a Scots artisan. Coillard led his first party from Basutoland through the Orange Free State and the Transvaal into the territory of the Ndebele (Ma-Tebele) under Lobengula (now Southern Rhodesia), from where they had to retreat to Khama's Ngwato (Bamangwato) in what is now Botswana, from whence they reached Barotse country on the Zambezi. After some time there, they returned to Basutoland and Coillard went to Europe. His second expedition succeeded in establishing mission stations in Barotseland and Coillard remained in Barotseland until 1896, when he took two years' leave in Europe, before returning to Barotseland where he died in 1904.

This book by Coillard, published in 1898 in French under the title *Sur le Haut Zambèzi*, is his personal record of journeys made and of the work of setting up the mission. It consists of gleanings from the pages of the *Journal des Missions Evangéliques*, of letters and notes in his journals, "jotted down in the interval of arduous toil, often by the light of campfires, cramped in a canoe, or jolted in a cart. . . ." As Coillard himself notes, they are "not a systematic history, either of my own missionary career of forty years, or of the Barotsi Mission". Written in the conditions thus delineated by Coillard, the notes have an immediacy and an urgency that would have been lost had he attempted—perhaps he had not the time to attempt—to write such a "systematic history". We are left therefore with an account of how the leader of a small party, moving intrepidly but with great difficulty through events which shook south-central Africa, saw what was happening. We receive no clear picture of the course of those events. This makes it difficult for a reader who does not know the history of south-central Africa to follow what was happening; I therefore begin by giving a summary of that history.

II

From at least the fifteenth century, and almost certainly for a long period before that, "Natal"[2] was occupied by a large number of small independent tribes, each under its own chief. According to tradition, they squabbled with each other periodically, but no tribe attempted to rule its neighbours. From some time between 1775 and 1810, such a process of conquest began on a small scale and a few chiefs, in what are now northern Zululand, Natal and Swaziland, began to subjugate their neighbours.[3] We can never be certain why this process began: I have argued that it occurred because the land became insufficient to support the human and cattle population under extant technological conditions, and Kuper saw the same causes in Swazi history.[4] Be that as it may, the process of subjugation continued until the Swazi nation was established north of "Natal", while in "Natal" itself the Zulu under Shaka in 1819 defeated and drove out their main rivals, the Ndwandwe under Zwide, and established an empire. Groups of defeated Ndwandwe fled northwards, to establish the Shangaan kingdom in "Moçambique", and the several Ngoni kingdoms in

"Zambia" and "Malawi".[5] Coillard (below, 36ff.) mentions one of the Shangaan under Mozila (Mzila), where Lobengula advised him to go since they had no missionaries.

The disturbances caused by these wars were thus spread far beyond the region of Zulu fighting, indeed as far as Lake Victoria in the north and Botswana in the west. Besides the Ndwandwe groups which escaped by fighting their way from "Natal", the wars started other tribes, driven by Shaka's threats or by tribes he had attacked, on a series of warlike migrations across southern Africa. In 1824 Mzilikazi (Moselikatse), a chief under Shaka over the Kumalo tribe and one of Shaka's generals, broke out of the Zulu kingdom and fought his way, absorbing people, into the "Transvaal", whence he was driven by the Boers in 1836. (These Boers were part of the Great Trek from the Cape Colony after the emancipation of slaves by the British in 1834.) He thereupon fled first west, then north into "Southern Rhodesia" where he conquered a kingdom over the Shona peoples, and raided beyond the Zambezi,[6] while threatening to invade Barotseland—rumours of these invasions are reported in Coillard's book, while he reports a savage Ndebele raid on the Toka, to the east of Barotseland. By that time, Mzilikazi had died, and been succeeded by his son Lobengula, with whom Coillard—almost a prisoner—tried to negotiate permission to evangelize among the Banyai, a Shona people tributary to the Ndebele.

While this turmoil had spread from "Natal" across southern Africa, in the Dragkensberg Mountains to the south-west of the Zulu kingdom, a minor Sotho chief, Moshesh, began to build the Sotho nation by a policy of accepting under his protection the Sotho peoples who had been broken by marauding bands moving across the mountains on to the inland plateau.[7] He was most successful in this policy, and the Sotho nation survived to form the independent state of Lesotho.

In 1835 the Paris Evangelical Mission was founded among the Sotho, and, as a young man, having felt the call to missionary work, Coillard joined it. He worked there for twenty years. And he started, unwittingly at the time, the mission in Barotseland by seeking a field where Sotho Christians could evangelize among their fellow-Africans: originally he planned to work among the Banyai, until Lobengula refused him permission. But while at Lobengula's capital, Gbulawayo, Coillard decided to shift his interest to Barotseland.

This shift in interest is related to yet one other of the tribal armies which marched on a career of conquest across south-central Africa. In 1824—the same year as Mzilikazi of the Ndebele left Zululand—a Sotho chief, Sebetoane (Sebetwane or Sebituane), left the "Basutoland" region, and fought his way west to "Bechuanaland" (Botswana), and then north: ultimately, in 1838, he succeeded in conquering Barotseland, where he, and later his son, ruled until 1866 when the Lozi drove out their conquerors, known as the Kololo. But though they were thus defeated in the end, the Kololo left their language as the *lingua franca* of the Barotse nation, and the main language of the dominant Lozi.

At Lobengula's capital in 1878, on his first expedition, Coillard (below, 40ff.) met some Lozi who had taken refuge there from their homeland, and found that they spoke Sesuto (Sesotho), "as we do. I knew already from Livingstone that the Makololo had introduced it on the Zambesi, but I did not realise the fact that it is still spoken there. 'Why do you not come to us,' they said, 'and save the nation?' But the Zambesi—that is a long way to go! As far as we can judge at present, there are only two alternatives for us—either to return to Basuto-land, or to seek other parts. Return to Basutoland! The very thought seems to us treachery and a temptation of the Enemy . . ." The journey to Lobengula's Gbulawayo had been arduous, with even a risk of being killed by the Banyai (according to Coillard's view), and the golden opportunity of beginning to work in a country where he and the Sotho evangelists could speak the language indeed seemed to him "heaven-sent", the answer to the obstructions which the Enemy, Satan, had placed in their way. As the reader will see, Coillard sought constantly for Divine guidance, and for signs that he was carrying out God's work in the right way. Given this new hope, he seemingly seized on it, if at first with doubts about the distance of Barotseland from Basutoland. His decision was confirmed when he necessarily moved from Lobengula's capital, but circumvented the turbulent Banyai by going south-west to the country of Khama, the Christian chief of the Ngwato, a Tswana tribe. Khama, and the Rev. James Hepburn, the missionary there, urged them to go to Barotseland.

Barotseland was well known in Europe from the writings of David Livingstone. He had reached it from Bechuanaland when it was ruled by the Kololo under Sebitoane, with whom he became good friends. Indeed, it was in effect Sebitoane who largely financed Livingstone's march from Makolololand first westwards to Luanda, on the Atlantic, and then after his return to Linyanti, eastwards to the mouth of the Zambezi River on the Indian

Ocean—the marches which made Livingstone famous.[8] The Kololo (like the Lozi later) lived under constant threat of attack by the Ndebele and Sebitoane was most anxious to help Livingstone open up trade with the coasts. Above all he was anxious to tempt Livingstone to settle with him as missionary. He was eager to retreat from the malarial Zambezi valley to the healthier plateau of Toka country to the east, from whence the Ndebele had driven him; and, as Livingstone's father-in-law, the Rev. Robert Moffat, was established at the Ndebele capital, he hoped that the relationship between the two missionaries would induce the Ndebele to conclude what we would call a pact of non-aggression.[9] Livingstone was too restless an explorer to settle thus; and when Livingstone persuaded his Society to send other missionaries in his place, they were not acceptable to the Kololo. Several of the party, under Rev. W. H. Helm, died, and the mission collapsed. Coillard had in 1868 met one of the party, the Rev. Roger Price, and in 1898 at a meeting in Wimbledon, London, he said publicly: ". . . A great deal has been spoken about my name here, and I am sorry that so much should have been said. . . . We have a custom in South Africa among the blacks—when a man kills a bird, he never eats it himself, but lays it at the feet of his senior; and if I had killed a bird tonight, I think it would be my duty to lay it at the feet of my dear brother who is here now and whom I have not seen for more than thirty years, the Rev. Roger Price, of the London Missionary Society—the true pioneer of the Barotsi Mission."[10] Later, a Jesuit mission proved equally unacceptable to the Lozi:[11] Coillard met the remnants of the mission at Leshoma, outside the southern frontier of Barotseland, and tells us of the sad end of their enterprise.

By this time, therefore, the Lozi, many of whom had lived under Kololo rule, including the king who had most to do with Coillard, were well acquainted with missionaries, even if they did not understand the purpose of their work. Moreover, missionaries entered into their foreign policies. This was particularly the position among the Tswana tribes, where the missionaries became important as the chiefs sought protection from the British against the Boers in the Transvaal. An important influence on the Lozi was Khama, who urged Coillard to go to the Zambezi. He may have done so as a Christian; but he also, I suspect, wished to extend his influence on his northern front. He too feared Ndebele attack. Shortly after Coillard went to the Zambezi, Khama entered into ambassadorial relationships with the Lozi king.

This was the record of missionaries before Coillard's first visit to Barotseland. While he returned to Basutoland, between his two expeditions, Frederick Stanley Arnot journeyed to Barotseland, and stayed there from August 1882 to May 1884. He apparently never contemplated settling in the Zambezi valley, though he was received with kindness by the king. He ultimately founded a mission in Garenganze (Katanga),[12] on the plateau to the east in the territory of the Nyamwezi freebooter Msidi who had conquered the Lamba. Arnot left the Lozi capital a few months before Coillard returned to the southeastern entrance to the country.

Explorers and hunters had also begun to enter Barotseland. After Livingstone, the greatest explorer was Emil Holub, who described Barotseland under the rule of Sepopa, the king who drove out the Kololo conquerors.[13] He later (1885–86) returned when Coillard was at the Zambezi, and went into Ila (Mashukulomboe) country, where he and his party were attacked. Coillard describes their plight when they reached his camp; and later the Lozi king Lewanika said he was going to attack the Ila to punish them for plundering a party which came to them from his dominions (below, 279, 292). Earlier in 1879, Coillard had succoured another explorer, Alexandre Rocha de Serpa Pinto, journeying from Benguella, who had been deserted by his porters in Barotseland (below, 71). In an entry not reproduced here, Coillard notes (presumably according to Pinto) that the king Robosi had detained Serpa Pinto's baggage. He gives no report of the gallant fight described by Serpa Pinto, himself pictured holding the Portuguese flag, against a sudden night attack by the Lozi, in his book *How I Crossed Africa.*[14] No Barotse, who was alive at that time, and whom I questioned in the 1940's, had ever heard of an attack on a white man.

Barotseland was relatively isolated, but it had for a long time also been reached by traders in search of slaves, and later skins and ivory, and by hunters. The first traders came from the Portuguese territory on the west coast, partly half-castes and Africans, but occasionally Portuguese, notably António Francisco Ferreira da Silva Porto, who was there in Livingstone's day. Arab traders also reached Barotseland from the east. When Coillard went there, more traders and hunters were coming up from the south, and one Englishman, George Westbeech, was well established at the Lozi court. Like Holub, Westbeech visited Sepopa (1873–74, 1875), and later he stayed from 1885 to 1886.[15]

Thus Coillard was not going to completely unopened regions; but it was still a difficult and hazardous journey to Barotseland, and travel within the country was most arduous. It was also a period of great political uncertainty within the kingdom: in 1878, in his first reference to the possibility of going there, when describing his meeting with the Barotse refugees at the Ndebele capital, Coillard noted (below, 40): "They have taken refuge here to save their lives; for their country, it seems is frequently subject to revolution, and human life is very cheap."

III

When the Kololo conquered Barotseland it was ruled by the Aluyi (now Malozi) from the great valley, a flood-plain which stretches along the Zambezi for 120 miles between $14\frac{1}{2}°$ to 16°S. at about 23°E. At its widest the plain is about 25 miles across.[16] The Valley has been scooped out of wind-blown sands by the Zambezi in its meanderings, which have left many water-filled depressions and ox-bows. The bordering scarps rise to some 50 to 200 feet and are covered now by gardens in scrub woodland, with occasional trees of stature. In the Valley the Lozi dwell on mounds, mostly raised by termites but some added to by the piling up of earth. The Lozi dwell on their mounds for most of the year; but when the rain which falls on the Congo-Zambezi divide floods the river for the period February-March to June-July, depending on the depth of the flood, they move to temporary camps or another set of villages at the margin of the Valley. Coillard repeatedly refers to this inundation and the ceremonial movement of the king, in the royal "barge" Nalikwanda (Nalikuanda), between his plain capital and his *mafulo* (camp) on the margin. Standing out on the plain are some villages where trees have been planted to mark the cenotaphs of dead kings, at which offerings and sacrifices used to be made. From this plain the Lozi conquered outwards in all directions, but mainly to the east and south-east, and at its largest the kingdom must have been well over 250,000 square miles in size and contained over 25 different tribes. The outer provinces were not directly ruled, but were controlled by what Coillard in French terms calls "préfets" who were responsible mainly for forwarding tribute to the king.

Coillard gives the Lozi an origin in the east and others have derived them from the south; but they themselves state that they are related to the Lunda to the north, indeed to the great Lunda kingdom of Mwata Yamvo in the "Congo". This legend is supported by the ecological, linguistic, and cultural evidence. But their myths relate their system of government to a voluntary rendering of the tithe of a catch of fish to Mboo, who was a son of God Nyambe (Nyambi) by his daughter Mbuyumwambwa. Mboo was buried at Ikatulamwa (Katuramoa) which Coillard mentions several times as a great national shrine. The giving of the tithe to Mboo established the kingship. Mboo quarrelled and fought with his young brother Mwanambinji (Moana Mbinyi) who established his rule in the south of the plain, where he ultimately entered the ground near Senanga, and where his cenotaph is still acknowledged as one of the most sacred shrines of the nation. Coillard (below, 170–171) describes how when he passed this cenotaph his paddlers wished to make offerings there and he refused: the paddlers therefore had to content themselves with giving it the royal salute. Travellers were still doing so, to my knowledge, as late as 1947.

This division of the plain into northern and southern kingdoms, according to Lozi legends, was later the precedent for a division of the kingdom between two capitals, that of the king and that of the Mulena Mukwae (Morena Mokwae), a day to the south, by Coillard's time permanently established at Nalolo. At this period, also, the king's capital was permanently established at Lealui, after a move from the Kololo capital at Naliele. Previously kings had continually built new capitals. The king was superior to the southern capital, but the latter had all the appurtenances of royal court, royal musicians, sanctuaries, etc., duplicating the northern capital, and it was entitled to be consulted on all matters and to take a share of all tribute passing it on the way north.

According to legend, the first re-established southern capital was under a princess (Mukwae), but early in the nineteenth century a prince ruled there. In 1838, after the death of the great king Mulambwa,[17] civil war broke out when the prince in the south contested the kingship of his half-brother who had been selected by the northerners. Lozi claimed that it was this civil war which allowed the Kololo to defeat them; and hence when they regained their homeland, they returned to the custom of placing a princess in the southern capital. Coillard describes meeting two of these princess chiefs,[18] as I have translated the term Mulena Mukwae: Maibiba, the sister of king Akufuna, a gentle and kindly woman, and Matauka, sister of Lewanika, a much fiercer and more turbulent person. She fitted better the character, since the princess chief is saluted as is a male king (below, 213). Maibiba was so well liked that after her brother was defeated, she was allowed, as she wished, to retire from "kingship" and live a more secluded life, though Coillard met her at the capital of her brother's conqueror.

The king and princess chief ruled, at least theoretically, through a council of what Coillard calls chiefs and *likomboa (likombwa)* attendants. The latter is now translated as stewards. When I studied the Lozi, and long before that, the royal council was disposed in three sets around the king: on his right sat the *makwambuyu*, Coillard's chiefs, whom I call councillors; on his left sat the *likombwa* stewards; and in front of him sat the princes of the royal family. Coillard makes no mention of this third set. Each set consisted of a number of titles, mostly of legendary importance but some newly created, in fixed order. If a councillor or steward was promoted deposed or died, a successor to the title was appointed who occupied the same position in the set. (Coillard describes the twelve chiefs sent to Sesheke to guard the south-eastern marches against the Ndebele and watch over entrants to the country as occupying titles in the same way.) Princes, and princesses who were represented by their husbands, also mainly succeeded to legendary titles. To each title, of councillor, steward or royal, might be attached a village or villages, people, cattle, productive sites, and claims on tribute. These were attached to the title, not to the incumbent; and if he vacated the title, his claims to them ceased. That is, under this system, neither chiefs nor stewards had bodies of followers permanently attached to them, save in their natal villages. The councillors-of-the-right were most powerful, under the leadership of the Ngambela (Gambella), whom we might call prime minister— a very powerful person.

Coillard brings out clearly that the stewards, who looked after the king's personal affairs, were expected to be, and often were, the spokesmen for the king, while the chiefs were expected to represent the interests of the nation.[19] One of the councillors, Natamoyo, was a sanctuary: a convicted person who could reach him in council, or his courtyard, was safe. He was one of very many sanctuaries, including the cenotaphs of kings, well described by Coillard (below, 223–224).

When the Kololo defeated the Lozi in 1838, many of the Lozi fled to Lukwakwa (Lekhoa Khoa) in the north, where they set up two kingdoms which became affected considerably by the Mbunda, a tribe, two chiefs of which with their people had settled long before in the Barotse valley to provide, among other things, the main diviners (see below, *passim.*). But many Lozi, including princes, stayed with the Kololo by whom they were well treated and often honoured. The reputation of the Kololo remained high among the Lozi, from Coillard's time until modern days, and hence Coillard's

Sotho evangelists were well received, and not rejected as he feared they might be. Sepopa was a Lozi prince with the Kololo, and he revolted in 1864 and drove them out, killing those of the men who did not escape to "Bechuanaland". Sepopa was a very generous king, but he killed men whose wives he coveted, and others, including children, for pleasure. The Lozi in 1876 (two years before Coillard first arrived) killed him and appointed as king Mwanawina II (Nguana-Wina). Coillard says (below, 56ff.) that Mwanawina was also driven out because of tyrannical actions; Lozi who were alive at the time told me that he had grown up among *mangete* (foreigners, often meaning non-Lozi—not a tribe as Coillard speaks of them); and the relatives of his wives treated them too familiarly, though they were queens. So in 1878 Mwanawina was driven out: he fled to the east whence he made essays to come back to regain the throne. Lubosi (Rubosi), later taking the name Lewanika, became king.

Coillard speaks (below, 148) of a quick revolution against Lewanika because he too ruled tyranically. My own informants said that this move against Lewanika had an entirely different cause. Under the Kololo, according to Sotho custom, the councillors of the king were great chiefs who "owned" many villagers and controlled many people; and they used to come to the council attended by their armed followers. Coillard describes this system at Sesheke, the gateway to Barotseland. Lewanika decided to return to the old system of Lozi government, where men filled titles as chiefs and did not have bands of personal followers: he aimed thus to weaken the power, or at least the armed strength, of the chiefs. He was helped in this plan for reorganization by an aged councillor, Nalubutu (Narubutu).[20] Nalubutu had grown up under king Mulambwa before the Kololo invasion and knew the old Lozi system: Coillard (below, 400, 408), describes him as "the preserver of ancient customs," who "worthily" represented "the conservative party". Secondly, Lewanika proposed that any Lozi returning to the valley should be able to reclaim land occupied by his ancestors, and displace from it the people settled there by the Kololo, and break the claims of those who had got control over land under the Kololo or under Sepopa. These two proposals were blows to the power of great chiefs, and, led by Mataa (Mathaha), they attacked Lewanika at night (1878) and attempted to kill him. He escaped, and fled to the Mashi where he found allies who supported him, with the people of the south of the valley, in a "counter-revolution". This was against Mataa, who had found a new prince to be king, in Akufuna Tatila (Tatira), previously ruling in Lukuakua, one of the Lozi kingdoms in exile. Lewanika won the battle (1879), allegedly with the help of traders from "Angola". But Mataa did not give up: and he went again to Lukuakua to obtain another king. By ridicule he forced Sikufele to go with him, though Sikufele refused to fight. Mataa was defeated and slain; and Lewanika, as described by Coillard, then proceeded to take revenge on the relatives of Mataa and others who had killed many of his immediate family and friends.

All of these events happened in a period of about eight years, so it is little wonder that Coillard found Barotseland to be a country of civil war and anarchy, suffering famine because people could not plant and reap, with those who could battening off the subject peoples. These could only murmur "Ke-lelumo" (It is the spear—civil war); or as they later said to me, "Mwandwa, mulao ulobezi" (In war, the law sleeps.) It does seem that there was more civil strife at that period than at other, legendary it is true, periods of Barotse history: we might find an English parallel in the period of the Wars of the Roses. But of course all these types of states, with simple technologies and weapons, in Europe and Asia as in Africa, have been marked by constant civil strife, wars and coups that are better called rebellions rather than revolutions. They did not aim to subvert the political system as such; it is notable, if the above record is followed, that no councillor essayed to seize the throne; it always went to a royal prince. Even the ambitious Mataa went twice to Lukuakua to find princes in whose name he could revolt against Lewanika; and it is not to be wondered that one of Lewanika's first moves was to subdue this source of "pretenders" for the throne.[21]

I have no space to give in greater detail an account of Lozi history, culture, and social organization, and must refer the interested reader to my other publications. I can only warn that Coillard does not seem to have been a good observer, or recorder. To bring out his inaccuracies I would have to edit his text page by page, and the conditions in which this new edition is reproduced preclude doing so. A few examples must suffice of how poorly he made observations, and of how indeed his biases about a degraded people misled him to paint a gloomy picture—a picture which justified to his supporters the high cost of his mission. When he protested against the pre-marital sexual play of the youth, their elders told him: "*babapala*". (They are playing.) This he describes as a measure of moral degradation. But he applies the same interpretation to people telling him, when he asked after the king: *"babapala"*. (They are playing.) But there was quite a different significance. He frequently describes the king's bands of drums and xylophone, and how they played continually day and night. They do so as long as the king is alive and well: the sound of the drums means that the king is well. Hence his respondents were in fact replying to his question by saying that as the drums played, the king was well—using a plural prefix, as Lozi always do for important people, or out of politeness. This is but one example of how inadequate understanding misled him.

So too, in view of descriptions by other travellers, I find it impossible to accept his statement that the Lozi never tried disputes by judicial methods, and had no idea of the value of witness and evidence, though they also used diviners and ordeals in some cases.[22] He does seem correct in his statements about the relative fragility of Lozi marriage, when compared with the Sotho marriage;[23] but he gives little information about marriages and how they worked. He writes (below, 424) about the custom by which every year "the finest boys and girls were taken from every village and brought to the capital, nominally to learn their duties, in reality to be distributed as slaves at the kings' pleasure", despite the banning of slave-trading. He added that "few ever saw their homes again". This was a Lozi custom by which the king staffed royal villages and founded new villages: I met many men and women who were thus "chosen" at this period, from the valley and outside, and they regarded it as an honour and maintained close relationships with their kin. These examples do not deny that Coillard gives considerable useful information about the Lozi and other peoples whom he met and among whom he worked, so that this book is an essential reference for Barotseland and all the areas where he travelled and worked; but what he says has to be carefully sifted with other information and screened for bias.

IV

I have looked at the Lozi, the people with whom this book is mainly concerned, the people mentioned whom I know best. I have not space to deal with the Ndebele, the Sotho and others. Let me therefore mention briefly the other events of crucial importance.

Coillard's was the second mission expedition from Basutoland to seek a new field in the north. The first was jailed by the Boers in the Transvaal. Coillard's expedition covered the period during which, between 1877–81, the British made their first temporary conquest of the Orange Free State and the Transvaal, a period of rule which ended at the battle of Majuba Hill. The mission's difficulties arose from Boer suspicion of the alleged political activities of missionaries, going back to the activities of Dr. John Philip in the Cape Colony.[24] It was also a period of travail in the history of Basutoland, involving resistance to British attempts to disarm the Sotho, and final establishment of a British protectorate over the Sotho. He describes well the debates in the Lozi council, the gathering of all Lozi when they came under the protection of the British South Africa Company in 1890, and the results of their disappointment that this protection did not come directly from Queen Victoria. That occurred at the same time as the Company entered Southern Rhodesia and defeated the Ndebele. When Coillard left Barotseland for Europe in 1896, the Shona/Ndebele revolt against the Europeans was about to break out: it had failed by the time he returned in 1898.

One matter I do draw attention to. This is the manner in which rumours, and accurate information, travelled through the subcontinent. Notably, Lobengula's refusal to accept Coillard's party is ascribed to Ndebele resentment against the Sotho evangelists who were taken to represent a nation whose chiefs betrayed Chief Langalibalele of Natal to the British when he was pursued by a punitive expedition for refusing to surrender a firearm. News travelled afterwards in garbled form; but by the time of Coillard's journeys, south-central Africa was a single field in which different kinds of whites were engaged in complex relationships with one another and with the various African peoples. An event far away could affect men's actions.

Rumours about Coillard help to explain why Lewanika's relationships with him blew from warm to cold, and back again, as Coillard repeatedly reports. He shows that Lewanika's council was divided as to how the Lozi should react to the entrance of missionaries at all, and to the political situation created by the entrance of European powers into the region. They were doubtful here about Coillard's role. Undoubtedly also, Lewanika tried to exploit the missionaries materially. But Lozi accounts of Lewanika indicate that he was very shaken by the sudden night attack on his capital and the killing of so many of his family and friends. He became vengeful and suspicious. Lozi told me that he was convinced that the revolt was inspired by drunkenness among the chiefs, and he therefore banned beer-drinking. Unhappily for Coillard he seems to have become involved in Lewanika's suspiciousness. Coillard had approached him during his first short reign, and after Lewanika fled to the south, Coillard continued these negotiations with the new king, Tatila. He did so against the advice of Westbeech, the English trader who knew the Barotse well. In fact, Coillard's first visit to the Barotse capital was paid to Tatila. When Coillard returned after seven years Lewanika was again on the throne: and reading these journals I think it may well be that the king felt that Coillard was one of those friends for prosperity alone, and therefore tried him before he gave his confidence. To Coillard one king or the other in a country of so-called "anarchy" made no difference: it was deeply felt by the king himself.

V

I turn finally to the book itself. Not surprisingly, it is dominated by long passages in which Coillard affirms his faith in his mission. He wrote at length about his feeling that he was carrying out the duty of a "soldier" of Jesus Christ. He seemingly did so both to feed his own faith that he was serving thus, and the faith of his audience whom he urged to support the work of missionaries, with money and material goods, and with volunteers. The book is largely an exposition of how great was the task and the duty of carrying the Gospel to men in "darkness". I feel that in a way he sought consolation in his letters for the sufferings he and his comrades endured—for the deaths of European and Sotho adults and children—when he described the faith that moved him. Yet at the same time he needed no consolation in general. His doubts, which struck him when Barotse approached him at Lobengula's capital, were about the distance of the Zambezi: might not the same expenditure of money and lives have brought more fruitful results elsewhere?—perhaps in Basutoland? As he determinedly struggled to establish mission stations in Barotseland, and particularly as the number of converts remained small, he wondered whether it was not vainglory that kept him at work among the Barotse.

This haunting doubt remained with him to the end; and it was touchingly documented in a story recounted by his dead wife's niece in her biography of him and his wife. She described his visit to Europe in 1896:

Another time, when he was visiting some friends, his hostess came to the supper-table excusing herself for being late. "I was putting my little boy to bed, and he kept me. When he was saying his prayers I bade him pray for M. Coillard, and he asked, 'Why does every one make such a fuss *(tant de cas)* over M. Coillard?' So I began to tell him why, and he said—what do you suppose? 'I think we must all ask God not to let him grow too proud!'" Everybody laughed except the subject of this remark, who looked very grave. The next day, in private, the hope was expressed that he had not been annoyed by such an embarrassing speech. "Oh no," he replied, "it was God's message to me, and He sent it by the mouth of a child so that it should not wound me."[25]

There was in Coillard some of the indomitable pride and obduracy which had moved David Livingstone to persevere despite all obstacles and advice. Clearly these qualities, with courage and faith in duty, enabled the Mission ultimately to achieve success. But when these qualities were curiously mixed with humility arising from the feeling that a man was carrying out a Divine task, when many occurrences could be seized on as an indication that God had selected him for the task he saw before him, questioning and self-doubt had to emerge. Was he pursuing, at such costs to others, a Divine task, or was he pursuing his own vainglory? I feel that it was to still these doubts that Coillard so often wrote down his praises of the missionary task, emphasized the ignorance of the Gospel and the cruelty and degradation of the people, and prayed for Divine supprt and the prayers of his audience. Much of this book is also taken up by the humdrum—but far from humdrum— accounts of travelling through arduous countries, with wagons sticking, their wheels breaking and oxen dying, of goods received belatedly in wrecked and wretched condition, of fever and other illness, and of problems of building and finding food: as he recounted each hazard and difficulty, he renewed his faith not in Christianity, where he was unshakeable, nor in the missionary duty to evangelize, but in the necessity to pursue and establish a branch of the Basutoland Mission among the Lozi.

The repetition of the arduousness of travel may seem as wearisome as travelling itself. I myself worked as an anthropologist in Barotseland nearly forty years after Coillard died. Travelling was much less arduous and was certainly safe. The civil wars and resulting anarchy which had beset Coillard with uncertainties and difficulties were long over. New treatments for malaria and other endemic diseases made health much more secure. But even then, moving afoot or on a horse with carriers, or up and down the Zambezi in a large barge, was not easy. Coillard (below, 255) describes the terrors of crossing the waterless sands to reach the river Mutondo (Motondo): those sands in the 1940's still worried my carriers. Anyone who has made such a journey can appreciate why so much of Coillard's letters—as he himself commented—was taken up with the problems of travel. When he finally returned in 1898 to Barotseland, he proceeded rapidly by rail where previously he had laboured for months by wagon, from South Africa to Bulawayo—he died in Barotseland just before the railway reached the Victoria Falls, but saw the start on building the bridge across their gorge.

But travel inside Barotseland remained difficult until the invention of the four-wheel drive. In 1965 I drove a Land Rover in three hours from the Barotse Valley to a village which I had visited twenty-five years before: then it had taken me two days on foot to reach the village. And the great majority of the population still moves on foot. So these long passages about the hazards of travel have to be read if one is to picture what central Africa was like—and still is for many of its people. The letters give a vivid picture of the conditions which beset not only the traveller, but also the local people; and they help to explain why so many kaleidescopically changing rumours of what was happening in the heart of the Lozi kingdom reached Coillard as he waited at its gateway for royal permission to enter. They explain the slow course of his dealings with the king, 300 miles away, and why the king could give orders in his capital but could not have them carried out by his chiefs in the provinces. Indeed only when we take into account these conditions of travel, do we realize how big, in terms of technology, was the Lozi kingdom—larger, at its greatest extent, than Germany. Reading of these difficulties, as I worked yet again through this book, I realized anew how right was W. M. Macmillan, the great South African historian, when he told a young colleague beginning on the study of Central Africa, to walk for a few days only along one of Livingstone's routes.

This book enables us to walk at least in imagination along a great man's spiritual and geographical journey. At times, he must strike us as hard: he had to be. I have cited above the story of his reaction to a little boy's prayer that he not grow too proud, to show that he had a softer and self-criticising side, and a readiness to forgive in others what he prayed might be forgiven in himself. Livingstone wrote that by carefully selecting incidents he could show the Kololo to be wholly good or wholly evil, but that, taking them all for all, they were "the same curious mixture of good and evil as men are everywhere else." Coillard occasionally uses a similar phrase, when he speaks of individuals, including himself. He rarely does so of a people; but in his final years he wrote several times of "my dear Barotsi".

He records his dismay at the sharpening colour bar and the refusal of apprenticeship to blacks in South African and Rhodesian life, particularly as enforced by church-going whites. He deplored the conditions in which African migrant labourers were housed in the growing towns.[26] He wished to work for an independent African church, self-sustaining and self-propagating. Hence he did not quote in this book what is reported by his biographer, that the Sotho evangelists at Lobengula's claimed that it was their mission and that he was the cause of their difficulties. And he reacted charitably, though deeply hurt, to the secession from the mission in 1903 of a Sotho evangelist, who set up an independent church. This was the first case of "Ethiopianism" in Barotseland. It ended with the Lozi king expelling this leader.[27]

Coillard surely would have welcomed the independence of the African church in Barotseland within an independent Zambia; and despite his weaknesses, when we read his book we can understand why President Kaunda showed publicly his appreciation of the work of the Paris Evangelical Mission Society.

Max Gluckman

1 September 1969

NOTES

1. Later the Barotse Province of Northern Rhodesia and then Zambia, now the Western Province. Modern spelling of the Bantu languages, and hence of the names of people and places mentioned below differs from the spelling used in Coillard's time: in Barotseland particularly the language has become less Sothoized, and Coiilard's renditions were greatly affected by his knowledge of Sesotho (Coillard's Sesuto). I have decided it would be most helpful to readers who do not know the names and places, if I used modern spelling, and at first mention put in parentheses Coillard's spelling. The main difference is that Coillard uses "r" for "l" and "o" for "w".

2. Hereafter, when I refer to territories anachronistically, I put them in quotation marks. This is convenient and brief.

3. On Swaziland, see Hilda Kuper, *An African Aristocracy: Rank among the Swazi of the Protectorate* (London, 1947). For an anthropological analysis of Zulu history, see my *The Rise of the Zulu Empire* (Lon-

don, 1970). E. A. Ritter, *Shaka Zulu* (London, 1955), is a popular epic about the first Zulu king, while D. R. Morris, *The Washing of the Spears* (New York, 1965), is a recent popular history of the Zulu from the creation of their empire to their defeat by the British. A recent compressed history is Monica Wilson and Leonard Thompson (eds.), *The Oxford History of South Africa, I. South Africa to 1870* (London, 1969). John D. Omer-Cooper has written on the events that followed on the rise of the Zulu: *The Zulu Aftermath: A Nineteenth-Century Revolution in Bantu Africa* (Evanston, 1966), pp. 336–364. There are many earlier histories dealing with the events, notably the classic by W. M. Macmillan, *Bantu, Boer and Briton: The Making of the South African Native Problem* (London, 1929). The recent books give references to earlier studies.

4. An argument discussed and criticised in R. F. Stevenson, *Population and Political Systems in Tropical Africa* (New York, 1968), 27–52. For the Swazi, see Kuper, *African Aristocracy, passim.*

5. The best analysis of these Ngoni is J. A. Barnes, *Politics in a Changing Society: A Political History of the Fort Jameson Ngoni* (Manchester, 1954).

6. A general account of this process, and of earlier "Southern Rhodesian" history, is Philip Mason, *The Birth of a Dilemma: The Conquest and Settlement of Rhodesia* (London, 1958). It contains references to other books.

7. On the process see D. E. Ellenberger and J. C. Macgregor, *The History of the Basuto, Ancient and Modern* (London, 1912).

8. Recorded in his *Missionary Travels and Researches in South Africa* (London, 1857). His second visit to Kolololand was described in the book *Narrative of an Expedition to the Zambesi and its Tributaries* (with also the name of his brother Charles on the title-page) (London, 1865). See also Isaac Schapera (ed.), *Livingstone's Missionary Correspondence 1841–1856* (London, 1961); *Livingstone's Private Journals 1851–1853* (London, 1960); *Livingstone's African Journal 1853–1856* (London, 1963).

9. See Max Gluckman, "As Men are Everywhere Else", *The Rhodes-Livingstone Journal: Human Problems in British Central Africa*, XX (1956), 68–73.

10. C. W. Macintosh (niece to Mme. Coillard), *Coillard of the Zambesi: The Lives of François and Christina Coillard, of the Paris Missionary Society, in South and Central Africa (1858–1904)* (London, 1907). On Price, see Edwin W. Smith, *Great Lion of Bechuanaland: The Life and Times of Roger Price, Missionary* (London, 1957).

11. See H. Depelchin and C. Croonenberghs, *Trois ans dans l'Afrique Australe au pays d'Umzile; chez les Batongas; la valée des Barotses; debuts de la Mission du Zambeze* (Brussels, 1879, 1880, 1881).

12. Frederick Stanley Arnot, *Garenganze: Seven Years' Pioneer Mission Work in Central Africa* (London, 1889; 2nd ed., Frank Cass, 1969).

13. Emil Holub, *Eine Culturskizze des Marutses-Mambundas Reich in Süd-Central Africa* (Vienna, 1879), and (trans. E. E. Frewer), *Seven Years in South Africa: Travels, Researches, and Hunting Adventures between the Diamond-fields and the Zambesi, (1872–79)* (London, 1881). (The Barotse are dealt with in volume II.)

14. Macintosh, *Coillard of the Zambesi*, 280. Serpa Pinto's book was translated by Alfred Elwes (London, 1881), II, 45. Macintosh, 280, quotes Coillard's journal as reporting that Serpa Pinto's people deserted him because they were afraid of the Barotse reputation.

15. "The Diary of George Westbeech", in E. C. Tabler (ed.), *Trade and Travel in Early Barotseland* (London, 1963).

16. For a general account of Barotseland and the Lozi ruling tribe see my "The Lozi of Barotseland in North-Western Rhodesia", in Elizabeth Colson and Max Gluckman (eds.), *Seven Tribes of British Central Africa* (Manchester, 1951). I describe the plain's ecology and productive system in greater detail in *Economy of the Central Barotse Plain* (Livingstone, 1941).

17. The ninth king according to legend, on a genealogy eleven generations deep. Anthropological analyses of genealogies have revealed how these are truncated, and, as we find genealogies in many tribes eleven generations deep, we cannot treat these as historical records. From Silva Porto's and Livingstone's evidence we can state that the kingdom was well-established by at least the end of the eighteenth century and probably much earlier.

18. I used "princesses" rather than "queen", because she was of the royal family, not married into it. Coillard (below, 213) says the southern ruler might be the mother of the king, but this only happened when she was born of the royal line. After a king's death, it might be his father's sister.

19. This is all I can now set out for lack of space: for fuller analyses see my *The Ideas in Barotse Jurisprudence* (New Haven, 1965), Chap. II, and *Administrative Organization of the Barotse Native Authorities* (Livingstone, 1943).

20. I cannot accept Coillard's statement that this is a corruption of Ma-Roberta, the name of Livingstone's wife, as reported in Macintosh, *Coillard of the Zambesi*, 343.

21. See my *The Ideas in Barotse Jurisprudence*, Chap. II, and more generally my *Politics, Law and Ritual in Tribal Society* (Oxford, 1965).

22. See my *The Judicial Process among the Barotse of Northern Rhodesia* (Manchester, 1955; 2nd enlarged ed., 1967): my own data collected in 1939–47, but citing earlier records.

23. See my "Kinship and Marriage among the Lozi of Northern Rhodesia and the Zulu of Natal", in A. R. Radcliffe-Brown and C. D. Forde (eds.), *African Systems of Kinship and Marriage* (London, 1967).

24. See Macmillan, *Bantu, Boer and Briton*, op. cit. passim.

25. Macintosh, *Coillard of the Zambesi*, 407.

26. *Ibid.*, 257.

27. These last incidents and observations are recorded, *ibid.*, 424–433.

Yours cordially F. Coillard

ON THE THRESHOLD OF CENTRAL AFRICA

A RECORD OF TWENTY YEARS' PIONEERING AMONG THE BAROTSI OF THE UPPER ZAMBESI

BY

FRANÇOIS COILLARD

OF THE SOCIÉTÉ DES MISSIONS EVANGÉLIQUES DE PARIS

Translated from the French and Edited by his Niece
CATHERINE WINKWORTH MACKINTOSH

WITH FORTY-FOUR ILLUSTRATIONS FROM PHOTOGRAPHS BY THE AUTHOR

LONDON
HODDER AND STOUGHTON
27, PATERNOSTER ROW
1897

To

THE BELOVED AND BLESSED MEMORY

OF HER

WHO FOR THIRTY YEARS

SHARED AND ADORNED MY LIFE AND MISSIONARY ACTIVITY,

JOYFULLY FACED THE WANDERINGS, HARDSHIPS,

AND DANGERS OF PIONEER WORK,

WHO

BY HER SUFFERINGS AND DEATH

CONSECRATED THE BAROTSI MISSION,

AND

NOW SLEEPS AT SEFULA.

" She hath done what she could."

CHRISTINA COILLARD (NÉE MACKINTOSH).

[*To face page* v.

AUTHOR'S PREFACE

TO THE ENGLISH READER

THE present work is not a systematic history, either of my own missionary career of forty years, or of the Barotsi Mission. These are only scattered leaves, collected, at the request of friends, from the pages of the *Journal des Missions Evangéliques*, where they have appeared from time to time during the last twenty years, and now published less for those who already know them than for the rising generation, for whom the Africa of the ox-waggon and the assegaï will soon be little but a name. Jotted down in the intervals of arduous toil, often by the light of camp-fires, cramped in a canoe, or jolted in a cart, they make no literary pretensions; they are but simple descriptions, which have already proved interest ng to some, and which God has deigned to bless. I should have liked to condense them much more, and above all to revise them ; but time and health have failed me to do more than glance over the proofs. After all, the untrammelled style of the traveller sits better upon an old African wanderer. In an academical garb, to which I have no title, my friends would not recognise me.

I am no painter, but I do admire Nature. Nowadays every one practises photography, myself amongst the number. The illustrations to this volume have been executed from very indifferent negatives ; they are the work of a tyro, hampered by adverse conditions of climate and the lack of suitable appliances ; and their sole value—if they possess any—is that they are instantaneous views. Though not artistic, they are *faithful*, and I would say the same of the letters which they illustrate. They, like the pictures, only profess to be *instantaneous photographs* ; not artistic, but certainly faithful.

I do not share the weakness of certain amateurs who are the sole admirers of their own performances, and who do not perceive that people only praise them out of good nature. I have far too exalted an ideal for that. I am fully aware of my own awkwardness and my own short-comings. If here and there I have succeeded, it is by sheer accident. But being only an amateur, I do not profess to work for the great public.

My heartfelt gratitude also is due to my niece, who, with her sisters' help, has spared neither time, pains, nor labour to make this volume presentable to the English Christian public, and thus serve the interests of the Lord's Kingdom. But if these pages can interest our friends, and win new ones for us ; give them a true idea of the country where we have travelled, laboured, and suffered ; and increase their love for the work to which we have given our lives ; if only they can comfort some hearts, and confirm some souls in the Faith ; give a fresh impulse to the Evangelisation of the Heathen World ; awaken and develop some new vocations ;—if, above all, they can exalt and glorify the Master Whom I serve, and Whom I love—I shall have succeeded, and my prayer will have been granted.

F. COILLARD.

September 12th, 1897.

NOTE

THE heartiest thanks are due from author and editor to Captain St. Hill Gibbons, whose generous courtesy has permitted us to make use of his own survey of the Barotsi country; and to all other friends, who, by lending photographs in their possession, or in various other ways, have helped forward the publication.

Except where otherwise stated, the footnotes have all been added by the editor—of course, with the author's sanction. No pains have been spared to verify every detail; but should the experienced South African detect any discrepancies or inaccuracies, they must be laid to the charge of the translator, and likewise all literary short-comings. The English version is wholly inadequate to convey the charm of the original and the delicate precision of its diction. But the chief practical difficulty has arisen in connection with the spelling of the African names. The strictly phonetic and grammatical French orthography looked so unfamiliar to English eyes that it was abandoned as likely to confuse the reader. Unfortunately, there is no rule in this respect among English writers on African subjects; and it was found necessary to retain the *é* to represent the sound of *e* as in *rein*, while *e* (without accent) represents that of *e* in *lean*. When the latter follows a vowel, it is marked with the diæresis *ë*.

The illustrations are all from photographs by M. Coillard, with the exception of the one facing page 17—" The Camp, near Harrysmith"; and this is also the only one that belongs to

Part I. in order of time. The others were all taken after his visit to Europe, when he first studied photography. That of Mr. Waddell and the leopard was not taken at the time referred to in the text, but on one of many similar occasions later on.

The portrait of M. Coillard is from a photograph by Vandyk, Gloucester Road, S.W.; that of Mme. Coillard from one by Penabert, Paris.

C. W. M.

CONTENTS

PART I

THE BANYAÏ EXPEDITION

1877—1879

ix

PART II

THE BAROTSI EXPEDITION

1882—1887

PART III

AT SEFULA

1887—1892

CHAPTER XVII

CHAPTER XVIII

CHAPTER XIX

CHAPTER XX

CHAPTER XXI

CHAPTER XXII

CHAPTER XXIII

CHAPTER XXIV

CHAPTER XXV

CHAPTER XXVI

CHAPTER XXVII

CHAPTER XXVIII

CHAPTER XXIX

PART IV

LEALUYI

1892—1896

LIST OF ILLUSTRATIONS

xix

MAP.

INTRODUCTION

THE banyan tree is the true emblem of the Church of God. Each one of its mighty branches bears roots ; each root that touches the soil, and grows there, becomes a new trunk, which in its own time must spread its branches farther, and strike new roots.

If the Church's mission begins, and *should* begin, at Jerusalem, it must not stop short there. Her movements are always tending farther and farther afield ; her aspirations are ever towards the " regions beyond," to the uttermost parts of the earth ; her spirit is the spirit of conquest and aggression. " Forward! forward!" is her never-changing motto.

Never has the Church grasped this more thoroughly than to-day. Modern missions sufficiently proclaim that. And what inspires us personally with joy and confidence is less the actual and immediate result which can be tabulated, than the spirit of reproduction and extension which animates the missions themselves. That has its root in the nature of things. It is the essential condition of vitality. Woe to us who conduct them, woe to the missions themselves, if we hold them too long in leading-strings, and if, kept thus in an abnormal childhood, they lose the power of independent action and of responsibility ! Their members acquire a false conscience, their development is blighted, and the moment their guardians are removed they are condemned to dwindle and—disappear themselves.

Perhaps this education presents peculiar difficulties among the natives of South Africa. Certain it is that among them, unhappily, it has not assumed those proportions which astonish us among the South Sea islanders and elsewhere. This is due in part to the local circumstances, to the immigration of the

white man, which undoubtedly changes the conditions of existence. But it is due also in part to a certain reserve in the
confidence we bestow on our still infant Churches, and in their
members, who have so recently emerged from the slough of
heathenism. Perhaps, too, we shrink from the personal responsibility of straying from the beaten track.

Yet which of us does not reiterate—sincerely reiterate—
the utterance, that, if ever Africa is to be evangelised, it must
be by her own children! What is so far only a beautiful theory
ought to become a *practice*. Our Churches and our Christians
must send out missionaries. There, as in Europe, that is the
thermometer of religious life. To give, and give *oneself* in the
spirit of Him Who loves us and gave Himself for us—that is
its essence.

The following pages form an account of a humble effort
in this direction. Up to what point the attempt has succeeded,
it is for the reader to judge.

The Banyaï Expedition, which eventually led to the founding
of the Barotsi Mission, was proposed and undertaken by the
native Christians of Basuto-land—a fact which must never be
lost sight of in following its history.

The question is often asked, why, when France has such
extensive colonies of her own, the French Protestant missionaries
are found labouring in British colonies. The answer is two-
fold. First, that, in the early part of the present century,
the Protestants of France were prohibited from missionary
work in their own colonies. Secondly, that the two fields
they now occupy within the British sphere of influence were
not under the protection of any European power when they
first entered upon their labours. About 1830, a wave of
missionary interest swept over the Reformed Churches of
France. But where should they find a field? While they
were discussing this question, they received an appeal from
Dr. Philip, of the L.M.S. in Cape Town, to which they at
once responded ; and this led to the establishment of the
Basuto Mission, at the request of Moshesh, the supreme chief.

Of the three French missionaries who came to Basuto-
land in 1833, one name stands out pre-eminently—that of

M. Arbousset. The more his work and character are studied, the greater the reverence they inspire. He belonged to that race of giants whose exploits in the first half of the century have shed such lustre on our African missions. He possessed in a rare degree the gift of evangelisation, and of communicating it from the very first to the native Christians. In his flock, men always formed a remarkable proportion of the congregation; and each of them, in his own degree and capacity, took a share in the propagation of the Gospel. Not content with this home mission, M. Arbousset more than once sent his catechists for short excursions on foot, with a baggage animal for their provisions, to spend an indefinite time among the Bapeli, in the country now known as the Transvaal.

Some of these catechists had been noted warriors before their conversion : their consciences were burdened with the depredations they had made upon these same tribes, and they wanted to atone to them by bringing them the Gospel of Peace. Later on, in 1863, Isaiah Seëlé went, with the approbation of all the missionaries. Seëlé was a man of high social position, of rare intelligence and remarkable character ; he spoke French and English and several native languages, and possessed an extensive knowledge of medicine. He spent several years evangelising those tribes among whom the Berlin Society of Missions has since founded and carried on a prosperous work. Many of these tribesmen were in the habit of passing through Basuto-land on their way to and from Cape Colony, whither they went to earn money and buy guns. Thus they had seen something of the benefits of missions, and their chiefs were willing and even anxious to have permanent stations.

But this movement was checked by the long and disastrous wars of the Orange Free State with the Basuto. In 1865, all the French Protestant missionaries were expelled from the country, ourselves among the number. The only exception was the one at Thaba Bossiou, a stronghold which the Boers had not been able to take. Armed men brought waggons to our door, and carried us off in such haste that Mme. Coillard had not even time to take her bread from the oven! It was with very heavy hearts that, bidding good-bye to our weeping flock, we set out, exiles from our only home on earth, and followed the waggons, where they had hurriedly piled up our property. The church bell, carelessly packed, sounded a funeral knell all along the road. "Make the best of it," said the commandant, M. de Villiers, who was a personal friend of mine, and who did his best to cheer us up in his own way. "Leave nothing behind, for you will never come back here."

So the Government of Orange Free State had decreed; but the Master we served had ordained otherwise, for three years later, in 1868, when Basuto-land became a British colony, we did come back. We had spent part of the interval in Natal, working with the American missionaries among the Zulu, and gaining a knowledge of the language, which, later on, was to be of the utmost service to us.

It was during this forced exile of their pastors that the Basuto Christians awoke to a sense of their individual responsibility, and gave themselves up to preaching the Gospel most zealously, and with remarkable results. On their return, the missionaries, who had suffered so bitterly at being torn from their field of labour, found it completely transformed. It was a garden which the Lord had watered and blessed.

Their first care was to organise and consolidate the movement. They selected among the Christians those whom they judged most worthy of confidence, placed them here and there as evangelists, and began to cover Basuto-land with a network of stations, which have gone on multiplying year by year ever since.

It was impossible that religious life should thus develop among the Christians without their desiring to spread still farther the Name of Jesus; and this missionary spirit was ardently fostered by my friend Mabille, the worthy successor of M. Arbousset. Before long their spiritual and material prosperity had alike reached such a pitch, that they desired once more to send native catechists to other heathen tribes, and to equip and maintain them. This gave the first impulse to the Banyaï Expedition.

But whither should they carry the Gospel? The Berlin Society had asked and obtained permission from the Boer Government to carry on work in its territories among the tribes they had previously visited, and it became necessary to look farther afield. Accordingly, M. Mabille, accompanied by M. Berthoud, went on an exploration in the extreme north of the Transvaal, with a view to finding there a field for the Mission de la Suisse Vaudoise, of which MM. Berthoud and Creux were the pioneers. They left the Basuto catechists Eliakim and Asser among the Magwamba tribe. Others afterwards joined them, and together they carried on a work of perseverance and devotion, of which the Swiss missions have since reaped the blessed fruits.

The station of Goedgedacht, in the Zoutpansberg Mountains, was occupied at this time by Mr. Hofmeyr, the first missionary ever sent out by the Dutch Reformed Church of the Cape. He, like M. Mabille, was an ardent evangelist ; and a year or two later, by their joint advice, Asser, the leader of the Basuto catechists, undertook a missionary exploration in the Banyaï country, in the neighbourhood of Zimbabye. He started in 1874, accompanied by Jonathan, from the Leribé Church, and two members of Mr. Hofmeyr's flock.

Asser was a very remarkable man, for a native. He had the true pioneering spirit, and would not allow any hindrance, sickness, or danger to turn him back or break up his little band. Moreover, he kept a regular diary, in which he noted not only their adventures, but the hours and distance of their travelling, the water-holes, names of chiefs, and similar details, important for the future. His report was that three great chiefs gladly gave full assent to the coming of missionaries, and had at once chosen sites for the stations. Some of the Banyaï had, on hearing the Gospel, found a striking analogy to one of their ancient traditions—namely, that the son of one of their great chiefs had disappeared mysteriously, and that every tenth day ought to be observed among them in his memory until he should come back. They also shaved their heads at the new moon in his honour. He added : " The Banyaï cultivate maize, rice, etc. *Very industrious, but they say they never wash themselves.*"

Asser's return to Basuto-land in May 1875 was the electric spark which kindled into flame the missionary zeal of his fellow-Christians there. It would be difficult to exaggerate the effect of his addresses. " Ah ! why could I not cut off my arms and legs," he cried, " and make every limb of mine a missionary to these poor Banyaï ! " At one memorable meeting, an old man rose at the back of the church. " Enough of talking," he said ; " let us do something." And, advancing to the communion table, he put down a modest half-crown. The impetus had been given. The whole assembly followed his example ; and the movement spread to all the other stations. On a Communion Day one saw men, women, and children, even babies at their mothers' breast, pressing reverently round the communion table to lay down their offerings. The sum of £500 was raised in a very short time, without counting quantities of cattle, great and small. The Missionary Conference could no longer hesitate. At its next session, in August of the same year, the mission was unanimously decided upon. The money found, the men offered themselves. Four were chosen, and they at once prepared to start with their families.

While these outward events were in progress, circumstances were taking place unobserved which had far-reaching and undreamt-of effects upon the future of the mission. Several of us, especially my friend Mabille and myself, were feeling dissatisfied with the state of things in our respective congregations: there were few conversions from among the heathen ; and though there seemed plenty of zeal among the converts, we were conscious it was not all spiritual energy. Just at this time, we received a visit from Major Malan, whose name is affectionately remembered by many both in England and South Africa. He was the grandson of Cæsar Malan, of Geneva. Having resigned his commission in the British army in order to devote himself more freely to the service of the King of kings, he had undertaken a tour among the South African missions ; and God made use of him as a channel of the greatest blessing. His journey through Basuto-land was the occasion of a fresh revival. He did great good to us poor labourers as well, choked with the dust of our clods, as is so often the case, alas ! and he bestowed on us an affection which we cordially returned.

Later on, at his instigation, a great " consecration meeting " was convened at King William's Town. Mabille and myself urged by a common need, resolved to make the journey, of over three hundred miles, on horseback, in order to be present at it. The subjects were :—

> 1st day.—Christ—Emmanuel. " In Him dwelleth all the fulness of the Godhead bodily."
>
> 2nd day.—Ourselves—believers. " Ye are complete in Him."
>
> 3rd day.—The necessary consequence of these two facts —complete consecration to God. " Your bodies . . . a *living sacrifice*, holy, acceptable unto Him, which is your *reasonable* service."

To Mabille and myself it was more than a spiritual feast ; it was a *revelation*. There we approached the sunlit summits, the Tabor of Christian life, which had always been represented to us as inaccessible : we had, as it were, a vision of the Lord. It seemed to us that we had never given ourselves, that we did not even know the A B C of renunciation, and we were haunted by the sense of this.

On the other hand, our project of extending the mission, which everywhere attracted attention and interest, occupied a very large place in our thoughts. It was the one theme of our conversation as we rode back with our honoured friend, for Major Malan was specially interested in mission work by native agency. One day, we were crossing the River Key, and climbing the slope, when, in obedience to an irresistible impulse, we all three sprang from our horses, knelt in the shadow of a bush I still see before me, and, taking each other as witnesses, we offered ourselves individually to the Lord for the new mission—an act of deep solemnity which made us all brothers-in-arms. Immediately we remounted, Major Malan waved his hat, spurred his horse, and galloped up the hill, calling out, ' Three soldiers ready to conquer Africa ! "

Mabille and I said to each other, " *We* are the soldiers : *he* is an officer—one of the 'thirty' perhaps, like David's mighty men. But, by God's grace, we will be true till death."

And we meant it. That marked a new era in our Christian life, and was, in so far as we were concerned, the true origin of the Barotsi Mission.

On our return, in the autumn of 1875, the Banyaï Expedition was preparing to start. We had at first intended to send our native missionaries alone. But the Transvaal Government, which had got wind of it, opposed their passage, on the ground that the Basuto, coming as foreigners among the Banyaï, might stir up trouble on their northern frontiers. Upon this, it was decided that one of us should escort them. But which one? Mabille urged that he should be sent, but the Conference could not agree to this, in view of the important position he held, not only as pastor and evangelist of a large district, but as the head of the Training School for Evangelists at Morija. Instead, it accepted the offer of a newly arrived missionary, young, unmarried, and as yet without a definite post. This was M. Dieterlen. His character as much as his talents inspired us with the greatest confidence, which subsequent events amply justified.

The third General Synod of our Churches took place at Leribé from the 5th to the 11th of April, 1876. Seventy-eight delegates, besides the missionaries and catechists themselves, represented the various Churches. Large numbers of native Christians, too, came together from all parts of the country, even from other Churches in Kaffraria and elsewhere, some of whom brought us tangible proofs of their interest in the form of subscriptions, besides their messages of encouragement and brotherly affection. Even the heathen chiefs could not remain indifferent to this great demonstration, and the British authorities of the country did not fail to come and bring us their good wishes.

It was under these happy auspices that, after numerous and deeply impressive meetings, we commended our pioneers, our dear brother Dieterlen and his four companions with their families, to the Lord's keeping. We were bidding them farewell in the very place whence in bygone days bands of marauding cannibals used to scour the country, and whence at the head of his clan emigrated the chief Sebetoane, the founder of the Makololo kingdom on the Upper Zambesi.   Survivors of those days were present, some converted, some still heathen, to see their fellow-countrymen, equipped by the freewill offerings of other native Christians, going forth on a mission of peace. It was a striking object lesson, and representatives from every part of the tribe were there to witness it.

Who would have believed that, scarcely a month later, this expedition would come to an abrupt end in the prison of a civilised and Christian state ?   Yet so it was ; and this is the story of the disaster.

M. Dieterlen had started at the end of April 1876.   He had expected some custom-house delays on the frontier, but, meeting with none, passed on to Pretoria, which the waggons traversed in broad daylight without being stopped.   Two days later, May 10th, they were arrested at nightfall by two field-cornets, the women and children sent to a farm several miles away, the waggons and goods confiscated and searched, the men taken back to Pretoria and imprisoned, one in the condemned cell. Owing to the kindness of a German missionary, Mr. Grüneberger, who bailed him out for £300, M. Dieterlen was free to plead for the release of his companions.   They were accused of carrying contraband, but this was proved not to be the case ; and the officials then said they did not care to have French missionaries settled north of the Limpopo.   M. Dieterlen pointed out that they had no jurisdiction over those territories, and that no white traveller had ever yet been asked for a passport.   " Do you know what our intentions are ?   Do you know what treaties we may have made with the natives or the Portuguese ? " asked the official.   They were ordered to leave instantly, on pain of confiscation and imprisonment.   M. Dieterlen, who acted throughout with the utmost courage and discretion, tried every expedient to move the Government, but in vain.   After being fined £14 ("costs"), he was allowed to take his waggons, and the catechists were released after two nights and a day of imprisonment.

It is only fair to say that many of the Transvaal burghers expressed their sympathy with the young missionary and his companions ; and indeed the kindness shown to the subsequent expeditions by all the Boers they met sufficiently proves that this treatment was only the work of a small political clique, hostile to foreign missions.

This unexpected check greatly distressed our young Churches, but without discouraging them. The missionaries, urged to some extent by their flocks, met in conference at Thaba Bossiou, and decided not to abandon the enterprise. The Transvaal Government itself had thought better of it, and let us know indirectly that it would place no obstacle in the way of a new expedition, provided that it were conducted by a man in whom they felt confidence, and that a formal declaration of merchandise were made to the authorities on entering the territory of the Republic.

But the man—where was he to be found ? M. Dieterlen had by this time received an important appointment to our Normal School, and we could not do without him. And then, too, we had to consider the susceptibilities of those whose consciences were already somewhat ill at ease on his account.

For such a delicate and difficult mission it was desired that one whose views had long been well known should offer himself. But he had not offered himself the previous year, neither did he do so now. Before " running," he felt he must be " sent." Thereupon, his colleagues unanimously addressed a pressing appeal to him.

What follows will show how he and his beloved wife *obeyed* this appeal, and what a new direction this angle of the road, which they had reached so suddenly, was to give to their lives.

The station of Leribé, which twenty years before we had been called upon to found, was an advance post in a province which the old inveterate paganism, elsewhere considerably undermined, had made its fortress. It was ruled by an intelligent chief, Molapo, a man of iron will, but long a renegade from Christianity, irascible and jealous of his authority.

Yet in spite of his incessant opposition, our labours had been blessed. A congregation, small in numbers, but rich in faith and works, had gradually grown up around us. The continual vexations, often amounting to persecutions, to which we and they were alike exposed, had specially drawn us together. We lived with them and for them ; we were one family.

For seventeen years, when not travelling, we had lived in temporary and very primitive abodes. We had often sighed for something better, but our life had been singularly chequered and adventurous. During the last year or two, however, our desires had been satisfied. Since the completion of our beautiful stone-built church, we had been able to attend to our own dwelling. We now inhabited a fine spacious house, in the midst of a lovely garden, the work of our own hands. " Shall we ever eat of it, I wonder ? " said Mme. Coillard one evening, as we were walking round our newly planted quince hedge. We never did.

Leribé, nestling in the shadow of its great mountain, with its picturesque gorge and its magnificent panorama, had become an ideal station. I moved in the midst of an immense district, making frequent evangelising excursions, riding for days and weeks together, accompanied by the young men of my flock, sharing their food, sleeping with them under the rocks or in hospitable huts. There was an unspeakable fascination in this life.

Yes, but the charm must needs be broken, innocent as it was. We needed another discipline in the Lord's school ; it was His will that, " emptied from vessel to vessel," we should learn the lesson that consecration, *a true and full consecration*, is not a mere doctrine, nor yet a single isolated act, but the fabric, the very principle of life. Vague presentiments haunted us ; for, as we started, my beloved wife said, not without emotion, " We have weighed anchor ; we are out on the wide ocean : God knows where we shall land. But," she added, with happy calm, " ' He knoweth my wanderings ; my tears are in His book.' " [1] And when we saw the column of fire rise, there was no more hesitation. God had spoken, " Arise, depart, for this is not your rest " ; and our hearts had responded, " Lo, I am continually with Thee ; Thou hast holden me by my right hand ; Thou wilt guide me by Thy counsel, and afterward receive me to glory." [2]

[1] Ps. lvi. 8.   [2] Ps. lxxiii. 23, 24.

Nor were we alone. Among those whose watchful care followed and surrounded us, my two friends—true comrades—Major Malan and Mabille held the first place. They envied the post assigned me in the mission to which they had given themselves equally with myself. " But as his part is that goeth down to the battle, so is his part that tarrieth by the stuff." [1] And from that honourable position they unfalteringly upheld us.

I cannot lay too much stress upon the fact that this mission, springing spontaneously as it did from the religious life of our native Christians, could not, even in developing, lose all traces of its origin. The natives, indeed, were very determined about this, and mingled with this determination a certain presumption natural to adolescence. But, in spite of this, from the very first it began to take on an eclectic character, which it has ever since maintained. This was partly owing to the unlooked-for wanderings of the expedition, bringing its members in contact with various other agencies, both political and religious, which all helped it on. But it was due, in the first place and above all, to Major Malan. He it was who aroused for it the interest of Christians, both black and white, in almost every denomination throughout Cape Colony and Natal. He also founded an association in England to promote South African missions by native agency, and edited a magazine with the same object in view. He *believed* in the mission, and through all its phases his confidence in God was always the same. He pleaded with God for it in secret, and with men by word and pen ; while at every turn, at every check and disappointment, he was ready with letters of sympathy and encouragement, and substantial help from himself or his friends. His ardent faith and love, which recognised no barriers between the different members of the One Family, won many friends for our mission in England, and especially in Scotland, who have been its faithful supporters ever since. In a word, his devotion ceased only with his life ; and shortly before his death, already in the grip of the disease which he knew would soon arrest his earthly activities, he wrote

[1] I Sam. xxx. 24.

to me, " Don't speak about it, but I do believe God will after all grant me my heart's desire, and let me go and join you. ' Be thou faithful unto death, and *He* will give thee a crown of life.' "

What Major Malan was in Europe, Mabille was in Africa. By evil report and good report, when we were borne forward on the waves of popularity and enthusiasm, and when we had to battle against the current, the enterprise almost stranded, and ourselves abandoned, criticised, and condemned by every one, he never forsook us. He was one of those true and valiant men one can always count upon. In our worst moments, he always had tender, hopeful words for us. How many times, when we were almost overwhelmed, has God not made use of him to rekindle our courage! It was not that he merely *interested* himself in the mission ; it was *his own* just as much as it was ours. For him as much as for ourselves it was a work of faith, and he caused it to be known and loved everywhere through the magazine he edited, *La Petite Lumière du Lessouto*, which circulates so widely among the natives of South Africa.

When, in 1883, I preached my farewell sermon at his church, he said to me, as I was entering the pulpit, " Speak, and the Lord bless thee. And if the best of my catechists should respond to the appeal, remember I give him gladly." As we came out, he said, " Yes, God *has* asked for my best ; it is Levi. Ah well ! I did not expect it ; but—*he shall go*." And from that time forth the evangelists of the Zambesi Mission were recruited almost always from his Church or his Bible School at Morija. From first to last, he never failed us.

Our hearts were knit like those of David and Jonathan by an uninterrupted friendship of more than thirty years. We had absolutely no secrets from each other, except between our souls and God. First as students, and later on in the ministry, we shared everything—our plans, our difficulties, our struggles, our encouragements. What he was to me personally, what the evangelisation of Africa, above all of the Zambesi, owes to him, God only knows. Even on the threshold of eternity, he could not forget either the friend of his heart or the Mission of the Zambesi ; and his solicitude for both shone out amid the prayers and exhortations, the almost prophetic utterances, that glorified his death-bed. He was eagerly awaiting news of the last reinforcement he had sent us, and suddenly he exclaimed joyfully, " Arrived at last ; they have reached the Zambesi ! " And it was so. Doubtless the Lord had granted him that mysterious and unerring vision He so often bestows upon His dying saints. Then, in a fresh transport of triumphant faith, he cried in the native tongue, " *Ohó Coillard senatla sa Molimo ! motsualle da ka* " (" O Coillard—my own friend ! "). . . . " *Quoi-qu'on en dise, tu as de la foi. Courage !* " These were almost his last words.

Now these two men, full of the Holy Ghost, mighty in faith and works, have passed away. God has taken them. Eternity will reveal their part in the Barotsi Mission : my own is probably the least. They were " true till death." May I be like them ! May I, as they did, glorify God by my life and by my death, and like them know but the one motto, " *To live is Christ* " !

F. COILLARD.

THE CARAVAN IN THE MAKARI-KARI DESERT.

[*To face page* 1.

PART I

THE BANYAÏ EXPEDITION

1877—1879

WHEN Israel by Divine command
   The pathless desert trod,
They found throughout the barren land
   A sure resource in God.

A cloudy pillar marked the way
   And screened them from the heat,
From the hard rock the water flowed,
   And manna was their meat.

Like them, we have a rest in view,
   Secure from hostile powers ;
Like them, we tread a desert too ;
   But Israel's God is ours!

ITINERARY OF THE BANYAÏ EXPEDITION

	Leribé Mission Station	... Left April 16th, 1877.
Arrived April 24th, 1877 ...	Harrysmith	,, ?
,, May 6th	Heidelberg	,, May 11th
,, May 19th	Pretoria	,, May 30th
,, June 15th	Marabastadt	,, ?
,, June 22nd	Goedgedacht	,, June 28th
,, June 30th	Valdezia	,, July 11th
,, July 13th	Goedgedacht	,, July 17th
,, July 26th	Crossed Limpopo River ...	,, July 31st
,, Aug. 8th	Michael's Fountain	,, Aug. 10th or 11th
,, Aug. 11th	Crossed Bubye River ...	,, ?
,, Aug. 18th	Crossed Nguanetsi River ...	,, Aug. 21st
,, Aug. 22nd	{ Nyamonto's (in sight of Bohoa Mountain) }	,, ?
,, Aug. 28th	{ Crossed Zingwesi and Lundi Rivers }	,, ?
,, Aug. 31st	{ Masonda's Mountain (near Fort Victoria) }	,, Sept. 3rd
,, Sept. 4th	Nyanikoë	,, Sept. 17th
,, Dec. 15th	Bulawayo	,, ?
,, Jan. 19th, 1878 ...	Hope Fountain, Bulawayo	,, end of Feb. 1878
,, about March 10th ...	Inyati	,, March 31st
,, April 27th	Shoshong	,, June 14th
,, July 26th	Leshoma	,, Aug. 19th
,, about Aug. 28th ...	Sesheke	,, ?
,, Sept. 6th	Leshoma	,, ?
,, Nov. 1st	Sesheke	,, Nov. 6th
,, Nov. 7th	Leshoma	,, about Nov. 18th
,, ?	Deka	,, Dec. 2nd
,, Dec. 31st	Shoshong	,, Feb. 25th, 1879
,, March 3rd, 1879 ...	Seleka (Old)	,, ?
,, about March 6th ...	Blaauwberg, W. (Thateli's)	,, ?
,, ?	Goedgedacht	,, ?
,, March 29th	Valdezia	,, April 17th
,, about May 8th ...	Pretoria	,, May 19th
,, July 16th, 1879 ...	Leribé	
	Left Cape in the *Conway Castle*	Jan. 13th, 1880.

THE BANYAÏ EXPEDITION

A VERY few words are needed to enable English readers to follow the history of the Barotsi Mission. As the foregoing pages have shown, it was an offshoot of the Basuto Mission, now so well known. François Coillard had come out to Africa under its auspices in 1857. Three years later, he married Christina Mackintosh, with whom he had become acquainted before leaving Paris. She was the daughter of a Baptist minister in Edinburgh, the Rev. Lachlan Mackintosh.

After twenty years' labour, they were in the act of preparing for this first European furlough, when the news of M. Dieterlen's disaster arrived. " The Gospel entered Europe by a prison. Forward ! forward !" were M. Coillard's words to the Synod, on hearing of it ; and little as they expected the call themselves at such a moment, there could be no question of refusing it. They had offered themselves once for all.

The expedition left the Leribé station on April 16th, 1877, and returned to it about July 16th, 1879. Besides the four Basuto catechists, Azael, Aaron, Andreas, and Asser, with their wives and families, it included four men as drivers and leaders for the waggons—namely, Fono, Bushman, Eleazar, and Khosana. Of these, the last three were Christians, who volunteered out of love for the work, and not one of whom lived to return. The number was completed by M. and Mme. Coillard, and M. Coillard's niece, Elise, a girl of eighteen.

It had at first been planned that they should go round by Bechuana-land, avoiding the Transvaal ; but this proved unnecessary. Already the Boer authorities had offered to let M. Coillard pass through ; and when he arrived at Pretoria, he found they had been superseded by the British Government, whose representatives at Pretoria gave the mission party every encouragement. After crossing the Limpopo, the party turned to the

north-east, and plunged literally into a trackless wilderness.
They had only the compass to steer by, and had to cut their
way, as they went along, through forest and prairie grass.
This route was pretty nearly identical with that now connecting the Chartered Company's line of forts, and was beset
with every peril, from swollen rivers to wild beasts and wilder
men. Masonda, a treacherous Mashona chief, almost succeeded in destroying the whole caravan. A few weeks after
their escape from him, they were seized by an armed band,
and carried off to Bulawayo, to Lobengula, the Matabele king,
who accused them of having entered his territories without
permission and by a new route.

Lobengula kept them prisoners nearly four months, treating
them with personal kindness, but constantly putting off the
official reception in which he must finally grant or refuse them
permission to settle among the Banyaï. He would not believe
they had entered his realms from the Transvaal. Queen
Victoria, he understood, was now sovereign of the Transvaal,
and consequently his next neighbour. How was it, then, that
she had not charged them with a present for him?

"No doubt she would have done so," incautiously remarked
a European who was present, "if she had known of your
existence."

"What!" angrily muttered the king, "who could there be
who does not know ME and the extent of my kingdom?"
Lobengula seldom raised his voice, even in anger.

"Yes," interposed Mme. Coillard, "difficult as your Chief-
tainship must find it to believe such a thing, there *are* beings
on earth so wretched and benighted as never even to have
heard of YOU." And Lobengula did not pursue the subject.
Indeed, he seemed rather overawed generally at the tone adopted
by these captives, helpless though they were, in the hands of a
chief continually surrounded by executioners.

In the end, he absolutely refused permission for the missionaries to settle anywhere within his dominions, and sent
them out of his country. For, although they had not known
of it, and the Banyaï strenuously denied his authority, he
claimed suzerainty over the whole of Mashona-land—a claim
which a few years later was to cost him dear.

They next went to Khama's town. A few days before

leaving Bulawayo, however, they met some refugees from the north, speaking the Sekololo tongue, which is identical with Sesuto.   At once the thought presented itself, " Perhaps this is to be our field " ; and when they reached Shoshong, both Khama and his missionary, Mr. Hepburn, warmly took up the idea.   The chief himself was in frequent communication with the Barotsi king, Robosi (since known as Lewanika), who, like himself, had to be always on the defensive against the Matabele, and he volunteered to send ambassadors with or before the expedition, setting before Robosi the advantages of having missionaries, and urging him to receive them.   Accordingly, the Coillards set off with Azael, Asser, Khosana, and Eleazar, leaving the families with the other two evangelists under Khama's hospitable care.   Six months later, they returned to Shoshong.   They had succeeded in reaching Sesheke, on the left (north) bank of the Zambesi ; but the delays imposed by etiquette had prevented their obtaining an interview with the king before the rainy season, when the whole Barotsi Valley is under water for some months, and Lealuyi, the capital, is practically inaccessible.   However, he had granted them leave to return with the evangelists and establish a mission there. Within these six months, the three devoted servants, Khosana. Bushman, and Eleazar, had passed away.

The expedition now left Shoshong, and cut across country to the Swiss mission station of Valdezia, in the north of the Transvaal.   Here two of the catechists were left temporarily ; while Asser, the hero of the original Banyaï exploration, was placed with Aaron at Seleka, a small heathen village on the borders of Khama's territory.   On July 16th they found themselves once more in Basuto-land, and in the following January the Coillards started on their long-deferred visit to Europe.

C. W. M.

A LETTER FROM M. COILLARD TO HIS COMMITTEE IN PARIS
RESPECTING HIS PROPOSED MISSION TO THE BANYAÏ.

LERIBÉ, *January 23rd*, 1877.

GENTLEMEN AND DEAR BRETHREN,—The Secretary of our
Conference has doubtless already informed you of the pro-
position which my colleagues have made—namely, to confide
to us the projected expedition to the Limpopo. This news
will have surprised you all as much as it did ourselves.
The reasons which have led our brethren to address this call
to us, fully realising what it would mean to us, have been
submitted to you, and you have been able to judge of them.
If this appeal, no less pressing than unanimous, had been
made last year, when it was first talked about in the mission,
it would have found my wife and myself *quite ready*. But
coming just at the moment when we were thinking of starting
for Europe, at first it overwhelmed us. The overthrow of all
our plans, an indefinite farewell to our station at Leribé, the
responsibility of such an undertaking, the strange new prospects
which it opened up to us, and all so sudden and unexpected,
stunned and bewildered us. We both felt the need for being
alone before God, and for seeking His will together at His feet.
The darkness which had gathered so swiftly round our path
seemed very mysterious. But light broke little by little ; and
then we saw that our road had taken another direction. From
the moment we realised that the foundation of the Banyaï
Mission was in danger, and that nothing less was at stake than
its postponement to an indefinite date for want of a labourer,
we understood what the Master demanded of us, and we no
longer hesitated to obey. After ten days of communion with
Him, we were able joyfully to silence the "counsels of flesh
and blood," and to say to Him once more, " Here we are ; send
us." He has deigned to accept our sacrifice, and in token
thereof He has filled our hearts with perfect peace.

It is an honourable and a confidential mission with which
He is charging us, one of which any one else would have been
more worthy than ourselves. We are haunted by the painful
sense of our own incapacity and ignorance ; but what upholds
us is that God is often pleased to make use of the weak things

of this world to confound the wise, *that no flesh should glory in His presence.*

The question of health is an ever-present menace, and not a little disquieting; but we keep reminding each other that if the Master is calling us, "He knoweth our frame"; and also that we do not belong to ourselves, but to Him Who has loved us and given Himself for us. But we shall not be alone in those unknown regions. You will identify yourselves with our work; your prayers will uphold us. God will send His ministers before us to prepare the way; and besides, *the Angel of the Lord Himself will encamp round about us,* as He did about the prophet, with His legions of angels, *and will deliver us.* That is our confidence, our strength, and our joy.

We are quite taken up now with our preparations for departure. I intend (D.V.) to ride over next week to Natal, to arrange about our waggons and purchases myself. My dear wife will stay here to prepare supplies of food and clothing, and set everything to rights, with her usual activity. Thus, on my return, we shall have nothing more to do, except to settle some details as to the catechists and the expedition in general. We hope to start in April at latest. Then, and till then, we shall have a time of fatigue and emotion. I dread the farewells. But the Lord will uphold us to the end. *He will be our strength.*

As to our itinerary, it is not yet settled. Availing ourselves of some indirect overtures from President Burgers, we have once more applied to the Transvaal authorities for a passport We have as yet received no answer. And, also, we are anxious to know what will be the result of the mission undertaken by Sir Theophilus Shepstone at the request of the British Government, both as to the Transvaal and as to Sekoukouni.[1] Up to the present, the news is anything but reassuring. The newspapers of these parts talk of irruptions made into the territory of the Republic by Cetewayo's savage hordes. Strange rumours, to which we cannot attach much credence, circulate among the natives. In case of that road being barred to us, I should not consider it a misfortune if we were obliged to go by way of Mangwato, and even to go as far as Inyati in Matabele-land. But there, too, the Lord will guide us.

[1] Or Seccocoeni, a rebel chief whom the Boers had in vain been striving to subdue. See "The Life of Sir Bartle Frere."

CHAPTER I

HEIDELBERG, *May 6th*, 1877.

YES, we are off to Banyaï-land, the Zambesi regions, the interior of Africa! It is almost a dream! These last three months have been so full of work, of preparations, preoccupations, and emotions of every kind, that it almost makes me giddy to think of it all; and I cannot help repeating with David, " It is God that girdeth me with strength, and maketh my way perfect" (Fr. Ver., *smooths my way*).

First of all, I had to go to Natal to purchase our waggons and provisions. I found our expedition excited the most lively interest everywhere. I arrived in Durban on a Wednesday evening, and immediately betook myself to the church, where, according to the custom of the country, a meeting was going on. I entered noiselessly, and sat down by the door. The pastor, Mr. Mann, who had caught sight of me at the close of his address, calling to me, bade me welcome in the name of the Church, invoked the blessing of God upon our enterprise, and begged me to close the meeting. On the following Sunday, in spite of rainy weather, the church was full, and I preached on these words : " And other sheep I have, which are not of this fold : them also must I bring."

At Pietermaritzburg, I also had several opportunities of pleading the cause of missions. Thanks to the general interest, of which my friend the Rev. J. Smith had set the example, I was able to procure waggons on extraordinarily moderate

8

terms, and yet as complete and comfortable as they could possibly be. In passing through Harrysmith, that little town in the Free State where ten years before we had been led as prisoners,[1] I found there was the same interest, so much so that on my return I was able to add nearly £70 to the Mission Fund, without ever having thought of making a collection.

One evening, I arrived at a farm ; the owner and his family, English people, were earnest Christians. They thought I was on my way to Europe ; but when I told them how the Master had suddenly changed my route, and was sending me into unknown parts, the old lady of the house, clasping her hands, exclaimed with all a mother's emotion, " Blessed servants of God ! carry the ark of the Lord ! go forward ! fear not ! And we, if we are not strong enough to go with you, shall at any rate follow you in thought ; we will shout with the sound of trumpets and timbrels " (2 Sam. vi.). Then, once more taking up this enthusiastic strain, she added, " My prayer is, that before you leave Leribé God may grant you a mighty revival. Then we will come and rejoice with you ; and while you and your dear lady are taken up with speaking to the awakened souls, I, who do not understand the language, will be preparing your food, and I too will have my share of blessing."

Directly after my return to Leribé, I had to ride off again to Morija, where special devotional meetings had brought most of our brethren together. We considered the choice of evangelists, for a new appeal had stirred up several new volunteers. Out of the four who took part in the first expedition, one was left to be employed in Basuto-land, because of an accident which has almost entirely deprived him of the use of his right arm. This was Onesimus, and great was his grief when he learned our decision. In his place they chose Aaron Mayoro, of Leribé, a young married man, the father of two children, and full of manly zeal. He has given proofs of his perseverance and self-abnegation in occupying the ungrateful post of Bouta-Bouté.[2] His wife, who is worthy of himself, was brought up in our house.

Next, I had to give my attention to the work of the district

---

[1] By the Boers. See Introduction.

[2] A very dreary village—the native place of Moshesh, the supreme chief, occupied since his death by one of his grandsons. An out-station confided to a catechist.

I was about to leave. I had recently sent some young men to occupy different posts as schoolmasters ; and now it was necessary to go and install them officially. One of them, Philemon, is a young man I should like you to know. A Mopeli by birth, he had fled from his father's house while still a child, in order to go to the white men, and earn enough to buy a gun. Although he lived with a pastor, his hatred for the things of God knew no bounds. On the journey back to his native country, he stayed some time among us with a troop of his fellow-countrymen. The truth made a deep impression on some of them, and farther on their way, they informed him of their determination to come back to Leribé and learn. He broke into a violent rage, and so far forgot himself as to spit in their faces. A fortnight later he followed them ; and standing at our door quite broken down, and even shedding tears, asked to be admitted among our pupils. His was one of those striking conversions which leave no room for doubt ; and he won the place of a son in our hearts as well as in our house. We prepared him for the school of Morija : he has just left it with his diploma. His gift for teaching is remarkable. In three months, in a place where he had scarcely four or five pupils, he has got together more than forty-five, all the children of heathen ; and what he has taught them in this short space of time astonishes us. His manners, frank and simple, but respectful, have won the esteem of all the neighbouring petty chiefs.

The dedication of the church of Tsikoane attracted a great crowd of people. There were some there whose presence added much to the solemnity of the occasion for me ; these were the evangelists from Morija, who were to accompany us to the Banyaï. They arrived at Leribé the next day ; and then, in the midst of meetings and private interviews with the members of my flock, we had to put the finishing touches to our preparations for departure, pack the cases, and load the waggons.

By the Saturday, everything was finished. Our friends Jousse and Mabille, and their companions, our brothers Duvoisin, Casalis, Preen, Dieterlen, and Christmann, and some Christians from other Churches, arrived. Those whom their age or other circumstances prevented from coming wrote us encouraging and affectionate letters. The presence of our dear Basuto-land brethren and their fervent prayers powerfully upheld us. It seemed like the angel whom the Lord sent to the prophet in the desert with food and the message, "Arise and eat, because the journey is too great for thee."

I ascended the pulpit for the last time. A ministry of nearly twenty years unrolled itself before me, with all its blessings, its few successes, but also its recollections of unfaithfulnesses and miserable mistakes, now, alas! beyond repair—a ministry the fearful responsibility of which I had never so fully realised before. We bade good-bye to each member of our dear flock. For us, the Lord's promise has not been empty. If we have left mothers, brothers, sisters, we have found them again in this life : it was from them and from beloved children in the faith that we were parting. We were leaving another fatherland, another France.

Besides the collection made in the church, our poor people came again on the Monday, bringing us their little presents with many tears. One of the most aged women of our flock came, just as we were getting into the waggons, and offered us a mat she had long been working at. " I wanted to spread it under your feet, servants of God," she said, bursting into tears. The sun was already close to the horizon ; we felt it was impossible to bear the emotional strain any longer. The brothers and sisters who had stayed with us to the last moment assembled in our parlour, and commended us once more to God and to the word of His grace ; and after a few private moments with my beloved wife in this house, which had witnessed so many struggles and benedictions, one last look at the garden that adorns this retreat, we entered the waggons and gave the signal to start. Dear Leribé, at once our Bethel and our Ebenezer, farewell, farewell ! Farewell, children of God, whose tender affection has given us citizenship among you, and made us forget the house of our fathers ! May our successors be as happy there as we have been, and still more blessed ! Did we make the mistake of looking on Leribé as our earthly home, and the work we pursued here as our *own* ? The Lord has dispelled that illusion ; but yet we cling to its very stones, watered by our tears and the sweat of our brows.

Most of the people persisted in following our waggons. I rode to bid good-bye to the poor chief Molapo, who was ill, exhorted him for one last time, and prayed with him. I had

just separated from M. Jousse. God only knows what I owe
him. Now I had to part from Mabille, the friend of my heart,
the witness of my conflicts and my weakness. We felt shaken
to the very foundations. But Jesus was there ; no separation
from *Him.* " I am with you alway, even to the end of the world."

The magistrate, the traders, and some Europeans of the
district also wished to give us a token of the interest they took
in our distant expedition, and sent us, together with a purse
of ten guineas, a letter, in which they were pleased to acknowledge our labours, and to express the warmest wishes for the
success of our enterprise and regret for our departure.

The next day, many of our people came to our camp to
renew the painful scenes of the previous day. Men on foot
and on horseback accompanied us for several days' journey. It
was at Harrysmith that we parted from the last, and among
them Nathanael Makotoko, to whom I am closely bound by
a friendship of more than twenty years, and whom only the
most urgent duties prevented from going with us. The many
kindnesses we received at Harrysmith did not succeed in
softening the bitterness of this last drop.

The caravan is composed of three waggons and three tents.
The expedition includes the four evangelists Asser, Azael,
Andreas, and Aaron, with their wives and some of their children.
Besides these, we have three young men from Leribé who have
volunteered to lead the teams and graze the cattle. Eleazar,
the driver [1] of our waggon, is the son of Luka Ntsaba, who, in
1833, guided the first missionaries to Basuto-land. He is one
of the evangelists from Morija. He was burning with the desire
to go the Banyaï in that capacity, but his wife would not hear
of it ; and it was thereupon that, with her consent, he offered
himself to drive our waggon. His is a merry, playful tempera-
ment, and he possesses in a very unusual degree the gift of
speaking well. Four Bapeli have joined us for the sake of
returning to their own country, and they try to make themselves useful, one of them especially, who has long lived in our
house, and has never ventured to declare himself converted,
although I believe him to be a true child of God. Finally,
a niece of mine accompanies us ; a strange concatenation of

---

[1] In Africa, the *driver* of an ox-team wields the long whip; the *leader*
goes before the team to show the way.

circumstances has brought her to us, and I hope she will be a blessing to us and to others.

Our rule is to start before daybreak, and to travel late into the night, resting for a few hours during the heat of the day to take a meal and graze the oxen, for whom we have to sacrifice our comforts, our habits, and our tastes. Besides family worship morning and evening, at our chief halts we have prayer meetings and regular services. The watchword which seems to have been given us from the beginning of our journey, and which constantly recurs in our conversations and our exhortations, is, " Let this mind be in you, which was also in Christ Jesus " (Phil. ii. 5). Needless to say, the most perfect harmony reigns amongst us. We cherish no illusions as to the difficulties, privations, fatigues, and perils that await us ; but for that very reason we feel all the more the necessity for strengthening ourselves in the Lord. We know we are followed by the prayers of God's children, and that the angel of the Lord encamps round about us and delivers us.

GOEDGEDACHT, July 17th, 1877.

It was from Heidelberg that I wrote last. An epidemic had broken out among our teams and carried off several oxen. After a week's rest, we were able to go on, and we arrived at Pretoria about May 19th. We halted for a moment before entering the town, just to compose ourselves, and look round upon the panorama before us. A beautiful valley, encircled by hills ; clumps of trees, through which we could descry a confused mass of white houses,—this was Pretoria, Dieterlen's prison, the great wall set up against the Gospel. But God has broken through the gates of that prison ; and when He opens, no man can shut.

We outspanned to the sound of cannon ; flags were flying everywhere ; the streets were filled with excited people, and the air with martial music. The town was holding festival. Sir Theophilus Shepstone and the members of his government were going to take the oath of allegiance to the Queen. The coincidence of our arrival with this circumstance seemed to us very remarkable. We set up our camp close to the prison, which was surrounded by the tents of the English ; and it was under the shadow of those very walls that on the Sunday evening we took the Communion together, our hearts overflowing with gratitude. " There is our prison," said one of the catechists to me ; " we must show you our cells." One time, when Asser was passing close by it with one of his companions, he took it into his head to knock at the door. " What do you want ? " asked the jailer roughly. " We should like to see the cells once more where they put us last year." " Get out with you, Kaffirs." This time the door was shut tight enough !

We went to pay our respects to Sir Theophilus Shepstone, whom we had seen a great deal of in Natal. He seemed pleased to see us again, and showed the greatest interest in our enter-prise, as did the gentlemen attending him. He gave us all the information and all the advice he could, and asked us to write to him as often and as regularly as possible. He pressed us very much to stay in Pretoria till the 24th, the Queen's birth-day, so that our catechists, to whom he came and spoke very kindly, might, as he said, realise that they had nothing more to dread from the prisons of Pretoria, but had rather to confide in a government which was friendly to missions and the protector of the blacks. The Baron de Salis-Fanson, the Belgian consul, also interested himself in our expedition.

Our stay in the capital could not fail to make a sensation. The employés of different grades under the late Government behaved very apologetically to us. One of them especially, now a servant of the new Government (in what capacity I know not), pressed me strongly to visit him at his house, " for he very much wanted to have a long conversation with me, not to make any *excuses*," he added, pulling himself up to assert his dignity, " but to give us some *explanations*." But as I did not want any explanations from him, I politely referred him to public opinion, to his conscience and his God. If I had one regret, it was that Dieterlen himself was not there to see with his own eyes the change that has taken place. Every one we met thought it the correct thing to talk indignantly about Burgers and his govern-ment, and the way they had treated first Dieterlen, and then our Swiss brethren, Creux and Berthoud.[1] It is a token of sympathy, which costs very little under existing circumstances ; one must just take it for what it is worth. We enjoyed the society of the German missionary and his wife, Mr. and Mrs. Grüneberger,

[1] See note on page 17.

and of Mr. and Mrs. Bosman. The latter friend, a young Dutch pastor, who, like most of his fellow-students, does credit to the South African School of Theology at Stellenbosch, has only been a few months established at Pretoria. He has the true " sacred fire," and assuredly his labour will not be in vain in the Lord. In view of the prejudices of his congregation, he would not have dared to offer his pulpit to a missionary ; but he had the courage to transform his Sunday school into a missionary meeting for us, and, as he had announced it at the morning service, a large number of adults assembled and seemed interested. I love the Dutch Church of the Cape, the asylum of the old French refugees ; and wherever I can meet with it, I love to report the Christian and missionary spirit that still dwells in its bosom. The wars and antagonisms of races, their continually conflicting interests, have stifled, but they have not quite extinguished it. May God cause His Spirit to blow over this Church and her pastors !

We were impatient to be off again, and on a Wednesday evening at sunset we inspanned. Some soldiers ran up to bid us good-bye, and wish us a pleasant journey : we had been neighbours for ten days, and had made acquaintance with several of them. " Sir," one of them said to me, " the behaviour of your people has been a wonder to us ; it has done us real good. We have never seen such honest natives, nor any that were so polite and religious. We often used to listen to their singing, and many a time we would have come to your services, if we had dared."

It was icy cold, and as we passed along the streets we could espy through the windows families sitting at their tea, or round sparkling fires. We could not see a step before us ; in fact, we lost our way. And how our thoughts did go back to our home at Leribé !—not regretfully though. We were only too happy to be going forward.

We were now crossing a wooded country ; the road was good, and so was the spirit animating all our people. They sang hymns, they hunted or pretended to hunt, and all along the road we kept meeting obliging people. We were the objects of special kindness in what they call the Bush Veldt—a district to which a great many Boers had betaken themselves in patriarchal style, with their families and flocks, for the winter. Here, where there is no telegraph, news flies at a surprising rate. Everybody knew about us, and the purpose of our journey, and all expressed good wishes for us. It was curious to see these forest camps. Often we would halt for the night, believing ourselves to be quite alone, and then suddenly in the middle of the night or very early in the morning we would hear the sound of psalm-singing. It was the farmers' families at prayer. These psalmodies, awaking sweet childish memories, and making me think of the " assemblies of the Desert," [1] thrilled strangely through us in the midst of these forest solitudes and the silence of the night. All the farmers behaved most kindly and obligingly to us ; they gave us milk, eggs, and meat, nearly always refusing to accept payment. Indeed, the Lord's goodness and mercy accompanied us like two angel escorts ; and when we came in sight of Mr. Hofmeyr's station at the foot of the beautiful Zoutpansberg Range, beyond which no messenger of Christ has yet carried the Gospel, we fell on our knees and gave thanks to God.

Our brother the Dutch missionary, Hofmeyr, was absent, and did not return till some days after our arrival, which, however, did not prevent his people from receiving us with touching affection. On his return, he lent us two teams ; and leaving our luggage and one of the waggons at Goedgedacht, we left for Valdezia. The journey occupied three days.

It would be impossible to describe the delights of finding ourselves once more with our dear friends Creux and Berthoud, the pioneers of the Mission de la Suisse Romande (as the Mission Vaudoise is now called). The meeting of our catechists with their brethren at Valdezia was a sight worth seeing. Here, it was like being in Basuto-land ; the hamlet which the evangelists occupy at the station even bears its name. Every one talks Sesuto ; they sing our hymns, and among these beautiful mountains the illusion is complete. Our arrival was quickly noised abroad, and the same evening some young men converts and a great many heathen came together to bid us welcome. We spent ten days with our brethren—days too quickly passed. One little excursion we made with M. Creux to visit Mr. Schwellnus, a German missionary. Our Swiss

[1] Assemblies of Protestants during the revolutionary period at the end of last century and beginning of this, in the district of France known as the Desert, around Nîmes and the Cevennes.

THE CAMP, NEAR HARRYSMITH.

[*To face page* 17.

friends have fraternised with the representatives of the Berlin Society, and they share the mission field with each other in a friendly spirit. Travelling through this country, I have been struck with the influence of our Basuto Mission, its language and literature, among these tribes, and in the Transvaal. Our three waggons might have been loaded with books, and we could easily have sold them all. Everywhere we were beset with demands for books, especially New Testaments. Our friends had put off a festival for our arrival. A modest and primitive church was completed for the occasion; the bell rang for the first time to call both faithful and unbelievers together; and six young men, pagans not long ago, publicly confessed the Saviour's Name, and received the seal of baptism. Generally in South Africa women are more easily attracted to the Gospel than men; servitude has prepared them for it. Here, it is principally among the young men that it is working, young fathers of families; and this is the true future for the Church. Asser in his address made a touching allusion to the time when, all alone with Eliakim, he first broke ground in this garden of the Lord. In the evening, we took the Communion together. Valdezia is the Elim of our journey. We parted from our friends, feeling rested, refreshed, and encouraged. I say nothing of their kindnesses to us; and for a very good reason—I should not know where to begin. They placed everything at our disposal, even the provisions they have such difficulty in procuring for themselves. They had not even waited for our arrival before buying some cattle for us, and picking the best out of their own teams to exchange them for our sick or worn-out oxen. The Lord had used their captivity at Marabastadt[1] to make them even more popular than they were before. Berthoud is a doctor, and his success in this branch has won him as much consideration and influence among the whites as among the blacks. Creux is above all an evangelist, and his thorough knowledge of English opens many doors to him. He preaches in this language to the farmers, visits them, and keeps an especial look-out on the spirits, which are the curse of the country. And, indeed, people hereabouts stand considerably in awe of him.

---

[1] They were taken from their station and brought there by the Boers, who objected to their missionary work. The same Government which had arrested M. Dieterlen kept them prisoners for several weeks.

Goedgedacht is a mission entirely sustained by the children of the Dutch Church at the Cape. It is here that MacKidd died, a Scotchman, and a true servant of God, whose name the natives never pronounce even now without the most profound reverence. At present, Mr. Hofmeyr is at the head of the work.[1] He is an Afrikander, a man mighty both in faith and works, his heart burning with love and enthusiasm in his Master's service. His spirit has communicated itself to his people, and for them this expedition is the answer to ardent prayers. He had always been on fire to see the Banyaï evangelised, and he would have started himself, if some one could have taken his place. He has all the affection and admiration of the pious Cape Dutch for our mission (the S.M.E.P.).[2] So you may think what a reception they gave us when we came back. They loaded our waggons with flour, maize, and sweet potatoes, not forgetting fowls, pigs, pigeons, cats, and I don't know what not! Our people said, " Look, master, how our waggons are growing ! " As for me, I thought of Noah's Ark.

It was a solemn Sunday, the last we spent with our friends. From the pulpit went forth pressing appeals to consecration and devotedness, which we took home to ourselves. In a special Church meeting, our friend said to his flock, " Who is going to the Banyaï with our brothers from France and Basuto-land ? Let each one examine himself." The next day at dawn, he came to me and said, " Dear brother, the Lord is asking my right hand for you ; but it is all right ; you shall have him." At midday two other men, the pillars of the Church, presented themselves. " The Lord is taking my best men," he said, " but they are His." On the eve of our departure, there was a fare-well meeting in the evening, which went on far into the night, and brought back to us all the sorrowful scenes of Basuto-land. One could feel the beating of hearts full of faith and devotion. " We are going to the wars," said those who were going with us, " like the Israelites against the Amalekites. You stay here, hold up the hands of God's servant, and pray for us." " My beloved brother," said Mr. Hofmeyr, quite overcome by his feelings, " here are three of our children, whom we are commit-

[1] Son-in-law of the Rev. F. and Mrs. Neethling, and nephew of Mr. Andrew Murray.

[2] La Société des Missions Evangéliques de Paris.

ting to you, to go with you and carry the Gospel to the Banyaï, for whom we have prayed so much. It costs us much to part with them, because of the position they occupied among us. But the Lord is calling them ; and if I have any regret, it is that my sons John, Henry, and Christopher are too young to go too." Then turning towards these three men, who were standing up in the midst of the assembly, " Remember," he said, " that the fertiliser which makes the seed of the Gospel grow is the flesh and bones of Jesus Christ's disciples."

But I do not feel capable of telling you any more about it. This is not the moment to be trembling and giving way to emotion. It is the moment for us to draw near to God, to gird ourselves with strength and courage, and go joyfully forward. We are taking the desert way, which we do not know anything about. The Creux have accompanied us thus far. It is like the gangway that still joins us to the shore ; once raised, we shall be cut asunder from all our friends, and deprived, no doubt for a long, long time, of all intercourse with them and the civilised world. But the Lord is our light and salvation. Of whom should we be afraid ?

CHAPTER II

On the Banks of the Limpopo—Palm Tree Fountain—Crossing the Crocodile River—Lions—Arrival in Banyaï-land—The Chief Nyamonto—Adventures at Masonda's Mountain—Cattle carried off—A Great Deliverance—Messengers sent from Maliankombé at Nyanikoë to Lobengula.

ON THE BANKS OF THE LIMPOPO, *July 27th*, 1877.

YESTERDAY we crossed the Limpopo, only a few days after leaving Mr. Hofmeyr's station ; but they were days that certainly counted for something. We had slept at a little distance from the river, near a beautiful fountain with no name, where, for the first time, we found palm trees laden with fruit. We have given it the name of Palm Tree Fountain ; it recalled to us the Elim of the Israelites. We would willingly have stayed beside it for some days, for we were very tired. During the last two or three days, we had been obliged to cut our way with axes. But knowing that the Limpopo was so near, we struck our camp. We reached the river about eleven o'clock, and outspanned on the north bank, when the last rays of the sun were disappearing on the horizon. We had great difficulty in crossing this river, because it flows over a bed of deep sand ; and, once over, we were so exhausted with fatigue, that all we could do, after penning the donkeys and tethering the cattle, was to give thanks to God. Then we perceived that three sick oxen had been left on the other side of the stream. Who would go to fetch them ? The moon rose late. The crocodiles have such a reputation in these quarters, that not for worlds would one of our people have risked making a night excursion across the reed thickets that fringe the river, nor would we have dared to take it on ourselves to send them. We laid the matter before the Lord in all confidence. Lions and hyænas roared and howled in various directions ; nevertheless, next morning

we found the three oxen walking about in the forest. To-day
is Thursday, and we are going to rest till next Monday. We
have killed an ox, a present from Mr. Hofmeyr, so that we shall
not want for occupation in cutting it up and drying it. Every
one in the camp is happy. We bathe in the river and admire
the baobabs, which form a perfect forest hereabouts. The lions
have often sent us their salutations, but have never yet honoured
us with their visits. Our waggons are beginning to look very.
deplorable ; their canvas covers are all so torn, that it seems
as though we should soon have to sleep *al fresco*. Passing the
bushes and thorn trees of these parts is no joke.

August 9th.

You will notice on Baines's map a group of hills through
which the Bubye River flows ; we are at the angle of those to
the south-west of this river. Till now we have followed the
waggon tracks of an elephant hunter, Mr. Foster. Now we
must leave these tracks, for they would lead us too far from our
route. We shall have to cut our way through the woods, guided
by the compass. When we reach the Bohoa Mountain (Baines's
Wochua), we shall not be far from the first Banyaï villages. We
hope to find a Makalaka chief on our way named Mathipa, at
whose place we shall be able to renew our stock of native
provisions, which is sensibly diminishing.

The country we are traversing is very dry, but God has so
guided us till now that neither we nor our cattle have suffered
from thirst. My wife always has a provision of cold tea in
bottles, so that from time to time she can give a draught to
a thirsty axeman, or a team driver hoarse with shouting. We
got no sleep last night : we had scarcely outspanned, and had
not had time to pen our beasts, when a lion came out of the
thicket and fell upon one of our dogs. As he only succeeded
in leaving the traces of his claws upon the poor creature, he
prowled round the camp all night, defying the gleam of our
fires and the firing of our guns. He was not alone : the laughter
of the hyænas mingled with his roaring ; anything but a soothing
serenade for us.

All is peace and goodwill among us. The serpent of ill-
humour has not yet come in to poison our intercourse with one
another.

NYANIKOË, BANYAÏ-LAND, *September 17th*, 1877.

We have been, thank God ! nearly a fortnight in the Banyaï
country, which is locally known as Bombé, and have pitched our
tents near the residence of the chief Maliankombé.   We crossed
the Bubye at its junction with the Mokokoë, a river whose bed
is fairly wide, but just then it was dried up.   Our journey had
become extremely laborious and fatiguing.   When we had with
great difficulty forced our way through a scrub, covered with tall
grass and brushwood, we found ourselves in an immense forest,
so thick that we could only advance very slowly, valiantly though
we hacked out a road for ourselves with our axes.   We were
nearly two days without finding water, but a cloudy sky veiled
the full ardour of the sun's rays from us; and when the last drop
in our barrels was exhausted, we came unexpectedly upon a pool.

The point we aimed at was the Bohoa Mountain.   I shall
never forget the view that met our eyes on the day when, in
order to discover it, we climbed the first hills we came to.   From
the bosom of this immense forest, in which we had been
burrowing like moles, wooded slopes rose billowing before us,
and mountains of bare rock, to which trees were nevertheless
clinging and struggling for existence.   Always keeping to the
northward, we at last reached the Nguanetsi at the confluence
of its two streams, and then wandered about for two days before
we could find a fordable spot among the enormous rocks that
encumber the bed of this river.   And then it was only by filling
up the interstices of these blocks with stones and trunks of trees,
and covering a very slippery boulder with sand, that we were
able to get our waggons across.   It was near there that we met
our first Monyaï, a man of middle age.   At the sight of us, he
fled ; but seeing we were upon his heels, he sat down and
saluted us, trying to smile, but still gripping his bow and arrows.
Friendly words and a piece of meat reassured him.   He gave
us some information, and showed us, quite close by, a trap for
wild beasts, a deep pit with sharp stakes at the bottom, and
lightly covered with grass.   We shuddered at the thought of the
frightful accident that might have happened to us, if God had not
caused us to meet this native.   The next morning, the flour sack
was shaken out for our people's breakfast.   But He who sent
ravens to the brook Cherith to feed His prophet there could not
forget us.   That very day, in this forest, which has hitherto been

so solitary, we caught sight of black figures hiding behind trees,
who cast furtive glances at us, and disappeared like shadows.
Others, growing bolder, approached us little by little, and before
evening they brought us flour, peas, groundnuts, rice, etc. The
Lord had sent us abundance. From this moment, our waggons
were besieged by natives from far and near, who escorted us day by
day, and bivouacked beside us at night, to satisfy their curiosity.
The news of our coming had spread, it seems, with lightning
speed through the forests and mountains, and the strangest
tales were told about our heavy white machines, our waggons.

Between the Nguanetsi and the Bohoa Mountain, we arrived
close to the village of a petty chief named Nyamonto. Like all
the inhabitants of this region, he lives on a steep hill, strewn with
an avalanche of rocks ; it is on these heights that one spies the
huts of the villages, perched there like eagles' eyries. Our arrival
was greeted from afar by the shouts of the whole population.
After exchanging a few messages with this chief, I climbed his
mountain, accompanied by Asser. Never could I have believed
that human beings could inhabit such a spot ! To me, it seemed
too dangerous even for baboons. But the terror with which the
Matabele inspire these poor people is such that they never feel safe
except in these inaccessible places. Agreeably to the etiquette
of the country, I offered a piece of stuff as a present to the old
chief, who seemed to be in a bad temper. "That is all very well
for a child," he said ; "it is unworthy of Nyamonto"; and he
left us abruptly to confer with his council. Then sending for
me, he offered me with much ceremony a small elephant's
tusk. "The eyes of Nyamonto," he said to me, "have seen the
man of God, but thou hast not seen Nyamonto." "Of course
not," I replied, "since Nyamonto has not visited me yet at my
waggon."

Upon that, the chief, calling his men, took his bow and arrows,
and gave the signal for departure. He descended, sliding and
leaping over the rocks in a way that made me giddy. I paid
my respects to him with a cotton blanket, and his face lighted up.
"Now," he said, "thine eyes have seen Nyamonto." Then he
proceeded to inspect our vehicles, our beasts, etc., to the accompaniment of clappings and cries of astonishment, very amusing
to hear. My knowledge of Zulu was a great help to me on this
and subsequent occasions. My interpreter, who was also the

chief's right-hand man, had worked in the diamond fields, and had brought back some very undesirable notions therefrom. He absolutely refused to convey to his chief what I said about the benefits of the Gospel. " If God loves us, why do the Matabele destroy us ? We want nothing of that sort here ; we will have none of it," said he, with a significant gesture.

A little farther on, we met six or seven men, sent by a chief named Masonda, who called himself the son of Maliankombé, and strongly urged us to go to his place, adding that it was our best road and our shortest. We had no reason to doubt his veracity or refuse his invitation ; so we followed our new guides, gladly resigning to them the hatchets which had grown so heavy in our hands. We crossed the Singezi, and then the Lundi, a little way above their junction. But the difficulties presented by these rivers, where the waggon wheels sank up to their naves, and thirty oxen could scarcely stir them, can only be understood by those who have travelled in similar countries. While ascending the steep bank, just at the very moment we thought ourselves out of our troubles, the *trek-tow* (the chain to which the oxen are attached) broke, four times over ; and four times the waggon rolled violently back into the river. We closed our eyes in terror, but it was neither upset nor broken.

Arrived at Masonda's, we outspanned under the shade of a gigantic tree in a lovely glade. We could have fancied ourselves in some magnificent park. Above the labyrinthine valleys rose tier upon tier of heights, colossal piles of granite boulders interspersed with tropical vegetation. It was on one of these apparently inaccessible summits that our new friend had fixed his residence. He received us with abundant protestations of joy and friendship. "You are weary ; you come from afar," he said : " here is a kid " (it was really a bullock) ; " eat and rest." I returned the compliment by sending him a fine woollen blanket, which he seemed to appreciate.

The next day at his request we went to visit this chief, Masonda, accompanied by our ladies. The ascent proved steep, almost impracticable, and under the burning sun we felt utterly exhausted. We duly announced ourselves, and the petty potentate kept us dancing attendance out on the rocks in the noontide blaze so long that at last I protested. They then led us into a cave, formed by a chaos of heaped-up rocks. A crowd

[*To face page* 25.]

ON THE LIMPOPO (CROCODILE) RIVER.

gathered round the entrance, and increased to such an extent that it aroused the suspicions of our evangelists. "We are blocked in," one of them whispered in my ear. "Blocked in? Let us get out then!" And the Banyaï fell back to let us pass. Thereupon a brother of Masonda came up, who said he was commissioned to do us the honours of the capital. This personage, who had the most unbounded sense of his own importance, was filthy, scowling, blind in one eye, and deeply pitted with small-pox—the very personification of a demon! He seized Mme. Coillard by one arm, whilst another took her by the other, under pretext of helping her to climb a steep, slippery rock ; and two more of equally forbidding aspect led off my niece. I followed just behind them, full of vague uneasiness. We were slowly and painfully toiling up, when one of the evangelists, unable to contain himself any longer, said to me in terror-struck tones, "Where are they leading our mother?"

I started, as if out of a trance. In front of us rose the sharp peak ; right and left, no sign of a habitation ; beyond, nothing —an abyss! In less time than it takes to tell, I had sprung forward, seized my wife, and snatched her from the hands of the savages. Aaron did the same for my niece, and we promptly redescended. The Banyaï offered us no opposition, and without further parley we regained the camp. A messenger followed close upon our footsteps to tell us how annoyed Masonda was at our hasty departure. "I have not seen you," he added, "but I have something in my heart, and I will come myself."

This he did ; and his easy manners, and his countenance sparkling with intelligence, made a good impression upon us ; while in the minute and studied etiquette with which he approached us, there was something quite novel, and very interesting to us. In the evening, we had a meeting for praise. "O God," said one, "how good, how faithful, Thou art! Thou hast led us through the desert ; Thou hast fed us and quenched our thirst ; Thou hast made us pass over great rivers ; and now Thou hast brought us to the Banyaï land. We are in good health, our axes are keen, our waggons light, and our oxen have grown fat under the yoke. Thy benefits are very many : who can count them?" Our hearts responded "Amen."

The following day, which was Sunday, messengers came from Masonda to ask for gunpowder. This was what he "had in his heart." " Masonda does not like the blanket ; he wants a canister of powder and a box of caps." I explained to them that I was not a trader, but a messenger of peace, and that I had nothing to do with selling powder ; but it was so much breath wasted and they went away discontented. Not a soul came near us that day. In the evening, Masonda arrived with some men, reiterating his demands more or less imperiously. Then I perceived we had fallen into a trap. To prove my amicable intentions, I offered the chief another present. He refused it with disdain and sat down sulkily near our fire. After we had retired into our tent to have tea, one of our people came and said in a low voice, " We are surrounded, and the natives are still coming down from the mountain." We immediately turned towards Masonda, who was devouring a piece of meat we had given him, and in friendly tones tried to persuade him to go away. Although the night was very dark, we were able to discern the black line our man had spoken of. The chief beset us with demands of all sorts, but would not go away. He wanted a dog, then he required two, then he wished to choose one himself, and so forth. At last he took a sudden resolution and departed. " I shall come back to-morrow," he said with emphasis.

The next morning at sunrise, our waggons began to move, for we felt we dared not delay. It proved the signal for a great tumult on the neighbouring hills. Troops of men rushed towards us, uttering fierce cries, and armed to the teeth with assegaïs, hatchets, bows and arrows, and sharp knives, which they carry in a sheath on the left arm. Some few even had antiquated firearms, and these were by far the least formidable ! Having arranged the waggons side by side, and made the women and children go inside, I went up to the chief, who was trembling with rage. " Powder ! caps ! a gun !" he shouted. At last I made him accept an ox in place of the one he had given us ; he must needs choose it for himself, and it was only the fifth we took from the yoke that would satisfy him. After that, I made the waggons go on, dividing the crowd. " May Masonda sleep sound and in peace !" cried some of our people, who were now hoping to be delivered from the claws of the lion. I could not say as much myself. A crowd of armed men continued to press round our waggon in a way that was anything but reassuring. We were advancing with difficulty, when, all at once, my waggon sank in the muddy stream, and all our efforts to drag it out were unavailing. I let the other waggons pass over the spur of a hill and outspan at a stone's throw (for we had started so early the oxen had not had time to graze, and were weak for want of food) ; and while we were working to disengage the first one, my wife and niece sat down under a tree to sew. An ever-increasing circle soon formed around them ; and a native standing behind the tree began jeering and brandishing a hatchet a few inches above my wife's head. It was time to tell these people to withdraw ; but the young man, who gave himself airs of great importance, answered me so insolently that our ladies immediately yielded the place to him.

During this time the agitation rose higher and higher around us. Now the valley was overflowing with people, and re-echoing with their savage cries. It was Masonda returning. Then ensued a scene I feel incapable of describing. Masonda, standing on a rock and foaming with fury, disposed his troops so as to surround us, ordered them to take away our oxen, and dictated his terms to us. "So many sacks of powder, so many caps, so many blankets, so many guns, and you shall go."

I had great difficulty in restraining our people, who were already running for their guns. "We will die for our wives and children," they said, "since there is nothing else for it, but at least we will die like men."

"Like men, yes, my friends ; but like Christians too. Lay down your guns. Put your trust in God, and remember 'they that be with us are more than they that be with them.'"[1]

They submitted—with an ill grace it is true ; but I thanked God, for the first shot would have been the signal for a general massacre of our party.

I tried in vain to persuade Masonda to bring back some seventeen oxen he had carried off ; but when he saw I was having the rest yoked, he ordered me in the most peremptory manner to desist. However, I held out, and the oxen were inspanned. But during this time, the tumultuous crowd, led by a "seer," a magician, who declared himself inspired, rushed towards the waggon, shrieking wildly, and apparently bent on pillage. "The night is falling," they cried, "and you are in our hands. We will have

---

[1] 2 Kings vi. 14-17 : "The mountain was full of horses and chariots of fire round about."

your blood and everything you possess, and we shall see if your God will deliver you."

I trembled at the thought that one blow from a hatchet might explode the chest lying outside the waggon, which contained our whole provision of powder. Seeing me suddenly reappear with a sjambok[1] in my hand, they withdrew a short distance ; but for a moment I thought I should not be able to hold them off any longer. The sun was going down, and our position became more critical every instant. My wife on her side was doing her own work ; she had assembled the wives and children of the evangelists round her, to besiege the Throne of Grace, and gather strength and calmness in prayer.

When once the bullocks were inspanned, we thought the cry of "Trek!" would be the signal for a hail of arrows and assegaïs. But no! It only provoked the yells of the infuriated mob, and the bullocks were so excited thereby that they gave a vigorous pull at the yoke, and dragged the waggon out!

The effect upon the natives was magical. Those who were blocking the way fell back to let us pass ; the others made no attempt to pursue us. But while we had been inspanning, a troop of them had carried off seventeen of our other oxen. All my efforts to obtain another interview with the chief were in vain, for it was only in the forest he would grant me audience, and there he summoned me imperiously "to confer with him." Not judging it prudent to follow him thither, I in my turn sent him this message : "Understand that these seventeen oxen are not mine ; they are the property of the God Whom we serve, and Who has delivered us. Beware of slaughtering them ; tend them well ; and one day it will not be I who will send for them, but you who will bring them back to me yourself—*every one.*"

Meanwhile, what was to be done ? Night fell, and the natives would not retire. All around us, their fires were glowing along the edge of the forest ; we could even hear them commenting with much animation on the events of the day. And then it was that the plot revealed itself, which laid bare the horror of our adventure two days before. To throw our ladies down from the crag we were climbing, and then fall upon us, massacre every one, and plunder our possessions—such had been their design.

[1] Pronounced *shambuck* : a riding-whip, usually made of hippopotamus hide, short, and tapering to a point.

"And why did we not do it?" they kept asking each other, clacking their tongues.

Still, when we considered it calmly, we found we had more reasons for thanksgiving than for murmuring. Our lives were safe ; though our goods had been looted, our cases had not been rifled ; and although we had lost a good many bullocks, thirty remained, ten for each waggon. We could not go far, for the night was very dark ; and at every difficult place we had to double the teams. We had to resign ourselves to wait till the morning. The natives surrounded us, but did not attack us. Thus " the angel of the Lord encampeth round about them that fear Him, and delivereth them."

Next day, a troop of men from Maliankombé came to meet us, and brought us to Nyanikoë without further adventure. The chief received us with great reserve. We were arriving like mariners escaped from shipwreck. Maliankombé sent to Masonda to enquire what had just been happening, but a man whom I sent with his messenger was not received. What came back to us were Masonda's claims. " Give me ten sacks of powder, and a waggon loaded with your baggage, and you shall have your oxen." Now, the chiefs of the place where we were began to carry out a system of spoliation on their own part, beyond all reason and ruinous in the highest degree. Our relations narrowly missed being broken off altogether. We discovered that the Banyaï pay tribute to Lobengula, supreme chief of the Matabele, and any Matabele who comes this way holds his head high and permits himself to insult chiefs and subjects with impunity.

(Extract from a letter of Mme. Coillard's, dated September 15th.)

"Yesterday forenoon I was lying in the waggon (the thermometer was 92° ; I felt quite overcome), when I heard a loud noise behind, and saw a native leap over the fence which we have had put round our camp, to keep our importunate visitors off, who come by hundreds before daybreak, and only leave after sunset. I saw in a moment, by the polished ring this man had on the top of his head, that he was none other than a Matabele warrior. He gesticulated and shouted, 'Here I am ; I have arrived at last. How dare you come here without our consent? Lobengula has sent me to claim tribute, and to tell you Masonda did well to despoil you, for you have no business here unknown to us.' F. put him out of the enclosure, and told him if he had any just claims they would be listened to, but there must be no noise. We see that this man has right on his side, but that he tried to frighten us by exaggerating : we think he is one of Lobengula's numerous spies, but we wish to have to do with the chief, not with each one of his subordinates, and we fear that we must ourselves go to Inyati."

(F. Coillard's narrative continued.)

Thereupon I decided to send messengers to Lobengula, and to take advantage of this opportunity to open communications with the missionaries of Inyati. But you have no idea of the prudence, patience, and perseverance demanded for dealing with the various susceptibilities of these Banyaï. Finally, Asser has gone off with one of our young men who speaks Zulu, and the chief has sent his brother to accompany them. For a moment, we had been on the point of going ourselves ; but the thought of leaving our people and property here, and the fear of being surprised by the rains, made us give up the idea. The impossibility of our travelling with so few oxen also seemed to us a manifestation of God's will. When Asser comes back, we shall place him here with Aaron, and we think of then going as far as the chief Zemito, where Andreas and Azael can be installed, and where we ourselves shall pass the rainy season. I can say no more about our plans. We desire to be led step by step.

I send this letter by Mr. Hofmeyr's people, who are returning home. They have been a great help to us, and have so thoroughly identified themselves with us, that it costs us a great deal to part with them. They have quite won our hearts.[1]

[1] As far as it can be identified on modern maps, with which Baines's chart does not correspond very clearly, the scene of this adventure seems to have been what is now called Providential Gorge, near Fort Victoria ; but it is not quite certain that it was not a valley which runs parallel to this. When the B. S. A. Co.'s pioneers passed through the ravine, and gave it its name (some ten years later), the Banyaï assured them that no white men had ever been there before ; but this in itself would not disprove the identification, for the Banyaï seem to have extraordinarily short memories ; and besides, their statements, to say the least, are not to be implicitly relied upon.

M. Coillard's official intercourse with the Banyaï chiefs was conducted by an interpreter, but he managed to understand their language fairly well, from its affinity with Zulu, and these too could follow him when he spoke the latter tongue. Asser, the catechist, of course knew the Senyaï quite well, from having lived in the country.

CHAPTER III

BULAWAYO, *January* 18*th*, 1878.

IT was on December 15th that our waggons stopped before
Bulawayo. It was not till to-day that the chief, Lobengula,
would consent to discuss our business officially.

For two months, we awaited Asser's return from Bulawayo.
It would take a volume to recount our various experiences
and distresses during this time. We were exposed to the
greatest dangers. The country is a perfect slaughter-house ;
and there is no central authority of any sort. The independent
villages, perched as they are upon the most inaccessible heights,
are constantly at war with one another.

The prevailing insecurity is such that a Monyaï never
ventures into his fields alone, nor yet without his weapons.
By night as by day, at home or abroad, he always carries his
assegaïs, bow and arrows, and on his left arm the terrible cutlass, which, on the slightest provocation or suspicion of danger,
is instantly unsheathed. If he is not called upon to defend
himself, he is all the better able to attack other people—a
proceeding from which he is never deterred for want of a pretext.
It was a hard time for us, alone among these savages, of whose
language and customs we were alike ignorant. The Banyaï,
who go almost completely naked, have few wants ; a bit of
calico or a bead necklace is all they need. Nevertheless, if
we refused to buy their sky-blue milk or the siftings of their
flour, we could not escape violent altercations, wherein the

cutlass gleamed among their flowers of rhetoric! The chief Chibi nearly murdered me, and would have succeeded, had not Aaron flung himself between my person and his knife.

And with all that, what cowards they were! Did but the shadow of a Matabele darken the horizon, cries of terror resounded on all sides. A general stampede took place, and each man fled with his small cattle, and hid in the caverns and underground passages of his mountain.[1] For us, as for themselves, the alarms were of daily occurrence.

At last, one day, they had real cause for panic. An armed force of one hundred and fifty men, commanded by three chiefs, took up its quarters beside us. It had been sent by Lobengula, who, furious at our having penetrated unknown to him into a country which it was his interest to keep closed to Europeans, had scornfully refused to accept my presents and salutations. After forcing Masonda to give back everything he had stolen from us, including the seventeen oxen to enable us to travel faster, the chiefs ordered us to raise our camp, and, in fact, made us their prisoners.

Poor Banyaï! When they saw us going, they understood that they were losing friends; and in spite of their terrors, we saw them there grouped about the rocks, and heard them lamenting.

How shall I describe what we went through, during those three weeks of forced marches, across a country without roads, rivers without fords, marshy valleys, and rocky wooded hills! Our every movement was watched. If we dared to wash ourselves in a wayside stream, it was a crime. Did we not know that we must appear before his Majesty covered with dust and sweat, in proof of our eagerness to obey him? If we dared to pluck a flower, we were accused of taking specimens, in order to seize the whole country afterwards. Writing? Who could say what black art we might be practising against them, and what calamities we might not be bringing down upon them! And every day runners were despatched to the capital.

At length, we came in sight of Bulawayo. We were already climbing the furrowed slopes of the ravines, when a messenger

---

[1] See Colonel Baden-Powell's "Matabele War" for more detailed description of these "mountains," and a sketch "elevation" and "section," showing the caves and subterranean passages.

came with the order that we were to stop just where we were, without taking a single step farther to choose a more suitable spot. Towards evening, one of those magicians, whose repulsive aspect is pretty familiar to us by this time, arrived at the head of a company.

Our soldiers instantly rose, formed ranks, and stood at attention. The witch-doctor, dipping a gnu's tail into some slimy greenish mixture, sprinkled them with it back and front. This was a ceremony of exorcism. Then, turning abruptly towards us, he made us all pass through the same disgusting rite; our waggons, our oxen, men, women, and children, no one escaped. "And this man," he said, fixing his gleaming eyes upon me, "give him a double dose; he is the arch-sorcerer." And a double dose I had, right in my face, and all over my clothes. All this was not calculated to reassure us.

We spent two days thus, carefully watched and guarded. No one dared approach our vehicles; and every one went a long way round to avoid us. The third day was Sunday, and in the afternoon a messenger came to summon me to the king's presence. "Run, white man; the king is calling you."[1]

But the nearer I came, the less I felt disposed to hurry myself.

I passed from one court into another. Naked men, with crowns of polished leather encircling their heads in token of their manhood, were squatting in dead silence all around. In the centre stood a waggon, and I noticed a corpulent but pleasant-faced man, carelessly leaning on his elbows upon the packing-case which served as a coach-box. His smooth hands, his nails of exaggerated length, the monkey skins he wore about his loins, the men who approached him bowing, all told me that this was Lobengula himself. I saluted him; he saluted me in Sesuto, and an embarrassing silence ensued.

"Where is your wife?" he asked me at length, using the second person singular.

"At our camp."

"Why didn't you bring her here to see me?"

[1] The insulting terms of the message can hardly be translated. An equivalent on our part would perhaps be, "Look sharp, nigger, or it will be the worse for you."

"Because amongst us it is not customary for ladies to visit gentlemen first."

Another pause.

" Moruti, where is your wife ? "

" Morena " (chief), " she is at my camp."

" Why have you not brought her to see me ? "

"Because with us it is the gentlemen who go to pay their respects to the ladies, and not the ladies to the gentlemen."

" *Yé bo !* Is that possible ? "

A third pause, followed by a third repetition of the same conversation, and another interval of silence.

Feeling that this interview was quite as uncomfortable for his Majesty as for me, I took leave. I had seen his face, and thenceforward our escort left us, and we felt more at liberty.

My strange conversation had much impressed me. I had indeed tried to say a word about our expedition, but Lobengula silenced me at once, saying the moment had not come. The idea occurred to me that Mme. Coillard might be more successful. It cost her a good deal to appear before this tyrant, not knowing what his intentions towards us might be; but she yielded.

On her arrival, he came out of his hut, and, taking her hand, escorted her to the shadow of his waggon. There he took his seat upon a soap-box, saying to her, "Sit down there on the ground, and let us have a chat."

" On the ground !" I exclaimed. " With us, ladies do not sit on the ground. Is there not a box or a block of wood somewhere ? "

" Certainly," he replied, and rose with great alacrity to fetch her a seat. " You have come a long way," he said, looking very straight at her. " You must be very tired."

"Yes," replied Mme. Coillard. " We have come a long way, and we are very tired." Then, with her habitual calm and charm of manner, she recounted our journey and the object of it, our experiences among the Banyaï, and everything else. Not once did he interrupt her, unless it was to ask a question. He was conquered.

" I did not know all that," he remarked ; " but we will talk about it later on."

Since then he has been very friendly. He made us camp

quite near him, and always sends us meat, "the portion of honour," which no one else but himself may touch. But he would not discuss our business, and kept putting it off for the Council of Chiefs which will assemble later on.

We do not regret this delay. On the contrary, we are very glad of this opportunity of making acquaintance with the king, and making ourselves known to him, although it obliges us too often to be the unwilling witnesses of his hideous cruelties. One day, for instance, I was sitting in his court, when a little herdboy came in, and, on being questioned about some trifling offence, began to prevaricate. Lobengula ordered him to come and crouch down before him, while he sat silent, every now and then glaring at the cowering boy. Presently he sprang up and said, "That lying mouth must be punished." He ordered four men to hold him down backwards on the ground, and, seizing a glowing brand, himself knelt on his chest, and applied it to his lips. In vain I pleaded for a milder punishment. Next day the poor little fellow's lips were quite burnt away.

However, to ourselves personally he has shown himself very affable. He has often come to see us, apparently finding as much pleasure in chatting with us as in drinking a cup of coffee. What gave us chief pleasure, however, was that he sent for Mr. Sykes (of the L.M.S.), so that he should be present at the discussion of our business. This friend lost no time in responding to Lobengula's summons ; nevertheless, he was kept waiting for ten or twelve days. At last the chief decided to deal with a question which he evidently finds a very thorny one. His pride had been hurt to think we could possibly have been ignorant of the fact that the Banyaï were "his dogs," his slaves. He understood this, however ; but he does not wish, he says, that his slaves should be taught. His own country is already provided with missionaries. He will soon have four, and he does not want any more. He questioned me closely as to who had sent us, and what part the Basuto chiefs had in this expedition. My reply was perfectly straightforward. I tried to make him understand that it was the Churches which had sent the catechists, and that the chiefs had shown their goodwill by contributing like others to the good work. As he was insisting that we should return to those who had sent us, I pointed out to him that such a proceeding would not be understood. It might have passed if he had sent us back from Nyanikoë ; but it was no longer possible, after his having sent for us, accepted our salutations, and treated us with kindness. He then said that he would not give his reply yet, and that he would refer the matter to his headmen, who were to assemble for some great ceremonies at the end of the month. My impression— and Mr. Sykes's too—is that the chief is personally very favourable to us, but that he finds himself in a difficult position. He has his hands full this year. Some European hunters have been maltreated by his people, and have gone away with anger and threats. Expedition after expedition arrives, asking permission to go to these same Banyaï, one to explore the country, another to look for gold, etc. He has refused each request peremptorily, without even giving them the satisfaction of a discussion. So how could he grant ours? But all the same, it costs him something to refuse us. I fear that if he proposes to consult his headmen, it will only be as a pretext for shirking his responsibility. They are all opposed to our going to the Banyaï; "for," they say, "if Lobengula once allows that, where shall we go raiding ? " That is the root of the matter.

I hope that the chief will consent to a compromise, and allow us to settle among the Makalaka, who are more immediately under his power, or who at least recognise it and submit to it. The L.M.S. missionaries would approve of us, and would not say we were encroaching on their territory. But I doubt whether Lobengula will consent even to that. " Go to Mozila's," he says, " where there are no missionaries." The River Sabi is the frontier between Mozila and the Matabele. Apart from the Matabele and Mozila's people, all the other tribes are reduced to the same state of slavery. Such are the Banyaï, the Makalaka, the Mashona, etc., which once formed part of the powerful kingdom of the Balotsoë which Moselikatse ruined. Please take particular note of this fact : there is no independent tribe on this side of the Zambesi, except the people of Lobengula and of Mozila. It is said that this latter is very hostile to the white man. The question of going to him would require the most serious consideration. Another fact which I should point out to you for your guidance is that the region we were in is evidently a hotbed of fever. It was not the country which was represented to us as being perfectly healthy, and people here consider it providential that we quitted it in time.   The L.M.S. is going to begin a work on Lake Ngami at Sechulatebe's.   On this side of the Zambesi, from the lake as far as the gold mines Baines discovered in Mashona-land [1] (at the north point of the mountains marked on his map), the Matabele have devastated everything ; there is no longer the vestige of any population. I have heard this on good authority.   There still remains the other side of the Zambesi ; but before daring to cross it, even in thought, let us pause and pray !

I assure you, I have great difficulty in resisting the current of discouragement which is bearing down every one around me. But I have a profound conviction that God will open some door for us, and that all the sacrifices which the poor Churches of Basuto-land have made, all the prayers which have been, and are still being, offered, will not be unavailing.   We ourselves are ready for anything, but less for returning to Basuto-land than for any other course.   We are in the field, and not thinking of our hearths just yet.

My wife has been threatened with rheumatic fever, which has kept her in bed for several days.   I myself have been suffering from nervous ophthalmia for nearly a fortnight.   But now we are well, thank God ! and so are all our people ; and they would be perfectly happy, were it not for the heavy cloud lowering over us.   This is only natural ; indeed, it would not be right, if joy and singing could go on in the camp as usual.

MATABELE-LAND, *March 5th*, 1878.

The gloomiest predictions of those who profess to understand the true state of affairs here have been more than realised.

After the great national festival, the sacrifice of fifteen human lives and the customary purifications, Lobengula remembered us.   He sent for our friend Mr. Sykes, of the L.M.S., who, in spite of the incessant rain, hastened to come with all his family.   We went together to the new camp of the Matabele king, who leads a semi-nomadic life.   We still had to await his good pleasure for three or four weeks.

The Great Ones of the Nation at last assembled.   They had a private conference with their master, which lasted a whole day—

---

[1] The Fort Salisbury region.

and I do not suppose it was the first one. The next day the chiefs held their assembly, to which we were admitted, at our camp. We expected all the etiquette and decorum which are so rigorously exacted in Basuto-land under similar circumstances. But it was with Matabele we had now to do. Every one spoke at once, each one louder than the other. They rained questions upon us, without giving us time to reply. We were reproached with the road we had made for ourselves into the Banyaï country ; then with the fact that we had no official character, not having been sent by the supreme chief of the Basuto. We were prepared for all that, but these were only the preliminaries. The stalking-horse of these wily diplomatists was the affair of Langalabalélé.[1] " Tell us his crime ? In what country, in what place, by whom was he betrayed and made prisoner ? " In vain we attempted to explain to them that the Basuto have lost their independence that they cannot be held responsible for the acts of the English Government, and that, as regards ourselves, we have absolutely nothing to do with political questions : in vain Mr. Sykes told them, in language they could not fail to comprehend, " Who can know the heart of a king and sound its depths ? Did you know Moselikatse's ? " It only brought down on us a volley of such abuse as made our people tremble. In fact, it was really against them that they had a quarrel. They put me on one side, and made me all sorts of professions of confidence and consideration and goodwill. " But you Basuto," they cried, with threatening gestures, " you smell of Molapo, that unworthy son of Moshesh, who betrayed and sold Langalabalélé ! We fear you. We shudder at the very sight of you. Allow you to settle in our territory ? Never ! Never ! There is the road which leads out of our country—begone ! "

[1] Langalabalélé, a chief of the same race as the Matabele, but living in Natal, where they themselves originated. Four or five years ago, this chief, having, by purchases of arms, drawn upon himself the suspicion of wishing to revolt against the British in Natal, was summoned to appear before the Governor. Instead of obeying, he crossed the frontier with all his people, and took refuge in the territory of Molapo, son of Moshesh. The British authority in Basuto-land then ordered Molapo to help in the capture of Langalabalélé, which he was obliged to do, or else be treated as a rebel himself. Molapo effected this capture, however, in the most treacherous way possible, inviting Langalabalélé and his followers to a friendly reception, and then delivering them over to the British.

Strange to say, Mr. Sykes and I did not lose all hope even then. We tried to persuade ourselves that the Matabele dignitaries wished to make us appreciate their favour, and at the same time to put in their place those people whom they despised while yet feeling their superiority. Cruel illusion! The chief called us, for this conference had taken place at our camp, and he had abstained from taking part in it. We passed long hours there in his court, sitting on the ground in the full blaze of the sun, silent and gloomy, as if awaiting the hour of a burial. Lobengula was in his shed, as silent as ourselves, but in the shade! It was only towards sunset that he broke the silence. This audience was but a painful repetition of the morning's conference, with no more decorum and a good deal more abuse. The king gave the keynote, and the great chiefs, vying with each other, fell upon our evangelists like dogs unchained. Lobengula insisted upon the distinction he had already striven to establish between our people and ourselves, declaring that, if I had been alone, neither he nor his people would have had any objection to treating with me, but that, as for the Basuto catechists, he would under no consideration permit them to remain in his country—entirely, as he said, on account of this unhappy affair of Langalabalélé, and of the odious treachery of Molapo. Our brother, Mr. Sykes—let me say it to his honour—did not leave me alone in the breach; and he too received his share of insults.

And so ended this official audience which we had waited for so long. We fancied ourselves under the influence of some frightful nightmare; we could no longer recognise the son of Moselikatse, who for more than two months had treated us with so much consideration and cordiality. We might well repeat, "The heart of a king is unsearchable!"—especially of a Matabele king. We stood as if nailed to the earth; but when all the chiefs one after another had done homage to their master and taken leave, we too were obliged to salute him and depart. We met in a tent to pray, but only tears could have eased our hearts.

Four days have passed since then. The chief and his sister, surprised that I had not visited them as usual, asked for me. They are evidently very ill at ease. Lobengula tried to throw all the responsibility of the affair on to his chiefs, and reiterated

his protestations of benevolence towards me personally. I felt
all the advantage of my position. I had never spoken his
tongue with such facility ; and to this potentate, surfeited with
the most abject flatteries, it was given me to use a language
full of respect certainly, but full also of truth and plain-dealing.
" Chief, I also am a Mosuto. I am one with my people ; I am
at their head. The blow which strikes them strikes me first.
What grieves me, and will grieve all our friends, is that, after
permitting us to see your face, and treating us with so much
kindness, you are now driving us ignominiously out of your
country, and for an affair with which we have absolutely
nothing to do." He was silent and hung his head ; then, as
if to acquit his conscience, he added in a low voice, " If I had
known all that, perhaps we should have spoken otherwise."
Yes, perhaps ! Nevertheless, the verdict of his council remains,
and we are now preparing our waggons to take the road pointed
out to us, which leads " out of the country." So this is what
our missionary expedition has come to ! After nearly a year's
travelling, what is the result ?

And now, will you ask what we are going to do ? The first
thing is, not to lose courage. And why should we lose courage ?
There is nothing extraordinary in our circumstances. Jesus
and His Apostles have gone through the same, as their blood-
stained traces testify. The ways of the Lord are not our ways,
and His thoughts not our thoughts. Should we forget this ?
We spoke of the Banyaï, and their name was already dear to
us. But who knows if the Lord has not other views than ours,
other people for us to evangelise ? If Lobengula had simply
and frankly refused to allow us to go amongst his slave
tribes, it seems to us that our horizon would not have been
so dark. But this unhappy affair of Langalabalélé, which his
people make the pivot of all their abuse, almost hopelessly shuts
for us the door of nearly every Zulu tribe. It is impossible at
present even to think of knocking at the door of Mozila, this
other Moselikatse, the terror of all the tribes from the Sabi
to Sofala.

It is true we have met some people at Bulawayo who come
from the north side of the Zambesi. They have taken refuge
here to save their lives ; for their country, it seems, is frequently
subject to revolutions, and human life is very cheap. What struck

us about them was that they speak Sesuto, as we do. I knew already from Livingstone that the Makololo had introduced it on the Zambesi, but I did not realise the fact that it is still spoken there. " Why do you not come to us," they said, " and save the nation ? " But the Zambesi—that is a long way to go ! As far as we can judge at present, there are only two alternatives for us—either to return to Basuto-land, or to seek other parts. Return to Basuto-land ! The very thought seems to us treachery and a temptation of the Enemy. Our camp is not exactly joyous these days, and no one thinks of parading his stout-heartedness. But I have no doubt that, when our dear travelling companions have recovered from this terrible blow, energy and enthusiasm will revive in their hearts. They feel as we do, that to return to Basuto-land in the present circumstances would be disastrous to the cause of the mission. I am full of courage, and have good hope. For the moment, what we have to do is to leave Matabele-land, and go to Shoshong— alas ! a considerable retreat in the direction of Basuto-land. There we will mature our plans, and await the counsels and directions of our brethren. All the members of the expedition charge me to send their salutations to you and to the Churches of France. "We are not discouraged," they say ; " but, O brothers and sisters, fathers and mothers, do uphold us ! " I join with all my heart in this message.

In leaving these parts, I think of the return of the Ark from the land of the Philistines. Our thoughts and hearts constantly return to the Banyaï country, to Nyanikoë. I tell myself that a miracle is not impossible, though it seems very improbable, and that the Lord may still open the doors of that country, which have been closed to us. The spark which has glimmered in the darkness of that unhappy country may one day produce a great light. No doubt we have done little during our stay of six months ; nevertheless, I have the conviction that our testimony will remain. They will long remember those whites and blacks in strange garments, with their rolling houses drawn by oxen. Will they forget the bell which daily summoned all to prayer? Will no recollections remain of the history of the Creation, the Fall, and the Redemption, which we have tried to make the Banyaï understand, stammering their language? Among our memories of Nyanikoë are the moments when, surrounded by these poor people, I tried to fix in their minds, by making them repeat it, that text which is the very essence of the Gospel : "God so loved the world, that He gave His only begotten Son, that whosoever believeth in Him should not perish, but have everlasting life."

May God have pity on the Banyaï and remember them ![1]

[1] The Banyaï are now being evangelised by the missionaries of the Dutch Reformed Church.

CHAPTER IV

Departure from Matabele-land—Final Interview with Lobengula—Misery of
Africa—Ferocious Character of the Matabele—Barrenness of Mission
Work—Tati Gold Fields—"Ruined Cities"—Ethnological Problems—
Sickness in Camp—Accidents on the Road—Arrival at Khama's Town
—Warm Welcome—Khama's Character and Government—Missionary
Meeting—Future Plans discussed—Decision to go to Barotsi-land.

MANGWATO (SHOSHONG), *May 22nd,* 1878.

YOU see now that our last ray of hope has vanished! We have
definitely quitted Matabele-land, and here we are among
the Bamangwato, some hundreds of miles to the south. After
the stormy conference with the chiefs which I told you about,
our evangelists, terrified (and not without reason) at the hostile
attitude of the Matabele, would have liked to leave without
delay. I thought it better not to hurry, for fear of giving our
departure an appearance of flight. After having written to
Basuto-land, so that the directions of our brethren might reach
us at Shoshong without loss of time, we went to visit the stations
of Shiloh and Inyati, which took us three weeks. Our people
will never forget Shiloh. It is a bright spot to them, the only
one, indeed, in this hard experience of Matabele-land.

I went, as etiquette required, to pay Lobengula a last visit.
My presence evidently embarrassed him greatly, and he found
it difficult to receive my farewells with a good grace. He took
refuge once more in explanations and professions of personal
friendship; he pressed me to settle in his country (without the
Basuto catechists, of course); he showed displeasure on learning
that I and my people were going to make some stay with the
Bamangwato chief; he even went so far as to offer me a passage
across his own territory, and some guides to conduct me to
Mozila, on the other side of the River Sabi. I told him I would
reflect seriously on all he had told me, and I took leave. Shall

43

I confess it ?   I had till then buoyed myself up with a vague
hope that at the last moment the path to the Banyaï might still
be opened to us.   It was now evident to me that the Lord
Himself, for reasons that we cannot yet understand, had signed
our passport to turn us away from our chosen field.   It only
remained for us to depart, and we left without any more idle
regrets, conscious of having left no stone unturned to make our
mission succeed, and strengthened by the conviction that in
going straight to the Banyaï we had not strayed from the right
way, and that to-day, in leaving Lobengula's kingdom, we were
still following the path of duty.   Yes ; but these countries,
which only a great black stain can adequately represent on the
map of Africa, are immense catacombs, which we cannot think
of without shuddering.   There, be it not forgotten, vast popula-
tions live in constant terror, ruthlessly given up to pillage and
destruction.   There is so much misery that the world knows
nothing of ; but *we* are pursued by stifled cries, and that of the
Macedonian has never rung so loudly in our hearts : " Come over
and help us."   But the door is shut.   " How long, O Lord,
how long ? "

The treacherous and cruel character of the Matabele is well
known.   But no ! it is not.   The atrocities which form their
pastime and delight defy all description.   Their thirst for rapine
and pillage respects absolutely no one.   They are a people *sans
foi ni loi.*   The king can have his subjects massacred without
distinctions of rank, and he does so, remorselessly ; but he has
not the power to govern them.   Here, indeed, is a country where
Satan has his throne.

You will ask me what influence the Gospel has had up till
now on this savage nation ?   Alas ! apparently none whatever !
I confess it is the most perplexing problem of modern missions.
The Revs. Thomas and Sykes have laboured for twenty years in
the country.   Mr. John Moffat first,[1] and then Mr. Thompson of
Ujiji, consecrated to it the first-fruits of their ministry.   In spite
of all these efforts and sacrifices, there is no school, no church,
not a single convert—*not one !*   In fact, I do not know which
ought most to astonish the Christian world, the barrenness of this
mission field or the courage and perseverance of these noble servants of Christ who have for so long ploughed and sown in tears.

[1] Son of Dr. Moffat.

It was at the beginning of April that we finally turned our waggon booms towards the south. Each day's march took us farther from the country where we had hoped to unfurl the Gospel standard. Now everything had grown hard. Our men were weary and discouraged, and the journey was one of the most difficult imaginable. To add to our troubles, fever broke out among us. Six of our people fell ill at once. Our waggons would have reminded you of European ambulances. Ours had two patients in it, whose grass beds we renewed at every halt. It was thus that we slowly and painfully arrived at *Tati*. Several times, I thought we should be obliged to dig a grave for my faithful Bushman (by name, not by race). He survived, however, by a miracle of God's goodness.

We remained several days at Tati. Indeed, everybody seemed in want of rest. A Boer was returning from hunting, his waggon covered with wild-beast skins, and from him I bought the almost entire carcase of a giraffe, at a moderate price. It afforded a pleasant occupation for our people to dry it. I myself profited by this respite to explore the neighbourhood. You know what a talk the gold mines of Tati made a few years ago. Hundreds of Europeans flocked thither to seek their fortunes, and I am assured that numbers of cottages occupied the slopes of the hills and the banks of the river. I visited with great interest the quarries and deep pits whence the auriferous quartz is extracted. Now everything is changed, and the population has disappeared, owing to a quarrel among the promoters. The pits are abandoned, grass and bushes cover the roads again, the white houses have been swept away, and the few stores which survived them are in ruins; finally, the engine, overthrown by torrents, partly destroyed by the natives, who have stripped off all the copper to make ornaments for themselves, lies there, rusting and half buried in the sand. Ruins are always mournful, but for the Christian and the missionary there is something peculiarly melancholy in the abandonment of the Tati mines. No one can tell what the diamond mines have done to open the interior of Africa, and no one can say what might have been done by the mines of Tati and of Walta,[1] at least three hundred miles farther north, which Lobengula allowed Baines to exploit. However this may be, God directs all

[1] Fort Salisbury.

events. The flood of civilisation advances slowly, but surely, and with a might which Lobengula fears, but cannot arrest. Yet a little while, and the waves of this flood will have rolled over the whole of Central Africa, and swept away all obstacles.

Curiosity also led us to visit the ruins that are found almost everywhere in these parts. These particular ones crown the hills around Tati.[1] The walls, which are four feet thick at the base, are built, without mortar, of stones roughly squared and reduced to the length of a brick. In the interior, and at certain heights, rows of little stones are arranged so as to form zigzags, and they display a taste which prevents me from attributing them to natives.[2] Within the enclosure of these walls, one can still see the traces of the furnaces where they smelted iron. All the surrounding country and a large part of Matabele-land is auriferous. In the environs of Tati, they still show some very ancient mines which have been more or less filled up by time. It would even appear that, while digging the shafts I visited, they came across some galleries, evidently of very remote date. All this raises the most captivating of all the problems in this mysterious Africa—the ethnological.

What are the origins of the African families? . . . Several people have attempted to solve this, but no one has yet done so satisfactorily. It would be as presumptuous as premature on my part, were I to express an opinion. What strikes me, in reading the books of modern travellers, is that the Banyaï or the Makalaka form part of an immense family whose branches under different names extend as far as the region of the great lakes. Although their language presents some affinity with the Zulu tongue, their customs and habits would rather seem to

[1] Similar in character to the celebrated ruins of Zimbabye. Those at Tati have now completely disappeared.

[2] Mr. Selous points out that the designs found in the ruins of Mashona-land bear a strong family likeness to those in fashion among the highly industrial Barotsi, whom M. Coillard knew nothing of at this time. The traditions as well as the language of the Barotsi point to their having once lived in Banyaï-land; and the ground plan of their huts, which never varies (two concentric walls, surrounded at some distance by a stockade), has a rudimentary resemblance to that of the Zimbabye ruins. Professor Raoul Allier of Paris, however, following out a suggestion of Semper (in the latter's "Studies of Primitive Architecture"), inclines to the belief that the Barotsi zigzag and wavy patterns are derived from wickerwork, in which they are very expert.

connect them with the Bechuana, though without entirely assimilating them to the latter.

But let us return to Tati. Seeing no change in the state of my poor boy, and fearing the others would get worse, we decided to resume our journey. We were now crossing a water-less country, so it was impossible to halt, and we were obliged to travel by night as well as by day. We had more than one accident in these forests, partly through making sharp turns to avoid large trees, and partly through lack of sufficient hands to lead the waggons. Now it was our canvas tilt that was torn, now the dessel-boom that broke ; the outside cases that were smashed, or the wheels wedged between trunks of trees. Never-theless, we are surprised and thankful that we were able to bear it so easily. We expected to arrive here on Saturday, April 27th, and in order to do this we had made a good night's march ; but suddenly, in the middle of the morning on a beautifully level road, one of our waggon wheels sank, and completely splintered up. What should we have done, if this had happened a few days earlier ? Two of the catechists had to remain with the waggon. We left them our water kegs well filled, and our day's provisions, and hastened our march towards Mangwato, whence we could send them help. We were not expected till two days later. The Rev. and Mrs. Hepburn (of the L.M.S.) and the chief Khama received us with a cordiality which at once put us upon the footing of old acquaintances.

"You have stolen a march upon us," said our brother Hepburn : "do you know that the chief and I had planned to go and meet you, together with his people ? " " Oh," replied my wife, laughing, "think what a deplorable figure our ragged waggons would have cut in such a demonstration ; and our-selves too, we should not have known where to hide our heads." I too asked myself if such an ovation would not have turned our heads. On Monday a wheel was sent to the friends we had left out on the veldt, and by the evening we were all together again.

The tribe of the Bamangwato is governed by a man who is still young, Khama by name (the gazelle). Through the civil wars which have often desolated this country, the population of Shoshong, which might rise to thirty thousand, does not

number now more than from fifteen to twenty thousand, so I
am assured. A remarkable feature is that one sees very few old
men here. Those that war and epidemics have spared have
emigrated with the old rival chiefs Sekomi and Macheng. But
the young men are quite devoted to their chief ; and it is not
surprising, for in him they find a protector and a father. Last
year, there was a terrible famine : the people were dying of
hunger, and subscriptions were organised. Khama, in addition
to his quota, distributed ostrich plumes and ivory to the value
of about £3,000 sterling,—so the traders themselves tell me,
and they are well informed in this matter. This year there
is abundance ; and, according to custom, each man brings his
chief a basket of corn, the first-fruits of the harvest. In an
assembly of the tribe, I was touched to hear Khama thanking
his subjects and directing their thoughts towards God. " My
friends," he said, " this is neither Khama's corn, nor yet the
missionaries' ; no, it is the corn of Jesus, that King of kings
Who, this year, has given us rain and a fruitful season." This
corn, sold by auction under his eye at 35s. the sack, produced
a sum of more than £80, which was devoted entirely to the
building of a church. And, mark this ; only a little time before,
Khama had given something between £24 and £28 out of his
own pocket. A Christian who knows how to give is a Christian
who knows and feels how much he has received.

The European population of the place, which is more or less
fluctuating, numbers about thirty fixed residents. They also
respect Khama's power. As soon as he succeeded to the throne,
he promulgated a decree against the sale of spirituous drinks.
Here, then, is a community entirely transformed, as if by magic,
and one may say in spite of itself, into a total abstinence society.
No one regrets it : every one feels the benefit. Moreover,
Khama is just, kind, and obliging to all. Thus, when some
European drunkards, whom he had expelled, sought to revenge
themselves by slandering him, all the residents at Shoshong
were so ashamed and indignant at it, that they published two
letters in the Cape newspapers (unknown to Khama, of course),
in order to refute these odious calumnies, and vindicate the
noble character of this Christian chief.

Mangwato is the chief centre for the commerce carried on
in Matabele-land, on the Zambesi, and round Lake Ngami. The

traders have calculated that last year more than one hundred and fifty thousand pounds of ivory passed through their hands, being the tusks of more than twelve thousand elephants. At this rate, one need not be a prophet to predict the early extinction of these animals. One can understand that, in a community where such great interests are at stake, more or less serious commercial complications sometimes arise. When this happens, all the Europeans form themselves into a court of equity, under the presidency of the missionary; and their decisions, with the sanction of the chief, have the force of law.

Mr. and Mrs. Hepburn, warm-hearted Scotch people, have succeeded Mr. and Mrs. Mackenzie, who have been called to direct the Moffat Institution at Kuruman. Our friends have been blessed in their work. Six months ago, they returned from Lake Ngami, whither they had gone to found a new mission like ours, and install two evangelists with Moremi, son of Letsulathébe. During their absence, it was chiefly Khama who evangelised his people. The Spirit of the Lord has breathed upon the dry bones, and they are beginning to stir. There could not be a finer sight than the compact crowds of men and women coming to the services every Sunday, all clothed, and a great many of them very well clothed too. When shall we see such a thing among the Matabele?

Mr. Hepburn and the chief Khama wished to have a special missionary meeting the same week, at which we were to speak in detail about our expedition. It was the middle of harvest-time; notwithstanding, from 8 a.m. on the appointed day an audience of some five thousand people began to assemble.

I left the speeches to our evangelists, who all spoke very interestingly, each according to the natural bent of his mind. The assembly hung upon their words. I only gave a general sketch of our expedition, and filled up the gaps in their story. Mr. Hepburn gave us a beautiful address of welcome and encouragement. But I should have liked you to hear Khama in a quiet but powerful address, plead the cause of the Truth among the heathen, and that of missionary duty among the Christians! It is a curious thing that whilst, among all the Sechuana dialects known to us, that of the Batlapi is the furthest removed from Sesuto, the Semangwato is the one which most closely resembles it. They assure me that every one understands me very well, although I am a foreigner. You may imagine how happy our people are; they feel themselves quite among their own people, *at home.*

After having enjoyed the hospitality of our devoted friends the Hepburns for ten days, we installed ourselves in Mr. Mackenzie's house, and our people occupied the former apartments of the students. Our evangelists were longing for a little family life. The public and common life which we had led for thirteen months had become as distasteful to them as to ourselves. At Mangwato, they resolved at all costs to make-believe, and act as though they were in Basuto-land. For reasons of economy, I should have liked to go on having only one fire and one common pot; but with one exception, they either could or would not understand my reasons, and I had to give in. To tell the truth, I cannot find it in my heart to begrudge them this.

We heard of M. Arbousset's death [1] indirectly, whilst among the Matabele. In him, another giant has fallen, or, rather, another warrior has entered into glory, there to receive the crown of life. Africa has few missionaries of his stamp. Another source of trouble to us is what you tell us about the deficit of £2,400 which still weighs on the Society. I infer from this that we must be as economical as possible. From Basuto-land, too, we hear of famine there—another lesson in frugality. It has cost me some sleepless nights. Alas! we are badly situated for practising economy. First of all, our people are tired out, and I do not know where to cut down our expenses. A year ago, the matter would have been easier. And then the necessaries of life have risen to fabulous prices here. Thus, unsifted flour, which is often damaged or adulterated, is sold at £5 15s. the sack; coffee at 2s. 7d. the lb.; sugar at 1s. 6½d. the lb.; potatoes and onions at £3 10s. the sack; sorgho at £2 10s.; an ordinary cow is worth £10; and everything else in proportion. Vegetables are a luxury we can dispense with, but one cannot live without bread. Our conveyances too, whatever we do, and wherever we may go, *must* be repaired. All this, I repeat, is a nightmare to me. I find myself between two fires I ask God for wisdom and faithfulness, so that, on the one hand, our caravan may not have occasion to murmur, and that, on the other, we may not be too heavy a burden on the Churches.

[1] A pioneer of the S.M.E.P., sent to Basuto-land in 1833.

June 8th, 1878.

Since I began this letter, I too have had to pay my tribute to the fever of the country, and feel much shaken by it and very weak. I must, nevertheless, tell you something of our plans. You will remember that we only had two alternatives—to go to Mozila, or to the Zambesi. It is a question which we have weighed before God, and we have always been awaiting (so far in vain) some light from Basuto-land. After mature consideration, we have given up the thought of going to Mozila's : first, because of the pretext which Lobengula made use of to expel our Basuto ignominiously from his country ; and, secondly, because of our ignorance as to the nature of the political relations between Lobengula and Mozila ; finally, and above all, because of the inveterate hatred between the Matabele and Basuto. I knew this antipathy existed, but I had no idea it was so deeply rooted.

Hence our faces naturally turn towards the Zambesi, and our Mangwato friends, Khama and Mr. Hepburn, urge us to go in that direction. Even though the Makololo no longer exist as a tribe, we are told their influence has left its trace. The Barotsi, who have now the upper hand, have adopted the customs of their former masters, and speak their language— namely, Sesuto. These are advantages which it would be difficult to exaggerate. I do not ignore the fact that the affinity of the Basuto to the Makololo may possibly prejudice the Barotsi against our evangelists. But the Barotsi have seen Livingstone, and have heard missionaries spoken of : if, therefore, a European missionary could win their confidence, the position of our native catechists could be established without difficulty. The journey would be very long, but no longer than it would be to go from here to the Banyaï, perhaps not so far.

The great, great objection which I expect you will raise is that the whole district is a fever country. But the Banyaï country is quite as unhealthy ; and if the door had been open, we should not have hesitated to enter it on that account. We should have sought out the most favourable localities there. For a long time, the Bamangwato country was looked on as such a hotbed of fever that traders did not dare to pass more than one season there. Now, from twenty to thirty are in permanent residence. Lake Ngami surpasses all that one can say in point of unhealthiness, and the frightful desert, which has to be crossed before reaching it, has become sadly famous through the sufferings of the Helmores in 1859, and yet a mission like ours is being formed there by the L.M.S. But forgive this pleading : it is premature. *Our object at present is not to go and found a mission, but simply to explore.* We are going as scouts ; and if God brings us back in health, we will tell you what we have seen, and it will be for you to decide what we can do.

We are thinking of starting in a few days with Asser, Azael, and Eleazar, my leader. We are leaving all the families here with Aaron and Andreas, under the care of our friends the Hepburns. The chief Khama gives us his co-operation ; he has procured two guides, and has sent messengers[1] to the chief of the Barotsi to announce our arrival and recommend us to his kindness. It is a very solemn moment for us, dear friends ; we cannot refrain from asking ourselves, as we look at one another, "Which of us will return?" We foresee difficulties and trials which make us tremble. But the sympathy and prayers of the Churches, the sense of duty, and above all the approval of our Divine Master, will sustain us as in the past.

[1] *I.e.* an envoy with an escort.

CHAPTER V

SESHESKE, ON THE ZAMBESI, *August 30th,* 1878.

THE date of my letter cannot fail, I am sure, to give you joy. Here we are at the Zambesi, thanks to our kind heavenly Father, who has led and protected us as He did His people of Israel long ago. I will say little of our journey from Mangwato across the most dreary of deserts. In the beginning we missed the way, and travelled for three days without water, through the fault of a guide who said he knew the road. Happily, just at that time we had the company of Liponkoë one of the evangelists whom the Bechuana Mission (an offshoot of the L.M.S.) is sending to Moremi at Lake Ngami. This excellent and energetic man had some horses, and, thanks to his help, we were able to retrace our steps, and spend the Sunday near a pool. Muddy and repulsive as it was, this water saved the life of our beasts. A few days later, we separated from our friend Liponkoë, after committing each other to God's care. Alone with his family, he was making a journey which had proved fatal to more than one white man : the place where he is going to carry the Gospel is the most malarial spot in the whole country round. He and his excellent wife showed such spirit and cheerfulness we could not admire them enough. Their colleague Konkoë had already preceded them to Lake Ngami.

The only human beings we met afterwards were Masaroa, the Bushmen of these countries, miserable creatures, who only live on roots, wild berries, and the produce of the chase. If they happen to kill an elephant, a buffalo, a giraffe, or some other game, the whole community emigrates, and sets up its quarters near the slaughtered animal, till a new success induces them to transport their penates elsewhere. Our waggon tracks brought them to us. They thought we were hunters, and dreamt of good living. Finding their hopes disappointed, they revenged themselves by making us take a direction which would have brought us to the Mababe Swamp. This made us lose several days, and it was not without difficulty that we found the right road again. The monotony of the country, coupled with our own anxieties, made this part of the journey tiresome and fatiguing.

It was towards the end of July that our waggons stopped at Leshoma, the nearest place to the Zambesi known to us, and thence we were able the very same night to send our cattle beyond the belt of forest infested with tse-tse fly. On hearing of our arrival, Khama's envoy came to us with the discouraging news that he had not been able to penetrate into the Barotsi country because of the political troubles which were convulsing it. I sent him back with a present for the new king, requesting the subordinate chiefs to despatch it without delay. Supposing they did so, it would be at least six weeks before the answer could reach me. We resolved to turn this regrettable delay to the best possible account by making an excursion to the Victoria Falls.

We set out—my wife in a litter of my own construction, carried on the shoulders of four stout natives, my niece on a donkey, the rest of us on foot, with a dozen porters, loaded with a small tent and our provisions, all walking single file, camping every evening in a shelter made of branches, and surrounded with large fires to keep away wild beasts, starting off every morning before sunrise, and only resting in the middle of the day to prepare a meal, picnic fashion. Our porters, and the visitors of whom there was no lack, belonged to various vassal tribes of the Barotsi, and came from different quarters. We had Masubia, Matolela, Matoka, Mashapatane, etc.; and, would you believe it? *all* understand and speak our language—that is, Sesuto! Every morning we prayed with them, and every evening we taught them a passage of Scripture, and that beautiful hymn of our brother Duvoisin, "*A re bineleng Yesu*" ("Sing the praises of Jesus"). It is a pleasant thought that this is no doubt sung now in more than one hamlet where the name of Jesus had never before been heard.

It was on August 1st that for the first time we contemplated the majestic current of the Zambesi, its banks and islets clothed with forests, dominated here and there by baobabs and palms. We followed it as far as the cataracts, six days of moderate marching. The beauty of the various points of view, the magnificence and vastness of the panorama, which every turn and every rising ground renewed, struck us dumb with admiration. The cataracts themselves are formed by a fissure, which extends from one bank to the other, about a mile across. The waters of the Zambesi, calm and tranquil like a lake, are suddenly precipitated into this gulf, leaping and breaking over enormous rocks, raging, boiling, and sending into the air clouds of vapour, which have earned for the falls the Sesuto name of *Musi oa Tunya* (The Thundering Smoke). From these sombre abysses, in which the eye can scarcely distinguish the green foam of its waves, it escapes, enclosed within another fissure equally deep, which yields it a narrow passage near its left bank ; and, forming numerous zigzags, it rolls into the distance with a muffled roar. One can scarcely gaze into these depths for a moment, or follow for an instant the tortuous and restricted current of this river, without turning giddy. The beholder's first impression is one of terror. The natives believe it is haunted by a malevolent and cruel divinity, and they make it offerings to conciliate its favour, a bead necklace, a bracelet, or some other object, which they fling into the abyss, bursting into lugubrious incantations, quite in harmony with their dread and horror.

The news had spread that the missionary announced by Khama had arrived and was in these parts. Scarcely had they caught sight of us or heard our gunshots before canoes crossed the river, bringing us little presents and great salutations from the chiefs, and provisions, which their people sold at famine prices. It is not their fault ; it is the education they have received from some of the traders, and from travellers to the cataracts. Our intercourse with the Barotsi chiefs has been most pleasant. Some put their canoes at our disposal, so pressingly that we could not have refused them without offence.

But it required courage and good nerves for a lady to entrust herself, not merely to these savage strangers (above all, with our experiences of Masonda fresh in our memories), but also to this roughly hollowed tree trunk, scarcely wide enough to crouch in, and rocking at every stroke of the oar in anything but reassuring fashion. Our boatmen, however, soon won our confidence. Not only did we make a very pleasant trip in one of their *mekoros*, but on our return, at the request of several petty chiefs, we crossed the river and visited a large and beautiful island, with many villages, inhabited by people who have sought a temporary refuge there from political troubles. We were received there with demonstrations of great joy, and much clapping of hands, accompanied by the salutation of the country, " *Shangwe, Shangwe*," which answers to the primitive meaning of " Sir." Imagine what I felt on these islets of the Zambesi, surrounded by a crowd understanding and speaking Sesuto! It was with full hearts that we spoke to them of the love of God and sang the praises of Jesus. They were all eyes and ears ; and when we stopped, our primitive congregation, still open-mouthed with astonishment, expressed its pleasure by renewed clapping and renewed " *Shangwes*." Then they followed and preceded us noisily to the neighbouring village ; and if they thought we were silent too long, they would say, " Are you not going to sing about Jesus to us ? " We left the island with all sorts of small presents, escorted by a little flotilla of canoes. When we were in the middle of the river, clappings and cries of " *Shangwe* " still reached our ears from the crowd assembled on the bank.

This was one of the red-letter days of our journey. You will understand, from what I have said, that the whole population is beyond the river. The Matabele have exterminated or driven away all the little tribes who lived on this side, and have reduced the country to a frightful desert.

On returning to our waggons, which we had left in charge of a native, as all hunters do (a fact which speaks volumes for the honesty of these savage children of Africa), we heard all sorts of contradictory reports about the troubles of the country. About eighteen months ago, the Barotsi, driven to extremities by the tyranny and cruelty of their king, Sepopa, expelled him, and sent him to die of hunger and his wounds, abandoned on

SUNRISE IN THE DESERT.

[*To face page* 56.

the banks of the Zambesi.[1]   He had made himself odious by
his want of respect for the wives and property of his subjects,
although otherwise very popular.   His nephew, Nguana-wina,
seized the power, and so abused it that, at the end of eight or
ten months, a new revolt forced him to flee.   Robosi, the son of
Sepopa, was then chosen chief, to the general satisfaction, and
Nguana-wina has vainly striven to stir up the vassal tribes to
re-enter the capital and restore him to sovereignty.   This is
the origin of the troubles which I speak of, about which we
hear but few credible reports.   The most influential man of
the tribe is Gambella, better known by his official name of
Serumbo, a man of whom every one speaks well.

Having established our camp on one of the sandy, wooded
hills of Leshoma, the highest point I was able to find, I decided
to start without delay for Mpalira.   Eleazar and Asser accompanied me.   We had long dreaded this moment of separation,
and not without reason.   I bade farewell to my dear wife, whom
I left quite alone with my niece and Azael, in the Lord's
care.   I did not know, under present circumstances, whether
I should be allowed to cross the river ; but I was quite determined not to turn back, if the door were only opened the least
little way.

Mpalira is a sandy isle at the confluence of the Chobe and
Zambesi.   Three Barotsi chiefs, whose powers are subordinated
to one another, are established there, governing the tributary
tribe of Masubia, and guarding the principal ford of the river,
the entrance to the country.   No one can cross it without
special authorisation.   I had no difficulty whatever.   Livingstone has left the name of *missionary* in such high honour that
my character as such was a sufficient passport.   The chief,
Mokumba, a man of unusual intelligence, received me with
many attentions.   Still, before consenting to let me pass on
to Sesheke, the headman of which had sent me a pressing
invitation, he had to forward a special message, and obtain
formal permission, as all entrance to their country, and even to
the left bank of the river, is absolutely forbidden to strangers.

---

[1] There was a fitness in this fate.   One of Sepopa's favourite amusements
had been to kidnap children, and cast them to the crocodiles, sometimes
dismembering their living limbs one by one, sometimes throwing them in
whole.

I must tell you that Sesheke has been the theatre of political troubles, and that, it being at the very entrance of the Barotsi valley, strangers have been forbidden to approach it. When all the formalities had been gone through, which took a week, Mokumba, assured of the Sesheke chiefs' favourable disposition, conducted us thither himself. The journey generally takes a day and a half by canoe. We took longer, and passed a delightful Sunday on an islet of the Zambesi. There, the river flows across a flat and denuded country ; one can only see the woods in the distance ; zebras and antelopes of every kind abound to such an extent that in the distance, and above all at sunrise, one might easily take them for an immense forest.

On approaching Sesheke, several gun-shots announced our arrival, and gathered a curious crowd on the bank. Mokumba was proud of his canoes, which cleft the water like fish. Each had for rowers five or six vigorous young men, standing up, one only at the stern, and the others at the prow, exactly as they are represented in old Egyptian paintings.[1] Sesheke, from its position, is one of the most important posts in the Barotsi country. It is the residence of twelve petty chiefs, the principal of which, the Morantsiane, has all the attributes and powers of a viceroy. One of these dignitaries came to receive us and conduct us to the *lekhothla*, where they came with the greatest solemnity to bid us welcome. The discourses of this person and that, and the minute scrutiny to which my poor person was subjected, seemed to me very long, all the more so as I was very tired, and was sitting on a drum, which would persist in rolling away from under me. During all this time, young men were executing grotesque and noisy dances—in our honour, no doubt. At the end, the Morantsiane placed a hut at our disposal, and gave orders for " my bed to be made."

I had scarcely retired, when all the chiefs, even those who had arrived from Naliele[2] with their sovereign's ivory (which they were going to sell at Mpalira), came one after the other to visit me. The ice was now broken, and we felt at ease, like old acquaintances.

---

[1] See Livingstone's " Travels." He points out that the pestle and mortar used by the Zambesians for pounding their corn are exactly the same as those in the Egyptian paintings.

[2] Higher up the Zambesi ; it was the capital of the Makololo in Livingstone's time, but is no longer a place of much importance.

I must say that this was not difficult, for the Barotsi are true Basuto. All their chiefs have been the servants or slaves of Sebetoane and Sekeletu. It is from these Makololo potentates, of whom they always speak with affection and the highest respect, that they received their education, and formed their ideal of the dignity, manners, and power of a sovereign. The warrior tribe of Barotsi, once subdued, had become the most devoted of all to the interests of the Makololo ; and if Mpololo, the cousin and successor of Sekeletu, had not shown himself so capriciously cruel, they would never have thought of revolting. But once they had resolved to free themselves, there was no atrocity they would stop at. I had feared they would look with suspicion on our Basuto evangelists ; but no, it was quite the reverse. The Barotsi have nothing more to fear from the Makololo, of whom they have exterminated the whole male population. When they heard us relating our journey, they said, " You are true Makololo : no distance frightened them." They surround me and my people with the greatest attentions. They bring us the usual presents of food, with all the delicacy of the Basuto. " This pitcher of milk is only a little water to moisten your lips " ; " This basket of flour is only a crumb of bread to beguile your hunger." The influence of the Makololo over the tribes they subdued has been extraordinary : it would be interesting to compare it with that of Moselikatse and his Matabele. And when we hear every one around us speaking Sesuto, when we find here the same customs, the same manners, the same costumes, the same sociability, the same code of official politeness, great herds of cattle, and abundance of milk, it really requires an effort of mind to believe oneself at the Zambesi, and not in some retired and still heathen part of Basuto-land. If the door of this country is opened, and the Churches of Basuto-land enter courageously, they will have reason to admire the ways of that Providence which has made use of Sebetoane and his Basuto bands to prepare these numerous tribes to be evangelised by the Basuto Christians of to-day. Could we pass lightly over the fact that, from six days' march below the cataracts up to the north-west extremity of Barotsi-land, and as far as Lake Ngami, Sesuto is the medium of communication between these diverse tribes, each of which has, nevertheless, its own private dialect ?—and that, if ever this field becomes *ours*, all our books, our institutions, and our workers would serve for this mission as well as for that of Basuto-land? This is an incalculable advantage. And what is still more remarkable is that the Barotsi and all their tributary tribes *belong to the great family of the Makalaka*; their dialects prove it. So it cannot be without reason that the Lord has removed us from amid the Makalaka of Nyanikoë to bring us to the Barotsi country, to these Makalaka who are half Basuto.

From another point of view, this is a classic country for me. I have found the traces and memories of Livingstone here. This man had guided his canoe, and was there when he planted the seeds of the trees on the island above Musi oa Tunya; that one was his cook; a third his factotum. Some had gone with him on his perilous journey from Loanda; others had accompanied him to the Zanzibar coast. In Europe, people admired the intrepid traveller; but one must come here, where he has lived, to admire the *man*. If some travellers have engraved their names on the rocks and tree trunks, he has engraved his in the very hearts of the heathen population of Central Africa. Wherever Livingstone has passed, the name of *Moruti* (missionary) is a passport and a recommendation. Must I confess that I have been humiliated not a little to see myself fitted with a doctor's cap by these gentlemen of Sesheke? Whether I will or not, I am *Nyaka* (doctor), Livingstone's successor. Thus it is that the first missionary that comes by is invested with the boots of this giant.[1]

[1] This was in 1878. M. L. Jalla, writing in 1893 from Moru in the Batoka country, says: "Among the inhabitants was a native whom Livingstone had once taken to the east coast and brought back in 1860. I got some interesting details from him about this long journey: how the Doctor had inspired the Mashukulumboe with salutary terrors, when they were about to pillage him, by firing ten revolver shots into the air; he had put another band of natives to flight by sending rockets into their camp. At that epoch, a gun still passed for a great marvel. Of all Livingstone's teaching, this worthy man had retained only one thing—namely, that at the coast they would all grow rich. You see legend is already beginning to mingle with history in all that concerns Livingstone. For instance, all the Batoka maintain that the Doctor entered the abyss of the Victoria Falls, that he held converse with the deity who hides there and calls the water down, and that he brought pearls up from it, with the news that whoever penetrated thither would find great treasures. In a little time, the great Doctor will not fail himself to acquire a halo of legendary divinity."

LESHOMA, *September 20th*, 1878.

A great disappointment awaited me at Seshéke. In the official interview which took place the day after my arrival, I discovered that the message from the chief Khama, in passing from one mouth to another, had been so garbled that it was reduced to purely political salutations, and there had been absolutely no mention made of our expedition. The supreme chief of the Barotsi was completely ignorant of my arrival. The present I had sent him had never been despatched. For this, they alleged a multitude of reasons, the validity of which it was quite impossible for me to gauge. After six weeks' waiting, therefore, I had to do everything over again, and send new messengers to the king to announce my arrival, to request an interview, and to transmit to him my gift of salutation. In vain I pleaded to be allowed to follow them at some days' interval : that might have cost some of the chiefs their lives, as it is against the law of the Barotsi. So I had to renounce the idea, and accept with good grace my hosts' excuses and protestations of goodwill. They sent a messenger immediately, whose return is expected at the end of the month.

During our stay at Seshéke, we of course occupied ourselves with evangelisation. Every day we had numerous congregations, chiefly of *men*, for the women kept themselves at a distance, or hid themselves in neighbouring courts. You would be astonished at the difficulty one experiences in teaching the rudiments of the Gospel to heathen, with whom everything is still to be begun. They understood our language perfectly ; but what we said of God, of His greatness and His love, left them bewildered. Prayer seemed a great mystery to them, and a terrifying ordeal. " *Yuala,*" they said to one another on kneeling down, " *hoa shuoa*" (" Now we are going to die "). When they asked me the hour of prayer, they said, " *Re thla shua néneng ?* " (" When are we going to die ? "). If they were counting the days since our arrival, they said, " We died so many times." This unfortunate expression comes from the Makololo, of whom certain chiefs, hostile to the missionaries, could not decide to kneel down and close their eyes in silence, while the *lekhoa* (the white man) remained standing and spoke alone. They feared his evil designs. To banish all suspicion, I knelt down at first with the evangelists, and then made them repeat the Lord's Prayer all together. As for the singing, it excited their curiosity in the highest degree. Livingstone, it appears, did not sing. Simple as they seem to us, our Sesuto hymns were far above the heads of these poor people. So I composed two or three very short ones. The first, which we sang to the tune of the Old Hundredth, became so popular that the words were soon repeated by the whole village. The native songs are composed of recitatives and choruses of a single syllable, "Hé, hé! ha, ha!" *ad libitum*. And the great difficulty was to get these people to sing the *words*. They thought it was sufficient if *we* sang them, and they repeated in chorus some monosyllable rhyming with the end of each line.

The Morantsiane and his counsellors, fearing I should be discouraged by their delays, pressed me to wait at Sesheke for the return of their messenger. The temptation to do so was very great, on account of the work we had begun there; but after ripe reflection, I came to the conclusion that duty recalled me to those I had left at Leshoma. So they supplied me with canoes, and I started off. My principal object in returning was to make the necessary arrangements for bringing my wife to Sesheke, which I believe to be healthier, and where she could easily await my return from Naliele, while devoting herself to the work. The sand-hills and woods of Leshoma are a melancholy solitude which has lately revealed unsuspected dangers. It is infested with lions. We did not know of this; all the same, prudence had prompted us to fortify our camp with a strong palisade. This did not prevent the lions from penetrating it, and tearing the last of our watchdogs to pieces at the very door of our tent.

Natives are not always a help in these circumstances. Once, when we were travelling, and a lion had helped himself from our peripatetic farmyard, a servant of ours, named Jons, worked himself into the greatest state of excitement. He always did, when there was any hunting in prospect; but he had so far never had a chance of exhibiting his prowess. "Master," he said, "you *must* let me help; there is not my equal for a lion hunt. I never lose a bullet!" And this proved to be no idle boast, for the excellent reason that Jons was never known to fire one off: at the first alarm, he invariably fled, usually leaving his gun behind him. On this occasion, as the lion was not likely

to return for a few hours, I sent him with some of the others
to rest, while I watched.   He seemed very unwilling to yield to
such unsportsmanlike laziness, but complied.   I had the greatest
trouble to wake him.   When he could no longer, with any show
of decency, pretend he had not heard me, he opened his eyes a
little way, and said, " Oh, master, I am *so* disappointed I cannot
join in the lion hunt ; I really have such a dreadful headache ! "
" Nonsense ! " I answered :   " who thinks of headaches when
there are lions about ?   Take your gun like a man, and come
along ! "   He followed me, trembling, and allowed himself to
be posted like the others in position to shoot.   The lion crept
towards us, and the signal was given, " Fire ! "   But at the
critical moment, we heard no shot from Jons's direction ; indeed,
he was nowhere to be found.   We finally discovered him,
clinging panic-stricken to the back of the women's waggon in
the darkest and remotest corner of the kraal.   But that was on
another journey : we have no skulkers this time.

While returning to Leshoma, I fell ill, and had much difficulty in doing the ten or twelve miles between this place and
the Chobe.   I reached it only to take to my bed, and for some
days they believed my life to be in danger.   Thanks to God
and to the skilled nursing of my dear wife, the crisis proved
favourable, and I am now quite convalescent.   One of our young
men, Khosana, fell ill at the same time as myself.   The same
cares were lavished upon him by my wife as well as by our
men, but the disease went to his head ; though not delirious,
he kept uttering heart-rending groans.   All remedies proved
unavailing, and at the end of three days he passed away.   This
was on the morning of Friday, September 13th.   The next
day we sorrowfully carried him to his last resting-place, under
the shadow of a beautiful mahogany tree, there to await the
resurrection dawn.   Passers-by may not know the whereabouts
of his tomb ; but the Lord knoweth them that are His, and
their death is precious in His sight.   It is the first death we
have had among the members of this expedition during the
eighteen months we have been travelling ; and it has taken us
by surprise.   The Lord has baptised us by affliction.

This tomb at the entrance of the Barotsi country is a serious
call to the youth of Basuto-land.   Khosana was a young man
from Leribé, who volunteered for this expedition.   His conversion

dates from the visit of Major Malan. He endeared himself
more to our hearts every day, through his unfailing obedience
and respect; while his gay and lively character made him a
universal favourite. He was very fond of singing; and his
sweet, unostentatious piety made him a popular evangelist.
Exhortation was not exactly his province : he left that to his
elders. But, after the meetings, he loved to sit in the midst of
a group of heathen, and teach them to repeat a verse of God's
Word or to sing a hymn. He leaves a blank among us; but it
is of his father's and mother's grief we are thinking. May God
sustain and comfort them !

LESHOMA, *November 9th*, 1878.

I have once more returned from Sesheke. The first part
of my letter will have shown you already that the Barotsi like
to take their time, even when dealing with business affairs.
Thus the messenger sent to the capital, whose return they led
me to expect at the end of September, only arrived at the end
of October. The king had not understood the message, and
politely refused to let me enter the country, under pretext of
the civil war which was threatening it. He sent me a tusk
of ivory at the same time, evidently mistaking me for a trader.
The chiefs of these parts, surprised at such an answer, invited
me to Sesheke, whither I betook myself immediately with Asser.
Eleazar had already preceded us thither, and had been awaiting
us for six weeks.

The Morantsiane, while officially delivering the chief's
answer, told me that since then the officers who had come
to sell the ivory had returned to the capital, that they had
represented the affair to Robosi, and that they were expecting
another messenger every day. In spite of the slender confidence
with which these fresh proceedings inspired me, I was detained
longer than I wished, as much by Eleazar's illness as by that
of the Morantsiane himself, and by the impossibility of getting
a canoe. Thereupon, one of the Sesheke chiefs came from the
capital with a new message. Robosi, the king, informed me
that he much regretted not having received the first, and
put all the blame on his officers, who had sent it by a slave
instead of by one of themselves. He expressed a great desire
to receive us. But he added, that if the missionary were in

a hurry to leave the country before the rainy season, it must only be on the condition that he returned before the beginning of winter in June, when the corn would be ripe. He himself was building his town just now, but by that time he would be in a position to receive me. He was already giving orders that, on our return, we should be brought to him without delay. By cross-examination, we assured ourselves of the veracity of this message from the supreme chief ; and after freely discussing it with all the headmen, we are quite satisfied with it. We have arrived at the conviction that he and his people are sincerely anxious to have us, and that they are frankly opening the door of their country to us. Unfortunately, the fact still remains that I have not been able to have an interview with the king himself. This will always be a matter of keen regret to me, and perhaps in your eyes it may invalidate the invitation of the Barotsi. If they are counting on our return, it is of course understood that it means with the families of the evangelists, in order to establish ourselves definitely in the country.

I did not dare to make any promises. The advanced season, the low state of our stores, which threaten soon to give out, and, above all, the condition of our people's health, make it impossible for me to attempt any further steps, and make it our duty to turn back to Mangwato. I foresee that we are going to find ourselves once more in a position of extreme embarrassment. I know the establishment of a mission in these parts presents immense difficulties, and raises grave objections. One of the greatest, besides polygamy, will be slavery, which is at the very foundation of the social edifice. The great question certainly is that of fever. Livingstone has already made known the Barotsi Valley : it is unromantic, and the climate is deadly. To be convinced of this, one need only remember that, when the waters of the Zambesi rise, the whole Valley is inundated, and the villages are nothing more than islets. They are then left to the care of slaves, while the owners establish themselves on the hills, and give themselves up to feasting and hunting. But the Banyaï country is quite as unhealthy, if not more so. Without going into any further questions, it is evident that the Barotsi and their dependants, who all speak Sesuto, should be evangelised : they ought to be, if the Saviour died for them too. This post will evidently be a perilous one, a post of self-devotion.

But let us say at once, if the post of danger be the post of honour, here it is. The question is a very serious one, when one thinks of the precious lives which may be sacrificed there. But where shall we find a missionary sphere which unites the conditions of being easy of access and healthy and everything else we desire? For my part, I see none. It is for you to judge if young Churches which are making their first missionary efforts, and a society like ours, always poor in resources, both of men and money, can or cannot undertake such a work. You know the opinion of our evangelists. Mine is, that it is a question of time. When I think that God in His providence made use of the Basuto (then called Makololo) to subdue these tribes, and make them adopt their customs, and, above all, their language, I cannot resist the conviction that He was then preparing them for the Basuto to go and evangelise them, and thus complete the work of Sebetoane.[1] It is an important fact, and one which I ought not to pass over in silence, that the very nationality of our evangelists assures them an influential position among the Barotsi. The latter have exterminated the Makololo out of policy, not out of hatred. They never speak of Sebetoane and Sekeletu but with the greatest respect, and the Barotsi chiefs still pride themselves on the civil posts they held under them. The women and children who survived the massacres of the Makololo, far from being reduced to slavery, occupy honourable positions.

I have another piece of news to tell you, but I can hardly bring myself to speak of it. We have just lost another member of our expedition, Eleazar Marathane. When we returned from our first visit to Sesheke, he, knowing how prone the Barotsi are to let things slide, begged me so earnestly to let him go, first to Mpalira, and then to Sesheke, to look after our affairs, and hasten them as much as possible, that, after several days of hesitation, we ended by letting him start. He enjoyed our full confidence, he let us know all he was doing and all that happened, and great was the joy of seeing him again, when we reached Sesheke a fortnight ago with Asser. We found

[1] The conquering chief of a Basuto tribe which invaded and subjugated the Barotsi country a generation or two before Livingstone's day. The Barotsi gave the name of Makololo to him and his people. Sekeletu was his son and successor.

he had been doing the work of a good evangelist ; he had gained the affection and esteem of the Barotsi chiefs and their people. " He is no longer a Mokololo," they said ; " he is a Morotsi, a brother." This pleased me very much. The same day he fell ill ; the next day, feeling a little better, he was able to help us with our business ; and seeing that the chiefs, trembling for their lives, refused to give me permission to go to the capital (this was before the king's second message), he entreated me most urgently to ask this permission for himself. " They won't object," he said ; " I shall only be a letter." It took more courage than we thought, perhaps, to make such an offer, for the Barotsi have the reputation of being incorrigible poisoners and traitors. A few days before my arrival, a fire had reduced two of the chief's huts to ashes : I had lost thereby all the clothes, books, medicines, provisions for the way, etc., which I had left there for the voyage which I counted upon making to the capital. Nothing had been saved. Happily, I had brought with me some of the most necessary medicaments. In spite of all my care, the disease made such terrible progress, that I saw the Lord was going to take our friend. If only I could have procured a canoe, and transported my dear patient to Leshoma ! But the chief, who was ill himself, wanting to keep me till the arrival of Robosi's second message, always put me off till the next day.

As the malady increased, our superstitious visitors became fewer and fewer, and we were left to ourselves. The Monday morning, the 4th instant, we made one last effort. They had supplied us with two canoes, and our luggage being on board, we had to move our patient. He had such a desire to see my wife again that he begged us every instant to start. It was too late ; he almost died in my arms, and we had to give up the thought. He sank rapidly ; he knew that the moment of departure was near for him, and he was happy. Only, he said, he suffered on our account, who were nursing him, and on that of my wife, who was alone at Leshoma.

Incessant drowsiness and difficulty of speech already prevented him from telling us what was passing in his mind. But his radiant face, and his lips, which often moved, showed us he was in communion with his Saviour. When I repeated a verse to him, he would say, "*Ki teng!*" (" It is well !") ; and until

a little while before his death, he still replied to my questions,
" *Ntate !* " [1] (" My father ! "). The Tuesday evening at eight
o'clock, he yielded the last sigh without an effort. I had some
difficulty about the funeral. They wanted us to have it at
night. I obtained permission, however, to have it in broad
daylight, and even succeeded in getting all the chiefs of Sesheke
to attend it. Of course, everything fell upon Asser and myself.
But in spite of all the fatigues and emotions of the preceding
days and nights, the Lord upheld us. We were enabled to sing
a hymn, and myself to explain very calmly to my trembling
auditors the mysteries of Death and Resurrection. Instead of
a hastily dug ditch, far in the forest, the tomb of our dear
Eleazar is five minutes from the village, on the edge of a wood,
under the shade of a tree. He had said to me a few days
before, when he heard the king's second message, " God be
blessed ! The door is open ! My tomb will be the finger-post
of the mission—a *tebeletso !* " (the earnest of what one expects).

The next day we were descending the river ; the weather
was in perfect harmony with our feelings—it was raining. But
news from Leshoma had made me uneasy, and I was hurrying
to arrive.

Eleazar was a friend to us all. His heart was thoroughly
in this expedition. He wanted to go with us as an evangelist ;
but not being able to overcome the obstinate resistance of his
wife, he had eagerly seized the offer I had made him to come
with us as driver. Three days were enough for him to make
his arrangements. With him the sacrifice was complete. I
asked him before his death if he had never regretted, or if he
did not now regret, having come. " Master," he said a little
sadly, " you have forgotten my salutations to the Church at
Leribé. I have offered my life to the Lord ; it is for Him
to say where my grave is to be dug. For me it is all one : at
the Zambesi, as in Basuto-land, heaven is near to us."

SHOSHONG, *January 30th*, 1879.

What did you say, when you received my last from Sesheke
and Leshoma ? Those are dates in our missionary life which

Ntate, a Sesuto word used for " father," really meaning " The one who
loves me," a term of affection. *Monere*, or *Monare*, also meaning " father,"
is a term of respect, usually applied to missionaries.

neither my wife nor I can ever forget. Beyond all our sufferings and experiences, it is there that the pioneers of the Basuto Churches sleep. It is very mysterious that God should have taken to Himself Eleazar, Khosana, and Bushman, three out of the four helpers whom I had taken from my flock at Leribé. Fono is the only survivor. It was in response to an appeal made to my Church that they offered themselves to accompany us. It was a solemn meeting, and a memorable, in which these three men, placing their persons and their lives at God's service, addressed to the deeply moved assembly their last exhortations and farewells. The Lord has accepted their sacrifice.

In Eleazar we have lost a sure counsellor, a precious friend. If at Leribé my official relationships with him occasionally left something to be desired, because of a misunderstanding, in travelling it was quite the reverse. Would you believe that, during the eighteen months we have been travelling together, not the slightest cloud has even for an instant troubled our intercourse? I told you he had a high standard of *duty*. His warm affection, his devotedness, his delicate attentions to my wife and niece, especially had endeared him to us. His death-bed, so calm and radiant, was the worthy crown of such a beautiful epoch of his life. His memory will always be blessed to us. It was a great privilege that the Lord permitted me to tend him and close his eyes. What an ardent soul was his! How much he had at heart the success of our expedition! It was at his own entreaty that I yielded and sent him to Sesheke all alone. When we rejoined him, he renewed his entreaties, this time that I would send him quite alone, to carry my message to the Barotsi king. And when I set before him the dangers of such an enterprise, he replied, with a smile and a depth of conviction that were alike irresistible, "It is the Lord's work: what does it matter, if we do die for Him?" He had at least the joy of learning before he died that the Barotsi country was open to us.

Khosana was a remarkably intelligent lad. His parents were Christians, and all his father's pride was centred in this son, whom he wished to send to the south for a first-class education, so that he might become a schoolmaster. My heart misgave me, when I heard him volunteer for Banyaï-land in the midst of a crowded congregation in our church at Leribé.

I thought his father would never allow him to go. Outside
the church door, I said to him, "You heard your son to-night?"
"Yes, I heard." "And will you let him go?" He answered
with some surprise, "My son has given himself to the
Lord, the same as I have: what right have I to hold
him back?" "Ah! but if we return without him?" "My
father, the journey to heaven is as short from there as from
Leribé."[1] At Leshoma, our last care was to carve the name
of our dear Khosana on the trunk of the tree that shadows
his tomb. We left that place on November 13th, at ten o'clock
at night, in wet and windy weather. We had to stay some
time at Deka, near the sources of the river so called. We
travelled under great difficulties, for want of experienced hands.
Fono, though unwell, took Eleazar's whip, and a young
Morotsi (Seajika), whom I had hired, took Fono's place at the
head of my team; while another of the same nation, Karumba,
took Khosana's. Half-way on our road, Andreas came to meet
us from Shoshong with the oxen, and with the sad news that
Bushman, whom we had left convalescent, had also died.

My poor Bushman! I could not believe he was dead. He
had been more than twelve years with us, having followed us
to Natal, when we were in exile. I had sent him with our
faithful Jonathan, who was returning to his country, near
Valdezia; and when our expedition was preparing to start
thence, he offered himself to "graze our cattle." "I am a very
stupid boy," he said; "I can't teach; but won't you take me to
feed your beasts?" And it was not an empty offer on his part.
Never were cattle better cared for. At whatever hour, in whatsoever weather, we might outspan, he cheerfully took his spear
and his book, if it were daylight, his cloak, if it were night, and
set off. It was not a rare thing for him to spend whole nights
quite alone, tending and feeding our cattle in the lion-haunted
forests. He never complained either of the cold or of the heat,
nor of fatigue, nor even of hunger; and I sometimes found that
people might have been more considerate of him. If he were
dull, a word of affection cheered him up, for he was sensitive to

---

[1] On his return to Leribé, M. Coillard scarcely knew how to greet the
bereaved father. "You see," he said, grasping his hand, "we have not
brought him back." "My father," replied the old man, "do not grieve. I
offered the Lord the best thing I had, and He has accepted my sacrifice."

affection. He was faithful in little things. How many times in watching him have I not wished from the bottom of my heart to be as faithful a shepherd as he! Bushman did not shine like Khosana by his intelligence and gaiety; and though he had already reached a certain age, he would sit down in the school with quite little children, and preferred to educate himself rather than to earn money. All his relations were, and still are, heathen; and although he was without resources, without friends, and often ill received even by some Christians, he had won a place among them by his astonishing perseverance. As I have already told you, he fell very ill near Tati, and had to be left at Shoshong while we went to the Zambesi. Being very weak, he was carried every day to the prayer meeting. One day, when they came to fetch him, he shook his head, and said, " I have done with prayer—I praise." A few hours later, he had gone to another meeting—no more to pray, but to praise.

What a sad return to Basuto-land these three bereavements are preparing for us! But if these graves are our title-deeds, as Machpelah was for Abraham, we must be prepared to see our men fall, and also to replace them. I am happy to say Fono has grown more serious, and seems to be sincerely seeking the Lord.

I was forgetting to speak to you of a travelling companion whom we have had on our return from the Zambesi—namely, a Portuguese explorer, Major Serpa Pinto. He had entered Africa by Benguella at the head of a scientific expedition. His two partners left him at Bihé to go more northwards, while he went to study the sources of the Chobe. He arrived at the Barotsi country, and was preparing to direct his way to the Lualaba, when all his porters, to the number of one hundred and fifty, abandoned him. He had no one left with him but three men, three little boys, and two women. Not being able to procure an escort from the Barotsi, and being attacked by fever, he found himself in the greatest straits. It was then that he heard us spoken of, and obtained from the chief some canoes and rowers to come and find us. While I was acting as head nurse to our dear Eleazar at Sesheke, my wife lavished her care on Major Serpa Pinto. He was very ill. But assiduous care, better diet, and rest at length brought about a happy change of mind and body. We offered him such hospitality as travellers can : a place in our waggon. His culture and natural amiability made him a pleasant travelling companion. We considered that it was a real privilege to be able, in the name of our society, to show some attentions to so distinguished a man. He left us ten days since to go straight to Pretoria, and thence to the coast for Europe. We parted from each other with the keenest regret, and his departure leaves a blank among us. He is one of the warmest friends to Africa that I have yet met. The importance of his work cannot fail to attract the attention of the scientific as much as of the religious public.[1] Since he left us, he has had all sorts of adventures. The rains have come on—torrential rains : the Limpopo, the Marico, all the rivers are overflowing ; and the country on the other side is nothing but one frightful quagmire. And he took great trouble to inform us of this, so that we should take a different route. Our tents are worn out, and the canvas of our waggons is in rags. All the same, we are preparing to start next week, making an immense *détour* by Sechele's country, Nylstroom, Marabastadt, etc. Although we were in such sorrow, we left the Zambesi full of hope for this mission. Once at Valdezia, we shall see what we can do.

[1] See Major Serpa Pinto's book " How I Crossed Africa," vol. ii., pp. 131-276, for a detailed account of the journey from Leshoma to Shoshong, and a generous tribute to the Coillard family.—TR.

CHAPTER VI

NEAR PRETORIA, *May 6th*, 1879.

IN my last letter, I took leave of you before two alternative
routes, and in a great perplexity. In proposing that our
evangelists should remain temporarily at Shoshong, so as to
allow of our conferring together and maturing our plans, the
Basuto-land Conference (at bottom unfavourable to our projects)
might seem to have solved the difficulty. But, for several
reasons, the catechists positively refused to remain there. And,
sooner than return with them to Basuto-land, we decided to
follow the directions our brethren had first sent, and go together
to Valdezia, to seek in the north of the Transvaal the field of
labour we had once caught a glimpse of.[1] It was against the
grain, I admit, for we saw no light in that direction, but we were
afraid of straying from the path of duty and missing our way.

We therefore left Shoshong on February 25th. It would
be impossible to tell you all the kindness showered upon us
by the Bamangwato. Mr. and Mrs. Hepburn set the example:
Khama and the Christians followed. During our journey to
the Zambesi, they supported the families who remained with
them, and did so with a liberality and delicacy that touched
us deeply. On our departure, they loaded our waggons with
provisions, and overwhelmed our evangelists with presents,
clothes, and rich furs. We too had our share of attentions

---

[1] The missionaries at Valdezia would seem to have pointed out a corner
to them on their previous visit.

from the chief and other persons. The little community of Europeans, to whom I had the privilege of preaching the Gospel during our stay at Shoshong, also made a point of testifying their sympathy at the moment of our departure.

As the rainy season was already well advanced, we ventured to take the most direct road—if, indeed, there *is* any trace of a road in these deserts. Six days later, we were at Seleka's. They say we ought to have made the journey in four days, which I somewhat doubt. Seleka is a small tributary chief of Khama's. His village is picturesquely placed just where a wooded gorge opens out: his power extends over several hamlets scattered along the banks of the Limpopo. We had scarcely outspanned in the forest at the entrance of the gorge, when a number of people on foot, on horseback, and on oxen hastened to visit us. The old chief was ill; nevertheless, I saw him. He ordered one of his sons to collect his people and bring back my words to him. When the preaching of the Gospel was over, I was quite surprised to see the men consult together, and then, in concert with their chief, implore us to settle near them. Something they had let fall the day before ought to have prepared me for this. "For a long time," they said, "we have been wishing for a missionary, but we don't know to whom we should address ourselves, and no one thinks of us. Surely God has sent you to us; do not go away." This appeal moved our catechists deeply; but you will easily understand that I did not feel free to respond to it just then, as Khama had told us his missionaries of the L.M.S. thought of making Seleka an annexe to Shoshong. Still, we promised to confer with the one whose right it was to decide—namely, Mr. Hepburn—and to let them know our decision later. Poor things! how regretfully they watched us inspan and go away! They gave us guides to replace Khama's; and in the hope of being able to cross the Limpopo, we travelled by forced marches, through deluges of rain, and across a flooded country.

We crossed the river at a spot where we were assured the waggon of a hunter had once ventured: trees have grown and the banks have deepened since then, and I should not now recommend this ford to anybody. We took nearly all day to effect the crossing, firing our guns now and then to scare the crocodiles. Thence our guides had to conduct us through the woods, towards the top of a mountain in the Blaauwberg where a petty chief named Mapena lives. After having wandered in this desert for several days, we found ourselves entangled among hills, gorges, and brushwood, so thick and thorny that we could hardly get through them. We had missed our way.

Knowing myself to be in the neighbourhood of the chief Malebogo, I sent to the nearest village to ask for guides. A troop of armed men soon appeared; their bearing and their dances were hardly calculated to reassure us. At Shoshong, one of our friends who came from Potchefstroom had informed me the tribes of the Zoutpansberg were rising against the English Government, and that a regiment of volunteers was being raised to subdue them. But my desire to take the most direct way had silenced the voice of prudence in me. What I saw now gave me food for reflection. Very soon, these wild-looking creatures dashed tumultuously towards us. Thateli was their chief, and he addressed me haughtily : " Who has given you right of way here ? You must pay. Let us see what you have in your waggons." You can easily picture the scene of confusion which ensued. Nevertheless, I succeeded in calming our importunate visitors, and in keeping them at a respectful distance, while I led Thateli away with me to explore the rocky flanks of the mountain and to open a way with hatchets.

Unfortunately, in the dusk, my waggon was thrown violently against a clump of thick trees, through a sharp turn they obliged us to make. I thought it was completely smashed up. There was nothing for it but to outspan there in these thickets, one behind the other.[1] It was no small labour to cut down these big trees, and clear away the undergrowth by the light of a lantern ; but I was able to discover, with gratitude to God, that the damage was much less serious than I had feared.

While we were working, our pretended guides had left us, and I now perceived that they had plundered us : tent, bedding, blankets, clothes, hatchets, even the food on which we had counted for our people, exhausted with fatigue—all had vanished. " Will they attack us during the night ? " we asked each other. We committed ourselves to the Lord, and in spite of the barking

---

[1] African travellers always try to form an enclosure (or laager) with their waggons when halting for the night, for greater security.

of our dogs (we had been given new ones at Shoshong) we slept in peace. Next morning, thinking we were intimidated, Thateli's men came back in a body, noisily claiming wages for what they called their *services* the evening before! But torrents of rain soon delivered us from their incessant importunities. We were not deterred from pursuing our way all the same, harassed and hungry; and at nightfall we reached the mission station of Blaauwberg, where Mr. Stech (B.M.S.[1]) received us cordially. But we had great difficulty in getting there. The waggon of one catechist had the tilt utterly destroyed; the other had lost the tire of a hind wheel, and only reached the station next day with a borrowed one. Mine was also a pitiable spectacle; and several of our oxen had fallen lame. Nevertheless, we had much cause for thankfulness; for, in a country where fever rages pitilessly, we were all in life and health. Still, we had to separate for a few days, and send the useless waggon to a farmer of these parts, who in case of need works as a blacksmith. This pious and interesting man, a descendant of Huguenot refugees, would not accept a penny for his labour. The extraordinary rains, which delayed us five days with our friends the Stechs, had soaked the soil to such an extent, that there were nothing but bogs to be found, out of which we could scarcely tug our heavy mud-clogged waggons, though we yoked thirty oxen.

Directly our brother Hofmeyr heard we were in these parts, although he was ill, he harnessed his waggon and hastened to meet us. Like most pious Africanders, he is a warm-hearted man. Let us not try to tell the emotions this meeting called up. When we saw this friend once more, who had been the last to wish us God-speed two years ago, we felt indeed that we were coming from a far country, and that we had not all returned. Yes, but we must not weep for those whom the Master has so honoured.

We found our friends the Hofmeyrs in trouble: they had all been visited by fever at once—father, mother, and children; so that their friend the blacksmith farmer had sent a waggon and taken them all to his own house. Mr. Hofmeyr had been unable to move, and his wife was so weak she seemed a mere flicker that a puff would put out. In the village, too, many people were

[1] Berlin Missionary Society.

laid up. We only stayed two days with them : our desires were towards Valdezia—that Valdezia we had left overflowing with life and health, flooded with light and refreshed by the dew from above. Alas! we found it buried in the gloom of sickness : our arrival was scarcely noticed. Mr. and Mrs. Berthoud were both ill in bed ; nearly all the six little children of the two families had fever ; and all called for ceaseless care. Add to all that the isolated position of our friends, each with a new-born infant, and the lack of good servants, and it would be difficult to conceive a more deplorable situation than theirs. It was certainly time we came. My niece Elise lent a helping hand for the children. My wife, the sick nurse of our expedition, who has never found time to be ill herself the moment there was any one else to be tended, took her place beside Mrs. Berthoud—only for a brief time, alas! The sickness had already made terrible progress, and five days after our arrival our sister passed away. The lucid moments that lighted up her last days will ever leave sweet memories in the hearts of those who were privileged to be near her : her words bore witness to her inward peace, her faith and perfect confidence in her Saviour.

As for me, I had not the comfort of being with our friends in these solemn circumstances. Two days after our arrival at Valdezia, I had set off with two of the evangelists to Mochache's, to see if the little field of work every one had seemed so sure of were really accessible. The journey took us a fortnight : half the time the rain fell pitilessly ; the roads were frightful. Mochache, you must know, is the high priestess of the neighbouring tribes. She has her sanctuary in a wooded gorge, where the rites and sacrifices are performed which she ordains and presides over. With the exception of a few privileged " ancients," none dared approach the sacred grove ; and if by chance some head of cattle venture across the boundary stream, whoever the owner may be, they at once become the property of the priests in charge, and are sacrificed without appeal. No stranger is allowed to penetrate into the village of this chieftainess : it can only be seen from afar, perched upon the mountain side like an eagle's eyrie, on the edge of a black forest. She herself is invisible, so that certain individuals take it upon themselves to doubt her existence. Those best informed assert that Mochache really exists, and they even add that she is immortal !

All I know is that, like all the fraternity of magicians, she is gifted with a penetration which sets her far above the common herd. For two days, she made us wait, in order to heighten her dignity : then when pressed by my messages, she refused to see us, asking haughtily the object of our visit. Her answer was already prepared. " I have my god, and I am his priestess ; I do not want you or your God. Besides, your week has only seven days ; mine has eight : so how could we ever come to an understanding ? If I allowed you to come to me, either you would be in prison, or you would ruin my authority."

All our arguments struck against this rock without shaking it. In vain we warned and pleaded ; in vain we had prayed and hoped : the door was indeed closed. They ordered us to leave. While once again turning my waggon pole from this door, at which I had just knocked in vain, I was, in spite of my sorrow, too deeply conscious of the presence and sovereign will of God to yield to discouragement. I thought of the strange remark my friend Mr. Buchanan had made, after the check we experienced from the Matabele : " God has sent you as an advertisement through the heathen tribes of tropical Africa." An *advertisement !* Well, so be it ! And then those words of my Saviour took hold of me : " What I do thou knowest not now, but thou shalt know *hereafter.*"

On my return to Valdezia, I found two letters—one from a German missionary inspector of the Berlin Society, whom I had acquainted with my projects, and whom my brother Creux and I had jointly invited to a fraternal conference. Not being able to come himself, he reminded me that all that part of the Transvaal was the field of labour of their Society, and that a division could not take place without inconvenience. The other letter was from Mr. Hepburn, burning with affection. He deplored our departure from Shoshong, and told me of two important decisions of their conference, by which they invited us and our American brethren to share their field of labour, pressed me to occupy the post of Seleka, and welcomed us there in advance in God's Name.

What light in our darkness ! Was this to be the *hereafter* of the Master ? After having conferred with our companions, it was decided that Asser and Aaron should go immediately to Seleka ; that for reasons of economy and prudence Azael and Andreas should follow them later on ; but that for the present they should remain at Valdezia, under the care of our friends Creux and Berthoud. It must be clearly understood that the post of Seleka is not an important one. It would make a fine annexe to Shoshong, but it is too restricted for an independent field. For us, alone, it would be a forlorn hope. But *it is a finger-post planted on the road either to the Banyaï or the Barotsi.* What will you think of it, dear friends ? For my part, when I see how the Lord has led us by a way that we knew not, and when I try to discern His holy will, I am filled with gratitude. We have knocked at all the doors pointed out to us ; we have found every one of them barred—all, with one exception ; and it seems as though the Lord would force us to enter there. Perhaps you will say it is only half open ; but at any rate it is not quite shut. We have no choice : the field of Barotsi-land is certainly, in my opinion, the only one the Master indicates for our Basuto Churches.

The moment of separation from our evangelists was a solemn one. For two years we had lived together in perpetual contact ; we had shared the same fatigues, the same trials, the same blessings ; we had run the same risks ; we had experienced the same deliverances. We were one family. We had learnt to know one another—not always, perhaps, to each other's advantage ; but our mutual affection had never faltered. To say that we had been able to travel together for so long, without having had any serious misunderstandings, is I think the greatest praise I can give to our evangelists and their excellent wives. In their last prayer with us, while casting themselves on the Lord, they asked that to us " might be given eyes that looked backward, that the window of our secret closet might be always open towards the regions whither they were returning." Could it be otherwise ? May He who is sending them, to Whom all power is given in heaven and on earth, accomplish for them also His promise : " Lo, I am with you alway, even unto the end of the world."

It was thus that, comforted, but heavy-hearted, we separated. The society of our friends Creux and Berthoud, who are going as far as Pretoria with us, softened the parting for us. We are travelling by short stages—a dismal ambulance hospital. My wife took the fever at Valdezia, and has been very ill ; she was eight or ten days in bed. She was scarcely convalescent when it was the turn of my niece. There can be nothing more dreary than travelling by waggon with invalids ; but our friends Creux and Berthoud are a living lesson to us in devotion and Christian resignation.

NEAR POTCHEFSTROOM, TRANSVAAL, *May* 29*th*, 1879.

We are hastening back to Basuto-land. It is important above all things to know whether our Churches there are prepared to charge themselves with the responsibility of a work at the Zambesi, and to face all the sacrifices it will involve. Without first knowing this, it would have been *absolutely impossible* for us to leave Shoshong with the catechists to begin the Barotsi Mission, so the placing of these latter at Seleka will permit of our plans ripening. And we are not deserting the cause we have at heart ; indeed, I am sure that in the present circumstances our return to Basuto-land can but promote it. You will see we are making an immense *détour*. The temptation to go straight to our station at Leribé and rest was very great ; but we felt it was our duty to visit the Churches, and learn their inclinations. If we can thus do some good, we shall not regret this extension of our journey in mid-winter.

You would, I am sure, be astonished at the interest our expedition excites all through this country. The Zambesi is the end of the earth ; evidently we must have seen everything, and every one makes it his business to bombard us with questions. You know that in the Transvaal there is a strong party of discontented Boers, who chafe under the British Government. The newspapers will perhaps have told you of the hostile demonstrations in this country at the time of the British High Commissioner Sir Bartle Frere's visit, a few days before our arrival at Pretoria. It seems that two emissaries have gone from here to explore the Banyaï country, and that their reports represent it as a perfect Canaan. Consequently, if the discontented Boers go to these parts, we may expect the wars of extermination necessary for the conquest of this second Land of Promise. Hence the questions with which we are plied incessantly, as to the natives, the country, the resources, etc. Already, two years ago, there was an exodus of six hundred Boer families who would not submit to English domination.

Unhappily, this caravan of warrior patriarchs was badly commanded, and plunged recklessly into the frightful Kalahari
Desert, seeking its way towards Lake Ngami. The tale of their
sufferings goes to one's very heart. Tortures of thirst decimated
their teams and scattered 'their flocks ; it is said that their way
is strewn with baggage, thrown out to lighten their waggons—
furniture, utensils, tools of every kind. They found all the
pools emptied or dried up : then men and beasts, maddened with
thirst, threw themselves pell-mell into the mud and fought for
it, and there at last found death. One day, at the last extremity,
their chiefs assembled a meeting for prayer : they had scarcely
finished when a transport waggon arrived loaded with barrels
and leather bottles full of fresh water. Mr. Hepburn, the
zealous missionary of Shoshong, who had preceded them by
several days, had heard of their distress, and sent them this help.
The remainder of this unhappy expedition directed its course
towards the west of the lake, and was further reduced by fever,
privations, and the attacks of the natives ; dissensions broke out
among themselves ; and since then no one has been able to give
any news of them.[1] But we who come from the Zambesi are
supposed to know everything, and it is touching to hear these
poor peasants asking us for news of the *trek-menschen* : one has
a brother among them, another a cousin, every one has some
relation, more or less distant.

At Pretoria, our friends the Bosmans constrained us to
accept the most cordial hospitality at the Dutch manse. It
was insisted that I should give a public lecture on our journey-
ings in what we should call in France the *Palais de Justice*.
The governor, Sir Owen Lanyon, whom imperative duties
summoned to the seat of war, expressed his regret that he could
not be present, but all the civil and military authorities honoured
us with their presence. Although the newspapers spoke very
indulgently of this lecture, I had the feeling it had not been
a success. I could not feel at ease in that same hall where
Dieterlen and our evangelists had been cited to appear as
prisoners three years before.

At Potchefstroom, to which a week's journey brought us,

---

[1] The survivors reached Damara-land and Benguella, where they are still
living under the German and Portuguese Governments. See Mr. Hepburn's
" Twenty Years in Khama's Country."

we found the same interest. We arrived there on a Saturday evening. Not only had I to preach the next morning in the Wesleyan church, and at night in one of the Dutch churches, but they prevailed upon me to stay over the Monday, and in the evening I was obliged to do the best part of the talking at a public conversazione, convened for the occasion. The Wesleyan, Dutch, and English pastors were present. We were told it was the first missionary meeting ever held in Potchefstroom ; and they might have added—in the Transvaal. I felt happy to plead the cause of missions before such a sympathetic assembly.

KLERKSDORP, *June 2nd.*

We arrived here on Saturday evening (the day before yesterday) in time to pass a pleasant Sunday, but a little too late to meet a party of Zambesi traders who had just left again. They bring news which gives me great concern : it is that since my departure Nguana-wina, the expelled king, has returned at the head of troops from Makumba-Kumbe, fallen upon several petty Barotsi chiefs of my acquaintance, and put them to death. He then went to attack Robosi in his capital. It seems that the latter had time to gather his forces to resist him. What will be the end of this civil war ?

LERIBÉ, *November 12th,* 1879.

How I wished for telepathic communication, so that you might know my delight on learning the deficit had at last been wiped out ! The spirit of conquest is the vital principle of mission work. The Church of our day has certainly grasped this, and no part of the world offers a more striking spectacle of emulation, enterprise, and zeal than our Dark Continent. Doubtless science, by the intrepidity of its explorers, gives a powerful impulse to this movement. But, let us say it to the glory of God, the Christians of England and America show themselves no less intrepid, no less devoted, than the geographers and traders. And shall not we take a part, however humble it may be, in the evangelisation of Central Africa ? Could we not from now onwards create a special fund for this new mission ? You will have learnt officially the decision of our Synod about it. The urgency of this work seems to impress itself on every one. We *must* go forward ; everything drives us But it is felt at the same time that such a work ought not to be undertaken lightly. And it has been thought that, instead of going straight back to the Zambesi regions, as I begged to be allowed to do, it would be better for me to visit France first. This decision would have pained my wife and me very acutely, if we had not witnessed the good spirit and perfect harmony which have reigned all through the discussions of the Synod. So we are going to France, as we should have gone to the Zambesi, in the spirit of duty and obedience. The Lord shows us the way so clearly that we have no right to hesitate.

December 7th, 1879.

Starting for France ? We must believe it, though we cannot realise it. It seems to us that this is only taking up our expedition again, and our prayer is that our journeys in Europe may be yet more blessed than our peregrinations in tropical Africa. And that is saying much, but not too much. If we should live to be very old, these two and a half years would always stand out for us like summits flooded with sunshine in a panorama where dark shades abound.

The spirit of the Leribé Churches is excellent. A little movement which had shown itself recently has added some members to our class of catechumens, and what rejoices me is that these are conquests over paganism. Another proof is furnished by our collections. We have had three in three months. The first produced a little more than £5, the second nearly £9 15s., and the third nearly £10. The collection with us is a part of the service. Each brings his offering to the table, and the whole is afterwards consecrated to the Lord by prayer. Nothing touches me like seeing with what eagerness and what radiant faces the little ones bring their mites. Even the babies in their mothers' arms have their threepenny-bits, which their little hands put into the Lord's treasury. They have told me of children crying because they had nothing for the collection, or because they had only a threepenny-bit, the *sou* of this country, where the copper of Europe is not yet known. It is impossible that this education should not bear fruit in the future lives of these little creatures.

Our meetings, like all our farewell meetings, were solemn : especially the last, that on Monday morning, where several spoke.   A thrill passed through me, when I saw my old friend rise, Nathanael Makotoko, whose friendship of more than twenty years has never faltered.   At first, he could hardly control himself.   Addressing M. Dormoy, my successor, " Young servant of God," he said, " we receive you with love amongst us ; but it is needful you should know what we are passing through to-day.   You see us assembled here, a great company : we are saluting our spiritual father ; we know him, and he knows us.   Do you know where we were and what we were, when, young like you, he came here, twenty years ago ? Where we were ?   Lost in the world !   What we were ?   Wild beasts ; yes, beasts of the field ! "   And he burst into tears.

This moment of parting had awakened memories.   Nathanael is no longer the young man of old, vigorous and valiant.   Of those bygone days, nothing is left him but the scars which recall the dauntless courage he displayed in fighting for his country, and defending the fortress of Moshesh.   To-day, he is growing grey, he is shattered ; the persecutions he suffered from another chief, to whom he had devoted himself, have, while fostering his piety, left a shade of melancholy upon his character. He is a chief too, and yet he works on the roads that his house may maintain its position ; and as he does nothing by halves, he works like a convict.   No evangelist has done more than he. He speaks of nothing but his approaching departure for the sky, and of the little hope we can cherish of seeing each other again down here.   However that may be, the meeting-place is sure, and it is not far distant.[1]

After the private and official farewells, and a last interview with Molapo, to whom it was given me to speak once more some serious words, we at last left Leribé.   We spent the first night at the district magistrate's, Major Bell, who had specially invited us.   The report had gone about that in the evening I was to give a lecture on our journeys in the Court-house, which had been arranged for it.   White people had come riding and driving from great distances, in spite of the late hour.   The room was packed.   Some Basuto, too, moved by curiosity, had

---

[1] Nathanael Makotoko is still alive (1897).

collected outside, and impromptu interpreters repeated to them
all that was being said inside. We went on to Cana and
Berea ; and there too, as at Leribé, we met good Christians, who
brought us, some their shillings, others a little flour for the road.

ON BOARD THE "CONWAY CASTLE," *January 20th*, 1880.

Our journey through the Colony, after crossing the Orange
River, was by no means devoid of interest. We did part of it
by train, a novelty to people like ourselves, who had not heard
the puffing of the iron horse for twenty-three years! And
here the railway did not lack local colour. Once the engine
stopped short on a mountain-side. There was no station near,
and every one ran to the doors, not without alarm. But our
minds were quickly relieved. Right down in the valley a
farmer's wife was waving her umbrella, and signalling to the
guard to wait for her. Soon she began trying to run up the
hill with her daughters—no easy task for a lady of her proportions, under a burning sun and the relentless gaze of her future
fellow-travellers. But she got there all the same, and was
received with a storm of hurrahs. After which episode we
continued our journey.

At Kimberley, we were received with the greatest cordiality
by Mr. and Mrs. Calvert of blessed memory ; it was of him,
if I mistake not, that it was said, " He arrived at the Fiji Islands
without finding a single Christian ; he quitted them without
leaving a single heathen."

There is a kind of free-masonry—the real kind this—which
unites the Lord's builders ; but one feels it an honour to be
in the company of such devoted men—men, too, whom God
has so honoured.

Here, too, we were invited to hold a meeting, over which Sir
Charles Warren presided, and the audience was both numerous
and sympathetic. We have carried away the happiest memories
of Kimberley. A black evangelist, the pastor of a large and
active congregation, pressed us very much to visit him. He
sent a conveyance for us, and, when we arrived, we found he
had arranged a perfect festival for us. When we left the meeting, the evangelist put a number of little diamonds into my
hands. " M. Coillard," he said, " these represent a day's work
of my men ; choose which you like."

I took a long time to look over them ; there were yellow, black, and white. At last I chose a black one.

" Oh, but that is the least valuable," he said.

" Perhaps so, but I like black diamonds ; they are the jewels I am seeking myself for the Saviour's crown." [1]

Not far from East London, seething with the feverish activity of civilised life, Dr. Stewart and his excellent wife offered us the warmest hospitality at Lovedale, that splendid establishment with its thousands of Kaffir pupils. Our voyage through the Colony was fatiguing in every respect. I could not shake off a feeling of lassitude, which overcame me to such a point that all the sources of life and thought seemed dried up within me. Dr. Stewart said it was one of the sequelæ of the Zambesi fever ; and he himself, since his return from Livingstonia, has experienced the same thing. We stayed a fortnight at the Cape. I did not feel capable of going on. And then, too, we wanted to leave my niece at the Huguenot Institution at Stellenbosch until our return. I need not speak further of the interest our mission aroused in all the Churches, especially among the pastors of the Dutch Church.

We left Cape Town on January 13th in the *Conway Castle*, and spent two weeks at Madeira, where our dear friends the Rev. Mr. Buchanan and his wife received us with open arms. It was a time of physical rest and deep spiritual refreshment.

Madeira, with its wonderful scenery, its beautiful sky, its magnificent climate, but also the human misery which displays itself everywhere, and the shameless beggary which accosts you at every step, is a ruin and a petrifaction. That is what the phylloxera and Romanism have done between them. There is no hope for the poorer classes but in emigration.

[1] This was before the days of I.D.B. and other mining regulations. One day during this visit, Mme. Coillard was making friends with a dog in the street, when the owner, a prosperous-looking lady, invited them both into her house. In the course of conversation, she told them her husband had been a tailor, and, after bringing her and their children to Kimberley, they had found themselves in a state of destitution, not being able to get work. Sitting in their wretched hut one day, he began turning over the earthen floor, for want of better occupation, and found *diamonds*. It was the site of a mine, supposed to have been worked out ; but, by diligent search, they found enough small diamonds to ay the foundations of a comfortable fortune. Such things would not be possible now.

Dr. Kalley, of Edinburgh, came to settle there about 1830, curing the sick and preaching the Gospel of the Kingdom, after the example of his Saviour. Eighteen years later, a minister, also Scotch, Dr. Hewitson, came to help him. But incessant and terrible persecutions in the end forced these servants of the Lord to leave the isle, and the Madeira Christians to exile themselves. A vessel conveyed the latter to Trinidad, and thence most of them went to America, where they founded prosperous Churches. There are only about thirty of them left in Funchal, all very poor, but rich in faith and life.

PARIS, *March* 11*th*, 1880.

Bless the Lord with us! He has led and guarded us ; He has brought us here in health and peace. We can sing the 23rd Psalm with overflowing hearts.

We reached Paris the evening before last. After twenty-three years' absence, we could not believe we were once more in the capital of the world, the centre of modern civilisation. The next day, we went to a mission sale. I would not have missed it for worlds ; the object lies too near my heart. It was for the education of missionaries' children. We have no children of our own, but we are all the more interested in those of our little colony in Bastuo-land.

Shall I confess it ? In the midst of all these people who thronged the hall, we experienced at first a feeling of sadness and isolation. We recognised no one : no one recognised us. We were strangers in our fatherland!

But, after all, it was only the faces that had altered : only the " earthly tabernacles " had grown old. Directly our presence was known, we found ourselves in the midst of friends and acquaintances. " Is it really you ? How glad we are to see you back again ! " And some added, " But I thought you were much taller and bigger." It is always the same, you see : at a distance, people as well as things assume abnormal proportions.

CHAPTER VII

London—The Whirlpool—A Reminiscence—Coffee Palaces and Cabmen—
Mildmay Conference—The Sunday-School Festival—Pleading the Cause
of Africa—Molapo's Death—A Contrast.

LONDON, *August 6th,* 1880.

LONDON! Another landmark! A few more stages perhaps, then the last, and the journey will be ended. Thus every milestone we pass makes life more solemn. London is the centre of the whirlpool of modern commercial life. And this life seems to incarnate itself in this maze of iron roads, among these trains which whistle, cross, and intersect one another, from the roofs of the houses down to the bowels of the earth, under the very foundations of this feverish city, everywhere casting out floods of human beings. A stranger from the deserts, seeing these multitudes hurrying, hustling one another, and running breathlessly after their business, receives a painful impression. After all, London is a desert to him, if he knows no one there. It seems that in this perpetual movement a poor man is not allowed to stop. The moment he sits down on a doorstep to rest his tired limbs, a policeman comes up and says pitilessly, " Move on, move on." He moves on, only to hear the same imperious order, until at last he seeks a refuge in the grave.

And yet London attracts me. Twenty-three years ago, I passed through it on my way to Africa. At that time, I did not know a word of English. On the eve of our departure, I had made an important purchase of books; but when they were brought to our hotel that night, I found, to my dismay, that I had lost the banknote into which I had changed *all* my French money. The manager of the hotel, who was a Christian, paid my bill; but we were to leave next day at eight o'clock. I spent all the night praying, unpacking, searching, and ransacking every imaginable thing—in vain! As early as possible, I went with a friend to all the shops where I had made any purchases the previous day; but they laughed in my face at the idea of enquiring after a lost banknote in a London shop. I was at last returning sadly to our hotel, where the cabs were already waiting, when I heard a voice calling me. I turned back, and went into a stationer's shop. "Excuse me, but did you not buy something here yesterday?" "Yes; some paper and an ink-stand: but why?" "Did you not lose anything, sir?" "Yes, indeed; I lost a banknote: have you found it by any chance?" "Here it is, sir; you dropped it out of your purse yesterday."

My emotion may be imagined. To recover a banknote lost in London—in the City—seemed to be a miracle! The young man who restored it to me had no need to tell me he feared God. He was a member of the Y.M.C.A. A few moments later, we left London and embarked for Africa.

My impressions of London, this time, have by no means effaced the first. It is true that side by side with great wealth exists abject misery, but nothing is more touching than to see the generosity and activity displayed by Christians. I shall not easily forget the warm reception given to us two or three times in Temperance Coffee Palaces, and with what uncere-monious heartiness they applauded all I said. The poor people wanted to make a collection. I only expected a few *pence*, and they handed me over more than £2. After the meeting, a cabman came up to me and said, "I am going to take you home in *my* cab," and nothing would induce him to accept a fare from the hands of a friend. We met several of these cabmen, whom we recognised as brothers in Christ; and such meetings are especially pleasant in London. Let those take courage who "go into the streets and lanes of the city," as well as those who search "the highways and hedges." Their work is not in vain in the Lord.

The meetings that specially interested us were those of Mildmay. One of the characteristic features of these meetings is the part taken by laymen, such as Mr. Stevenson Blackwood. What power there is in the piety of such men! I noticed the same thing wherever I went: laymen have broken through all barriers, and carried the position, even in the Church of England.

And what astonishes me no less is their knowledge of the Holy
Scriptures. In fact, wherever you go now, you hear nothing
talked of but "Bible readings." You would think people had
only just struck on this diamond mine ; and certainly never
were such riches dug out of it.

The Mildmay meetings were scarcely over when those of
the Sunday-school centenary began. We were present at the
great demonstration at the Crystal Palace. Such an event is
an epoch in a man's life. I seem still to hear that choir of
five thousand picked voices within the Palace itself, and then
that of thirty thousand in the Palace garden, singing, not music
written for effect, but hymns in praise of the Saviour. In such
demonstrations, and their popularity, there is not only something profoundly impressive, but something, too, which reveals
the secret of this nation's power. At every step this secret
betrays itself : even the public monuments proclaim it. With
us, you see everywhere " *Liberté, egalité, fraternité.*" Here,
inscriptions like this, " Not unto us, O Lord, not unto us, but
unto Thy name give glory " ("*Non nobis, Domine*") ; or even,
as on the front of the Royal Exchange, " The earth is the Lord's,
and the fulness thereof."

After the meetings of which I have just spoken, I found
my work had been cut out for me ; so, with our devoted friend
Major Malan, I bravely took the field, and pleaded for Africa
and the Zambesi wherever I was given the opportunity. We
began with the House of Commons, where Captain Gosset, the
Serjeant-at-Arms, had brought together in his rooms some
Christian friends, eminent men, who took a great interest in
the evangelisation of Africa. Afterwards we had drawing-room
meetings here and there, and then made a tour in the country :
Aldershot, Guildford, Weymouth, Dorchester, Wareham, Wool-
wich, Wimbledon, and Sevenoaks were thus visited. Everywhere
we had interesting meetings, each having its own special stamp.
Here, it would be a colonel who presided in true British fashion,
and the meeting had a martial tone ; there, it would be the
mayor in a public room, or even in the townhall itself ;
elsewhere, again, it was a Church of England clergyman who
had put himself to expense for the occasion had had a large
marquee erected on his lawn, and assembled all the *élite* of
the place ; once, it was even a bishop, Mr. Moule, who has

laboured for long years in China as a missionary, and is going back as a bishop. Just think of China pleading for Africa, and the Church of England giving a token of affection to the Reformed Churches of France and Switzerland! Going from place to place like this, making fresh acquaintances and seeing new faces every day, is very fatiguing, and requires more courage than one would think. But beside a gallant officer, who would feel cowardly?

The time of our visit to England was very ill chosen. It was the end of the season; every one was tired of meetings and collections; and I dare say more than one person, on seeing the notices announcing the Rev. F. Coillard and Major Malan, said to themselves, "What! another meeting! another collection!" But what would be the use of our collecting the money needed, scraping it together no matter how, and then finding ourselves left in the lurch as soon as the work was begun? The money will find itself: the great thing is to awaken a living interest which will sustain us when we have gone to the front.

Meanwhile, I received a telegram one day, announcing the arrival of my friend Mabille at Southampton. He brought me sad news. First, of the disarming of the Basuto, and since then telegrams have been arriving one after the other, causing us the greatest anxiety. Now, it seems the excitement is dying down. The Basuto will not revolt, thank God! All the more crying is the injustice to which they have been subjected; and nothing can extenuate it, unless it is the fact, as they, poor things, suggest themselves, that they have black skins. "And yet," they add in their prayers, "it is Thyself, Lord, Who hast made us black."

Another piece of news which went to our hearts was that of Azael's death.[1] What a loss! He was the oldest of the band. Converted late in life by the instrumentality of Eleazar Marathane, he was but little developed intellectually. But, on the other hand, he was one of the most pious men I have ever met in Africa. He was a kindly man who did not know how to be angry, everybody's friend, full of simple faith, always the same, always feeding on the Word of God and prayer. And

[1] See pages 78, 79.

God has taken him! Well, well! We are always trembling for the Ark of the Lord, always ready to cry out and stretch forth our hands to keep it from falling! He knows what He is doing.

The other day, at an underground railway station, I happened to take up a newspaper, and read this: "The chief Molapo of Basuto-land is dead." I felt stunned; the words seemed to swim before my eyes. What! Molapo dead! How mysterious, how inscrutable, are the ways of God! No one who did not know what Molapo had been to me, and what I had perhaps been to him during my missionary career, could understand what I felt. Alas! I was his Micaiah! He thought that in religious matters I never prophesied anything good for him. As a man he possessed fine qualities. He gave signal proof of intelligence and bravery in his youth, thus gaining the favour of his father Moshesh, and obtained great influence in the country. He was born to command, and could not brook opposition. He made every one tremble before him, and the spell of his name lay heavy as lead over his whole district; not the remotest hamlet but felt its weight. Immensely rich in cattle, as later on in specie, he made use of his wealth as a means of subjugating all wills to his own. Like all tyrants, he would take the lead in everything, and rule the progress of civilisation and the Gospel according to his own caprices. Nevertheless, his opulent nature had beautiful impulses of generosity, that set him in happy contradiction to his usual self; but, jealous of his authority, and intoxicated with his power and the flatteries of his petty courtiers, he had grown suspicious, irritable, unjust, and extraordinarily suspicious. No one who had read the touching story of his conversion would doubt its reality. If he had remained a Christian, he would have been the salvation of the tribe. Unhappily, he relapsed into heathenism, and became the most implacable and formidable enemy of the Gospel. Shortly before my arrival in Basuto-land, he had persecuted the Christians of his district as much as lay in his power, stripped the most conspicuous of their cattle, and deprived others of their fields: he was always on the alert to stop a sinner on the way to conversion, if possible. And yet his conscience still spoke, in spite of all his efforts to stifle it. It is asserted that, for a long time, he never went to rest without reading the Word of God and praying, even while he was living in sin. At times, the struggle was such as to affect his reason. Then he would flee to the mountains, and retire with a few attendants to a cave. I often had most intimate conversations with him ; and one day I asked him, during one of these private talks : " Tell me frankly, Molapo, what did you feel when you were converted ? Do you believe that you were only a Christian in name then ? or did some real change take place in you ? "

He looked fixedly at me. " My pastor," he said at last, sighing, " it was not any illusion of my imagination. In here," pointing to his breast, " there was a fire that devoured me—I could not hold it in ; but now," he added in a tone of bitter sadness, " it has all gone out—there is nothing left but a heap of ashes. As to the things of God, I no longer understand them : it is like the sound of a chariot that has disappeared into the distance."

Another time, when I went to him to beg for the liberation of six of his wives, who were to be baptised, he said, after a long discussion, " I will set free four of these women, but not the two others. I know what it is to be converted ; my own baptismal name was Jeremiah. These four women are really converted ; the others are not ; and if you baptise them, you will one day see I was right." And, as a matter of fact, one of these latter, after some years of Christian profession, did fall into sin, and returned to paganism.

On my return from the Zambesi, I found him attacked with a partial paralysis, which had affected his face. But our prayers had not been granted : his heart was in no way softened, and he still kept harassing our Christians. M. Dormoy wrote to me again only a little time ago that another of our members found himself obliged not only to leave the station, but to emigrate from the country, on account of the perpetual injustice of which he was the victim. And the next news was that of Molapo's death ! In spite of all our exhortations, all our prayers, and those of the Church, in spite of his own conflicts, and the cries of his conscience, can he have died an apostate, only " breathing out blasphemies against Christians and the Gospel," as they wrote to me a little while since ? Who can penetrate the secrets of a soul with his God ? and who can say whether at the last hour this wandering child did not fall into the arms of his Father ?

My position towards him, and my deep affection for him, make me feel the anguish of David over the death of Absalom.[1]

Another friendly face at Leribé had also passed away some weeks before, that of Elia Mapiké, also one of the first converts of MM. Casalis and Arbousset. He was a weak man, and, like David, had a deplorable fall ; but he was restored, and always remained a faithful Christian, in spite of the terrible temptations which beset him. He was an elder of our Church ; and his peaceful, happy end contrasted with that of Molapo, the man who had persecuted him so malignantly, and with whom he was to appear before God. His last words were characteristic. He had, like Moses, chosen rather to suffer

---

[1] Molapo and his brother Letsie were the two first Basuto to welcome the French missionaries in the name of their father, the chief Moshesh, in 1833. Seven years later, Molapo, the younger, declared himself a Christian, and was baptised. His was not a nature to do anything by halves ; and nothing was lacking either in his conduct, his astonishing knowledge of the Scriptures, his complete abandonment of heathenism, or his zeal for the progress of the Gospel. He made a Christian (*i.e.* not a cattle) marriage with Lydia, the first woman baptised in Basuto-land. His courage, generosity, and great intelligence made him the idol alike of his father, his tribe, and all the missionaries. But his abilities being greater than those of his elder brother Letsie, Moshesh, to avoid collisions between them, assigned him the district of Leribé to govern, the only condition being that he should have a resident missionary, which he too desired. Unfortunately, the Paris Society had not a man to send, nor yet the means to maintain one. Hence, it was settled he should only make administrative tours in his province, delaying his establishment there till he could have a missionary. Gradually his visits grew longer and longer. He got into the habit of doing without the ministry of a pastor. His district, too, became the refuge of those who wished to escape from the missionary sphere, and their influence was too strong. First tolerating pagan customs, he next yielded to them, and became a polygamist, and by the time M. Coillard was appointed to the district the mischief was done. Incessant conflicts with the Boers on his frontiers, while all the missionaries were exiled, fostered in him a hatred of everything connected with white men. Before long, he was actually persecuting all Christians. On his death-bed, he was jealously guarded by two attendants, who would not allow the missionary or any other Christian to come near him. But his first and still faithful wife, Lydia, was summoned with Rahab, another Christian woman, and they daily read the Bible aloud and prayed with him. One night, he burst into tears, and begged that they would remove him from where he was, and take him *to the missionary's*. But he was dying of paralysis, and before the missionary's arrival he had already lost the power of speech.

affliction with the children of God than to enjoy the pleasures of sin for a season, and he had a foretaste of future bliss. Though he was a happy Christian, yet, when the first rays of heavenly glory were lighting up the tomb, he went down to it with a joy never felt before, which he expressed in these words: " *Kalo hasé phetho !* "   " The beginning is nothing to the end ! "

M. Coillard.   Mlle. Coillard.   Mme. Coillard.   M. Jeanmairet.

Mr. Middleton.   Levi.   Levi's wife.   Ma-Ruthi (Aaron's wife).   Isaiah.   Aaron.   Mr. Waddell.

THE MISSION PARTY, MAY 1884.

[To face page 166

PART II

THE BAROTSI EXPEDITION

1882—1887

O GOD of Bethel, by Whose hand
   Thy people still are fed,
Who through this weary pilgrimage
   Hast all our fathers led !

Through each perplexing path of life
   Our wandering footsteps guide,
Give us each day our daily bread,
   And raiment fit provide.

Oh spread Thy covering wings around,
   Till all our wanderings cease,
And at our Father's loved abode
   Our souls arrive in peace !

97

THE BAROTSI EXPEDITION

January 1884 to January 1887

CHRONICLE

Aug. 1882	Return of M. and Mme. Coillard to Leribé.	
Jan. 2nd, 1884	Expedition started for Barotsi-land.	
,, 30th	,, reached Pretoria.	
Feb. 11th or 12th ...	,, left Pretoria.	
,, 23rd—March 3rd	,, delayed at Saul's Poort.	
March 15th—30th ...	,, ,, ,, Marico River.	
April 8th	,, reached Shoshong (Khama's).	
,, 15th—26th ...	M. Coillard to Seleka to fetch the evangelist Aaron and his family.	
May 21st	Expedition left Shoshong.	
,, 24th—June 1st ...	,, delayed at Kané.	
July 15th (about) ...	,, reached Pata-matenga.	
,, 26th	,, ,, Leshoma (right bank of Zambesi).	
Aug. 10th—Sept. 24th	M. Coillard starts for the capital, and is turned back by news of revolution deposing King Robosi (Lewanika).	
Dec. 12th	M. Coillard, with Aaron and Middleton, starts for Lealuyi by canoe.	
Jan. 8th, 1885 (first voyage)	M. Coillard officially received by King Akufuna (Tatira), and invited to establish a station as soon as floods permit of transport.	
Feb. 11th	M. Coillard returns to Leshoma.	
Aug. 14th—21st ...	Expedition crosses Zambesi to Kazungula.	
,, 29th	Catechists Aaron and Levi stationed at Mambova.	
Sept. 24th	Expedition reaches Sesheke—Station established under M. Jean-mairet's charge.	
Nov. 4th	Marriage of Elise Coillard and M. Jeanmairet.	
,, ,,	News of counter revolution restoring Lewanika to power, and preventing establishment of a station at the capital.	
Dec. 20th (about) ...	Middleton sent to Pretoria to renew exhausted supplies.	
March 6th, 1886 ...	M. Coillard's second voyage to Lealuyi (alone).	
,, 23rd	Official reception by King Lewanika.	
April 17th	M. Coillard returns to Sesheke.	
June 15th	Middleton returns from Pretoria, and is detained six weeks at Kazungula.	
Aug. 16th	M. Coillard and Waddell, Aaron and Middleton, start for Sefula to found station, taking the waggons, and travelling over-land.	
(Sept. 22nd	Birth of Marguerite Jeanmairet at Sesheke.)	
Oct. 11th	Expedition arrives at Sefula—Station founded.	
Dec. 2nd	M. Coillard returns to Sesheke to fetch Mme. Coillard.	
,, 15th	M. and Mme. Coillard start for Sefula.	
Jan. 10th, 1887... ...	,, ,, ,, arrive at Sefula.	
March 4th	Foundation of school at Sefula station.	

THE BAROTSI EXPEDITION

IT was in August 1882 that M. and Mme. Coillard returned to Leribé. During their furlough (it could scarcely be called a holiday) of two and a half years, they had travelled through France, England, Scotland, and the Protestant communities of Switzerland, Italy, Holland, and Belgium, awakening interest in the new Barotsi Mission. The Paris Committee felt unable to accept the onus of so risky and costly an experiment, but it was sympathetic and encouraging, and undertook to receive any contributions subscribed to a special fund for the purpose. The sum of £5,000 had to be collected: an English friend headed the list with £1,000; the rest was got together little by little. Basuto-land was to maintain its own evangelists, and Europe the Europeans, the whole responsibility being cast upon M. Coillard, for the field seemed highly unpromising. The country was generally believed to be the unhealthiest in South Africa; and it was inhabited by about seventeen different tribes, nominally under the sway of the Barotsi kings, but perpetually at war with one another. The difficulties of getting there were almost overwhelming. Nevertheless, when the Coillards left Europe, it was with the intention of starting immediately for the Zambesi.

But they found the state of things in Basuto-land very different from what they had left two years before. The war which followed the Disarmament Act had changed everything. Many of the Christians had died or apostatised; Churches had been broken up; civil war was raging between the loyal and the rebel chiefs; and the people were so impoverished, spiritually as well as materially, that to rely on any substantial help from them was out of the question. Before going farther afield, it was absolutely necessary to reconstruct the work at Leribé, and a year and five months were thus spent. In December 1882,

Mr. and Mrs. Weitzecker arrived from Italy to take up the work of the station. They were the first missionaries the Waldensian Church ever sent to the foreign field, and their coming gave the first impulse to the movement which has since led that Church, poor as it is in wealth and numbers, to send ten workers to South Africa from its fifteen parishes. In January 1884, the long caravan at last set out for the Barotsi Valley.

The party consisted of M. and Mme. Coillard, their niece Elise, and M. Jeanmairet, a young Swiss missionary, with the evangelists Isaiah and Levi and their families, and two artisans, Middleton and Waddell, the former English, the latter Scotch. The start was made under depressing circumstances. The indispensable drivers and cattleherds were no longer an eager band of volunteers, as in the first expedition, but merely hired servants. Moreover, during the long delay, the enthusiasm of many supporters, both in Europe and Africa, had cooled down ; and so deplorable was the state of Basuto-land, that many of their colleagues and other equally devoted friends of missions thought they were forsaking an immediate and a crying need for a mere quixotic enterprise. But the Coillards felt too strong a conviction of their call to hesitate. When they passed through the Transvaal, the Boer Government, by this time reinstated at Pretoria, at first made great difficulties ; but in the end it gave way, and remitted all customs duties. At Shoshong, the party was rejoined by the catechist Aaron and his family, who had been left to carry on mission work at Seleka ever since the previous expedition had halted there, in March 1879.

At the time of the first expedition, trade with the Barotsi Valley had been entirely in the hands of native and half-caste Portuguese merchants, but it had since then been opened up to white traders from the south. The devoted missionary explorer Mr. F. S. Arnot had been over two years at Lealuyi, keeping the place open, in spite of terrible difficulties and privations.[1] The mission party reached Leshoma on July 26th, 1884, and was preparing to cross the Zambesi, when news arrived that Mr. Arnot's health had obliged him to leave for Benguella, and that immediately after his departure a revolution had

---

[1] See Mr. Arnot's book "Garenganze" (Hawkins & Co.).

broken out, by which the king, Robosi (Lewanika), had been driven into exile. The country was in a state of anarchy, which continued until his restoration in October 1885 ; and this obliged the missionaries to stay thirteen months at Leshoma.

In August 1885, the expedition crossed the river, and a station was established at Sesheke, under the charge of M. Jeanmairet, whose marriage with Elise Coillard took place in the following November. Soon after Lewanika returned to power, he sent for M. Coillard (March 1886), received him very cordially, and pointed out a site for the station ; but meanwhile supplies had run out, and the missionaries had been obliged to send all the waggons to Pretoria to renew them. Consequently, it was not until Mr. Middleton returned with them, that the materials necessary for founding the new station could be transported to the interior. It was on August 16th that the pioneers started, and the journey of two hundred and twenty miles occupied exactly two months. They followed the native paths, cutting a road through the forest, step by step, to allow of the waggons passing. Sefula, the site of the future station, nineteen miles from Lealuyi, the capital, was finally reached on September 11th.

As soon as the work of installation had been put in train, M. Coillard hastened back to Sesheke for his wife (who had been obliged by the state of Mme. Jeanmairet's health to remain with her for a time), and together they reached Sefula on January 10th, 1887. This date marked the conclusion of the Barotsi Expedition, and the commencement of the Barotsi Mission.

C. W. M.

CHAPTER VIII

The Return to Africa—Arrival at the Cape—The Huguenot School—
Stellenbosch—Wellington—Natal—Travelling New Style and Old Style
—A Trying Journey—Arrival at Leribé—Disastrous Effects of the War—
Jubilee of the S.M.E.P.—Disappointments—Tour with M. Jeanmairet
among the Churches—An Appeal to the Friends of Missions—Arrival of
the Weitzeckers—Departure from Leribé.

LERIBÉ, *August 26th*, 1882.

BY God's goodness, we have at last arrived at Leribé. We
had to regret five or six days delay at the Cape ; but we
profited by it to go to Wellington, and shake hands once more
with that venerable veteran M. Bisseux,[1] who still represents
the heroic days of the beginnings of our mission. We also
visited the Huguenot School. The creation of this establishment, due to the efforts of a truly apostolic pastor, Mr. Andrew
Murray, has initiated an important reform in the system of
education for young girls in South Africa. It is a *home* rather
than a school. Every day the pupils there devote about an hour
to domestic work ; but the hour is reckoned in *minutes*, to
remind them of the value of time. At the same time, they
carry on really serious studies there. To me, one of the best
fruits of the system and the influence of the house is the fact
that many of the pupils on leaving feel the desire to do something for others, and in their turn devote themselves to teaching
Already, institutions of this kind are arising in the principal
towns of the Colony, the Free State, and the Transvaal. It

[1] M. Bisseux, one of the first party of French Protestant missionaries to
land in South Africa in 1829, died in 1896. These missionaries, when they first
arrived, were welcomed by the colony of descendants of French Huguenots
at the Cape, who begged M. Bisseux to stay with them and be a missionary
to their native servants ; and to this work he devoted his whole life, never
returning to France.

was a beautiful thought on Mr. Andrew Murray's part to connect this work with France, by calling it the Huguenot School. It is a homage to the memory of our persecuted forefathers, many of whom sought refuge at the Cape, and whose names are still met with among the pupils of the school at Wellington.

We also visited Stellenbosch: it is a little Edinburgh, a centre of education. There is a girls' school of the same kind as the one at Wellington—two, indeed, one of which belongs to the Rhenish Mission, and is very prosperous. Above all, there is the Theological Faculty of the Dutch Church: it is thoroughly evangelical, and has been a source of great blessing to the country. What especially rejoices us is to see the missionary spirit developing in the Dutch Church, and gradually dissipating the prejudices of former days. Thus among the theological students, at the same table and on the same benches there is actually a young man of colour. This is a victory indeed. The Rev. Th. Ferguson has also carried on for some years a missionary school, which has already sent out workers, and which numbers many pupils, all Dutch or colonists.

At the Cape, I was naturally occupied with Basuto-land business. I saw the Governor, the Ministers, and some members of Parliament. Then, after eight days' coasting in the Indian Ocean, we were at Natal, and were cordially welcomed at Durban by old friends. We next started for Pietermaritzburg. It was not in ox-waggons that we did the fifty miles this time, but on a real railway, still a great novelty. The line is simple and very narrow—no tunnels; it follows the contours of the mountains, and gently climbs the slopes when necessary, and then the unpleasant rocking makes one feel sea-sick, and calls forth loud abuse from the passengers on all sides. But in imagination we were going over the adventurous journeys of olden times; we were enjoying the grand panorama that unrolled itself before us, and were thankful and happy. A farmer was sitting beside me; and in the evening, when we stopped at a station, and every one had run into the buffet or the bar, my neighbour came to me, as I was walking up and down the platform. "Sir," he said, "will you share my food?" It was biscuit. I was not hungry; indeed, I have no particular fancy for that kind of bread.   But his invitation was so cordial, that I broke the brick, and began to nibble it, chatting with him meanwhile.   It was truly a bit of Africa—hospitable Africa! I do not remember such a thing ever happening to me in all my European journeys.

Many changes have taken place in the fourteen years since we left Natal.   The Zulu, who inhabit it or have sought refuge there, are reckoned at nearly four hundred thousand.   For the sixteen or eighteen thousand colonists, the great question of the day is the labour question, as at the Cape.   The Zulu are so proud and independent that they only work to get the means of obtaining wives for themselves.   Thus, people are obliged to import *coolies* from India.   And to-day, these coolies are everywhere : on the railroad, in the shops, the hotels, the private houses, the market, and the prisons.   Their shops and their Oriental costumes impart a distinctive character to the towns of Natal.   People say they are born shopkeepers; and their stores, thronged with customers, are looked on with no favour by those tradesmen who cannot compete with them. The Wesleyan Church carries on a work of evangelisation among them, but it must be owned the soil is singularly arid.

At Maritzburg, it was my old and intimate friend Mr. Smith, the pastor, who gave us hospitality.   We thought it would only be for a few days, and it was for weeks.   No waggons anywhere— we must have them made to order ; no oxen to be had either. At last, we managed to procure some ; but at what a figure! We had to take them ; there was nothing else for it.   One day, I was in the garden, watching some soldiers go by : I never see them without feeling the strongest sympathy.   Out of the black rabble that followed them, two individuals emerged, and dashed up to me, gesticulating, laughing, and shouting, as soon as they could get near enough—and indeed a good deal sooner : "*Lumela Ntate, lumela Ntate*" ("I greet you, father").   It was Gideon and Fono.[1]   They were bringing my waggon from Basuto-land!   The sight of it, our home on wheels, filled me with sadness.   It had been left out of doors for two years and a half without shelter, exposed to sun and rain, and was in a

---

[1] Two black servants.   Fono, it will be remembered, was the only survivor out of the four Basuto who volunteered for the first expedition.

pitiful state of dilapidation. It was no use to think of selling
it ; no one would have given me anything for it. The repairs
alone cost me about £36 !

But the oxen are bought, the waggons are ready. Let us
load up and set out. How delightful to sit cosily in a corner
of one's chariot, and look at the long team winding before one ;
to hear the "Trek" of the leader, and the crack of his long
whip ; to make one's way leisurely on, camping like gipsies ; in
a word, living the real African life again ! Alas ! the charm
is very shortlived. A cattle plague, which has made terrible
ravages in South Africa, prevails also about here. Even before
we left the town, two of the oxen sent from Basuto-land had
succumbed. I had scarcely sold their skins, when others
dropped on the road. We halted on a rising ground about
three miles from the town. It was a complete disaster : care,
rest, remedies—nothing was of any use. In a few days, I lost
twelve. To-day, at the moment I am writing, they are cutting
up the seventeenth. I made myself perfectly wretched about
it ; and every ox that died drew from me the lament of the
prophet's son, when he lost his axe-head : "Alas ! for it was
borrowed." But that did not repair our losses. The journey
had no lack of other adventures of all sorts : we had gales that
carried everything before them ; dust-storms overwhelming the
waggons ; rain, snow, and rotten roads. It was one of the most
wearying journeys I ever made.

I hasten on to our arrival at Leribé—our dear Leribé. Alas !
it is no longer what it was five years ago ! We knew that well
enough ; and yet I confess the reality surpasses the darkest
pictures our imagination had conjured up. True, some few
people came to meet us, and are happy to have us back ; and
Nathanael Makotoko, grown somewhat greyer, but with all his
habitual friendliness and courtesy, was there too with a troop of
young men. But there are gaps among those who surround
them, both Christians and pagans. The station, deserted and
dilapidated, might be a tomb, were it not for the presence of a
few women, and above all of our friends M. Marzolff and Mlle.
Louise Cochet, who did all they could to give us a welcome.
The village, once so neat and gay and smiling, is now nothing
but a heap of silent and desolate ruins. I cannot speak of the
mission garden ; it is the emblem of the Lord's vine, though

wasted by a very different enemy.[1] War, and the worst of all,
civil war, has sown the seeds of implacable hatred and revenge.
The life of the camps, those camps which are the sink of the
worst and most shameless corruptions of our civilisation, has
given such an impetus to the current of demoralisation that few
of our Christians, I fear, have been able to resist it.   Some have
openly returned to wallow in the mire of paganism ; others, and
perhaps the greater number, have taken to brandy.   The ranks
of the young men, those young people on whom we had founded
so many hopes, have been broken up by the violence of passions.
The Christians, whose profession had resisted so many attacks,
have come under such hurtful influences that their life seems
paralysed.   In the presence of so many disasters and such ruin,
the heathen mock at the Gospel, the church is deserted, " and
the highways of Zion mourn."

Here, the district is torn between the two principal sons
of Molapo. Jonathan, the legitimate heir of the power, whom
our Christians have followed, has obeyed Letsie's orders, has
remained loyal to the British Government, and has lost everything, like his partisans.   Joel, son of his father's second wife, by
raising the standard of rebellion, carried with him the greater
part of the tribe, and thus acquired an imposing position in the
eyes of the British Government, but one which the latter cannot
respect without trampling on all its promises and engagements,
and mercilessly sacrificing Jonathan and the loyal Basuto.   The
situation is still most strained.

It is springtime here. Let this lovely season spread her
mantle of flowers and verdure over all our ruins and desolations.
Doubtless the contrast is painful to the heart ; but it also
inspires us with confidence and hope for the future.   The winter
will not last for ever.   It was in the midst of the smoking and
deserted ruins of Jerusalem that Jeremiah exclaimed : " It is
of the Lord's mercies we are not consumed, because His com-
passions fail not ; they are new every morning : great is Thy
faithfulness."

LERIBÉ, *July* 10*th,* 1883.

In a few days, we shall have been back here a whole year.
And we were only to stay *six months !* But the Zambesi

[1] Ps. lxxx. : " Thou hast brought a vine out of Egypt : Thou hast cast out
the heathen, and planted it. . . . The boar out of the wood doth waste it," *et seq.*

Mission will lose nothing by this forced delay. It has pleased
God to put our faith in the crucible of sorrow and disappointment. Now I understand it : after the noise and publicity of
Europe, we needed these humiliating reverses, we needed this
time of silence and solitude, to draw us near the Saviour, in
deeper communion with Himself.

The conference at Hermon in March did me good. It was
wholesome, after such a long separation, and such a crisis as
we have passed through, to see our colleagues again, whom we
love and respect, and to talk with them. We were counting on
the festival for the jubilee of the mission [1] : we had quite set
our hearts upon it. We would have liked to pass a few days
en famille with our missionary colony once more, before our
departure for the interior. More especially did the occasion
seem to me a unique one for pleading the cause of the Zambesi
Mission before the assembled Churches, and proposing it to
their hearts and consciences as a monument worthy of their
raising to the glory of our God. And it was all the more
necessary because during these last years there has been a
cooling down of missionary zeal, a step backwards, due in great
part to political preoccupations. We were making plans. But
we were on a volcano : it erupted ; the civil war broke out ;
our unhappy district was once more given up to pillage and
destruction. And farewell to our happy prospects—farewell
to our harvest of blessings—farewell our jubilee ! You know
the rest : the last hamlets of the district destroyed ; Molapo's
town and its beautiful European houses, built and furnished
at great expense, reduced to ashes ; old men massacred,
children mutilated, women ignominiously stripped and maltreated before our eyes, on the very station where they
had sought refuge, in " the shadow of the house of God."
Alarms, panics, isolation, suspense, and perplexity augured
ill for the jubilee. It was impossible for me to absent
myself, and our longed-for festival seemed nothing but a
mirage. We could not attend it.

We were fortunate in having with us my future colleague,
M. Jeanmairet, a nice, earnest young fellow, and also a friend,
a young lawyer from Geneva, M. Gautier. We were expecting

[1] 1833—1883.

the visit of Mr. and Mrs. Boegner [1] and their cousin, Mr. Gustave Steinheil. God did not allow us to be disappointed, and we thank Him that no alarm took place during our friends' stay here. We took advantage of it to study certain questions once more which affect the Zambesi Mission. The moment, indeed, has come when our plans must take a definite shape, and we must at last set to work. Jeanmairet and I are going to ride round to visit the Churches by invitation of the Conference, and take leave of them. Our programme is full. Our journey, which will take six weeks, is to begin the day after to-morrow. I confess I dread it a little, particularly now in the middle of winter; and it costs me much to go so far away from the station and leave my wife alone with my niece. There is a truce just now; we cling to the hope that it is the presage of happier times, and not the calm that precedes the storm.

LERIBÉ, *August 28th*, 1883.

Our journey occupied six weeks. On the very eve of our departure, people came at nightfall to tell me skirmishes were taking place at three or four places. Blood had already flowed; there was going to be more fighting—so much was certain. How could I leave my wife and niece in such circumstances? After reflection, I resolved to abide by my decision, whatever might happen; only I took precautions, and the magistrate promised to let me know if the civil war should break out seriously again. Well! the armistice lasted the whole time we were away, and they scarcely experienced one of those alarms which had been so frequent before. And then, such splendid weather! You know our little missionary colony well enough to know up to what point the duties of hospitality are understood here. I fear we imposed that privilege rather too onerously upon our brethren: I had a very bad conscience on the subject, for certainly I should not have liked any one to take it out of my horses the way we did with theirs! But we could not help it; and I only hope that when it comes to their turn, they will meet with friends as generous and obliging as they were to us.

We had few adventures. The good hand of the Lord was

---

[1] The Director of the Maison des Missions in Paris and his wife, daughter of the late M. de Pressensé, who were making a tour in Basuto-land at this time.

upon us, and we were able to carry out every item of our programme as arranged beforehand. We had experiences of various kinds, both encouragements and discouragements. But, on the whole, it was the encouragements that predominated. It was then that we could appreciate the full extent of evil that the war had worked among our Churches. What a difference between the dead calm now, and the thrill of enthusiasm that was electrifying them in 1876 and 1877! How easy and delightful everything was then!—so it seems to me now, looking back on it. I could have gone to the ends of the earth, borne onwards by such fire. To-day, when sometimes the voice finds no echo, how one feels the need of God's mighty hand to gird one with strength for going forward! We found on our path here just the same objections over again that I was combating in France, against outside missions. "How can we make collections? How can people go to the Zambesi, when there is still so much to do in Basuto-land?"

Still, we had some good meetings; and though we cannot as yet say what the results will be, we brought back more than good words, which cost nothing—tangible tokens of interest. You can guess how impatient our Zambesians are, Seajika and Karumba (who had been left at the Morija School all this time since the first expedition). Poor boys! after the service at Morija, they came to my room and beset me with questions. They would have liked to know the day of our departure, to leave the school instantly to come and get ready, as if they had any great preparations to make! Karumba pretends to be tired of his studies, and he seems to fancy if he can have a rest, the moment for departure will come all the quicker.

Good news awaited me on my return. My wife handed me an envelope: "In reply to our prayers." It contained nearly £100, of which £50 were from our friend Mr. Arthington. So the waggon is provided for: now we are only waiting for the team. Oh, if we only had more faith! And yet it does not need much, does it, to remove even mountains?

LERIBÉ, *October 24th,* 1883.

Our farewell meeting with the representatives of the Basuto Churches is fixed for November 25th, and our final departure for December 5th. We are already in the midst of our preparations, just as though we were going to take the train for the Zambesi. It is not the express, and still less is it the Flying Dutchman, that will carry us into those far-away regions, but our bovine servants, who are the symbol of *patience*. It is a time of fatigue and anxiety, for one has to decide what must be done with the things we leave behind, as well as what we take with us, and to foresee the future wants not only of ourselves, but of every member of the caravan. Every day we look to God for the wisdom we so greatly need. The members of our flock are no less sad than ourselves at the approaching parting, but the arrival of Mr. and Mrs. Weitzecker will console them. We now have the four waggons we require, and are only waiting for our last team.

The moment, then, has come to put our hands bravely to the work. But it has also come to make a serious appeal to all our friends, and all the Churches whose messengers we are. When we were in France, the Zambesi Mission was popular. You were heart and soul with us, urging us on. We believed this, and counted on you. Now the moment for action has come : before charging the enemy, we cast a backward glance ; we are looking for the main army corps, those who follow and support us. One would think it had receded from us ; and we tremble at the thought.

Beloved brethren, wherever you may be, in France, England, Scotland, Italy, Switzerland, Belgium, or Holland, rich and poor, we appeal to your affection for the cause of missions, to your love for the Saviour, and we adjure you to uphold us, pray for us, work, and give cheerfully. God will do the rest. Adieu !

LERIBÉ, *December* 19*th*, 1883.

Our friends the Weitzeckers have at last arrived. And then, at the very moment we were thinking of inspanning, a new and totally unexpected difficulty arose. The small-pox broke out in some parts of Basuto-land, a long, long way from where we are. But, unluckily, it is in Basuto-land all the same ; and so great is the panic, that the whole of this unhappy country has been placed in quarantine. Three days earlier, no one would have opposed our passage ; but the Weitzeckers had not arrived then. I took certain steps with the authorities of the Orange Free State, and I am awaiting their reply. Our whole caravan is ready, waggons loaded and all ; and yet we have to ask ourselves if we can possibly get off by January 1st !

Last Sunday, we had such a congregation that they could not all find room in the church ; and I presented my successor to the tribe. They gave him such a cordial welcome as leads me to hope he may be spared many of the difficulties we apprehended for him. Mr. and Mrs. Weitzecker will soon win the love and confidence of our people. Next Sunday, we shall have their installation, several baptisms, and our farewells. From the political point of view, we hope for much, since we know that England is going to take the country under her protection again. Evidently God has views of mercy for this nation.

You know how many difficulties have arisen to hinder us, one after the other : sometimes the darkness has seemed so thick that we could only have groped our way, if we had not heard the Master's voice going before us. That voice has never failed us, and we have discerned it amid all the noise, more or less sympathetic, more or less hostile, which has echoed around our projects. As for the work we are undertaking, I have it too much at heart to compromise it by lack of precaution. Apart from that, the question of success lies with God. If I should die before I even have the joy of seeing the Gospel banner finally planted in these distant regions, and without the comfort of seeing the Churches of my Fatherland march resolutely to the conquest of Tropical Africa, what are man's judgments to me ? I shall die with the conviction of having done no more than my duty. Do not think what I am saying is mere bravado. There is not a shade of that in my mind. I am neither an enthusiast nor a lover of adventures. The very prospect of such things would be enough to discourage people of our age and tastes. I am a soldier ; my marching orders are signed ; I obey and start : if I fall, others will take my place. In any case, with Christ, the victory is certain.

BETHLEHEM, *January 6th*, 1884.

Starting for the Zambesi ! Yes, at last we are off. It is no longer a prospect, but a reality, since our departure on January 2nd. Our preparations, our last farewells, with all their fatigues and emotions, are behind us. At fifty years of age, we have once more taken up the pilgrim's staff, and our faces are turned towards the regions beyond the Zambesi. Already Leribé, our Bethel and our Ebenezer, the work of our youth and our maturity, is a thing of the past. Already the blue mountains of our second fatherland have vanished from our eyes. And when our dear Mikea, Zakea, and Mareka, who are accompanying us to Bethlehem, have taken leave of us, the last cable will be snapped, and we shall be launched upon the open sea. But Jesus is and will be there. Nothing will remain but the pain—the wrench we do not speak about, but which every one understands. Once more, He will count our wanderings and guide us with His eye.

Our departure was the end of a long agony of several months. Up till the last moment, our faith was on the rack, and Satan was doing everything he could to hinder us. Scarcely did we see one difficulty smoothed away than he raised up others still more formidable and embarrassing. We had the satisfaction of installing our friends the Weitzeckers, and of passing a few days with them—busy days, of course, but happy and blessed too. Their arrival swept away many fears and prejudices. Our flock had been afraid of falling into the hands of an inexperienced young man ; and, far from concealing their discontent, they murmured loudly. From the moment they had heard Mr. Weitzecker, and found him a full-grown man, the opposition died away. We are starting without the slightest misgivings. We have the warmest affection for our friends, and the fullest confidence in the experience they have already acquired. We joyfully bequeath them the fruit of our labours : no one could more worthily enter into them. The material labours necessary to a mission station are all finished. They will have nothing to do but to maintain them. We are confiding to their care a cherished flock, which, in spite of all the disasters of the war, has never ceased to be affectionate and interesting.

I envy my young colleague Jeanmairet going to the Zambesi without having lived long years in Leribé. *We* have cleared the ground ; *we* have sown, God only knows with what tears ! Our friends are going to continue our work and reap. Oh, may the sheaves that they bring to the Saviour's feet be rich and abundant! And after the burden and heat of the day those who sowed and those who have reaped shall rejoice together. No one but the Master knows what it is to leave Basuto-land, the mission and the missionary family, all so united— those beloved brethren from whose views and feelings we may sometimes differ without ceasing to love and admire each other. As a member of such a body, one feels strong. My departure will leave no empty place here ; but when I think of the isolation that awaits us whither we are going, a shuddering depression sometimes comes over me. God bless Leribé! We will speak no more of it. Forbid that we should seek to magnify the little we have had the privilege of doing for Jesus! Yet should we offer Him what cost us nothing? There must be no weakness now the moment has come for action. The Lord Who sends us has girded us with strength and crowned us with peace and joy ; and He has promised, " Thy shoes shall be iron and brass, and as thy days so shall thy strength be." May He pardon me if this be the language of presumption! We leave it to others to discuss and find fault with our enterprise. We ourselves have nothing to do but obey : it is our simple duty— nothing more. And I trust my Master will render me always invulnerable, whether to adulation or to the most hostile criticism.

We certainly need to fortify ourselves in God as we face that vast unknown called the Barotsi Mission. An icy blast which has blown since we left France has, alas! destroyed in many hearts the confidence and interest once bestowed on us. And I fear it has dried up more than one source on which not only our work but that of the whole mission was depending. It is hard for soldiers who are storming the breach, and cannot possibly draw back, to hear those who had urged them on shouting, " Forward! but it is highly improbable we shall be able to follow you." You Christians who daily pray, " Thy kingdom come," will you forsake us ? Is it with this prospect saddening and overwhelming our hearts that we must go forth to struggle with all the difficulties bristling before us, and contend with all the most formidable powers of paganism, with sickness and with death? No, you cannot, you will not ; and before we reach the Zambesi, you will once more give us proofs of your co-operation, and those words which spring from the heart to the heart, awake its courage, and sustain its faith.

CHAPTER IX

PRETORIA, *February* 5*th*, 1884.

PRETORIA ! This is a stage to be noted. When you have already been living gipsy fashion for a fortnight, when you find yourself here and the Vaal at your back, you begin to realise that the journey has begun in earnest, and that you have really gone part of the way—and a bad part too. Indeed, the Caledon kept us two days, with its banks and shoals, in spite of the vigorous help of our people from Leribé ; then ravines, sloughs, marshes, where our teams, though doubled and even tripled, could not always drag our over-loaded waggons. I do not know how many times we had to unload our baggage to get out of a bad place, and carry it on. Distance might lend some enchantment, some halo of romance, to these adventures ; but we are quite *blasés*, and we have no longer the same elasticity as some years ago.

Our departure from Bethlehem was an agitating moment. Some friends had agreed to meet at our camp ; and tears flowed while we stood and sang our farewell hymn in Sesuto, and, kneeling together, heard the Wesleyan pastor commend us to the grace of God in an earnest prayer. The Dutch pastor, Mr. Théron, had recommended us by letter to the Boers of his district, and assuredly not in vain. At Heidelberg, where we did not know a soul, we were surrounded on all sides with interest and attentions. It was the Dutch pastor himself (whose views are the antipodes of mine) that sent us a fine fat sheep: traders, the butcher and the baker, poor people, touched at hearing the object of our expedition, sent us milk and fruits of every kind. It makes one feel very small and unworthy to be the object of so many kindnesses. But we believe it is the Lord making His face to shine upon us.

If we had trouble in getting into Pretoria, we certainly had no less in getting out. I had asked the Government to exempt us from the heavy duties levied on all kinds of merchandise. After much trouble, and a correspondence which threatened to compromise all our interests, I obtained an audience of the Executive Council. Some hours after, an official despatch announced to me that, in view of the essentially evangelical character of our mission, and in order to facilitate it as much as possible, we were exempted from all duties. We owe this favour, in great part at least to, our indefatigable friend Mr. Bosman. He even contrived to organise a missionary meeting. The hall was full, and it was General Joubert, the Vice-president of the Republic, who took the chair. He presented us to the public of Pretoria in a speech full of fire, in which he took care to emphasise his views on *evangelical* missionaries, and on those who, while preaching the Gospel, also mingled in politics, and made trouble between the blacks and whites. We ourselves were classed among the former, and the wishes his Honour expressed for the success of our enterprise, equally with the news of the favour the Government had that day accorded to us, were received with loud applause. On our arrival, we had once more pitched our tents beside the prison, that same prison where our first expedition was incarcerated nearly eight years ago. Who could ever have prophesied the welcome they gave us to-day? God be praised!

One difficulty overcome, another confronts us. The drought is such that we do not know how we are going to travel to Mangwato. And then they tell us there is a frightful famine there. At such a time I remember having bought a sack of flour for £5 10*s*., and maize and potatoes at £3 the sack. What a prospect for our expedition! At the last moment we had to do violence to our feelings and renounce the plan of passing through our brother Gonin's station. It is such a dry country that we should risk serious losses of cattle for want of water and pasturage during days together. I have past experience to go by ; so I hastened to make sure of some sacks of flour the traders here were haggling over, and to procure three huge tuns for our water supply. These tuns have lock taps, and I shall keep the keys in my own pocket, so that we shall be sober and moderate !

Our present expedition differs materially from the first. Seven years ago, not only were we carried along on a wave of enthusiasm which made everything easy, but all those who accompanied us, with few exceptions, formed part of the mission and shared my responsibility to some extent. To-day, the enthusiasm has died down, in France as in Basuto-land : our staff is almost entirely composed of men, devoted enough no doubt, but whose services we have to pay for at a very high rate, and who have no responsibility.   Isaiah, an excellent young man from Bethesda, and Levi, a worthy evangelist from Morija, are the only ones who have given themselves to the mission. But this latter is scarcely more than a passenger with his family, since he is incapable of wielding a whip. But I hasten to say it would have been difficult for us to choose a better staff. All our men, except one or two, profess to know and serve God. We have characters of every shade. One is earnest, almost melancholy, and taciturn ; another talkative, sparkling with fun and high spirits. This man is gentle and submissive ; that one energetic and full of resources. During these six weeks of travelling, we have studied each other well, and the conclusion I have arrived at for my part is that each one has not only, as they say, the faults of his good qualities, but the good qualities of his faults. It is not hard to recognise this, if one but sets one's mind to it. We had, however, to get all these diverse elements into working order—by no means an easy thing at first. To speak only of a very prosaic matter which plays so large a part in our lives—namely, food ; one person cannot eat cold millet cakes ; another pretends that maize upsets his stomach ; a third even asserts that wheaten flour makes him quite ill ; pork does not suit one, nor curdled milk another. What is to be done ? One cannot do violence to these good people, nor yet give in to all their whims and fancies. But now they have all got into step—myself included, I suppose ; and if it were not for those *expenses* that haunt me like a horrible nightmare, the task would be fairly easy.

We had the joy of meeting our friends the Creux here, on their way to Switzerland. We took the Communion together last night. To-day, we must bid each other farewell—a long farewell. We should like to charge them with all sorts of affectionate messages for a multitude of our friends in France and Switzerland.

PRETORIA, *February* 11*th*.

I cannot write much to-day, as we are just off for Mangwato ! Do not forget us. And above all, say to the " wise " : " Wait for the end !" I do not pretend to possess a monopoly of light and wisdom, but say that " God hath spoken *once* ; yea, *twice* have I heard His voice " (Ps. lxii. 11, Fr. Ver.).

MANGWATO (SHOSHONG), *May* 18*th*, 1884.

What I dreaded is just what has happened. The interminable delays before our departure have brought us to the worst of the bad season. Our very start from the capital seemed ill-omened. We had scarcely left the last of its streets before a pelting rain suddenly came on—it was a perfect waterspout, inundating the country, and transforming the stream, which flowed in front of us, into a raging torrent. It was only with the greatest difficulty we could cross it, grumbling all the time at the municipality of this city, if there be one, whilst sinking knee-deep in the mud, doubling the teams and shouting to the creatures till we were hoarse. Our friends, the Creux, Constançons, and others—quite a little cavalcade—were with us in their summer clothes. The rain did not look like leaving off, so we hastily took leave of each other—they to get back to their homes and change to dry things, we to continue our journey. No supper, no fire for us ; no one even thought of it. Our poor boys passed the night under the waggons, with their trousers tucked up, trying to sleep, like herons, on their legs. When we rose the next morning, the whole country was nothing but one immense sheet of water. And thus the expedition from Pretoria to Mangwato was inaugurated ! Oh, how we should appreciate the benefits of a railway now ! When will it extend so far ? Patience ! it is coming on. Major Machado, a Portuguese officer whose acquaintance we had the pleasure of making, has been working for months at a report for a proposed

line to put the Transvaal into direct communication with the
sea through Inhambane. That is not the Zambesi yet, but it
is a step towards it. Whilst waiting for the accomplishment
of this beautiful dream, we poor tramps slowly work our way
along, with heavy hearts, between the showers. Oh the roads!
the marshes! the mud-holes! the bogs! And to face all that
with heavily charged waggons! Even if I had the leisure, I
should only weary you very needlessly were I to relate all our
adventures. Every time the oxen stuck in a bad place, we said,
"Now we are in for it!" We looked at the sun, doubled,
tripled the team, and finally put our shoulders to the wheels.
If it would not budge, and the oxen turned refractory, the
men simply unloaded the waggon, carried the contents on their
backs to *terra firma*, and there reloaded again. At such times,
fatigue was forbidden! The shortest road—though not quite
the best—crossed the River Apies, skirted the Mathlabase, and
crossed the Limpopo ; this we had decided to follow, but during
the night we went astray, and found, too late to turn back—
which, by the way, we never do—that after all we had taken the
road passing through Saul's Poort, M. Gonin's station. We
saw the hand of Providence in this, and had no reason to
regret our mistake. Our friends, the Gonins, received us with
open arms for the few days we could spend with them. Their
kindness touched us deeply ; their devotedness and self-
renunciation did us good to witness.

Outside Saul's Poort, the road—save the mark !—had become
impassable : advance was out of the question. Scarcely were
we out of one slough, before we fell into another. One day,
thanks to our good Jonathan's vigorous arm and chest, my
waggon had safely covered a mile or more of a fearful morass ;
but Levi's, which followed ours, sank up to the understel. Four
teams, of sixteen oxen each, failed to stir it, the poor beasts
sinking up to their bellies, and being thus incapable of pulling.
We worked in vain till night fell, and finally had to abandon
the attempt. The next morning, after a few hours' heavy sleep,
the first thing we did was to go together to the Throne of Grace ;
and we did so with confidence. "Send Thine angels to our
help," prayed one of our party. We were just arranging our
plans with renewed vigour, and full of courage, when some men
arrived on foot and on horseback, some with oxen, others with

waggons. They were the Christians of Saul's Poort, who, hearing of our distress, were hastening to our help. They were the angels of God for whom we asked. When have we ever cried in vain to this Father of ours, so full of tenderness? The waggons were soon unloaded, and the bad place passed. These kind friends of their own accord travelled with us for a fortnight, cutting out a new track, in order to avoid the marshes of the Limpopo as far as possible. They took us right to the junction of the Marico (Malikoë) with the Limpopo, and would have come even farther. Unfortunately, both rivers were overflowing, and the ford at the Marico was more than forty feet deep ! When should we be able to cross it ? Fearing to become an additional burden to us in this uncertainty, our friends found there was nothing to be done but establish us there, and return to their homes.

When they had bade their last good-byes, their waggons had disappeared into the woods, and the rumbling of their wheels no longer reached our ears, a kind of horror came over me. I saw the enormous impassable river before us ; the clouds gathering over our heads, threatening more than once to over- whelm us ; the marsh whose pestilential neighbourhood I dreaded, yet could not escape. And famine stalked there ; that hideous spectre showed its teeth at us. To crown our misfortunes, the Bushmen stole our two goats. Good-bye to the drop of milk we enjoyed so much ! Our horses, too, died one after the other, and so suddenly that we could do nothing to save them.[1] What was to be done ? The most experienced had long been at their wits' end. The loss of our two saddle horses was bad enough, undoubtedly ; but to see our draught oxen die off like flies was a much more serious matter. It was the change of pasture which proved so fatal to them. The flocks of vultures, which never left us day or night, fought over their carcases, and bands of Masaroa disputed the fragments of putrifying flesh with our horrible guests. As a finishing stroke, first Levi, then Isaiah, had to struggle with dysentery ; Middleton, too, who could not understand that the fever would dare to attack him—*him*, so active and so necessary. And on the top of all that, every

---

[1] Six horses were lost at the Marico, three belonging to members of the expedition, and three which some Basuto chiefs were sending as a present to Khama. Only one remained.

one had to be put on rations.   It was easy enough for ourselves,
but less so for our people, one or two of whom were rather
perverse.   But when they saw my wife merrily kneading a
small loaf of bread with all the siftings and all the bran, this
loaf, baked in a brass pot, being the allowance of bread for
six persons during a whole week, they understood, and even
pushed the economising of our few remaining provisions to
a further extent than we would have dared to insist on.

In such a situation, everybody vied with each other to bring
the first news of the river in the morning.   They went to look
as soon as dawn appeared, and twenty times more during the
day, to examine the pieces of wood stuck the previous day
at the margin of the water.   One day, it was declared to have
sunk a great deal, and already we began to make plans for
fording it, but the next day it had risen again.   A fortnight
passed thus, and we were obliged to devise something to pass
the time.   Some looked after the cattle, others took their guns,
searched the woods, and frightened the game ; a third party got
some fishing tackle ready, and went to—watch the water flowing,
and look out for the crocodiles, which, however, kept out of
sight !   We also unpacked the splendid boat given us by the
African Society of Paris,[1] and thus we could visit travellers
on the other side who were stopped like ourselves, exchange
provisions with them, and even procure a little milk for ourselves
from time to time.

At last the day of our deliverance came.   A messenger
whom I had sent to Mangwato brought us some oxen from the
chief, and some waggons which the traders had sent to lighten
ours.   You may guess how eagerly we seized our pickaxes and
spades to level the steep banks, and our hatchets to fill up the
mud-holes with trunks of trees and branches.   The river was
still deep ; the oxen had to swim : the current was rapid too,
and washed into the waggons.   Never mind ! we shut our eyes
to all danger, launched the waggons one after another, and
crossed without further mishap.   We thanked God, and began
to breathe freely.   On seeing the rotten roads, and the ruts
made by our predecessors, we understood Whose hand had
stopped us at Marico.   If we took six weeks to cover a distance

---

[1] The *Messager de Paix*, unfortunately wrecked later on.

CROSSING THE MARICO (MALIKOË) RIVER.

[To face page 120.

which usually took from twelve to fourteen days, other people, who were accustomed to the business, and had taken the most direct route, did not arrive before us. As to our oxen, we were thought lucky to have lost no more. Poor consolation, is it not? But still that is all the consolation travellers exchange!

We travelled more rapidly now, and at the end of a fortnight saluted the hills of Mangwato. One day, during our midday halt, whilst breakfast was being cooked we were sitting in the shade and practising an appropriate hymn, when we heard a horse's trot behind us. I looked round; it was Aaron coming to meet us with Khama's son-in-law. We shook hands with the warmth of old friends; then we sat down and bombarded each other with questions. The good man had left Seleka eleven days before, and had come to meet us on foot. He told us about the death of his daughter Caroline, a short time before. This dear little girl, who was eight years old, and had contributed not a little to the enlivenment of our party, had been bitten by a snake one night in bed, and died after two days of agony. She was every one's pet, and she seems to have been a child who loved the Saviour. When her mother saw she was dying, she said to her, "What would you say, if that snake were a messenger from the Lord to call you to Him?" "Oh, mother!" she answered, "I should say nothing, and only be very glad: I do love Him so."

It was pleasant to meet such friends as Khama, Mr. Whiteley, Mr. Musson, and others at Mangwato. Khama is always the same, and he was overjoyed to see us again. He had his "fatted calf" all ready—a great sheep of the African breed, with a tail weighing from ten to fifteen pounds or more, the fat of which is very much appreciated. He also provided for our cattle, and sent us two large loads of firewood, immediately. Every morning, he used to come to our camp with a smiling face to ask after our health. On the day appointed for our official salutations, we went in a body to the *lekhothla*, where the chief was awaiting us, surrounded by his suite. He received my little speech, sentence by sentence, with an emphatic "*E Rre*" ("Yes, my father"). I delivered messages to him from a number of European friends. Then came the climax—the presentation of a fine musical box, playing six hymn tunes, made expressly for him at Geneva. It was handed to me, and I uncovered it. Every head was craning forward, and every eye was fixed on me and the mysterious object. I put my hand in my pocket for the key : it was not there ! I searched—searched everywhere, and searched again—all to no purpose : the key was lost ! *Tableau !*

A little coolness and presence of mind saved the situation, and indeed the unlucky incident only had the effect of sharpening curiosity, for the next morning the crowd and excitement were greater than ever, when suddenly the melody and charming accompaniments of that hymn " Safe in the arms of Jesus " were heard ! Of course, after that, every one wanted to hear the box sing !

Four or five days after our arrival, M. Jeanmairet and I left for Seleka. The chief gave us some oxen ; and one of his brothers, his waggon. We made the journey, there and back, by forced marches, so as not to spend a Sunday on the road, and we were not away more than a fortnight. Our object was either to relieve, or, preferably, to definitely suppress, the station at Seleka. Asser had returned to Basuto-land with his numerous family ; Andreas has received a call from our Swiss brethren at Valdezia, and is only waiting till they send for him. Being a near relative of certain Makololo chiefs, and especially of a man who quite recently gravely compromised the name of the tribe, and who died while heading some Matabele hordes against the chief Moremi, he rightly feared his presence among us might give offence to the Barotsi. As for Aaron, he is coming with us. We arrived at Seleka on Saturday, and were to leave on the Tuesday. But, in the meantime, we could not sit with our hands folded. Our first interview with the chief Kobé was characteristic. No one but ourselves might enter his court. As a precautionary measure, his son squatted down in front of the door, which was tiny enough as it was ; and the entrance to the royal hut having been carefully closed, we did not enjoy the privilege of seeing his Highness's face. He was there, however, inside ; for at every pause in my speech we heard a sulky grunt from a hoarse voice, which, when I had finished, cleared itself sufficiently to say, " Go away with the rain, and may the rain follow you wherever you go ! May God deluge you with rain !

Thank you!" And that was all the regret he felt at seeing the evangelists depart.

The next day, the whole village assembled for the morning gathering—two hundred persons at the most, all told. M. Jean-mairet baptised Aaron's infant and that of Andreas; and I baptised a boy about fourteen years old, Mosenéne (a serpent or adder), who took the name of Zacchæus. This was the only actual fruit of the mission at Seleka. Three men have returned to the world, and three others have emigrated to a German station. We hesitated at first, on seeing Mosenéne's youth; but when we had heard him confess his faith, and answer all our questions intelligently, we were quite satisfied. It was touching to see this young lad rise in the midst of the congregation to make a public declaration of his profession, and then kneel to receive the seal of baptism. The most absurd reports had been circulated about this ceremony, and consequently every one was eager to see with his own eyes what would happen to Mosenéne when we gave him children's flesh to eat, and human brains to drink! Since then, Kobé has sent the boy to us here at Mangwato with two other men, so that we may send him on to the school in Basuto-land. "He will come back and teach us in a year," he said.

The afternoon service was less well attended, though it was then that the evangelists were to make their farewells. Aaron did so in the style of a true Boanerges; Andreas with no less authority, but more gentleness. One could quite feel these men had taken up a position, and that they were regarded by the natives much as the Basuto regarded us. Moreover, our evangelists had passed through experiences which had been wholesome to them, and had made them understand our own situation. They have worked hard at Seleka; and if there have been few conversions, I was struck by the number of those who knew how to read and write, and the spirited way they joined in the singing. We had the painful impression that the natives of Seleka were hardened, and that our taking away these witnesses for the truth was a relief to them. Already they were beginning to dispute the thatches of their huts, and to worry them with begging.

It was at Seleka that we had to part from Filipi, a man from this district who was converted at Berea, and above all from Jonathan, who is returning to Valdezia with his son and another boy who accompanied him from Basuto-land. It costs us much to bid good-bye to our dear Jonathan; he is our son in the faith, and I believe he feels towards us as much affection as we have ever had for him. With him, too, the expedition loses a part of its very soul, if not its right hand too. His energetic, sometimes impetuous character brings him always to the front. He wanted to accompany us here, and would not accept more than half the wages the others demanded, either for himself or for his two boys. Six men left us here, according to our previous arrangement. Who will replace them? Khama assured me that I must not look to him, on account of the rumours of war. This was another of those waves that break against our faith, yet without shaking it too much. On our return, Khama showed that he had not forgotten us. He is lending us three men; and to spare us too great an expenditure, he is sending three messengers with us, who, besides the message entrusted to them for the Barotsi king, are commissioned to help us on our way.

There was also news from the Zambesi. Two young men, who had been there on a commercial enterprise, were returning with their health shattered by fever, and they brought us quite a budget of correspondence. Mr. Arnot, in a long letter teeming with interest, gives us every detail about his work. He is still at the capital, and has started a school, which has already passed through all sorts of ups and downs. Robosi himself writes to Khama [1] asking him for his alliance; and as a proof of friendship, for one of his daughters in marriage, and a black dog! He announces that the Jesuits have been to him, but that they are not after his heart, nor yet after his people's heart, and he has forbidden them to come into his country. "The one we are looking for is M. Coillard," he adds. "I am told he is on his way hither, and I ask you as a favour to help him, so that he may come as quickly as possible." Do not found too many hopes on the favourable disposition of a heathen chief who knows nothing of the Gospel. Paul, in obeying the Macedonian's call, found a prison in Macedonia. But what did it matter, since that prison proved to be the door of Europe?

[1] Of course by Mr. Arnot's hand.

We wanted to wait for Mr. and Mrs. Hepburn's return from England before presenting the Church at Shoshong with the beautiful set of communion plate which the Comité des Dames de Paris had procured for us. As our friends did not arrive, however, we had to do it without them. The presentation took place the day before yesterday—a very simple but very cordial ceremony. The vote of thanks brought home to us the fact that we are no longer in Basuto-land, the Greece of South Africa, but it was none the less appreciated on that account. Khama's speech consisted of two draught oxen which he sent the next morning! Another gave us a cow, and a third two sheep. Friendship (*setsualle*, as we say in Sesuto) is a great institution here. Numerous as we are, each one has his *motsualle*,[1] or *tsala*[2]—his friend. This friendship entails all sorts of duties and privileges, especially in the way of gifts. Even though there is a famine at Mangwato, our " friends " do not let us want for water-melons, sugar-cane, curdled milk, etc. Naturally, my special friend is Khama. He had prepared a fine jackal-skin kaross against my arrival, and a leopard skin for my wife. We shall be rich when we leave Mangwato!

I forgot to mention the post. The post! How it makes our hearts beat! A friend of ours, knowing we were at Marico, had taken the first opportunity of sending us a packet of letters. The man to whom they were entrusted proved friendly to the last degree ; he spent a whole evening with us, chatting on every conceivable subject—except the post. On arriving at Mangwato, four days after, we heard that this good man had had our letters! He had quite forgotten to hand them over. We had our compensation though ; for besides the express messenger he sent on a fortnight later, Mr. Dawson, when he came to greet us, was followed by a man carrying on his head a large basket full of newspapers and more correspondence. You should have seen how we all pressed round it, and how all eyes sparkled at the sight. The postal service is interrupted now, because of the small-pox which is raging in the direction of Zeerust. The two postmen, who are sent every three weeks, take a fortnight to accomplish the journey, and it costs £3. In order to defray the cost of the service, a tax of £3 10s. is imposed upon every European without distinction who makes

---

[1] Sesuto word.   [2] Sechuana word.

a stay in the country, and it means therefore £14 for us. But the Europeans of the district have held a consultation, and unanimously decided to make us pay only half that sum.

We are now on the eve of starting again. We have been obliged to deposit some of our baggage here, and consequently there has been a great deal of work to do, in unpacking and repacking, and much cause for lamentation over the damaged and broken articles. But the waggons are reloaded at last, and they have been covered with ox-hides, to protect them a little from the spikes and branches that obstruct the path. Even dead oxen are still good for something.

KANÉ, ON THE WAY TO THE ZAMBESI, *May 25th*, 1884.

As we had to lighten our waggons, because of the deep sands we have to plough through in the desert, we have been obliged to unload, sort, repack, often to load, unload, and load again, and make all sorts of combinations. We must inspect every case, and weigh the importance of every article. Our clothes and personal effects gave us little trouble. By this time, we have learnt to strip ourselves by degrees of what we like to call *necessaries*, and to content ourselves with very little. Our friend Jeanmairet has left a good part of his own property to make room for objects of more general utility. He has proposed it so heartily, and done it with such a good grace, that it is really quite a lesson for us all.

In spite of all this selection, we still have a great deal of cargo which gives us anxiety. The purse of the Zambesi is unfortunately very cumbersome. Oh those bales of stuff, those cases of glass beads, that Parisian bazaar on a small scale! What would we not give to reduce it all to £ s. d. ! Then, again, we are carrying the granary and the grocery of the whole caravan, which are no trifle. Do you know how many of us there are? Twenty-nine, without counting the Masaroa Khama has placed at our service, the number of whom is left to our discretion. The family of Aaron has linked itself to us, with all the indispensable adjuncts of an additional waggon, and a team of cattle. But Aaron is not the man to sit enthroned on the box in front, with a white sunshade and a pocket-hand- kerchief to fan himself. He brings a valuable element of energy into our midst, and has taken upon himself a great part of the

A leafless Baobab Tree.

A NEW SORT OF TEAM.

[To face page 127.

responsibility, so that he is a great relief to me. He has left the care of conducting his own waggon to Ezekiel Pampanyane, and has bravely taken charge of the cart. This is no trifle, for it is drawn by two oxen, which support the pole, and by six asses, which he has had to train. Nothing could be droller than this team. The oxen, feeling themselves disgraced, shake their heads and try to gore their new yoke-fellows : the donkeys do not disturb themselves in the least ; they are placid to excess. You may yoke them, you may push them, you may thrash them— nothing ruffles them. They do not stop short at a bad place, neither are they to be hurried on a good road. If you have not learned patience, they will teach it you. Karumba, the trumpeter of the caravan, has taken upon himself to help Aaron conduct this equipage, at which everybody laughs. But Waddell, Middleton, and even M. Jeanmairet, also lend a hand very readily.

Our departure from Mangwato has been, like all departures, profoundly sad. One does not separate from friends like Khama without a pang. And yet I leaped for joy when we descended the hills that hide Mangwato from our eyes, and breathed the air of the Kalahari. The evening before, we took the Lord's Supper at nine o'clock, in the room of our much-respected friend Mr. Whiteley, who is at the head of one of the first houses of business here. The elders, the chief Khama, and a few Europeans joined with the members of the expedition. Solemn moment, which none of those present will ever forget ! Among this number was Zakea Mosenéne, the lad we had baptised at Seleka. He had arrived a few days previously. After the departure of his evangelists, the chief Kobé, realising then the consequences of our abandonment, sent Mosenéne and two men to us with the request that we would complete his education and "make him grow," so as to make an evangelist of him for himself. He will go to the Bible School at Morija, when our Basuto return thither.[1]

[1] After four years spent at the public school of Morija, Zacchæus Mosenéne returned to his own people, who, however, were no longer to be found at the old place: they had emigrated to the Transvaal, and a new Seleka had arisen on the banks of the Limpopo. Zacchæus followed them, and is still with them. He has remained a steadfast Christian, and his letters show that as a schoolmaster and evangelist he is doing a good work. He has indeed " grown," and he has the true *feu sacré.—Author's Note.*

We could not be ready till the evening of the next day, Wednesday, 21st. You might have seen us there in the public place, our six waggons inspanned, surrounded by all the European population of the neighbourhood, and a crowd of Bamangwato. According to our daily custom, directly the oxen were yoked, and before the signal was given to start, we all stood with heads uncovered, and amidst profound silence raised *our* hymn—the hymn that inaugurates *every* day's march :

Ka linako tsotle	(I need Thee every hour,
Morena ka!	Most gracious Lord !)

Then, kneeling down, we commended each other to God, and to the word of His grace ! Then came the handshakings, the last farewells ; falling night hid the general commotion ; but some electric current, I know not what, seized us irresistibly, and made the most secret fibres of our hearts vibrate.

After having passed the last huts of the town, and bidden farewell to the last of our friends, we passed on our way in silence. The sky was starlit, the air fresh and bracing. One heard not a sound but the groaning of the wheels, the crack of the whip, and the conductor's " Trek " ; and no one felt in the mood to talk. " Khama : what a noble man he is ! And Kuate : what a friend ! " said one or other from time to time, without comment. Yes, indeed ! Do you see those two draught oxen ? They are Khama's salutation. That beautiful black heifer ? Kuate's. Those three milch cows come from Mr. Whiteley ; this sack of maize and this salt meat from Mr. Beaumont, the butcher of Mangwato. Those eight hens come from the yard of a young clerk ; and fowls are scarce here. These goats, these broad-tailed sheep, are an expression of good wishes from Mr. and Mrs. Clark and the principal members of the Church. Here also are pumpkins, water-melons, curds, millet, and I don't know what besides.

And these kind people have given us all this, telling us in every tone that they will be so sorry, *so* sorry when we are gone ! Each wanted to show us that we were loved for the sake of the work we were going to do. " Since I have known the Lord," one friend said to me, " no work interests me like yours. It is a delightful privilege to help it on, and I hope with all my heart that the day will come for me to serve it more effectively." He is a trader, who makes our mission a constant subject of prayer ; but he is not the only one who has shown us how much he sympathises with us in our serious enterprise. This is worth something in a community where travellers and missionaries are judged otherwise than in Europe. Note, moreover, that Mangwato is one of the driest and most arid of places. It is a bitter irony for a missionary to glorify the enclosure before his house with the name of *garden* : it is nothing but an area burnt up by the sun, in which only thistles and one or two stunted mimosas will grow. Those who have a passion for gardening try by unremitting care to rear a syringa, an oleander, or a passion-flower ; a cabbage that never comes to a head ; two or three bunches of salad which are hard even in sprouting. Can you believe it? We have had vegetables at Shoshong ! Every one who could deprived himself so as to send some to us. However, it is the rule here never to sell these delicacies—they are sent to friends ; and if by good fortune any one brings potatoes, onions, or dried fruit to Mangwato, they are bought for the whole community.

Unhappily, things are going badly ; times are hard. Trade, which here is exhausted, will go to seek its fortune on the banks of the Zambesi. Ostriches and elephants carry their plumes and their ivory farther away. The terror inspired by the name of Matabele keeps the Bamangwato always on the alert, and forbids them to hunt. The traders declare openly that they are only living on what they have saved, and each is trying to wind up and quit the country. Khama, too, has plans of his own.[1]

[1] Every one knows that Khama has since transported his capital with its whole population to Palapye.

CHAPTER X

KANÉ, *May 25th*, 1884.

KANÉ is the Beersheba of the desert : there are at least seven wells. They are not springs, however ; and when we passed here five years ago, we found only a little mud in the holes, and I was forced to buy water from the Bushmen, bartering tobacco for it.[1] Now the wells are full. I had intended going farther to spend Sunday ; but we had so much trouble to get through the sand, even when doubling the teams, that we did not arrive here till midday ; and then rain came on, which has never stopped since. The thermometer, which a few days ago stood at 95° Fahr., fell to 58°, and we were reduced to curling ourselves up the best way we could in our damp waggons. "There aren't any tropics ; I don't believe in them," says somebody, muffling himself round in his cloak ; and nobody contradicts him, but we all have a good laugh, which warms us up. Such a great and sudden change of temperature is exceedingly trying. One can never, in this country, lay aside one's winter clothes. Among the comforts I enjoy is a pair of sabots with wooden soles and leather uppers, which I brought from France. I pity those who have none, and I cannot think how I did without them for twenty-three years.

---

[1] The Bushman's method of obtaining water is as follows : A man or woman (usually the latter) holds in his or her mouth a long reed and a bent of grass ; the other end of the reed is inserted in the mud-hole : the water is sucked up and ejected ; it runs *along* the bent of grass into a gourd. The Bushmen thus act as human syphons ; they keep gourds of this water by them to sell to travellers. See Livingstone's "Travels on the Zambesi."

Just now, as I am writing, a messenger is arriving from Khama. He has come eighteen or twenty miles through pouring rain to bring us a little packet, and the salutations of the chief. He will return to-morrow with this letter. In answer to a communication from Robosi, king of the Barotsi, who asks, among other things, that Khama should help us on our road, the latter sends Makoatsa and four men to accompany us as far as to Robosi himself. One takes charge of the led cattle, another of the sheep, a third of the donkeys; the fourth looks after the beautiful horse Khama is sending to Robosi, with a fine carbine; and Makoatsa is to watch that they do their work well and take care of us. "If you neglect your duty, if you annoy the Chief's friend, *he* will not lay his hand upon you, because he is a man of God. But I am Makoatsa, and I will make you eat some stick; and when you return, it is the Chief you will have to do with!" This was his speech in presenting these men to me, whom Khama gives us without wages. Meantime, one of them who acted as guide during the night nearly made us lose our way in the wood, which might have led to serious accidents; and to-day, he has allowed the oxen to stray.

Every day we have to congratulate ourselves upon having my wife and niece with us. The complications their presence occasions are nothing in comparison with the benefit it brings to us all. My wife has taken her place as mother and hospital nurse among us; and she is often our providence.

(F. C. to personal friends on his fiftieth birthday.)

PATA-MATENGA, *July 17th*, 1884.

I know that if any one thinks of me to-day, it will be you. Well, dear friends, the wishes and prayers you offer for us are placed in a safe bank—you may be sure of that. And we respond to them by those electric lines which centre in the heart of the eternal Father. The fiftieth year of my life is now accomplished. How much longer is left me to serve my Master here below? I am quite ready, if He should wish me, to glorify His name, either by life or by death. The desire of my heart, subject to His Divine will, is nevertheless that He may still grant me a few years in which to establish the work we are beginning. What joy it would be to me to see some Barotsi converted, and the Gospel spread among other tribes, before my departure for heaven. If you only knew the happiness I felt when I arrived here! We are not at the Zambesi yet, but we are not far from it; for early in the morning one can almost see from here the clouds of spray rising from Musi oa Tunya. Another four or five days' waggon journey, and we shall once more pitch our tents at Leshoma. We shall then be only three or four miles from the Zambesi, the course of which we have already been following at a distance, and which we are now approaching diagonally.

Pata-matenga, which five years ago we thought so fresh and charming, has become dreary and desolate. Westbeech's establishment is still there, surrounded by a few native huts, and supplemented by the Jesuits' buildings; but the Mapane Wood is half destroyed, the grass dried up, and partly burnt (for it is winter); and as there have even been frosts, the palm trees too are withered up. However, there is still one little corner on which one's eyes may rest with pleasure; it is the corn fields, with their delicate green, belonging to Mr. Westbeech and the Jesuit Fathers, and the latter's kitchen garden. To see a piece of ground at Pata-matenga, well cultivated and tended, the borders neatly marked out, and filled with straight rows of cabbages, potatoes, peas, and lettuce, is a delightful sight to those who have been travelling for nearly two months, through sand, sloughs, and tracts of forest land or desert.

Mr. Westbeech, informed of our approach by the natives, was awaiting our arrival. Till ten o'clock in the evening, he stood at his door with lanterns to encourage us. As for us, we, alas! were stuck in a fearful bog, where our waggons had sunk up to the axle-trees. After struggling, toiling, belabouring and shouting at our oxen till midnight, we succeeded in bringing them to a less muddy spot, where we had no choice but to remain till daybreak. Mr. Westbeech came to meet us, and the news he gave us from the Zambesi was encouraging. "All the chiefs are in your favour," he said; "but I confess, while I was doing my best to persuade them to have patience, I had given up all hope myself. It was impossible to understand your delays."

The Jesuits have established themselves very well here; they have a chapel, a simple but cosy little house, huts and sheds for storehouses, a fine poultry yard, and a pretty garden : it is a little village which would be prosperous as a mission station if there were any evangelisation to be done here. But what can they do where there is no population ? A few waggon-drivers and servants may chance to travel by with their employers, and these gentlemen catch them on the wing ; but this does not amount to much, for they are few and far between.

What I do admire about the Jesuits is the completeness of their staff. They have a gardener, cook, steward, carpenter, etc. It is the " brothers " who are entrusted with the material things of the establishment : the fathers will concern themselves with the spiritual when occasion offers. M. Jeanmairet and I went to see them one day. Their garden is a little oasis, beautifully watered and tended, and there are all sorts of vegetables in it, with which their owners are most generous. What they complain of is that most of them will not set their seeds, so that every year they have to renew the supply for fresh sowings. One of the fathers had gone with a brother to see the Victoria Falls ; but the Superior was there, Father Kroot, a Dutchman, with two brothers, a Milanese, who is the gardener, and the steward, an Englishman. These gentlemen were very courteous to us, and presented me with two bags of native wheat to provide for my people. This was indeed a very great boon, for we had already come to an end of our provisions, and Mr. Westbeech had nothing to spare for us either. They even extended their kindness so far as to send me some vegetables, a fine cabbage, a few leeks, and some lettuces ; and these, unknown to themselves, provided us with a little treat for my birthday. But as soon as they did learn this, Father Kroot insisted on bringing out a bottle of Bordeaux, and making every one clink glasses and drink my health. Their behaviour was all the more noble since our presence here must be a thorn in their side. I warmly appreciate it, and wish them well. I feel more and more that principles and doctrines must be contended for, but persons respected. However, I do not think we have ever neglected this maxim in practice.[1]

---

[1] *Author's Note.*—The staff of this mission had had a series of disasters. Out of seven members, one died by a fall from his horse, two were drowned, two died of hunger and fatigue, another of consumption, the seventh died of fever among the Batoka, and some believed he had been poisoned.

Our intention is to push on to Leshoma, install my wife there, and then leave for the Upper Zambesi. You can understand that this three months' separation, which would be a slight matter in Basuto-land, is a serious and solemn thing for both of us. My wife will be left with no light burden. If you only knew what it is to have to provide for a troop of natives like ours! From the moment the drivers lay down their whips, not only is all work at an end, however little that work may have been, but some one has even to cook their food and draw their water for them, and it is not at all easy to content them. I wanted to send them all back to Basuto-land or Mangwato. But how was it to be done? My oxen are all worn out. I tremble at the thought of all the expense and all the worries of their continued sojourn with us; but in spite of it all, I am glad they should have come as far as the Zambesi, and I hope they will not go away with a bad impression of it. I tell you all this, that you may not imagine we made a triumphal progress across the desert, along a path strewn with flowers. There were thorns, and sharp ones too, besides those in the bushes, which mercilessly tore our garments and our waggon tilts. But all that is over now, and we have to face the new difficulties which await us. What we lack more than anything else is a good gardener, for our diet is one of the first things to be considered, and it is a very poor way of living to have nothing but millet and rice, never seeing a potato or green vegetable. We shall certainly try to do something in the way of gardening, but it will necessarily be very little. We did not come for that purpose.

LESHOMA, *August 7th*, 1884.

Leshoma! This is our Bethel. We stopped here in our wanderings six years ago. In the midst of struggles and distresses which God alone knows, new horizons opened before us, lighted by a ray of hope. It is an important date in our career. It is good to come back to Leshoma, and pause to adore the ways of Jehovah, His goodness and His faithfulness.

The journey across the desert was long: our oxen were travel-worn, our waggons heavy, own people weary and dispirited; and so, in spite of all our determination, we travelled more slowly than one usually does. Indeed, our first stage to Kané

A MOSAROA OR BUSHMAN (FULL AND PROFILE, SHOWING CHARMS AND TATTOOING).

was made with so much difficulty that I decided to send part of
our baggage back to Mangwato, and this necessitated fresh
sorting, and fresh reductions in our ideas of the "strictly
necessary." Our friend Mr. Whiteley hastened to come himself
with a waggon and team from Khama. During this time it
poured with rain, and throughout the desert we have scarcely
known what it was to suffer from thirst.

The sight of the Makari-kari Desert somewhat raised the
spirits of our fellow-travellers. They felt, as we did, that we
had made progress. And then, too, there is something new
and attractive in the wild panorama spread before our eyes
with its *vleys*[1] and sands, its immense plains sprinkled with
clumps of trees, and its silent, lifeless solitudes. Only at rare
intervals does an ostrich or a fleeing gazelle interrupt the
monotony of the picture. Even the lion has not deigned to
honour us with more than his nocturnal roarings : only hungry
hyænas have seized our donkeys, and caused commotions.

The Masaroa,[2] children of the desert, knowing that we had
people from Shoshong with us, hid themselves at our approach.
They scarcely dared to come and sell us a little honey. To
judge from what we saw, the Bamangwato treat them very
cavalierly. Doubtless without the knowledge of their chief, they
rob them of the little they possess, seize the booty of their chase,
the wild fruits and herbs, and even the large caterpillars and
chrysalides which these poor wretches look upon as dainties.
It is in these plains that certain rivers lose themselves : the
Nata, for example, which after a short course disappears under
the name of Sua. The soil of the Makari-kari is so soft our
waggons sank till we were almost in despair. Scarcely had
we emerged from these morasses, when we had to work our
way through those deep sands which will always be the
traveller's nightmare. It was pitiful to see our poor oxen, with
their galled necks, lolling out their tongues and sinking under
the yoke. It was bad enough when we ploughed our way
through the open country. But in these literally impenetrable
thorn thickets, where it was absolutely impossible for the driver
to use his long whip, the oxen had their revenge, and we only
triumphed at the cost of shouting ourselves hoarse.

[1] *Vleys*: a Dutch word applied to the shallow lakes in the deserts.
[2] Name by which the Bushmen are known in the Zambesi basin.

In these virgin forests, the road has not been traced by an
engineer! The first waggon threaded its way through as best
it could, making endless zigzags to avoid the large trees, and
all the others followed, ours last of all. Think of getting round
all these obstacles with our enormous teams! Our poor Levi
knows what it is, by this time. He was obliged, though much
against the grain, to take his turn at the whip. Did we propose
to do a long stage of our journey by night, or early in the
morning, so surely did we hear the cry of alarm behind us,
almost before we were fairly off, "*Hihu! hihu! Koloï e tsueroe!*"
("The waggon has stopped!"). We had to retrace our steps,
hatchet in hand, asking ourselves how serious an accident
it was likely to be. Alas! we would find a box of hats quite
crushed, or a case of haberdashery in pieces. We would pick up
the hats and reels of cotton, mend the torn bales, and start again.

Every one has his share of damages. A dead branch made
a hole in the tilt of M. Jeanmairet's waggon, and the boughs
swept out everything they could reach—books, a dressing-box,
a case of dental appliances, etc. But no one has been so badly
used as our friend Waddell. A portmanteau, a trunk, and tool-box
comprised all his belongings. The portmanteau and the trunk
disappeared one after the other. "At least my chest of tools
has escaped," said our young Scotsman with satisfaction. He
was proud of this mahogany chest, with its ingenious com-
partments, the first work of his apprenticeship. It received
many blows and fractures, but our carpenter always found some
way of repairing them. One day a new "*Hihu! hihu!*" from
Levi made us run breathless to his waggon. The precious
chest was no longer; its splinters lay scattered on the ground!
This time the damage was irremediable. Poor Waddell! He
used his hatchet with all his might to disengage the rest of
his tools from the trunk of a great tree. As for ourselves, we
could only look on, sorrowful and silent. Waddell's face was
flushed, the tears starting to his eyes; yet he tried to smile
in spite of all. "Never mind, sir," he said; "the chest is broken,
but the tools are saved. Give me some boards and time enough,
and you'll see if I don't make something better." There is
grit in a man like that. It is easy enough to give him time;
but where were the boards to come from? They will have
to be made first, and no one knew that better than he did.

In other ways, too, I must say our two artisans have thoroughly entered into the spirit of the expedition. They cheerfully accept our privations : they are always happy, always ready to make themselves useful. It is seldom that Waddell does not find an opportunity of using the saw, the hatchet, or the plane during the halt in the middle of the day. It is a pleasure to see him at his work, for he loves it ; and if no accident demands the dexterity of his vigorous arm, he goes away, axe in hand, to explore the forest, and returns with specimens of wood of every kind and colour. " There is mahogany, sir, real mahogany," he exclaims, radiant with delight, " and here is teak, and a kind of cedar, and another thing like ebony. If God spares us, you'll see what good use we shall make of all these treasures." And when we hear him smoothing away all difficulties, felling trees and sawing planks (actually planks !), we already see a cottage raised as if by magic, with furniture all complete, which the dear fellow delights in prophesying will make Mme. Coillard quite forget the mission-house at Leribé ! One feels that Waddell has always been his mother's boy ; he needs to be surrounded with much affection, and to find a quick response to his own, which he gives back unreservedly.

Our two evangelists Aaron and Levi form an admirable complement to each other. Like all of us, they have their defects and their good qualities. Aaron is active, energetic, and animated, but also sensitive and quick-tempered. Levi is an intelligent man of a very even disposition, sober in his speech as in his habits. He is better educated than Aaron, and one soon discovers that he is the son of a Christian (the first in Basuto-land), and that he only knows heathenism by contact or tradition. What he does, he does well ; but he has not much enterprise. His little addresses do us real good, and I do not think I can give you a better idea of his character than by quoting part of a letter he wrote me before our departure :

" This is to tell thee," he says, " that thy letter reached me safely. I received it with joy. Yes, my father ! one who is charged with a mission like ours ought to be worthy of the greatest confidence. If even the chiefs, who are only men, find obedient and faithful messengers to send into the enemy's country, who am I, that I should have misgivings when the

King of kings sends me? The chiefs send their messengers,
but they remain at home. My King does not remain behind.
He says, 'Follow thou Me!' Then He walks in front. Oh,
if only I could bring myself to roll all my burdens upon Him!
If I but possessed the full confidence that He would guide me
and work by me—by one who was lost without hope, and only
became a *man* by His grace! O man of God! May the
journey, undertaken in His name alone, be blessed! My wife
and I have consented to our Father's employing us in His work.
We are weak, but we hear Him say, 'My strength is made
perfect in your weakness.' We have no intelligence, but we
are told Jesus has been made our wisdom; we are sinners,
but He has been made our righteousness. Who then has
brought us forth that we should thus be made complete? I
praise the mercy of God, I praise His grace, Who has made
of *me* a messenger of salvation—of *me*, *Molatlegi* (lost)!
Molatlegi—that was the name of my childhood; it was the name
of all others that befitted me, for I was lost."

The wives of our evangelists contrast with one another
quite as strongly as do their husbands. Levi's wife is quite
young, and has little experience. Aaron's wife, Ma-Ruthi, has
grown up in our house, so our mutual affection is no new thing,
and the grace of God has already done its work in her heart.
She has the soul of a missionary. Every day during our
journey, she taught her children and Levi's to read and sing;
and she never loses an opportunity of speaking about the
Saviour to the heathen that she meets.

Knowing us to be in the tropics, no doubt you think of us
as being half roasted. Make your minds quite easy on that
score. It is winter-time here. The thermometer, which by
day rarely rises to 68° Fahr., frequently falls to 40° Fahr., even
inside the waggon. Those only who know how chilly the
natives are can form any idea of the trouble we have had every
morning to stir up the caravan. Oh, my poor clock and the
bugle! How they did hate them! They did not know how
I, through my continual sleepless hours, weighed, so to speak,
every minute of my people's rest, and never sounded the horn
till the last moment. One of the benefits of Sunday was that
the clock and bugle were silent, and the poor fellows profited
by it to their hearts' content in the intervals of our services.

It was on July 26th that we arrived at Leshoma, the same date as six years ago. We had no intention of camping on our previous site. Nevertheless, leaving the waggons behind, my wife, my niece, and I made a loving pilgrimage thither. We descended into the valley ; then turning to the left, we climbed the well-known hill, and searched some time for our former camping-ground. The clearing, the hut, the fence, all had disappeared in the luxuriant growth of bushes ; the ashes that covered the ground were all that remained. No—I am wrong. There is a gigantic mahogany tree near ; and its trunk still bears, clear as on the day it was cut into its fibres, this simple epitaph :

KHOSANA

DIED

13—IX—78.

That opens a large chapter in our souvenirs.

The deadly tse-tse fly, which formerly infested these woods, has retired, following the buffalo in its flight before the hunter's rifle. So we were able to camp farther on, only ten miles from the Zambesi. The site where we have pitched our tents is charming, and is certainly the least unhealthy we could have chosen. It is a sandy hill, about ninety-eight feet above the valley, and one thousand feet above sea-level. Delightfully shaded, yet not overcrowded with trees, it stands on the edge of a limitless virgin forest, a splendid park, of which no one has disturbed our enjoyment—not even the lions. Before us, to the west and on the right, following the valley, stretch wooded hills, as far as the long blue line which limits the horizon. This blue line, on which our eyes fasten instinctively, is Trans-Zambesia, which is to be our field of labour, the second home of our adoption. A stream, the Leshoma, flows through the valley, loses itself, and reappears, forming beautiful limpid pools, which promise us the inestimable luxury of baths at small cost.

One disadvantage of this place (and no doubt we shall find others) is a fine black sand, which penetrates our garments, enters the very pores of our skin, renders all our measures for cleanliness terribly insufficient, and threatens us with an extraordinary consumption of an article all the more precious here because impossible to procure—*soap*. We must learn to make it ourselves ; and our poor housekeeper, on whom all the care falls, has already armed herself with recipes. For neighbours, we have at two hundred paces from here a trader named Blockley, and across the valley some native hunters. The establishment of the former and the huts of the latter fit into the landscape very well.

Mlle. Coillard has soon found the makings of a very interesting school, among the children of the expedition, and the Zambesi boys who work for us. She teaches morning and evening with an energy all her own, and with as much interest as at Leribé.

Who can say with what feelings of relief, joy, and gratitude we at last outspanned our waggons and pitched our tents ? Yes, the journey has been long, costly, and difficult ; and its chief legacy is an utter lassitude, both moral and physical. It seemed to us sometimes that the springs had been over-strained, and the very sources of life dried up. But day after day, and in every circumstance, God has given us the needed measure of grace. All along the way we have found sympathisers among both black and white, Boer as well as English. Even where enmity and obstacles were predicted, we have been heaped with benefits, and surrounded with interest. We have had no bad illness, no serious accident, not even trying adventures. We saw the famine spectre, and dreaded thirst, but God provided for all our needs and filled the desert pools for us. Our greatest difficulties have been the channels of the most precious benedictions. At the Ebenezer which we raise here to the name of Him Who has told all our wanderings, the past inspires us with adoration, the present with perfect confidence. Guided by His eye, led by His powerful hand, one step at a time suffices.

CHAPTER XI

SESHEKE, *August 9th*, 1884.

SESHEKE! How can I write that name without emotion! Here my Master brought me six years ago, and showed me the new field of labour that we sought. Here He stopped me—His own time was not yet come. Here our dear Eleazar Marathane ended his career, and here he sleeps. All the experiences of my first visit rush back upon me. Time has softened all that was bitter and sorrowful in them: only the blessings remain as sweet as ever.

I cannot refrain from glancing forward. Yet what use is it? The future is God's; ours is the present. The present! it is dark. Our path bristles with difficulties; I had foreseen them indeed, but it was impossible to appreciate their gravity. But never despair! It was when the patriarch, a fugitive and alone, rested his weary head on a stone that the Lord raised for him a corner of the veil, and in a glorious vision gave him a glimpse of the multitudes who should bear His name. "Be not afraid," said the Lord to Paul in Corinth, "but speak, and hold not thy peace, for I am with thee . . . *for I have much people in this city.*"

But let us return to Leshoma. Once we had pitched our

camp, and sent our oxen to Gazuma, two days' journey off, to graze and rest, we felt we must see the Zambesi : we were too impatient to wait any longer.

We left my wife and niece to rid themselves as best they could of a nightmare which had haunted them ever since leaving Mangwato—*the washing!* After twenty-five years' missionary life, Mme. Coillard had still to go through this apprenticeship, one which she dreaded, for so far she had never been reduced to the necessity of doing it herself. And think what an accumulation of linen during our journey! The catechists' wives, out of pity as much as affection, consented to lend a hand ; but evidently it is not an aid on which we can count. So M. Jeanmairet and I left our laundresses at the edge of a stream and started, accompanied by some of our party, lightly equipped, and somewhat lightly provisioned.

We followed the valley, which a recent prairie fire has covered with a dreary pall. Two hours and a half of walking, and then, just as we emerge from the brushwood, a wide ribbon winding over the plain and threading its way through impenetrable jungles appears before our eyes. It is the Zambesi. Arrived at the official ford of Kazungula, we announced ourselves by firing our guns, in accordance with the custom of the country. No answer. We fired again and again with no more success. We said to each other that with such a strong wind blowing the river was too rough for the canoes to cross without danger ; and satisfied with this explanation (quite gratuitous on our part), we passed the rest of the day hunting birds, admiring the majestic river, looking for hippopotami and crocodiles (which, however, made themselves invisible), and watching the curious antics of the king-fishers. Night fell, and we tightened our waist-belts, for we had counted on better entertainment, and protected ourselves as best we could under a rough shelter of reeds, swarming with mice and vermin. The cold was so intense (40° Fahr.) that all, with one or two exceptions, sought the garment of the poor—*the fire.* There was no sleep for any of us. Directly morning dawned, we began firing again ; but still no answer. And yet not the slightest breeze to-day, not a ripple on the water ; it is like a polished mirror. What does this silence mean? Tired of waiting, and by this time half starved, we folded up our rugs and trudged back to Leshoma. Such has been our first visit to the Zambesi—a bucket of cold water thrown on all our joyous anticipations. But later on, all was explained. The ferryman, Singandu, not having received any orders about us, had run to his chief. He was returning with positive commands to bring us over immediately, when the rumour arrived that the Matabele were coming. Panic had seized every one.

A few days later, messengers came from Sesheke. The letters by which I had announced to the king our arrival first at Shoshong, and then at Pata-matenga, had been stopped by the "lords of Sesheke," and were waiting there for the "salutation," which should have accompanied them. And I thought they were at the capital! What a stunning blow! I positively refused to give any more presents till I had seen the king. Since then, I have been told that the chiefs sent on my letters, but by a slave on foot, as if it were a matter of small importance. How will the king receive it? When will his answer come? To fill up the time, we organised an excursion to the falls of Musi oa Tunya; but, at the last moment, I was obliged to give it up, and let our friend Jeanmairet go with Middleton and Waddell, accompanied by our Basuto and some porters.

And we—we look northwards to the blue line beyond the forests, till sight is lost in the depths of the immense perspective. And as days go by, we wonder if the horizon is not growing darker. Troops of Zambesians come to Leshoma, but they bring no news; they are slaves come to barter. They bring millet, sorgho, ground nuts, beans, and sometimes a little wild honey, all in calabashes of various sizes. Every calabash costs so many strings of beads, or a *setsiba*, two long ells of calico, which is exorbitant. And so it falls on my dear wife to bargain with these noisy and sometimes impertinent gangs: she has to answer quietly, buy with prudence, and explain gently in order to send them away satisfied. It is hard drudgery; and Levi and Joel, who had at first willingly accepted the office of helping "their mother," soon saw that, and backed out of it one after the other, leaving her to manage alone. It is not simply a question of providing for our evangelists and their families, the drivers and native helpers, but also of getting together the necessary provisions against the return journey of our men, who

have come from Mangwato and Basuto-land, and of laying up
in store for the whole expedition against the rainy season.   And
buying sixty sacks of corn in this way, to speak of nothing
else, represents a formidable expenditure of energy and patience
to any one not hardened to this petty haggling with beads and
bits of calico.   But in spite of weariness and sadness at such
waste of time, the missionary's wife never complains.   Even
while longing for a few days' respite she says to herself, " It
is for the Lord."   Yes, and " for the Lord " she faces all her
other duties, and appears next morning at the market forced
upon her, strengthened in secret for the day.   When the purchases come to an end early, our proper work begins.   We
make these Zambesians repeat a Bible text, and sing a verse
of a hymn, which we explain to them.   They go away astonished,
and we follow them in thought beyond the blue line where we
would be.

One day (it was the afternoon of Sunday, August 9th), we
saw in the valley a long file of men winding their way towards
us.   At their head, we soon recognised Karumba,[1] who had
returned to visit his parents.   He announced that the thirty
young men he brought had been sent by the chiefs of Sesheke
with canoes to fetch us.   Here was a ray of light in our dark
sky !   My preparations were soon made, and I went off without
any misgivings.   I leave you to guess how happy I was as I
crossed the Zambesi.   The sun was just setting ; its flaming
disc was bathing itself in the ripples, and colouring them with
its fire ; while the wooded banks, tufted with palm trees, were
reflected as in a mirror.   All was peace and harmony.

Next morning, when I rose, I found the charm broken.   My
boatmen had struck, and were noisily refusing to move till they
had received *setsibas* to their liking.   Without giving in, I
managed to calm them down, and had a most enjoyable journey
with them.   We were not pressed for time, so they fished and
hunted birds in the jungles, and in the evening I taught them
to sing.   At our last stage, I distributed *setsibas* of red calico.
After a bath, they dressed themselves up in them, each according
to his own fancy, and all alike grotesque.   We were announced
by gunshots ; and when our little procession arrived at the

---

[1] One of the two Zambesians whom M. Coillard had brought back from
the first expedition.

[*To face page* 144.]

LESHOMA—A MARKET DAY.

entrance, and went to the *lekhothla*, great and small turned out
to salute us with, "*Lumela Monere! Shangwe! Shangwe!*"
("Hail, father! we are your servants ").[1]

You will remember that Sesheke is the residence of twelve
or fifteen chiefs.   In European language, they would be governors
or prefects.   These are Barotsi, promoted to the government of
the numerous tributary peoples.   They assume the names and
titles of their predecessors, and form a council, presided over
by the principal chief, the Morantsiane.   The Morantsiane of
to-day is no longer the old man whom I knew and liked six
years ago, but his son, besotted with beer-drinking and hemp-
smoking.   Even the village is no longer the same.   It was
burnt down during the war of Nguana-wina ; and though it has
been rebuilt since, it looks dirty and dilapidated.   I no longer
see those double huts, so spacious and airy—*for huts*, that is to
say—that I admired there.   Otherwise it is still Sesheke, with
its dignitaries, the Rataü, the Mokhele, the Katukura, the
Nalishua, etc.   Some of these titles are borne to-day by new
heads ; still, I find a number of old acquaintances among them ;
and, to judge by their demonstrative salutations, they are
pleased to see me.   When the little official speeches were over
on both sides, we talked together for a long time.   They related
all that had happened in their country since our journey through
it.   I answered the questions they showered on me, and talked
to them of my travels and my mission.   After all, it is pleasant
to come to Sesheke.

Then I was told my baggage had been taken to the hut
destined for me, so I bade my friends good-night, and went
home to rest.   But, at the door, Aaron and I started back in
disgust.   The hut and court were no better than a kennel, and
so filthy that no one would even put out a hand to clean it.
I sat down on one of my bales outside, intending to pass the
night there.   At last one of my canoe-men, touched with pity
fetched a poor little slave-girl, whom he pushed into the hut to
clean up the worst of the dirt, and the next day Aaron and Ben
finished it.   Decidedly, our dear Zambesians are not hospitable.
We lay down hungry before this uninhabitable hovel.   Next
morning, before rising, I was assailed by a crowd of noisy
vendors, and by the principal chiefs, who had held a council

---

[1] *Shangwe*, literally " Sir," meaning "your humble servant."

during the night, and now brought me the result. They regretted having sent my letters by a slave, and to repair this error one of them would start immediately for the capital. I urged them to take me with them. But there is the law, which bars our way like the great wall of China. No alternative— we must have patience.

We have set to work to visit the people in their homes, and have to submit as best we can to the assaults of these insatiable beggars. They will certainly contrive to rob us of everything we possess : they are absolutely shameless. M. Jean-mairet, who has joined me, helps me to gather the people every morning under the shade of a great tree near our dwelling. We tell them Bible stories, speak to them of the Saviour, and make them repeat a verse and the Lord's Prayer. We teach them to read—that is, to repeat the alphabet. They look at us with astonishment, and mimic exactly every movement they see us make ; they beat time like us, speak in the same tone, and repeat our every word. Some lie down, others sit ; they take snuff, chatter, laugh, and salute each other by clapping their hands. We tell them to be quiet and behave properly, and continue our work as earnestly as before. What troubles us most is the terrible rapacity of these people. How shall we get to the Valley. robbed as we have been already ?

Meanwhile, a messenger came from the king. He was one of the sub-chiefs, and brought a numerous retinue. Mr. Arnot having gone to Benguella with Silva Porto [1] to seek medical advice, no one had been able to read my letter. (This explains why no measures were taken to conduct me to Lealuyi without delay.) The message brought back by Mosala came to this : If the Jesuits wrote the letter, the king gave them permission to fetch their baggage (chiefly tools and merchandise), which they had left in his country last year, but declared he would not give them any help, neither canoes nor men ; they could come in waggons. If the letter were from me, Mosala was charged to bring us to the capital at once. But the joy this gave us, though keen, was shortlived. The same day the rumour spread that the Matabele had crossed the Zambesi, and there was universal panic. The canoes which were to have brought

[1] A well-known Portuguese trader. See Serpa Pinto's "How I Crossed Africa," vol. ii., p. 66.

us to the king were sent laden with ivory to buy powder and
guns from Mr. Blockley ; the cattle were taught to swim for
safety, and all prepared to flee.   In these circumstances, what
shall we do without canoes or rowers ?   And to think that I
have charged myself with seven or eight cases of Mr. Arnot's,
to oblige him !   How shall we get back to Leshoma ?   How
can we remain alone at Sesheke ?   " My soul, wait thou only
upon God."

SESHEKE, *September 4th.*

Still at Sesheke, the Slough of Despond.   Through what
alternatives of hope and disappointment we have passed in a
few days !   At such times, the Saviour's presence is a precious
reality.   Amid the chaos of our last adventures, it is difficult
for me to take up the thread of my narrative.   Behind us, these
waves seem but small things, though they made my faith quiver
like a reed in a pool.

I was saying that the canoes sent to fetch us went back with
powder and guns.   Jeanmairet and I were now only thinking of
leaving.   Unhappily, the reports brought back by the scouts
only tend to show that the threatened Matabele war is more and
more imminent.   The chiefs have been consulting auguries and
casting lots, inoculating themselves with a specific to render
themselves invulnerable, seeking out every sort of charm, and
passing the rest of their time in drinking and teaching their
cattle to swim.   No one concerned himself about our journey.
In the absence of the Morantsiane, I gathered the old chiefs,
and told them we had decided to leave on foot.   They approved,
and promised us porters.   On his return, the Morantsiane was
alarmed at this news.   It was a reflection on him.   Through
the clouds of drink that obscured his brain, he came to offer to
" his friend " Jeanmairet a calabash of honey, and to me two
monkey skins.   Then, growing bolder, he said, " Moruti, you
will not make this journey on foot, at your age, and in such
heat ?   What would the king say ?   To-morrow you shall have
my canoe."

We yielded, but several days passed, and we were still there,
waiting for the rowers who were " coming every moment."   At
last they arrived.   It was Saturday.   Rataü and Tahalima
loaded our " dug-outs," prepared our seats with great care, and

made our rowers take a trial trip, before they declared themselves satisfied.   After a few words of farewell to the assembled
crowd, and a prayer on the bank with Aaron and Josefa, who
were going on foot under Mosala's guidance, Jeanmairet leapt
into his boat, I into mine, and we pushed off into the open
river.   At this place, it flows round an islet, making a fine bay.
We had not been embarked five minutes, when our skiffs began
to fill with water to an alarming extent.   The two men who
were baling could hardly keep them afloat.   The danger became
more imminent every moment.   It is not in my nature to turn
back, so I also began to bale ; and we succeeded, though not
without difficulty, in gaining the opposite bank.   All my baggage
was wetted—absolutely soaked.   Nothing vexed me more than
the loss of my medicines and three dozen photographic plates.
Rataü immediately sent a second canoe ; and having dried our
baggage, we pressed on to Tahalima's cattle farm, where we
passed a well-employed Sunday.   Very early on Monday morning, while we were busily at work, mending our canoe with
papyrus and palm leaves, the lords of Sesheke sent me an
express messenger with an order to return thither immediately.
The messenger entreated me privately not to hesitate, telling
me that similar orders had been sent to Aaron and even to
Makoatsa, Khama's envoy.   What could have happened ?

Rataü was commissioned to tell us.   A revolution had
broken out in the Valley ; and the king, whom they wished to
assassinate, had fled.   This was serious news.   It seems the
chiefs had expected it : no doubt it was the reason of their
delays.   But what could we do now ?   How could we make
such a long journey in a country where anarchy prevailed ?   If
even in ordinary times there was so little security from pillage
and rapine, what would it be now with no recognised authority ?
And then, to whom should we go ?   Who were the leaders of
the revolution ?   And so. we had to follow the counsels of
prudence, and decide—*to wait !*   What a hard lesson that is !

It is difficult for us to find out the real causes of the
revolution.   This only is certain, that Robosi held the lives
of the Barotsi chiefs very cheaply.   He murdered seven in one
day, at a banquet to which he had invited them.   Lately, he
caused a respected chief and one of the late Sepopa's wives to
be put to death.   Then he was taking measures to get rid of

most of the lords of Sesheke, when his schemes were discovered. A plot was hatched, and Robosi only owed his safety to his coolness and flight.

The lords of Sesheke could not contain their delight. Every one killed oxen and made beer, and for several days there was nothing but a series of orgies. After 10 a.m., it was rare to find a man sober. We had to suffer for it in more ways than one. Our man Ben had made friends with a chief named Kanyanga. "Here are my two daughters," said this man to him ; "they are your wives." Ben took this as a joke, but not so their father. One day, Ben passed in front of Kanyanga's wife without clicking his tongue, which is their way of saying "Excuse me." Kanyanga was furious that a son-in-law should thus fail in respect towards a mother-in-law. He rushed straight to our hut, entered and seized my finest gun, vociferating threats of fire and murder. And this was one of our best friends ! We passed a night of misery. Quite recently, and in broad daylight, this same Kanyanga had killed one of his wives and her brother for as slight a cause. Poor Ben ! he stripped himself to redeem my gun ; cloak (the cloak he was so proud of !), rug, shirt, calico, everything was given up to satisfy the rapacity of this man blinded with passion.[1] You can understand the serious consequences this incident might have had for us. So I brought the matter before the council of the chiefs, and the result of this public investigation was to clear Ben, and consequently the mission, of all blame. In spite of this, not a voice dared to raise itself in condemnation of Kanyanga's conduct.

The Barotsi chiefs, always exposed to secret assassination, are naturally suspicious and afraid of one another. The sword

---

[1] Ben, a characteristic specimen of one kind of "mission Kaffir." A Batoka slave, he owed his freedom to Khama, at whose capital he was educated by the missionaries, and professed Christianity. He developed unusual ability, and earns an excellent livelihood by acting as guide to European travellers. At home, he is a most respectable member of society and a pattern of domesticity. With his quondam employers he shows himself full of skill and resources, invariably gay and good-tempered, generous, affectionate, and even faithful, but quite free from inconvenient scruples of any kind. The fact that natives of this stamp generally lay themselves out for the service of travellers often leads the latter to think they are the only existing "mission Kaffirs."

of Damocles always hangs over their heads; and when ambassadors come from the capital, no one knows whether, besides the ostensible message they bring, they may not have a secret commission to murder some one. Moreover, when the chiefs come to the *lekhothla*, they are always accompanied by a numerous retinue, armed, not with assegaïs, for these are not allowed in the African forums, but with clubs. If they have the slightest ground for such suspicions, they sleep outside, and surround themselves with all kinds of precautions. This will give you an idea of the land of cut-throats to which we are bringing the Gospel of peace.

In this respect, our experiences at Sesheke have been hard. In relating the incident about Ben, I skirted an abyss of Zambesian paganism, of which the sight alone fills one with horror. Our evangelists need a special measure of God's grace to preserve them in the midst of the universal corruption which flaunts here in broad daylight, and the shameless temptations with which men and women assail strangers. I have studied heathenism at close quarters in Basuto-land, as among the Zulu and among other tribes, and horrible it was. But here it surpasses all conception. A historian, speaking of George IV., has said that if he had been stripped of all the waistcoats in which he had a mania for muffling himself up, you might have searched in vain for the *man*. I would not say the same of the Zambesians; I believe that under the pile of all that is hideous and odious in paganism we shall find *men*, and men whom we can love. Besides, we are doing the work of Him Who "came to seek and to save that which was lost," "not the righteous, but sinners": let us not forget that.

LESHOMA, *October 15th*, 1884.

To divert our minds from political matters, and turn the interminable visits of my "unemployed" friends, the chiefs, to useful account, I proposed to them that we should make a net. This is the privileged work of the chiefs, and in no way beneath the dignity of a king. They alone have the right to fish with a net: the people must content themselves with weirs of reeds, and other equally primitive contrivances. This gave me an opportunity every day of learning things myself, and of evangelising. Our conversations were sometimes so deeply interesting when we spoke of Nyambe (God) that all hands stopped work, and all eyes were fixed upon us.

Unhappily, my friend Jeanmairet was out of sorts, and, without being confined to his bed, gave me a great deal of anxiety. I dosed him well with Dover's powder and quinine, and the fever was checked. Our severe diet of sorgho and black coffee was not of a nature to restore either appetite or strength to my dear convalescent. So we profited by the calming of the political atmosphere to return to the camp.

How beautiful Leshoma is, on returning from the burning sands of Sesheke! All is so fresh, so verdant here. It is spring, and the woods are putting on their festival array of the most varied and luxuriant tints. They only do it once a year, so that we may never weary of admiring them. Leshoma is a hive of bees. At dawn, the bell (for we have a bell) calls every one to prayer ; then each goes to his work. No one is idle. Aaron and Levi already occupy their own cottages ; those of M. Jeanmairet and of our two artisans are nearly finished ; our own two-roomed cottage, the exclusive work of Waddell and Middleton, is also making great progress : so that besides our tents (which the heat makes so unbearable that we must put them by for other campings), quite a rustic hamlet is being raised. These shelters of stakes and grass are a sanitary measure ; and scanty as they are, they seem to us, after our gipsy life of nine months, to be everything we can wish for in the way of luxury and comfort in our present circumstances. The whole will cost but little. Besides, we count on Leshoma's being the headquarters and sanatorium of our mission for a long time to come.

I have brought back deep impressions from Sesheke. The more closely we see the work before us, the greater seem its proportions. After my arrival, I set myself to study the Serotsi tongue. But I soon discovered that this language is only understood by a very limited number of people, principally chiefs. It is the same with other dialects. Only the Setoka appears to be of any importance, and recommends itself necessarily to our study. The language of the country within three hundred miles of the Victoria Falls in either direction is Sesuto. All the tribes of serfs understand it : they speak it rather as the peasants at home speak French : it makes us laugh sometimes. But they quite understand good classical Sesuto. I knew this already, and yet it is always striking me more and more forcibly.

There is one social question I have never yet fathomed ; it is more complicated than I thought at first : it is the question of slavery. According to Serpa Pinto, it is one of the fruits of the commerce between the Portuguese and the Barotsi. I do not know if this be the case. But one always experiences a strange shudder on first seeing this horrible sore with one's own eyes. At Sesheke, I was offered a child of eight or nine years. They wanted in exchange a gun worth £6. I could have had him for less. The other day again I received the following note :

"DEAR MR. COILLARD,—Here is a little boy offered for sale. If you want him, you can have him, for I have enough of them. His price is, a hat, a waistcoat, two or three handkerchiefs, and some beads. If you would like to have him, tell me, and I will send him to you. He is the same size as my little Jonas."

I had the boy brought. He was about twelve years old, and had been torn from his parents and his home during one of the raids made by the Barotsi on the Mashukulumboe. His beautiful eyes and ivory teeth were thrown into relief by his ebony face. His hair was thicker and less woolly than that of the people here. His back was all scarred with the blows he had received. The man who wanted to sell him praised his good qualities : he was well built and robust ; he was a good herd-boy, and he would certainly make an excellent servant.

My wife could not turn her eyes away from the poor child. Her heart was moved. The slave-trader perceived this, and took advantage of it. He pushed the child roughly. " Tell the lady you like her very much," he said. " Madam, I like you very much, and I should so like to stay with you," said the poor little slave, fixing his melancholy eyes upon her with a supplicating look. We had to put an end to this pitiful scene. A hat, a waistcoat, calico, and beads—the price of a human being for whose ransom the Son of God shed His own blood ! If we had only consulted our feelings, we should not have hesitated ; but to open a new slave-market, that was impossible. The slave-dealer, who had been sent by a chief of Sesheke, was displeased, and went away at once, very angry with the little Moshukulumboe. We followed him with our eyes, poor child ! across the valley till he disappeared into the woods with his cruel guardians. What would they do with him ?

There was a great surprise for us on our return from Sesheke—*the post!* Yes, the post, which we had not received for over five months. Even I, hardened old African as I am, felt my heart beat quicker on opening a packet of some sixty letters. No newspapers, for the obliging trader who acted as our postman had left Mangwato on horseback to rejoin the waggons, and had not been able to burden himself with a bag full of gazettes and reviews. So we must postpone hearing news of the external world, political, religious, and literary. Besides, we must not complain, for our friends have supplemented them most carefully. No bad tidings have come to sadden us, not even any bills to pay. If only I had sixty pens at my disposal to tell all these friends at once the good they have done us ! A letter from Europe is at a premium when it reaches the Zambesi. We turn it this way and that, we examine the stamps and read, then we put it carefully on one side to read it again at our leisure. It is a *tête-à-tête* that we promise ourselves with such and such a friend. Unfortunately, the post goes out again in a few days, so all our letters must be written at once. Our friends must not be too exacting with us : they must be good enough to take their share of this long letter, in writing which so many names present themselves to my pen. When shall we get the next post ? And later on, how many times in the year ? Once, or twice ? I do not know. But write to us *all the same*, dear friends ; write to us *all the more*. You pray for us, you work with us, you have an affection for us ; but we want you to *tell us so*. We place the Barotsi Mission on your hearts. Remember, we are on the threshold of the interior ; before us stretches a field which only your resources and your zeal will limit. Meantime, we are happy and united. Although we are at the Zambesi with our Master, we are not martyrs yet !

October 30th.

Our Basuto left the day before yesterday, with the people returning to Mangwato. The Zambesians, who are uncomfortable at home, and who have heard from some privileged persons like Karumba and Seajika that the world does not precisely end at the river, nor even at Pata-matenga, are devoured by the desire to emerge from their shell, and see what happens outside of it. We had to be very firm, almost harsh, to prevent a legion of young men from joining their little caravan, in the capacity of vampires. But I am afraid a good number have taken short cuts, to reach the waggons farther on. The same day, about fifty young men arrived, sent by the lords of Sesheke to fetch us. A new king has been elected—Maïna. An embassy is on the way to Sesheke to send for the chiefs. A messenger went in advance, so that they might prepare without delay to go and render homage to the new sovereign. Hence the canoes and this tribe of rowers that they send us. Unfortunately, it is summer ; rainy weather has set in ; we have constant storms, and pass rapidly through great alternations of temperature. The beautiful winter season has passed. It is not exactly an attractive programme to make this long journey of two months under such variations of heat and rain, in canoes which are always leaking, and we thought it would be better not to expose M. Jeanmairet to such a trying journey, and, humanly speaking, to certain fever. So I shall go alone with Aaron, our evangelist. We hope to start to-morrow. It is not fever I fear in this journey, nor the difficulties, but the rapacity of these poor Zambesians, who consider it nothing out of the way to deposit you upon an islet, till they have extorted plenty of presents from you. We need to keep close to the Saviour, and draw love and patience from Him.

LESHOMA, *December 1st,* 1884.

At the date of my last letter, I was sending away our Bamangwato and Basuto drivers, and was starting again, rather hurriedly, for Sesheke. From all appearances, I ought by this time to have been at Lealuyi. This is just a specimen of the hopes and disappointments of which we have perpetually been the playthings since our arrival here. We must not yield to the temptation of dwelling only on the dark side of things. We

have not been made to stay in the sylvan solitudes of Leshoma
to take root here, though no doubt we thought we should have
been much better placed and much more useful beyond the river
in full active service, than reduced to the passive service of
simply sitting under our gourd to wait.

At Leshoma, the days follow each other without much
change. Only our constant activity makes them pass quickly,
and breaks their monotony. We have folded up our tents, and
in their place huts have been built, which, though simple, afford
us undreamt-of comfort. Our establishment, now three months
old, astonishes every one, and represents as many *years* of
labour in Basuto-land, where the building materials are lacking. Middleton and Waddell have tried to make a saw-pit.
M. Jeanmairet has thrown off his coat, and begun his apprenticeship. Such a good example has inspired Aaron to follow it.
Unfortunately, our saw is too thin, and the wooden frame too
weak ; and poor Waddell has been racking his brains to try
and make planks a foot wide with a saw designed for quite
a different purpose. Perhaps one day we shall have a circular
saw turned by the waters of the Zambesi. What a dream !
Alas ! the making of planks is a nightmare which has never
ceased to haunt my mind since we first spoke of the Mission to
the Zambesi.

My niece's school has been enriched by some Masaroa
children. But it is only with great difficulty that we have
brought them to it. " Just think," said the half-caste wife of
a hunter, "that little girl always wants to accompany me when
I go to hear the preaching ! What has a Mosaroa to do with
the things of God ? As if He troubled Himself about these
Bushmen ! " These poor children were perfectly delighted when
they were allowed to come to school ; but Mlle. Coillard had
a great deal of trouble at first in making them sit down with the
others, and submit to the same discipline, easy as it was. The
first visit of all the Zambesians who come, slaves and chiefs,
is to " Missi's school." M. Jeanmairet, who works hard with
her at the evening class, is learning to cast his bread upon the
waters. Many young men only remain a month, and then
return home. They have learnt a few letters of the alphabet,
a hymn perhaps, and a verse of the Word of God, and they
go away, apparently to forget everything ; while our friend begins

all over again with others, probably with the same result.   It is schooling for him too.

The post will always be an event at the Zambesi.   The very evening before I left, two messengers came from Pata-matenga, bringing us a great packet of letters, which a trader had been so obliging as to bring from Mangwato ; and what was more, the good man added that he still had "a whole bag of news-papers and a pile of letters for us, with which he had not been able to load the porters." How tantalising ! But never mind ; we shall enjoy what we have. Adieu, dinner ! Adieu, sleep ! The silent hours of the night fly by while we listen to the news !

Thus cheered up, Aaron and I started for Sesheke.   The crossing this time was as disagreeable as possible.   I was so tired, I could not keep awake : it rained, and the wind blew, in the intervals of burning sunshine.   The river was as beautiful as ever, but "wrathful," and we did not cleave its troubled waters with impunity ; they revenged themselves by breaking over us.   We spent the whole day huddled up with our feet in the water ; and when, in the evening, we undid our rugs, we found them, alas ! perfectly soaked.   It is nothing short of a miracle that we did not take fever.

At last we reached Sesheke.   The village was silent and deserted : there were no longer children playing noisily, no more busy slaves, women building huts, and chiefs discussing business in the *khothla*[1] or round pots of beer.   Grass was growing in all the courts.   The Morantsiane was alone, with a few other persons and some slaves.   What had happened ?

A few minutes' conversation explained all.   When the lords of Sesheke sent us their canoes, they were awaiting messengers from Lealuyi, whom they knew to be on the road, and expected every moment ; they were hoping that on my arrival we could all go together to the capital.   Not only did the messengers fail to arrive, but sinister rumours were spread on the subject of their acts and deeds.   It was whispered that these men were secretly charged with a mission of murder ; the intended victims even were pointed out ; it was known that on the way they had put to death one of the chiefs of their own band.   We were assured that several important persons had shared the

---

[1] *Khothla* and *lekhothla* are nearly synonymous, meaning court of justice. *Khothla* refers rather to the *place*, *lekhothla* to the court in session.

same fate, and that even Makoatsa, Khama's ambassador, who
had been going to the capital on foot with his suite, had been
first robbed and then ruthlessly murdered. Terror had seized
on everybody ; and they had all, under one pretext or another,
taken their household goods and fled into the woods and fields,
thence to watch the course of events.

At our arrival, Rataü, Tahalima, and others ventured out to
see us, surrounding themselves with all kinds of precautions.
We held a council, and at the first glance were able to judge
of the situation. It was out of the question for any of the chiefs
to conduct us in person to the Valley ; all declared themselves
incapable of giving us the slightest protection, of which fact
we were even more strongly convinced than they. Besides,
although they put rowers and canoes at our service, our journey
under the existing circumstances was an impossibility. The
time had not yet come. And for Aaron and myself to remain
alone in the deserted village was likewise impossible. So we
had no alternative but to return to Leshoma. What I regret
is not our trouble, but the *setsibas*, measured by arm's length,
which we must distribute to the rowers. In spite of this, we
have brought back pleasant impressions from Sesheke. Every
time we see the chiefs, it seems to us that we have gained
more of their confidence. They are more communicative, more
thoughtful for our comfort, somewhat more hospitable, and,
above all, less *grasping*.

A little incident closed this journey of a week. When we
came to the rapids of Mambova and Mpalira, Aaron, who is not
very fond of travelling by canoe, wished to take a short cut on
foot, with his gun on his shoulder, accompanied by Karumba.
I descended the rapids in the canoe. When we came to the
meeting-place, I searched, but Aaron was not to be found. I
left a canoe for him, passed on, to wait for him at the Kazungula
ford, five miles farther on. Judge of my astonishment, an hour
later, to see the boat arrive without Aaron ! The canoe-men
assured me that they had searched, shouted, and waited for
him a long time in vain. I made them cross the river and go
back on foot to meet him. It was the middle of the day,
and suddenly one of those storms came on such as one only
sees in the tropics. The flashes of lightning blinded us, the
thunder rolled from hill to hill, and the rain beat down with

extraordinary violence. The crystal surface of the river was broken up; the waves rose like those of the sea, swept up and tormented by the wind, which drove them along, while the great raindrops riddled them like shot. The spectacle was a new and wonderful one for me. But my baggage! I had huddled myself up under a deceitful mackintosh, which absorbed water like a sponge—I have never yet found one which would resist the African climate. Suddenly I felt something fall on my head. It was a mat, which a kind-hearted boy was depriving himself of, to cover me. True, he had not much clothing to get wet! But all the same, this kind deed gave me a great deal of pleasure.

Two o'clock! Three o'clock! Four! Five! It was still raining; the sun was going down; it was equally impossible to go to Leshoma or to build a shelter for the rapidly approaching night. And Aaron, where was he? In the dusk, we discovered an abandoned shelter of branches. All at once, Aaron appeared on the opposite bank; and as soon as the wind went down, he crossed and rejoined me. Poor fellow! it seems that when he reached the rendezvous he could not find us; and no one having seen us pass, he thought we must have been wrecked in the rapids; so the poor man returned with Karumba to Mambova, following the banks, questioning the passers-by in vain, and searching for the fragments of our canoes with an anxiety better imagined than described.

LESHOMA, *December 9th*, 1884.

The moment we have so long waited for has at last arrived. A new king, Akufuna, has been elected. He is a young man who has grown up in exile, and has been obliged to act prudently at first, and to initiate himself into the duties of his position. As soon as he felt himself thoroughly settled, he thought of us. He wishes to see us even before the lesser chiefs of the country, hoping, he says, that we may be able to give him good advice, to guide him in the exercise of the power confided to him. Two bands of messengers have arrived at Sesheke, each with more pressing messages than the last. The chiefs of Sesheke have sent them on to us, without losing any time, and three of them have come down by canoe to wait for us at the ford of Kazungula. They have sent twenty young men to carry our baggage. But the honour was too great! I was frightened at the thought of the *setsibas*, so I bade them a friendly farewell! I shall put our packages on the backs of our donkeys: it will be humbler and more economical. We do not wish to expose more men than we can help, so M. Jeanmairet and Levi will remain at Leshoma. Aaron, and Middleton at his own request, will go with me. We need not assure our friends that we will be prudent and take every precaution, so do not fear.

Oh, if you could only know what one feels on finding one-self on the threshold of this Central Africa, where the least ray of the Gospel has not penetrated! If those friends who blame our imprudence could see from afar what we see, and feel what we feel, they would be the first to wonder that those redeemed by Christ should be so backward in devotion, and know so little of the spirit of self-sacrifice. They would be ashamed of the hesitations that hinder us. These innumerable tribes, of which the Barotsi is only the first on our way, are sitting in the shadow of death : they perish as pagans amid horrible and bloody superstitions, while we have the Light and Life which we owe it to them to impart. We must remember that it was not by interceding for the world in glory that Jesus saved it. *He gave Himself.* Our prayers for the evangelisation of the world are but a bitter irony so long as we only give of our superfluity, and draw back before the sacrifice of *ourselves*!

LESHOMA, *December 10th*, 1884.

The sun touches the horizon. A few hours ago, we were all activity, finishing our packing and loading our donkeys— rather a difficult task, as we have only two pack-saddles, and our donkeys are so small that we can put but very little on their backs. I have sent Middleton and Aaron on with our baggage : they will camp at Kazungula, and communicate with the chiefs who are to conduct us to Sesheke. This allows me to remain here till the last moment. These last days have been a time of visitation. Most of the members of the expedition have had fever. During three days my dear wife gave us much anxiety. I did not know what turn her illness would take. And message after message kept coming for us from the river, where the chiefs were waiting for us. Poor people! they could not understand that the illness of a *woman* could interfere with my departure, when it was "the king, *the king himself*," who was calling me. At last the chiefs, Rataü, Tahalima, and others, came themselves to see us. It was an act of great courage, for they never venture on this side of the river, where they always fear the Matabele, and now Robosi, who, they say, is somewhere about the Quando River. It was a civility for which we were much obliged to them, and they showed a sympathy, too, which gave us pleasure. So far from importuning us, they showed us the greatest deference. "Do not think we have come to worry or interfere with you. Our mother is ill, and it is she whom we have come to visit. Take care of her, and when you are ready to go, you will find people and canoes waiting for you at the ford." Happily, my wife is better.

Are you not astonished to see how the enemy impedes our every step, and contests every inch of the road? He is not yet at the end of his resources. The hindrances which postponed our departure from Leribé have been renewed under other forms at Pretoria and Mangwato. Now we have passed four long months of waiting and hoping and disappointments at Leshoma, and at the last moment illness came and caused fresh delays. I suppose these are not the last trials which will assail our faith before we are definitely settled among the Barotsi. But *to doubt would be unworthy*.

It is a bad season, and God has permitted this journey to be robbed of everything that could make it attractive; no doubt, in order that we might judge more calmly, both of men and things. Our delays have already had this advantage, that we have been able to make close acquaintance with the chiefs of these parts. This can only be to the advantage of our mission. They are so many *friends* for us. I should astonish you if I confided one of my cares to you. I am going to Lealuyi like a bird that every one tries to pluck, in spite of the pecks and scratches they will certainly get. In what sort of state shall I return? God only knows! That is very much of the earth, earthy, is it not? But how can I help it? The traders, with the sole object of gaining a monopoly of the ivory trade, have scattered their presents lavishly. Now, in spite of so many ruinous sacrifices, the monopoly threatens to escape them, but the education they have given the tribe is bearing bitter fruit. We cannot expect the Barotsi to understand our mission and make a difference between us and the traders. And as we absolutely cannot imitate their extravagant liberality, we are looked on somewhat disdainfully. To establish our position here, we have to destroy an entire education which has already borne seed, and to struggle against the trend of public opinion ; and it will be hard work at first.

SESHEKE, *December 15th*, 1884.

And so I have left my own people. My dear wife showed herself equal to the circumstances. I should have left a week sooner, only she fell ill. "To-morrow I shall be better," she said, "and you can go. I will never be in your way, when God opens the door and calls you." So there was a rainbow over our separation, for He had answered our prayers. Dear Jeanmairet accompanied me part of the way, and then, as Serpa Pinto has jokingly represented me in Europe, I continued my way alone with a Zambesian, "my stick in my hand." Aaron had taken my gun. They were all ready for me ; but the wind blew so hard that we had to wait till evening, and even then we were not quite free from danger as we crouched down in our pirogues. We passed the night with one of the two chiefs who were to conduct us to Sesheke. I was struck by the respectful and considerate manner of the other. Every time I looked at him, I found his eyes fixed on me ; he listened to all I had to say with remarkable interest. He was Mahaha, a petty chief, whom my wife and I and the catechists had met on an islet six years before.[1] The good man had received us with the greatest cordiality, and was so desirous to hear about the things of God, that immediately after the customary saluta-tion he demanded, "Sing to us about Jesus." And we sang together the hymn we used then to sing at every stage :

A re bineleng Yesu,	(Sing the praises of Jesus,
Hoba ke eena Moloki.	He alone is our Saviour.)

The impressions of our visit and our singing have not passed

---

[1] See page 56. Mahaha is not to be confounded with Mathaha, a rebel chief afterwards killed.

away, it seems; and Mahaha, reminding me of every little incident, added, with his face radiant and his eyes fixed on mine, "*Yesu* has blessed us! We have had plentiful rain and splendid harvests. We have had maize *so* high, *so* big" (making a significant gesture with the hand). "Such millet! We have never seen anything like it!" Directly he had heard of our arrival at Leshoma this year, he had made haste to send a boy to help us in our labour of settling down, and during my absences he had frequently sent my wife corn, honey, etc. So you may judge of his delight in escorting us to Sesheke. Everything at the Zambesi is not bad, thank God!

At Mpalira, we meet Makoatsa, Khama's messenger, who was said to have been murdered; he was returning laden with furs for his master. We also found there three petty chiefs, sent by the king to fetch us—pleasant enough and full of consideration for us : they won our hearts from the first. They were going to Leshoma, where they knew I was detained by my wife's illness : they wanted to have the satisfaction of seeing us, and personally transmitting the messages they were charged with. I decided to remain at Mpalira that day and the next, which was Sunday, so as to converse at leisure with them, and above all with Makoatsa, and to evangelise. We had no cause to regret the delay, for we had large gatherings and interesting conversations.

On our arrival here, the chiefs worked like horses to make us comfortable. They gave us a new hut, roomy and clean; they have brought us provisions for the journey; and morning and evening they love to assemble in our courtyard and talk. We profit by this to talk to them of the things of God, on which subject they ask the strangest questions; and to collect information about ethnography, ethnology, etc.; and to study the Serotsi language. When I am tired of talking, I simply begin to read or write : that is all. They are never tired of watching my pen run over the paper; and they ask what mysterious medicine can initiate into this wonderful art. Aaron also has begun to study Serotsi, and now it remains to be seen which of us will make the most progress. See my pretension in matching myself against these African philologists, who seem to learn a language without thinking about it! Their memories are like iron : everything is engraved; nothing effaces itself. All

MASATOANE—A CHIEF OF SESHEKE (FULL AND PROFILE).

the same, I do make some progress, to the great satisfaction of my professor. Let me take advantage of it to pass a little lesson on to you, very elementary, but very useful. The name of the tribe is not *Barotsi* at all—that is the name the Makololo have given it, corrupting the real one, which is: *Aruyi, Moruyi, Morotsi,* pl. *Aruyi* ; *Seruyi,* the language ; *Boruyi,* the kind ; *Lealuyi,* the country, and not *Lua-lui,* nor *Lua-luyi,* as I wrote it at first. The confusion in African geography resulting from the way in which travellers attempt to render the native names in English, French, and Portuguese is such that I am determined to render the native pronunciation as faithfully as possible. Livingstone himself, whom I admire more than ever since I have read his life, has fallen into more than one error ; but then he acknowledges that he has no ear for music. So I shall write Lealuyi, pronounced Le-a-*lou*-yi.

Since I began this letter, they have brought me three cases and the packages I left under the care of that excellent man the chief Tahalima. What was our horror to discover that everything had been opened ! Some one had helped himself liberally to beads, powder, calico, red and black woollen caps, etc. The thief had amused himself by trying on my woollen shirts and a white flannel suit, covered as he was with grease and ochre, and, finding them no doubt too small for him, had dragged them off as best he could, and put them back into the chest, pell-mell, with lead, bottles of medicine, etc. The shirt business only amused us, and we said laughing, " If the rascal had only been obliging enough to leave us a bit of soap ! " But the loss of our beads and stuff—our pocket-money for the journey —puts us in a great difficulty. You see we made no mistake in bringing the Gospel to the Zambesi !

In one of my former journeys, I took the portraits of several chiefs, and succeeded fairly well in printing them. Some young men to whom I showed them in Leshoma have published it abroad. And now, in all the villages we pass through, you should see every one rush out and ask me to show them " the chiefs that I have in my pocket." And you should see the excitement of the women, and hear the noisy exclamations of the men. " Eh, Rataü ! you can see his charms, and his fillet, and his wrinkles ! What a nose ! Yo ! yo ! Yu, there's Masatoane. Don't you see him, with his closed eye ? Just look at his torn

ear! You see his earrings and his beads? He is going to
speak ; now you'll see him wink his eye, and say in his squeaky
little voice, '*Ka Sebetoane! Koenyama!*' Oh! lumela Masatoane!" Here the interest seems at the highest pitch. What
will it be if I ever make copies and exhibit them with my magic
lantern !

But a crowd is coming into the court. The chiefs are
bringing the young men who are to conduct us to Lealuyi.
So I must put up my traps and get ready in earnest !

CHAPTER XII

LESHOMA, *March 5th*, 1885.

YOU read in our last letters of our departure for Lealuyi.
And now I hasten to announce our return, and to give
you some details of our journey. I confess we rather dreaded
it in the rainy season ; but as the events which delayed us were
quite beyond our control, the path of duty was clear, and
we had the right to count on God's blessing. We were not
disappointed. The journey was as happy and as prosperous
as possible. It lasted two months to the very day, instead of
three or even *four*, as was predicted. Aaron and I kept wonderfully well ; only Middleton was ill. At the very beginning, he
got his feet burnt by the sun in his boat ; and not only was he
helpless for a whole month, but his constitution received such
a shock that his state gave us much anxiety. On the return
journey, thank God ! he quickly recovered.

Under the escort of chiefs, who surrounded us with attentions,
and with an old man like Mokhele, one of those venerable
pagans that one loves to know, a voyage on the Zambesi could
not entirely lose its charm. The river itself is always beautiful
with the monsters that sport in its depths, the clouds of water-
fowl that animate its sandy shores, its verdant isles, its rapids
and cataracts, its banks, here bare and irregular, there bordered
with wooded hills. At every turn there is a new panorama.
There is nothing exactly picturesque ; the vegetation itself is

nothing remarkable, but it is there, reflected in the mirror of the water and fringing the horizon. At certain places, I could have believed myself on Lake Como or Maggiore.

But after all, it must be frankly confessed that the charm of novelty soon passes off. Leaning against one's baggage, huddled up on a damp mat, in the small space left by five or six canoe-men, the traveller wearies of admiring, gets tired of reading, struggles against sleepiness, and ends by giving way to fatigue. It is no longer Basuto-land, where you bestride your horse, and guide it as you will over hill and dale. At a certain age, the apprenticeship to a Zambesian canoe is rough ; but one gets accustomed to it. It is difficult not to be impatient when the oars work listlessly, and the boatmen coolly give themselves up to a deafening chatter, and no progress is made. But when navigation becomes difficult and dangerous, then interest revives, gossip is at an end, and there is not even an answer to an inopportune question. Nothing is heard but the cadence of the paddles frothing the water. They are on the alert, for the Zambesi is easily irritated ; a whistle suffices to rouse its anger, to call up the wind and the catspaws on the water, and to capsize the canoes.

We generally start at break of day, when we have had public prayer, and when every one is at his post. Except for a few short halts on the bank, we only stop to encamp. At two in the afternoon, they are already discussing a site ; then we moor the boats, build shelters, and prepare the evening meal and the food for the next day. I speak of the shelters ! These are simply kennels of reeds and straw, where our young men lie heaped together. If a hurricane comes on in the night, they inevitably collapse. The Zambesians are accustomed to it, and take it stoically. Some hide themselves under the masses of wet grass ; others cover themselves with the mats they have been lying on : one dozes in a crouching position, and marks time—a wooden bowl on his head by way of a cap ; whilst another, wrapped in the rags of a skin garment, snores beside him. If their stomachs are not empty, they have only to exchange glances on waking up, and all roar with laughter.

The Zambesi would be one of the greatest arteries of commerce, if it were navigable. And it would be so, except for the rapids. But those rapids ! We have passed no less than twenty-four between Ka-tima-Mollo and Seoma of Ngonye, a distance of eighty miles (more than a hundred kilometres) according to the pedometer. We admired the prudence and solicitude of the chiefs no less than the dexterity of the canoe-men, both when rowing painfully up the river, and in descending it; the canoe shoots like an arrow through the foaming billows that dispute its passage among the obstructing rocks. The attempt looks like sheer madness. Woe betide the canoe which turns broadside on among these reefs in the midst of the irresistible current! One of these rapids bears the sinister name of Loshu (Death), because of the numerous accidents there. This was where the Jesuits going to the capital in 1881 lost one of their party. The unfortunate man, not understanding the language, and seeing the canoe-men jumping into the water to right the boat, imagined that there was danger, leapt from the canoe, and instantly disappeared in the boiling whirlpool. They did not even succeed in finding his corpse. The *Rapids of Death!* We passed a dreary night there, camped in the rain on an islet, in the midst of a fermenting jungle,[1] and swarms of the most venomous mosquitoes, having to listen, willy-nilly, to the descriptions of the misfortunes that had given these parts their sinister celebrity. It made us shudder. One could almost catch a glimpse of Charon and his bark in the shadows of the darkness. After this, you will not be astonished at our Zambesians' noisy delight, when they found themselves safe and sound on the other side of these dangerous places. They hastened to land on the first sandy shore, seized each other by the two hands, and threw themselves into a passionate dance; then pressing round us and their chiefs, they all clapped hands on their bended knees, saying to each other, "*Shangwe! Shangwe!*" then rising, and drawing up in line, as if in the presence of a divinity, real, but invisible, they shouted with all the strength of their lungs, "*Yo-sho! Yo-sho!*" This is the salutation, the thanksgiving, strictly reserved for the sovereign. To flatter us, they added with beaming looks, "You see, Jesus has taken care of us!"

Above Sesheke and beyond Katonga, I was struck by the

---

[1] Mr. Selous speaks of the *sour smell* rising from the wet and rotting jungles in the Barotsi Valley.

beauty and fertility of this region, which I believe to be the healthiest in the country. To judge by the quantity of ground lying fallow, it was relatively very thinly populated. At present it is nothing but a vast solitude. The chief Mokhele assured me that it was the Barotsi, while travelling, and, above all, their subordinates, who by their exactions and general behaviour had driven away the population into the interior of the country. We were soon able to convince ourselves of this. No sooner was the solitary canoe of a Mosubia fisherman seen, than there was a race, a regular pirates' race. "I'll have his spear! I'll have his fish! I'll have his food!" they cried, each louder than the other, pouncing upon their victim. If we came in sight of a Makalaka village, our young men, deaf to all remonstrances, invaded it like a horde of brigands, seizing everything they saw. They forced the unhappy people to take the roofs off their own dwellings and bring them to their camp. If the Makalaka offered them food, they placed it before these petty tyrants, and kept at a distance, prostrated, and clapping their hands. "Dogs of Makalaka!" the boatmen would cry: "how dare you insult us with this handful of maize, and this wretched fruit! Do you not know that we serve the lords of Sesheke? If it were not for the *Baruti*" (missionaries), "we would strangle you on the spot! But wait a little; we will pay you out." And the unhappy creatures, trembling with fear, would redouble their clappings and their "*Shangwes.*" We had more than once to interfere, to prevent their coming to blows. What must it be when there is no moral sway exercised! At the sight of our canoes all the men in a village generally fled. It was heart-rending!

There is another thought that besets one in crossing these regions, so vast, beautiful, and fertile, so rich, and yet without inhabitants, except for a few Makalaka hamlets here and there. One's thoughts involuntarily turn to a corner of our globe where man, struggling for existence, scarcely even finds a place under the sun. These African solitudes, and our great European cities, those monstrous antheaps of human beings, where, side by side with opulence, there is so much poverty and misery, tell me do they really enter into His designs Who said, "Be fruitful, and multiply, and *replenish the earth*"?

On December 26th, we came to Seoma of Ngonye. We

FALLS OF NGONYE, UPPER ZAMBESI.

[*To face page* 169.

had to wait four days before it was possible to collect the Makalaka (whom famine had dispersed into the woods), to transport our boats above the falls. I profited by the delay to visit them. You will remember that Major Serpa Pinto gave a poetic description of them, which, on the whole, is a fair one. The cataract is formed by a wall of basalt, over which the river rolls, and falls fifty feet, making many beautiful and widely spreading cascades. These foaming waves, these sheets of silver, are brought into relief by the black rocks on which they dash themselves, and by the beautiful belt of vegetation in the background, which breaks between the azure of the river and the sky. The dazzling light of the tropical sun flooding the picture throws the contrast into strong relief.

We must not compare Ngonye with Musi oa Tunya. There are no two Musi oa Tunyas in the world. There everything takes colossal proportions ; the whole makes one dizzy, and inspires one with terror. One would say it was the entrance to the infernal regions. Still, the Ngonye Falls would be admired in any country ; they form an enchanting picture. There is a stunning roar, but none of those thunderbolts or cannonades which make everything tremble under one's feet. Nevertheless, the natives of these parts have as high an ideal of their divinity, as their neighbours have of theirs at Musi oa Tunya, and never dare to approach the abyss without an offering. I was rash enough not to conform to the established custom. And whilst scrambling from rock to rock, looking for a point of view to photograph, I slipped, fell, and rolled to the edge of the torrent, which would have swept me away like a straw if I had not clung to a projecting rock in time. I escaped with a sprained hand, but the accident made a great sensation. On my return, I went to the opposite bank, to get another view of the cataracts. On the way, one of my guides asked me confidentially if, this time at least, I had not armed myself with an offering. I said "No." He was horrified, and I had some difficulty in persuading him to follow me. As soon as we were in sight of the falls, he threw himself down on a rock, and, clapping his hands, began a long incantation in a tone which testified sincerity no less than sorrow. " O Nyambe,[1] thou who inhabitest these abysses,

---

[1] The Supreme Being.

appease thy wrath! These white people are poor, and have nothing to offer thee. If they had stuff and beads, we would know it, and I would not hide it from thee. O Nyambe, be not revengeful, do not swallow them up; appease thy wrath, Nyambe!"

What a comfort it was for this good Mokalaka, when we took our way home, safe and sound! I am sure that he never even noticed that I had taken the precaution to remove my boots, so as to move about on the rocks, polished by the action of the water!

But we must hasten on. The first day of January, we were going up the river, admiring the forests which bordered it, under the impression that they would soon disappear. And sure enough, to use the native expression, these beautiful forests suddenly fled away to the right and left, as far as the hills, barely discernible on the horizon. Before us stretches a plain, as far as eye can see. It is a vast prairie, where the limpid Zambesi winds, sending out an arm here and there, and, at the entrance of the Valley, spreading out like a lake. The view is a strange one, but not as dreary as I should have thought. The rich carpet of verdure somewhat redeems the monotony of the landscape. One could almost believe oneself in Holland, if it were possible to see a steeple and a windmill in the midst of a village of proverbial cleanliness.[1] The annual floods have already begun, and invaded the lower parts of the plain. At this point we leave the river, and nothing is more curious than to see our canoes gliding over the grass, and to hear our people asking the passers-by which is the *road* to the capital.

But softly! It is not thus, clandestinely, that we enter the Barotsi Valley. One evening the chiefs came to see me, surrounding their visit with all the official forms possible. Addressing themselves to Aaron, who was at my side, they counted on him, as a Mosuto, to explain to me the important business which brought them. "There is in the neighbourhood the tomb of *Moana Mbinyi*, one of the most ancient kings of the country. No one passes without making a pilgrimage there, with an offering of white beads, or calico of the same colour. All travellers, even the white ones, submit to this

[1] See Mr. Selous's book "Travel and Adventure in South-East Africa," pp. 254-258, where he makes the same remark.

national and sacred custom; they count upon our doing so too, and declare that, considering my age, they will accept a compromise, and will go themselves to place my offering on the tomb of Moana Mbinyi." My answer may be easily guessed. The chiefs, seeing they had nothing to gain, predicted all sorts of misfortunes, for which, they said, our obstinacy alone would be responsible. Next morning, our whole party was gloomy and silent, and they burst into invectives when we passed at a distance before the old king's tomb. But in the evening, when we camped, thanks to a great abundance of meat, green maize, and curdled milk, that some hospitable chiefs had given us, every one had forgotten the tomb of Moana Mbinyi, and all were gay as usual.

Let me remark in passing, that the Valley is sprinkled with these tombs of Barotsi kings. One can recognise them a long way off by the magnificent clumps of trees which shade them. Some chiefs, with a certain number of people, live there, and keep them up with much care. The reigning king, alone, with his *Gambella*, or prime minister, has the right to enter the sacred enclosure, formed by beautiful strong reed mats. And in every way, the king, dead for generations past, is treated with as much deference as if still living and reigning. They present him with libations of milk and honey, and offerings of beads and white calico. They bid farewell to him before starting on a journey, and on their return they come to salute him, and to tell him the news. So here is a powerful lever for us to use in preaching the resurrection of the dead and eternal life. It is one of the numerous questions which it will be interesting to study from a scientific as well as from a missionary point of view.

On January 5th, we arrived at Nalolo, the second capital of the kingdom, that of *Khosi ea Mosali*, the queen. This is an ancient institution of the people of these parts, to which Sebetoane gave quite a fresh impulse by placing his daughter, Ma-Mochesana, in the position of queen of the Barotsi country.[1] I hope one day to have the opportunity of speaking at greater leisure about the various attributes of this important personage. At present it must suffice for me to introduce you to *Maïbiba*.

[1] See Livingstone's " Travels on the Zambesi."

She is an amiable and gracious woman, who has passed her first youth, and is both intelligent and talkative. Her dignity is no burden to her ; she sits in the *lekhothla* with a great deal of grace, and transacts her business surrounded by her councillors. None of them has the right of sitting in her presence, not even her husband, who bears the title of *Mokwe Tunga* (Son-in-law to the Nation), but yields precedence to the principal councillors. Every one gives her the royal salutation, standing at a distance, and shouting, " *Tautôna* ! "—that is, " Great Lion " ; properly speaking, the *male* lion.

Maïbiba received us with the greatest affability. When she had recovered from a slight embarrassment, very natural under the circumstances, she asked all sorts of questions about the country whence we came, and the object of our mission. She pressed us to stay over the next day, to make her better acquaintance, and to speak to her people of the Gospel of peace which we brought. She listened to me with an intense interest, mingled with surprise, when I spoke to her of God's sovereignty, and of her own duties towards herself and towards her nation.

" Ours is a land of blood," she remarked sadly ; " kings and chiefs succeed each other here like shadows. They are never allowed to grow old. If you come back in a few months, shall we still be in power ? After all, one might envy the Makalaka " (the serfs and slaves) ; " revolutions do not touch them. Ah ! " she added, sighing, and addressing herself to her councillors, " Robosi is no longer king, and he has lost all ; but if he has been received by people like these" (pointing to me), " he may think himself happy ; he has nothing to regret."

How can one refrain from a feeling of pity in the presence of a person like Maïbiba, over whose head—and to her own knowledge—the sword of Damocles ever hangs ! All the nation joins in praising her good qualities—her kindness, her horror of blood, her intelligence in business, her princely hospitality. We are the last to contradict this ; for, in spite of the famine which desolates the Valley, we had abundance in the camp, besides the ox, which is *de rigueur*. The queen had the success of the mission so much at heart, that, unknown to us, she immediately sent a confidential message to her brother the king, proposing to come herself to him. Of all the chiefs, she is the only person who seriously enquired into the robbery of our goods at Sesheke, and who has deplored it. All that is said of this interesting princess, and all that I have observed myself, has filled me with esteem for her. One would like to see her invested with supreme power ; then there might be some hope for this unhappy country.

I had a strong desire to take her portrait. But she did not care particularly to be exhibited like the chiefs of Sesheke, whose portraits, at first sight, startled her considerably. Also, she was the only one who did not seem inclined to sit before my mysterious camera. People came in crowds from all the villages. Ten times a day, I had to recommence the exhibition of the photographs, and hear the same remarks, and the same bursts of laughter. Then I had to show the "sun," *i.e.* the watch, that I had in my pocket ; then the portrait of my wife, which I had in a locket. Fancy a man caring sufficiently about his wife to travel with her portrait ! And then my mirror, which the young women never forget ; for these black ladies, too, have a little spice of vanity; they fancy themselves beautiful, very beautiful even, and do not at all think that the white race has a monopoly of the æsthetic ! One old woman, who could not believe that my whole body was as white as my face, on seeing my bare arm, cried out, in a tone of compassion which quite touched me, " Is it possible? He is like a new-born child ! "[1]

One day's journey after leaving Nalolo, and the next we arrived at Lealuyi. My first impression was such as one would prefer to forget. Certainly war, and civil war above all, drives men mad ; it turns them into wild beasts. Here, as in Paris, it brought forth the Commune, and the Commune has left its traces. Of all Robosi's beautiful native town, nothing is left but two large huts in ruins ; all the rest has been totally destroyed, and a thick jungle has overspread everything. The capital to-day is nothing but miserable shelters, half buried in luxuriant grass. One can scarcely discover the winding paths leading from one quarter of the village to another. After Lewanika's[2] flight, the chiefs looted his treasures, the people and slaves joining in. The sole remains of his riches I was able to discover

---

[1] It is generally known that negro children are not born black.
[2] Robosi's other name.

were an armchair (his throne!) and his footstool covered with
leopard skins. It seems that even the state barge, a masterpiece of industry according to the accounts given, was sunk, so
that nothing should remain of the expelled king. The property
of the Jesuits suffered the same fate. These gentlemen had
asked me to look after it, and to collect what remained, if it
were worth the trouble. I found nothing but some pieces of iron
of no value, and a medicine chest, of which the bottles had been
emptied for snuff-boxes : that was all.

The report of our coming had spread, and we found the
greater number of the most important chiefs waiting for us
at the capital. The day after our arrival there was a grand
official reception. The young king, draped with Portuguese
calico of a large pattern, sat in the public place. Behind him
were his servants, in front the musicians playing on the *serimba*,
and on drums, making a deafening noise, while all the chiefs
with their suites were seated in a circle round him at a distance
of about two hundred yards. The spectacle partook both of
the serious and the comic, and recalled what I had seen at
Sesheke at the time of my first visit. Mathaha, the Gambella,
or chief minister, had put on a black suit and a white shirt!
Others were dressed up in uniform, tunics of every kind : here,
one of a Kimberley policeman ; there, a dragoon, or a naval
officer ; and a little farther on, the coat, long worn out, of a
high official of the Portuguese Government. We had leisure to
make our observations while the royal music was splitting our
heads. At a given moment, all the chiefs were commanded to
approach the king one after the other ; and when once the
council was complete, the *serimbas* and drums became silent,
and the ceremony began.

The chiefs Mokhele and Warubita introduced us, and gave
an account of their mission by describing our voyage minutely.
Then it was our turn to greet the king and his council, and
to explain the purpose of our mission and its character. All
the chiefs answered one after the other by speeches very inferior
to those we should have heard under similar circumstances in
Basuto-land, but in which we detected an undercurrent of great
satisfaction and sincerity. " You are welcome, servants of God,"
said Mathaha, " you who bring us rain and slumber, peace and
abundance. It is in the name of the whole nation that we

AKUFUNA (TATIRA), THE USURPER

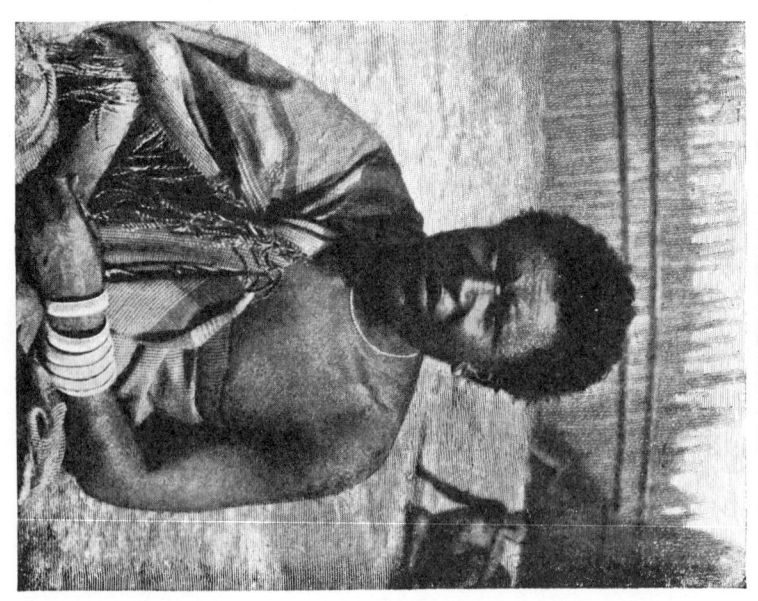

MATHAHA (SEFANO), THE REBEL CHIEF.

[To face page 175.

receive you.   We have waited long years for you, and thought
you had forsaken us ; and it is with joy that we see your faces,
and hear you say that you are now come, not merely to visit
us, but to live among us, with your families.   You will soon
discover that we have *yellow hearts*, and that our country is a
country of blood.   The nation is weary ; it sighs for peace, it
languishes.   Here it is ; we place it before you ; save it.   You
see, the king is only a child : be his father ; uphold him with
your counsels.   We do not ask for presents ; we do not seek
your goods, if you have any.   What we ask for is your teaching ;
what we wish for, is peace ! "   The others spoke in the same
strain.

The day after, another scene was enacted, but one which
nearly ended in a fiasco.   The business in hand was that of
giving our presents to the king.   The Barotsi chiefs insisted on
its being done according to the rules of etiquette.   They formed
a long procession, which the old Mokhele headed with great
dignity, followed by Warubita, carrying the precious parcel.
But, unfortunately, the king was suffering from ophthalmia ; he
had left the *lekhothla*, and retired into a hut—a royal hut, but
only a hut, after all.   And it was there, crouching down, huddled
together, and half suffocated, that we accomplished this important ceremony.   The privileged public filled the court, and
blocked up the doorway.   I was vexed, for I had counted on
this occasion to give Akufuna, the young king, some advice,
publicly.   While I unfolded the great " St. Cyr " military cloak,
which I had bought at the Belle Jardinière, the Gambella,
perspiring profusely, tried to get his feet into a pair of boots
which he had coveted.   The mantle astonished everybody ;
and the Gambella, throwing aside his boots, put it round the
shoulders of Akufuna, who strutted about before us for a
moment.

They listened to me in silence when, addressing myself to
the king, I endeavoured to show him that before God he was
only a servant, who had to render an account of his administration ; that his subjects were God's creatures ; and that he,
Akufuna, king as he was, had no right to put any of them to
death, without preliminary trial.   " It is well said ; that is the
counsel of a father," whispered the chiefs.   But when I spoke
of theft, and the necessity of extirpating it, every one burst out

laughing. "What are you laughing at? Did I say anything funny?" "Eh! Moruti! you talk of punishing and putting down theft, but every one steals here!" And even while laughing, they were in earnest. Here is the proof. A few days later, I had to be absent a whole day; no one would undertake the responsibility of my baggage, although I left two boys to look after it. "Here," they repeated, "people steal by day as by night; nothing is safe." I was obliged to carry the packages to a young man of Scottish origin who was passing through Lealuyi.

That day we left early with the Gambella and Mokubesa, to inspect the site offered to us for the station. Livingstone, it seems, had cast his eyes on it, and later it had been offered to the Jesuits. We found that water was at a great distance from the hill, which complicates matters for building and for the housekeeping, and that the hill itself was covered with planted fields, a source of interminable strife with the natives. The Gambella, offended because I did not share his admiration for the scenery, killed an ox, which he divided, and then leapt into his canoe, in order to reach the capital by daylight, if possible, for it was already late, and left me. We soon lost sight of him in the jungle, where we forced our path with difficulty. The sun set; no twilight here, no moonlight, no landmarks to guide our way. We wandered for a long time in the darkness, without being able to find the channel which we had followed; we came to dry land everywhere. At last, much against our will, we took the direction of a fire; it belonged to a fisherman. The isle was not a hundred yards square, and the smell of putrid fish was unbearable; but we had no choice; so we stuck our oars into the ground, to make a shelter. With one blow they went in a foot, and the water spurted out; clouds of mosquitoes whirled and trumpeted round us, stabbing us pitilessly; hunger gnawed our stomachs; and the handful of reeds the good fisherman gave us scarcely sufficed to roast one or two cobs of maize.

What a night! and with what joy we greeted the first rays of dawn! At last, at eight o'clock, we were at the capital, and put an end to the anxieties of our new friends. We heard that Mokubesa had fortunately arrived in the evening, astonished at not seeing us. As for the Gambella, he had passed the whole night with his crew completely at a loss, wandering in

their canoe, and it was only in the morning that the sound of
drums reaching his ear enabled him to take the right direction
and arrive a short time before us.

The chiefs designated another spot, and two of them took
us to it.   Arrived at the village nearest the place in question,
we killed an ox, and, while it was being prepared, explored the
proposed site.   We had to wade through pools and cross the
Sefula River three times, up to the waist in water, and then a
pouring rain came on, which soaked us through and through
in a moment.   Don't talk of waterproofs ; I have never found
one that was any good.   Our guides were muffled in long shirts
of Portuguese calico, which dragged at their heels, and clung
to their limbs ; one of them had indulged in an umbrella of
the same material, half worn out, and with a frame of impossible
construction, letting the rain through like a sieve.   But what
did it matter ?   It was an umbrella, and our Morotsi was proud
of it, and would not let it go for a moment.

The next day the weather was perfect, and Aaron and I
were able to examine the place more at our leisure, and to
convince ourselves that, for an establishment like ours, it presented incalculable advantages.   There still remains the question
of its salubrity, which only a stay at Sefula can decide.

In any case this will be our headquarters when we first
install ourselves at the Valley.   It has been arranged, that in
the month of May, when the floods are over, and the country
dry enough for travelling, the chiefs will send canoes to transport our baggage.   We shall divide into two parties ; and while
one will go up the river, the other will make the journey by
land.   It is no small enterprise ; but we shall have the whole
winter before us.   One last request the chiefs made while
accompanying us to our canoes was that we should not leave
the Basuto behind ; they wish to have them at the Valley.
The respect and esteem that the Barotsi still have for their
old masters is something extraordinary.   A chief would not
consider himself a chief, if he had not a *Mokololo* for his first
wife ; and when you visit him, he never fails to introduce her
to you.   This explains how the Sesuto language has kept its
pre-eminence in the country.   All the important chiefs wished
to have Basuto evangelists.   One understands their motives,
but the fact is none the less significant, especially after the

rumour which was spread, to the effect that the Barotsi were,
very suspicious of some Basuto coming to settle in their
country with a number of strangers.   Aaron's presence in the
capital created quite a sensation ; the chiefs courted him, their
wives sent him food, and people came from far to see him.
This popularity has its dangers, but such is the fact ! If only
the Churches of Basuto-land understood the mission that God
has prepared for them !

On our return journey we had incessant rain, which delayed
us a good deal.   We were impatient to reach Sesheke, for we
knew we should find tidings of Leshoma there ; and we were
not disappointed.   We had scarcely reached land when a stupid
young fellow came towards us and said, without any other
preface, " Your little daughter Philoloka died a month ago."
Poor Aaron, petrified, fell back on his stool, unable to speak.
As soon as possible, he retired to our hut, and there burst into
tears, which somewhat relieved him, and we were able to pray
together.   A letter from my dear wife confirmed the sad news ;
the Sesheke chiefs who had paid a visit to Leshoma gave us
a very sad picture of it.   Every one there was ill, and we
wondered *who* would still be found alive.

We lost no time, and February 11th found us once more
at Leshoma. . . . Such moments as those do not bear description.   Only our friend Jeanmairet had come to meet us.   At
the sound of our guns the others dragged themselves out of
their beds and their huts to receive us.   Leshoma had become
a hospital ; we were horrified by the cadaverous faces we saw.
During my absence they had been cruelly used by the fever,
which had spared no one, my dear wife less than anybody.   And
it was upon her that all the anxieties fell—the commissariat,
the charge of the workmen, the care of the cattle.   " I thank
God," she said in her letter, " that my head has always been
clear, and that I have been able to come and go, and to give
advice and medicine to whoever needed them."   We have one
or two desperate hypochondriacs amongst us, who were a great
source of trouble ; but my niece, always gay, busying herself
with the housekeeping and the school when she was well
enough, and M. Jeanmairet, struggling energetically against the
depression left by the fever, have done their best to provide
some distraction, and beguile this trying time.

Soon after my arrival our patients recovered, and now, in spite of ups and downs, the sanitary condition of the caravan is satisfactory. Although the fever has continually attacked us, at least it has been in a very mild form.

And now, shall I sum up my impressions in a few words?

1. To tell the truth, the political condition of the country does not inspire me with much confidence. Mathaha, the chief of the revolution, is blinded by ambition. The king is a beard-less boy, born and brought up in exile. He is a perfect stranger among the tribes who have called him to govern them, and does not yet speak the Serotsi language, nor the Sekololo. To him power means pleasure, and he occupies himself very little with business. Discontent is already making itself felt. Some regret the expelled king ; others think of a new chief. I am no pessimist, but I think I foresee another revolution. But there is room for hope that it will not break out before we are in the Valley, and that there will be no bloodshed.

2. The nearer one sees the Zambesians the blacker they are, and it is impossible to make them more so. But we must not be discouraged ; we must look the work which is before us straight in the face, in all its prosaic reality. The work which is done with such admirable devotion amongst the dregs of society in our large cities shall be done here by us. May we do it in the same spirit! But what a task! What clearings to make! How many things to demolish and uproot. But how good it is to know that if we are bringing the Gospel in earthen vessels, that Gospel is still the power of God.

3. Lastly, how vast the field is! While I was pleading in Europe for this mission, the Jesuits came into the country ; and apart from any external influence, they managed to make themselves unpopular, and to close the door. But though the Barotsi have received us so heartily, it is not because they have any true idea of the Gospel that we bring. They sigh after something they have not, and which they do not even know. They are feeling after the One Who alone can give peace and save—" Jesus, the desire of all nations."

March 25th, 1885.

We and our catechists have some plans of evangelisation, which are constantly being upset by slight attacks of fever in one or the other; and now that the chiefs are gone, we must postpone them. I regret it on account of the evangelists.

Our friend Jeanmairet, who has changed the night school into a day school, has tried to get them to take a share in his work. But the natives have not quite the same notions of duty as he, and do not find it at all interesting to make these Zambesians, whose brains are still fallow, repeat A, B, C. You must not be surprised at this, for our natives have not much elasticity. When all goes well, they are cheerful enough; but they are soon discouraged. Evangelisation will be tiring and laborious, because the population is so scattered. If only I had a horse, one of my horses that died on the way! There are some here. But do you know the price? From £76 to £80! These are no horses for a missionary! While admiring them, one has to repeat the Tenth Commandment. It is not easy, when one sees them grazing without doing anything, or mounted by urchins, who tire them out to show that they can make them gallop better than their masters, who are afraid of them, can do.

LESHOMA, April 9th, 1885.

Ten or fifteen days ago, we wrote till we nearly split our heads and put out our eyes, in order to send a good budget to Mangwato. I had hired a Griqua very cheaply, a hunter out of work, who promised to come back in less than two months. We rubbed our hands with joy, for in addition to the consolation of having paid off our debts of correspondence, we had the delightful prospect of receiving, before our departure for the Valley, the post which had been accumulating at Mangwato for months. A few days went by, and one morning, when I woke, a shadow passed before my door. I rubbed my eyes to see better; but I had made no mistake—it was indeed Yantji, my postman, who had returned, bringing back our letters. And we thought he was already in the middle of the Kalahari Desert! What a blow! A merchant, to whom I suppose Yantji was in debt, foreseeing that elephant-hunting, which had been closed by the Barotsi revolution, would soon be reopened, had stopped my man on his way, and sent back our letters. The Fathers of the Jesuit Mission, who shared our disappoint-

ment, sent their condolences, and informed us that they were
sending a waggon to Tati or Mangwato at the end of May or
the beginning of June. Thank you! At this rate, with African
delays, you will get our letters in October or November.

Meanwhile, the waggons we expected arrived, with a great
deal of news, a number of letters, and a bag quite full of
newspapers and publications.

The news is not cheerful. Our young Zambesians, who
returned radiant, informed us that of their fellow-countrymen
who, in spite of all we could do or say, obstinately persisted in
following Makoatsa on his return to Mangwato, five are dead of
hunger and thirst. Two of them had left our service. One of
them was called Molilima. One evening, throwing himself
down under a shelter in the desert, he said to his companion,
"This is the end; I can go no farther; I am dying. It is your
fault, for you tempted me away against my will." The others
rose up in the night and left the unhappy boy there, still
sleeping! Can one imagine his awakening! A few days later
it was his comrade's turn.

There were new disasters, too, among our draught oxen.
Our waggons would still have been at Mangwato, without any
possibility of moving, if our dear friends Musson and Whiteley
had not lent us oxen, to the detriment of their own commerce,
to bring them back to the Zambesi. This deed has touched
us all the more, since the presence of English troops in the
country has considerably raised the price of oxen, and that
Mr. Musson himself has just been robbed by some adventurers
from Stella-land.

The death of some of our bullocks makes fresh complications
for our journey to the Valley, and caused us grave anxiety.
Surely our heavenly Father would not permit such serious
embarrassments if He Himself had not provided. "*Jehovah
Jireh*"—that is our motto.

And the bag of newspapers—with what pleasure we open it,
sort the different publications, and arrange them according to
their dates! If you knew how we sigh after something new,
something *fresh* to read! Our library is so limited that we
wander intellectually, too, in the arid solitudes of the desert.
This is not the least of our privations. We hope those friends
will not be displeased who have too good an opinion of us, and

think we are above such things ; but everything which keeps us abreast of the times in Europe, as regards politics, literature, or religion, has a lively interest for us. From a distance, your world seems to us to be more agitated than ever ; it travails. We are not impassive spectators, believe me.

I have just been reading the Report. What attracts my attention above all is the list of donors, and of their gifts. I analyse it, diary in hand. Do you blame me ? I seek, one after the other, all the localities I have visited—above all, those where they beat the big drum to attract the public. They were so proud to exhibit a Protestant traveller, a lion recently returned from the Zambesi. How beautiful the French language sounded, when, in a generous burst of enthusiasm, an orator laid on the hearts of a sympathetic assembly the evangelisation of Tropical Africa ! . . . Much was promised, and I have the right to ask from the Report, " What has been done here ? What has been done there ? " . . . Here a *little*, there *nothing*. A missionary enterprise is not a balloon, filled with gas, launched into the air before an admiring crowd, and left to take its chance. No ; it is a work which demands energetic co-operation, both personal and constant. I have felt this deeply during my travels, and I know where our strength lies. Though Churches, like those of Marseilles and Nantes, which assist us collectively, are rare, there are *men* friends, and *women* friends, some rich, and many poor, who have laid our work upon their hearts ; orphanages, Sunday schools, dear children who wish to take their share in our work. Every gift, however small it may be, every message which tells us silently that they love the Zambesi Mission and pray for it, is a powerful tie which unites us. With all these beloved fellow-workers, great and small, French and foreign, the burden of the day is less difficult to bear, and success appears to us more certain.

April 17th, 1885.

To-morrow I shall send back the oxen belonging to our friends at Mangwato. (We have already lost two, and I fear greater losses.) So this is an opportunity for sending letters, and I must close this one. I can scarcely hold the pen, for I, too, have just had a rather severe attack of fever. Since the foregoing was written, I have been across the river with our two catechists, intending to make an evangelising tour, lasting a fortnight. But the state of my party at Leshoma made me so anxious, that after having publicly blessed Karumba's marriage, I left the evangelists, and came back. My wife was as ill as ever; you would hardly know her, she has grown so thin and weak. She is no longer at an age when her constitution can stand such frequent shocks.

CHAPTER XIII

Winter at Leshoma—Kamburu and Nguana-Ngombé—Soap-making—
Neighbourly Intercourse with the Jesuits—Fresh Political Troubles and
Delays—A Bargain in Goats—British Protectorate of Khama's Country—
Engagement of Mlle. Coillard to M. Jeanmairet—The Passage of the
Zambesi—Life at Kazungula—Death of Little Monyaï—Arrival at Sesheke
—The Jesuits—Dr. Holub—Revolution and Civil War—Treachery and
Robbery—Perils of Waters and Perils of Wild Beasts—Marriage of Elise
Coillard and M. Jeanmairet—A Wedding Party under Difficulties—
Building the Station—A Reign of Terror—Middleton sent to Pretoria.

LESHOMA, *June 24th,* 1885.

WE only hear distant echoes here, and often confused ones,
of what is happening on the other side of the Limpopo,
and even at our door. We have been staggered by the news
about Angra Pequena and Santa Lucia. Are we then to have
the Germans for neighbours ? And, who knows ? perhaps one
day for masters ? Commerce can only gain by a vigorous
competition. But the African tribes, what will be their destiny ?
There, as in the countries of the Bechuana and the Zulu,
England is reaping the fruit of her policy of expedients. She
has sown the wind ; she now reaps the whirlwind. It is to be
regretted, for, in spite of all her hesitations and all her blunders,
England has always shown herself the protectress of the
aboriginal races.

Disastrous news comes to us from Saul's Poort. On their
return journey to Basuto-land, our conductors, and the evangelist
Andreas and his family, have lost several oxen. A thunderbolt
killed seven. Andreas and Josefa were thrown down and
stunned. When they came to themselves, young Zakea
Mosenéne,[1] at the head of the team, was also on the ground,
and regaining his senses, he cried, " Lord Jesus, receive my

---

[1] The convert of Seleka : see page 123.

spirit"(!). No one was killed, thank God! But these losses, added to others, haunt our pillow with sadness and care.

We are now in the middle of winter. The thermometer, in the morning down at 44° Fahr., rises in the middle of the day to 77° Fahr. The bright light and the great heats of summer have passed away, and, with them, the fever, that importunate guest of whom we have not been able to rid ourselves for the last six months. When the wind comes from the north-east, it comes impregnated with the miasmas around the Victoria Falls. Then appetites flag, and headaches, shiverings, and all those dismal symptoms with which we are now so familiar, attack us, several at a time, or all at once. But the fever is mild, and only lasts a short time, and then courage and energy revive ; the future even brightens before us, as if there were to be no more spring and autumn—that is to say, no more bad seasons. Undoubtedly, at the Zambesi, one becomes a little bit of a Trappist in spite of oneself. Everything repeats every day the solemn warning, " Brother, remember that thou must die." However good it may be for us to think of this, we share the illusion with the rest of the world, and we believe that the moment has not yet come, since we have not yet done our work.

When one asks a Mosuto if it is going to rain, he puts on the air of a sage, looks at the clouds, considers the wind, and replies invariably, with all the gravity of an oracle, " If the rain likes to fall, it will fall ; if it does not like to fall, it will not fall." And there you are, so much the wiser. I asked the traders the other day if they considered this year had been good or bad as regards the fever. " Well," they replied, " after rainy seasons, as after dry seasons, we have had good years, and we have had bad years also." With my eyes shut, I could have thought it was the answer of some wiseacre in Basuto-land. My impression is that we have had a good season. When, on our first journey in 1877, we passed the best part of the year here, we lost two men. To tell the truth, I have the conviction that if this " deadly pestilence " has not approached our tents, it is because they have been surrounded by the prayers of God's children.

Life at Leshoma is necessarily dreary and monotonous. Waiting and the uncertainty about the future would make it unbearable, if each one had not his regular occupation. Our " park " has neither avenues nor paths. Under the stunted trees there is nothing but brushwood, haunted by serpents.   One hears but the raucous cry of the parrots, or the twittering of a flight of birds, attacking occasionally some belated owl surprised by the day.   The population in the neighbourhood is composed, as you know, only of a few families of half-breed hunters, and that of the trader Blockley, together with the Masaroa and Zambesians attached to their service.   Bands of Masubia, Matoka, Mananzoa, Mashapatane, come and go constantly to seek work and sell their produce.   It makes our heart ache to see these poor things performing a journey of six days or more (coming and going), to exchange one or two calabashes of millet or earth-nuts for a piece of calico or a few necklaces of beads.   When our supply is complete, we have to send them away, which they do not understand.   We seize these opportunities to let them hear something of the Gospel.

We have two young men in our service who are rather more advanced.   One of them, Kamburu, is our factotum, and also our washerman.   He rubs our linen remorselessly into holes, or else brings it back much in the same state as he took it away.   He has never been to Paris, and knows nothing of *eau de javelle*.[1]   He is the despair of our housekeeper.   The other is our scullion, wideawake and intelligent : he is Nguana-Ngombé (the calf).   Like Kamburu, he was lent for one month, and now it is ten since they both came to us.   Nguana-Ngombé has developed a taste for cookery, which he carries on in the open air.   He fetches his fuel from the forest, carries his water, and crushes his maize, which he boils every day, all without a frown.   When he is called, he comes hopping on one foot, and one knows he is in a good humour : the contrary is exceptional.   He has a clock in his head which never goes wrong.   At seven o'clock to the minute, every morning, the coffee (mixed with roast maize) and the polenta are on the table, and at five o'clock the dinner.   I must not praise him too much, otherwise he might give me the lie.   That has happened to me more than once.   What gives us most pleasure is that these two boys, under the care, first of my niece, and then of M. Jeanmairet, will soon be able to read fluently, and already they write quite nicely.

---

[1] A solution of chloride of lime.

Our life here is of course rather more primitive than in Basuto-land. Making beer, vinegar, candles, etc., presents few difficulties ; but one of our great troubles is *soap*. The bad soap which a trader sometimes sells you as a favour costs 1*s*. 8*d*. a pound, often more. This is serious for such an expedition as ours. We have had therefore to procure the necessary ingredients by degrees—ashes, lime, tallow ; and then Mme. Coillard serves her apprenticeship. What a business to make this mixture boil six or eight days, but also what a satisfaction to take out of the pot (for we have no cauldron) these bars of precious soap ! Every one is interested and congratulates us on our success.

Our aim is to make use as far as possible of the resources of the country, both for food and the household requirements. We could cultivate our own corn ; we might even grow our coffee, and roughly manufacture our sugar, if we had hands and time. I have the impression that, once installed, we shall not be too heavy a burden for our contributors in Europe. The precarious thing, the black spot, is the transport, the journey. Doubtless we shall not have such losses in cattle every year, but it is distressing that our disasters should pile themselves up like this at the outset. We feel it keenly.

The Jesuits are definitely leaving the country. They have completely renounced their project of a mission to the Barotsi : they have already abandoned Tati, which the miners have once more deserted, and they are going to retire for good from Pata-matenga. These gentlemen have been very kind and obliging to us. Our intercourse with them has been most agreeable—I might almost say friendly. They let me know that they could make over to us cheaply certain things we might need. I took my cart, and started with Middleton : this journey took us a week. Father Booms had had to conduct Father Kroot to Tati, as the latter had fallen seriously ill. I found the brother Saadeleer all alone. He is Flemish, a warm-hearted man, full of energy, and a true Christian. With my cart I was quite independent ; nevertheless, this good man rivalled Mr. Westbeech in his attentions to us. You would have been very much astonished to see me, a descendant of the Huguenots, holding serious converse with this disciple of Loyola, on the experiences of the Christian life, the evangelisation of the world, of Africa in particular, on the approaching Coming of our Saviour, on true conversion, and on the most effective way of treating the natives.

We could not agree on all these points, of course. For the natives, these gentlemen do not recoil from "muscular Christianity," even the bastinado occasionally. We repudiate that system; we believe rather in moral suasion, which we must necessarily exercise if we walk with God. The traders, like the Jesuits, think us too indulgent. It is said everywhere on the other side of the river that we do not beat people, and it is possible that the poor slaves, who believe in nothing but brutality, take advantage of it. They certainly possess the secret of provoking one. Still, it is a serious thing to take the law into our own hands, and be judge, jury, and executioner all in one. Father Booms has come back to Pata-matenga to help with the move. At his invitation I am starting again to pay him a visit and see what business I can do with him. Is it not extraordinary that the Jesuits should retire, leaving us a clear field, when for six years they have been alone in the country, and threatened to shut the door to us?

Since I wrote last to you, fresh troubles have arisen in the Valley. A strong coalition has been formed against the young king Akufuna, whom all despise, and tax with being a stranger, a Mokalaka. The two parties have come to blows; that of the king has triumphed after a bloody battle. As usual under such circumstances, massacres of chiefs have taken place, and sinister rumours spread terror throughout the land. The survivors have taken refuge on a large island with their followers. Thus the river highway is no longer safe. It is even doubtful if the canoes which were promised us, and which ought to arrive this month, can be sent. We are still waiting. It is rumoured that the lords of Sesheke, who have been to pay homage to the new king, are returning—on foot of course. However, we shall soon have news. We dread fresh delays. The season is advancing, the only one in which we can travel and build: to lose it is to expose ourselves to losing a whole year. But we are thoroughly determined to cross the stream at the very earliest opportunity. Messrs. Westbeech and Blockley promise me their help.

If you should meet some friend who wants to do something

LESHOMA—M. JEANMAIRET'S SCHOOL.

[*To face page* 188.

special for us, it will be a good thing to know that what
we most need is some *canoes* to travel in and evangelise. A
good canoe costs (in barter goods) from £7 to £8. We need
four to begin with.

LESHOMA, *July 11th*, 1885.

We are still awaiting the return of the lords of Sesheke.
They left two months ago to render homage to the king Akufuna.
Perhaps—who knows ?—they may be already fighting for him.
As soon as they come back, we shall take over one or two
waggons, and make the journey by land. We shall take very
little luggage, for, in the present state of the country, there
is less security than ever.   And, moreover, to clear a path
through the sands and the bush is no trifle, especially if, instead
of crossing the river at Kazungula, at the confluence of the
Linyanti (Chobe) and Zambesi, we are obliged to ascend and
traverse these two streams one after the other, taking our
waggons to pieces each time.   But that is a small worry.   What
is really almost turning our hair grey is the question of our
oxen. They are nearly all dead. For us, it is a very painful
consideration, because it is a question of finances.

However that may be, in some way or other we are going
to install ourselves in the Valley. Our friend Waddell, who
is now looking and feeling quite strong again, has courageously
set to work, sawing mahogany, and making little windows for
our future establishment at Sefula. Oh the luxury of a window
with glass panes ! Now we shall begin to appreciate it. During
six months of the year, the south-east wind blows towards the
Equator : that is the fever wind. Nothing can screen us from
it, neither the mats nor the blankets which we nail to the
openings of our cottage. With Middleton's help, we have sorted
our packages afresh. We are ready.

I have just come back from another journey to Pata-matenga.
The Jesuits showed us the most cordial hospitality. But that
did not prevent us from catching fever, just as on a former
occasion. Leshoma is decidedly the healthiest spot we could
have chosen. And who knows? these delays which have kept
us all boiling over with impatience may have been purposely
designed to acclimatise us—if indeed it is possible to get
acclimatised at the Zambesi   I was able to procure corn,

sheep, and goats from the Jesuits, and some other things which M. Jeanmairet and I required. What do you think I paid for the goats? *Three shillings!* These gentlemen made a very good bargain of it, and so did we. They are of so degenerate a breed, such rickety, microscopic creatures, that you could put a whole one into the pot to make *soupe maigre*. When, as now in winter, they are in bad condition, you can literally see the light through their ribs, and their small amount of flesh has a disgusting flavour.

The season has been extraordinarily dry : all the pools have evaporated, and to cross the Kalahari Desert is almost an impossibility. Mr. Westbeech tells us that more than two months ago Khama became a British subject, and that the frontiers of the British possessions now reach right up to the Zambesi! Now commerce and prosperity will revive together with hunting, and the country will enjoy the security hitherto disturbed by the Matabele. On the other hand, rumours as to Lobengula's intentions towards the Mashukulumboe and the Barotsi are far from reassuring. But we can rest calmly in the knowledge that " the Lord reigneth."

I have some news to communicate which I am sure will give you pleasure—namely, the engagement of my dear niece to M. Jeanmairet. The date of the marriage will not be settled until we get news from the Valley. This event will enable us found two stations from the very first—one at Sesheke, and the other at Sefula. But I tremble at the prospect of losing our dear Elise. My beloved wife is, among us all, the one most subject to fever ; she is no longer the robust person you used to know. We have not a daughter of the house. What shall we do in case of illness, and when I am obliged to be absent ? And the school—who will take charge of that ?

KAZUNGULA, *August 23rd*, 1885.

Kazungula and the left bank of the Zambesi ! One step farther in our long pilgrimage. We have crossed the river and we are at last in the country which for more than six years has been the object of our thoughts and the goal of our aspirations. I leave you to guess how our hearts overflowed with joy and gratitude. And will this country prove to be the

Land of Promise for us, or the den of lions? Both, no doubt;
but the God of Daniel was the God of the Patriarchs, and He
is also ours. We distress ourselves very little about the future;
the present is enough for us.

If I remember rightly, there was a little cloud hovering
over my last letter. We were expecting canoes which did not
arrive, and were impatiently awaiting the return of the chiefs
of Sesheke. We would fain have kept the favourable weather
which was fleeting with the winter season. The sojourn at
Leshoma, which threatened to lengthen itself indefinitely, was
becoming more intolerable every day. Moreover, our prayer
meetings had acquired a character of extraordinary earnestness
and unity. The moment we heard the chiefs had returned,
we sent Middleton and Aaron at once to demand from the
Morantsiane help for crossing the river, and to study the route
we should have to clear. In spite of our ardent prayers, we
were expecting every kind of objection and hindrance. It is
always the history of the Church at Jerusalem, praying for
Peter's deliverance, and refusing to believe that he was already
there, knocking at the door. "O ye of little faith!" The
Morantsiane replied that the chiefs would hold themselves at our
service as soon as ever we wished it.

At the same time, the chief expressed a wish that one of
us should stay at Sesheke. Our friend Jeanmairet was quite
marked out for this important post. In a solemn meeting, it was
proposed that Aaron should go to the Valley to found a branch
station, while Levi should stay at Mambova, Mokumba's place,
within easy distance of Sesheke. "Have pity on me," Levi
said: "I am not stout-hearted; I am a coward. I am not afraid
of sickness which God sends, but I am afraid of living all alone
among those savages." We did not press him, wishing to give
him time to think over it. But after prayer, and before we
separated, Levi said to us, "I am ashamed of having spoken
as I did. It was want of faith in God. I am ready to go,
no matter where. I shall abide by your decision." It was a
beautiful triumph of faith in such a pessimist as our friend.

As for Aaron, he did not seem to have the slightest mis-
giving. He said to Levi, "My brother, God is almighty to protect
us. If we are just as ill again next season as we were last, I
shall say, 'We shall *always* be ill, it is our lot, and we will

accept it as from God.' And as for the Zambesians, even if they *are* terrible savages, God will touch their hearts, and we shall find among them pitying friends who will stand by us. That was our experience at Seleka. God will not forsake us."

The question of Isaiah was more difficult to solve. We have decided that for the present he should stay at Sesheke and help M. Jeanmairet to install himself. Aaron will stay this year at Mambova with Levi, and will rejoin us in the Valley next year, if God will.

These arrangements made, and the sorting and packing of our baggage finished, we were not yet at the end of our difficulties. Our men fell ill—my niece had erysipelas. . . . They got well ; and it was now the turn of the oxen to drive us desperate. One of our teams has gone with our Basuto conductors and Andreas the evangelist. Out of the four others, only one is left—namely, the one which has just arrived with our waggon, and which I bought at Mangwato; but the oxen at Leshoma are dying of hunger, and those which have just been travelling are nothing but skin and bone, and are so weak that every morning we have to lift several of them to their legs to make them graze. How could the poor creatures pull the waggons, to say nothing of cargo ? Our perplexity is extreme.

One bright spot was the last Sunday we spent at Leshoma. It was what in Basuto-land they call a festival, the baptism of Levi's wife, and of Aaron's little daughter, born on our return from the capital, and shortly after the death of Philoloka. The dear child was baptised by the significant name of *Matseliso* (consolation). A large number of Zambesians, about a hundred, were present. How much did they understand of this ceremony which we tried to explain to them, and what impressions did they gather from it ? I cannot tell. For us, it was very solemn. But still more solemn was the sacred feast, of which we once more, and for the first time in public, partook together.

At last the day of departure arrived. It was Friday, the 14th. We had already sent two small loads of luggage to the ford of Kazungula. Now they pile up all that is left in the family waggon, and in a transport van. Two yokes borrowed from our two teams are going to draw the cart, which is transformed into a perfect Noah's Ark ; puppies, cats, fowls, ducks, pigs, all have a place there—a Babel which would have amused any one who had time to notice it. The sun has disappeared from the horizon ; time presses, for the tse-tse fly still haunts the pathless woods we have to cross. The big waggons once inspanned, we think of the cart. It will be a moment's affair. Our Zambesians, who are afraid of the oxen, have hidden themselves, and it is not without difficulty that we bring them back to their posts. But in vain we search : only three oxen are to be found ; the fourth has taken it into his head to tumble down our saw-pit. We break down the margin ; we raise the beast ; they bite his tail, and pull him by the horns,—all to no purpose. He will not lend himself to any of our efforts. We are forced to give up the game, and to leave the cart for another journey.

It is half-past eight when the conveyances start, and no moonlight. " Ho ! ho ! " What has happened now ? My waggon has bumped against a post which supported my rain-gauge, and this rascally post has smashed a foot-rest we had arranged for my wife. After that, we roll hurriedly to the foot of the slope. We are off. . . . Patience. Cries of alarm are resounding behind us. Oxen and waggons, they shout, have precipitated themselves into the hog-pen ! Poor Isaiah ! he is by no means past-master of the art of conducting. At half-past one in the morning, we were still only half-way. I should have liked to perform the converse of Joshua's miracle, for we were in the thick of the fly district. We had plenty of laughable incidents in that short stage. But they did not prevent us from arriving at the ford of Kazungula, worn out and chilled to the bone, at 4 a.m.

That bit of the road really counts for something. Happily, in a little while the tse-tse will have completely disappeared, and it will be possible to do it by daylight. The road is open, and it is good, thanks to our hatchets and spades. The merchants have done everything they could to induce us to take another. They feel that they run the risk of losing the monopoly of commerce ; and one of them already speaks of coming to establish himself here. Otherwise I must say that they have shown themselves obliging. Mokumba, Rataü, and other inferior chiefs arrived before long with a multitude of people. Our first interview convinced me very shortly that they intended to fleece us without mercy. We agreed to give

all the work to seventy men for an equal number of *setsibas*.[1]
But after two days of some hours' work, they claimed their pay.
There was a general strike, and we had no alternative but
to accept a compromise.   Foreseeing the recurrence of similar
annoyances, we engaged a certain number of more tractable
men, who in their turn raised another levy, and from that time
everything went with order and spirit, so much so that we could
even enjoy the novelty and strangeness of the animated scenes
which shifted every moment.   It was interesting to see the
canoes crossing one another, loaded with our trunks, transporting
our goats, making every ox swim, while his head was held up
out of the water by the horns ; but still more imposing was it to
see floating among the Zambesi canoes the tilts of our waggons
transformed into rafts by means of the understel, and towed
behind our boats.   So far, the passage has taken place without
the slightest accident.   But it lasted no less than eight days,
for the wind interfered ; and when the wind blows and the river
rages, no canoe dare venture into mid-stream.

It was on Friday last, the 21st, that we all crossed, except
the evangelists and their families.   We were taking our evening
meal in a shelter, exposed to all the winds, when the chiefs
raised the mat which serves us for a door, and squatted down
among our bales of luggage.   They brought us news, and not
good news.   First of all, Rataü announced that one of his
villages was burnt, and, strange to say, it was the village and
the very hut where the luggage had been deposited that I
brought for Mr. Arnot.   It is destroyed ; but that is the least
thing that troubles our friend Rataü, who demanded that I
should console him for his own losses by a large present.   The
same thing happened to me, seven years ago, also at Sesheke.
Then the luggage was at any rate my own.   Much more serious
is the news that Robosi's partisans have retreated, that those
of Akufuna have taken up arms, and that there is fighting in
the direction of the Ngonye Falls.   An express messenger has
come to call the chiefs who were here, but with the order to
leave us a certain number of men under the authority of a
brave old fellow named Pelepele.   We shall lose nothing by the
change.   But the horizon is dark.   They say to us, " Now you
are in the country, go and settle wherever you like."   But

---

[1] Two and a half yards of calico.

where? In the first place, we must get to Sesheke, and then we shall see. In this den of lions, we enjoy as much, or as little, security in one place as in another. When I complained to Rataü about the behaviour of his people, "Ah, *Moruti*" (missionary), he replied, "we *marena*" (chiefs) "have power to strangle and kill these slaves, but not enough to make them obey us."

All this does not disturb us out of measure. We all bless God that such news did not come to detain us at Leshoma, for it would have been difficult for most of us to believe in the sincerity of the Barotsi in their relations with us. God can keep us in a den of thieves as well as in a desert. We believe that our lives will be respected ; as to our goods, that is another question.

Tuesday evening, the 25th.

Last Sunday was the first Sunday we passed on Barotsi soil. It was a most glorious day. The wind which had blown all the preceding week had calmed down ; the sky was serene. After the morning preaching, we all started in a boat and went to visit our old friend Mahaha, whom you remember. He is ill, and does not leave his courtyard. What a lovely trip it was! The great island that we skirted seemed to float upon the waters, wearing like a diadem the palm trees with which it was studded. A light mist veiled the whole panorama, giving glimpses of distant prospects. The worthy Mahaha could not contain his joy at receiving us in his own home; at every turn he saluted each one of us afresh. He wanted to know what I thought of Akufuna ; and for his part, he made no secret of his own opinion. "He is the stuff *batlankas*" (slaves) "are made of," he repeated, "but kings—no!" We understood each other without any further explanation. The court is full of village inhabitants, who are enchanted to see us again.

After a short service, suited to our audience, Mahaha cried, "Shall it be said that our Mother came to see us, and found nothing but hunger?" Immediately the women rose, and each brought a little dish of sorgho, and placed it at my wife's feet, clapping her hands. It was charming. Then all these people escorted us to the bank ; and long after we had taken to our oars again, their noisy remarks, their hand-clappings and their "*Shangwes*" still reached our ears. It was not the only

pleasure of this happy day.   The first thing in the morning we
had fetched Ma-Ruthi and the children of the two Basuto
families in a boat.   It was a treat indeed for the children to
be on the Zambesi stream at last, and to cross it in our pretty
boat, the *Lengosa la Khotso*.[1]   We enjoyed their delight, dear
little things!   When we brought them back, and deposited
them on the steep bank, "Oh, wasn't it nice!" said Monyaï; "if
only we could do it again!"   Who could have dreamed that
this dear child was on the point of embarking for heaven and
eternity?   The next day he complained of internal pains.   The
complaint advanced by giant strides, and the following morning
he breathed his last, in spite of our medicines and our nursing.
When we had done crossing the river, we had to retrace our
steps, and there on the right bank of the great stream, in the
shadow of a grove, to dig a grave and tenderly lay his mortal
remains there.   He was nine years old, sparkling with intelligence, and with his father's gentle disposition.   But the frequent
enteric attacks from which he suffered had stamped a look of
precocious maturity upon his little face.   Once more, the
opening of our work must needs be consecrated by suffering.
Dear Monyaï! it was touching to see him lying in his grave,
his only coffin a light cotton blanket.

> He lay like a warrior taking his rest,
> With his martial cloak around him.

KAZUNGULA, *August 29th*, 1885.

Is it not splendid that the passage of the Zambesi has been
effected so easily after all, and without the smallest accident?
It was a great mountain before us.   God has made a plain of it.
Not one boat has been capsized; not a piece of our waggons
is missing; not a single boat has been lost or even injured!
And we had some cases, chiefly of tools, which were very big
and heavy.   We were not obliged to unpack them, and this was
a great point gained.   It was pretty to see our waggon tilts
with their understels floating between two canoes.   Three men
on each side were enough to keep them afloat while the others
rowed.   By midday on Monday we had brought over two,
with all the pieces and the gear.   In the evening our three

[1] *Messenger of Peace*—not the iron boat previously mentioned, page 120.
which had, unfortunately, been destroyed in transport, but an old worn-out one.

waggons were put together, and the cart as well. They were ready to start. To-day they are loaded. But as we have not enough oxen, and those we have are in terribly poor condition, we are sending two small loads with M. Jeanmairet and Middleton to Sesheke, and we shall remain here till the poor beasts return to seek us. The evangelists are already with Mokumba at Mambova, where we brought them. Now, you see, our expedition is coming to an end.

So we shall no longer be all together. It may be that the state of the country, or the no less serious state of our oxen, will force us to prolong our stay at Sesheke, where M. Jeanmairet is going to begin his work of installing us ; but I have great hopes of at least *reaching* Sefula before the rainy season. How we sigh for the moment when we may at last stop our waggons ! We sometimes find our pilgrimage rather long.

If the expedition has succeeded, it is not because Satan has let us alone. Often we thought that he would triumph, and that the whole thing would burst like a bubble. God allowed all that to purify and strengthen our faith. If the expedition has succeeded, the mission also will succeed : we are sure of that. It was an epoch in the history of the evangelisation of Africa, the day when we, with our waggons and families, crossed the Zambesi,—this barrier hitherto insurmountable to strangers ; above all, to strangers who wished to settle north of the river. Will great sacrifices of men and money be demanded of European Christians ? It is possible. But the Gospel will not retreat. They may rob us, they may kill us, yet in a few years the messengers of salvation will become a great army, penetrating even to the heart of the Black Continent.

Say and repeat to our friends, that the strength and development of our mission depend entirely upon their co-operation. Do not let them wait till death weakens our little staff before sending help. I pray God that our mission may not be one of those rickety ones, always hovering between life and death, only uttering sighs and groans of distress. The Christian world has the right to expect more than a fire of straw in the Barotsi Mission. We must not only maintain ourselves, but develop. We *must* go on. This country is only the door of the interior. The field before us has no limits. It is not only to people of education and fortune in my own country that I appeal, but to those of *any* nation and *any* denomination.   Christ *must* be preached ; the Good News *must* be published.   Time presses. Do not let the traders outstrip us !   Let us show that the disciples of Christ also are capable of noble enterprises and great sacrifices.   Speaking of the regrets expressed by Queen Victoria for the death of John Brown, whose devotion she praised, a critic remarked, " Is there, can there be devotion in serving a Queen ? "   Ah, how can *we* then speak of sacrifices and devotion, when it is the King of kings Whom we have the signal honour of serving !   The very angels envy us.

SESHEKE, UPPER ZAMBESI, *December* 12*th*, 1885.

This letter, which will show you that we have advanced a step in our pilgrimage towards the interior, must be confided to the kind keeping of the Jesuit Fathers, who have just definitely quitted these regions.   What a disastrous mission theirs has been !   Quite recently, we have heard of Father Kroot's death, that warm-hearted man, with whom we had such pleasant neighbourly intercourse.   He had gone to Matabele-land to die of an illness which had long been undermining his health. As a matter of fact, the Jesuit Mission only existed in perspective.   In 1879, Father Depelchin visited the Barotsi capital, and had a reception which promised full success.   The following year, Father Burghergge went to begin the new mission, with two " brothers," of whom one was drowned in the Loshu. Unfortunately for them, neither he nor his companion understood the language.   They were reproached for their lack of sociability, which was taken for suspicion and contempt ; and the king—purposely it is affirmed—showed himself exacting and rapacious.   Then came misunderstandings, brought about by the ill-will of certain chiefs, and the duplicity of the missionaries' servants.   In short, after a sojourn of several months at Lealuyi, and without having been able to do anything towards settling down, the Jesuits found themselves obliged to evacuate the country.   They retired to Pata-matenga ; and after five years' isolation, they at last left this forlorn hope.   If they have not succeeded, they have at any rate left behind them the recollection of a generous hospitality, which they exercised on every occasion with the greatest cordiality, together with several tombs, as pledges of their devotion.

Before the Jesuits, the L.M.S. had, as you know, martyrs among the Makololo at Linyanti in 1859,[1] and had been obliged to retire.   And now our intrepid young brother, Mr. Arnot, in his turn, has just definitely quitted the Barotsi country to visit other tribes farther north.   All these checks are not exactly of good augury for ourselves.   We do not pretend to more devotion, nor to more wisdom, than our predecessors, neither have we very great resources in men or money.   This is true. May God grant us so much the more the *audacity of faith*!—for we need it.

The Jesuits, who are leaving Pata-matenga, remind me of Dr. Holub's expedition, which has just arrived.   May the sacrifices of the Church not be eclipsed by those of science!

As for ourselves, we have now been at Sesheke for nearly three months.   If we had had draught oxen, Aaron and his family would not have remained at Mambova, nor we here. We should have been at the Valley long ago, working hard at the foundation of our establishment, and the mission would already have occupied four instead of two important posts. God knows how we sigh for a more settled life and more regular work.   The gipsy life which we have led for two years has a wonderfully withering effect on heart and soul.   It is difficult to accustom oneself to it.

You will recollect that several chiefs came to preside at our passage of the river.   The alarm which suddenly dispersed them was not unfounded after all.   A counter-revolution had broken out in the Valley, and there had been fighting.   Robosi, who had taken refuge and established his headquarters on an island of the Mashi, one of the tributaries of the Linyanti, re-entered the capital, and seized the throne.   Akufuna, surprised, unpopular, and half deserted, fled with Mathaha, his prime minister.   Quite recently, having rallied his partisans, he came and took his rival by surprise.   The battle, which lasted a whole day, with alternating successes, was a most bloody one.   Nearly all the chiefs of both parties perished : Serumbo, Mathaha, etc.   A troop of black traders, come from Bihé or the coast—*Mambari*, as they call them—threw themselves into the fray, and assured to Robosi a decisive victory.   But

---

[1] See Livingstone's "Travels."

the slaughter, even for those accustomed to bloodshed, was
awful. And even after this, we fear we must expect new
massacres. It behoves royalty to be vindictive and bloodthirsty :
public opinion, paralysed by terror, does not protest. How
can one explain the fact that so many tribes, groaning under
the yoke of the Barotsi, do not profit by such circumstances
to regain their independence? Certainly they give themselves
up to pillage and to acts of vengeance and cruelty, but that is
all. Nothing proves more clearly how degrading are the effects
of slavery.

The political disturbances have their counterpart at Sesheke.
From the first rumours of Lewanika's (Robosi's) return, the
chiefs divided into two camps ; and their tempers growing
heated by jealousies and personal grievances, a small civil war
became imminent. Either from fear or distrust of each other,
or from the necessity of ripening their plans of attack and
defence in secret, there was a general scattering of forces.
Some took refuge in their respective villages, or the woods,
whence they could, if necessary, retreat with more security, cross
the river, and leave the country. Others collected in the
islands, which they look on as natural fortresses. All communication was interrupted, and then began a system of spying,
false rumours, brawls, and panics such as are only known in
Africa. Jeanmairet, who had preceded us to Sesheke, witnessed
all this confusion. He needed some courage to remain all alone
with Seajika in a deserted neighbourhood, with baggage that
invited robbery. For the rogues and vagabonds who always
abound here do not lack audacity in such times as these, you
may be sure. But God has watched over our friend, and over
his lonely little hut, with no protection round it. Our arrival
did not alter this state of things in any way. The chiefs showed
us much deference, sent regularly to enquire after us, and came
themselves with presents to welcome us. We also visited them
in their various camps, and they listened respectfully to our
counsels. But all our efforts towards a reconciliation proved
abortive. " Your intentions are good," they said ; " you are
servants of God, men of peace ; you have seen countries where
justice reigns. But you do not know us Barotsi yet. We are
men of blood ; we murder each other drinking, talking, and
laughing together." Which, alas! is only too true.

Nevertheless, it is something, if, as they assure us, our presence here prevents the two parties from coming to blows and killing each other. The station is neutral ground, a city of refuge. Both parties feel that, here, they would not dare to kill anybody. When the chiefs of the two parties meet, it is not to the village (a stone's throw from here) nor yet to their own houses that they go ; they prefer to stop just here, and make shelters if they have to pass the night. To see them sitting together under the shade of a large tree, without arms— except for a stick, which in their hands is a formidable weapon— taking snuff, clapping their hands, scattering the usual "*Shangwes*" and every possible token of politeness, you would think them the most inoffensive people and the most intimate friends. But as soon as darkness succeeds to twilight, they take their arms and flee, each distrusting the other. It is a *sauve qui peut* on all sides. It is sad to see this great village of Seseheke deserted and falling to ruins. In spite of the visits I have just mentioned, we feel the isolation keenly.

One would think the very wild beasts knew we were unprotected. Crocodiles swarm in the river-bend ; they attack everything ; our pigs fell victims to them long ago, and our dogs too—those beautiful Newfoundlands that every one admired so, and that kept such good watch. So valiantly did they hold the wild beasts at bay that their barking gave us no rest by night ; now, the hyænas prey savagely upon our goats. For us, it is an irreparable loss. There are fresh alarms every night : we fire, but kill nothing : and if it goes on, we shall be forced to have recourse to strychnine.

And if it were only crocodiles, hyænas, and leopards that we had to combat ! But the thieves give us no respite. Doubtless, they are not more numerous than usual ; but since there has been no supreme authority recognised, their audacity baffles description. In the daytime, they come to see us, ask for snuff, talk, and are as friendly as possible ; and contrive there, beneath your very eyes, to slip a knife, a hatchet, napkins, or calico under their armpits.[1] In the night, they force the strongest locks, and the best padlocks. They respect nothing.

---

[1] This feat would not be difficult to the large number who draped themselves in a piece of stuff, passed under one arm and knotted on the other shoulder. Socks hung out to dry were irresistible for the purpose of pockets.

Did they not even take one of our tents to make *setsibas*?
And to whom should we complain? Who would do us justice?

The other day our shepherd, a charming boy named Sakulala,
came all out of breath to tell us that a thief, and not the first
one by any means, had come in broad daylight, and within gunshot stolen one of our sheep, and taken to the woods. I sent four
or five young men after him, who worked for us; and nothing
could have pleased them better. In the evening, they returned
in triumph, carrying the remains of the sheep, and leading the
prisoner by a halter round the neck. He was a sturdy young man,
but he had a wound in the head from a club, and his face was
covered with blood. Poor wretch! there he was, kneeling before
us, silently enduring the invectives his excited countrymen were
raining upon his head. But for us, they would have beaten
him to death. "A thief is a dog! Have no mercy on him!"
Such honest fellows as they were themselves! My wife, moved
with pity, took him aside, washed his face, and bound up his
wounds. The Zambesians could not get over their amazement.

The thief, having recovered from his fright, tried to work
upon my dear wife's feelings. "I am an honest man, my Mother.
I have even been in service with your friends the Hepburns"
(of the L.M.S.). "What happened to-day was an accident. It
was God who willed it." I put the rascal in a boat with the
remains of his booty, under the guard of his captors, and sent
him to his chief. The latter, furious, ordered him to be put
to death. I had foreseen this, and sent Seajika to intercede for
him. They were already strangling the unhappy man, when the
chief allowed himself to yield. "Go," he said to him; "it is to
the *Moruti* you owe your life." He went, and threw himself
into the river, and dived several times.[1] He had found grace
in the sight of the gods, as the crocodiles did not devour him.
Then he came and knelt before his master, clapping his hands,
and crying, "*Shangwe! Shangwe!*" The chief responded by
clapping his hands too, and all was over.

The affair only cost me the sheep, the fragments of which
were given to the worthy Lekhoa, who had so bravely captured
the thief. This Lekhoa was a good worker, and a respectful,
obedient young fellow, whom we greatly liked. We had never

---

[1] In accordance with the Barotsi custom, when a guilty man has been
spared the punishment of his crime.

had a better Zambesian in our service ; and when his month was up, and he left us to go home, we very much regretted him. But what was our astonishment to discover after his departure that he had not gone empty-handed either. He had been tempted by a pillow-case, some towels, and I know not what besides. Let us close this chapter, and return to it no more. . . .

On our arrival here, on September 24th, after an adventurous journey, it had been our intention to go on, and try to reach the Valley before the rainy season. No one opposed it, and there was no time to lose, for we had to make a road through thick woods, infested with tse-tse, through deep sand, rivers, and morasses, for a distance of three hundred miles. We shall only take one waggon, for want of oxen ; and for the sixth time since leaving Leribé, we shall leave our baggage behind, and only take what is *indispensable*. With grass and reeds, a shelter is soon made.

A great question upon our minds was the marriage of our dear Elise. We decided to have it on November 4th, and we gave it all the publicity possible. The chiefs of Sesheke, delighted at the news, sent us beforehand some presents of food for the occasion. We even hoped it might be a means of reconciling the two parties. On the eve of the great day came messengers from Robosi, who stopped at the station, and sent for the chiefs on both sides. Everything promised us a beautiful festival. I killed two oxen. We had decorated the woodwork of the mission-house (which was in course of construction) with foliage and French flags. The hour approached, when all at once sinister rumours began to fly. The chiefs were not coming ; they only spoke of fighting. Panic seized everybody, even the king's envoys, and in a few seconds we were left alone.

We looked at each other in silence. What was to be done? Our resolution was soon taken. I was just going to ring the bell, hung for the occasion, when I saw clouds of dust at the entrance to the woods. It was the Morantsiane and his people. All those who had fled returned ; and the ceremony took place before a grand assembly. Raw meat was then distributed to the chiefs, which was quite in accordance with the custom of the country ; and while their slaves huddled, around flaming fires, were cooking or roasting it, chattering nineteen to the dozen, and the chiefs were talking in the *lekhothla*, we had our wedding breakfast in the hut. The customary speeches were not lacking. Aaron and Middleton each had a good word for the occasion. We were quite a family party. There was little excitement amongst us, but we enjoyed an atmosphere of serenity and happiness, such as doubtless the guests at Cana experienced. Games and races filled up the afternoon pleasantly enough, and in the evening we showed the magic lantern. Just as we thought all was over, we found Middleton had prepared a surprise for us, in the shape of fireworks—a Roman candle, one or two Bengal fires, a little Catherine wheel ; and when, for a finale, he let off a splendid rocket, there was a deafening explosion of surprise and excitement. They had heard the old men tell of Livingstone's exhibitions, and these legendary tales had whetted their curiosity, so that the effect produced by the evening's entertainment was quite indescribable. " Look, there is God's gun ! " they cried, following the rocket in the air, with its shower of many-coloured stars. In the midst of the uproar, some of the chiefs came to me and said confidentially, " Moruti, you know everything : which will win, Lewanika or Tatira (Akufuna) ?   Surely you love your son, the Morantsiane, too well to hide it from him. You can count on our discretion." [1]

Robosi, who thought we were still at Leshoma, sent orders that we should be brought to Sesheke at once. We made arrangements with the chiefs to continue our journey ; but, unfortunately, the king's messengers had scarcely left us when the situation became worse—nothing was to be h ·rd but alarms. Those who had ventured to till their fields fled again, and all our people deserted us. From the Valley came confused and contradictory tidings : the spring rains, which we had greeted with such delight, became incessant deluges. In ten days, I collected 9.75 in. of rain, and then my rain-gauge had been twice upset by the oxen. We are assured that the rivers are full, that the valleys are now morasses, and that no chief would dare to leave his post under present circumstances. Less than all that would have told us that, whether we would or no, we were detained at Sesheke till next winter.

[1] The wind-up of the day's pleasure was that the boys and young men crowded up, and demanded payment for their exertions in playing games, and it took half-an-hour's discussion to silence them.

Shall I tell you what feelings of grief and discouragement came over us? But we cannot give way to them for long : the torrents of rain force us into action. Our tents, burnt by the sun, and constantly drenched, no longer shelter us. And when the sun shines, and the thermometer rises to 112° Fahr., they are equally uninhabitable. So we *must* build. They are cutting posts, collecting grass and reeds, and in three weeks we shall have a two-roomed cottage, which will be a little palace for us when it is plastered and dry. This disappointment enables us to give a good deal of help to our friend Jeanmairet. We have only been here three months, and we have already three buildings with kitchens and other adjuncts. All this is only for the time, but the time may be years. Are you not astonished to see how quickly we build? I think we leave the Paris masons far behind. We will not say anything about the architecture.

With the blankets and stuffs bought in Europe, we have been able to buy ten young bullocks, which we have broken in, and some cows. In Basuto-land, nothing is more difficult than to buy a cow or a nanny-goat ; they are the banks of the flocks. Here it is quite the contrary. What is the use of keeping herds for the future, when one may be killed from one day to another? It is much better to enjoy what one has, kill the oxen and sheep, and sell the cows and ewes. A good thing for us! With plenty of milk, appetites and strength have returned. Our friend Waddell has regained colour and flesh ; and except for some slight indispositions, the health of your friends at the Zambesi has never been better. A simple but regular diet is, I believe, one of the best febrifuges, and we owe this to the presence of our ladies.

Our political horizon is also clearing. Robosi's position is stronger. New messengers have come from him to arrange matters here, and to call the chiefs and ourselves to the capital. So it is very probable that I may leave at the beginning of January. And now, if you ask me what are our dominant feelings, I will say that they are cheerfulness and gratitude. Now that we have crossed the Zambesi, we are among the Zambesian tribes ; we are at work, and so are our evangelists at Mambova, near the confluence of the Zambesi and Linyanti. Aaron wrote us the other day that public prayer and the

Sunday preaching have been well attended. They have even tried to organise a day school, and have had encouragement.

SESHEKE, *January 1st*, 1886.

The other day, I wrote from Leshoma, whither I had gone to repair our buildings, and send off our waggon to Pretoria. I had an adventurous journey, and returned after ten days' absence. To my joy, I found all my dear ones in good health. Our political horizon has suddenly darkened again. The repeated messages of the king assured us he had proclaimed a general amnesty, and regretted the massacres which had taken place. Several times he had sent gracious messages to the Morantsiane, who had been compromised by his relationship to Mathaha, the chief of the revolution; he ordered him to return to Sesheke, to till his fields and dwell there in peace. Robosi's sister, *Khosi ea Mosali*, the queen, had declared herself willing to marry the Morantsiane, and to settle at Sesheke, in order to consolidate the alliance of the two parties. Peace was apparently re-established. People went from one camp to another to visit; the chiefs exchanged tobacco, ground corn, and were actively preparing canoes and provisions for the journey, as the moon was "darkening." All the chiefs were going off together to pay homage to the king.[1] There was life and stir everywhere. The chief Rataü and the others had left their island, and returned with their wives, children, and cattle. The alarms had come to an end, and we began to breathe freely. During my absence, a chief came from Robosi, with a numerous retinue, and established himself at the station, declaring that, as he was commissioned to escort me to the capital, he would wait patiently for my return. Would you believe that all this was only to hide a plot?

Just before the new moon, in the nights of December 26th and 27th, the chiefs of Robosi's party, who had assembled their people in the woods, fell upon the Morantsiane's village, and there gave themselves up to rob and murder to their hearts' content. The Morantsiane fought his way through the chiefs that surrounded him, and escaping the sight of the Barotsi chiefs, succeeded in reaching the forest. But they have seized all

[1] As soon as the new moon should appear.

the canoes on the river, and are vigilantly guarding all the
fords ; and on the tracks of the unfortunate chief they have set
troops of young men, who will hunt him down like a wild beast.
Will there be found no compassionate soul to save the life of
this unhappy fugitive, who has now neither hearth nor home ?
It seems that Mathaha committed atrocities which the pen
refuses to describe, not only on Robosi's partisans, but also on
his wives and children. Robosi has sworn to avenge himself,
and to spare neither position, age, nor sex in any member of
Mathaha's family.[1]

Terror is at its height among the aristocracy of the country.
The slaves rejoice ; for them it is only a change of masters,
and they press after the " conquerors," as they call them, and
want to take their own share in murder and robbery. The
young men in our service—except Nguana-Ngombé and
Kamburu, have not been able to resist the general impulse,
and have left. The country is in a fearful confusion. We do
not know when these massacres will stop, nor what will come
out of this chaos. Living among such people, whose feet are
so swift to shed blood, one feels one's dependence upon God.
In these times, we pass through hard and humiliating experiences.
The chiefs are generally very pleasant to us, and many boast
of our friendship. But we are entirely at the mercy of their
slaves, who deceive, insult, and rob us, without any authority
bestirring itself to do justice and protect us. This is, perhaps,
the darkest point in our life on the Zambesi. But there it
stands, " He that dwelleth in the secret place of the Most High
shall abide under the shadow of the Almighty."

The individual who came from the king to fetch us is the
same who was charged to deliver him from those he calls his
enemies. The rains have begun early this year, the river is
rising, the low parts of the country are already submerged, and
travelling by canoe is becoming more and more dangerous and
difficult. On the other hand, Middleton is on the way to
Pretoria [2] (this letter will catch him at Leshoma), and it is
doubtful if Aaron can accompany me this time. The same
prudential reasons as last year will again keep Jeanmairet here.

[1] See later on, page 214.
[2] For supplies, business at Pata-matenga and Shoshong being at a standstill.

So I must go alone with this Barotsi chief when he has accomplished his bloody mission. God will protect me. May He soften Robosi's heart! All they say of him conveys the impression that he is an intelligent man, generous on occasions, but also a vindictive, suspicious tyrant, and alas! thirsting for blood. It is absolutely necessary for me to see him before we all definitely leave this place for the Valley. In spite of all the messages, full of amiability, which he has sent us since he has returned to power, we clearly foresee that our position near him will not be exactly a bed of roses. But do not be anxious on our account.

CHAPTER XIV

Second Journey to the Capital—A Zambesian Charybdis—The Hunter's Paradise—Boat lost in the Rapids—Vandalism—Nalolo and Queen Mokwaë—An Unexpected Meeting—King Lewanika—Lealuyi—Visit of the Chief Moremi—The Barotsi *Lekhothla*—Conversation with the King—Barotsi Legends—The Natamoyo—Sunday Service—Back to Sesheke—Visit to Mambova—Murder and Cattle-lifting—An Appeal— Middleton returns from Pretoria—Dr. Holub.

SESHEKE, UPPER ZAMBESI, *April 19th*, 1886.

I HAVE just returned from a second journey to the capital. Since the counter-revolution which brought him back to power, Robosi (or Lewanika) has sent us message after message, earnestly entreating us to visit him. We ourselves desired no less earnestly to do so, not only in the interests of our mission, but also because of the pillage and murder which are desolating the country. Having no canoes ourselves, we were at the mercy of the chiefs of Sesheke ; and they, demoralised by the execution of the king's vengeance, kept vacillating and putting us off from day to day. Weeks passed thus. I had patience till February 26th, which, to tell the truth, I was not sorry to pass in the family circle, as it was the twenty-fifth anniversary of our marriage. But when once this day was over, I decided to start on foot, with two or three donkeys, and quietly made my preparations. The chiefs got wind of this, and were roused. I soon obtained my crew and two canoes, one for me, and the other for the petty chief who was to accompany me, and the baggage belonging to his people. It does not take much to crowd one of these troughs that they call boats. Each man has his mat, his gourd, his bowl ; and when everything is piled into the dug-out, it seems as though it *must* capsize.

Our dear Jeanmairet's place was clearly marked out ; he had to remain at Sesheke. I did not care to hamper myself with

Levi, who is not a good traveller ; and Aaron, in spite of his great desire to accompany me, could not. The chiefs did not fail to make a great fuss, and protest their uneasiness at seeing me start alone ; but I easily soothed their anxieties ! On reviewing my crew, I was glad to see they had apparently made a good choice. My ten Masubia [1] were mostly full-grown men ; and my mentor, still a young fellow, was a neighbouring petty chief, with whom we had had very pleasant intercourse.

A separation in this country always has something particularly sad and solemn in it. But this time it was very far from being what it had been the year before. Circumstances have changed. We are in the country, and are all well. So we can say good-bye with all the serenity that comes from obedience to duty and utter confidence in God.

We left on March 6th. I was not mistaken in my Masubia. They showed unflagging good-will, and made it a point of honour to give me pleasure. Mokumoa-Kumoa, the chief, set the example. As soon as we disembarked, he was always the first to set up my little tent, construct the shelters, and search for wood. I hunted waterfowl ; he supplied big game— a zebra, or an antelope ; so we never lacked meat. In the evening, at the camp, I taught them a hymn, and we talked of the things of God. Our conversations were often very long and deeply interesting.

At this season, when the waters are rising, the navigation of the river is difficult, and particularly dangerous at the rapids. So, faithful to the promise I had given at parting to my dear wife and the chiefs of Sesheke, who seemed anxious for the safety of my person, I conscientiously went on dry land at every dangerous place. At the beginning, we had to lose some time in hunting ; but when once our purpose in so doing was fulfilled, I wished to push on, and my people were quite willing. One day, we arrived at Matomé's little village, in the neighbourhood of the rapids. In the twinkling of an eye, all my people vanished ; and when at last Mokumoa-Kumoa and the boatmen did reappear, it was to tell me, with long faces, that we must spend the night there. It was only two o'clock. In vain I protested : not one oarsman would take his place in the boat,

---

[1] Nearly all the canoe-paddlers are drawn from the Masubia tribe, as they are considered the most expert.

and I had at last to give in. I could not understand this
singular strike; but when we were once encamped, Mokumoa-
Kumoa came and sat beside me. "My Father," he said, "this
is Matomé's village; and with the best will in the world we
cannot pass beyond. Perhaps you don't know that a serpent
dwells in these parts, an enormous monster with several heads.
If any one is unlucky enough to pass close by its lair, it suddenly
makes the water boil in the most terrific fashion; and then
swallows everything up—canoes, oars, baggage, and rowers.
Nothing escapes. As we don't know the monster's whereabouts,
Rataü and the lords of Sesheke ordered us to take Matomé
to guide us. Unfortunately, Matomé is away. What shall
we do?"

Next day, in default of Matomé, two of his sons acted as
our guides. They sat in a tiny canoe, which the current carried
away like a cockle-shell, when we passed from one bank to
another. Near the junction of the River Lumbé, they slackened
their speed, then stopped, and showed us on the opposite shore
a great sand-bank, saying in low tones, "That is where he lies."
I wanted to ask a question. "Hush!" they said; "you must not
speak of him while on the water." I asked later on if *they* had
ever seen the monster. "Seen him? No! He is only known
to the king, and to the great ones of the realm. They possess
a medicine, but they keep it secret. If the hydra attacks one
of their canoes, the master at once offers it his belt.[1] Then you
see the canoes shoot to the bank like an arrow."

Mr. Westbeech, who had preceded me up the Valley, told
me that his canoe one day ran into a bank of quicksand.
Every stroke of the oar made the water boil in an extraordinary
manner, but did not advance the pirogue. All his people were
paralysed with terror. Mr. Westbeech seized the paddle, and
succeeded, though not without difficulty, in floating the canoe
off; and his rowers began to breathe again. And then, to hear
them relate the adventure!

One can never tire of admiring the region of the rapids
which I described last year. One would think that the river,
wearied with its leaps and struggles among the rocks, was
gathering itself together for fresh combats while flowing limpidly

---

[1] The chiefs wear as charms belts made of an entire snake skin.

between its verdant banks. The arborescent vegetation, though
not at all tropical in character, is nevertheless relieved here and
there by wild date palms, of which the natives are very fond.
This is the hunter's paradise, haunted by elephants, buffaloes,
and other big game. Often, at the sound of a low whistle,
we run our boats into the reeds, and stepping on land very
cautiously, we catch sight of troops of buffaloes or antelopes,
which gallop away at the slightest sound. I have also met with
more villages than last year ; which, however, is not to say
that the country is populated.

The news of my arrival had spread abroad, and the poor
Makalaka, instead of fleeing to hide, were happy to come and
speak to us. One day, we met three little canoes ; it was the
head of the village going to do homage to his new chiefs, and
the worthy man immediately turned back to prepare provisions
for our journey. We had to sleep at his village, which upset
all my plans. But I had no reason to regret it, for, besides the
reception he gave us, it was an opportunity for speaking of the
Gospel. The next day, another Makalaka chief was waiting for
me, at the entrance to his village, with a dish of pumpkin, and
pressed me to pass the day with him. I had to refuse. " In
that case, why did you not come to spend the night with
Matokomela ? " (his name). " Do you think that I don't know
how to receive strangers as well as he does ? "

We must beware of generalising from such facts, and giving
them an importance they do not possess. These poor people
have no idea of the Gospel, but they feel that those who preach
it are men of peace, and protectors of the unfortunate.

At Seoma, we met two large canoes and some men, whom
the king, in his impatience, had sent to fetch us. In the
night, one of my boats, which had remained below the falls, was
carried away by the current. At family worship, I asked God
to give it back to us. " It is no use for you to trouble God
about it," said my Masubia ; " the Zambesi does not play hereabouts. The boats it carries away one never finds again." I
took one of the king's canoes, and we pursued our way.

In two days, we came to Senanga, the entrance of the Valley.
The inundation, though very late this year, was nevertheless so
high that we left the river, and took a short cut to Nalolo,
across the plain. We soon found ourselves entangled in

QUEEN MOKWAÉ—SLAVES BRINGING HER FOOD.

[To face page 213.

masses of reeds and inextricable jungles, where we were buried
upright, and from which we only escaped with many scratches.
Where the grass and reeds were shorter, every stroke of the
paddle stirred up clouds of mosquitoes, flies, and insects of every
kind, which filled our eyes, ears, and nostrils. A veritable
plague of Egypt! There were also fish leaping, water-tortoises
exploring their new domains, and from time to time a snake
swimming, which invariably tried to get into our boats. All
this caused some excitement among us, and broke the monotony
of the voyage. The sun was scorching. To keep on sitting,
that is to say crouching, in the canoe was to condemn oneself
to suffocation ; so I stood up, at the risk of a ducking. Not a
village, not a hamlet, to be seen ; before, behind, right, and left,
nothing but the plain, with its reeds and rushes, and the water,
which in some places rose above them, and reflected the sun as
in a mirror. Nothing could be more melancholy than this
journey. But from time to time we suddenly entered a pool as
if by surprise—a perfect garden made by God to bloom in these
solitudes, doubtless for the admiration of His angels. The
surface of such a sheet of water was invariably covered with
water-lilies, blue, pink, and white as snow. There were yellow
and even green ones. Some were large and double like roses,
others coquettishly displayed their petals like five little miniature
feathers of fairy-like delicacy on the green background of their
leaves. All scented the air with their perfume. My Masubia
had no appreciation for this picture which charmed me so. They
fell upon the aquatic plants, and tore off the stalks to mix
them with their tobacco, and the roots to regale themselves
with. Alas! vandalism rages everywhere.

On March 20th we reached Nalolo. You remember this
is the second capital of the kingdom. From ancient times,
it has been the custom of Barotsi kings to collaborate with one
of their sisters in the government of the realm : sometimes
it is their mother. This queen has her court, her drums, her
serimbas, and surrounds herself with all the ceremonial in usage
at the king's own court. She sits in the *lekhothla*, discusses
state affairs, judges lawsuits. She is saluted like the king with
" *Tautôna* "[1] and " *Yo-sho*," the salutations reserved for royalty

---

[1] Lion (*not* lioness).

alone. People prostrate themselves before her, and nobody has the right to sit in her presence, not even her husband, the *Mokwe Tunga* (Son-in-law of the Nation), who is only a servant, and can be dismissed at her pleasure. Perhaps it would be going too far to say she was polyandrous!

When her majesty is not sitting in the *lekhothla*, she retires into a hut surrounded by two courts. There she grants private audiences. Whichever way one looks, the eye falls on some kind of charm. In the court, there are generally young slaves attached to the queen's service, and occupied under her direction in weaving fancy mats or working in beads. It was here that Mokwaë[1] received me. She was not a stranger to me. I had seen her the year before, a prisoner at Mathaha's, where she would have been reduced to the condition of a slave, if it had not been for that good Maïbiba, who at that time was queen, in spite of herself. I had managed then to have a little conversation with her, and it seems this had consoled her and raised her courage. This time, I found her sitting on a mat, under a thatched roof. As soon as she saw me, she began to laugh; she held out her hand, and made me sit opposite to her. Still laughing, she looked fixedly at me for a few moments, and at last, betraying the course of her thoughts, she cried out in a tone that startled me, "Mathaha! Mathaha! We have slain him and all his!"

She introduced her children, who, by the way, never call her mother, but *Morena*,[2] always sit behind her, and never on her mat; and then, while a charming little girl stood between my knees, playing with my watch-chain, we soon found ourselves engaged in a most captivating conversation. She related to me all the vicissitudes of the revolution—her flight from Mathaha's village, the devotion of her partisans, who, while the fortunes of war were against them, brought her by forced marches to Seoma, and thence for greater safety to the River Mashi, a tributary of the Linyanti, where, later on, her brother joined her. She continued her tale of thrilling interest, to the great victory at Lealuyi, which confirmed Lewanika's power, and concluded by exclaiming with loud peals of laughter, "We have

---

[1] Pronounced Mō-kwy-ee, sometimes written Moquai.

[2] *Morena* means "chief"; it is exactly equivalent to "lord." The queen's dignity is indicated by her always being addressed with *masculine* titles.

utterly destroyed Mathaha and his gang, and their bones are
bleaching in the sun. And the insolence of these sorcerers to
beg for mercy! Mercy indeed! We threw them out on the
veldt to the vultures. That was our mercy!" These shouts
of laughter, these exulting tones, and the insatiable vengeance
they proclaimed, made me shudder. My eyes were riveted
on this woman: I listened as in a dream. I knew her of old.
Rather more than two years ago, her prime minister, named
Pakalita, offended her. One day, when she was giving the
people a feast of *yoala*,[1] she had Pakalita called to her private
house, talked to him for some time, gave him a pot, and left
him alone with a band of men who were to murder him.
But the slaves were intimidated by the presence of this
venerable old man, so universally respected. For a long time
Mokwaë awaited the execution of her orders in the court, and
at last re-entered impatiently. "What!" she cried; "you are
given orders, and this is the way you carry them out! Seize
him!" Then, arming herself with an old Portuguese sabre,
she herself, with one stroke, cut the old man's head off. She
made them throw the corpse into a neighbouring court, and
then seated herself in the *lekhothla* as usual. Towards evening,
the public crier announced: "The queen informs you that
she has pulled a troublesome thorn out of her foot." It was
understood, and it made a great impression. This was one
of the causes of the revolution. Yet Mokwaë has her partisans
and admirers.

She received us cordially, and in the evening she sent us
the ox of welcome—a fine, fat one. The next day, a large
assembly met at the *lekhothla* to hear the preaching of the
Gospel. They were astonished, serious, and attentive. I felt
myself to be upheld and blessed, and both preached and sang
without fatigue. Afterwards, Mokwaë invited me to her house.
In the court, what was my surprise to see her take off her
calico robe before three or four traders from Bihé! These
gentlemen were evidently tailors. One examined the sleeves;
another pinched her about the shoulders; a third fitted the
bodice. "I only hope," I said to myself, "that they won't
ask *my* advice." During this scene, I did not know which

---

[1] Native beer.

way to look, and felt relieved when I found myself alone
with Mokwaë. She invited me into her house, a spacious one,
and admirably clean. While some young girls waited on her,
I sat opposite on a roll of mats. She handed me a cracked
old accordion. "Now," she said, "play me something." I
willingly played a tune, then another, then a third. Memories
of childhood, sacred ones to me, thronged into my mind, and
melancholy stole over me. At last, I returned the instrument
to Mokwaë. She seized it triumphantly, ran her fingers over
the keys with surprising agility, drawing from them a cacophony
which evidently enchanted her. Then, growing excited, she
began to sing. I passed half an hour listening in utter amazement to this strange serenade. Surprised at my calmness,
she ended by putting down the accordion, and saying with
much satisfaction, ".You see I know how to play too." I
should think so, indeed! She had quite eclipsed me.

She then asked permission to visit the islet where I had
camped. I took the precaution of sending some one to hide
the objects which might excite her greed. I gave her my
very best reception, and a cup of black coffee without sugar,
which she forced herself to swallow out of politeness; and I
made her a present of a pretty striped blanket, which she received
with her usual brusquerie. But you should have seen her face
and her excitement when I showed her my photographs. At
the sight of Mathaha's, she started back in terror. "Sefano!
Sefano!"[1] she cried; "the infamous wretch! These people"
(meaning me) "are dreadful: they carry the living and the dead
in their pockets." Then taking fresh courage and smiling
cynically, she repeated, "But we have destroyed this Sefano."

What a contrast between her and her cousin Maïbiba, whom
I introduced to you last year. Poor Maïbiba! After the fall
of Tatira (Akufuna), she took to flight; but Lewanika, who
respects her very highly, was easily moved to clemency, and
sent to bring her back to the country.

On Monday, March 22nd, at daybreak, our canoes were
laded, and we started for Lealuyi. It was a beautiful morning,
with a fresh breeze and a radiant sun which revived every one's
spirits after the rains of the day before and the damp tent.

---

[1] Mathaha's other name. Most of the Barotsi have several names.

Towards two o'clock in the afternoon, as we approached a village, we noticed groups of men and canoes, and great animation. It was the king, Lewanika,[1] who had been making a great pilgrimage to the tombs of his ancestors during the last few days with a considerable retinue. We had been hearing the drums all the morning. As we approached, a canoe shot across the water, and was soon alongside of us. "Stop! do not go on! The king wishes to know who you are." I was astounded to see that the man who addressed me was none other than *Mokano*. Now this Mokano, during one of my absences from Leshoma, had so grossly misconducted himself towards our ladies that I had had to bring him before the *lekhothla* of the chiefs at Sesheke, and reprimand him sharply. "Do you recognise me?" he asked, as he saluted me. "Oh yes, Mokano; go and tell the king that I am here." He returned a moment later. "The king orders you to come to the village, and pray to one of the gods of the nation. Take an offering of white calico with you; a very little will be enough."

"Go and tell the king that we do not pray to the dead. I have come to teach him to pray to the only true God, the *living* God."

Mokano seemed to fly; he soon returned. "The king understands your reasons, and excuses you from praying at the tomb. He only asks a yard of white calico, and he will pray for you."

"Tell him," I replied, "that I wish to see him, and speak to him myself."

My canoe-men could hardly contain their indignation any longer; they could not understand my obstinacy. Mokano went off with a triumphant grin. I had not long to wait for Lewanika's answer. "The king cannot see you; you must first give the little piece of calico he asks for; he must have it." So there I was, involved in a broil which Mokano did not fail to foment, without the possibility of a personal interview with Lewanika to explain my reasons. I gave the yard of calico, and soon the noisy "*Yo-shos*" which echoed through the air told me what had been done with it. The Barotsi gods

---

[1] Hitherto called Robosi, or Loboshi, "the escaped one," because he was born while his mother was fleeing from the Makololo. On his accession to the throne after exile, he retained only the name of Lewanika. The Barotsi make scarcely any distinction of sound between *l* and *r*.

are satisfied with very little, a rag of calico, a necklace of beads, only they must be white—no other colour is tolerated in their Elysium.[1]

Soon a boat, covered with a tent of mats, glided alongside of mine, and a man of about thirty-five glided out of it. He was strong, well-built, and intelligent-looking, with prominent eyes and pendulous lower lip. His whole clothing consisted of the skins of small wild animals, attached in bundles round his loins. He held out his hand, smiling: "*Lumela, Moruti oa ka Ntate*" ("I greet thee, my missionary, my father"). This royal apparition took all my people by surprise. "Prostrate yourselves," cried those in the canoes that now surrounded us, "*mo shoaelele.*" But no! they were abashed, each kneeling at his post, nervously clapping his hands. Only Mokumoa-Kumoa in the bows of his canoe did it according to rule. Standing up, he raised his hands and cried out for every one, "*Tautôna! Yo-sho!*" then knelt down, and taking water in his hands, tossed it over his arms and chest, rubbed his forehead at the bottom of his boat, clapped his hands, and poured forth a stream of laudatory epithets to Lewanika. This is what they call the *shoalela.*

The king did not seem to pay any attention to all these demonstrations. He expressed the pleasure he had in meeting me; enquired after our health and my voyage; offered to share a roast goose with me; and then, as he had to continue his pilgrimage, he arranged to meet me at the capital. We then formed a procession of boats. The king had fifteen, his wife's was manned by nine rowers. All these men were decked out with the skins of wild beasts and bright-coloured stuffs, floating from their shoulders. At the end was the canoe carrying the enormous drums and kettledrums, which the men beat furiously. They are only sounded in war time, or on occasions like the present. The noise is deafening, and can be heard to a great distance. We followed the royal procession for some time, and then, as it turned off to other tombs, we went on to Lealuyi, where we arrived towards five o'clock. The arrival of the king

---

[1] See Miss Kingsley's "Travels in West Africa": "White cloth is anathema to the missions, for it is used for Ju-ju offerings, and a rule has to be made against its being given to the unconverted, or the missionary becomes an accessory before the fact to pagan practices."

later on in the evening put the whole town in a flutter, but I
was too tired to come out of my hut.

The official reception took place in the morning of the next
day at the *lekhothla*. Mr. Westbeech was there. The king
made us place our chairs one on each side of his, while the
Gambella and his principal ministers knelt before him. This
ceremony was a very simple one. Lewanika listened patiently
to all I had to say on the aim of the mission, our delays, losses,
etc. In his turn, he expressed the joy he felt in seeing me
at last in his country after having so long expected me, his
displeasure at the delays to which we had uselessly been
subjected, and his indignation on the subject of the thefts.
He also spoke of his gratitude for the kindness we had shown
towards certain members of his family and some of his adherents
in his misfortunes. He introduced to me with visible satisfaction those of the chiefs, and even of the servants, who had
accompanied him in his exile, and then, with an excitement
almost amounting to passion, related his flight and exile,
Libebe's[1] hospitality, his first meeting with those of his partisans
who had sought him out, his battles and his victories, his
unconquerable suspicions even of those on his own side, and
the hunger for vengeance which gnaws his heart. He also
described the visit of Moremi, chief of the Batawana of Lake
Ngami.[2] Moremi is Lewanika's friend. For many years they
had exchanged ambassadors and presents till the revolution broke
out. Then later, when Moremi learnt that Lewanika wished to
re-enter his kingdom, he hastened to come in person and bring
him help. He arrived too late, however ; Lewanika had already
conquered his enemies. The visit of the son of Letsulathébe[3]
was therefore of a purely pacific character ; but that is not to
say he did not considerably alarm the Barotsi, coming as he did
at the head of a hundred well-armed cavaliers. One day he
played a little comedy which nearly ended in tragedy. A great
pitso was taking place. Moremi and his poeple were on one

---

[1] The hereditary name of a tribal chief on the Linyanti or Chobe River.

[2] For an interesting account of this chief, see Hepburn's " Twenty Years in
Khama's Country." See also former letter, page 53. The Batawana are a
Bechuana tribe.

[3] *I.e.* Moremi. African chiefs are often designated by the names of their
fathers.

side, Lewanika and his Barotsi on the other.   Moremi, using the
great freedom of speech possessed by the Bechuana in their
pitsos, began to taunt the Barotsi openly on their revolutionary
tendencies ; then, advancing towards Lewanika, he said to him,
" You are my brother and my friend ; those people will kill
you some day. Rise up, take your gun, and come with me."
Lewanika rose and took his gun. The Barotsi were touched, and
protested their attachment to their king. Moremi, improving
upon his original speech, made a fresh attempt to take Lewanika
away, and there was a new demonstration. The third time, the
Barotsi, wounded to the quick, seized their arms, and surrounded
the Batawana, heaping abuse upon them ; and blood would
certainly have been shed but for Lewanika's intervention.

Before passing on, let us say a word about the *lekhothla*,
which differs essentially from that of the Basuto and
Bechuana, as much in the ceremonial as in the way of treating
affairs. Liberty of discussion does not exist here, and in the
lekhothla, as everywhere else, the potentate of the Valley can also
say, " *L'état, c'est moi*." At seven in the morning and three
in the afternoon, the king, followed by the drums, the *serimbas*,
and sometimes by his ministers, goes in procession to the place
where he sits in the shade. He is generally clothed in a long
red cotton shirt, with large designs, coming down to his heels,
and the cap of striped cotton, so dear to the Barotsi. It seems
that etiquette demands he should frequently change his attire,
but his wardrobe is of the smallest ; and as he has no ivory, he
is in poverty. The few European garments he has been able
to procure, he has given to his ministers, and to the *Mokwe
Tungas* (the husbands of his sisters) ; and he owes to Moremi's
generosity the white serge suit, the white shirt, the shoes, and
the hat which he put on in my honour. As soon as the drums
make themselves heard, all the men run to the *lekhothla*, and
sit down before the king at an interval which varies according
to their rank. Those who come from a distance perform all
the servile ceremonies of the *shoalela*, like our Mokumoa-
Kumoa ; then they come in single file, and, kneeling down,
place an offering at his majesty's feet—an otter skin, a shell
called *mande*,[1] very highly esteemed, or a simple bead necklace.

[1] Called by Livingstone *omande*. He gives many interesting details of
superstitions connected with it in his " Travels."

But an offering is absolutely necessary; and while they recommence the *shoalela,* one of the officers calls out, *"Puma noka"* (" The king is satisfied "). And I thought of God's word to Moses which we Christians are apt to forget, " None shall appear before Me empty." The king himself seems quite unconcerned about all this : he does not reply to any of the salutations ; he gives his orders, sends his messengers, distributes his work ; he listens to the cases submitted to him by his ministers and issues decrees. If he cites some one to appear, he simply pronounces his name, and immediately four, five, six men rise and call the name in every direction. Those who hear it repeat the name, till it is sounded all over the village.

Great animation reigns in the *lekhothla* about the king's person. In the intervals of the sittings, he retires to his own home. On one side of the public place is a vast enclosure—of course a circular one. This is his harem. The huts of his wives are ranged round the inner wall, and separated by reed courts. In the middle is a fine roomy hut surrounded by a court, which is his private room. Nobody has the right to approach it, except his ministers, and they may only enter with his express permission. And there, almost every day, when he did not come to me, I passed hours with him, teaching him the alphabet and talking. Perhaps you would like to be present at one of our conversations. Lewanika, pleased with his progress, was laughing heartily, rolling on his mat. Then, becoming more serious, he said :

" I had thought of coming to see you to-day. I have all sorts of things to ask from you : candles, coffee, medicine for the eyes, medicine for the head, and so on."

" It would be no use coming to me for them. I have only brought necessaries ; and even if I wished to, I could not satisfy your demands."

" But when you come with your waggon, then you will have all your riches, will you not ? "

" I hope we shall have what we want for our own use, and for barter."

" And if I want shirts, trousers, a hat, and shoes, you will have to get them for me if I need them."

" Not necessarily ; I am not a trader. And besides, our exchange goods only consist of beads and calico."

" What ! you have not brought any clothes ?   What will you do when your own are worn out ? "

" I have what is necessary for my own use ; nothing more."

" Do you mean to say that, if I need clothes, you will *give* me your own, as you do not sell them ? "

I told him he must get them from traders, like Mr. Westbeech, as he sells them his ivory.

" But," he said, " who gives you these things ? "

" I buy them."

" What with ? "

" With money."   (He then wished to see some money.)

" But where do you get this money ? "

I explained to him that the " believers " in my country gave us part of their possessions to provide for our needs.   He uttered an exclamation of surprise, and remained silent for some time ; then began again.

" Moruti, you are old ; give me counsel how I shall rule my country, and strengthen my government."

" First put away your assegaï, and let it sleep, and renounce vengeance once for all.   Set yourself to win the confidence of your people, and inspire the smallest with a feeling of perfect security.   Punish theft ; and, above all, accept the Gospel for yourself and for the nation."

" What are the riches of a country ?   The riches of mine is ivory.   But ivory diminishes every year ; and when all the elephants in the country are exterminated, what shall I do ? "

I thought of Colbert's great saying.[1]   But there is no industry here from a commercial point of view.   I pointed out to him the fertility of his country, and that if the chiefs would give themselves up to the cultivation of cotton, tobacco, coffee, sugar-cane, etc., they would soon find that it would be an inexhaustible source of riches for them.

He then questioned me about Lobengula.   Had he missionaries ?   Were there believers in his country ?   Was he himself a believer, like Khama ?   Why was he not a Christian ?   Then, evidently alluding to the intentions of invasion with which Khama is credited, and to his own raids on the Mashukulumboe, he said :

[1] " La France a deux mamelles : l'agriculture et l'industrie."

" Is it true that Khama, who is a Christian, still makes war, and invades other people's countries ? "

" I could not say, for Khama is only a man ; and then he does not govern alone—the council of the tribe is there."

" But is it wrong to make war ? "

" Not to defend one's country."

" And if I found myself engaged in a warlike enterprise, would you accompany me ? "

" No. Our mission is a mission of peace."

" At least you would lend me your guns, and give me ammunition."

" No. That would still be taking part in it."

" What ! and you live in my country, and are my father ! And if you had been here when Mathaha revolted against me, what would you have done ? When you heard guns firing, would you not have run to my defence ? And if I had sent back for arms and ammunition, would you have refused me ? "

" Yes, but I should have prayed for you."

" Oh yes ! " he said, with shouts of laughter ; " and while that was going on Mathaha would have killed me. That would have been a fine way of helping ! And if I had fled to you, what would you have done ? "

" I would have received you into my house ; I would have given you food and clothes ; and I would have taken the place of your servant, and would have made your fire myself."

" That is well. But if Mathaha's people had pursued me, and said to you, ' Deliver Lewanika to us, that we may kill him ' ? "

" Then I would have stood at the door, and said, " This is a city of refuge. If you wish to violate it, you must kill me first.' "

" That is splendid ! "

This outline of a conversation lasting several hours will give you some idea of the man. He seems to have a great wish to resemble Khama. Like all small African potentates, he has an extraordinarily exaggerated idea of his own dignity. Man has never appeared to me so utterly degraded as in his presence. They attribute to him a magic power : he can render himself invisible and invulnerable, and ensure success in hunting by certain medicines known to himself. And I have heard him claim this singular power, in the open *lekhothla*. He is religious in his own way—that is to say, extraordinarily superstitious. Near his harem is a "grove," carefully screened round with mats, where he offers prayers, sacrifices, and libations to the manes of his ancestors, and to the sun. I have witnessed strange customs and ceremonies at Lealuyi which I cannot relate. I have been particularly struck with the feast of the *new moon*. It is kept *strictly* as a day of rest, and celebrated by peculiar dances and songs, in which all men without distinction of age or rank take part, while the women, at a distance, applaud them with shrill cries. Oxen are killed, cooked, and eaten on the public place, and the silver disc is noisily greeted as soon as its outline appears. Whence come these customs, and many others, which remind us of the Levitical laws?[1] These are very interesting questions to study, but to do that would require patience and prudence.

Where do the Barotsi come from? They themselves say from the east. They came up the Zambesi, conquered the Bawewe tribe, which they found in this country, and mingled with them. What I have told them of the Banyaï leads them to believe that they are the stock from which they have sprung. And strange to say, they perfectly understand my little vocabulary of *Senyaï* (the Banyaï tongue)—in fact, it is the same language as the Serotsi.[2] They relate that on their arrival in this country, a god married *Buya-Mamboa*, and that this woman gave birth to the Barotsi kings. Their tombs, and those of the queens, are scattered over the country to the number of about twenty-five. Many are shaded with woods, and kept up with great care; all are sacred places, *cities of refuge*, which were even respected during the revolution. Another no less important city of refuge is that of the queen, at present Nalolo. I met there a chief of Sesheke, seriously compromised, whom Mokwaë kept till she obtained Lewanika's pardon for him. At the capital itself, Gambella's hut for his peers and the enclosure of the king's court are respected refuges. But it is above all to the *Natamoyo* that they look in case of danger. This Natamoyo is entrusted with the duty

---

[1] Especially being "defiled by the dead" and by contact with blood.

[2] It must be borne in mind that the Barotsi have their own language, though they also speak the Sesuto, learned from the Makololo.

THE YOUNG MORANTSIANE.

[To face page 224.

LEWANIKA AND HIS CHIEF WIFE MA-MORAMBOA (1886).

of appeasing the king's anger, of restraining it, and of protecting its probable victims. The enclosure of his house, always near the *lekhothla*, is sacred. Should any one be accused by the king's order, and pursued by a crowd of his emissaries, if he can put his foot inside the court of the Natamoyo, he is saved. Moreover, when the king wishes to assure himself of a man's death, he takes measures to prevent the Natamoyo from knowing anything about it, so that the man may not escape.

Alas! in spite of all these wise precautions, there are few countries more stained with human blood. Sitting at the *lekhothla*, I passed in review these hundreds of men, without recognising *one* of those whose acquaintance I had made the previous year. "We threw them out to the vultures : their bones are bleaching in the sun." One scarcely ever sees a grey head among the chiefs. They do not grow old here. They have committed crimes upon women and little children which only the language of Elisha to Hazael can describe (2 Kings viii. 12). The women who have escaped these hecatombs have been shared as part of the booty, and have fallen into the power of their husbands' murderers. But they seem to console themselves easily, for some of them who have passed thus from hand to hand are now at their fifth, sixth, or even tenth master. It is heart-rending. Oh, dear friends ! if you only had an idea of heathenism such as we see it here !

After our conversations, Lewanika was anxious to hear the public preaching of the Gospel. Following Khama's example, upon the advice of a chief who had been to Mangwato, Lewanika, on Friday evening, made the public crier proclaim that the next day every one was to prepare, for the day after was the Lord's Day, and no one could grind, nor go to the fields, nor travel, nor work. On Sunday morning, he came to the *lekhothla* without his drums, and collected his people by calling them publicly. There was a fine audience, serious and attentive. I sang and preached, as at Nalolo ; and here, also, I felt myself sustained and blessed. I have never in my life wished so much for a good strong voice. There was, I assure you, something electrifying and profoundly touching in speaking of God and the Saviour to this mass of pagans. The paraphrased reading of the Ten Commandments struck Lewanika, but I remarked that he remained seated when every one else knelt in prayer.

Whatever his motives may be, Lewanika has a great desire
to see us established in his kingdom. " How many are you ? "
he asked. " Two missionaries, and two helpers." " Is that all ?
But how can you teach my whole nation ? " He showed me
Mokwaë's son, quite a young man, whom he destines for the
office of Morantsiane at Sesheke. " Very well," he said, "your
colleague must remain at Sesheke to instruct and direct this
young man. There must be another *moruti* at Seoma, another
at Nalolo, another at Libonta. *When will some more come to
help you ? "* I underline the question and pass it on to you,
dear friends, and to the Churches of Basuto-land.

He showed himself very kindly disposed as regards the
choice of a site, so much so that he wished to come with me
to visit the different places which he believed best adapted to
our establishment ; but he was hindered from so doing, and
the Gambella accompanied me instead. Besides Sefula, which
may one day be occupied by the Nalolo missionary, I was
favourably impressed by *Kanyonyo*, a place which last year we
found encumbered by corn and manioc. It is a little valley
close to Mongu, not far from the capital. The annual floods
never come there ; and the south-west wind, which blows during
the worst six months of the year, drives away the marshy
miasmas, although it is this same wind which, sweeping afterwards
over the swampy valleys, becomes impregnated with malaria.
Sefula enjoys the same conditions. And these are, I think, the
least unhealthy parts of the Valley that I know, relying on our
experience of Sesheke on the north and Leshoma on the south
of the river. Sesheke is as healthy as Leshoma is the reverse.
This year, while we all enjoyed excellent health here, all the
members of Dr. Holub's expedition were ill at Leshoma, and
one died there.

Lewanika, hearing of our losses in bullocks, sent an order
to the chiefs of Sesheke to give me seventeen. Will the order
be carried out punctually ? That remains to be seen. At
Mr. Westbeech's suggestion, he has sent gangs of men, so as to
save us the expense, to clear a road for the waggons through
the forests which we must traverse. He himself wished us to
start immediately, but we shall be obliged to wait till the waters
dry up, so it will be July before we are able to leave.

The return journey only took us eight days. In passing

Seoma, I enquired after my boat, and learnt that it had been found below the first rapids, among the reeds, where the current had carried it. Judge of my people's astonishment! They all came to shake hands with me in congratulation. The same ceremony was repeated at the port of Sesheke, where we disembarked on April 17th. All our beloved ones were there, well and radiant with delight, and the news I received of our evangelists was also excellent. How good the Lord is!

The cost of my journey may perhaps interest you. Here are the details :

	£	s.	d.
Ten cotton sheets at 12s.	6	0	0
" Tips " in calico for the rowers	1	10	0
Calico and beads for presents and purchasing food	2	10	0
	10	0	0

The sheets were not a new purchase ; we had them before. If among our European purchases there are some which have not been as useful as we expected, our stuffs on the contrary have been of the greatest possible service, and a great economy. It is the purse which has supported the expedition till the beginning of this year, which has paid for our buildings at Leshoma, then at Sesheke, all our journeys and expenses of communication, and the exchange of twelve draught oxen here.

SESHEKE, UPPER ZAMBESI, *May 4th*, 1886.

It is to avoid confusion that I write to you from Sesheke. In point of fact, it is some days since we left it, Jeanmairet and myself. We had a great desire to visit our evangelists at Mambova, for they have had a monotonous and difficult life since our departure for the Valley. Poor fellows ! what a sunbeam for them ! Once at Mambova, we made a flying trip to Leshoma with Aaron to visit our baggage, and took advantage of a moment's respite to complete our mail.

You know that the counter-revolution which brought Lewanika back to power was of the bloodiest. Unhappily, the insatiable vengeance of the king pursued, and still pursues, to the uttermost the rebels who sought salvation in flight, or who ran the risk of throwing themselves at his feet and imploring pardon. He has sworn to exterminate the last scion of the house of one Kuanosha. For months, his emissaries have been overrunning the kingdom in every direction with secret missions: then chiefs who are in the plot fall in the night upon such and such a community, pillage and massacre to their hearts' content, and return triumphant, with troops of horned beasts, of women and children. They share the women among themselves, while waiting for the king to dispose of this human booty.

As to the cattle, masters and slaves vie with each other in stealing and squandering it. No one is astonished, and no one would dare to raise his voice in disapproval. " *Ke-lerumo !* " (" It is the spear " ; civil war). It seems that then anything is allowed. I have said elsewhere that the pen refuses to give details as to the atrocities committed at Seseheke itself on women and little children. It is sickening. And do you imagine that the savage behaviour of these men, who habitually bathe their hands in the blood of their chiefs and of their brothers, is such as to inspire us with terror? Not at all. These are the most polished people in the world, and I think they even outdo the Parisians. A master always calls his slaves " *Shangwe*," [1] even the youngsters. A slave would never address another without making use of the same expression, and calling him *you*, not *thou*.

No later than last week, at Seseheke, they murdered a petty chief, who for months had been flattered and nursed into a false security. He was fed, and ostensibly received into the confidence of the *lekhothla*. Lewanika, fearing the matter would come to our ears, had commanded that this man should be carried away on a hunting expedition, and executed far away from us. Rataü, with the other chiefs (some of them his relations), did not approve of these precautions. " What is killing a man ? " he cried. " The affair won't take long. Besides, the missionaries know that ours is a country of blood." The evening of the next day, on their return from a visit which some of the chiefs paid us, with the unfortunate Makapane, they gathered themselves at Rataü's, where they had organised a feast of *yoala*. They drank, they chatted gaily ; then suddenly a man rose behind Makapane and struck him on the

---

[1] " Sir," or rather " Sire."

temple with a club ; they next disembowelled him, and threw
him out for the vultures to feed on.   Rataü felt he must come
and tell us about it ; but to prevent our giving the poor man
burial, he assured me that they had flung his corpse to the
crocodiles.   Alas ! the vultures that hovered over the forest
gave him too visibly the lie.   While I was trying to make
Rataü understand the enormity of this crime, and while I was
applying to him the Divine word, " He that killeth with the
sword shall perish by the sword," he clapped his hands before
me as heartily as though I had loaded him with praises.   The
hypocrite !

Amid this appalling outbreak of passions, we ourselves have
had, and still have, to suffer.   By day, as by night, we are
exposed to the most barefaced thefts.   They respect neither
our waggons, nor our folds, nor our houses.   Without protection, without any defence as we are, it is truly a miracle
of God's goodness that we have not yet been completely
stripped.   The slaves steal audaciously for their masters.   The
chiefs themselves come shamefacedly each time to mumble a
few words of excuse or of sympathy.

It is hard to see our sheep and cattle stolen and killed in
broad daylight at a couple of hundred paces from the village,
and to recognise our own shirts and stuffs upon the greasy backs
of chiefs of the second and third degree.   What can we do?
Pray that God may enable us by His grace to " take joyfully
the spoiling of our goods," and may deliver us from all feeling
of bitterness.   That will one day come to an end ; and meanwhile our Master will never let us lack for necessaries.

One word more and I close.   What do you think of
Lewanika's remarks about our small number ?   This " *when
will they come*" *:* is it not the cry from Macedonia ?   Is it
not something abnormal, and extraordinarily abnormal, that
revivals in France should produce so few missionary vocations ?
See what is happening in England ; this host of labourers who,
their own salvation once assured, invade the Lord's field in
China, in the great African Lakes, on the Congo, etc.   The
experiences of the year which has just elapsed show us that
we must have each an evangelist with us.   Levi will go and
join Jeanmairet, and Aaron will accompany us to the Valley.
Thus there will be two stations only in this immense country

—*two !* As long as the Churches of Basuto-land do not freely
enter into our work, by sending us evangelists, and *supporting*
them themselves, we hesitate to call for such evangelists.   The
position of Aaron and Levi, who have no connexion with
the Church of their own country, and who are exclusively
supported by Christians of another race, with whom they
have not the slightest communication, is most painful.   They
feel it, and I should not be surprised if one day a deep
discouragement seized them.   What gives us *our* strength is
the bulk of the army of Christ which is behind us and upholds
us.   This subject has acutely occupied us, and I believe that by
different lines of argument Jeanmairet and I have arrived at the
same conclusion—namely, that the native part of our mission
staff, if it is to continue to exist and develop itself, ought from
the financial point of view to be entirely the work of the Basuto
Churches.

A dear brother, whose affection for me personally has stood
the test of many years, wrote me lately with a frankness for
which I thank him : " You must not be surprised if you do not
find the enthusiasm you would like everywhere.   People will
accord you a support *based not on faith, but on success*."   But I
have never promised *success*.   FOR US, OBEDIENCE AND FAITH :
SUCCESS LIES WITH GOD ALONE.   I appeal to you, dear
unknown friends, to give a striking contradiction to these
words of our venerated friend—a contradiction that shall redound
to God's glory.

SESHEKE, *July 1st*, 1886.

I confess that I am sometimes stupefied when I see the
aspect under which the Barotsi display human nature.   Hitherto,
I have witnessed nothing like it.   The Zambesians have nothing
in common with the Bechuana, but a basis of superstition, a
black skin, and a dialect of their language.

The farther I go, the more I believe that tribulations await
us.   The martyrdom of Bishop Hannington in Uganda gives
one food for reflection.   We feel more and more the need to
cling to God and His promises, come what may.   If God be
for us, who can be against us ?   In such surroundings as these,
the presence of that glorified Saviour Who has sent us, and to
Whom all power is given, not only in heaven, but on earth

(hence on the Zambesi too), is a glorious reality ; and we feel it.
Therefore have no uneasiness on our account. We follow the
Man of Sorrows. Should we follow Him *afar off*, and with
divided hearts ? But this Man of Sorrows, *every knee* must bow
to Him, *every* tongue must confess His name. I do understand
that the world calls those enthusiasts who follow the Saviour
with love. I do not understand how I could have followed Him
so long without enthusiasm.

We love to reckon up the blessings of God as David did.
They are far more abundant than we dared to hope. Can you
believe that, thanks to the Jesuits' corn, we have never yet
wanted for bread ? It is true that we are not so extravagant
with it at the Zambesi as in Paris. We also have milk, which
in a household like ours is an immense resource. And then,
above all, we enjoy good health. This is, no doubt, in answer
to the prayers of many friends. My dear wife is the least
robust of us ; and she, among us all, has the hardest and most
active life.

I have just been away for a fortnight. Our friend Middleton
had sent word to me of his arrival from Pretoria at the ford
of Kazungula, after five months' absence. He seemed no less
happy than I at our meeting. The wind blew so hard that
the canoes could not be navigated for a fortnight. But at last,
with a score of willing men, and an armful of *setsibas*, I managed
to get oxen, waggons, and baggage across without too much
fuss. Then I returned to Sesheke, leaving Middleton to watch
over the baggage, till the country should be dry enough for the
waggons to trek. Alas ! we wish we could keep the lovely
days that are speeding away. Why are we not already at the
Valley to begin our work, and shelter ourselves, before the
rains ? They are burning the grass over the surface of the
country more or less everywhere. Will they also burn the
stubble which we need as thatch for our buildings ? That is one
of our anxieties, and not the only one.

At Kazungula, I met Dr. Holub, who himself had just
crossed the Zambesi, and was waiting for porters, in order
to start towards the country of the Mashukulumboe. His
expedition had been severely tried. He had had great losses
of cattle, like ourselves, and had spent a great deal. Two of
his best men have died, one at Leshoma, the other at Pata-

matenga ; a third had to return to Austria ; all the others have
been much tried by fever. The expedition is thus reduced to
three Europeans, Mrs. Holub, and the Doctor himself. They
have got rid of everything that was not absolutely necessary
to them : their regimen is severe, but all are full of spirits. I
learnt more than one lesson of courage and self-denial from
them. It is touching to see this young woman following her
husband on foot, through savage tribes and in a cruel climate,
in order to share his fatigues and dangers. I offered her one of
my donkeys. Ah, why has not the Gospel more of such intrepid
missionaries as those of geography? Why do not the young
Christians of France awake? They are asleep, and the heathen
are dying. In response to my expressions of sympathy, Mrs.
Holub coloured, and her feelings overcame her. The Doctor
said, " Yes, it will be hard and difficult ; but," he added with
a beaming face, " *if* we succeed, and *if* we can return to Austria
—oh ! then our fortune is made ! "

Well, I thought to myself, I am better off. For us, there
is no *if*. In the service of Jesus, success is certain, whatever
men may think ; if only our obedience be implicit, for the
fulfilment of His will *is* success. And after the burden of the
day, when we arrive at the end of the journey in the Father's
home—oh, then ! . . .

CHAPTER XV

SESHEKE, UPPER ZAMBESI, *July 29th*, 1886.

AT this date—who doubted it?—we ought certainly to have arrived at our final destination, Lealuyi, and there vigorously pushed forward our temporary structures. And alas! here we still are, helpless prisoners at Sesheke. The winter, the good, the only good season for health, for travelling, and for work, is rapidly passing; indeed, it is already gone. We are sometimes tempted to stamp with impatience, like naughty children. If these delays go on much longer, it will be a question whether it is possible to make the journey, and install ourselves at the Valley, before the rains which begin in November.

Our friend Middleton was absent six months to renew our supplies. At Mangwato, where, at the present time, commerce is nearly ruined, he found nothing, not even a piece of calico, the *indispensable money* of the Zambesi. He had to push on to Pretoria. On his return, I hastened to meet him at Kazungula, so as to bring over the baggage, oxen, and waggons, always a great affair. Unhappily, the great plain of Kasaya was still submerged and quite impracticable. Middleton, therefore, had to wait six weeks at Kazungula. This delay causes us the greatest embarrassment. My niece, Mme. Jeanmairet, who hopes shortly to become a mother, was to have gone with

us to the Valley. Her husband would have joined her there a
little later, which would have afforded him the opportunity of
making the acquaintance of the king and the principal chiefs
of the country. Now we must give up this plan and all its
advantages. But what can we do? To prolong our stay here,
and thus retard for a whole year the foundation of our station
at Lealuyi, is absolutely out of the question. For us, *now*, one
year is worth ten. We only see one alternative, and we shudder
at it, but only for a moment. The duty is clear. I shall start
alone for the Valley with our two artisans to begin the work
of installation: the waggons will come back to fetch my wife,
who must also make the journey alone with Aaron and his
family.

Middleton having at last arrived, our preparations are quickly
finished, and our carriages loaded. On the four, we have put
scarcely the equivalent of two loads. We are dividing our oxen.
Last year, just after our journey from Kazungula to Sesheke,
we lost many of them from the tse-tse fly. The generous forethought of kind friends has happily enabled us to renew our
teams to some extent. Now, by counting the old, the lean,
and those we have to lift to their legs, we have just the minimum
of oxen required. But it will not do for a single one to die by
the way. And now for the drivers! My waggon has never
lacked for an arm, when it has had to roll in the King's service.
Here are two men of Mangwato, who will each take charge of
a waggon.[1] The evangelist Aaron has offered himself to lead
mine; Middleton, helped by Kamburu, will take the fourth; and
Waddell, with Nguana-Ngombé, the cart, transformed once more
into a Noah's Ark. We did not arrive at this solution all at
once. Last year, our evangelists stood a little on their dignity;
doubtless they feared the Zambesians would misunderstand
their position relatively to ourselves—a small weakness which
we understood and easily excused. Thus we are all the more
pleased at the right spirit which has led Aaron to offer us his
services, not only for my journey, but also for that of my dear wife.

We have still to find "leaders," boys who run before the
teams to guide them. But where shall we find these boys?
Sesheke and the villages of the chiefs are still abandoned and

---

[1] Franz, frequently mentioned in subsequent letters, was one of these.

in ruins. Those of the Masubia round about are also at this
season completely deserted. Men, women, and children are
all dispersed in the woods and islands for hunting and fishing.
Do we by chance meet some one and speak to him of our
journey? "*Borotsi ke naga ea lerumo,*[1] *lerumo le teng*" ("The
Valley is a country of blood and murder"), he replies, with
agitated looks; "we are afraid to go there." The terror which
the Barotsi inspire is such that even our shepherds wished
to leave us. The parents of Kamburu and Nguana-Ngombé
also hurried hither to stop them. But they remained faithful
to us, although their engagement had expired.

Kamburu is going to adventure himself with the conductor's
long whip. "How could he forsake his father in difficulty?
He doesn't know the business, but he will do his best." One
cannot ask more. He is somewhat ambitious, is Kamburu.
What with the odds and ends of every sort of apparel in which
he rigs himself out on occasion, he is on the way to transform
himself into a *mothambezi*, a dignity assumed by the Hottentots
and half-breeds who follow the Europeans in these parts. One
day, his aspirations will lead him to Mangwato, to the Diamond
Fields, to Basuto-land—who knows?—to seek a little work,
civilisation, liberty—and a great deal of money.

As to Nguana-Ngombé, he wishes to stay with us. Contrary
to our expectations, he was able to resist the importunities of
his elder brother, and above all those of his chief Mokumba's
wife, who sent messengers and left no stone unturned to get him
away from our house. "I shall wait for my master to come
back from Lealuyi; *I* want to be educated," he replied respectfully, but also with characteristic firmness. And do not think
that reading, writing, and arithmetic are the only things that
enter into his programme. No. For him to be educated means
to acquaint himself thoroughly with every kind of work he sees
performed: to knead and bake the bread in a pan; to make
candles, saw in a saw-pit, plane boards, sew, iron linen, wash
photographic plates, and what not besides? No false shame!
His great energy makes every kind of work easy to him. His
merry laugh and helping hand often give us a lift forward in
undertakings which by no means come within his province.

[1] *Lerumo,* spear or assegaï, equivalent to "murder."

This dear child eagerly listens to the preaching of the Gospel. During my last journey to the capital, I sent him a little letter, which he received while ill. " My mother," he said to my wife, " I understand. I too would be a child of God. I would like to be converted." Up to the present, he has not yet made the decisive step. If he left us, it would probably be an irreparable loss. We tremble above all at the thought of this boy, so gifted as he is, and of such an open joyous nature, being dragged back in spite of himself into the brutality and misery of serfdom. But we must not interfere. Our business is to confide the interests of this dear soul to the Saviour Who has given His life to save him.

SESHEKE, *August 8th.*

The lords of Sesheke, so long announced and awaited, at last arrived yesterday. The fugitive population took courage, and assembled here for the occasion. One way and another, a great deal of powder was exploded. They are bringing us a perfect legion of new dignitaries, the new Nalishua, Liamine, Mokoro, Lesuani, etc., all of Sesheke—young men of our acquaintance, who, to put it mildly, make us tremble for the future. Kabuku, the Morantsiane elect, is himself a boy of eighteen or twenty. He is the son of Queen Mokwaë. At Lealuyi, Lewanika had confidentially pointed him out to me as the viceroy destined for Sesheke. Poor boy ! he is lost among such as Rataü, Tahalima, and Mokhele, whom the contrast makes even older ; and he scarcely knows how to bear the weight of so novel a dignity. He makes grimaces like a coquettish girl ; he winks, twists his mouth, trifles with a rhinoceros horn to occupy his hands, which he does not know what to do with ; he drinks *mpote* (a honey beer said to be as strong as brandy), and surrounds himself with the ceremonies observed at the court of Lealuyi. He had not been half an hour on the station before he exhibited the cloven hoof of a practised beggar. He had all sorts of wants to satisfy. Above all, he coveted one of our wooden chairs, and would not take " No " for an answer, even after repeated refusals. He returned to the charge with such importunity that I ended by giving in. And now this seat, shining with grease and ochre, is borne before him, as the symbol of his high office !

The old chiefs, our former friends, are as vile and cringing before the young beardless prince as they were haughty. They seem to us like high functionaries who are now disgraced and degraded, but who cannot as yet be dispensed with. At the time of their visit to the capital, the king would not kill a single head of cattle for them ; he only gave them fish to eat. Moreover, they are gloomy and uncommunicative. Lewanika divided up the wives of all the chiefs who have fled or been massacred ; but the children—those dear little children, some of them so intelligent and loveable—have all been pitilessly put to death, to the very last one. They bring us heart-rending details of this horrible tragedy.

We talk business with them. The king is still sending pressing messages, and the chiefs, who have received their orders, promise us men without delay. For the moment, the great preoccupation of their lordships is the site of the new Sesheke. They have consulted the *litaola* (divining bones)— "cast the dice," as we should say ; they have sacrificed oxen to the manes of the ancient chiefs of Sesheke ; they have gone at daybreak in procession, ceremoniously led by a woman, to pray at the important tombs ; and then, on Sunday afternoon, they have come in a body to pray to the God of the missionaries ! So nothing is wanting to assure the prosperity of the new capital of the province. What lessons these poor heathen teach us, all the same, in their ignorance !

Mokumba, too, has returned. He hastened to come and see us. Nguana-Ngombé laid at his feet his own wages for two years' service, and kneeling before him, clapping his hands, he said in a supplicating tone, " My master, my time is up ; but I would like to stay with the *Baruti*" (missionaries) " and be educated—my master." He was trembling with emotion, and great drops of sweat ran down the transparent skin of his face. It was a scene of extreme psychological interest. Mokumba kept silence for some time ; then choosing for himself a fine woollen blanket of flaming colours, and passing the rest to him, " My child," he said at last, " I am Mokumba. I would not be the one to take thee from thy father and mother. They love thee, thou lovest them ; thou art happy ; stay with them. Later on, thou wilt return to me." Our boy's face brightened like lightning ; he gave thanks, and clapped his hands ecstatically. It seemed as though he already breathed the first sweet air of liberty, and caught a glimpse of new horizons. All his friends came to congratulate him. As for ourselves, we blessed God.

SESHEKE, *August 14th.*

The chiefs have kept their word, and they have astonished us with their eagerness to oblige us. They have brought us a troop of men and youths, and promise us a still larger number. It is in their own interest, for the wages of a slave or serf belong by right to his master, and each of these is to receive a cotton blanket and some calico. By this reckoning, a bale will not go far. Besides, we know our Zambesians well enough to be certain that it is not the greatest number which does the most and the best. Therefore we choose, and inscribe very solemnly the names of those we require, and we dismiss the others politely. That does not suit the chiefs ; they discuss it excitedly, and testify their disappointment and displeasure by half turning their backs to us, frowning and clicking their tongues. But we take no notice of it ; we are used to whims of this kind.

August 18th.

It was the day before yesterday that our vans at length set off, in the midst of a noisy assemblage of the whole population now at Sesheke. They did not go far. They stuck in the sand two miles from the station. The young Morantsiane, perched on the cone of an ant-heap, and escorted by some youngsters, pretended that it was he who checked us in this way, to avenge the affront I had put upon him by refusing him my pocket-knife. The next day, he sent me a rather more polite message. He had consulted the *litaola,* and the oracle had replied that Sepopa (a famous king who had restored the Barotsi power after the fall of the Makololo) was incensed against me because I had not yet rendered to him the homage due. What he now requires is the offering of an ox, a goat, a sheep, some calico, etc., and then " he will give me the road." To the stupefaction of my Sesheke friends, I simply unloaded part of the luggage, which I brought back to the station ; and while the waggons, thus lightened, continued their way without hindrance, I stayed to pass the

day with my own people. The house was very empty without
Middleton and Waddell. What will it be when I am finally
gone away too? This day went by on wings. Four o'clock
struck. We threw ourselves on our knees. And then—was
it a dream? I found myself all alone, ambling slowly with a
heavy heart. My looks involuntarily turned back, and sought
yet to distinguish certain forms: the waving of a handkerchief. . . . But no! it is weakness. Forward! And striking
my spurs, I plunged resolutely into the wood.

My excellent nag speedily brought me to the waggons.
We travelled a great part of the night, and before dawn we
were already on the march again. But what was my dismay
on discovering this morning that, in spite of tolerably recent
repairs, the two right wheels of my waggon threatened to
collapse. The naves are completely rotten ; you can plunge a
knife-blade into them like cork ; the spokes work up and down
like pistons, one after another. To console me, they say and
repeat and shout in every key all round me, that it will assuredly
break up, and will never reach the Valley. I could have boxed
the ears of these prophets. Not only must my waggon take me
to the Valley, but it *must* come back and bring my dear wife
there too. And then it will have deserved well of the mission
and of its friends. There are few missionary waggons which have
rolled as far—few which have given so much satisfaction to
their travellers. Ten years' service in a country without roads,
among woods and rocks and burning sands, without ever being
sheltered from the wind, the rain, and the rays of a tropical
sun, is much—very much. How shall we replace our good old
waggon, our *home* of so many years in the desert? Meanwhile,
let us repair it as best we can. It is the work of some hours
to shorten the circumference of the wheels, to tighten the iron
tyres and the spokes with wedges of wood. With this lame
arrangement, we continue our way, often casting uneasy looks
at the unlucky wheels.

MOSIKILI, *August 22nd.*

Only fifty miles from Sesheke after a whole week of toil !
But patience ! Once we are fairly off, we shall travel better. We
made a sensation passing through the villages of Rataü, Katukura,
Kuenane, etc., for the poor people have never seen oxen under

the yoke, nor houses on wheels. On the 20th, we reached Loanja, of which we have heard so much. It is the granary of the country. At certain seasons, the Loanja is a stream, or rather a lake ; now it is an immense morass along its whole course, averaging half a mile in width. Its valley is extremely fertile. All the cereals of the country are cultivated there. For the manioc and sweet potato, they make beds on the borders of the swamp, and surround them with deep trenches to drain them. It was not easy for us to avoid either these deep ditches or the traps for big game which abound on the skirts of the woods. Happily, these pits are not furnished with pointed stakes, as those of the Banyaï are. What a rich country this would be in the hands of European agriculturists !

Having reached the confines of the tse-tse country, we ask in the king's name for help and a guide from a petty chief, who simply laughs at us. Of our pretended guides, not one knows the way, nor has the power, with which we believed them to be invested, to procure us the help we require. They are nothing but a torment to us with the airs they give themselves. Monibotale is quite an inferior village chief ; but when he talks of himself, which happens not infrequently, he is a *Nguana-Morena*[1] (a prince), a *Khosi e Kana-Kana*, such a very great personage ! Why did the chiefs of Sesheke insist so strongly on our taking this route, rather than the one Lewanika was to open on Sekhosi's side ? Our people see in this nothing but a malicious and sordid ruse.

As we have to travel by night now, Middleton and Waddell, with two natives, offered to go on in advance, to clear the road. Thinking they were too few for so heavy a task, I was inspired with the unlucky idea of starting too, with my hatchet over my shoulder. Waddell had an attack of fever, and dragged along painfully. We hacked vigorously away. Here and there we lighted great fires to show the direction of the road. At ten o'clock, we reached Mosikili, where we were to wait for the waggons. My companions, tired out, curled themselves up round the fire, for it was cold, and quickly dropped off to sleep.

Alone, I stood to keep watch, plunging my gaze into the thick darkness, straining my ear at the least noise, until I

[1] *Nguana-Morena* = child of a chief, *i.e.* prince ; *Nguana-Ngombé* = child of cattle, *i.e.* calf.

fancied I could hear the bells of the oxen, and see confused shadows looming up before me. At two o'clock in the morning, I sent a couple of men to learn what had happened. They came back at five, saying that Aaron, having missed our road, had got his waggon stuck in the mud of the swamp. Having at once made the oxen cross to an islet where they could graze all day in safety, I returned to the waggons. Mine was indeed there, almost lying on its side in the slime—an accident which would have been impossible by daylight. The men were gloomy and depressed. The exchange of some friendly words, and a good meal which we hastily prepared, quickly brought them round, and the poor fellows worked all day in the mud with admirable spirit. The waggon having been raised out of this fathomless quagmire with infinite difficulty by means of levers, we paved the spongy ground with sunken stones and branches of trees. Happily, we were able to do it all by daylight. At eight o'clock in the evening, the oxen arrived. I do not understand how these people can sort the different teams, and then the oxen belonging to each yoke, on such a dark night, for there was no moon. By ten o'clock, we were out of the marsh, and by 2 a.m. at Mosikili. There, alas! a new stoppage. Mosikili is an island. To reach it, one must cross an arm of the Loanja, about three hundred and fifty yards wide, with water above one's knee. And of course our last waggon must needs stick there. In vain we double the teams ; in vain everybody, chilled to the bone, stands and shouts at the full pitch of his lungs. The first streaks of dawn are already lighting the horizon, and, willy-nilly, we must give up the job until the next night, and save our oxen.

How capricious this murderous fly is! Can it be believed that swarms of it abound in the forests which skirt the Loanja, while on the islands, about five hundred yards off, there is no trace of them? These islands are sure and well-known refuges, where the Barotsi in travelling always pen their cattle.

I could not help smiling when I heard of a curious and original theory. It would seem that people had been strangely mistaken as to the nature of the *Glossina morsitans*. Its sting, we are given to understand, is perfectly innocuous. The disasters attributed to it are simply the effects of a malarial climate. Thus the oxen are subject to marsh fever like their

masters! Well, what tons of quinine we should need to save
them! And if, after all, it were true, what fatigues and
anxieties would be spared us! It is a fact that very little is
as yet known of the tse-tse. It follows the buffaloes in their
migrations : so much is certain. My own opinion is that it
lays its eggs in their dung, and that it sucks their blood ; for,
according to the hunters, the moment they have knocked over
a large animal, its carcase is instantly covered with swarms
of tse-tse.

August 22nd (? *23rd*).

How difficult is the education of our Zambesians ; above all,
of the Mathambezi![1] River people, passionately addicted to
fishing and canoeing, all other kinds of work they abominate,
and this kind especially. They are afraid of the oxen ; they
abhor the waggons and the night journeys. And here are two
successive nights that they have not slept. They are chilly,
and that makes them cross ; one can only stir them by scolding.
Provided they have food, fire, and sleep, nothing else matters
much to them. Whether we progress or not, whether the
cattle stray or the waggons stick, they care very little. A
scene took place this morning, during which all the bitterness
of the Mathambezi overflowed. The Zambesians struck very
decidedly : they rolled up their mats, and prepared to go
home.

"Be off!" cried all the drivers at once. "Be off, quick!
If it were not for the *Moruti*, we would thrash you all like dogs.
Begone with you, foxes—run!"

And if they *had* gone? . . . I called the recalcitrants, and
addressed some sharp reprimands to them, which they received
with a fawning air, repeating at every sentence, "*Ntate, Ntate*"
("Father"), and then went back to their work.

Thus for the time the storm was calmed. But it did not
make the boys do their work with any better grace. The
stuck waggon kept us the greater part of the night, and we
are forced to stay here over Sunday.

KALANGU, *August 24th*.

Kalangu is the name of a petty Matolela chief, extended
also to his village. This worthy old man, learning that we

---

[1] Half-civilised people.

were at Mosikili, sent a band of young fellows to meet us and
guide us, for fear, he said, we should be surprised by daylight
in the midst of the tse-tse. We were travelling royally : it was
a treat. Suddenly the cry of alarm sounded from behind. We
ran with our lanterns. "The oxen won't go on," Kamburu
said piteously; "we can't manage it." A moment's inspection,
and we discovered that several had got the traces under their
bodies, and were being dragged along by the rest of the team.
No wonder they would not go on ! This little incident did not
damp the spirits of the caravan. Our Matolela ran on ahead
with blazing firebrands ; they screamed, bellowed, and yelped
like a troop of jackals. Was it to frighten the wild beasts, or
to announce our arrival from afar? Our principal guide has
adopted the motto that you must never give a white man
exact information about the road. And he has so thoroughly
indoctrinated the others, that when we ask how far we are
from Kalangu's they invariably reply, " Oh, it is still far, far, *very
far !* " " Well then, let us outspan, so that the oxen may rest
a little." "What ! outspan ? " cried my mentor, quite taken
aback ; "but we are just there ; it is here, close by." And he
was right. It was now 2 a.m. As usual, we crossed the oxen
to an island, and sought a little sleep. When I awoke, curiosity
had brought the whole population together : a grand opportunity for preaching the Gospel ; and it was not the only one,
for we had to pass two days at Kalangu's, while they were
clearing the road before us. Two pleasant days with such
sociable people ; but, alas ! two days of delay.

August 25th, 1886.

Twelve hours under the yoke—from 6 p.m. to 6 a.m. ! In
all my missionary life, I only remember a single circumstance
in which such a thing has befallen me, and that was when
the Matabele took us prisoners among the Banyaï. Kalangu's
people conducted us with lively clamour for about ten miles,
and handed us over to the petty Matolela chief Moanza, who
was expecting us. He furnished us with men, and we continued
on our way. Now it is that our difficulties begin. The road
here has not been cleared at all, and we are obliged to make it
as we go along. We are bordering the forest on the left, and
the swamp on the right in the direction of N.N.W. Our new

guides say it is cold ; they light fires, and take a nap, while we are working, or while our chariots stick in the inevitable bogs. Impossible to procure the slightest assistance. I consulted my watch ; we looked at the stars with ever-growing anxiety. " Make haste ; the daylight will overtake us." This was the universal cry. In fact, the dawn appeared, and we were still at some distance from an island that had been pointed out to us. While our Zambesians were roasting themselves by the fire, we hastily outspanned ; and Aaron, with another conductor, made our exhausted oxen run towards the island in question.

We were close to a deep rivulet whose marshy banks filled us with fear. After a necessarily frugal breakfast, we were obliged to seek a ford, and pave it with wood and branches. In spite of all our precautions, the following night we were not out of it before one o'clock in the morning. So there was a whole week of great exertions all consumed in crossing the tse-tse regions. And we thought we should have done it in two nights ! Thank God, however, here we are at its limits. But still we have to inspan before dawn for safety, and travel all day under a fiery sun and through burning sands to reach the water. This journey utterly finishes both men and beasts : they can march no longer, only drag themselves along. And with what a cry of joy we salute an open glade that gives us a glimpse of a sheet of water ! It is *Matsa*.[1]

AT THE RIVULET SIBOYA, *August 30th.*

Moanza's people give us infinite worry ; they will not do anything. At night, " *they* are not going to travel, not they " ; in the morning, it is too cold to wield the hatchet ; at midday, it is too hot. I have tried in vain to get rid of these greedy vampires ; they are on the look out for *setsibas*. However, they succeeded in making us lose our way in the woods, on purpose, far out of our course, near another belt of tse-tse. Heaven knows where they would have brought us, if some chiefs of Sesheke, who in their turn were going to pay homage to the king, had not sent us some good guides. The forest was thick, the sand deep, and our oxen exhausted ; it was Saturday, and it was necessary at all costs to reach the water. We left two

---

[1] Plural of *letsa*, pool—" pan " or " vley " in Cape language.

waggons, and took all the oxen to pull the two others. We courageously hacked our way through the thickets ; but it was impossible to know the general direction we ought to follow, and from east to west, and *vice versâ*, we zigzagged round all the points of the compass.

However, towards twilight, we came out by a charming rivulet which flows north, and bears its waters to an affluent of the Njoko. Our young men, tired out, struck, and refused every kind of service. The next day was a miserable Sunday, for we had to fetch the other vehicles left in a waterless desert. A deep sadness possessed me. At four o'clock in the afternoon, we enjoyed the imposing spectacle of a total eclipse of the sun. It was splendid. Our boys, hidden in the woods, rushed up quite thunderstruck. "Yo ! we are all dead men !" The fowls went to roost ; the dogs bayed ; the stars shone in the sky. In the midst of my cares, I had quite forgotten the phenomenon, for which I am angry with myself. We had a good meeting afterwards. I also spoke seriously to my boys, and threatened to complain to Lewanika about them. I felt that *that* bolt missed the mark. However this may be, they promised amendment. The day closed better than it began.

August 31st.

What a surprise ! The messenger I sent to Sesheke last Friday has returned already. Three hundred miles in four days and a half is not bad. It took us two weeks. I joyfully gave him his *setsiba*, and retired to enjoy by myself the precious missives he brought. Good news of my people, thank God ! My dear wife, who had been ill for a week after my departure, is better, and tries to carry on her little widowed household. The Jeanmairets are going on as usual. The new Morantsiane promises to be a thorn in their side, and, as my wife remarks, they will need all the grace of God to know how to be both firm and kind.

And what news of Dr. Holub's expedition ! Pillaged, completely pillaged, by the Mashukulumboe, not without bloody reprisals ! It has returned to Kazungula in a deplorable condition of sickness and destitution. No calico, no blankets, to send them, for I had taken them all. They are our purse But our good Dorcas, with the help of our "children," succeeded

in making up a good parcel of dresses, linen, soap, etc., to help
Dr. and Mrs. Holub.   In this check, there are some details I
cannot well understand, but the sympathy of those who have
hearts will not be wanting.   I can easily put myself in Dr.
Holub's place, for our Matolela and our Mangete are no better
than the Mashukulumboe, and they would treat us worse if
they dared.   "Oh, how I think of God's mercy!" writes my
wife; "He does not leave us to ourselves—He guides us by His
counsel.   And when darkness surrounds us, such darkness that
we really do not know whether to turn right or left, He says
to us, 'This is the way; walk ye in it.'   The contrast between
our expedition and the Holubs' is quite a sermon to me.   I
think a great deal of what happened to us at Masonda's,[1] and
I tell myself how easy it would have been for us, by the slightest
imprudence, to put ourselves into the same position as that
in which the Holubs now find themselves."   It is perfectly
true.

RIVER SEBA, AN AFFLUENT OF THE NJOKO, *September 2nd.*

We have worked all these days, until the axe was ready
to drop from my hand.   We are all as black as sweeps, and
can scarcely look at each other without laughing.   Since we
left Sesheke, the country (woods and plains lately burnt) is
quite covered with ashes, which, being stirred up by the oxen,
envelop us in a thick cloud.   We can only breathe when
here and there we find grass of last year spared by the general
conflagration.   We do not get on.   When shall we arrive?
Will it be possible for my wife to make the journey this year?

NJOKO, *September 3rd.*

We were making our way slowly and painfully through the
woods to reach a distant ford, when the chiefs from Sesheke,
of whom I have already spoken, and who acted for us as a
volunteer vanguard, sent us information that they had found
a passage close by—a very good ford, stony bottom, no
shoals, very little water, and above all no mud-holes.   We went
to inspect it; and although it was not precisely all that they
said, we believed it to be practicable.   The river at this place

---

[1] See chap. II.

is eighty yards wide, with a very rapid current. We launched
my waggon, drawn by thirty-two oxen. It was eight o'clock
in the morning. We thought all would be finished by ten
o'clock, and that, after the ordinary midday halt, we should
start, and travel by forced marches, so as to pass Sunday at
the Lumbé. Unhappily, as always happens in such cases,
hindrances arose : oxen unharnessed, yokes detached, yoke-
keys broken ; and then, at the moment of coming out of the
water, the hind wheels stuck so fast that one of the naves
disappeared in the mud. Before us a short but steep slope ;
the oxen refused to make any effort : cries, blows, altering the
angle of the traces—all was in vain. The waggon twice
dragged backwards into the middle of the river, now lurched
to the left against a sand-bank, while trying to avoid a quagmire
on the right. But we put chiefs and Matolela to the wheels ;
a few strokes of the spade, a long pull and a strong pull, and
we shall easily be out of it ! Yes ; only the oxen have turned
obstinate and pig-headed : they neither hear nor feel any longer.
Some pull backwards ; others, by a dexterous movement of
the neck, slip the yokes over their heads, and stare defiantly
at the execrable waggon. One detaches himself and escapes ;
another lies down, strangles himself out of pure contrariness,
foams, bellows, and stretches himself out for dead. " Bite his
tail ! " In vain they bite his tail ; he remains insensible.
Order being at last established, and each man at his post, before
unloading we make one last effort. Our Matolela find it is
less trouble to work with the tongue than with the shoulder ;
they make an appalling hullabaloo. The exasperated oxen
fling themselves to the right with such impetuosity that no one
can stop them. We see the left wheels rising ; the danger is
imminent ; the frantic people lose their heads completely. Some
throw themselves upon the wheels, others upon the oxen. And
in less time than it takes to tell you, the van had lost its
centre of gravity, and lay on its side, upset in the river. A
blank silence succeeded ; the natives, stupefied, nailed to the
spot, with their hands on their mouths, looked at one another,
and looked at me. Certainly it was not the time to lose one's
head. We outspanned the oxen, and rushed to the capsized
waggon. My heart is sore at the sight of this wreck, and at
the thought of my wife's journey. And the river current,

churning up the sand amid the chaos of our baggage, laughs aloud, as if to insult our misery.

To extricate our packing-cases, flung together pell-mell, to fish out our bedding, our bales, our sacks of provisions, was a laborious task, lasting some hours : Waddell and Middleton imposed it on themselves.   It was three in the afternoon. Waddell looked as white as a sheet ; he staggered, and I thought he was going to faint.   I then remembered that we had had nothing since the evening before.   I ran and fetched him some wine to give him a spurt.   I would fain have fled the sickening sight, when our baggage was out of the water. Here is my case of scientific instruments turned upside-down, the lid broken, the instruments scattered ; here is my bedding, my change of garments, my linen, everything dripping with water and full of sand.   There are our provisions, coffee, tea, lard, honey, with which our good housekeeper had taken special care to provide us ; vermicelli, arrowroot, very carefully kept for times of illness,—all that spilt, mixed up, trampled in the mire.   A sack of flour is drawn from the bottom of the river which was to have lasted us for months ; then the salt-bag and the sugar-bag.   But the bags are empty, salt and sugar completely melted !   Then, again, my little travelling library, Bibles, hymn-books, scientific works, books of medicine, literary works, journals and reviews from the last post, stationery—all a mass of muddy pulp.   And to put the finishing touch, the whole of them thrown on to a bank newly swept by fire, and covered with thick layers of black ashes.

But let us leave the baggage, and think of the waggon.   We take the understel to pieces, bit by bit, which is easy.   Next, we have to extricate the tilt, which is less so.   The important thing is to carry it, to raise it at arm's length above the great wheels, so as to put it back on the understel ; and that almost surpassed our strength.   The sand and water had doubled, tripled its weight, and our Matolela left us almost alone to make those efforts which threatened to break us in half.   By dint of entreaties, scoldings, and patience, however, we at last accomplished it, and finally the tilt fell into its place, amid deafening cheers.   So there is my poor waggon once more erect.   Good old friend, our home on wheels during so many years in these far-off and unknown countries, in the midst of such diverse adventures, what a crushed and melancholy look you wear, with your sides forced in, porch in rags, windows[1] smashed, tilt torn and muddy, box and brake all to pieces !

It was now twilight. Everybody had dispersed over the neighbouring hillock to bivouac. I was left quite alone, in the midst of my wreckage. The one thing that shone out amid the tumult of my thoughts was a lively sense of God's goodness. Undoubtedly, I shall have to pay, and pay rather dearly, for the services of the Sesheke chiefs. But these services were a great help to us ; their behaviour gave us pleasure. What should we have done without them, at the mercy of the Mangete and Matolela? Above all, what should we have done, if such an accident had befallen us in the swamps of Loanja, at night, in the midst of the tse-tse country, my wife with us, far from any village and any possible help ? The accident might have been ten times, a hundred times worse, and quite irremediable. At the camp, the Barotsi had made me a shelter against the blowing wind with some branches and a little grass. Waddell offered me his Scotch plaid, which I could not accept ; Middleton procured me one or two cotton coverlets ; Kamburu had found me some grass for my couch ; Aaron gave me his pillow ; and Nguana-Ngombé, ill as he was, had furnished me with the garment of the poor, a blazing fire. Thus cosseted by all my people, and exhausted with fatigue, I lay down and slept profoundly till morning. Then we had to begin our task over again ; carry all our luggage in our arms to the plateau ; and, in the midst of a curious and ever-increasing crowd, who have no honesty to spare, nor discretion either, to empty the cases, spread out dresses, clothing, linen, remnants, utter rags, the colours coming off on one another, articles of barter, provisions, groceries—all damaged and already fermenting ! What an exhibition ! It was then that I could take stock of our losses. How priceless henceforth will everything be which reaches the Valley safe and sound ! It was in the midst of this dismal drying-ground that I preached the Gospel to an audience of two hundred and fifty people. The men listened attentively, but the chatter of the women knew no respite : their ears were closed to the preaching. It was our frippery that absorbed their looks and thoughts. It saddened me deeply.

[1] Of four small panes—an unusual luxury in a waggon.

AT THE LUMBÉ RIVER, *September 11th.*

The journey is most laborious. Our axes do not grow rusty, but our arms grow weary. The sand is such, and our oxen are so tired, that we scarcely make two miles an hour. Middleton's team is reduced from fourteen to ten ; we are obliged to leave his waggon behind to fetch it later on, and that doubles our stages. At Lake Kambe, Waddell knocked down an antelope, a *khokong* (gnu). I was proud of it for him, for it was his first piece of big game, and pleased for ourselves because of the meat.

Directing our course N.N.W. through a wood, we came out on the dried-up lake of Isemvu, thence into the spongy valley of a stream, tributary to the Lumbé. At its source, it is nothing but a marsh ; two miles lower down are pools ; and farther on, joining itself to another affluent of the Lumbé, it forms impracticable swamps, stretching away out of sight. Impossible to get near the Lumbé. At 9 p.m., we halted at the edge of a forest, to pass Sunday there. " The Lumbé," said our enlighteners, " has only one known ford, and this ford is deep : the water reaches to the neck." This was sad news indeed. A visit that we paid it next day convinced us that this report falls far short of the truth. To reach the river, we must cross morasses, and skirt deep pools, treading a soft, saturated soil. At first sight, it seems physically impossible. Must we unload everything, take it all to pieces, carry luggage and waggon in our arms, and transport the whole in canoes? And how many days will that take us ? I dare not think of it.

ON THE LUMBÉ, RIGHT BANK, *September 20th.*

What a delicious day of rest we had here yesterday! The first since we set out. One must work all the week as we do to know with what joy we greet the Lord's Day. After breakfast and worship, each one seeks out a shady, quiet corner, and sleeps—sleeps as though he had never slept before. I read, write, meditate, and with one bound behold me travelling in every part of the world. I am in Leribé, . . . in Europe, . . . in France. I see those happy meetings which from afar seem to me like spiritual feasts. My sky darkens a little ; the solitude around me grows vaster ; I feel myself in a dry and thirsty land where no water is. Satan is not far off. But while I am letting my thoughts rove, a vision suddenly illuminates them. Rising to a higher plane, I see no longer merely the places known and loved, the Bethels of my pilgrimages, but I review the countries of the whole world where the preaching of the Good News resounds. I seem to hear it mounting towards the sky, from populous cities and deserts, from towns and hamlets, from continents and isles lost in the sea, a universal symphony of praise, wherein the diversities of human tongue are harmoniously blended. It seems to me that the day is about to break, in which every knee shall bow to Jesus, and every tongue confess that He is Lord, to the glory of God the Father! Then I take courage and leap for joy. Around me, it is true, all is yet silence and darkness. But what will it be when these tribes of the Zambesi and the nations of the interior see the Great Light, and join their voices to this mighty concert?

From here, we can still see our camp of last week : we have, however, made a great step forward, for then we were on the left bank, and here we are on the right bank. The Lumbé is a deep stream, and its banks cannot contain it. It spreads into a denuded plain, several miles wide, where it divides into an infinity of branches, separated by impassable swamps which are characteristic of the rivers in the intertropical and equatorial regions of this continent. It flows parallel to the Njoko from north to south, and thirty leagues from here throws itself into the Zambesi from the top of a basalt wall, where it forms a series of cascades. I have tried to determine its geographical position. For two days, we explored its course, some of us on foot, and some on horseback, without finding any ford but the one in front of us. However, discovering a less marshy place, where the waggons could approach the river without too much danger, we decided to pass our baggage over in canoes, and afterwards risk our empty vehicles at the ford already mentioned. Some petty chiefs, attracted by the bait of *setsibas*, soon ran up with some men. " The river was almost empty," an old man said to me ; " but since that terrible marvel of the other day, it has filled up again." Unlucky eclipse ! what calamities are not attributed to it? The canoes they brought were quite small : a single person with an oarsman can kneel in one, if he keep his balance very nicely. The idea occurred to me of coupling

them two and two, and thus we transported all our baggage
without the least accident. The passage of the ford was much
more dangerous. But we had taken our measures. With the
help of the thick cords of the country, we succeeded, not without
trouble, in preventing the teams and waggons from being carried
away by the current. There you have the work of a whole
week. With a bridge, it would have taken a few minutes. Poor
Africa ! Happy civilised countries !

Our provisions were at the lowest ebb, and there is a famine
in the country. Impossible to procure victuals before reaching
Ruyi.[1] And how get there with exhausted oxen ? We took a
great resolution. We chose the best oxen, took two waggons,
and left the two others, which we shall fetch later on. We gave
Franz and Kamburu the remainder of our food, calico, and
beads, and bade them good-bye. We travel much better now.
We have made seven leagues to-day towards the north-east,
still following the valley, or rather the plain, of the Lumbé. It
is not less than five or six miles across, and is bordered on both
sides by woods, sending out sandy spurs which we could not
avoid. The soil is rich in minerals, and we find here and there
the remains of former smelting furnaces. We are not far from
the celebrated mines of Kachenje, whence the Matolela[2] of
the whole country extract iron for their own use, as well as
for their small commerce and the tribute they owe to the king.
It would seem that, formerly, mining operations were seriously
carried on in the Lumbé Valley, as in all the tributaries of the
Zambesi. Evidently a dense population once dwelt there,
judging by the fields lying fallow, and the raised beds surrounded
by trenches, now covered with grass, where the manioc and
sweet potato were cultivated. From a distance one would take
them for tombs.

What has become of this population ? A melancholy problem. When I travelled by canoe on the Zambesi, and wondered
at the depopulation of so rich a country, my guide told me
that the inhabitants had retreated towards the interior for
greater security. And now the still more remote north is
pointed out to me as their whereabouts. At Sesheke, they told

[1] Or Luyi.

[2] This tribe has almost the monopoly of iron-smelting and working, the
making of knives, assegaïs, etc.

us that we should travel among numerous tribes—*Machaba-chaba*. Where are they? Here and there a village, a hamlet hidden in the woods—that is all. The conquest of the country by the Makololo has begun this work of destruction which the insatiable rapacity of the Barotsi still carries on.

In the hands of European colonists, this country would prove inexhaustibly rich. Everything could be cultivated there, the products of tropical as well as those of temperate climates. The drawback is the question of *markets*—that is, ways of transport. At any rate, even now there would be a work for commercial philanthropists to do. From the missionary point of view, if we were rich in men and means, there is room for a missionary establishment in the environs of Njoko. Already there are several villages there ; and one is justified in believing that the scanty population would group itself round a station. It would be a connecting link between Sesheke and Lealuyi.

September 22nd.

Misfortunes never come singly. First it is a sheep that dies, then a goat, then a calf. Good-bye to milk. Then it is an ox that breaks its leg, and must be slaughtered. All that is nothing. But here is my watch, my inseparable companion night and day, my repeater, the memento of a friend now in heaven, my only watch, which is broken and will not go. In vain I look at it, coax it, wind it ; its pulse has ceased to beat, and here I am without a watch. I had another indeed, but I was constrained to give it away in recognition of services rendered to us. I feel quite at sea. How can such a misfortune have befallen me ? Could it have been at the Lumbé, in wielding the hatchet through the woods ?

Another vexation. The guides given us by the chief Moana-Moari have led us astray. Having reached a path that they assured us was the right one, we left the Lumbé to plunge into the forest. We worked without intermission all the afternoon and the next morning to open the road. But the path swerved from south-west to south. That was not our direction ; I began to have my doubts. Close by a leafy shelter a fire was still burning, and we found there the remains of a recent meal. Evidently it was some travellers', who had just fled at our approach. In a moment, Aaron had mounted the horse. Oh that good horse, what services he has rendered us! God bless you, unknown friends who gave him to us. Aaron reached the travellers, allayed their terrors, and learnt from them that the path we were following led to the mines of Kachenje ; the road to Ruyi[1] is farther on. Good : there is so much labour lost! We retrace our steps, and push twelve miles farther on. Some travellers, who were bringing a troop of young girls for the service of the king's house, reassured us. " It is the highway to the capital ; there is no other." This highway is not two feet wide. It is because the natives, however numerous they be, never walk abreast, but always in single files, strictly observing the rules of precedence. We set to work again, and came out at the Isiki Pan. This is one of the numerous lakes dotted about between the Lumbé and the Ruyi, very shallow depressions of the soil, which partly dry up in spring, but which, at floodtime, form immense sheets of water from the surplus of the Zambesi. I succeeded in buying a little corn from the travellers we met, and even salt. Salt! Aaron, who scented it out before I did, went off secretly, and bought a tiny little calabash of it, which he presented to me. This salt is still quite full of sand and earth : all the same, it is salt ; and when one has been deprived of it for days, one could crunch it up like sugar.

AT THE RIVER MOTONDO, *September 29th.*

Nambora ka nkoli ! This was our nightmare ever since Sesheke. Every one spoke of it with terror. *Nambora ka nkoli*—that is, the forest "where one only drinks the water in his gourd." It is all thickets, sand, and thirst. The Zambesians have a terrible fear of thirst, and endure it very ill. The water of their river is delicious, and they drink it for pleasure. To be reduced to what is in one's gourd spells calamity. It took two days to make a passage through this ill-famed forest. Happily, Middleton, now that he no longer has his waggon, can take my hatchet and help me. It is only thirty miles across ; we entered it at two o'clock in the morning, and at

---

[1] In a private letter, M. Coillard says : " The Zambesians make a remarkable confusion of the *l* and the *r*. The natives do not seem to make mistakes, but the shade of difference still escapes us. We hear *Loboshi* and *Robosi*, used indifferently for king Lewanika's youthful name ; *Rumbé* and *Lumbé*, *Ruyi* and *Luyi*. Euphony seems to give the preference to the sound of *l* in Lealuyi." Major Serpa Pinto uniformly calls Robosi *Lobossi*.

night we had left it behind us. " No more difficulties ; we
have passed *Nambora ka nkoli.*" We came out upon an open
glade. It is neither a valley nor a plain. It is partly both—
an immense grassy track four miles wide, which appears on
the horizon north-north-east between little hills, and disappears
in the distance on the north-west between other blue hills—
a wide marsh, where the Motondo, without banks, spreads
out over a soil which it saturates like a sponge. Here and
there it forms deep pools, divides and subdivides into several
branches, which try to hollow out a channel each for itself.
On the banks of this immense swamp, a light crust forms,
elastic to the tread. Woe to the ox or the wheel that breaks
through it ! It will find a fathomless quagmire. Alas ! that
is just what befell us ; and though we had crossed our luggage
bit by bit in the cart, my empty waggon fell through, all four
wheels, as high as the floor ; and it was only after two days'
unspeakable labour that we got it out, almost by miracle. On
the principal arm of the Motondo, there is still to be seen
a confused mass of cleft stakes. These are the ruins of a bridge,
a rustic one indeed, which Lewanika in one of his expeditions
had made for his army to cross over.

AT THE RUYI RIVER, October 1st.

After the Motondo, here is the Ruyi, separated from us
by a wood eight miles broad. The Ruyi is an enlarged
edition of the Motondo—a marshy plain of similar appearance,
where the Ruyi meanders, spreads out, forms pools, ponds,
lagoons, and brooks. I rode on ahead, and directed my steps
towards an islet covered with huts, like straggling beads on
a rosary. At the sight of my extraordinary quadruped, some
big boys, who were herding cattle, broke off their games,
collected their cows, and fled with piercing cries. The men of
the village were more reasonable ; they came to meet me, and
led me across that labyrinth of ponds and watercourses which
they call the ford. The alluvial deposit having been carried
off by the rise of the waters, there is nothing left but a layer
of sand on a bed of clay. We should thus have passed without
any difficulty, if, at the principal stream, we had not fallen into
a quicksand. The chief, Kuangu-Muné, soon came to our help
with men and canoes. This venerable old man immediately

threw himself into the water, and, without saluting us, broke into voluble prayers and imprecations towards the gods, who are hostile to us. He sprinkled his arms, his chest, his forehead ; he spat on the oxen and spat on the waggon to exorcise them, while everybody looked on reverentially. The ceremony concluded, " You will come out of it now," he said, saluting me good-humouredly ; " I have conjured them away." Indeed, I gave him reason to think so, for, with the help of his canoes and his people, I immediately unloaded the waggon. When it had got free from the sand-bank, the night was advanced. I discovered the next day that the water had penetrated our cases, and caused us fresh losses ; and also that, favoured by the darkness, Kuangu-Muné's people had robbed us. That cast a cloud over our interview. He brought me food by way of salutation, and I made him a present worthy of his own. But I peremptorily refused the *setsibas* these people asked for their services of the day before, until the thief should be found and the things given back. We spent Sunday there to rest man and beast, and with the guides furnished by Kuangu-Muné we continued our tiring journey on Monday.

AT THE SPRINGS OF SEFULA, *October 9th.*

This is a date that thrilled us with joy. One more stage, they tell us, a long one, and we shall be there. It is like a beautiful dream. They told us, " Ruyi is the last river, the very last." But they did not tell us we had passed the last bad places. But let us speak no more of them. The long night journeys with waggons sinking in mire, or bumping against thick trees ; the day marches under a fiery sun, where the oxen bore the yoke so mournfully, and so painfully ploughed the sands, while the drivers dragged themselves wearily along, and guided their teams as if they had given up the last hope of being obeyed ; the unreasoning murmurs, and the agonising cares,—all these will now be over. Perhaps we shall have the consolation of finding ourselves in conflict with difficulties of another sort.

From Ruyi, bearing to the north-west, we pass Lake Mokangu, a fine expanse of water, then Kataba, then the brook of Moale, separated from one another by zones of forest, and communicating with the Zambesi, whose overflow they receive.

SEFULA—MR. WADDELL AND HIS UNWELCOME VISITOR.

[*To face page* 256.

The country itself presents the same aspect almost everywhere from Seskeke hitherto : plains, sands, denuded clearings,
and marshes—vast solitudes, so silent by day that it is hard to
believe they are inhabited, a melancholy panorama of extreme
monotony, in which it is difficult to find one's bearings.   The
dunes which run along the Njoko, and keep it confined in its
bed, form the sole exception.   With the intelligent Mangete
these interminable woods are not entirely without interest.
They readily acquaint you with the great variety of wild fruits
one finds there, the different kinds of honey, etc.   They show
you the india-rubber tree, a magnificent tree of the fig family,
which the Barotsi are fond of planting on the tombs of their
kings, and many other species of which they do not know the
commercial value.   You are especially struck by the grand
proportions of certain trees which are covered with a cork bark.
Not that this cork is good for anything ; but intelligent culture
might improve it.   I do not speak of the gums, nor of the wild
cotton one finds everywhere, nor yet of the precious fibres
which European industry could not fail to turn to account.   But
these Zambesian forests must not make you think of the
equatorial ones, still less of those in Europe or the New World.
No, our forests are what the English in Australia call *bush*—a
mass of trees and shrubs, torn about by the winds, stunted, and,
in general, prematurely old.   Life there languishes and easily
flickers out.   The sands of which we have to complain so much
cover up a very hard and impermeable layer.   That explains
at once the astonishing fertility of this sandy veldt where
irrigation is impossible, and the paralysis of aborescent growth.
There are exceptions to this.   By infiltration, all these depressions of the soil, these natural reservoirs they call *matsa*,
communicate with one another, and give birth to numerous
watercourses, like the Seba, the Siboya, the Sefula, the
Kanyonyo, etc.   Geology will one day reveal to us the mineral
riches of these countries, if any exist.

SEFULA, *October 16th to 23rd.*

From the Springs of Sefula, it took four days for a band of
twelve men to open a passage for us through the forest of
Kanyonyo.   And then, what a disappointment to find that the
little valley and the neighbouring heights were all covered with

springing fields, and that it was not possible for us to find a place to settle in. Thence consultations and new delays. Lewanika, annoyed with his people, sent word to us, " Establish yourselves at Kanyonyo ; the valley is yours ; they know it. Shut your eyes and ears ; graze your oxen among these fields ; don't disturb yourselves on that account." And in five or six weeks these starving people—for there is a famine—will be beginning to eat their maize, their sweet potatoes, and their pumpkins !

Without further hesitation, I steered for the place we had chosen two years ago. We arrived there on October 11th, in the evening, after a fatiguing and adventurous day. First, we had to cross the little river, which loses itself in a marsh. We spent the whole day beside it, unloading and reloading the waggons, dragging them through the morasses, carrying baggage on our backs across the bogs, waist-deep, among reeds and rushes, whose young shoots wounded the feet of our poor people.

Night fell. But a darkness deeper than that of night oppressed my spirit. I was seized with an awful and over-powering sense of helplessness, distress, and mental anguish. As soon as possible, I retreated to my waggon.

The cries of a fowl soon reached me ; then of another, then of a third. It was time to see to it. I took for granted that our rabble of Matolela were indulging in one of their favourite exploits—wringing chickens' necks. Waddell, always ready for anything, bravely took his mat and his gun, and posted himself behind the cart. Scarcely had he lain down than he detected a stealthy rustling. He listened with all his ears ; stared into the darkness ; and lo ! it was not a man, but a beast. He fired ; every one rushed up, and we found he had killed a leopard. What a reception, and what a prospect for us !

And so, after taking two months to cover about a hundred and fifty leagues, we have at last ceased wheeling. It seems strange to us. Neither my wife nor I have any taste for waggon journeys ; and that of course makes them so much the more tedious and prosaic. The tossing, wandering missionary life we have led has not been dictated by choice. We sigh for a few years' halt in our pilgrimage, for a little corner which we may yet be permitted to call our *home* on earth, and above all

for some work other than piling up bricks and mortar, clearing
and planting for our successors.

Our camp stands upon a sandy slope, covered with a layer
of ashes and with thick brushwood recently burned, in the midst
of a wood they have mercilessly rifled, shadeless, and most forbidding in aspect. From an elevation of a hundred feet, the
sight falls upon the Sefula, whose jungles and thickets hide the
stream ; it follows the verdant undulations of the woods beyond,
and then wanders over the distant hills whose blue mingles
with the sky. That is the south. On the west, it passes through
a few dried stumps and mutilated trees, then over this vast bare
expanse they call the Valley. Barotsi-land is not Basuto-land ;
still less is Sefula Leribé. . . . We shall get used to it. Busy
people do not know what home-sickness is. But alas ! at Sefula
everything has to be created, and we are no longer young. Shall
we ever have a single fruit tree there ?—a house ? We shall have
plenty of time to think about them. The great question which
preoccupies and absorbs me for the moment is the possibility
which threatens my wife and myself of being separated for a
whole year. By what means can I fetch her, make her travel
in the midst of the rains, and bring her here before the floods
overtake us in the desert ? How can we shelter ourselves in
the rainy season ? We should need to fly, if we are to make the
journey to Sesheke in a month, go and come back again ; and
an ox waggon on such roads cannot fly. I dare not think of
the river with its rapids, its dangers, its canoes always half full
of water.

The famine is such that we cannot find workmen. Every
one betakes himself to the woods, or goes fishing to provide
for the needs of his own. We ourselves are only living, like
every one else, on dried fish, which we buy at high prices, and
on cassava. The country is burnt up, the season advanced,
and we have not yet been able to find thatch to put a roof over
our goods, or even our own heads. All is dark. But I know
Him Who has said, " Call upon Me in the day of trouble : I will
deliver thee, and thou shalt glorify Me." He always keeps His
word. When the Christian is at the end of his resources, and
casts himself entirely upon God, help is not far off. " It is good
that a man should both hope and quietly wait for the salvation
of the Lord."

CHAPTER XVI

The Station of Sefula—Clearing the Ground—Lewanika's Palace—Industry of the Barotsi—Departure to fetch Mme. Coillard—The Thief of Time—An Ardent Sportsman—Justice at Sesheke—The Shadow of the Almighty —The Source of Weakness—A Ten Years' Pilgrimage—An Anxious Parting—Prosperous Journey to Sefula—Miseries of the Vassal Tribes—A Natural Phenomenon—Rapid Progress of Mission Buildings—The King's Tribute—A Visit from Lewanika.

SEFULA, BAROTSI VALLEY, *November 10th,* 1886.

HERE I am then at Sefula, on the little sandy plateau I spoke of, in the midst of a devastated wood, and under a tiny tent, which is riddled like a sieve, and lets in wind and rain by turns. I have planted it under a great mahogany tree for the sake of shade. Round me all is activity. Here are two boys tearing up clumps of bushes by the roots to make room for our cottage ; there is another charring uprights for our walls, that will preserve them from damp and from white ants. In the midst of the group over there, some young men are measuring, with noisy satisfaction, the *setsibas* they have just received, for having built a hut ; here are some more in single file bringing stakes and grass to make a second one. It will cost me ten yards of calico, the same as the first : five boys will have got all the materials together and finished it in three days ! A hundred paces off, a fold is being built ; and nearer at hand, in another direction, our friends Middleton and Waddell are sawing away with an energy it does one's heart good to see. As for me, I come and go, direct and superintend, lend a hand where it is most needed ; I buy reeds ; I bargain for millet, pumpkins, and manioc, exchange some words with my visitors, and resume my work. No more fish now, and the rains have spoilt all our provisions. The kitchen, which day after day repeats almost the same bill of fare, gives me little trouble, thanks to Nguana-Ngombé, who understands better than I how to make cassava with water, and boil pilled *mabele*. *His* watch never goes wrong, and our meals are almost as regular as if we had our good housekeeper.

Already our plateau looks rather less wild. We shall get used to it. Little by little the horned stumps and the brushwood will disappear ; eucalyptus trees, already sown, and other trees will take their place. And if ever we are rich enough to have a hydraulic pump, and bring water from the river to our slope, you will see what a pretty kitchen garden we shall have. *Flowers* we must seek for elsewhere, and fruits too.

Our relations with the king are most agreeable up to the present. Two days after our arrival, he hastened to visit us, accompanied by his headmen on horseback, and by numerous attendants on foot. He seemed really pleased to see us, and went away without having begged, and without his followers having robbed us of a single thing. That is saying not a little. After that, I spent Sunday with him, and had good audiences. I noticed, however, with pain that the women, at the morning service, hid themselves behind the wall of the *lekhothla*, and not one of them came to the afternoon service. Contrary to the established custom, Lewanika wanted to receive me at his own place, instead of letting me go to the Gambella's, the prime minister's. I must be the first to make use of his house. It is quite a recent construction, the work of Mambari merchants,[1] and he is not a little proud of it. The sentiment is thoroughly shared by all his people. Some one of whom I asked the road said to me, " Go straight on, and upon the other side of these shrubs, even before you see the town, a great house will rise up before you, and *call you*." When Lewanika beamingly introduced me to this palace, I said to him, joking, that I was tempted to take possession of it for my wife. He responded laughing, with all the courtliness of a high-born gentleman, " That is but natural : the house is yours, my father." It is composed of three apartments, sixteen or seventeen feet square, daubed and plastered by the hand, with ceilings of rushes, so well made and so strong that one could use them for granaries. One of the rooms has a pavilioned ceiling. The whole building is constructed of stakes and reeds, without *a single nail*: for where in the country could you find a nail ? There are

[1] The half-civilised negroes of the Portuguese coast.

instead forks which dovetail ingeniously into one another, and are held in place by withes of bark. The walls are fourteen feet high, with a little verandah, which gives the buildings a somewhat imposing appearance. None of the Mambari understand thatching, so the Barotsi had to do it in their own fashion—that is, the reverse of ours.

Lewanika would gladly overwhelm us with apprentices, grown-up men, whom he would like to see learning in a couple of months or so to accomplish every possible handicraft of the whites. We have had to check so much zeal, for "famine is the mayor of our commune." The king himself tries all the tools he sees. He was making a ladder when I was there; but he is so rough, he broke an auger of mine. Of course I did not scold him, but neither did I thank him.

It was last Monday that I finally succeeded in sending off the waggons to Sesheke to fetch my wife. I am going to follow by canoe to save time. It was not our original plan. I was to stay here to prosecute our work of installation, while my dear wife made the journey all alone. It was at her suggestion that I submitted to this arrangement. But the journey proved far more difficult and laborious than we then supposed, and the season is so far advanced that it is absolutely necessary to sacrifice something and make a desperate effort.

The king came to see the waggons start, and give his instructions to three petty chiefs and their people who are charged to conduct us, to show us the fords, and above all to call together the Mangete and Matolela to clear the road through the woods. He brought me a fine young ox, which was at once put under the yoke to break it in, and another which he killed. He had much to say, and spent the night with us. We especially discussed the question of his capital, and the next day we rode together to explore the surrounding parts of the Valley. He chose a place, three or four miles from here, where he will install himself in January during the floods; and if it answers to his requirements, he will then settle permanently there; and this is almost certain.

SESHEKE, *December* 10*th*, 1886.

Behold a grand leap of three hundred miles (400 kilometres) from Sefula to Sesheke! But it took me some time to accomplish it. After having sent off my waggons, built my hut and my "kraal," made my arrangements, and put the work in hand, I began to think of my voyage. "Nothing easier than to have canoes," said Lewanika: "you want two; I will give you four." But the days passed quickly, and—no canoes. To every message I received the same answer, "To-morrow," and next day it was still "To-morrow," but no canoes. I was on thorns. If I had had two horses, I should have set out and rejoined the waggons. But what could I do with only one? At last, on November 16th, in the evening, arrived Luchanana, one of the king's favourites, who has charge of my person, and of the expedition. The 17th, at daybreak, Middleton harnessed the cart, and brought me to the ford—ten miles at least across pools and deep puddles. What was not our dismay to find only one canoe! The second we were to find on the way; the third would follow us later; and the fourth—mine—was left behind, and we must go and fetch it, fifteen or sixteen miles from here.

So there I was, on a little sandy islet, roasting in the sun, every day repeating the A B C of patience—a hard lesson for such a scholar as myself. My voyage is very queerly organised. If it be thus that our friend Lewanika directs the affairs of the realm, I do not wonder there are revolutions. The boat having arrived—a royal barge, thirteen yards long, but so old and leaky that we could hardly keep it afloat—we started. In passing, I paid an interesting visit to the queen.

Now we really are on the way. But no! My mentor is a passionate devotee of hunting; and although he has promised me to make forced stages to redeem the lost time (which never *is* redeemed), he slips unperceived from the boat, and disappears for the whole day: he hunts to his heart's content, and then goes on a pilgrimage to some tomb to pray for rain, and for the prosperity of our voyage. He receives my reprimands respectfully, but his passion for hunting prevails over his promises. How should he resist the temptation of pursuing a troop of buffaloes! And how can I look sourly at him, when he returns to camp triumphantly with two or three fine antelopes? One evening, a troop of elephants came to drink, quite close to our bivouac. Instantly, all fires were put out; every one was on the alert. "Bang! bang! bang!" A plaintive cry made us think the shots had told. The animal, evidently

left alone, was about to bathe.   Once more, firing—more groans.
Next day the pools of blood declared we had not been mistaken.
The spoor was followed, and an hour later the creature lay on
the ground, riddled with balls, and pierced with assegaïs.   Good-
bye to our journey, for we must cut up the monstrous pachyderm
—a big affair.   Moreover, besides hunting, my rowers never
pass a village of Makalaka without requisitions, by which we
lose an immensity of time.   They do not understand that I am
in a hurry.   " If we don't arrive this month, we shall arrive the
month after : patience, we are getting along comfortably."

At the Falls of Ngonye, we had to leave my barge, which
threatened every moment to founder, and transport the others
down the cataract.   From the first moment they perceived us,
the Makalaka dispersed and hid in the woods ; and it is
incredible what threats, what abuse, our people must resort to,
in order to bring them together and force them to perform their
corvée.   And that causes fresh delays.   One part of the company
goes on foot ; the other must wait for it ; and the stages are
short.   And then the river is at its lowest ; the navigation of the
rapids is perilous and fatiguing.   We do not get on.   And I so
wanted to arrive on November 28th for a little family festival.
Spurred on by the thought that every day's delay threatened to
render our waggon journey quite impossible, I sent an express
to my wife—two boys with a little canoe.   They promised me
to be at Sesheke in three days.   Eight days later, we found
them in a village at one day's distance.   A hippopotamus had
upset the canoe, and broken it to pieces ; the boys had barely
escaped with their lives ; and my letter with the leather case
lay at the bottom of the river.   And during this time, the
waggons having arrived at Sesheke, my dear wife and all our
small world conceived such alarm, that they sent people to
enquire after me as far as Sekosi, and were preparing to take
other steps.

I found my wife a perfect skeleton, but otherwise in good
health, as well as all the other members of our little colony.
No fever this season : we bless God for it.   During my absence,
the thieves, whom nobody punishes, became bolder ; they even
entered by night the hut where Aaron's wife and children were
sleeping, and stole some clothes, all they could lay their hands
upon.   On my return, we brought the affair before the *lekhothla.*

The chiefs laughed at our complaints, and spoke of a fine which we could demand—*we ourselves !* But as we insisted that the culprits should be punished, they promised to send and search for them, and the matter rests there.

You will rejoice, will you not, to learn that Lewanika proposes to settle close to Sefula? We can, I think, have a fine school as soon as we have a house. But who will take charge of that school? Aaron is better gifted for evangelisation than for teaching. We have no longer my niece with us; and my dear wife, who is no longer strong, has the whole charge of a great household on her hands. As for myself, I must be a little free to direct the works and visit the villages. We must still lift our eyes beyond the Everlasting Hills, whence cometh our help.

Our hearts sink at the thought that we are going to leave the Jeanmairets alone with the Levi family. What troubles us so much is the difficulty of communications. I hope, however, that we shall be able to exchange letters every two months. But in two months how many things might happen! We ought to be two families on each station *to begin with.* It is a measure dictated by prudence and safety; and the needs of the country oblige us to have a station at Sesheke as well as at the Valley. Our circumstances are not exactly brilliant, and I dare not say anything as yet of the prospect before us. We are without human protection in this land of murder and rapine. It is in God alone that we must place all our confidence. He never leaves us. Oh, how many times we too can say, " He strengthened me *with strength* in my soul," and when we are assailed by swarms of doubts, "The Lord will perfect that which concerneth me "! As to the heathen themselves, we cannot be disappointed, for we know beforehand they have never had the Gospel.

Who has such a good reason as the missionary for believing in the communion of saints and the power of prayer? The angel of the Lord encampeth round about them that fear Him, and delivereth them; and in the midst of such an army, we have more—we have the prayers of saints, which form a mighty wall round the servant of God, and descend on him in a dew of blessings. What a privileged position! Ah, if we only had faith like a grain of mustard seed—real, daring faith—faith which believes in miracles! In theory, it is certainly there ; but in practice, in the details of life, where is it? I am always under-standing better how odious in the Lord's sight is the sin—I will not say of infidelity, but of lack of faith ! He has made us such glorious promises ; He has never broken His word. How then dare we doubt? Do you know a painful impression I have brought away from Europe ? It is that scepticism, like a subtle poison, has injected itself into all the veins of the Church. *Strong* convictions are rare. People float about in uncertainty, and pity those who still have profound and decided convictions, as though they were behind the times. Thence springs the weakness of the pulpit. I feel urged to repeat to young men the words of the Apostle, " Let the word of Christ dwell in you *richly*."

SEFULA, *January* 15*th*, 1887.

Sefula is not precisely an El Dorado ; neither is it the end of our difficulties—far from it ! But Sefula is the terminus of a three years' journey, and of a wandering life of ten years. It was in 1877, indeed, that we left our peaceful home in Leribé, for the unknown country of the Banyaï. We little thought that this journey, which was only to last some months, would end at the Zambesi, at the sacrifice for us of a much-loved work, and at the foundation of a new mission. Since then, we have never laid down the pilgrim's staff. If we had foreseen all that lay before us, courage would probably have failed us. But God in His great goodness has led us step by step. It was by degrees, and, so to speak, insensibly, that we arrived at the angle of the road where our missionary life took a new direction. God thus condescends to the weakness of His children. He spares them, while He is carrying on their education ; He hovers above their path, and makes it easy for them ; and they, borne up by the Everlasting Arms, " going from strength to strength," are quite astounded, when they look back, to perceive the progress made and the results obtained.

It is not without emotion that I inscribe this date, which opens a new era in the history of our mission. It will figure there for a long while in the future, I am certain of it, as our Jehovah-Jireh, and as an international monument of faith and unity. It is also our Ebenezer ; in setting it up, we can truly say, " Hitherto hath the Lord helped us " ; and we gaze into the future without anxiety, with serene confidence.

Let us, now, beware of a spasmodic zeal, subject to the caprices of fashion and vanity. For you who give and pray, as much as for us who are at the breach, the work confided to us is pre-eminently a work of patience, of perseverance, and of faith. Let us be ready to do it in the midst of the most serious dangers, the most acute disappointments, and the most costly sacrifices. Let nothing turn us back. The disasters of Dr. Holub's expedition, the martyrdom of Bishop Hannington, that of a Wesleyan missionary and his wife on the west coast, the massacre of Count Porro, and of M. and Mme. Barral, and other like facts, clearly tell that not with impunity can science, civilisation, and Christianity attack the Black Continent, one of the principal fortresses of Satan. Let us lay aside all timidity and mere human modesty ; let us be bold and audacious. Adolphe Monod has said, " Let us pray as though we could do *nothing*; let us work as though we could do *everything*!" The work is ever increasing before our eyes, in extent as well as in difficulties. We feel more than ever our weakness and our insufficiency. But the immutable promises of God are there in all their reality, and without other limits than our faith and the power of the eternal God. The conversion of the most degraded and brutalised souls, and the transformation of nations by the preaching of the foolishness of the Cross, are no longer miracles which the most sceptical can call in doubt ; they are accomplished facts, which history has many times set forth since the beginning of our century, without going further back. Therefore let us expect *great things*. " *If thou wilt believe*, thou shalt see the glory of God."

You will perhaps remember that it was on August 16th that I left Sesheke to make the first journey to the Valley by waggon. My dear wife and I had never been separated for so long a time and in such serious circumstances, and this widowhood was a hard trial. We have suffered terribly from the endless obstacles cast in our way, which almost made all our plans miscarry. If any one had told me beforehand that we should only leave Sesheke finally on December 15th to go to the Valley, I should probably have shared the pessimism of all those who declared the impossibility of such a journey at

that season ; for last year, at the same date, my waggon had
not been able to cross the inundated plains of the Kasaya and
the Nguesi to go to Mambova. They called my undertaking
madness, and said aloud what I apprehended secretly—namely,
that the floods would overtake us on the way, that we should
not be able either to advance or retreat, and should be held
in the swamps till winter.

Our departure from Sesheke was most dismal—a dark night
and pelting rain. For some days, the rise of the Zambesi waters
increased our uneasiness. I will say nothing of the parting
from our dear niece and her husband, with the prospect of a
hundred and fifty leagues' distance dividing us, and of a reunion
which climate and circumstances will render difficult, if not
impossible. Sesheke, as the capital of an immense province,
and as the door of the country, is a post which only yields in
importance to Lealuyi itself. It is simply absurd that there
are only two of us to occupy it. We wait impatiently for the
reinforcements we have desired of God and of yourselves. May
God watch over Sesheke and His servants !

In spite of the most sinister predictions, we made a rapid
and prosperous journey. It rained a great deal—it was the
season for that—but it was generally either in the night, or on
Sunday, or during our halts, and it did not make us lose a
single stage. The rivers overflowed and gave us trouble : we
expected that. At each we had to have our luggage brought
over in canoes, and once even to take our waggons to pieces,
as at Kazungula ; but everywhere the Mangete and Matolela
showed good-will and eagerness to help us. They greeted us
joyfully as old acquaintances. Not only were they satisfied with
very small remuneration, but they stole nothing from us, which
is saying a good deal.

We ought to put a boat on each of these streams. Taking
advantage of some special donations given us for the purpose,
I have ordered several ; but boats are difficult to find as long
as the king and the chiefs of the nation are not provided.
Besides a dozen men, Lewanika had sent three petty Matolela
chiefs " to take care of my wife, and bring her in safety to the
Valley." They belonged to the clan of the *Mayela-fatse*, the
earth-eaters, so-called because they eat on the floor instead
of using the usual dishes. The king Sepopa, whose personal

THE LEKHOTHLA AT LEALUYI—MATOLELA BRINGING TRIBUTE AND SALUTING THE KING.

attendants they were, used to feed them by throwing on the ground the remains of the royal dishes, or rather bowls. They contrived to win their master's confidence to such a point that he established them in the midst of the *Makuengoa* tribe, which he was not sure of. These little dignitaries, proud of their mission, held their heads high, talked big, and forced the Mangete to give them abundance of food and to carry their packages. Poor Mangete! how sorry we feel for them! Kalangu, who is one of their principal chiefs, and a very worthy man, confided his troubles to me, and implored me to use my influence over the king—for he thinks I have influence—to ameliorate their lot. The chiefs of Sesheke had just had a grand hunt, lasting ten days, in this neighbourhood: "they had passed like a cloud of locusts, leaving nothing behind them." "We do not complain," he said; "they are our masters." Next came one of the principal officers of the king's household, a *sekomboa*, who, displeased by the quantity of the victuals Kalangu had hastened to send him, seized those who had brought them (Kalangu's own son among the number), and throttled them in the Barotsi fashion.

On January 10th, in the morning, we entered the rich and beautiful valley where the Sefula takes its rise. You should have seen the sensation produced by our appearance! People, great and small, ran breathlessly from all parts, women especially. They came in front of us, and blocked our way, the better to see the white lady, a natural phenomenon, which had never before been witnessed in the country; and then there was a storm of hand-clapping, a perfect bombardment of "*Shangwe! Khosi! lumela ma rona!*" ("Your servants, master! We greet you, our mother!"). It was in the midst of a noisy crowd, which swelled at every step, that we arrived at the station. Since then, fresh troops succeed each other at every hour of every day. Some people bring little presents of welcome, the products of their fields, and all bring cordial salutations. On the whole, our impressions are favourable in studying the faces (which study us too). We seek involuntarily among these people the "brothers and sisters" who are promised us, and whom the grace of God will reveal to us one day. We seek also to discover among them resemblances to those we have left, but always bear on our hearts, and we mentally place names that are dear to us upon their heads. We shall love these Barotsi, not only as human beings for whom Christ died, but as sociable fellow-creatures. We could even hope before long to win their confidence and affection, were it not for the rule of tyranny and mutual suspicion under which they live.

Our dear friends Middleton and Waddell were in good health. Their life had been hard during my absence, and it was not astonishing that they had had several attacks of fever, though light ones. It was with ill-concealed emotion that they bade my wife welcome to Sefula. They had lost all hope of her arriving before the winter. In spite of incessant rains and great difficulties, they had succeeded in putting a thatched roof over a cabin of two rooms, made with stakes and reeds. We have now to daub it, to make a mud floor, and to let it dry, which will take weeks. Meanwhile, the waggon is our sleeping apartment; we take our meals in a grass hut, open to all the winds, and infested in the evening with mosquitoes and every sort of insect pest, making all work and even reading impossible. The forest where we are building, which I had left quite black, charred with the fire, has become a thicket of brushwood, which is still growing vigorously. One can hardly distinguish the roof of the cottage at fifty paces, in the midst of this undergrowth. It was stifling. I wondered that our helpers could live there during two months. These thick bushes, where a little black snake abounds (said to be very dangerous), are at the same time haunted by the hyæna and the panther. They have made frequent incursions into the camp by night; and we had to organise a regular hunt after them. You ought to have seen the delight of Nguana-Ngombé, and of my other boys, when they related to me how they had killed two of these monsters at a few paces from our doors.

Alas! in a neighbouring village, a young slave, who was dying of hunger, had stolen a few stalks of maize in the night. She was roasting them by the fires of our sleeping shepherds, and devouring them noiselessly, when all at once a hyæna sprang upon her, and carried her off into the woods. The next day, nothing was found of her but some fragments of flesh and scattered bones. Consequently, we must fortify ourselves with good palisades, and clear away the brushwood—a considerable work. Will you believe that it costs me a pang to uproot even one of these trees ?—for in Basuto-land I planted trees during twenty years, hoping to bury myself in them as in a forest.

No more famine now; there is abundance of food since harvest. Our young men can always be nibbling some stalks of green maize, which people passing by give them. We can provide ourselves chiefly with field purslane, pumpkins, young gourds, etc. Only it runs away with calico. A piece is no sooner begun than we tremble to see it finished. Whatever one may think, the system of barter is not economical. The cost of transport is considerable. Our small change is pocket-handkerchiefs, and above all *setsibas*. One can scarcely buy anything or obtain the smallest service without the *setsiba*. It is an obligatory present with what I may call the *bourgeoisie* of the country: the aristocracy is naturally more exacting. You can understand that we consume a considerable quantity of calico, and that, in spite of our calculations, we often run short. The age of money, which Lewanika invokes with all his vows, though without understanding it, has not yet dawned for us.

Just now, one sees in every direction long strings of people laden with burdens. As in the time of Solomon, it is the king's tribute: honey, pelts, wild fruits, fishing tackle, mats, etc.—the produce of the fields, of the chase, and of industry. The queen has her tribute like the king. The whole, brought to the *lekhothla* with great ceremony, is divided among the chiefs of the nation.[1] This gives Lewanika plenty of occupation and preoccupation, for he has to deal tactfully with jealousies and rivalries, as well as with the rapacity of those persons who make and unmake kings, according to their own caprices.

Saturday, January 22nd.

On Thursday morning, the drum and the *serimba* announced from afar the arrival of the king. Such was the panic, that the people who had come to work, to sell, or to visit had almost all disappeared in the twinkling of an eye. Notwithstanding this, soon afterwards there was a crowd, and one which renewed itself every instant, to do homage to the sovereign. The coming and going, the bivouacs, the fires, the animated conversations, the games full of originality—and the royal music

---

[1] The king's own portion is carried at night to his establishment: nobody but the confidential officer in charge must see it.

which by day makes one dizzy, and at night ruthlessly drives away sleep along with the evil spirits—all that confusion, uproar, and mob, while they do not lack interest, did not spare us fatigues of more kinds than one.   And now that the royal party has gone back towards the capital, it is a comfort to find ourselves peacefully alone.

Lewanika came to pay a visit of ceremony to Mme. Coillard, and he thought no doubt that it was the correct thing to surround himself with court ceremonial.   Poor man! he is not free from cares, and he needs a friend to whom he can freely confide them, and on whom he can lean.   He is suspicious of everybody, even of those who have brought him to power, and unfortunately he does not conceal it.   Thus he has confirmed the vague apprehensions which haunted us—namely, that there exists among the chiefs a party hostile to strangers, which sees our presence in the country with an evil eye.   May we have the wisdom which comes from above, so that, whether at Sesheke or Sefula, we may know how to conquer and to maintain our position, and even to gain influence!

Gloomy and careworn in private, Lewanika in public is chatty and gay.   He had brought with him not only his detestable band of music, but also his clowns.   One of them, dressed in a hyæna skin, imitated so perfectly the cries, the laughter, and the gait of this wild beast, that the very dogs were taken in, and rushed out at him.[1]   Plays of this kind are very popular here, and the actors are always sure of their fees; moreover, they never give up their *rôle*, even though it should knock them up for days afterwards.   The Zambesians do not know how to speak in public, nor to treat business with the decorum of the Basuto: they like jocularity; no one is safe from the keen shafts of their mockery and ridicule.   One can scarcely imagine that people of so playful a nature can be so cruel.   Alas! we cannot take even a few steps without striking our feet against a broken skull, or some burnt human bones.

---

[1] It seems that some tribes, who believe in the transmigration of souls, decide during their lifetime what animal form they will adopt after death. The medicine-man undertakes that their wishes shall be carried out, and on every possible occasion, especially new moons, funerals, and public festivals, they *practise* in their future character of lion, crocodile, jackal, etc.

Lewanika showed us the remains of the fuel which, quite recently, ten paces from here, had been used to burn the sorcerers. Yes, " the dark places of the earth are full of the habitations of cruelty " (Ps. lxxiv. 20).

A Letter to the Committee of the Société des Missions Évangéliques de Paris.

Sefula, Upper Zambesi, June 1st, 1887.

Gentlemen and honoured Brethren,—The missionary expedition which you did me the honour of confiding to me has now fulfilled its purpose. After the vicissitudes known to you, it has crossed the Zambesi, and installed some of its members at Sesheke, while the others have at last attained its final destination, the Barotsi Valley, three years after leaving Basuto-land. It is to God, first of all, that Mme. Coillard and myself give thanks, for having caused an enterprise to prosper which we had at heart, but which we knew bristled with difficulties, and for which we felt ourselves little qualified. But we feel urged to express our very sincere gratitude to you also, gentlemen, to our revered president, and our dear director. We know that, besides your confidence, you have given us your affection. You have borne us up in your prayers ; you have watched over us ; and in the midst of our difficulties and our isolation, your words have ever been able to reach us, to reanimate our courage and strengthen our faith. You have worked side by side with us when the stream was pushing you in another direction. Moreover, while we look up to you as the representatives of our Churches and our directors, we may also recognise in each of you a friend and colleague.

You will surely have seen the hand of God which has led us so marvellously during our long pilgrimages, and you will have seen His holy will writ large in the success He has granted us.

Therefore it is without the slightest hesitation, and with the greatest confidence, that I point out the Zambesian countries as a new field of work for the French-speaking Churches, and lay their interests on your hearts. Do adopt this new work, with the increase of responsibility, but also of blessings which it may bring you.

You have already anticipated me by sending us reinforcements. Blessed be they in the name of the Lord ! I will take my place among these young labourers, *pars inter pares.* I do not ignore the fact that there are many problems to resolve, many difficulties to conquer, many sacrifices to be made and dangers to be faced ; but such a noble task is not beyond you, since God confides it to you. Therefore accept this work of the Barotsi Valley unreservedly, and watch tenderly over it, as over a newborn babe. And may it be an immense blessing to the tribes of Central Africa, and to the Christians themselves who support it ! Such is the ardent prayer of yours truly in the Lord,

F. COILLARD.

PART III

A T   S E F U L A

1887—1892

BATTLE SONG OF GUSTAVUS ADOLPHUS.

Fear not, O little flock, the foe
Who madly seeks your overthrow;
    Dread not his rage and power;
What though your courage sometimes faints,
His seeming triumph o'er God's saints
    Lasts but a little hour.

As true as God's own word is true,
Nor earth nor hell with all their crew
    Against us shall prevail.
A jest and byword are they grown:
God is with us; we are His own;
    Our victory cannot fail.

C. Winkworth—*From the German.*

AT SEFULA

JANUARY 1887 TO OCTOBER 1892

CHRONICLE

Jan. 12th, 1887 ...	...	Arrival of M. and Mme. Coillard at Sefula.
March 4th ...	...	School established at Sefula.
Aug. 20th ...	...	Arrival of M. and Mme. Louis Jalla from the Waldensian Valleys, and of Dr. Dardier and M. Goy from Switzerland —First Missionary Conference (at Kazungula).
Feb. 23rd, 1888 ...	...	Death of Dr. Dardier.
Oct.	...	King Lewanika proposes to place Barotsi-land under British protection—Proposal negatived by chiefs.
Dec. 1st	...	Departure of catechists Aaron and Levi.
June 1889 ...	...	Mr. Ware obtains from Lewanika a large concession for a British mining company.
Aug.	...	Second Missionary Conference (at Sesheke).
Sept.	...	Arrival of M. Adolphe Jalla at Sefula from the Waldensian Valleys.
Oct. 31st ...	...	Establishment of a station at Kazungula under M. and Mme. Louis Jalla.
April (end) 1890 ...	...	Arrival of Mr. Lochner, the agent of the B. S. A. Co., to treat with Lewanika.
May 25th ...	...	Baptism of Nguana-Ngombé (Andreas).
June 27th ...	...	Lewanika signs a treaty with the B. S. A. Co., granting mining concessions in return for protection over the whole of Barotsi-land.
June	...	Departure of the Jeanmairets.
July	...	Arrival of Mlle. Kiener from Switzerland—M. and Mme. Goy placed in charge of Sesheke.
Oct. 8th, 1891 ...	...	Arrival of catechist Paulus Kanedi.
March 1891—June 1892		M. A. Jalla's journey to Europe.
Oct. 28th, 1891 ...	...	Death of Mme. Coillard.
Sept. 5th, 1892 ..	...	Return of M. A. Jalla with Mme. Jalla.
Oct. 28th 1892 ..	...	M. Coillard removes his headquarters to Lealuyi.

CHAPTER XVII

Beginnings of the Work at Sefula—A Council at Lealuyi—The Barotsi's View of Missions—The Execution of a Sorcerer—The Marriage Question—Poison *v.* Bloodshed—The House built—School established—Difficulties of Discipline—Trial by Ordeal—"Thou shalt not kill"—The Missionary's Daily Life—Industrial Skill of the Barotsi—Their Character—Arrival of Reinforcements—Plots and Counterplots—MM. Dardier and Goy—An Equestrian Adventure—A Tragedy.

SEFULA, *February 1st,* 1887.

WE have been three weeks at Sefula. It is a pause, but no repose. My dear wife is utterly worn out with fatigue. It cost us a good deal to set off on wheels again so soon to visit Lealuyi, the capital, nineteen miles from here. But we had promised to do it; so on Monday, very early, we started. Kamburu was our official conductor. Nguana-Ngombé, in short breeches, with my old felt hat on his head paddled along through the puddles, and frightened the birds with the report of his gun; he was aspiring to be a hunter. From the hamlets lining the Valley, the people came running, as much to see the house on wheels as to greet us. Troops of men, returning from the capital, kept crossing the path of other parties, who were betaking themselves thither, laden with bundles and baskets of cornstuffs for their masters. The waggon was empty; the plain, and the pools of water studding it, presented no difficulties whatever; the weather was superb; so we could enjoy this little journey as a holiday. The king was expecting our visit; but we were none the less obliged to send Narumango to announce us, conformably with etiquette. Long before he had come back, a turbulent crowd had rushed to meet us, flung itself upon the waggon at the risk of being crushed, taken it by storm, and, in spite of us, invaded it on all sides. It was thus escorted, and harassed by this ever-growing mob, that we drew up on the public square. Here we

277

must needs wait for his Majesty. It was not pleasant; the sun was scorching.

Here comes my messenger at last, with a *sekomboa* from the king : one of his chamberlains we should say. "The king is still seeking a house for you, and begs you to wait." Before long, another message : "I am commanded to conduct you to your lodging, a few steps from here." It is a dilapidated hovel, almost unapproachable for filth. When will these Barotsi, these lords who are so exacting when we receive them, understand the rudiments of hospitality ? I feel provoked : but what is the use ? The best thing to do is to take a spade, and with my boys set to work and clear it up. Thereupon arrives the king, accompanied by his councillor, to wish us welcome. "What!" said he, with some embarrassment, "they have put you in a wretched place." "That's all right," I said to myself; "the lesson has not been thrown away." A little later, I was obliged to yield to his importunities : our waggon was dragged, almost carried, by all the men of the village, chiefs and serfs, close up to a grand royal hut, surrounded by a wide courtyard, and situated in the shade of a thicket.

This little grove is a sacred place, carefully surrounded with mats. It is composed of *mothata*, indiarubber trees, euphorbias, bananas,[1] some climbing plants, etc. ; an infinite number of gazelles' horns are to be found there, filled with mysterious specifics and charms of every sort ; a cord, stretched like our telegraph wires, seems to be for the purpose of showing out evil spirits and spells into the open veldt. It is Lewanika's sanctuary ; it is thither that he repairs regularly, to hold communion with the gods.

Poor Lewanika ! in his pillow thorns are thicker than feathers. His projected expedition against the Mashukulumboe

---

[1] In the Barotsi Valley, the bananas were planted only for "medicine." They had been introduced by a sorcerer from the West Coast, and the king alone had the right to plant them and sit under them. One day, M. Coillard asked the king for some of the fruit of the banana in whose shade he was sitting. "What do you want it for?" asked Lewanika. "To eat, of course.' "Why, is it good to eat?" M. Coillard recommended him to try ; the immediate result being that bananas were classed, with honey and some other natural products, among the dainties only royalty might enjoy. There are no other fruit trees in the Barotsi Valley.

meets with opposition, and opposition irritates him. He was greatly agitated ; he paced up and down, and ended by staying at the waggon till a very late hour. From time to time, he would address to me some commonplace in Sesuto ; next, with surprising volubility, pour forth torrents of Serotsi ; then, all at once, burst out with something in Sesuto again, with great peals of laughter, which were greeted by incessant hand-clappings from his favourite servitors, kneeling before him. " Well, Moruti," he exclaimed, turning towards me, " it's all up with my expedition ; you disapprove of it, and my people won't have it. . . . Ah ! " he added bitterly, clicking his tongue and sighing deeply, " everything is difficult with these people. If I speak of a field to be tilled, *ba nyanda*—they grumble ; of a house to be built—*ba nyanda* ; of a hunting expedition —*ba nyanda. Ba nyanda tsotle. Ba nyanda ka metla. Ba nyanda kaofela, bontsu boo !*[1] They always grumble, they all grumble, they grumble at everything ! That black rabble !" I felt really sorry for him.

Next morning, from seven o'clock on, the drums, *serimbas*, and an uproar of salutations announced that the king was sitting in the forum—the *lekhothla* ; so there we betook ourselves. A *pitso* had been called together in our honour ; it was crowded. At the request of Lewanika, I opened the proceedings with a speech, in which I was at pains to set forth the character of our mission, and the benefits of the Gospel to a nation. I expected the king would speak in his turn. What was our stupefaction to see the Gambella (the prime minister) rise next, and begin thus : " Barotsi, you see the *Baruti* before you ; you have heard them. If you do not wish for them, fear not to say so, and they will return to their own home. Speak freely ; now is your opportunity. Do not say that the king imposes on you a thing you dislike. Speak ! "

The silence only lasted a few minutes ; but these minutes seemed hours to me. Could it be that we had fallen into a trap ? Why should our very acceptance be called in question ? And how if they were going to declare publicly that they would none of us ?

---

[1] *Bontsu boo* = " that black thing " : a term of contempt used by the Barotsi in speaking of the populace—the *canaille*. " Those blackamoors " would perhaps be the nearest equivalent.

Happily, we had not to wait long. The first orator was indignant, that there should be any doubt of the friendly disposition of the tribe. "Gambella," said he, "your insinuations are an insult to us and to the king. When did he ever bestow anything bad upon us? If he sent for a *Moruti*, was it not because he knew it was a good thing? Do we not hear it said that all the black nations have their missionaries, to teach the young, and those who govern, the wisdom of the white men? And would you wish us Barotsi to stay in a dark hole? You cannot think it. Rather let us thank Robosi for having brought us light. *Na ke ithumetse Morena*" ("As for me, I approve the king's deed").

The keynote had been struck; several spoke in similar terms; and we were beginning to breathe more freely, when a little bit of a man, pitted with small-pox, cried, "What! you speak like this, Barotsi; what cowards and liars you are! No, you do not like these foreigners, you do not like to see them in your country; you fear them; but you have not courage to tell the king so to his face. Well then, I will speak myself. These foreigners bring the curse with them. Is it not they who made the sun to rot?" (the total eclipse)—"and who distress us with drought? Cease your lies and flatteries; speak out, and declare you will have nothing to do with these whites; and without hesitation, send them back whence they came."

"No," replied another, "we will not drive away the missionaries; they bring the *Lengoalo*" (Scriptures, a corruption of the classical Sesuto *Lingolo*, literally writings or instruction), "and wisdom, peace, and prosperity. I understand myself that we shall have a mine of stuffs and of waggons: but how shall we draw them, since we have no oxen, and the *Moruti* disapproves of our expedition against the Mashukulumboe?"

"That's just it," interrupted a new orator: "learning is a thing that is only fit for women and children" (*ntho ea malapa*); "cattle is the business of men and of the *lekhothla*. So let us leave Litia" (Lewanika's heir) "and the boys of his age with the *Moruti*; and as for ourselves, let us go and get cattle; our families are starving."

"You understand nothing about it," spoke Liomba, a wise man, who has seen the world, during a stay he made at Mangwato. "Our expedition against the Mashukulumboe has nothing to do with the question of the missionaries. The *Baruti* are the fathers of the nation. I saw that well enough at Mangwato. Every day in the *lekhothla* the great chief Khama was stitching furs. ' It is for my missionary and friend,' he told us, ' M. Coillard, who has gone to the Zambesi.' Khama is a Christian, and so are all his people. (You don't believe that, do you?) They are all dressed European fashion; they all have breech-loading guns and rifled cannon. They don't marry there in the same way as here. But just wait. When our son Litia takes a wife, it shall be a great national festival. We will bring them to the *Moruti*, both arrayed in magnificent garments; and the *Moruti* will have all sorts of good things promised them, and will give them fatherly counsels. Then many oxen will be slaughtered, and every one will rejoice. Let us greet the *Baruti* not as foreigners, but as Barotsi and as benefactors. Let us help them, let us give them our children, but let us begin by listening ourselves to their teaching. It is to us, chiefs, that all our tribes look."

I replied to this speech by a closing address. In conclusion, I related certain incidents of the journey, which raised a laugh at the expense of the rain-makers, and of those who made us responsible for the drought and the eclipse of the sun. They laughed, it is true; but we do not disguise the situation to ourselves. An element of latent opposition has come to light, with which we may one day find ourselves in conflict. But to foresee the struggle and prepare for it is not to be discouraged.

I have tried to give the complexion of this *pitso* as faithfully as possible. It is interesting and instructive from more than one point of view. In three hours, twenty orators had spoken: that will tell you that they are brief at the Zambesi. The forum of the Basuto does not exist here; the Zambesians, who crawl before their tyrants, have neither public life nor political initiative. The parliamentary notions which, among the Basuto, form, or rather have formed, orators and personalities are unknown here. We are not among those who think a more liberal government would satisfy this nation, which is not prepared for such progress. What it wants is a strong and benevolent government of such a kind that the Gospel can develop the people and prepare them for a better life. And the existing government, despotic but feeble, is scarcely worthy of the name.

The four or five days which we passed at the capital were well filled. As Mokwaë, the queen, and several chiefs from outside had come for the occasion, the town overflowed with people. But how keep order when hundreds of famished slaves are there, and have nothing to eat but what they can pick up? This is how it was done. Every evening, as darkness fell, the public crier was to be heard, " Ho! ho! Barotsi with yellow hearts " (*i.e.* full of covetousness); "hearken! You have yellow hearts; but know that any one who approaches the *Baruti's* waggon at night will be fired upon. And if any one should steal the smallest thing, I will put him to death. I have sworn it. So be warned, O yellow-hearted Barotsi!" But make your minds quite easy; no one was fired upon, and no one was put to death, in spite of one or two alarms, which threw the whole village into the greatest possible excitement.

February 10th, 1887.

Never before have we felt as in these last days that we are in the midst of the kingdom of the Prince of Darkness. Lewanika has a child of nine years old, born epileptic. They believe him to be bewitched. He had several attacks while we were there. Also among the chiefs, during the last few months, there were several inexplicable deaths. The very morning of our departure from Lealuyi, the sudden death of a chamberlain was announced, who the evening before, in perfect health, had acted as our cicerone round the village and the king's harem. They kept the news secret till after our departure. Then there was an outcry of witchcraft; they designated aloud another *sekomboa*, Moeya-nyana, a pleasant, intelligent fellow, still young and much beloved by the king. There was a tumultuous assemblage at the *lekhothla*; a pot was set on the fire, and one of the slaves of the accused, by proxy, plunged his hands into the boiling water. The effects did not take long to declare themselves. Therefore Moeya-nyana must be a sorcerer. Who could close his eyes to the evidence? Who could continue to doubt it after this " judgment of God," which our forefathers practised in the same way during the Middle Ages? Immediately those present seized the poor wretch, bound him strongly with cords, extorted pretended confessions from him by means of all sorts of indignities, and led him to execution. He passed the night bound to a post. The next morning—a fine Sunday—the scaffold, a rough rack four feet high, was quickly set up; the fire lighted; the *moati*—a violent poison—prepared and administered; and the unfortunate chief soon struggled with death in the midst of the insults and curses of the excited crowd. The king had forbidden them to burn his favourite attendant. So they dragged him away, and threw him into an adjacent pool. During the night, the victim thus executed came to himself. In vain Lewanika endeavoured to save his life. Those who were to take him back to his own people at Sesheke murdered him close by here, in the most revolting manner.[1] Alas! it is not an isolated case. One's heart bleeds at the mere hearing of such horrors. They assume an appalling reality when they are committed, so to speak, under one's own eyes, and when one has personally known the victims.

February 28th.

Our Sundays are growing interesting. Our neighbours begin to count the days of the week, and to remember the Lord's Day, "the *tsipi*," *i.e.* the bell (although we have no bell), or else "the day one dies."[2] Yesterday we had one hundred and fifty auditors. The great attraction is our little harmonium. But how difficult it is in the open air to hold these restless spirits captive! It may be the wind, or the sun, or the rain. It may be a bird flying past, a fowl cackling, or dogs barking and fighting. They greet each other, too; they chat, laugh, take snuff, come and go. One must gently repress these liberties, and maintain order; but it is scarcely inspiring. It would be enough to sweep the whole sermon out of one's head, supposing one had written it. However, it sometimes happens that these poor people do listen. Yesterday I was telling the story of the Deluge; they understood me; their attention was riveted. And when, after having spoken of that deluge of fire predicted by St. Peter, I appealed to my audience, and cried, "Whither

---

[1] The Barotsi always cut open the body of a murdered man to let the spirit out, fearing, if it be left in, that it may haunt and injure the murderers.

[2] In allusion to the solemn attitude taken in prayer.

will you flee then from the wrath of God ? " " To thee, O Moruti,
our father," replied several voices at once. " And why should
we flee ? " asked an old man seriously ; " we are not sorcerers." [1]
Oh, how long we have to wait to see one soul open to the
beams of grace ! Nguana-Ngombé sometimes gives us hope.
I have several times surprised the dear boy hidden in the
bushes and praying aloud. Will not God, Whom he is thus
groping after, hear him ?

As for Kamburu, he seems under a spell. Did he not announce to me last night that he was married ! " Married ! Since
when ? To whom ? Impossible ! " " Oh yes, I am married,"
replied my boy, with his pleasant smile and his face all lighted
up. " And that's how they do things with you ? " " Yes, my
father." In his journey from Sesheke here, he met a young
woman who was by no means at her first husband ; she pleased
him ; he found a matron for her in the neighbourhood, sent for
her, and—the marriage was concluded. It is simple enough.

In Basuto-land, and among other African tribes before the
introduction of Christianity, " marriage by cattle " was a blessing.
It was a barrier against corruption, and a civil contract.[2] Here,
no such thing. A wife leaves her husband for another, a
husband sends his wife away with the greatest ease in the
world, and nobody is astonished. Should a man take a fancy
to some one else's wife, he has an interview with her, brings her
home, and all is said and done. If it is a chief, the matter is
even easier. In many cases, it is the women themselves who
take the initiative. A very remarkable fact, which I can only
indicate here, is that the Barotsi in general have small families.
It is true, though, that the mortality among children is very
great.

March 28th—April 2nd.

The disquieting political news which comes to us from
Sesheke has lately procured us a visit from Lewanika. His
person was neglected ; he was gruff and uncommunicative.
Discontent is breaking out here and there. He has not yet
been able to organise his great annual hunt : those who can,

[1] It is only sorcerers who are put to death by fire.

[2] In cattle marriages, the bridegroom has to buy his wife from her father
with cattle, and also to give back cattle to her relatives if he repudiates her.

evade his orders on the pretext of famine. His messengers make murderous descents on the villages : every one flees at their approach. What a people !

Here is a messenger from the king ! Surely it bodes some good news, for he comes quite beaming ; he is laughing with pleasure. Since the affair of Moeya-nyana, which Lewanika has taken the trouble to tell me in all its details, I am rather suspicious about the laughter of the Barotsi. Kambinda perceives this, and, like a good actor, puts on a serious air. " The king," he said, " is not indifferent to your counsels. You have rebuked him for governing with an assegaï under his cloak " (killing people clandestinely) ; " you have told him that God hates the shedding of blood. Well, he makes known to you to-day that he has cast the hidden assegaï far from him, and will shed no more blood. The other day seven children were discovered in the woods and captured : among them was a wife of Mokabesa, one of the chiefs of the revolution. Lewanika had them brought into the full council, and served them with a pot of beer, poisoned in their sight. ' You are of an accursed race,' he said to them ; ' your fathers have killed the kings who loaded them with favours ; they have massacred my own children. My day of vengeance has come. I will not break your skulls ; I will not pierce you with the spear ; but you shall all drink this beer, poisoned with *moati*. And if your god can save you, that is his affair.' They drank, or rather were forced to swallow, the fatal drink ; they were put into a canoe, and abandoned upon a desert island, to die there."

Since our arrival here, my dear wife has been extremely weak. The waggon journey tried her very much. We have long lodged in our old van, which no longer ensures us against either wind or rain. Our reed hut is finished, well plastered within and without ; it does not dry easily ; but though they are infested with white ants, our two little rooms are a perfect palace for us. We are surprised at the number of things we possess to make it comfortable and cosy, and we are filled with gratitude towards our heavenly Father. Mokwaë, the queen, first of all, and then Katoka, her sister, have come to spend some days with us. More than once, we had to show them round our two rooms with all their suite. They were quite astounded, as were we, once upon a time, in the palace of Versailles. What astonished them most was our casement windows, our glass, and our chairs. Pausing in ecstasies before each separate object, Mokwaë asked, " Have you given anything like this to my brother the king ? " She strutted about, or sat proudly enthroned on her mat in a large-patterned print dress, given her by my wife. They appreciated our little presents, behaved discreetly on the whole, and left a favourable impression upon us.

May 4th.

The great event of this month is the school. We would have wished to begin it on arriving here.   But, first of all, we had to make ourselves at least a temporary abode.   Even now, the school is carried on in the open air, in the midst of the constructions which are absorbing us ; but, at all events, it *is* carried on, and that regularly every day.   Already, it numbers twenty scholars on the books.   It was on March 4th, in the presence of the queen, that we opened it.   Lewanika has sent us two of his sons and five of his nephews : other chiefs have followed his example.   A hut has been erected for Litia, not without difficulty : the others have made themselves shelters, the whole surrounded with a palisade.   It is perhaps the embryo of our future Normal School.   You would not believe what an interest we take in this school, and with what joy Aaron especially, and my wife and I alternately, devote a part of our time to it every day.   Our two most advanced pupils will soon be able to read ; they all have some notions of Bible history and of geography.   But they are villainous singers.   Each of our little people has come with a number of slaves, more or less ; some of these attend school, and place themselves behind their masters.   But we have not yet arrived at making them understand that the teaching is for them too.

What is much more serious, is the question of how to feed all these mouths.   The young chiefs, by dint of threats, at first obtained abundance.   But the source became exhausted ; Litia's people spied upon the passers-by to rob them, or else pounced upon those who ventured to bring us their produce.   We were often forced to intervene.   The terror which the presence of these princes inspires is such, that our little Sunday audience has broken up : we have had to experience a dearth of food ; and it has been almost impossible for us to procure workmen.

Our dear pupils did not spare us. By way of thanking us for the provisions we gave them to the fullest extent of our power, they set to work to eat up our sheep; but they did it *delicately*, like artful pickpockets. To obviate all these rascalities, we ought to have a boarding school, where all the pupils would be on the same footing and constantly under the master's supervision. That too will come. Meanwhile, let us not despise small beginnings, but give thanks to God.

May 25th.

A fortnight ago, the king came back from his hunting expedition—an unlucky hunt, if ever there was one. In vain had his emissaries scoured the villages, and by their own peculiar methods carried off recruits and sowed terrors broadcast. The hunt was unpopular—I know not why. And then the floods this year are of the smallest; only the lowest parts of the Valley are submerged. It is a calamity from more than one point of view; and from that of the chase more particularly. The antelopes run all over the veldt, so they cannot be penned up on an island by hundreds of canoes, as is usually done, and slaughtered easily. And as the Barotsi count on this great annual hunt of a month or two to lay in their store of skins, one can understand their dismay this year. Hunger brought them back to their own hearths. Some were nothing but living skeletons. Within the memory of man, no such thing had been seen. How explain it, unless by sorcery? Certain incidents of the chase, moreover, had put the king and the principal chiefs in ill-humour. The day after his return, he found the floor of his house all sprinkled with blood. This time there could be no doubt his own person was aimed at. But who was the author of these misdeeds? Lewanika went no more to the *lekhothla*, and saw no one.

Terror seized on every one, and spread everywhere like a tidal wave. The recalcitrants who had not taken part in the hunt hid their corn and their little property by night, and escaped into the woods. The Gambella, the other ministers, and all the chiefs of the capital did not feel themselves safe from suspicions. Every one made it a point of honour to wash his hands of it by submitting to the ordeal of boiling water. So, on a given day, they set on the fire in the *lekhothla* as many pots as there were chiefs, and their slaves, always as proxies, plunged their hands into it by turns. The thing which so far I find inexplicable is that nobody was scalded. The women of the harem then had their turn, and next it was that of the female cooks and scullions.

Directly this news reached us, I took a canoe and went to the capital. It was Friday, the 20th. The king seemed pleased to see me—his heart was full ; he passed a great part of the night in my hut, talking. I spent the whole of the next day in private interviews with his principal councillors, and in the evening they were all assembled at my place with their master. But that did not suffice. The next day, Sunday, at the two meetings, I preached on the sixth commandment : " Thou shalt not kill." I leave you to imagine how they opened their eyes, when they heard me enunciate and develop this truth, here so new and strange, that man is the creature, the *exclusive* property of God, that kings and governors are only the shepherds of the people, and servants who will have to render an account of their stewardship. However much I shrank from the task, I had to denounce the atrocity of a superstition which so lightly sacrificed so many human lives, and the intrigues which have produced these last events. I felt the full importance of the occasion, and the grandeur of the ministry committed to me. Oh, how tremblingly I had gone to Lealuyi !—how I besought my Master for fidelity, for strength, and the power of a burning love ! They understood my address quite as well as the purpose of my visit. The people, astonished, said, " Ah yes, indeed ! " The king hung his head, and said to the Gambella, " The words of the *Moruti* have sunk into my heart." The councillors came to me in private, to beg me to repeat them to him ; and he himself in his turn asked me to say them all again to his ministers. They made me all sorts of fine promises ; no more ordeals by boiling water, no more poison, no more burning at the stake.

On the Monday morning, a man planted in the midst of the assembled *lekhothla* two pieces of reed with tufts of poultry feathers at the top. The fowls they were plucked from had gone through the preparatory ordeal of the *moati*, and had succumbed to it. These people (their owners) were sent back, and told that they were disturbing the public peace and the security of their villages. I do not know whether I succeeded in saving the life of one old woman, one of the cooks, who found herself scalded. But let us not deceive ourselves : it is not at the first blast of the ram's horn that one can overthrow or even shake the walls of superstition. It is one of Satan's chief strongholds. But we shall redouble the blows, we shall dig mines, and happy shall we be if we succeed in making a breach !

You see what an atmosphere we live in. Our sky would indeed be leaden, without the light of God's face ; our isolation would be unbearable, without the communion of the Saviour— and I would add, the communion of saints.

SEFULA, *November* 1887.

A chance for the post is the opening of our prison doors. Our benumbed thoughts spread their wings and flutter out. They fly into the open air, towards the countries of light, and move in the great world of the living. But the pen is duller and more dilatory. It has to reckon with all sorts of circumstances, which hamper its movements and chill its ardour. Oh, how we should fling it down, if we only had a telephone at our service ! Our isolation, without the faintest glimmer of social enjoyment, is a severe trial. We are stifled in this atmosphere of corruption, and we run a terrible risk of growing rusty and settling into a groove. No intellectual or moral movements sustain or uplift us ; all our surroundings drag us down ; and alas ! when we are in the dust, even then we are still far above the level of the darkness and foulness encircling us.

The material occupations and the cares which crush and absorb us are a heavy cross, which we often carry with an ill grace. The missionary, whose position, unfortunately, renders him conspicuous, and whom your affection puts upon a pedestal, does not live at that level at all ; it is only statues that stay there. His is not the contemplative life of the monk, nor that of a lover of adventures, full of dazzling heroism. No ! It is humdrum to a degree that would amaze you. It is a tissue of humble duties and little details, which fritter away his time, patience, and strength. In the evening, a sense of sadness often seizes him, when he makes up the account of his occupations, and has nothing to show for it but disappointments and fatigue. Even in his sleep, he is often haunted by the prospect of the struggles awaiting him next day. Is that, I ask myself, the ideal life of an apostle? When Paul stitched at his tents, was he sometimes beset by the cares which torment the most ordinary of human beings?

It is now just a year since I arrived here, accompanied by our friends Waddell and Middleton. My wife had remained at Sesheke. We pitched our tents in the midst of some clumps of brushwood and mutilated stumps, on this sand-hill, covered with a thick layer of ashes. This year must have seen at least twenty moons!

We began our work of installation in the midst of the most unfavourable circumstances. Satan was not the only one to make sport of us. But our God, ever good and faithful, has succoured us according to our needs. That formidable journey of my wife's, which was thought to be madness, proved quick and easy. Her health, shaken by the rough life we had led for three years, has gradually been restored. We have again had losses of cattle, which have seriously complicated our difficulties, and hampered our work ; but we have all enjoyed excellent health, and the attacks of fever have been as rare as they were mild. We still have to walk in thick sand : the brushwood, the stumps of decapitated trees, our jungles and our marshes, are still there—the haunts of serpents, hyænas, and leopards. The place will never be picturesque : our immense bare plain, the bed of a dried-up lake, with its miry swamps, will never be a Swiss canton, nor even a Basuto-land. We must just make the best of it. But Sefula may become habitable, and one may live happily there.

While drainage works are being actively carried on in the dale, we have begun to clear away the thickets, and already on the plateau, where formerly sorcerers were burnt alive, four little European buildings are rising, which are the great wonder of the country. They are very modest, just temporary cabins of stakes and reeds, which the termites are already eating out. But they have little windows, light and air. You would not believe the interest we have taken in setting them up, plastering them, and making the most of what we have to furnish them cosily. Is it not an emblem of life, which we know to be so short, and which we strive to make so fair?

Our material labours are only just begun ; the greatest

are still before us, and we contemplate them with a kind of stupefaction. Still, we must have more stable constructions than those which shelter us now. There are no stones that I know of within a radius of a hundred miles, and in order to build we shall be forced to make bricks. Middleton has made an attempt in the Valley, which has succeeded tolerably well. But he, to our great regret, is leaving us to return to Europe; and unless we find some mechanical means of prosecuting this work, the difficulties it presents are such that I should feel unequal to undertaking them. I should be unjust if I did not render public testimony to the devotion of Waddell and Middleton.

So much for material things. Now, what shall I say of the mission work itself? We are still at the day of small beginnings. We are clearing the ground. It is a very uninteresting period, for we have nothing as yet to show for it but our clods and the sweat of our brow. But we must clear the ground at all costs, if we would one day sow, and later on reap the harvest. For the present, the great thing is, not to lose courage; above all, not to lose faith in the work.

Let us first of all visit the school, which is carried on yonder under the scanty shade of a hollow tree. It has gone on regularly since the beginning of April. From thirty-five, the number of scholars has declined to twenty. The slaves (already rather big) of our young chiefs have gradually wearied of this passive service, so uninteresting for them, and of a discipline which, however light, is irksome to these children of nature. With one or two exceptions, of which we carefully keep count, we have found it impossible to make voluntary recruits among the surrounding villages. The school is still considered exclusively that of the young princes; and those who attend it are, or by the mere fact become, their serfs and their slaves. That is enough to frighten the parents, and the children themselves. With time, this will alter; but for the moment it is unfortunate.

Our young men's establishment leaves much to be desired in every respect. Its morality is not exemplary; hunger is its habitual guest, for these princes live at the charges of a public which loves them not, and this is the source of great disorder, which we are not in a position to ameliorate. They have nearly finished up our little flock of sheep and goats, and we do not know which way to turn for a little meat. Lately, during my absence, they stole my two aneroid barometers, probably to make snuff-boxes of them. Poor children! they little thought what mischief they were doing me. We have even had for a time to forbid them access to the workshop, whence nails, screws, and tools were disappearing with alarming rapidity.

And yet, if you but knew with what cares and prayers we surround this school! People would not believe in Europe, no, not even in Basuto-land, the amount of patience and perseverance needed to teach this class of young men, who believe that everything is permitted to them, and who turn everything into ridicule. In spite of all our occupations, my wife and I devote a certain time every day to helping Aaron in his irksome task. Happily, he is gifted with a strong will and plenty of energy. But he is not equal to the task. Five of his pupils already read fluently, and some others are making progress. What we need here, and what would do enormous good, is an industrial school. The Barotsi are industrious in their own way. They do wicker-work, and manipulate wood and iron with much taste and skill. The king pesters me to take apprentices. First of all, it was a dozen grown-up men ; then " his sons " (*i.e.* the boys of the royal family, including his nephews), whom he imagined he had thoroughly equipped with tools, when he had got them a plane ; then others again, who, he expected, would in a few months become as expert as Mr. Waddell himself. He does not understand how reasons of economy (for all these mouths must be fed) and the press of work together oblige me to refuse these amateur apprentices, and he never misses a chance of reproaching me with it. I was forced in the end to yield and take two intelligent men, although they are a burden and a hindrance to us.

We tell ourselves that this too is a work. I cannot blind myself : I see ever more clearly the immense services that industry and commerce, in upright and Christian hands, could render to the evangelisation of this country. The civilising side is perhaps the one that our poverty has led us to neglect too much. It is a subject which deserves the attention of Christian philanthropists.

Our Sunday audiences are subject to all sorts of fluctuations. We had succeeded up to a certain point in restoring the confidence of the people who came to sell their produce. One day, the king pays us a visit, finds his children have grown thin, assembles the chiefs of the neighbouring villages to rebuke them, and there is all our work of several months crumbled away at a touch. While our little chiefs profited by one of my long absences to give themselves a free hand, their guardians and followers lay in wait for the people who came to sell their produce or to be present at the preaching of the Gospel. They ruthlessly despoiled the former, and brutally forced the latter to perform the hardest and most servile labour. The work is not easy, you see ; more briers than down in our nest. Perhaps, in this dark picture, I have not sufficiently allowed for circumstances. How can we attract a regular audience, and see a school prosper, when we have not even a roof to shelter us ? Day after day, teaching and preaching go on outside, in wind, sun, and rain, and in the midst of a multitude of distractions, each more alluring than the other.

I do not know in what language to express my thoughts, to make our friends understand that the savages—ours, that is—are not in the least the sweet, simple, affectionate, confiding creatures they are represented to be in Europe ; that they have not the slightest desire to hear, and still less to receive, the Gospel. Here, as with us, the carnal mind is enmity against God ; but here—and do not lose sight of the fact—this enmity often expresses itself in the grossest and most humiliating guise. Do not misunderstand us. Even the most intelligent chiefs have very vague and very false notions about us and about our mission ; and if they call us into their country, it is generally for political objects and from personal interests. For us, whatever may be the key God uses to open the door, it is our duty to step in, even though it were the door of a prison. We cannot expect to be received with enthusiasm or triumph ; all that we ask, or have a right to ask, is toleration. Missionaries are often reproached with colouring their pictures too highly. Would you like me to add deeper shadows to mine ? It is never without a pang at my heart that I dip my brush in dark colours, to acquaint you with those we have come to evangelise. If I did not owe it to you to tell the truth I would rather cover

them with the cloak of charity. We only give you glimpses.
Now they are gloomy and sad. What would you say to the
reality, such as it is, alas! with which, moreover, we have to live
in continual contact?

I have told you already that I made a journey to Kazungula
to meet our friends the Jallas and MM. Dardier and Goy.
These long and repeated absences, without any communications, are painful trials among so many others which assail
us here. We do not get used to them. During my journeys,
Mme. Coillard, already weighed down by her own duties, has
further to charge herself with a part of mine, and to assume
all the responsibility. It is not an easy task with Zambesians.
At Sesheke, the sinister rumours of a new revolution are flying
about the country. In certain places, they were talking to each
other confidentially about a plot, which they asserted the Gambella himself was concocting, and which was to break out immediately. The sudden alteration in the behaviour of my oarsmen,
their insubordination, the rapacity and arrogance of Mokumba
and his men, and other equally disquieting symptoms, gave
additional substance to all these rumours. It was even asserted
that at the Valley, since our departure, the insurgents had twice
surrounded the capital, but that, finding themselves numerically
too weak, they had quietly dispersed. Would the revolution
break out during my absence, and the country be thrown once
more into anarchy? What would my wife do? How could I
rejoin her with this band of "brigands," as they called them,
being, as I now found myself, absolutely at their mercy? But
one is calm when one really confides oneself to God: "I will
both lay me down in peace, and sleep," said the Psalmist: "for
Thou, Lord, only makest me dwell in safety."

My return journey was accomplished without misadventure,
notwithstanding ; and I was bringing reinforcements. My
travelling companions, MM. Dardier and Goy, seemed so happy,
and enjoyed themselves so much, I felt quite young again.
At less than two days from Sefula, they fell ill. I thought
at first it was simply an attack of fever. As a matter of
fact, in Dr. Dardier's case, it was a sunstroke, slight enough
in itself, but it proved an exciting cause for other disorders.
My wife, being warned in time, sent the cart for the last stage.
It was the saddest part of the journey. The children of the

school, led by Aaron, came to meet us, singing hymns. I alighted to shake hands with our dear pupils. This simple reception in the Barotsi country moved me ; but our patients scarcely noticed it. M. Goy soon got over this first tribute paid to the unhealthiness of the climate, and recovered his energy and spirit. Not so Dr. Dardier. After a serious illness, he seemed to be fully convalescent, when certain symptoms arose and alarmed him. Now he is leaving us, and returning to Sesheke, partly for a family event which the Jallas are expecting, but more especially on account of his health. Will he ever come back to Sefula ? Our sorrow and disappointment are great, and they are in proportion to the immense joy which the arrival of this reinforcement had afforded us, and the hopes we had conceived.

The question of evangelisation is one difficult to resolve satisfactorily. What method can we invent ? It is evident that that of Basuto-land will not do here. There, you spring to the saddle, and gallop whither you will ; you visit one, two, or three villages, according to the time at disposal ; or else organise a campaign lasting two or three days. It is magnificent. Here, it is different. The villages, scattered over the undulations of the plain or in the midst of the cultivated marshes, are all difficult of access. You can neither reach them in canoes, because there is not enough water, nor on foot, because of the peat-bogs, unless you relieve yourself of all your clothes, which is not always practicable. I generally ride along the edge of the plain. I call the chiefs of the hamlets and the people whom I know, and many run up eagerly. But it is not always a house-to-house visit, and I do not reach everybody I should like to.

The other day, I wanted for the fifth time to attempt a visit to Namboata's village, which we see three miles from here. I had made arrangements, and had procured a man from among my friends to come with his sons and act as a guide. Everything went well for three-quarters of the way. Then I found myself involved in a miry swamp, crossed by a sort of canal. At the edge of the deep artificial rivulet, the horse, which was every moment sinking deeper, obstinately refused to go on. He grew restive ; threw himself first to one side, then to the other ; kicked furiously,—all to no purpose. I stuck to the saddle. All at once, he plunged, dropped his head

between his fore-legs, and began bucking so violently, that
before long I was rolling in the mud, while my mount had
bolted across the morasses, and was galloping over the veldt,
my two guides after him. In vain I approached him quite
gently, my hat in my hand, just as when he is being fed in
the evening. The ruse did not succeed this time; and the
horse was off like a shot, far away over the plain. So I must
needs paddle humbly through the pools, and reach home a
pitiable object.

There is a comic element in this little adventure, which is
not the only one of its kind; but it leads up to another which
I must tell you about—alas! a very different one. A week ago,
one of our little boys was leading my horse to water, and turning
it out to browse (it is a stallion, which always tries to bolt in
the direction of the capital). He was playing with the tether,
when suddenly the animal took fright and galloped off with
the child after him. M. Goy's workmen were instantly pursuing
him, shouting to the boy at the top of their voices to let go
the bridle. The horse, kicking furiously, disappeared into the
woods at full gallop. When, a few seconds later, it was found,
quivering and covered with foam, in the open, the child was still
there—but alas! nothing but a lifeless and mutilated corpse.
It was found that, in playing with the tether, he had made
a running knot, and passed his arm through it, when the horse,
suddenly frightened, had galloped away. We are in great
sorrow. Dear little boy! poor Samochese! He might have
been twelve years old. During the two months he had been
with us, he had won everybody's affection. He was so active,
so careful, so loveable. We had built such hopes upon him.
Now his sudden and awful death has destroyed them all. It
is the first burial which has taken place at Sefula: it was on
Sunday morning, the 13th of this month. Forgive me for
dwelling at such length on this bereavement, which we shall
long remember. To us, it seems very great; and when we
think of his father, above all of his mother, we do not know
how to be comforted.

BAROTSI WARRIORS ON THE WAR-PATH.

[To face page 296.

CHAPTER XVIII

SEFULA, *January 25th*, 1888.

A TIME of revolution among the Barotsi means anarchy in its fullest development. It is the hour for personal revenges. Every one pillages and massacres without running the risk of ever being called to justice. *"Ke-lerumo!"* ("It is the spear"—civil war). That justifies every passion, every disorder, every crime, and every atrocity.

Can one form the least idea of what this country becomes, whose inhabitants, even in time of peace, are so swift to shed blood? One might truly say, that it was over these tribes of the Zambesi that the prophet Hosea was lamenting, when he said, "There is nought but swearing and breaking faith, and killing, and stealing, and committing adultery; they break out, and blood toucheth blood."[1] I have already had occasion to speak of this; forgive me for recurring to it; but, be it remembered, we shall never tell everything; our confidences will always—yes, always, alas!—come short of the reality.

One detail. The Barotsi are not at all a pastoral people. Formerly, when they could "lift" an ox from the Mashuku-lumboe, they made a public feast of it, roasted it on the embers, flesh and hide together, as they still do with the zebra; it was exquisite, the singed hair flavouring the dishes. The Makololo initiated them a little into the pastoral life, but without imparting to them anything of their veneration for the bovine race. Except in very unusual circumstances, such as a marriage, a purification for burial, or a sacrifice to the

---

[1] Hosea iv. 2 (R.V.).

297

ancestors, it is rare for a Mosuto to allow himself the luxury
of killing an ox. A calf—a cow, never! It would be sacrilege.
Here all are immolated, without distinction and without special
reason—bulls and heifers, oxen and calves. They kill and
eat, like greedy children beginning with the best. When the
herd has vanished, each man looks at his neighbour and raises
the cry, "To the Mashukulumboe!"

During the recent troubles, the bovine race has been almost
literally exterminated in the country. I could never have
believed it, if I had not had the proofs before my eyes. It
was—I am speaking more particularly of the Valley—a
universal butchery. Every one tried to outdo the other in
slaughter. There were no more masters. No one's property
was respected, not even that appropriated by the chiefs who
held power. And we experienced something of it ourselves.
To this unbridled prodigality, a famine succeeded ; it was only
to be expected. Then, as always, the cry arose, "To the
Mashukulumboe!"

Lewanika wanted to yield to these clamours, thinking it a
good opportunity for winning popularity. But famine raged
through the kingdom, the political horizon was not clear, and
he was obliged regretfully to yield to the counsels of the wise
men, and give up the expedition. It was only deferred. Since
then, it has become *the* topic of conversation, the dream of the
populace.

Now the favourable season has arrived ; the rains are falling,
the streams are overflowing, the pools and ponds have become
lakes, and soon the Valley will be submerged. That will last
till June. The south-east wind will then begin to blow, the
waters will abate, and the earth will dry. Until that moment,
the Barotsi believe that their country is sufficiently protected
by the waters against an invasion, and that they have time to
go and make their contemplated raid. Lewanika, who at first
communicated his plans to me, now shows himself more reserved,
since he knows my opinion. It is the public talk, that he keeps
us informed of all that is going forward.

On a certain day, all the chiefs of the country were assembled
together at Lealuyi. The queen, Mokwaë, whose advice has
great weight in questions of this kind, also attended there, after
keeping every one a long time waiting.

Some days afterwards, we went thither also, at the entreaty of the king. It was M. Goy's first visit to the capital, and he will not soon forget it. The journey was full of adventures, Soaked through from the beginning, and that to the skin, we were obliged alternately to go through showers, through burning sun, and cold squalls of wind which were driving up the clouds. Night overtook us. We wandered long in these interminable sheets of water, without the smallest landmark. losing our way a dozen times, finding it only to lose it again. Utterly sick of it at last, we abandoned the canoe as soon as we could moor it in the reeds, set to work resolutely to paddle through mud and water again for more than half an hour, and we arrived at ten o'clock barefoot, *en caleçon*—begging your pardon—famished and exhausted.

The town was overflowing with people. Here and there were bivouacs, where they still talked ; the rush fires—for fuel is scarce in the Valley—occasionally shot out a flame that rendered darkness visible, and, dying out, left it thicker than ever. The enclosure of the *kuandu*—the king's private house in the midst of his harem—was packed full. Our arrival caused surprise, for no one here journeys at such unseasonable hours. Lewanika hurried up, laughing with pleasure, and we soon had one of his houses at our disposal, mats, a fire which made us shiver only to look at it, and to warm our empty stomachs a cup of some liquid. They told us, I believe, that it was coffee. Upon that, we could sustain conversation up to a late hour. Our royal friend, quite full of his expedition, felt the need of justifying it in our eyes. " They ill-treated Dr. Holub, who had just come from me ; it is my duty to chastise them. Besides, they are not human beings ; they are quite naked. And then . . . " he added hesitatingly, " and then . . . we have no more cattle, and we absolutely must have some. But you may be sure it is our very last expedition. On our return, we will give ourselves up entirely to your teaching ; and we will all become believers, all Christians . . . *all.*" Undoubtedly, he put the accent in the right place ; and if we are not convinced, he at least was consoled.

Next day, great animation reigned throughout the village. On all sides, the slaves and women were coming and going, jostling with busy messengers ; they were actively preparing food for the road. Everywhere one heard the cadence of the pesties, like the flails of many threshing-floors. The chiefs themselves held their little councils of war in twos and threes apart ; while the court fools raved deliriously, made music with the gourds, shrieked and bellowed, no one taking the slightest notice of them. Fresh detachments of armed men kept coming up every moment. In the evening, there was a grand military demonstration—let us not call it a review. The warriors, under their respective chiefs, massed themselves on the public square ; they were draped in flaming colours, decked out in ostrich feathers, in rags and fripperies of European clothing, in leopard skins, in every kind of wild beast's hide, great or small, which could give a man the semblance of an animal and a sufficiently ferocious aspect.

Little detachments would feign an attack upon an imaginary enemy, perform some evolutions which drew frantic applause from the spectators, and retire to their places ; then the whole black mass chanted lugubriously a wild war-song. Some of the commandants next came forward, and angrily harangued the king ; then advancing at the double, they fell on their knees, and planted gun and shield before the ministers, still declaiming with bitter words, and demanding that " this timid king, who does not know his own mind, should at last let loose his infuriated dogs."

What astonished me was the number of firearms possessed by these people. They had them of every calibre. To be sure, they are not of the most modern pattern ; the majority are flint-locks.[1] Never mind, they are *guns* ! And to a Morotsi the name alone is magic. No doubt the assegaï is still the national weapon—and a formidable weapon, too ; but the shields of hide—copied from those of the Matabele, which the Makololo themselves had adopted—are few in number and ill-kept.

Here, as elsewhere, all that is purely national is dying out. This is to be regretted, for it is not always a sign of progress.

As we are here to make observations, let us cast a glance upon the Sunday-morning audience which the public crier assembles. The king, with his band of music and his " monstrous regiment " of *likomboa* (officers and favourites

---

[1] The Portuguese have two factories of flint-lock guns in South Africa.

attached to his personal service, who possess great influence), has made his entrance. Every one kneels and acclaims him. This is more than the usual greeting : it is because yesterday his Majesty did not appear at the *khothla*, and he is supposed to be angry ; and "the king's wrath," saith Solomon, "is as messengers of death." Little by little, the public place fills, and produces on me the effect of a kaleidoscope. I do not see, as I did at Sesheke ten years ago, the cast-off clothes of soldiers, of police constables, of naval officers and high functionaries, with faded braids and broideries, which the uttermost waves of commerce had tossed hither like foam. No. But the spectacle, though different, is not less curious. The many-coloured cotton cap so dear to the Barotsi is a rarity. Men of import-ance supply its place by wrapping the head in a handkerchief, which does not keep its freshness very long ; and to that they add, if possible, a felt hat, seldom very correct in shape.

In exchange for ivory, Lewanika had bought up the whole stock of merchandise brought him just now by Mr. Westbeech on the one hand, and on the other by the caravan of a Portuguese merchant from Bihé. Everybody, in varying degrees, had a share in the royal largesse ; and were it but a remnant of an elbow's length, he must stick it on somehow. So one sees nothing but new *setsibas* and tinsels of every colour. Well, they may pass muster, and so may the hats and the shirts and the motley blankets. But what of the garments of European cut ? Just look at this old man, whose withered limbs bob about like matches in the folds of a vesture made for a Hercules ; while the Hercules has succeeded—I don't know how—in hauling on a pair of breeches which are splitting. Here, a stout individual is rigged out in a waistcoat only, and nothing else ; there is another of similar proportions in a sailor's jumper—a real strait-jacket for him. No matter, he must raise his arms over his head to salute the king, and return thanks for his gift. Whichever way you look, the absurdities are enough to make you laugh till the tears run down your cheeks.

Suddenly, every gaze is directed towards a procession which advances with dignity. It is the queen, Mokwaë, who comes with her suite of young maidens, with the princesses, the daughters of Sepopa, and the wives of Lewanika. All are clad in robes of calico print, all pieces of the same brightly coloured

stuff, floating over their shoulders, and large handkerchiefs on
their heads, streaming behind like veils ; and, with all that, a
profusion of beadwork and jewellery from some Parisian bazaar.
They gravely take up their place behind us on their mats ; and
after the whole assembly has clapped hands, the service com-
mences. I speak from the text, " And this is the condemnation,
that light is come into the world, and men loved darkness rather
than light, because their deeds were evil."

The next day we wanted to start early, but Lewanika desired
that we should be present at the great National Council. We
yielded. We took our places with him in the spacious hut of
the *lekhothla*, a sort of shed open on all sides. The chiefs were
packed there together like herrings, while the crowd pressed
round outside and listened eagerly. The session lasted from
8 a.m. till one in the afternoon. It was a succession of little
speeches, going off like rockets. Decidedly, the Barotsi are not
Basuto ; they do not understand public speaking, and Lewanika
is no better than the others. Counsels were divided. The great
chiefs had consulted the bones, the oracle had condemned the
expedition, and they were hesitating. Lewanika had known
of this for two days, and he was furious. Now, they would be
setting forth every possible objection ; then, to pacify the king,
they would be vaunting his wisdom and the prowess of the
Barotsi, and conjuring him to start without delay. Others,
but very few, had the courage of their opinions, and frankly
disapproved, especially the Natamoyo and the Gambella. The
great majority loudly demanded the expedition, especially the
likomboa, the favourite minions of the king, who are always in
rivalry with the ministers : it was they who spoke loudest of all.

The occasion was a unique one for speaking some home
truths to these people, and I did so. I saw, after the king's
closing speech, that the expedition had died a natural death.
We rejoiced over it with M. Goy, and it consoled us for
reaching home late at night, churning up the water and trampling through the mud. But the *likomboa* were excited ; and
backed by the great mass of the warriors present, they waited
till our departure, convoked another council, and won the game.
A messenger came, two days later, to announce that the expedition was definitely decided upon, and that the king was getting
ready for the campaign.

February 16*th.*

Decidedly, the expedition is on its way. Up till the last moment, I had counted on I know not what eventuality to put a stop to it. But no! In vain had the king been told of the famine which is ravaging the Makalaka, on whom he counts for provisioning his army : all to no purpose. They beat the big war drums all night. The warriors, who had returned home to prepare their commissariat for the road, began to assemble. The king performed his devotions. Offerings of calico, of beadwork, water, milk, or honey, were sent to each of the royal tombs in the country, and at the same time a sheaf of spears, which remained lying there for forty-eight hours, to give these dignitaries of the other world time to bless them.

On the 8th, Lewanika left his capital by canoe, camped at Mongu, completed his religious ceremonies at the tomb of Katonga, and on Monday he came and encamped on the other side of the stream of Sefula with six or seven hundred men. As he had notified us in time, we all went to the foot of the slope to see his army march past. The dreary sound of the drum, and that of the bells which are used for bugles, soon announced its approach. First, we perceived through the trees a file of young men, carrying as standards the famous consecrated assegaïs, and shining with ochre. At their head, solemnly marched an aged man, and a young girl, of whom I will speak presently. Behind them, came the king, the Gambella, a troop of people curiously got up, and the *moïfo* (the royal guard) ; then the camp-followers, a mob of men of all ages, carrying mats, gourds, clothes, etc., marching in disorder, and pouring in from every side through the brushwood.

The young girl of whom I have spoken is not the sutler of the regiment : she is the Prophetess. Chosen by the divining bones, she is the interpreter of the gods. Nothing can be done without her. She carries the horn containing the war " medicines " and charms. She is always ahead of the vanguard, and no one is permitted to pass before her, even when a halt is called. If she gets tired or falls ill, the young men have to carry her. On arriving before the enemy, it is she who must fire the first shot ; and all the time the battle lasts, she may neither sleep nor sit, eat nor drink. When a halt is called, she lays down her horn; the young men of her bodyguard strike the sacred spears into the ground. "*Tu ka yoye, bakuetu*," she cries; and her followers cry, "*Tu ka yoye.*" And the whole army, at a respectable distance, acclaims them with the whole force of its lungs, "*Tu ka yoye! Tu ka yoye!*" ("Fellow-country-men, may we live long! May our countrymen live!"). She takes up the cry once more, "*Ba ka fe!*" and her followers and the troops roar, "*Ba ka fe! Ba ka fe!*" ("May our enemies perish!"). It is the war-cry which the echoes of the wood repeat twenty times a day for whole months together. On their return, as a reward for her services, the young prophetess will become one of the *maori*, or wives of the king. Now she is his concubine. Her title is the *sebimbi*, and she carries the *likurume* (the medicine horn).

When the halt had been called, according to the rules I have described, Lewanika and the great chiefs came to salute us. While we were talking, a commotion, which seemed to be upsetting the whole camp, attracted my attention. It was Litia himself, the king's son, with all the boys and all the young men going out to war for the first time, who were now running at full speed, plunging into the marsh and plucking rushes, which they came and laid at the king's feet, then retiring and returning to the charge without taking breath, crying out "*Kamarie!*" (literally, "a young girl"); that is to say, "You think we are girls unfit for war; well! you shall see that we are men, and despise fatigue." It seems this little comedy is repeated at every halt.

The *sebimbi* gave the signal for departure, entered the water, and sprinkled herself. The whole army acclaimed her loudly, rose, and followed her example. We had it encamped at the distance of a gunshot from us during two days. What a rabble! And to think that it will roll on like a snowball. Since then, bands pass incessantly, and go to swell this over-flowing torrent. I suppose that when the contingents of Motulo, Nalolo, Mboela, and the province of Sesheke are assembled at Machile, Lewanika will find himself at the head of from ten to twelve thousand men at least. Can you imagine what this multitude of famished men means—for they have no commissariat—thieves, pillagers, brigands by habit, unbridled and uncontrolled? For their subsistence, they are going to make a descent on their poor Makalaka ; and already, in their own country, " terror goes before them, destruction accompanies them, and desolation follows them." What will it be for the unfortunate Mashukulumboe ? It is not only their cattle they are after, but also their women and children, who will be reduced to the most abject slavery. As for the men, their business is soon despatched, and they are thrown out for the beasts of the field to devour. It is said that the Mashukulumboe, when exasperated, give no more quarter than the Barotsi themselves, and that they keep the skulls of those who fall into their hands to drink beer out of.

Our school is broken up. All our pupils are gone after the quarry—alas ! to complete their dreadful apprenticeship to brigandage. It seemed to us that their education had been already pretty thorough, for, after having eaten our sheep, killed our asses, and stolen my aneroid barometers, they contrived to bribe one of our little girls and to appropriate our best table napkins, without counting a thousand and one other exploits of which these light-fingered gentry boast themselves. And yet, we regret them. We think sadly of the months they have passed here, and the little influence we have gained over them. We are under no illusions about the zeal they promise to bring to their work when they come back to school. We also know the value of Lewanika's fine promises. Poor Lewanika ! Aaron, too, has spoken to him with the virile firmness of a Micaiah. He knows very well he is doing wrong. During our last interview, he wriggled about on his chair, and ended by saying, " Don't you see, my *Moruti*, I am not my own master ? I am driven to it—I am driven to it ! But if you love me, keep silence ; do not go and spoil my good name in the world by writing that Lewanika has gone to make a raid on the Mashukulumboe ; and when I return, you will see."

Ah ! but the thought of this return makes us tremble. Who can foretell the moral—or rather let us say the *immoral*—consequences of these five or six months of national licentiousness, the letting loose of passions among all these savage tribes, and that terrible frenzy which takes possession of man from the moment he embrues his hands in his brother's blood, and transforms him into a wild beast, a hyæna that laughs as it tears its prey ?

Lewanika, while draining the country for his expedition, has by no means taken all the thieves with him. Lately, on a dark night, some of these vagabonds paid us the honour of a visit; they made a breach in our *kraal* (stockade), and took out an ox of their own selection, which they killed and dismembered at leisure. Out of courtesy, they left us the skeleton, but it had been picked as clean as if a cloud of vultures had been included in the party. The king heard of it, and in his indignation sent and authorised me to seize the knaves, and have them soundly taken to task—by whom I don't know ! All very well, only he forgot that these gentlemen are not in the habit of leaving any address.

The queen, Mokwaë, one or two of the king's principal wives, and other princesses, have come from Nalolo and from Lealuyi to make a little stay here, accompanied by the old Narubutu. It was kind of them, for they thought, in the king's absence, we should be dull, and not know what to do with ourselves. They consoled me for the theft of my ox by saying, " Just like the Barotsi ; the Barotsi are made that way ; you don't know them yet." A charming prospect for our future connexion, is it not ?

Since he has been on the march, Lewanika has kept us regularly informed of his movements ; his messengers cross one another. It is quite a new amusement for him to send us little notes, to tell us that his horse is lame, that he has forgotten to ask me for such and such a medicine, that his army has passed such a river, etc. ; for now he has a secretary of state—nay, two. They are our poor prodigals Karumba and Seajika, whom he has promoted to this new dignity. He has them about him to teach him to read, to pray to the missionaries' God in case of necessity, to scribble messages, to keep him informed of the price of merchandise in the countries they have visited in their journeys, to tell him the value of the coins he has a fancy for getting hold of, and to assist him in his commercial transactions. The king makes rapid progress. Already he knows the whole alphabet, which he considers a great triumph ; he always carries in his pocket, carefully wrapped up, the two A B C's I have given him. He also knows that a sheep sells for twenty-five shillings at Mangwato, a head of cattle for £10, while trade goods are going for almost nothing. I do not yet know what

sort of character our two young renegades are giving of the
Gospel and of us. We stand pretty well at court ; they themselves cannot altogether do without us. The time has not yet
come to run us down openly. It would be bad policy. The
king loads them with favours. Seajika has already received the
present of a wife. Karumba is going to have one of his own.
On the return from the expedition, they will have cattle, slaves,
villages, at last ! . . . Now they are fairly launched. May God
have pity on them !

The last messengers from the king bring us sad news of
Sesheke. You will have had it from a better source. Here in
a few words is what we have learnt. You remember Sekabenga,
who occupied the post of Morantsiane at the time of our arrival in
the country, and who had fled since the Restoration. Threatened
with the same fate as the unfortunate Tatira (or Akufuna), the
creature of the revolutionary chief Mathaha, he had made
common cause with him, and ended by finding an asylum with
Sagitema, a petty chief of the independent Batoka, on the confines
of the Mashukulumboe country. There, his party was increased
by all the malcontents who fled from the despotism of Kabuku,
his successor. Even in exile, these people, hunted down like
wild beasts, had a semblance of a court. Tatira was king ; he
had his drums and his little ceremonial. He soon found a rival
in Karorongoë, a quite insignificant young man, but one of
royal blood likewise, who had joined the revolutionary party.
Karorongoë hatched a plot, murdered Tatira, sold his old mother
to some Makupakupe in exchange for ammunition, and from
that time was recognised as king without opposition. All was
settled. Nevertheless, it is the Morantsiane who is the soul of
the party. In spite of his fall and his disgrace, he is more
popular than ever. Not only have the Batoka lodged him,
hid him, and saved his life, but they favoured his plans of
revenge. Duly warned by secret intelligence when Lewanika
started on his campaign, the Morantsiane and Karorongoë
made their appearance at Sesheke suddenly and in broad
daylight. At first, they were taken for warriors, passing through
on their way to join Lewanika's army. The old Tahalima came
out to salute them, followed by one of his sons and an attendant.
At the sight of the Morantsiane, he stood quite dumbfounded.
" On your knees ! Clap hands ! Acclaim the king," they

shouted to him. "It is our turn to-day." "I only acclaim Lewanika," replied the chief, with his ordinary dignity. "Where is he?" Upon that, insults, assegaïs, and clubs rained down upon him and his followers, and in a moment their mutilated corpses writhed in the last struggles of a horrible death.

Lewanika, hearing this news, retraced his steps, and directed them to Sesheke. But they say the Morantsiane has already crossed the river. In that case, what will Lewanika do? Will he renounce his expedition?—or will he leave the country to the mercy of this desperate band? . . . The great province of Sesheke is bound by a mere thread to the kingdom of the Barotsi. The latter, considerably reduced by their wars and their continual massacres, are hated by the Batoka, and reviled by all the tribes whom they oppress. Lewanika's lax policy of *laisser-aller*, and the ineptitude of his nephew Kabuku, whom he has promoted to one of the most important and difficult posts, have irritated all minds. It only needs the man of the hour to bring about an irremediable rupture. Lewanika knows all that. An energetic measure might yet save the situation; but it demands a firmness, a determination, which he does not possess. The greybeards who ought to form the council of his nation have all been killed off, with one or two exceptions. Their places are occupied by young men, for whom governing means brigandage carried on wholesale and for private ends. No tie binds them together; they all bear grudges against each other. The king himself distrusts his chiefs, as the chiefs distrust the king. But God, who has sent His Gospel of peace and love to this barbarous people, certainly has purposes of mercy towards them. We judge of things from the human point of view, finite and subject to all sorts of influences. God reigns; He watches over the interests of a nation with no less solicitude than over the development of a plant. Out of chaos He will bring order; out of darkness, light. *Post tenebras lux.*

SEFULA, *April 24th,* 1888.

You have no idea how people invent things in this wretched country. The story got abroad that they had completely pillaged us and burnt our houses, and that we had taken refuge in a neighbouring hamlet, bereft of all resources, and even of clothing. Lewanika hastened to send me an express, requesting

me to proceed to his camp with my wife, and saying that on
his return he would reinstate us at Sefula! It is vexatious
that, at a time when the atmosphere is so charged with electricity,
the idea should have been circulated that we *could* be pillaged
and burned. That does not tend to inspire us with much
sense of security. If ever we are pillaged and maltreated, it
will be by slaves, to the profit of their chiefs, as usual. But we
are not uneasy on that point ; we have other cares : the greatest
of all is the loss of our oxen. How bring our provisions from
Sesheke ? And yet, we must have them. We are short of
everything. And these losses, and these difficulties, will they
discourage our friends ? But God will grant to each of us
not merely to hold on, but to go *from strength* TO STRENGTH.
If the life here is a struggle every day, it is also a daily lesson
of unreserved confidence in God.

We are passing through one of those periods—should I
call it a crisis ?—when faith is a combat at every instant, and
when very often courage is no more than a smoking flax.
Material labours, with their incessant fatigues and their
gnawing cares, crush us down. Nevertheless, we must install
ourselves, however precariously. We feel that life is passing
without our having the satisfaction of doing much. But do
not think that I am pitying myself or complaining. A French
general once told his aide-de-camp that the politeness of a
soldier was *obedience*. And I myself hold that, in all circumstances, our duty towards our Master is fidelity. The witness,
too, of a good conscience is a great thing, and I understand
better and better why St. Paul returns to it so often in his
letters to Timothy.

CHAPTER XIX

The Return of the Army—Its Reception at the Capital—Distribution of Loot —"She"—Death of Dr. Dardier and the Jallas' Baby—Reflections and Hardships—The Basuto Evangelists—The Spirit of Missions—The King's Diplomatic Illness—Divining Bones—Blossoms in the Desert— Nguana-Ngombé's Confession of Faith—Visit of Mr. Selous—"Lost Whites."

SEFULA, *August 5th*, 1888.

WHILE we were having school in the courtyard, our friend Waddell ran up breathless, and cried to us from the end of the house, "The post!" The post! Is it true? With one bound, I am on the verandah, where three strapping fellows from Sesheke are setting down their bags, the first mail which has reached us since September 1887. The oldest dates are of one year, the most recent of only four months. Sefula is not the ends of the earth, after all!

The king has at last returned. His expedition against the Mashukulumboe has lasted five months—five weary months— while here, as in the time of the Judges, "there was no king, and each man did what was right in his own eyes." The thieves had a fine time of it; the women found it difficult to make their slaves obey them. They themselves, at such times, are not at liberty to leave their villages to visit parents or friends. They dare not even cut their hair. They plait and curl it—all to no purpose; it is a swarming forest, uncomfortable even for themselves; and in order to carry on effective warfare, they introduce unlucky beetles, which they keep captive there, and which die miserably.

The arrival of the expedition was ill-timed, for the moon was waning; and woe betide the man who, returning from a journey or from hunting, dare return to his own hearth when "the moon is going out"! The king therefore camped in the fields until the new moon, and then made his entry into the capital. The whole population of both sexes had come together there for this occasion, and I leave you to imagine how noisy the reception was. I saw something of it. It is true that, in spite of his importunities, I abstained from going to see him in his camp, when he passed quite close to us; but later on I went to spend a few days with him at Lealuyi. Mokwaë arrived there soon after; and not at all *incognito*, I assure you. It was a Sunday, and we had already had a service—that is to say, a preaching. Happily, it was over, for the whole village was soon in a ferment.

All the women of the capital have gone to meet the queen, and have swelled her procession; while the men, each with his peers and under his chief, are massed in different groups on the public square. And of course the drums and *serimbas*, so beloved by the Barotsi, must all be there, tintinnabulating as usual. What would these good people say to our European hurdygurdies, big drums, and kettledrums?

The procession slowly advances, and arrives; Mokwaë leading it, garbed in gaily coloured print: she herself performs recitatives, to which the troops of women escorting her respond in chorus. It is the praises of the king that they are singing; and I must say that these chants, mournful though they be, like all the songs of our poor Africans, are not devoid of harmony. The men acclaim her, one group after another, prostrating themselves, and clapping their hands. And this noise goes on for an hour,—without any confusion, however; all is perfectly decorous. The women will resume their performance at sunset; and Mokwaë, always the leader (*coryphée*), will sing with them all night. Meanwhile, at an order from the king, she retires to the spacious court of her own home. The chants have ceased; and the court now rises in due form. Lewanika invites me to accompany him to his levée. I quickly shake hands with his Majesty, and sit down close to the mat where he is enthroned. Lewanika kneels down; Mokwaë does the same: they kiss each other on the lips, take both each other's hands, and keep spitting upon one another; while the women of Mokwaë's suite, well greased with ochre and loaded with beads, ranged against the courtyard wall, repeat in cadence, " *Yo-sho! Yo-sho!* " in a minor key, which thrills through one. Then come the children and near relatives, who enjoy the privilege of being spat upon by royalty ; then the dignitaries, those highly placed personages who have a right to the privilege of kissing the king's and queen's hand, when they visit them ; then the middle class, who keep them- selves at a distance, and the common people outside the court, clapping hands with the greatest solemnity.

But the sun is sinking : the ceremonies are cut short, and at my request the public crier convokes an assembly which is double that of the morning. I preach on Gal. vi. 7 : " God is not mocked : for whatsoever a man soweth, that shall he also reap." While I interceded with God on behalf of this blood- thirsty nation, it was my duty publicly to denounce an expedi- tion which Lewanika himself calls an act of brigandage, and I did so. There shall be no mistake about the position we have taken up. Lewanika, full of consideration for his missionaries, had sent to our friends at Sesheke ten head of cattle he had just plundered, of which two were delicately offered to *Mme. Jeanmairet*, " our daughter " ; and I know that there was also a little herd kept back for us. But M. Jeanmairet, in a fine dignified letter, while thanking him warmly, set forth the reasons why neither himself nor M. Jalla nor Levi could as Christians accept such a present. Did Lewanika expect this refusal ? He contented himself with replying, " I understand : but what do the Barotsi possess that they have not obtained by pillage and robbery ? "

The number of cattle captured is enormous. We are assured that more died on the way than arrived here. It seems that the Mashukulumboe, at the approach of their enemies, drove their cattle into the haunts of the tse-tse. The king has reserved considerable flocks (as much for himself as for Mokwaë and the principal members of his family), which he has scattered through the country. They declare, however, that it will take another month to distribute the rest.

What makes one's heart ache is the young women and children who form part of this booty. They conceal the number from me ; they even declare that the king had given orders only to attack the cattle. But the truth will out. Of men, not one has been carried off. Walking through the village, I noticed here and there bundles of spears, most of them bent back—an indubitable sign that they had shed human blood.

Consequently, they had to be purified. The Gambella and others of my acquaintance ostentatiously showed me their sheaves of weapons—none of them bent. "They are pure," said they : "we remembered your injunctions." My friend Mahaha even sent me a similar message from Sesheke. Whatever these assertions may be worth, it is already something to hear a Zambesian boast of having denied himself the pleasure of disembowelling a poor Mashukulumboe. The king himself is not so far on ; for, seeing me come in, he said, trying to giggle, "Don't begin to scold me, if they tell you I killed a man with my own hand." Alas ! it would seem he had killed more than one. Wherever the Mashukulumboe made any show of resistance, he it was who directed the attack ; then, accompanied by some cavaliers, set off in pursuit of these poor creatures, terrified by the firearms, and by that nameless monster—a quadruped surmounted by a human form. Oh, what a terrible awakening is in store for that man, when the Spirit of God illuminates his conscience and touches his heart ! In this raid, Lewanika has, however, shown some magnanimity. Not only has he restored their liberty to several women captives of a certain age, but also their cattle, wives, and children to those who had courage to perform an act of submission.

They did not dare to attack a *chiefess* named Nashintu, whom the Makololo had once made prisoner, but afterwards liberated. On that occasion, they contented themselves with keeping her only son, who has since become one of Lewanika's principal workmen—and ours too, when occasion requires. This Samoïnda, like all the Mashukulumboe slaves, has distinguished himself by his cruelty towards his compatriots. Nashintu, like Mochache,[1] exercises power by means of her medicines and her charms. She has Pandora's box : she dispenses drought and hail, calamities and epidemics, at will ; and, shut up in an urn, she keeps the terrible scourge of small-pox. Finally, she possesses what many ladies of the great world would envy—the secret of perpetual youth.

You will be surprised to learn that, in this expedition, Lewanika has scrupulously observed the Lord's Day ! He kept about his person our two poor renegades Seajika and Karumba, to teach him to read. (Did I tell you he had sent for

[1] See Part I., page 77.

them from Mambova last year?) He made them his *Baruti* (missionaries), just as he appoints his scullions. Their duties are to pray, sing hymns, and *preach!* And to make them the more worthy of their office, he deprives them of intoxicating drinks. This still goes on at Lealuyi. Thus these two unfortunate young men find themselves in the most equivocal position. They have not the moral courage to confess that they are not qualified to preach truths which they belie by their return to paganism, and by an immoral life known to all the community, while their consciences accuse them no less than our presence. One need really be an African to play and sustain such an impossible *rôle*. The king, astonished at *my* astonishment, asked me, " What were we to do on Sunday, which we wished to observe, when you were not there? These boys know more about it than we do, and I rebuke them and send them away when they have drunk too much. Can they preach wrong things to us? "

The case requires prudence, simple as it may seem. We are too far from the capital for me to go there regularly and often. If we had established ourselves nearer—at Kanyonyo, which was not possible—the difficulty would have been just the same. It is in the actual village of the capital that we ought to be,—an absolute impossibility from the sanitary point of view, and no less impossible from the practical and economical standpoint; for the Barotsi do not live all the year in the Valley; they go and settle upon the heights around at the time of the floods. And then they readily change their place of residence. What would solve this difficulty and many others would be to have a band of devoted evangelists. But these evangelists we have not got. As to Karumba and Seajika, one of two things must happen: either they or Lewanika will get disgusted, and the movement will collapse of its own accord; or else the movement will develop, and they will feel their weakness, they will repent and return to their God. But how much greater would have been our confidence and joy, if their repentance and return had been the starting-point and motive of their activity! Let us not despair. God makes use of singular instruments sometimes, and it will not be the first time that the Gospel has converted the very people who preached it in their own fashion, without knowing it experimentally.

I speak of a band of evangelists whom we need; and alas! we have to record a loss among those we had. Our young doctor, M. Dardier, is dead. Poor young fellow! he did so enjoy his first canoe voyage. I can see him now, during a halt, jumping into one of our launches, and triumphantly reaching the open water, in spite of protestations from our crew, who, in their heart of hearts, enjoyed this exuberance of youth. One day, close to Nalolo, as I told you, while we were taking our frugal repast on the bank, he suddenly cried out, " How hot the sun is! "—putting his hand to the nape of his neck. He got back into the boat, and a sunshade was given him—too late! He was already suffering from the effects of a sunstroke. We did all we could for him, but he went from bad to worse. Alarming symptoms soon revealed an affection of the heart. He conceived a repugnance to Sefula, and could think of nothing but a prompt departure. But nothing is prompt in this country. He reached Sesheke, where also every care was bestowed on him. After a transient improvement, he grew worse again, and hastened to leave Sesheke. He had already crossed the Zambesi at Kazungula, where I had met him on his arrival from Europe a few months before, and was the guest of Mr. Westbeech, when death overtook him. Thus was cut short at the outset this career, on which we had founded so many hopes. The loss to his family is shared by the friends of missions: it is our loss too. It will probably, but wrongly, be a black mark for the Zambesi climate, which was beginning to reinstate itself in public opinion. Will it put an extinguisher on any newly kindled vocations for medical mission work.[1]

[1] Dr. Dardier, of Geneva, was the only medical missionary the Barotsi Mission has ever possessed, and the first European to lay down his life in its service. Hitherto the only victims had been its native helpers: three adults and three children. Now it was to be the turn of the white people: Dr. Dardier a few months after his arrival, four little children in succession, Mme. Coillard in 1891, and M. Goy in 1896. The last named came out in 1887, originally with the intention of devoting himself to agriculture and other industrial work in the interests of the mission; but as soon as he knew the language, he began to evangelise; and after his marriage with Mlle. Keck in 1890, he took charge of the Sesheke station, vacated by the Jeanmairets. During this year (1897), two more victims have been claimed—Theodore, a Basuto evangelist, and the only child of M. and Mme. A. Jalla: thus bringing the total number up to fifteen.

This dark cloud is not the only one that has shadowed our sky. M. and Mme. Louis Jalla will have told you that it has pleased God to consecrate their ministry through affliction, by taking back the child He had given them. Mr. Middleton has finally left us. Levi, the evangelist, too, can stand it no longer. It is now a long time since he wrote to me, " For seven months past, my wife has not left her room, scarcely even her bed." The poor man is nothing but a sick-nurse. He wishes to go back to his country for good, and we must from this year take measures with that object. Aaron is still one of us ; but his departure is only a question of time, and time shortly to expire. He too finds life hard at the Zambesi.

And for whom is it not hard ? The school of renunciation puts us under a discipline against which our old nature is always ready to rebel. One could accept willingly, even joyfully, for oneself, the privations which it goes hard with one to endure for one's own. To pass months without a drop of milk for the household, without a morsel of meat ; and to depend entirely upon a rapidly disappearing web of calico for the obtaining of a stringy fowl, which, but for its toughness, one could eat, feathers and all, at one mouthful ; fish that will not keep, and that one soon sickens of; and the vegetables of the country, millet or insipid manioc,—all this is not cheerful, it must be confessed, especially where there are children. The little flock I brought has melted away, cows and all, without our having profited by it the least bit in the world. At Sefula, we are all on the same rations ; and we generally share whatever we can buy to vary our diet. But our friend Aaron has to struggle against other trials peculiar to himself. He has a daughter of fourteen, to whom he is ambitious of giving an education which even Basuto-land could not afford her. And lo and behold ! the royal family has taken into its head that she shall be the wife of Litia, the heir-apparent. The Barotsi will never acknowledge themselves beaten, and in this matter they exhibit an exasperating persistence. Aaron, whose respect for them is no greater than it need be, is going to send his daughter to Mangwato, and has signified his intention of soon returning to his country.

Levi and Aaron are men with whom, as with ourselves, there is no need of a microscope to discover the flaws. But

BREAD-MAKING.

[*To face page* 316.

they both possess, each in his own way, qualities which make them valuable helpers, and we shall find it difficult to get better ones. I confess that for me it is a severe trial. Shall we ever have any other Basuto evangelists? I have said, " If Africa is ever to be evangelised, it must be by her own children." I counted on the Christian Basuto. As evangelists, I have always recognised in them special aptitudes which we Europeans do not possess. Their social and intellectual level brings them nearer than ourselves to the people we are evangelising. Were we mistaken then? No. The Spirit of God is working among the Churches of Basuto-land, and we know that there, as in France and everywhere else, the spirit of life is the missionary spirit. If distress has been great in that dear little country, it is not endemic there. The day will come, perhaps it is not far off, when the Basuto Christians will feel they owe a debt to these tribes of the Zambesi, who speak their tongue, after having borne their yoke—a debt which no one can discharge for them.

Meanwhile, who is to do the work ?

We have a perhaps unique opportunity of taking "possession of the land." All the chiefs, with few exceptions, seem well disposed ; the king shows a great desire to have instruction for himself, and for the tribes he governs—or, to speak more accurately, for the Barotsi tribe itself. How long will this good disposition last, if they are not converted? I have before me a list of twenty posts of evangelisation which we ought to occupy as soon as possible. The Barotsi would reserve to themselves the monopoly of education as well as every other monopoly, and that is why a day school open to all classes will encounter great difficulties for a long time to come. But if we had the staff and the means, and could open an establishment for boys, and one for girls, we should at once have such a number of pupils that we should have to limit them. All would submit to a discipline which that attending circumcision would enable them to understand. I do not pretend that it would be the easiest work in the world, but it is feasible. To undertake it, we should need a specially selected and experienced staff—men and women who would give themselves unreservedly to it, with all the physical strength they enjoy, all the talents they possess, all the force of their fullest love.

For the moment, the king's sons and nephews are coming

back, and I have reason to believe a pretty good number of the
sons of the principal chiefs also. For some time, moreover,
the king has been pressing us to receive Mondé, the eldest
daughter of Mokwaë. She will not come alone. But these
establishments, with a crowd of slaves of both sexes over whom
we have not the slightest control, are unspeakable dens of
licentiousness. And how, I ask you, can we carry on the school
and the evangelisation, and at the same time face the multi-
farious duties that make incessant claims upon our time and
attention? It is a serious thing to send out appeals, above all
when it is a question of coming to these climates. The Saviour
has shown us the surest way : " PRAY the *Lord* of the harvest
to send forth labourers into *His* harvest."

I do not share the fears of certain friends who think that
the Zambesi may well be set aside for the French Congo.
That may be a wholesome warning for our supporters. For *us*,
the work is the same, wherever it may be carried on. There
will be emulation, not rivalry, between us. At the Congo—as in
Tahiti, Senegal, and soon in Kabyle—we have the explosion of
Christian Protestant patriotism, so long suppressed and trodden
down by the ruling authorities. It is time for us to vindicate
among ourselves, in our own colonies, the right to serve our
country, and to contest with Roman Catholicism the monopoly
of patriotism and self-devotion, which she wrongly claims for
herself. Rome is not France, any more than it is the
Gospel.

But in the Zambesi Mission, as in the Basuto Mission, whose
daughter it is, we have the manifestation of the essentially
catholic, universal character of heartfelt Christianity. Like the
Good Samaritan, without any human calculations, Christians,
of no matter what country or denomination, unite their sacrifices
and their love to redeem the most brutal and degraded savages
who form part of the human family. Above all the prejudices,
interests, and flags of their respective nations, together they set
up the Cross, and spread its banner. And we, children of the
Huguenots, Protestants and Frenchmen to our heart's core, we
who have initiated this great work of elevation, in a country
where no European power protects us, say, shall we be putting
France to shame ? Shall we be denying our country, or—will
she indeed deny us?

For some weeks, the king has been ill. He has left the *kuandu* (his private apartment), and has secluded himself in a tent of mats which they have raised for him in the remotest corner of a back yard. Apart from his favourite attendants, no one has access to him, not even his ministers, the Gambella, nor even Mokwaë, his sister, so afraid are these poor people of what they call " bad feet." To arrive at the court he is occupying, one must cross three others, where night and day are found silent groups of slaves. The principal chiefs, who are at the capital, pass the night in the first, and in the second his *likomboa*, the most important members of the staff of the royal household. The third is reserved for his intimates. Men pass through the *lekhothla* like shadows, without stopping ; the chiefs sit there for a few moments out of duty, but no justice is administered, no business is transacted, no one speaks above a whisper. The evening fires are no longer lighted, the drums are silent (those beloved drums, how surprised they must be to rest !). No one dares go and work in the fields, though the season urgently demands it ; every one is melancholy and sus-picious ; fear has seized upon everybody. It was thus I found Lealuyi last week, when, alarmed at the turn things were taking, I betook myself thither in all haste.

Might it not be that this illness was only a pretext for attain-ing a political end—namely, to have an ostensibly good reason for getting rid of suspected persons ? My apprehensions, alas ! seem to be only too well founded. It is neuralgia that the king has, affecting half his face. He only gives orders in a whisper to the people crouching round his door ; but when once we were alone together, he could chatter, laugh, and in short let himself go as he always does. I asked him how it was that the divining bones chose precisely his own favourites to have free access to his presence. " Pooh ! " he said sharply, " the divining bones say what I wish." Evidently they do, and it is by no means reassuring.

While I was there, I was able to induce him and his ministers, the Gambella and the Natamoyo, to make some overtures to each other. Were they sincere ? We shall soon find out. The old councillor, Narubutu, whose portrait I have sent you, is laid up at the same time as Lewanika, and with the same sort of malady. I administered my sedatives with so much assurance that my patients confessed to a real improvement. I could not, however, persuade Lewanika to leave his tent, and sit in the courtyard, which is well sheltered, carpeted, and shaded with mats. It is whispered that a plot against Lewanika in favour of the Morantsiane has been discovered, and that the principal chiefs of the Valley, the Gambella at their head, are gravely compromised. I should not dare to deny it ; but I shudder at the thought of new massacres. I think Lewanika will not forget the conversations we have had during the four days I have passed with him. Oh, if only I could inspire him with a horror of bloodshed ! What I cannot do, the grace of God *will* do. There are great contradictions in this man. He is despotic, vindictive, and as cruel as possible ; yet, with all that, he has good sense, tact, generosity, and amiability. I could easily draw two portraits of him, which would have nothing in common. There is more than one Lewanika in the world.

I said some time ago that there were neither flowers nor fruits at Sefula. Last year, on my return from Kazungula, I found that all my eucalyptus trees had perished ; and this year, if we still have a score struggling on, it is only thanks to diligent watering. A single seed of sweet pea, which had somehow found its way here, was carefully planted and barricaded with thorns, in front of the bedroom window. It grew ; it sent forth a flower—only one ; but how lovely it was, and how delicious it smelt ! One morning, some Zambesi chickens—a dwarfish race, and hence all the more destructive—managed to slip under the thorns, and—pecked the flower to pieces and tore up the roots. Such a poor struggling little waif as it was, you would not believe the delight we had in it, nor our grief when we saw it withered and dead.

This makes me hesitate to speak to you about another flower, beautiful in a different way. But why should you not enjoy it with us, and help us to water it ? If it should wither (which God forbid), you will lament it with us, and your sympathy will be a comfort.[1]

On November 14th, 1887, I began my class of catechumens—

---

[1] Unhappily, the sweet-pea's history proved only too perfect a parable of Nguana-Ngombé's.

of *enquirers*, as the English more justly call them. This class
was, and still is, composed of only two members—Ruthi, the
daughter of our evangelist Aaron, and Nguana-Ngombé. It
is about the latter, whom you know already, that I desire to
speak. For more than a year past, we have had reason to
believe he was converted. He has always given us great satisfaction ; during the years (now nearly four) that he has been
in our house ; but that was not enough for us. To-day, he is
more than a good servant to us : he is a son. I believe I have
told you how often we have found this dear boy praying in
the thickets of the woods, and how one evening he came shyly
to ask in so many words, "What must I do to be saved ? " It
is a long time now, since he professed to have found the
Saviour. I wish you could see him, talking, in his somewhat
laconic manner, with the people who come to offer us their
produce, or calling together our children and work-people in
the evening. It is a pleasure to take him for an evangelising
journey. He is beside himself with joy ; he must needs stop
the passers-by, and shout to those working in the swamps
whom we cannot reach, and emphasise what I say, or repeat
it in the dialect of the country, in that genial way of his that
makes people listen to him. Everybody knows Nguana-
Ngombé, and every one likes him.

A fortnight ago last Sunday, we had a good audience of from
one hundred and forty to one hundred fifty people. I spoke
upon the Unknown God—Acts xvii. 23. When I had finished,
Nguana-Ngombé, under the influence of deep emotion, rose
and asked leave to speak. I took down his address, and I think
it will interest you. It touched us deeply.

" My fathers and mothers," he said, "you will be astonished
to see me stand up to speak in an assembly like this. It
is because I feel driven to tell you that I long sought the
Unknown God, of Whom the *Moruti* has just been speaking. I
have found Him ; He has revealed Himself to my soul ; I am
a believer. You look at me in astonishment. You all know
me. I am Nguana-Ngombé, a *moshimane*" (here, a slave). " My
father is a Mosubia, my mother a Motoka. I am the *moshimane* of the *Baruti*. Yes, but I am more than that—I am a
believer. I was lost : God has saved me.

" I was not always what I am now. Alas, no ! Four years

ago, I was a mere child " (he is now fifteen or sixteen). " I went
to Leshoma to ask the *Moruti* to take me into his service for
a month. It was a *setsiba* that I wanted. The month gone
by, I asked him to keep me for a gun. He consented. But
I did not like the things of God. When the hour for prayer
came round, I put my kettle on the fire, and ran off into the
woods. Those who knew me then, know that I was passionate,
and that I could not endure either insults or contradiction.
At Sesheke, I felt less dislike to the things of God, but I
understood them no better. The wish of my heart was to be
educated—that was all. When we arrived here, the *Moruti*
returned to Sesheke, to fetch our Mother, and left me with
Waddell and Middleton, and we did not know if he would come
back. Middleton gave us our food very regularly ; but there
were no more prayers, no more hymns, no more sermons.
These whites worked all the week ; on Sunday they rested,
and no doubt read the Word of God together. For us, the
bashimane, the Lord's Day was like any other day : we ate, we
slept. I did the cooking, and that was all. One day, my heart
was full of anger. I found our stock of insults too small ; and
I demanded of Middleton to teach me the biggest English
oaths and the most withering curses. He told me he had long
forgotten them.

" One Sunday, I asked him why he did not make us read.
He did it that day, but not after. I think he was tired. My
heart was very sad, and I mourned to myself, ' If only I had
profited by the teaching of my Father and Mother ! And how
if they never come back ? ' With these tormenting thoughts,
I wandered aimlessly in the woods. The idea suddenly came
to me, ' Suppose I tried to pray alone ! The *Moruti* says God
always hears.' I threw myself on my knees there, under those
bushes, and cried, ' O Thou, the great God Whom I know not,
have pity upon me ! ' One Sunday, it was raining, so that I
could not go into the woods, and I proposed to Kamburu and
the other young men to sing some hymns. ' Very well,'
replied Kamburu, ' but first we are going to sing *boyanga* ' " (a
heathen song " ' and to dance.' So indeed they did, and I went
away. They were displeased with me, made fun of me, and
called me all sorts of names : it drove me to pray all the more.
I was in a great agony. The counsels of Aaron and of my

Father" (the missionary) "helped me, and at last I found the pardon of my sins.

" Are you going to say,' Look at Nguana-Ngombé ; he wants to be a white man'? How can I become a white man, when I was born black ? God is not the God of the whites only : all white men are not believers ; we have seen some already who were bad like ourselves. The *Moruti* says it is the same thing in Basuto-land ; there are Christian Basuto, like Aaron, but there are others who have remained heathen. It is the Christian Basuto who bring us the Gospel which they have themselves received from the Christians of France.

" I hear people scoffing, and saying, ' Has the missionary been up into heaven, that he pretends to know God ? ' No, he has never been to heaven, he has never seen God, and, moreover, he has never said he has done so. But God has revealed Himself by His Son and by His Word. I shall never tell you that I have seen God, but I will tell you what I know of His Word, and how He has saved me. No, the *Moruti* has never been up to heaven. But he is going there ; and I, his *moshimane*, am going too. I am the first, and I should be very much afraid, if I were not a believer. Shall I be the only one to follow him ? You, my fathers and mothers, and you my *thaka*" (equals in age), " will you not come with us ? Question me as much as you like, as often as you like ; do not be afraid. What I wanted to say to you is, that I have found the Unknown God, the great God, and that I am a *believer*."

This simple story, which under my pen and in translation loses so much of its warmth and colour, was heard with the deepest attention. The men clacked their tongues ; the women remained motionless, with gaping mouths : we ourselves, taken by surprise, were deeply moved, and blessed God.

SEFULA, *September* 1888.

One Sunday morning, to everybody's great surprise, a gentle-man on horseback arrived. It was an Englishman, Mr. Selous, French by descent and education, and a well-known hunter. For fifteen years and more, he has been going after elephants, lions, and big game in the solitudes of the Linyanti, the Mashona, and the regions of the Southern Zambesi. In 1877, he crossed the river, and thence went northwards. We met at Mangwato the following year, and became acquainted. Mr. Selous arrived at Pata-matenga in the month of May, with two waggons of merchandise ; but, alarmed by the reports current in the country of an imminent revolution, he abandoned his hunting, and, with a troop of porters and guides, crossed the river above the cataracts of Musi oa Tunya, and went north, across the Batoka country. He hoped to work round the Mashukulumboe country where Dr. Holub almost perished, and to cross the Kafoné. But it happened that his guides brought him straight to a Mashukulumboe village. It must be said that, in that particular place, the connexion of the two tribes is so close it is difficult to distinguish them. The same nudity exists, the same customs, the same language. They seemed to receive him favourably. Mr. Selous killed two or three antelopes, and the Mashukulumboe performed some dances in his honour. But in the night that followed, the illusion was dispelled in a most unexpected manner for the travellers, by a volley of bullets full in their faces, and a hail of assegaïs falling on their camp. Amid the confusion that followed, and under cover of the darkness, Mr. Selous succeeded in escaping quite alone.

The same night, driven by thirst, he ventured into a small village, sat down by the dying embers of a fire, and felt himself dosing off, when in a neighbouring court he heard some one loading a gun. At the same moment, a handful of thatch, thrown on the brazier by a new-comer, kindled a flame, and lit up the form of a man, a few paces distant, who was taking aim at him. Instinctively, Mr. Selous put out his hand to seize his carbine. But the carbine was no longer there ; it had been taken away without his noticing it ! With one bound, he was in the tall grass, and escaped indeed, but quite alone, without arms, and stripped of everything. Fifteen days later, three of his men rejoined him, and he learnt then that twelve of his porters had been killed, and the rest scattered.

There is a sort of free-masonry among travellers. Moreover, kindness to a man who came to us in such circumstances was only our duty. While listening to him, as he related his adventures to us, I felt singularly drawn to him. He is a noble character.[1]

[1] See Mr. Selous's book "Travel and Adventure in South-East Africa" for an account of this visit.

A CROCODILE OF THE UPPER ZAMBESI.

[*To face page* 324.

It is a serious thing that the Batoka and Mashukulumboe
have got to the point of not fearing to pillage and massacre
the Europeans who have penetrated into their country. The
adventures of Dr. Holub and Mr. Selous are by no means
isolated cases. We hear of Portuguese traders, of the son of
a missionary we know, and of his partner, a young Englishman,
whom they have also massacred within the last few years.
For the moment, that country is closed to science and commerce, but I have faith that it is the Gospel which will open it
before long.

The Barotsi in full council (*pitso*) requested me to attend
before them, and asked with interested curiosity if the Europeans
who travel in these regions could be stripped and killed with
impunity—were they "lost whites," "adventurers whom
nobody cared for, even in their own country"? The Barotsi
themselves are only one step removed from thinking so, to
judge by the way they have treated some English gentlemen.
These had come from England for the pleasure of a few weeks'
hunting on the Zambesi; and they had made very valuable
presents to the chiefs of Sesheke and to the king. That did
not prevent their being pillaged, tormented, and harassed in
such a way that they left the country without hunting, carrying
away nothing but the bitterness of disappointment and disgust.
The king, who had been ill-informed and deceived, fearing
perhaps that he might make himself unpopular, did nothing,
said nothing even to condemn the evil-doers.

Our friends the Jallas and Jeanmairets at Sesheke will
themselves have told you the life of vexations and struggles
they have been leading, since the village was rebuilt on the
station itself. They can scarcely call their houses their own.
We, who know something about it, understand all the
difficulties of their position, and it makes me very sad. May
God give His servants and handmaids the needful courage
and strength, to hold their ground and finally triumph over
everything!

CHAPTER XX

SEFULA, BAROTSI VALLEY, *October* 1888.

I T is always with pleasure that I pay a visit to Lealuyi. There I find myself in contact with chiefs coming from all parts of the country, and I often meet also representatives of foreign tribes. I hope to do a little good there, and I always learn something. My one regret is that we are so far away, for each visit necessitates an absence of some days, and a considerable upset in the routine of station life. Still, this distance has its advantages too, and that consoles us. Since we cannot get nearer to the capital, we still hope the capital will one day come nearer to us. Lewanika had promised it; he had even chosen a situation and built a stable. The stable was never used—it has fallen into ruins; and since the Mashukulumboe expedition, the plan seems to have been abandoned—I do not know why. Other plans are in the air, and it is as yet impossible for me to predict what form they will take.

At the beginning of the month, I had passed two Sundays at Lealuyi—ten days well spent. Lewanika had convoked a grand *pitso*; but the chiefs delayed so much in coming together, that I went away, back to my sick wife. The couriers were soon after me, bringing their messages scrawled on sheets of paper carried at the end of a reed; for in our poor Seajika the king has found a secretary of state—not very deeply versed in the art of caligraphy, it is true, but of whom he is nevertheless very proud. He uses and abuses this functionary like

326

a child. " Every one has assembled," said Lewanika ; " hasten ; business is urgent, and the people are dying of hunger!"

People are dying of hunger! At the capital? Does it astonish you? It does not me, for I have never seen plenty there. In all South Africa, I only know one spot more sad and desolate—that is Morokoeng. Lealuyi is the residence of the king. His ministers live there usually, and the chiefs occasionally come to stay for a time ; but they all have their own villages at greater or lesser distances. In flood-time, it is an islet, where the masters feel so closely penned up, that in the end they leave it to a few slaves, and take refuge on the wooded dunes bordering the Valley. It is the time for grand hunts and masquerades :—the Barotsi are passionately fond of masquerades. It is also a happy time for the slaves. The canoes dart over the submerged plain : their service is easy. One rejoices to see the huts having a bath, and the filth disappearing : one only wishes this beneficent cleansing could be more complete. When the dry season returns, the village is repeopled. Then the slaves have a hard life. There are no fields in the neighbourhood ; all the food, like all the fuel, comes from a distance, and is carried on men's backs. The water—and such water !—is drawn two or three miles away. Only a few miserable cows are kept there for the little children of the aristocrats. The slaves, who swarm there, tighten their belts in vain ; they do not always succeed in cheating hunger ; and if they do not steal, they take to flight. If they are caught —and alas ! they always *are* caught, even if it is not for twenty years—they are no better fed ; they are simply strangled or flogged more liberally. Here, foreigner or traveller provides each for his own needs. Outside the village, he gathers reeds and armfuls of rotten grass, and makes a hovel for himself and his followers, and he vegetates there the best way he can, without anybody troubling about him, unless it be some of his relatives, if he has any.

If he is a person of some importance, the king gives him an ox, which is devoured in a couple of days, and then he fasts again in earnest ! If not, a pitcher of beer sometimes, a basket of millet, a bundle of manioc roots, or even a hoe, a mat, or some other trifle, and the duties of hospitality are fulfilled once for all. To see the bowing and cringing that follow, the exaggerated tokens of thanks, you would imagine there had been an unexampled display of generosity, if you did not know all about it.

And how false the world is with all its politeness and its adulations! If we try to apply this kind of hospitality to our own guests, we soon see we have quite a different race to deal with! How often I should like just for a moment to get inside one of these Zambesian skins, and see ourselves with their eyes, and judge of ourselves by their intelligence! Evidently here, a white man is not a being like another. With him, one may dare anything—one may permit oneself to be an exacting, imperious, even impertinent guest. And if he wants to barter for a *setsiba*, the Zambesian slave, following his master's example, sorts his fish, his sweet potatoes, or his weevilly millet, and brings the refuse. He laughs and says to himself, "That is good enough for the whites." He sifts his flour, keeps the best for himself, and unblushingly brings you the bran, pounded a second time. "That too is good enough for the whites." And it is the same with everything. For us, it is a chronic moral suffering. We say to ourselves, "They will change when they become Christians." We implore God to make love abound in our hearts.

What a digression about the capital, whither we are going! Let us hasten our preparations, and above all guard against hunger! This time, I determined to take my wife to Lealuyi. For a long while, she had desired it so much, that I think God must have put it into her heart. Perhaps too the change would do her good, I thought. Only, could it be done? The waggon was there, right enough; but the oxen and drivers were at Sesheke. No matter. Nguana-Ngombé, the man of all work, left the kitchen and took the whip; Aaron lent a hand heartily; we formed a miniature team of calves and heifers, and—set off. Our young cattle lay down, grew restive, struggled as though they would break the whole turn-out to pieces, bellowing with despair and foaming with rage under the yokes. In order to break them in for this little jaunt of six hours, we have been toiling and moiling for eight days under a burning sky in the sands of our dunes and the quagmires of our marshes. What scenes! I still laugh to think of them. No matter; we did not give up; we reached our goal—and that is the great thing. Our arrival at Lealuyi was a real triumph. For the moment, we preferred to forget about our return.

The next morning, I left my wife comfortably established in one of the king's fine huts with the queen, Mokwaë of Nalolo, her sister Katoka, and several princesses of the harem, as a sewing society in permanent session, and I betook myself to the *pitso*.

Although I have already spoken to you of a *pitso* among the Barotsi, I think this one merits a special description.

The king took his seat in the midst of a bewildering tintinnabulation of tom-toms and *serimbas*, the ministers crouching at his right, the chamberlains (if I may be pardoned for calling such small things by such big names) at his left. Troops of men, chiefs with their followers, were crowding from all sides into the public square. There was an incessant roar of acclamations like thunder, and, while the newest arrivals were prolonging it, the others were prostrating themselves, and taking their places among the groups already forming round the sovereign.

The drums ceased; silence fell. The Gambella (the prime minister), the upper part of his body unclothed, advanced into the space left vacant, saluted the king, and then made a speech. It was the " speech from the throne," as we should say. This speech was heard and received in such silence as seemed stupefaction. What do you think it was about? What indeed? You could never guess. Nothing less than the protectorate of " Satory "— Queen Victoria of England! In his exile, Lewanika had heard it talked about; he imagined that there he would find the panacea of all his ills. We had often talked it over together. I had tried to set his ideas right, and above all to inculcate wider and more disinterested views. I had resisted his entreaties, and many times refused to write to the authorities on the subject; and my reasons will be understood. I had counselled him to address himself first to the chief Khama, to take his ministers and favourite *likomboa* into his confidence, and then to treat of the matter in a council of the great chiefs of the nation. But Lewanika has the tendencies of an autocrat; he is a personification of the Divine Right. He was not sure of these great chiefs either, and he resolved simply to have recourse to a surprise. He counted on our credit and my goodwill, and thought he would be recommending his project

by identifying it with the mission. It is what the detractors
of missionary work do from another motive ; they take pleasure
in showing us up as political agents.

The Gambella spoke to the following effect : " Barotsi, we are
threatened by enemies from without and from within. I have
sought missionaries for you, so that you should not be behind
other nations. Did you welcome them ? Are you grateful for
them ? The chief Khama has missionaries, but he also has
masole " (soldiers). " They go together. So if you like to have
the missionaries, ask Satory to send us her soldiers. The *Moruti*"
(missionary) " will do it for us. To hesitate means to reject the
missionaries themselves. Would you like the missionaries to
leave us now ? Speak ; have no fear ; the *Moruti* is here ; he is
listening to you, and so am I."

Astounded like every one else, I was curious to see how
these poor people would take the thing up, and I held my
tongue. At length, a courageous orator broke the silence, which
had become decidedly embarrassing, " Lewanika, since we must
speak, see here : we are thy dogs. If those be thy words, we
have nothing to say—nothing. The *Baruti* are a blessing from
thyself. We have received them. They were foreigners ;
to-day they are Barotsi. We know them ; they are good people ;
they have not yellow hearts—not they ; they covet no man's
goods ; they pay for the services, we render them ; we all wear
their stuffs. They instruct our children, and give medicines
to our sick ; they are the fathers of the nation. We ought
to listen to their advice ; and if we absolutely must receive the
soldiers—well, let us receive them."

" But what are these *masole* of whom the king speaks ? "
burst out a second orator. " Are they missionaries too ? What
will they come to teach us ? The missionaries bring us the
Lengoalo" (that is, *the* teaching, properly *writing* which com-
prehends everything else). " Is not their teaching enough ?
Or have we refused to submit to it ? No, we have welcomed
them ; we love them : they pray for us ; they give us sleep and
rain. I ask, what are these *masole* ? "

The ball once set rolling, it was one series of speeches,
echoing and outdoing one another. Apart from a very
legitimate uneasiness on the subject of the *masole*—this thing
hitherto unknown, and now heard of for the first time—there

was nothing equivocal in the general confidence testified towards us. And they were all eyes and all ears when I explained that, as servants of God, we had absolutely nothing to do either with the *masole* or the British Government or any other government whatsoever. I dwelt on this, and I took care they thoroughly understood it. I added that, being perfectly disinterested in the question, as I am a Frenchman, I was ready to help them with my advice, and second them in the steps they took. I closed by explaining what a protectorate is, the liabilities it involves, etc.

Lewanika was stamping with impatience beside me. The speeches which followed showed I had made myself understood. " If you will have the *masole*," they said to Lewanika, " let them come, but not while we are here. We serve you because you are king and sovereign ; but if you become the *motlanka* " (the servant of rulers), " the subject of a master and a foreigner, that is a humiliation the Barotsi will never accept. We have welcomed the *Baruti* ; they have our confidence and our affection. Let us be docile and receive their teaching, and see what they will make of this nation ; it is worn out with bloody feuds. What we need is *teachers* " (*Baruti*), " and we have got them."

The chiefs demanded leave to shout and salute all at once, according to their usual custom for closing a great question, and thus to give a public manifestation of the nation's confidence in its missionaries. Lewanika was displeased, and withdrew.

At my suggestion, in the evening he assembled all the principal headmen at the *kashandi*[1] to discuss the question more freely. But discussion was no longer possible. The chiefs had laid their heads together and taken their stand. The king was on his mettle. Both sides were hurling provocations at each other, even while trying to keep up the traditional decorum. We were stifling in this electric atmosphere, and expected every moment to see the storm burst.

" The missionaries—yes, them we understand ; those are the men for us ; we will give our children to them ; but we will not have foreigners to rule over us."   " Why not ask me what I want them for, myself ? " retorted Lewanika.   Then turning to me, and pointing at them with his finger,[2] he added bitterly,

---

[1] The king's private office.   [2] A deadly insult to a Morotsi.

"It is to protect myself against those Barotsi. You do not know them; they are plotting against my life."

Thereupon, his *likomboa* launched boldly into abuse. "Now compel that base generation to confess its falsehoods and its plots! We know them all, and knew them long ago. To-morrow we will put you upon your trial; we will force you to unmask you schemes; we shall see how you will come out of it." Their vocabulary of insults is astoundingly rich, and there are some to suit everybody. I interposed with a few words of conciliation, and they listened to me. I thought the storm had subsided, but I was mistaken.

Early next day, the public square was full to overflowing when the king appeared. Seoli, one of the ministers, who owes his great influence as much to his own force of character as to his position, opened the *pitso* of the day with a violent harangue. He is, as every one knows, one of the most deeply compromised; and he took good care not to protest his innocence, but he boldly defied his enemies to prove his guilt. It was another minister, a member of his family, whom he denounced. Liomba, a man of weak character, protested, explained, and defended himself. "He had only warned Seoli, his relative, of the rumours current about him, and to put him on his guard." "Well now, it is for you to prove those rumours. Prove them!" they cried out on all sides. Already one felt that Liomba was to be a scapegoat, and that the failure of his cause was a foregone conclusion. Those most involved were the very ones to cry out the loudest against "this rabble who invent calumnies and spread them abroad, thereby compromising the king's safety, the life of his faithful servants, and the public peace." Liomba's adherents did indeed take his part at first; but they let themselves be intimidated, and ended by holding their tongues and hanging their heads. Then a perfect tempest broke loose. The popular excitement rose like the tide lashed on by a hurricane. He was forced to leave his place in the shade, and, stripped of his garments and bareheaded, to crouch down in the midst of the *pitso*, quite alone, amid the hooting of the crowd, on the burning sand, in a temperature of 104° F. in the shade.

This scene lasted from seven in the morning till four in the afternoon. I followed it with intense interest. Petty chiefs,

LIOMBA (FULL AND PROFILE).

[*To face page* 332.

parading their zeal, and thinking themselves free to do anything
to a defenceless man, overwhelmed him with abuse, pointed the
finger at him, and threatened him with their whips. "Bind
him with cords, and let us have done with this sorcerer," cried
one, whom I knew to be a thorough rascal. The Natamoyo (the
Minister of Mercy, protector of accused persons) was sitting
there, impassive and sanctimonious; the time had not come for
him to intervene. The king, in answer to a remark of mine,
observed severely, "Let them alone; they are bringing all his
slanders to light." The man was lost.

I rose and advanced towards him. "Barotsi," I said, "a
servant of God is a *Natamoyo*. You shall not kill that man—
you may kill me first. You have insulted him enough. What is
his crime? Say! Is he the author of your plots, or the inventor
of the reports that have filled the country, and reach us by letters
and messengers from Sesheke, from Pata-matenga, from Lake
Ngami, from Libebe's, and from everywhere else?" . . .

They listened in silence; little by little, the effervescence died
down. The Gambella and the Natamoyo spoke with modera-
tion. The cause was won. The king, by way of satisfaction
to the turbulent assembly, imposed upon Liomba the fine of
an ox, which he paid. While waiting for the beast to arrive,
Liomba took refuge with the Natamoyo, and for three days never
left his court night or day. At last, the fine was paid, the king
accepted it, and gave it to the *lekhothla*. Liomba submitted
to the ceremony of the *shoalela*; and scarcely had the king
pronounced his *pumenoko*[1] than the relatives and friends of the
poor man, his slaves, and even those who had abused him when
they thought him lost, crowded round him to kiss his hands.
We had already saved this man's life twice in the time of Tatira.

While all this was passing in the *lekhothla*, and agitating
the whole town, my wife, in spite of her great weakness of
body, had her own days well filled. She tried to pay two or
three visits to sick people; above all, they came to her. The
women and young girls besieged the hut, or filled the court,
from morning till night; and, whether they would or no, these
importunate visitors must needs be dismissed, if one would have
a little respite. The majority of women came with materials

---

[1] *Pumenoko*—"I am content." The royal acknowledgment of a salute.

to have dresses cut out for them and learn to sew ; the others looked on and listened to the chatter, which was by no means idle.   Others again were on the watch for a favourable moment to have a private conversation.   They had confidences to make, and advice to ask from the missionary's wife—a mother on whose discretion they could depend.   One gave a long explanation of her illness, another of her sorrows ; a third was enquiring about the things of God.

Those women who did not dare to penetrate into the harem enclosure where we were lodging, exchanged messages.   " I should so like to hear you sing ! " said one of them.   Happy thought !   My wife sent the three girls to her to sing hymns. From one court they were invited into another, then into yet another, and everywhere people crowded to hear them.

On Sunday, at evening service, as the shadows were lengthening, we were singing, " I have found, I have found the way " (" *Ke bone, ke bone tsela* ").   A silvery voice rose above all the others, and seemed to be hovering between earth and sky—a voice of charming sweetness.   Every one instinctively turned towards my wife with questioning looks.   It was not she. We discovered it was Sebane, one of our pupils, who was singing ; and a smile of satisfaction went round the assembly. No one will soon forget that silver clarion ringing through the mass of cracked voices.   Since then, we always associate that beautiful hymn with Sebane's voice.   This dear child, who is scarcely more than twelve or thirteen, is, of all our three girls, the one who at first seemed most unpromising.   She has become serious, active, lovable, and truthful.   May that hymn soon become the real expression of her own feelings !   These three children are only slaves ; but they are no longer what they were a month ago.   They are properly dressed ; they can sew and read and perform all sorts of little household tasks ; they have, in short, acquired a little air of civilisation, which raises them to such a point, that the queen, Mokwaë, when they came to salute her, quite forgot herself, and gave them her hand.

We could have returned to Sefula with a number of young girls, if we had wished, and had been able to do so.   But how could we resist the entreaties of the king, who besought us at least to receive his own daughter, Mpololoa, a nice child of ten or eleven ?   We ended by consenting, on condition that she should come quite alone, without slaves, and should be entirely left to our discretion. Instead of one, *three* came, and with a suite of slaves suitable to their rank. "What!" the princess Katoka had exclaimed, "let our children go to Sefula without slaves? Never!" In vain we sent them back; some persistently remain, "lying low" at Litia's, and appearing now and then. We had to make an exception in favour of two little slaves of the same age as the king's children, who share their amusements and come to school; and one other exception for Sanana's nurse, who has never left her. You see we already have the nucleus of a girls' school; and in the same way we have all the elements of a boys' school; in fact, we are overrun. We have neither the strength, nor the resources, nor the staff necessary for so great a work, the urgency of which imposes itself upon us more and more.[1]

For the moment, without speaking of the labourers required by our works, we have our hands full with the boys and all the little girls who live under our roof. We have to dress, feed, occupy, and instruct all these little people, and maintain discipline among them, slight though the latter may be—all of which in itself would be a heavy task for a person in good health.

But the work imposed on us is so important, that it would be culpable to let slip the opportunity for doing it. Mpololoa, who, as I said, is scarcely eleven, is already betrothed to a man who might almost be her grandfather, and who bears the title of Mokwe Tunga.[2] She is a pleasant child, but with her inferiors she puts on all the haughty airs of a great personage. The youngest of our new pupils is only seven— a little rogue, if ever there was one. When Mme. Coillard gave her a piece of stuff for the first time to learn sewing, Sanana looked at her and said, "My mother, for whom is

---

[1] The training of these young people was no easy matter, since the sanctity of their persons was such that it was not permitted *literally* to lay a finger on them. One day, while some building was going on at the station, a serf, running round the corner with a bundle of thatch in his arms, met the king's little daughter, who was running in the contrary direction, and by accident the tip of a reed brushed her eye. In an hour's time, before M. Coillard had even heard of the occurrence, the man was dead, executed by the child's attendants.

[2] Son-in-law of the Nation, equivalent to Prince Consort.

this garment? Sanana does not sew for anybody else ; she only sews for herself." You see there is not only an education needed, but a whole education to undo.

November 1888.

Our school began again on October 1st with forty-eight scholars on the books. It is a numerical gain on last year. Thank God, it is not the only one. The boys who gave us so much trouble, and sometimes so much sorrow, have come back to us in a much better frame of mind and with an ardent desire to learn. When they saw the school-house—still only a temporary one—which we are building, they were much disappointed to learn that it was not for the purpose of receiving them as boarders. They had been counting on that—I do not know why.

" We will submit to any discipline ; you can do anything you like with us," said Litia ; "and the king will feed us."

The king indeed enters thoroughly into these views. He is very energetic himself, and wishes all these young men to learn to work ; he finds it difficult to understand that our friend Waddell has anything else to do but teach them joinery. He has procured them planes and saws ; he spares nothing for them. He speaks of sending them "to the whites" ; where, he does not know. Lewanika himself is learning to read and write most zealously, and makes astonishing progress. He in his turn has set to work to teach his wives and servants, so that there is quite a little movement at the capital.

What is lacking is an evangelist endowed with a strong head and a sound heart, who should reside there. Aaron and I make frequent visits there. But now that he is leaving, and that I have lost my horse, what shall I do ?

The work here is certainly encouraging as it presents itself at this moment. The preaching is generally listened to attentively—attentively, that is all. It would not do to fancy that our Zambesians have as yet any true thirst after the things of God. Alas ! it often happens that, when we are beginning to hope, the smallest incident reveals to us that our wishes have given false wings to our desires ; and such revelations are full of bitterness. The preaching itself is often a hard task. During our open-air services, we are exposed to all sorts of rude interruptions, which provoke uncontrollable laughter. If the king sneezes, there is a thunder of hand-clapping. Or strangers come, and cannot understand this strange agglomeration of people who sing without dancing, and who are listening to the white man standing and speechifying ; they can only venture awkwardly and timidly to offer the usual salutation. That too makes every one laugh. Perhaps it is a lunatic who sits in front of me, and imitates my voice and my gestures ; or the king's idiot child, to whom everything is permitted, who runs about, questioning everybody and hitting people right and left. All that went on during my last preaching at Lealuyi. And when, preserving my self-control, I thought I had suppressed the effervescence, lo and behold ! a chameleon, dropped from I know not where, but sent by the devil, convulsed half my audience with terror, and half with mirth ! Our poor Barotsi have a keen sense of the ridiculous ; they make fun of every-body and everything. Often it is with a terrible inward conflict that I prepare myself to meet such an audience. Oh, why have we not a Philip here, a Stephen, an apostle full of the power of the Holy Ghost !

December 14th, 1888.

So here we are quite alone. Our friends left us a fortnight ago for Basuto-land—M. Goy to be married there, and Aaron to take his children. There is always something sorrowful in separations, and our circumstances added to the solemnity of the moment in which we commended each other to the grace of God. We had quietly made the preparations for the journey, and in seeing Aaron demolish and pack up his effects ; we had suffered all the melancholy feelings awakened by the break-up of a household. We had brought his school children to sing a farewell hymn, and receive the blessing of the master who was leaving them. Poor Aaron ! he did not make a long speech. " My children—I leave you with my Father and Mother : they are no longer young ; make the task easy for them." His heart was too full to bless aloud the school he loved so well. We had also taken our farewell Communion. And yet, up to the last moment, I cherished the vague hope of seeing something extraordinary happen to keep our helpers back. Illusion ! The spider thread snapped ; nothing extra-

ordinary happened. On Saturday, December 1st, we finally
bade each other farewell, perhaps only to meet in heaven. Our
friends had already accomplished their first stage, and our
appalling solitude was a reality. That, for the time being, is the
hardest of our trials, and the most difficult to accept submis-
sively. Aaron says he will come back. Will he indeed? And
Levi—will he? Does their departure really mean the rupture
of the bond which still attached us to Basuto-land? For my
part, I say NO, and I say it unhesitatingly.

In Levi and Aaron, we are losing two earnest Christians
and choice evangelists. What with his wife being always
ill, and with the unfavourable inclinations of the people at
Sesheke, which made it impossible to have a regular school
there, Levi may practically have been of little use; but it
cannot be denied that he was a moral force for us—and that
is something. As for Aaron, it is ten years since he left his
country. On our return from Banyaï-land, he remained with
Asser and Andreas at Seleka, where he worked with rare
devotion, supplying the needs of his family by his own industry,
when the Basuto War deprived them of all help. He accompanied us to the Zambesi, where he worked hard.
Converted at too advanced an age to enter a school, he has
educated himself by his own efforts. He knows very little,
but he possesses the precious gift of imparting to others the
little he knows. He had acquired a great influence in the
country; he leaves many regrets behind him, but he also
leaves the beautiful picture of a native Christian family as a
souvenir. Our evangelists quit us with an affection we heartily
reciprocate. They will not be lost to us: in Basuto-land, they
will make the Zambesi known and the mission beloved.

SEFULA, *December 15th*, 1888.

Here we are all alone; and while writing these words, I do
indeed feel that solitude is stretching immensely—indefinitely—
far in every direction. If we were in want of immediate help,
whence could it come? Happily, we have long since learnt
that "God is our refuge and strength, a very present help in
trouble" (Fr. Ver.: *un asile fort aisé à trouver*).

I confess that, before the departure of our friends, the
prospect of remaining quite alone frightened me not a little.

Above all, I dreaded the school, with its implacable regularity. God had compassion on us. He has made the arduous task a source of enjoyment. The school could not very well lose anything in our hands, although I recognise in Aaron certain special aptitudes I do not myself possess. The number of scholars has increased, and continues to increase every week. We have now sixty-five pupils, who all, with few exceptions, live on the premises. The king has even permitted a few of his young servants to come to Sefula to attend school. An excellent and enthusiastic spirit prevails among our young men. You would not think they were the same brigands of last year. They are respectful, and full of attentions toward us. Instead of devouring our sheep (it is true we have no more sheep to be devoured), they go on Saturdays (which are always holidays) to hunt for us, and dispute with one another the privilege of rendering us small services. When they knock down an ox, or their slaves return from fishing, a portion is always reserved for the " Father and Mother." It would not do to attach too much importance to all that. I only draw attention to these good inclinations, to show you that God, in answer to our prayers, remembers that our courage is a climbing plant, which cannot sustain itself, and needs props ; and those props He has given us.

The three hours (we are going to give four) which we pass every day with these children are happy ones, and we always feel sorry when the moment comes to dismiss them. We always fancy we could have made better use of the time. It is a hard task, all the same, to teach sixty-five children with three blackboards (one of them a box-lid covered with wax-cloth), four books, and six slates. And all that in the open air, amid every kind of distraction. One has to make shift, and multiply oneself. The system of monitors suits us admirably. Sometimes comical incidents occur to infringe discipline, as when people come to sell their produce, and, emerging from the wood, are astonished at falling into the midst of these *bana ba Marena* (children of the chiefs), who were always robbing them last year. You would then see them set down their baskets, and begin to clap hands ; whereupon our young princes tell them that " at school there are no princes," and that they must not salute them.

Sometimes, too, there are serious occurrences. The Barotsi brought back a great number of dogs with them from the Mashukulumboe ; and all these dogs have been attacked with hydrophobia. They are running all about the country, attacking men and beasts. Already many cattle and several persons have in their turn died of rabies. One day, when I was talking to the king, standing in his court amid a crowd of men crouching round, one of these mad dogs came and bit my leg. Happily, I had on thick canvas trousers, and he only pinched me. Before he could return to the charge, they had already clubbed him to death. Here on the station, we have killed at least twenty of them. You can understand the agitation which the appearance of one of these dogs creates among our classes.

To return to the school. I fear we shall soon be quite overcrowded. The king, irritated by Mokwaë's intrigues to give Aaron's daughter to his son Litia for a wife, has seen to the matter himself, and has chosen their future consorts for him and his nephew : little girls whom we now have to put into shape and polish up. Our house will soon be crammed. These good people cannot understand that a missionary's wife can be crushed beneath so much work and so many cares. They beg us importunately, " Receive our children ; they have a multitude of slaves who will work for them, and we will supply their food." That is to say, one day's abundance for five days' famine. I hesitate very much about beginning an establishment for the young princesses like that of Litia and his companions.

I was owing Lealuyi my monthly or bi-monthly visit (according as you reckon by theory or practice). The king gave me no peace with his importunities. But who would take my place here while I was preaching over there ? After much hesitation, my dear wife summoned all her courage, and rather than send our little audience empty away, she bravely performed the services and explained the Word of God. And I know that all those who listened were very much interested. Henceforth, when I absent myself, I shall know that Sefula will lose nothing, as long as my wife is not laid up.

Nguana-Ngombé also took his little part in the second service, and said some excellent things. He spoke on, " Take no thought for what ye shall eat." "When I took service with the missionary," he said, "a gun was the object of all my desires. I often asked myself when my time would be up, and I should possess it. When I had got it, I thought myself the happiest man in the world. A gun! *My* gun! It was never out of my thoughts. I used to get up in the night to make sure I really possessed it. I was always admiring it. But now that I know the Lord Jesus, it is He who has taken possession of all my thoughts and all my love, and I almost forget that I have a gun. It is there, hung up at the head of my bed, for days and days together, without my ever looking at it. When I hear some one talking about a gun, I say to myself, 'To be sure, I have a gun myself, so I have!' When I began to care for instruction, I longed for a shirt. Now I like to have clothes, but they come to me without my having to worry about them." He is a dear boy. I should like to make a good evangelist of him.

The king, too, is well disposed ; but that is all. And yet his thirst for the things of God is very remarkable. When Aaron and M. Goy went to pay their farewell visit to him, they were to come back, and spend the last Sunday with us, and we were to have the Communion. Unfortunately, the rain kept them, and delayed them till Saturday evening at Lealuyi. The king counted on their staying for Sunday ; our friends did not feel free to do so, and came back. It was a mistake, for which I am in great part responsible, and which I have bitterly regretted. Lewanika himself could not understand it at all. He sent me a letter written by Seajika, in which he poured out his sorrow. "What ! two missionaries leave us on a Saturday evening, when we were rejoicing so much in having them for Sunday. I don't understand you ! "

This goodwill on the king's part makes many things easy, although we must not count too much upon it. The chiefs —those that live round us—make it a point of honour to be on good terms with us. Those who made us suffer most last year are the greatest help for our work. If only it were the same at Sesheke !

CHAPTER XXI

A Serious Talk with Lewanika—Queen Mokwaë—Ex-queen Maïbiba—At Death's Door—Improvement in the School—Sickness and Mortality—Hostility at Nalolo—Break-up of the School—The Mokwe Tunga and his Troubles—Nalolo to Lealuyi—The *Nalikuanda*—A Prodigal's Return —Losses of Cattle—A Mining Concession.

SEFULA, *December 19th*, 1888.

A VISIT of some days at Lealuyi with my oldest pupils. The king was affable and chatty as usual. If the Barotsi were not such flatterers and so false, I should think he was not far from the Kingdom of Heaven. We were speaking one evening of our life at Leshoma, and of the countless difficulties which the chiefs of Sesheke created for me. "There is nothing surprising in that," remarked Lewanika. "When you came the first time, ten years ago, the Barotsi, suspecting your intentions, hastily consulted the bones and administered the *moati*" (a virulent poison) "to a number of fowls. Some died; others did not: hence the ambiguous messages which reached you. They dared not frankly forbid you to enter the country, and yet they were afraid to receive you ; and they tried by every kind of device to block up your path and discourage you. The cloak you then sent me I never saw, any more than your subsequent presents. They were declared to be bewitched, and were stopped on the way. What surprises *me* is that you had the courage to come back, and that you are here."

I was speaking on the subject of my first journey to the Valley, and my visit to Tatira. Lewanika interrupted me, and asked in a tone which demanded a reply, " Tell me now, what did they say about me ? What was I being accused of ? I could get nothing but evasive answers out of the Barotsi who remained here. I know you will tell me the truth."

I looked steadily at him. "Do you really not know what they accused you of?"

"No, and I wish to know."

"Well, they accused you of killing people without cause and without pity."

"Is that really true?" His countenance grew dark. "How many people did they say I had put to death?"

"A great many. They especially related how you had starved one of your brothers to death in an enclosure made on purpose close to the village; and how, in a single day, you had had seven Barotsi chiefs killed while they were drinking the beer that you had given them in order to deceive them."

After a few moments' silence : "It is all true," he said, "but the fault lay with Mathaha himself and his party."

He then told me how his unfortunate young brother, at Mathaha's secret instigation, intrigued to get possession of the power, and how Mathaha and his partisans accused Livingstone's old servant Mashawana, and other chiefs, of plotting against the king, and gave themselves no rest till they could get sentence of death passed upon them.[1]

Poor Lewanika! I pitied him deeply; for even though we talked a long while and of many things, his brow was still clouded, and from time to time he let slip expressions which betrayed the agitation of his thoughts. At last, getting the mastery over himself, and affecting a tone of gaiety, he said, "I must speak to you of two absences I have in view. I am first going to Ruena to snare antelopes. My second absence" (with a questioning look at me) "is a pilgrimage to the tomb of Katuramoa. The guardian of this village has dreamt that Katuramoa—a former king—has called me, and demands the sacrifice of an ox."

"What! you to go and pray to the dead! The worthy man might just as well have asked you for an ox without dreaming, and without obliging you to bring it to him yourself! And then, you know now that praying to the dead is offending God."

---

[1] Lewanika had his brother swathed round and round in an entire web of cloth, so that he was quite helpless, then loaded with beads and other royal ornaments ("that he might go to his fathers," the king said, "in a manner worthy of his rank"), and placed under a tree which still shades the *lekhothla*. A high palisade was then built all round him, and he was left to starve.

" You are right. But when I am a believer, I shall not go
and pray to the dead any more, and you will see if I don't
keep my word. Meanwhile, I must yield to the Barotsi; they
don't understand your teaching, you know."

" And when will you become a believer, Lewanika?"

" When I quite know how to read, and when I am better
instructed in the things of God."

" Why should you wait, tell me? Has not your conscience
often told you that you have done evil, and much evil?"

He grew pensive and hung his head. " Ah!" he sighed, "it
is a terrible thing to be a king. When I was only a private
person, they said I was an exemplary young man. I delighted
in hunting; and when I was not hunting, I was carving wood.
As a child, I once thrashed an urchin of my own age; later
on, I sent away Litia's mother, my first wife, because of her
immoral conduct. And that was all. They ruined me when
they made a king of me. I have become a corrupt and blood-
stained man!"

He paused. After one of those silences which are more
eloquent than torrents of words, we fell upon our knees, and
I prayed for him.

I had scarcely returned to Sefula before Mokwaë came to
spend ten days with us—as usual with a numerous suite. If
only she could travel more simply! Her young girls are so
arrogant! They think themselves at liberty to do anything.
Mokwaë tried to make herself agreeable: I think she followed
the sewing lessons at school with interest. One day, the rain
surprised us, and we had to seek shelter in our "tabernacle,"
which is now half roofed in. To maintain order, I conducted
my pupils in procession; Mokwaë placed herself at the tail,
and behind her, first her husband, then her councillors, and then
her servants. We managed to keep our countenances all the
same. One evening, they came to call me in a great hurry.
" The queen has eaten fish, and she is choking!" A good
mouthful of bread-crumbs which I made her swallow soon produced the desired effect. Unfortunately, two of her men were
attacked with ophthalmia, which is raging here; and a third
had an attack of fever. That sufficed to frighten the queen and
fill her with apprehension. So, the next day at dawn, she had
packed up her baggage, and hurriedly took leave of us.

I once interested our European friends in Maïbiba, who had been made queen during the time of the usurper Tatira, and who pleased me so much on my first visit to the Valley.[1] I had often enquired after her, and Mokwaë always answered with ill-humour. The king, however, assured me that she was still alive, that she had fled to Lekhoa Khoa, where Tatira came from, and that he would send for her.

He kept his word. Imagine my astonishment the other day at Lealuyi, when I recognised her among a gang of women who were kneading mud to plaster the fine hut Lewanika has had built for us. Our eyes met, and her pleasant smile betrayed her at once. "What! is it you, Maïbiba?" "Yes," she replied ; "I saw you before, but you did not recognise me, and I did not dare to come and speak to you." Although Mokwaë's eye was upon her, she found an opportunity of coming to tell me her adventures.

The king had been kind to her. When he sent for her, he allowed her to choose a new husband. "Leave me in the shade," she had begged of him, "far away from the *borena*" (the governing class in all its ranks) ; "I have always dreaded it." She chose for herself a Mo-Mbunda, who is not even the chief of a village ; and she says she is happy, poor creature! She is still just the same, frank and amiable, and she is treated with respect.

February 1st, 1889.

Propping myself heavily on a stick, wrapped in my dressing-gown, my head swimming, painfully dragging one leg after the other, I feel I am coming back from the confines of another world. A glance tells me as much, on entering my study.

In the middle of our New Year's festival, I felt the first symptoms of what I thought to be nothing but an attack of fever. Three days after, I was betwixt life and death. Who does not know how wholesome it is to be thus taken out of the scenes of active life, where it is so difficult to retire into oneself, and to be suddenly transported into the isolation of sickness, even to the threshold of eternity? But who can enter into the anguish of that woman left alone to bear a load already too heavy for two—alone to follow and battle with the

[1] See Part II. p. 171.

rapid progress of the disease, and threatened with the prospect of finding herself yet more alone in the midst of these savage tribes, and so far from any help?

But God is good. I was not indispensable to His work; and yet He still desired to make use of me. He is gently leading me back to life. Every one is doing his best not to interfere with my convalescence. Our scholars have left off their games; our boys and girls are making themselves as scarce as if they were mice.

Nguana-Ngombé, meanwhile, took the command of our work-people. He kneaded the bread, churned the butter, and washed the linen overnight. At daybreak, he distributed the food to everybody, conducted prayers, served our breakfast, and, without even taking time to eat, went off, his spade on his shoulder, at the head of his troop. And in the evening, the good boy fed all our staff, and prepared and served the dinner as though he had not left the kitchen. I really do not know what he is made of. And all the time, he is growing taller and taller as fast as he can.

February 12th.

Sefula has become a hospital. My strength is only coming back slowly, and now my wife is ill in her turn. For a long time, she has been ailing, and now she is confined to bed. Our friend Waddell, who was so well before, is also out of health. In spite of my great weakness, you see I have to be sick-nurse in my turn, and doctor too. This evening, Nguana-Ngombé had lit a candle and served dinner as usual—a dinner such as we do not often have: for Litia had sent us some beef; and Sepopa, the result of his hunting. We had to cook it all, for nothing keeps here. But when I, a poor convalescent, sat down to table all alone, this profusion seemed to me like irony, and my courage failed me.

February 24th.

Began school again some little time ago. It is a great responsibility to have so many boys on one's hands. Forced idleness always engenders a bad spirit. I was afraid, too, that my boys would begin to be discouraged, and to disperse. I first got them together for half an hour, and set the most advanced to teach the others. Directly the news spread, all

the absentees came back, and our list rose to eighty-five. Is it
not singular that this remarkable development of the school
should coincide with all our illnesses, and with the departure of
Aaron, who is now making a wayside call of six or eight months
at Sesheke, where they did not need him at all?

My wife, too, is now able to drag herself as far as the tree
which shades our school, and takes her share of teaching.
Oh that school! how it has taken hold of our hearts, and
what a place it occupies in our thoughts and prayers!

The construction of our temporary chapel advances.   I
had the idea of setting our pupils to carry sand and collect
cow dung, to level the floor and plaster the walls.   That
occupies them for an hour every two or three days.   But you
should have seen with what zeal they set to work, Litia and
all the young chiefs at their head.   When they have finished
their small task, they form themselves into a procession, and
file past the door, singing in two parts—

> *Borotsi, fatsi la bontata rona;*   (Borotsi, land of our fathers;
> *Gar'a ma fatse, le lethle ke lona!*   Of all lands, it is the fairest.)

Certainly, one need be born a Morotsi to sing that as they do!
For the moment, there is no more popular ditty in Lealuyi.
At this moment, a house is being built for Mondé, the eldest
daughter of Mokwaë: she has reached a marriageable age,
so they are going to bestow a husband upon her; and then
she will begin her education.   Likokoane, one of the king's
nephews, is just married, and his wife, a gentle young girl,
attends school with him.   However, this can only be temporary,
for Likokoane's village is at Kanyonyo.   All our pupils, great
and small, who are born Barotsi, have their own villages.
Otherwise, I should say that ours, that of the mission station,
is growing in importance.   It is now an agglomeration of huts,
built round and round.   In the middle are the houses of "the
king's children."   Litia, by his father's orders, surrounds himself with an etiquette which forbids familiarity, and safeguards
his authority among this mob of boys and slaves.   But, in
school, it is now admitted that there shall be no distinctions;
masters and slaves mingle in the classes, and teach each other.
That is a decided step forward.   The principle is so well
understood, that the king's daughters, who live in our house,

have learnt not only to do without their maids, but even to do household work, just like the little slave girls they found here with us.

I have recommenced my Saturday excursions through the hamlets dotted about in the marshes surrounding the Valley. We have scarcely any audience unless I go and get it together in this way. The question of family life here is a fathomless qnagmire. If I ask a Morotsi to send his children to school, he sometimes replies that the school is not for the serfs (*batlanka*) ; most frequently, he pleads as an excuse that he has no children—he has had one or two, but *Nyambe* (God) caused them to die. It is perfectly true that our Zambesians have very small families, and that—in a certain class at any rate—the prospect of paternity is looked upon as such a misfortune that divorce frequently follows. But it is also true that these poor people hide their children, as the Basuto do their cattle, and one can understand why.

First days of March.

Mondé arrived at our place as a royal bride, her arms loaded with ivory bracelets, her head and neck covered with beads. Her retinue was worthy of her rank. Nevertheless, she quickly caught up with the rest of the school. Of her own accord, she discarded some of her ornaments, and put herself on a level with the others, contenting herself with a mat instead of pillowing herself on a slave ; and she was already triumphing over A B C, when some clandestine love passages with a cousin whom she would have liked to marry irritated the king, and he sent for her immediately. Poor child ! they have given her a young man she does not like for a husband. They have threatened her with duckings—an old wives' cure for such cases, which is said to be very efficacious. But it is all of no use. Mondé has a will of her own. The king asks for my advice. I tell him he should have done that sooner. Such cases are not uncommon in this country ; but as marriages are dissolved as easily as they are made, it does not matter much. There are no unhappy couples here ; if people do not get on together, the husband seeks another wife, and the wife another husband, and all is said and done.

Death is never idle at the Zambesi, and generally ac-
complishes his work with appalling rapidity. There is poor
Mr. Westbeech ; he has just succumbed, while travelling, at
the Jesuits' place in Marico. How many blanks during these
ten years, even during these five years, in this small world
of the Zambesi! All the Europeans I have known, and
almost all the half-breeds (who are also personages here),
have passed away : Westbeech, Blockley, Dr. Bradshaw,
Afrika,—that is a long list already. Mamochesane, too,
whom I saw when I first went to the Valley, the daughter of
the powerful Sebetoane, died last year, in a condition not far
removed from abject misery and neglect.[1]

I spoke to you about the mad dogs which have been the
scourge of the country since the Mashukulumboe expedition.
After the dogs, it was the turn of the cattle ; and with them
the disease is always fatal. But more serious is the fact that
a corresponding disease is now raging among the human beings.
With some, it is a passing insanity ; with others, it takes the
form of madness, such that they have to be garrotted. Several
have succumbed to it. Just at this time it is Seoli, one of the
most influential councillors. The same day, his first wife died
also ; and two days later, another of his wives. A cry of
witchcraft would have been raised for much less, and public
opinion had already identified the sorcerer ; it could only be
the unfortunate Liomba,[2] with whom Seoli had had a crow to
pluck, and they loudly demanded his trial and death. The
king, in order, I believe, to shield him from his enemies, sent
him with Karumba to sell ivory at Kazungula. Liomba was
afraid of falling into a trap, and confided his terrors to me,
as if I could help him ! Still, I hope that the era of clandestine
murders has passed away, and that the Gospel has brought
peace and security into this unhappy country.

April 5th.

We are passing through a crisis. The number of our pupils
had exceeded a hundred. The prevailing disposition was excellent : everybody exhibited interest and enthusiasm, an entirely

[1] See Livingstone's "Travels on the Zambesi."
[2] See pages 332, 333.

new spirit of submission to discipline, and of respect towards us. Our task had become easy; it was a real pleasure. Then, first we had a perfect epidemic of ulcers among our boys— those African ulcers, which resist all ordinary remedies, eat away the flesh in an appalling way, and often cause death. They were the despair of Livingstone, and they are the terror of the Barotsi. Strange to say, all the boys and girls living in our house have escaped it, but we have lost a score of other pupils, who have returned to their parents to be treated.

But here is something much more serious. Nalolo, which has never been favourable to us, is now opposing us openly. Mokwaë is ill; indeed, very ill, they tell us. What do the diviners say?—the bones and the gods? I do not know; but evidently it is nothing good about *us*. Mokwaë has sent for her children; and all her people, one after another, have done the same. And these children from Nalolo were the flower of our school! More than thirty have departed already, without even bidding us good-bye. They were watched for as they came out of school : people even came at night, hurried them into canoes, and fled with them. Poor Barotsi, they have not much moral courage. These proceedings, which have taken us by surprise, trouble us very much. How long will the others stay with us? Yet it does not do to show our grief too openly; we must keep that to ourselves. Discouraged as our hearts are, may God give us grace still to carry on this ruined school with energy and spirit!

Here is another letter from the king, the third, I believe, and little calculated to reassure us. The porters, being charged at the same time with verbal messages, enable us to read between the lines. " O my missionary," writes Lewanika, " the Barotsi say I am going mad. They scoff at Seajika and his teaching. They ask what good the *Book* has done them. Never have we had so many calamities as since your arrival : never have so many men died!" . . . I do not yet know the cause of this hostile spirit, but it is very real. Sepopa and Likokoane confessed to me that, during their last visit to Nalolo, Mokwaë forbade them to sing hymns in her village. Litia has confidentially informed me that one party loudly demands our expulsion, and that twice already it has been discussed in the *kashandi.* Hence the king's doleful letters. And poor Lewanika, whom we know to be so weak, will he stand up for us ?

April 10th, 1889.

The breaking-up of our school still goes on. Rather than let it melt away altogether, we are giving three weeks' holiday, and I am taking advantage of it to go and visit Nalolo and Lealuyi. I must get some light on the situation. It is *Munda* (flood-time) ; the plain is partly inundated. The moment she heard of my intentions, Mokwaë sent me one of her canoes. My eldest pupils, Litia the first among them, have insisted on paddling me, and do it with delight. They are not very expert, and my dug-out rolls and fills with water in such a fashion as to make one a little nervous. Never mind.

We arrived. I was not kept long waiting. Mokwaë sent for me with Litia. They conducted me through I know not how many courts until we reached her hut of mats. At each passage, a servant was waiting for us, to pour water over our feet, and spread burning embers before us. Thus we had to pass through fire and through water—the flames must touch our feet ; and after this ceremony of exorcism, we were fit to appear before Mokwaë. She was enthroned upon a mat, with all the dignity of an invalid of her rank, surrounded with favourite servants and courtiers. All their faces were stony. The *Mokwe Tunga* (the Prince Consort) spoke little and very shortly. I questioned my patient, heard to the end the graphic description of her illness, and, satisfied with my diagnosis, I took leave. In the evening, I returned, administered pills, and myself prepared a cup of cocoa, which her Majesty found very much to her liking. She had a good night, and the next day she was overflowing with admiration for my pills, of which she wanted a supply, and a good supply too.

The ice was broken ; faces had brightened up, and tongues were loosened. Mokwaë protested that she had only sent for her children in order to see them before she died, for she believed herself to be dying, and she assured me they should return to Sefula as soon as I did. From other sources, I learnt that one of the grievances against me was that I made the Barotsi children do the work of slaves.[1] And then my

---

[1] *E.g.* collecting sand, etc., for the chapel floor (see page 347).

evangelising tours offended the chiefs: they, who can only make themselves obeyed by force, cannot understand that people assemble at my simple invitation. Another grievance—to wit, my teaching. Just listen to this! We sing—

Molimo mong a lefatse.   (God the Master of the world.)

World and *country* are the same word. Then does the country no longer belong to the Barotsi? I have predicted all sorts of calamities, it seems; they are expecting a deluge of fire from the north, which will sweep over the whole country. I have promised that, if the Barotsi accept the Gospel, they will live eternally. Well, they have accepted it, and they die more than ever. Monaré is dead, Seoli is dead, and many other persons, and so on. And you cannot think how seriously they put forth this nonsense, and a great deal more that would make you smile.

My boys and I occupy the principal hut in the establishment of the Mokwe Tunga, the so-called husband of the queen—a hut infested with *tampanés*. The bites of these frightful vermin, which swarm on the ground and rain from the roof, forbid us to dream of sleeping. You sigh for the dawn, while writhing and tearing yourself mercilessly to pieces. When you have endured several sleepless nights of such torture, it is enough to make you really ill; you are fortunate if the aggravated bites do not degenerate into bad abscesses. The travelling and carnivorous ants and the microscopic fleas are terrible. But the *tampanés!* Don't let us talk about them.

Masiho, the Mokwe Tunga, has escaped for a few minutes from Mokwaë's presence to visit me. He wanted to confide his troubles to me, for he too had some of his own. His first wife, an excellent person, with whom he had never any fault to find, had had a quarrel with Mokwaë. The two women were jealous of each other, and execrated each other cordially. Mokwaë made use of her authority to wreak her hatred on her predecessor: happily, the king interfered in time. The unfortunate Makabana escaped with her life, but she was torn from her husband and sent into a different part of the country, where the king gave her to another man for a wife. " How sad!" I exclaimed, when Masiho had finished his story. He began to laugh. "That's how things are done here."—"Now it's over and done with," he added.

I was anxious to assemble the village people to speak to them of the Gospel. The chiefs did not dare to oppose this, but they did not help me either. I seated myself in the public square, surrounded by my pupils, and we began to sing hymns. The men stopped at a distance, and the women grouped themselves round the entrances of their courts, but no one joined us ; and when we knelt down, it was in the midst of great roars of laughter. At sunset, I hit upon another plan. I went to the *lekhothla*, and began to exhibit my photographs. There was very soon a crowd. People were pushing and scrambling, tumbling over each other, and even throwing down the reed partition, in order to see better. And you should have heard their sharp comments and explosions of enthusiasm at the sight of Lewanika and Mokwaë ! In the twilight, the photographs were put away, and I spoke to them about the Saviour.

April 15*th.*

Quitted Nalolo for Lealuyi. I have left my royal patient on the road to recovery. Her gratitude has reached such a climax that at the moment of my departure she offered me a calabash of honey. Once, under similar circumstances, she sent my wife a mat, gnawed through by white ants, and me a cake of mouldy tobacco ! Tobacco to *me !* Poor dear woman ! We laughed over it a long while.

What a journey, through the jungles of rushes and of thorny bushes, that scratch and slap your face and cover you with clouds of insects—spiders, flies, and caterpillars ! The sun was blazing. We arrived at Lealuyi the same day ; but, as often happens, I was so exhausted that I could scarcely speak. A cup of tea set me up a little. Although we quite understood each other, Lewanika and I had a long explanation. I reproached him with having set a trap for me in confiding his children to me. He had requested me to discipline them and to make them work as though they were my own children, although he knew how touchy the Barotsi were in all that concerned their dignity.

" It is true," he said, " but I counted on their goodwill towards you. Since then, there has been a great reaction. Even my wives and retainers, who were learning to read and sing, have grown tired of it ; and, like everybody else, they are mocking me, and saying I am going mad.   I am quite alone ; I have no one but Seajika.   I am unhappy and discouraged."

The king was on the point of starting on a pilgrimage to consecrate the new royal barge *Nalikuanda* to the national gods ; but he put off his voyage on account of my visit.   This construction of the new *Nalikuanda* is a grand event.   They have been working at it a long time.   The work is generally surrounded with great mystery ; no one but the workmen may penetrate into the timber-yard, which they take the precaution of surrounding with a palisade of reeds.   One fine day, when the plain is inundated, she is suddenly seen to glide from the enclosure as if by magic, and to float upon the waters. Lewanika is very proud of the one he has just built, and made a point of doing me the honours.   After we had minutely inspected her, a crowd of men, decorated with caps and scarves of every shade, lions' manes, etc., seized her, and to the sound of drums, bells, and harmonicas she made her trial trip.   This monster barge, bristling with paddles and escorted by canoes, formed a striking picture, as it moved majestically through the freshening green of the plain.   Excitement mounted to its highest pitch ; every group, that curiosity had drawn to the bank, was shouting, singing, and clapping hands.   All were anxious I should share this enthusiastic admiration.

" Well, Moruti, and what do you say to *Nalikuanda ?*   You see what clever fellows the Barotsi are, eh ?   Oh ! the Barotsi——— "   And a significant click of the tongue gives me to understand that they have no fellow in the universe. Dear good people ! they really believe I never beheld such a masterpiece of craftsmanship.

Given their circumstances, it really is a work that does the Barotsi credit.   The barge is sixty feet long, nine broad in the middle, and three deep.   It is made out of a number of little canoes, the pieces of which are joined, and bound together by strong ligatures, ropes or wads of soft bark like touchwood, covered over with fibres artistically plaited.   These variegated bands, crossing one another in every direction, form a real adornment.   In the middle is a false bottom, surmounted by a spacious pavilion of mats, and covered over with blue-and-white

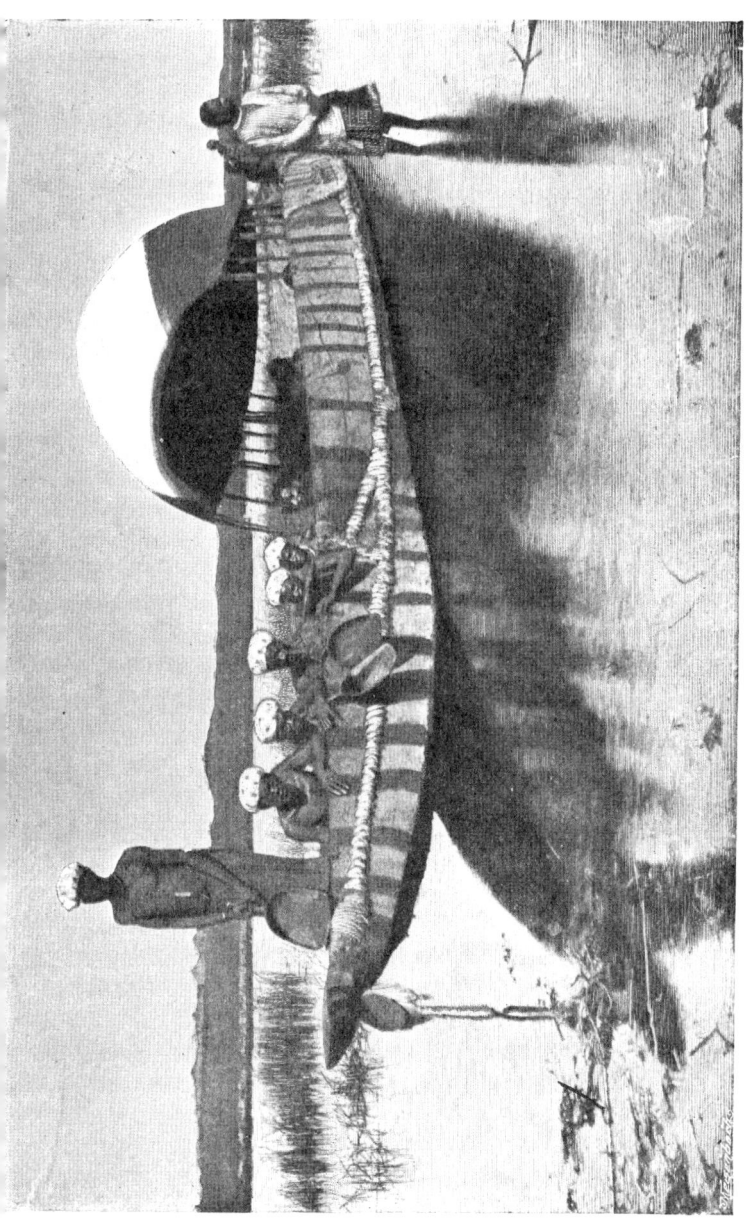

"NALIKUANDA," THE STATE BARGE.

[*To face page* 354.

stuff, which from a distance looks like the tilt of a waggon —not very poetical.

Besides the king and his principal councillors, *Nalikuanda* bears his band of musicians with the big drums, his kitchen, his scullions, and forty or fifty rowers, all exclusively Barotsi, and chiefs. It is absolutely forbidden for any woman to set foot in her. *Nalikuanda* must always arrive at her destined port on the same day as she starts. It is a great honour to take part in manning her ; but it is very hard work. It often happens that chiefs who are little used to exert themselves have the skin of their hands taken off. Woe to him who betrays his weariness ! An oar is passed between his legs, and he is tossed over into the water, whence a canoe fishes him out. It is a great disgrace.

The Sunday spent at Lealuyi was interesting. After the morning preaching, Seajika asked leave to speak. He related at great length the circumstances which led him to Basuto-land, ten years ago, and his conversion ; then his return to the Zambesi, and simultaneously to paganism. " I have fallen into every kind of excess," he said, " and you know it. I had become quite one of you again ; but know to-day that I for-sake you and return to my God." This return, which we were prepared for, while it causes us great joy, does not as yet inspire us with unlimited confidence. I took advantage of the occasion to address a few serious words to this poor prodigal. But if God receives him in grace, it is not we who would wish to play the part of the elder son in the parable.

May 22nd.

My excursion to the two capitals has not been in vain. Our school is mounting up again. Nearly all our pupils have returned ; the only absences are on account of health : so in this respect we are encouraged.

But here is Kamburu just come back from Sesheke with the overwhelming news that all the oxen that I had sent last year, the king's and mine, are dead. Consequently, no waggon, no baggage, no provisions ! All that, after all, is little in itself. It is the actual future of the mission that causes us anxiety. It is impossible long to go on running the risk of similar

losses. This new blow has crushed us. Is that the answer
to our prayers? Ah, what poor creatures we are! We were
quite ready to make the sacrifice of our lives, but I confess we
were not prepared to suffer so great a loss of cattle, representing
the sacrifices of so many of God's children, the shillings of the
rich and the pence of the poor. We could not pass through
these deep waters, if the arms of the Almighty did not bear
us up. "True faith is an active grace, and she always has both
hands full of work."

June 28th.

Repeated visits to the capital, from which I have once more
returned. A Mr. Ware, representing a mining company, has
come to solicit a concession from Lewanika for exploiting gold,
which is supposed to abound in certain parts of the country.
The thing was so novel, that the king and his councillors, taken
at a disadvantage, found themselves greatly embarrassed. They
feared a trap, and yet at the same time were fascinated by the
considerable presents of Martini-Henry rifles, of ammunition,
blankets, and garments, which Mr. Ware by no means forgot
to bring with him. There was nothing for it but to assemble
all the big-wigs of the nation, which took time; and then to
confer, which occupied no less.

A national assembly was convened, a *pitso*, to which the
Gambella proposed the question in the sombre, laconic fashion of
the Barotsi, just as if he were throwing a bone to a dog. To this
succeeded a volley of short speeches, all pointless and contradictory. It pained me to see the venal chiefs, already won
over themselves, allowing the poor people to ramble on in the
dark. I took upon myself to explain to the best of my ability
the real bearings of the question at issue, but I doubt whether
the chiefs around me liked it. No matter. The speeches took
a more reasonable form, and through the mazes of African logic
they nearly all arrived at the same conclusion. "We have
missionaries to teach us; and now that Westbeech is dead,
what we need is a trader who will bring us clothes, buy our
ivory, and go back home! Who are these white men? Whence
come they? Who sends them? Who has told them that there
is this red mineral in our country? Chiefs, are you very sure
that their gifts are honourable, and that you are not selling

your country in accepting them?" And the chiefs around me laughed.

It was merely a farce, repeated next day. I had an attack of fever. However, I was able to take part in the grand council of the chiefs, where the business was treated somewhat more seriously. The concession granted, the next thing was to settle the terms. Suffice it to say, that the concession is for twenty years, and that it includes the whole of the Batoka country (a tribe tributary to the Barotsi), to the east of the little river Machile and of the Zambesi, as far as Mashukulumboeland. It is immense, and Mr. Ware has reason to congratulate himself on so great a success. However, I think the interests of Lewanika and the nation have not been sacrificed. It is probable that other mining companies (there were more than eighty last year to exploit South Africa) will try to obtain some fragments of the country, for the region of the Rapids as far as the Ngonye Falls will certainly prove an irresistible bait. A commercial company is also endeavouring, by sufficiently seductive offers, to obtain a monopoly of the commerce. It proposed to place little steamers on the Zambesi, to canalise the Rapids, or to make a little railway there, and to establish *bi-monthly* communications with Mangwato. Just think of that! Lewanika had the good sense to refuse what it was beyond his power to concede. But he invited this company to establish settlements in his kingdom, promising his support and protection to them as to all honest merchants.

So there are the first waves of the invading ocean of European immigration crossing the Zambesi. Where will they stop? What will be their result for the nation itself, and for the tribes of Central Africa?

CHAPTER XXII

July 14th, 1889.

THE necessity for a journey to Sesheke becoming urgent,
we braced ourselves up to the decision. The king lent me
his aid with a good grace, collected my paddlers, whom he
placed under the orders of a chief and a sub-chief; and when
all was ready, he came to Sefula to present me with my little
fleet and to say good-bye. He spent Sunday with us, and put
on for the occasion the blue serge uniform with gold fringes
which Mr. Ware had given him. When he entered the church,
every one instinctively turned round, unable to restrain a flutter
of admiration. They even made an attempt at clapping hands;
but I instantly stopped it, reminding them that in this place
God only is great. Otherwise this was the only demonstration;
and it gave me great pleasure to see my dear Zambesians
reserve their customary noisy salutations till the end of the
service. In the house of God, the king takes the rank of a
motlanka (a servant). This is progress.

I left Sefula at 2 p.m. My poor wife, under the verandah,
surrounded by her little girls, followed me with her eyes till
the trees came in between us; and then went in, sad at
heart as one may imagine, to begin her three dreary months
of widowhood, while I moved slowly away, anxious and
preoccupied. Mr. Ware, the representative of the mining
company, was returning with me, and also a hunter, Harry Wall.
Nguana-Ngombé and Seajika accompanied me to the entrance
of the village of Letsuele, where the canoes and canoe-men

were awaiting us. They hastened to receive me, on their knees clapping their hands, which made my boys laugh. Litia, too, soon arrived with his own boats and his suite ; and the next morning, at eleven o'clock, we reached Nalolo.

We were on the shore, and were just about to begin the excellent breakfast with which our good housekeeper had provided us, when the queen, Mokwaë, appeared, followed by her inseparable Mokwe Tunga. Our men at once put themselves in position to give her a thundering salute. Would not one say they were the most faithful subjects in the world? I was taken by surprise, for we had intended presenting our homage to her after having satisfied our appetites.

Her Majesty, attired in a print gown and a shawl, with a handkerchief hanging from her neck, squats down on a mat, near the one we are using for a table. She looks at our food ; but one glance is sufficient. "What is the *Moruti* eating ? A bird ? " The Mokwe Tunga echoes her words. " The queen asks what the *Moruti* is eating ? Is it a bird ? " " No, my lord, it is a fowl." And the echo repeats, " It is a fowl." " What a pity ! " says Mokwaë sulkily ; " the queen does not eat fowl." I offer her, out of politeness, a cup of the black coffee, without sugar, which we ourselves are drinking. " Very well ; give it." And the poor woman, also out of politeness, drinks it, though not without many efforts and much grimacing.

Her son Kaïba was to accompany us ; and although he had known of my departure for three weeks, he was not ready ; it would have been vulgar to be waiting for me, and he required three days at least to prepare. I said I would give him till the next morning. Mokwaë smiled incredulously. I smiled too, and we changed the subject. We then went to inspect the new canoes which were being taken to the king. They had already passed the port of Nalolo without giving notice to the queen. Angry at this affront, she made them come back. She spoke loudly ; and the men, led by a chief of haughty disposition, seemed petrified. They crawled before this woman ; they swept the dust with their foreheads, and received her reproaches humbly, clapping their hands. She took possession of the two best pirogues, accepted as a fine the baskets of their provisions which the culprits hastened to offer her, and then dismissed them. To justify her conduct, which, as I knew, was not in the least arbitrary, she explained to me the custom of the country. When the queen's tributes pass Lealuyi, they must first be presented to the king, who takes what he wants ; and the same thing takes place when the king's tributes pass Nalolo—Mokwaë has the first choice. " But," she added sharply, " everything is altered nowadays, and these black creatures give themselves airs, and wish to set us at naught." While speaking, we arrived at the village, where we stayed some time. The queen gave us a quantity of curdled milk, and two oxen were killed, which my people spent almost the whole night cutting up and grilling.

In the evening, we returned to take leave of her, and I perceived that she was doing her best to get all she could out of my companion, Mr. Ware ; but as my presence evidently made her uncomfortable, I returned alone to the camp. It seems that she was wanting an endless number of presents. She had a long list in her head, but she feared my disapproval. What she wanted above all was a blue velvet dress with gold fringes, so as to be like her brother ; she had quite set her heart upon it.

The evening was beautiful ; the full moon flooded the sky with its silver light, and was mirrored in the waters. Not a ripple was on the river, not a breath of wind, not a sound, not the lightest murmur in the plain. Everywhere reigned a profound peace which charmed the soul. I wished I could have prolonged this little canoe journey of half an hour. My thoughts reflected the melancholy of this beautiful moonlight ; I thought of the work, and I thought of Mokwaë. I carried away from my last visit, as I always do, a painful impression. However amiable and chatty she may be, there is something, I know not what, which forms a barrier between us ; I have not yet gained her confidence. With her, I feel keenly the need of that wisdom that winneth souls. And I may say that the evangelisation of Zambesian women is the most arduous part of our work. We do not know how to reach them ; they do not take an interest in anything, and one cannot make them do so. It is heartrending. We are digging a very hard rock, and it is the sad experience of my wife too, in spite of the gifts God has bestowed upon her.

CARRYING CANOES PAST THE RAPIDS OF SEOMA.

[To face page 361.

The next morning, Mokwaë's son Kaïba, who is about thirteen years old, joined me with his suite, without making me wait too long. He has three canoes, and Litia two, which represent thirty men. We then travelled rapidly. On Saturday morning we passed Itufa, and were hindered by the chief of the place, who kept us waiting while he came with great ceremony to present Litia with provisions for the way, which the latter, out of deference, offered to me in his turn.

The same day we passed the tomb of Moana Mbinyi without taking any notice of it—a thing never done with impunity, according to the Zambesians. My boatmen did not dare to run the boats ashore, but they imposed silence on themselves, and bowed down as they passed, striking their thighs, as though in the presence of this great personage. In the evening, we went to camp over Sunday at Senanga, at the entrance of the Valley, where we had abundance of shade and fuel.

SEOMA, *July 18th*, 1889.

We arrived here on Tuesday, the 16th, at nine in the morning, with no other incident than that of a successful hunt, which delighted every one. We are encamped here near the water under a gigantic fig tree. The shade and coolness are delicious. But we had a terrible invasion of caterpillars—quite an Egyptian plague!

We found here a messenger from the king, who had out-run us, and was waiting for us. According to his orders, he had collected the men of the village and the neighbouring hamlets, and was watching to see they did not disperse—no idle precaution. The Makalaka of Seoma, close to the Falls of Ngonye and the neighbourhood (which is under the rule of three Barotsi chiefs), are obliged to transport all travellers' canoes up and down the river. It is a forced labour which they generally only perform when driven to it by threats and ill-treatment. As soon as they see a pirogue in the distance, they disperse secretly into the woods, and there the Barotsi have to search for days together, and collect them with the terrible African whip in their hands. I pity these poor people very much. I long with all my heart to found a missionary station at Seoma. You will understand how repugnant it was to me to receive a service from them rendered so unwillingly. But I could not help it. I had once thought of distributing calico among them ; but the king said to me, with justice, that this would be a precedent which they would certainly make use of to torment travellers. He promised to do so himself, to express his satisfaction, and this would not have the same bad result. What they are in want of. is a vehicle to facilitate their labour.

On our arrival, when they came to salute us, I announced that our whole party, sixty-five or sixty-six men, would help to transport the canoes. The poor people were so astonished, that the next day at dawn they arrived like one man to begin their work. By the evening, ten of our canoes were already below the falls, and to-day the seven others have followed them, as well as our tents and luggage ; and here we are at Mamongo. Only two days ! and we expected a delay of two weeks.

On the 17th, my birthday, what would I not have given for my wife to know I was at Seoma ! While our boats were being transported, I went with my lads to pass the day at the Ngonye Falls, and let them romp about among the rocks, bathe, sing, and amuse themselves like true schoolboys on a holiday. My gun furnished us with guinea-fowls, which we put into the pot ; some jam, a piece of stale bread, and the necessary cup of coffee, composed a picnic *menu* which left us nothing more to wish for. In the evening, I had a numerously attended meeting in the village. So much for external affairs. Inwardly, I was filled with gratitude and serene joy. In a few more years, the sixtieth will be here. One of my good friends had a theory, that at sixty years a missionary's work was done, that he was a worn-out tool. I kick against this doctrine ; *I* shall not subscribe to it. I believe in *youthful old age.* I do not ask God for a long life—my times are in His hand ; but I do ask the privilege of dying at my post, in harness, and of seeing the Zambesi Mission consolidated and prosperous.

MOLEMOA, *July 19th.*

We left Mamongo at eight this morning. Good humour and high spirits were maintained. The chiefs of my band are full of consideration and forethought. It is they who set up and pull down my tent, load my canoe, and preside at our daily installation. Litia, like a devoted son, puts his hand to everything ; no one but himself touches my bed. It is a privileged task which he himself has chosen. However, in other respects I do not sit with my arms folded. I have to see that everything is properly done.

What giants these Zambesians are ! I really must measure the feet of that good Moshowa, who is in the front of my canoe ; no shoemaker has ever fitted feet like them ! In the evening, while I am writing these lines, and the roaring fires are making the pots boil, our camp does not lack animation. The more serious love to relate episodes of national history, in which they take care to make the most of their own exploits. Others form a circle round a buffoon, who, with a gourd in his hand, is executing a new dance, full of astounding contortions. Later on, a voice is heard: "*Ako*" ("Guess"). Some one responds, "*Amba*" ("Speak"). Then comes an enigma, which must be included in a single sentence. Here is a specimen : "Mine is something found on the edge of a wood." "A bird ?" "No ; it is found on the edge of a thick forest." "A road ?" And so on. After several wrong answers, the speaker says, "*Ke shuile*" ("I am dead," *i.e.* I give it up). "You are dead ? Well then, it is the ear." Not very witty, is it? But it is surprising how excited they get over this kind of fencing. It sometimes happens that a man cannot sleep. Then he takes his *kangombio* (a little instrument of music five or six inches long, with metal tongues, stretched on a board over a calabash, to make it more sonorous), and there he sits, playing all night uninterruptedly, and singing those profoundly plaintive melodies peculiar to these black children of Africa. No one complains of it ; he is supposed to be in communication with the gods. It is quite an accepted thing.

We have passed the *Kalé* Rapids. One of the boats was wrecked, but we were able to save it. We bought two canoes from Matomé. He promised them to me a long time ago ; but although he had the king's authority, and had surrounded himself with every possible precaution, he thought it necessary to hide them on an island in the middle of the rapids ; and when he saw me with the young princes and Barotsi chiefs, it was not without great hesitation that he brought them. They are not particularly good ones, but they will be comfortable. " *Quand on n'a pas ce qu'on aime, il faut aimer ce qu'on a !*"

Saturday, July 20th.

An unlucky day! Litia went off in the morning with several men to hunt, and I told him to meet me at the confluence of the Njoko, where we expected to arrive early. It was so cold, that at half-past eight the men could no longer hold their paddles. However, we pushed on, and soon came to the Bomboë Rapids. The passage there was more difficult than dangerous ; but my men were afraid of it, and cast their eyes on another shute, far from the bank, where the current was deeper, but also stronger. A large canoe ventured, but they made a false manœuvre, and it was carried away like a straw, and caught among the rocks. Every one saw the danger, and every one thought himself wiser than his neighbour ; they began shouting orders and counter-orders ; and then, in the twinkling of an eye, I saw those terrible white breakers dash furiously over the pirogue and swamp it. Those within reach threw themselves on the floating baggage, and saved what they could. But what did the baggage matter? It was the canoe I wanted!

Can you believe that, while this accident was absorbing my attention, most of the other canoes had passed on, and all the men, squatting on the rocks below, were watching us and making fun of us? I had to bring all the weight of my authority to bear on them before I could collect ten men to help. I myself had found my way to the site of the disaster, and directed the operations. I wanted to disengage the canoe, and float it again ; but when we tried to lift it, the two sides, already stove in, remained in our hands! The wreck was complete. It recalled my sad adventures at Njoko. As for my Zambesians, they, of course, began to quarrel. They pointed at each other, shouted at the top of their voices, and I saw they would soon come to blows in the middle of the rapids. I managed, not without difficulty, to quiet them. An hour later, the current of our canoe life had begun to flow again, like the rapids over our wreck. They talked, took snuff, and laughed ; and if they still spoke of our misfortune, it was to lavish condolences on each other. "*Shangwe, ke noka, shangwe.*"

" Ah, my brother, it was the river ; the canoe was old and rotten." _Shangwes_ rained on every side, and those most to blame were the most flattered. I felt indignant. It is an axiom here, that, at all costs, you must conciliate the one whom you fear, or whom you have offended ; otherwise, beware of reprisals—the spear of the next revolution, or the sorcerer's stake !

NGAMBOË, _July 22nd._

Yesterday was a delicious Sunday, spent on a beautiful islet. Every morning we make it a rule to unite at sunrise for prayer ; then the tent is taken down, and the canoes loaded. In the evening, when the preparations for the camp are ended, they gather round my fire to sing hymns, repeat a portion of the Word of God, and pray. But our Zambesians have an invincible aversion to prayer, and are never in want of an excuse for getting out of it. On Sunday, there is no possible excuse, so every one is there. I felt very happy in explaining to them the good news of Salvation. A conversation the evening before, on the religious notions of the Barotsi, so captivating that it was prolonged to a late hour, had prepared us on both sides.

July 23rd.

Yesterday, Kaïba's [1] canoe nearly came to grief. Going down a rapid, it turned broadside to the current. In an instant, the white breakers leapt into it and filled it with water. A little fellow of his own age, who never leaves Kaïba, and was then sitting quietly at his feet, had the presence of mind to leap into the water, lift up the young prince, and deposit him on a rock level with the water. The men within reach flew to the rescue, floated the pirogue again, and fished up the greasy _karosses_,[2] which were none the worse for this little washing. To-day, there was a similar accident at the Lochu Rapids. It makes me rather nervous, not for my own life, but for those of the boys confided to my care.

Litia, who had received a fine Martini from his father, killed two beautiful antelopes. It was the first large game he had brought down, and the dear boy was almost beside himself

[1] Kaïba, Queen Mokwaë's eldest son, a young chief, pupil in the school. See page 359.
[2] Fur mantles.

with delight. Compliments—my own amongst them—showered
upon him like hail. A little later, Mr. Wall shot a buffalo.
What a treat! Everybody crowded round the beast; fires
were lit; and while some cut it up, others grilled strips of meat,
which were taken from the fire before they were even scorched.
We were obliged to bivouac. And even while I write the
fires are crackling; the meat is being baked and roasted; they
are singing, chattering, and teasing one another. Good-bye
to sleep!

SESHEKE, *July 25th.*

Fifteen days' journey from Sefula, including halts and
Sundays: that is not bad. Sixty-one hours' travelling in all.
Now we have arrived. My people have washed themselves,
fired their guns several times, and arranged the order of the
canoes; for they also aim at effect, and make the waves moan
under the strokes of their paddles, keeping time to the
monotonous chant of the rowers.

At first glance, the impression is a painful one. We enter
the bay of Sesheke by a side channel; the station lies in a
bend of the bank. But is that really the beautiful bay we used
to admire so much? It is now nothing but a lagoon, rapidly
filling with sand. Already grass and reeds have invaded it;
and when the waters are at their lowest, I think the little creek
by which we enter will be completely choked up. The buildings
too, which were never very imposing, have grown old. One
would think they were crumbling away. Nevertheless, here
is a pretty little cottage, with its reed-fenced court: it is the
Jallas'. And behind rises the woodwork of the Jeanmairets'
new house, telling of life and progress.

Shall I speak of our joy and emotion in seeing these dear
faces once more, after two years' separation? No; we will
only say that, after the first greetings were over, we had to
visit the graves where the darling children are laid.[1] It gives
me great pleasure to see the Jallas again, full as they are of
energy and spirit. A grain of optimism and enthusiasm is
a happy disposition in surroundings where everything conspires
to depress and crush you. There is so little poetry in a

---

[1] Two at this date—one of the Jeanmairets', and one of the Jallas'; later
on, two more of the Jallas'.

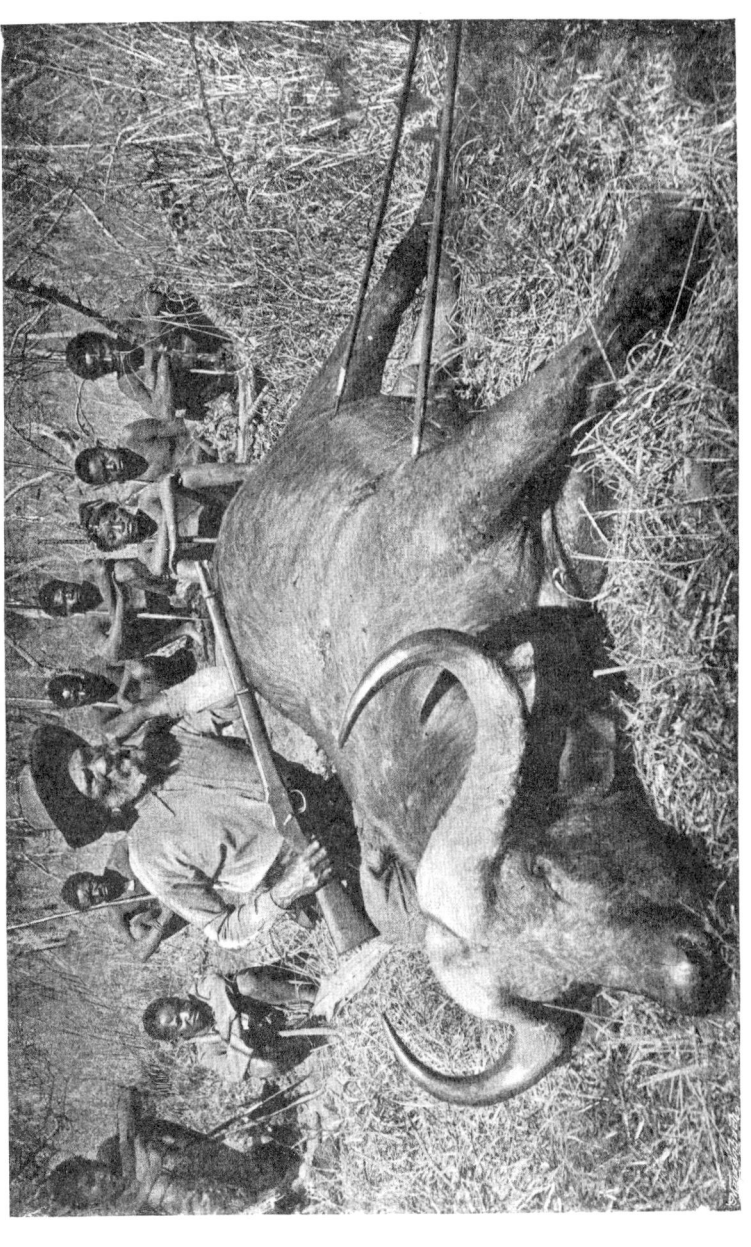

[*To face page* 366.

MR. WALL AND HIS BUFFALO.

missionary's life, that there is a risk of its turning to nothing but the saddest prose, if one once begins to give way. Already, I feel a warm affection for the Jallas; and they are a real acquisition to the mission.

KAZUNGULA, *August 3rd.*

Four days ago, I joined my nephew Jeanmairet, who had preceded me here. The waggons have come, bringing our baggage and provisions, and M. Jeanmairet has already begun to send off some cases by canoe. One really must have faith that angels escort these frail vessels, and watch over the precious chests, so dangerous is the navigation of the river. I cannot think of my return voyage over the rapids without trembling. My canoes are larger than those of Sesheke, but, even so, they are only hollow trunks of trees. And then, on the way here, all my people were very good-humoured, having the irresistible promise of a piece of calico, and we resolved to employ them by preference. This bitterly offended the people of Mambova and Sesheke, who thought their rights were assailed, and they put difficulties in our way.

The south-west wind has sprung up, and is blowing violently. We shiver under our cloaks and rugs. The air is darkened by clouds of dust, which penetrate everything. Our tents are blown about, and threaten every moment to be carried away. The river is as rough as the sea, the waves swelling and dashing against one another, white with foam. All communication with the left bank is impossible, and it is there that the chiefs of Sesheke are established, leaving us alone on the right bank, from the invincible terror they have of the Matabele. And the Matabele are fifty miles from here!

Yesterday, there was a grand beer feast on the Mpalira island. Every one went thither early in the morning, following the chiefs of Sesheke. But once there, they remained for the night, which was not at all in the programme. "The wind was so strong that no one would have dared to venture in a canoe!" What would not these poor fellows do for the sake of squatting round a pot of beer!

August 18th.

The wind has been blowing a great deal, but the Zambesians are quite good-humoured. They themselves watched for calm moments, and loaded the canoes early in the morning, or even in the evening by moonlight! Till now, everything has been done quietly, without accident. My nephew has left me, so that Mr. Jalla may come to join me. A question which urgently occupies our minds is the foundation of a large station here at Kazungula. It is the door of the country, and it is to M. Jalla that we would wish to confide this post. If Lewanika falls in with our wishes, and establishes a village here, to guard the official passage of the river, this station would be one of the finest and most important in the country.

September 2nd.

Our return to Sesheke has not been without peril, above all for our brother Jalla, whose canoe was too small to resist the force of the wind and waves. Since then, we have not wanted for occupation : we have had to dry the baggage and put it in order, load waggons drawn by untrained bullocks, and send off our canoes, which will deposit the baggage at Seoma, and return here. My time is naturally divided between the Jeanmairets and the Jallas, and in the evening we have earnest conferences. One day in particular, our conversation turned upon conversion and the missionary vocation, and we all spoke freely about our own experiences in these respects. Of course, these were different with each one. God does not lead all His children by the same road. I began to speak of the opposition I had met with, and of my own dear mother ; but it was too much for me.

SEOMA, *September 22nd.*

My stay at Seoma is already a thing of the past. We separated from our friends as those who may never meet again. But we feel strong, for we feel ourselves united. We understand and love each other. It is the greatest blessing we can desire, and it brings other blessings with it.

The crossing of the rapids was laborious, as I expected. Some of the canoes were sunk, chests and bales had to be fished up, opened, and the contents dried. But through God's goodness, we had no wrecks, as in coming down. We had some cases of sickness ; but it is always so on the Zambesi, and we do not complain of it. Here is news from Sefula at last.

My poor wife is always ill, and can bear the strain no longer.
Counting all the men who work with Nguana-Ngombé at the
canal, Mr. Waddell's workmen, our boys and girls, and the
Seajika establishment which has just been joined to ours, she
has fifty-three mouths to feed every day. The task is crushing.
A letter from Lewanika brings his answer about placing
M. Jalla at Kazungula. I expected some sulkiness on his
part, instead of which he fully enters into our plans, and
henceforward gives orders for the immediate foundation of the
village we advised him to build. It is the granting of our
prayers and the seal of God on our decision.

NALOLO, September 27th.

We have arrived here by forced stages, which our people
performed with a good will, in spite of the wind and waves,
which hindered us very much. One of my cares was the food
of every day, which I had to barter for in every village. Our
arrival at Nalolo was the signal for a great commotion, on
account of Kaïba's return. The poor child, muffled up in a
man's long shirt, made his entry at the head of a lengthy
procession, in the midst of a deafening tumult. The excited
women ran about, leaping and dancing, kissed his hands, and
made impossible contortions, uttering shrill cries. The men,
drawn up on the public place, noisily performed the royal
salute, *shoalela*. Our rowers caught the infection, and they
too began to *shoaelele*. After keeping them waiting for some
time, Mokwaë came out with her drums and harmonicas, and
sat down on her mat, while her son knelt before her to receive
the maternal *spitting*. Then we emptied the newsbag, and the
ceremonies were at an end.

Early next morning, we disembarked at Letsuele, where
our dear Nguana-Ngombé was waiting for me with my horse,
and soon afterwards I reached my home, from which I had
been absent nearly three months. My poor wife had been so
ill that she hardly expected to see me again. I found her very
thin, and utterly prostrated.

My canoe-men returned immediately to Scoma, to fetch
what they had deposited there, and ten days later all the
baggage had arrived. At last ! What a comfort and satisfaction.
These cases came from almost everywhere, from London, Paris,

the Cape, and Basuto-land, and had accumulated at Mangwato. Some are filled with provisions ordered three or four years back ; others have been packed at Leribé and in Europe five or seven years ago. We had given up expecting them. And now to unpack them ! It is the delight of sailors, and also that of missionaries in foreign countries, one of the keenest they can have. But no pleasure here is without alloy, and heart-breaks are often a discipline for the child of God, all the more necessary as they are harder to endure. Here is a case we have been expecting for two years. We cannot open it without a flutter. But what a spectacle ! The rain and the termites have got into it, and it gives out a choking smell. It is a mere heap of red earth turned into mud. In turning it over, we find in it rags of stuff, deplorable samples of dresses and garments which exist no longer, reels of cotton, haber-dashery, seeds in every stage of decomposition ; books too, whose leaves, gnawed into illegibility, do not even offer a clue to the names of the friends who have sent them.

Here is another. This is stationery, which has been no better treated, and now beggars all description. A third and fourth are provisions. The jams have fermented and run : this disgusting black mass, these tin boxes rusted into holes, out of which flows a kind of evil-smelling ink,—these are rice, macaroni, vermicelli ; luxuries for times of convalescence. Here are others again—— But no ! we must throw all that on to the dust-heap—these fermented fruits and these rotten biscuits, all those nameless vexations of which the transport alone has cost us so much anxiety, so much trouble, and, above all, so much money. Let us forget them, if possible. They were not necessaries, since our kind Father withholds them from us.

Let us stop at leisure before these well-made cases, carefully soldered, which have only joyful surprises for us. Here, indeed, are clothes, as fresh as if they came direct from the Bon Marché or the Belle Jardinière—all sorts of provisions in perfect con-dition. Here are photographic materials, precious gifts from some sewing circles, and numerous souvenirs of personal friends, overwhelming us with gratitude.

In the midst of our unpacking, a messenger has come from Franz, the conductor, to announce that my waggon has broken down at the Lumbé, half-way from Sesheke. One of the wheels is completely and irremediably broken. And there is no spare wheel ! All our waggons are in a pitiable condition. The two I bought at Natal on my return from Europe—and this is one of them—are completely done for. The climate dries and warps them, and the sand and the rain do the rest. It is heart-rending. We ought to have light iron carts, such as they make in England. In this case, the only alternative is to send our friend Waddell to do it up as best he can and bring it back here.

The question of our transports, above all from Sesheke to Sefula, will always be a mountain of difficulty ; the roads are very bad, the oxen die, the waggons get broken. But it must be clearly understood that the water-way will for a long time be only a last resort, as it is both unsafe and very expensive. I leave you to think how small a cargo can be put on one canoe, the length of which, on an average, is from twenty-five to thirty feet, by one and a half, never more than two feet at its greatest width, containing four or five men, or even *six*, encumbered with each one's personal baggage and food for a long journey. I had the king's canoes—his own, which he lends to nobody ; but one cannot always count on them. This difficulty will be smoothed away like all the others—I feel sure of it.

Before I close, would you like to read a little letter of welcome which Lewanika wrote on my return ?

" I salute thee," he says—" I salute thee with a joyful heart, since I hear thou hast returned, and in good health. Here, as usual, there are many sick, but I am pretty well. I am glad thy baggage has arrived without an accident ; I was afraid it might get wet. Thy boatmen have come themselves to salute me and *shoaelele*. They had all put on their white cotton clothes, the calico *setsibas*, and the red handkerchiefs thou hadst given them. Every one exclaimed, on seeing them, ' One can easily see they have been travelling with the *Moruti* !' But I knew how much had been given them, and remarked that they had hidden part. I ordered them to bring it all to the *lekhothla*, threatening to confiscate the whole if they disobeyed me. I would have every one to see that thou payest well those that serve thee. They obeyed me, and I rebuked them. The Barotsi are liars.

" As to public business, there is no lack of it here. There

are three questions which occupy me above all: they are,
sorcerers, beer, and adulterers.   The Barotsi of olden times, our
forefathers, did not turn sorcerers, they respected the wives of
others, and did not know beer.   We owe all that to the
Makololo.   I have summoned a *pitso*.   If the Barotsi will not
hear reason, it is as much as to say that I am no longer their
king, and that I am no longer anything.   In that case, there
will be trouble, for I am determined to act.   Will the Barotsi
kill me or drive me out of the country?   Thou wilt soon know.
Perhaps thy God to Whom thou prayest will hear.   Whatever
may happen, I am not afraid of a revolution.   But if I live,
and if I am king of the country, I must extirpate witch-finding
(by boiling water, poison, and fire), adultery, theft, and
drunkenness.

"Likokoane[1] troubles me ; he wishes to take a second wife.
I oppose it.   Sepopa, too, is always after Mondé, his sister"
(*i.e.* cousin).   "He will not forsake this wicked way.   It is Sasa
who encourages him to do wrong."

[1] See page 347.

RAPIDS OF NGAMBOÉ, UPPER ZAMBESI.

[*To face page* 373.

CHAPTER XXIII

SEFULA, *December 24th*, 1889.

YOU know we have been alone at Sefula for more than a year. The school absorbs most of my time. When I am not in the school, I visit the neighbouring villages ; and besides these two most important branches of the work, a mass of small duties fritter away my time. In an isolation like ours, it is certainly a great blessing to be very busy ; but it is distressing to feel that one is not equal to the task, that one does little, and nothing well. The time flies, one does not know how. Our spirits are often weighed down when we balance our accounts of the day's work, and yet we are both so tired that we long for bedtime. Is it the climate or laziness ? I often try to forestall things by getting up early ; but that is the sole hour I can call my own, and it is quickly past.

My dear wife cannot help me in the school as she did six months ago ; she is so often ill. The cares of our household tend always to increase rather than to diminish. Thus, we have this year two more daughters of the king's under our roof. Of course, these nine girls give a great deal of work and care to the mistress of the house. Here are already the materials for a boarding school. It needs a lady to give her whole time to it. Besides the girls, we have boys, as you know.

I am not speaking of our cowherds and servants, but of boys who are with us to be taught. Among them was a Mombunda whom we are very fond of; but the Mambunda are terribly savage and independent; they cannot bear to see one of themselves transformed, as they believe, into a white man. His parents have found a wife for him—a child—and they have succeeded in making the boy leave us. We have another, whom we consider as an answer to our prayers. He is a Moshukulumboe, who may be about fifteen or sixteen years old. As scullion to the king, he often accompanied his master on his visits to Sefula. When I went to Lealuyi, he never failed at the meetings. I cannot say that the dear boy has religious needs—they will come, I hope; but he has such a strong desire to learn, that he asked the king to be allowed to come to us. How can one close the door to him? He learns so zealously that he will soon read fluently. We pray much for this young man. Who knows if God may have chosen him to carry the Gospel to his native country and his savage countrymen.[1] Since I wrote to you last, several bands of Mashukulumboe have come to make their submission and to render homage to the king of the Barotsi. Lewanika generally sends them to Sefula, which gives us an opportunity of showing them some kindness. This is a tribe that interests us deeply, and among whom we hope to see the Gospel penetrate one way or other.

We have another, and no less interesting, young man in our house. He may be about sixteen or seventeen years old. It is Litia himself, the son of Lewanika.[2] He is hungering for instruction, and he has plenty of brains. For a long time, he has entreated us to receive him as a member of our large family. His father, who refuses him nothing, joins in his entreaties. You must know the natives to understand the reason of our refusal. We are afraid of this young man's retinue, and of his authority in the house beside our own. His persistence has won us over at last.

" I will be another Nguana-Ngombé for you," he said to me; " I will do all you tell me; I will not be a *Nguana-Morena*" (a

---

[1] This boy, Nyondo, eventually became a satisfactory convert, and is now preparing to be a catechist.

[2] Litia, though a pupil, had hitherto had his own separate establishment.

prince), " but a *moshimane*" (a serf), " if only you will receive me. Why have you taken Nyondo " (the Moshukulumboe referred to) " and not me ?   And yet I asked long before he did."   The poor boy, who is unhappy in his village, spent his whole days with us, taking part in all the manual work possible, interesting himself in everything like a child of the house ; nothing was beneath him.   His happiness, when he left me, was to read with Nguana-Ngombé, and to share his food.   Why not give way ?   With all this, Litia is not very communicative, and for a long time we have been lost in conjectures as to the real reasons that attract him to us.   We believe at times that he has religious needs, which he does not quite understand himself.   His father wants to send him to Mangwato to see a little of the world. My own desire is to send him to Morija.

After having told you about Litia, it is natural that I should speak a word about our school.   I reopened it on my return from Sesheke, but we have not yet succeeded in reassembling the hundred odd pupils that we had six months ago.   Our present number is only seventy.   In some respects, this diminution has its advantages.   The spirit prevailing among our children is excellent.   One very hopeful feature is their passion for reading.   A holiday to them is a day of privation, and generally they besiege my door and encumber my verandah to obtain the loan of the school books, of which I may say in passing we are obliged to take great care.

Among our luggage, I brought from Sesheke a little box of books—two Bibles only, of which one was publicly presented to the king, and the other reserved for our first convert ; but from the moment they knew that the New Testament and the hymns were for sale our pupils were jubilant.   One brought his ox, another went to demand a calf of his father, and for each we made a little packet of books and garments to the value of his animal.   You should have seen one charming little boy coming joyfully to tell me that his heifer had come ; and soon afterwards, sure enough, a pretty creature of two years old was gambolling in our court.   The whole school was present ; and when I brought the books, with a shirt and some pieces of stuff, there was a general exclamation of surprise.   The little fellow came up, his eyes sparkling with delight ; and he no sooner had the books in his hand than he jumped and skipped like his own heifer, and ran into the village, followed by all his companions. You must not exaggerate my thought, and see already an awakening among the children. No; but the germ may be there. For us it is a marvellous thing that these heathen children, who hardly know how to read, should desire to possess the Word of God. It is no less marvellous that their heathen parents should furnish them with the means of procuring it—they who know nothing of the Gospel. Then, again, they take quite a peculiar interest in our daily worship, and our meetings on Sunday. Each follows the reading in his book; each uses his own hymn-book. There is something real now in what we do, and these dear children take a personal interest in it. Last Sunday, we counted nineteen New Testaments and as many hymn-books at the service; and this movement continues. It will continue, probably, till all who know how to read are provided.[1]

Our intercourse with Lewanika is most agreeable. He has not yet had that awakening of conscience which we ask for him; but God has inclined his heart towards the Gospel. If we consented, and if we could, we should have all his children under our care. Not content to speak by example, he would *push* the Barotsi (not the serfs as yet; he is not so far on) into the right path. For that reason, he sought counsel from my wife during my absence. He wished, he said, to build a great prison. It should be composed, not of cells, but of three large wards; one should be for adulterers, one for drunkards, and the third should be for those who accuse others of sorcery (witch-finders). He has also convoked a *pitso*, the result of which he has communicated to me in an amusing letter. I had advised him to restrict his action with regard to the beer, so as not to compromise his authority.[2] It was decided that sorcerers were no longer to be burnt, nor to have *muati* administered, but that a special village should be established—and it is already founded—where the king will send to live all those accused of sorcery, whoever they may be, or to whatever part

---

[1] Eighteen calves were thus bought, and now form a team which has, happily, escaped the rinderpest (1897), and has been used to bring Mme. Goy (now a widow) out of the country.

[2] Lewanika of his own accord had decided to forbid the manufacture, sale, and drinking of beer throughout his kingdom. M. Coillard advised him to confine this edict at first to his own capital, where alone he could enforce it.

of the kingdom they may belong. How do you like the idea of a community of sorcerers? Generally, those accused of witchcraft are cantankerous fellows. The new village is not far from here. As to the adulterers, what a herculean reform! He has begun by acting with rigour against a young man of royal blood. At once, there is great indignation among the Barotsi. A serf laid by the heels may pass, but a Morotsi of pure blood, a connexion even of the king, what can Lewanika be thinking of? Katoka, his sister, publicly went and loosed the young man. The king, very indignant, had him bound again; but the opposition and murmurs passed beyond his powers of resistance; and when Queen Mokwaë sent messengers to deliver this Morotsi, Lewanika let her have her way.

You may remember that last year he had built his capital for the *Munda* (inundation) quite near here. Unfortunately, the rise of the water was so slight that he could not leave Lealuyi. This year promises better, and they are rebuilding the village. When these lines reach you, Lewanika will be still in our neighbourhood. I ask earnestly for the prayers of our friends that this season may be blessed, and that the evangelising may bear fruit. We do not cease to ask God for the conversion of Lewanika.

We have undertaken a formidable piece of work—*i.e.* a canal, which is to put us into communication with the stream, and by this means we shall make the evangelisation of the Valley easier. Into this work Nguana-Ngombé has put all the energy, the perseverance, and the strength of will with which God has gifted him. It is admirable to see him leading a band of workmen, and commanding their respect in the way he does. The canal is two-thirds done; we hope that the work will be finished next year. If only we were not so short of spades! We have also had to recommence the drainage works begun by M. Goy. For the third time, we have tried to sow European wheat. The first year, we did not reap as much as we had sown; first the dampness of the swamp, and then the sun, made our harvest fail. The second year, we reaped as much as we had sown, but not more. This year, we have succeeded a little better, and the harvest is double what we have sown. We have gathered a sack and a half of wheat. Next year, if God preserves us, our ground will be better prepared, and we shall have a little more experience. The garden—alas! no one has any time to think of it ; and even though Litia gives me a hand's turn now and then at need, we have no vegetables.

SEFULA, *January 6th*, 1890.

The great event of our little world is our New Year's school feast. This feast has been much talked of around us ; but I had little energy, and my wife was ill. I feared a fiasco ; but it is wonderful how a sense of duty masters you and spurs you on. It even forces you sometimes to forget yourself, which is a great blessing. The king announced his intention of coming with a crowd of people. He wrote jocularly to me the day before : "I am a great king, and I shall come with four of my princesses" (his wives), "with some grandees, and a numerous retinue. And I wonder how you will manage to receive all these people in proper style!"

Indeed, it was no small matter to be invaded by people so entirely destitute of discretion. The king graciously sent me an ox ; I returned the compliment by offering him one of mine. I killed two others ; and then, with a liberal distribution of millet, manioc flour, and curdled milk, we succeeded in meeting the exigencies of hospitality.

On New Year's Day, after a short service, we had a public examination, composed chiefly of reading, singing, and recitations. Lewanika, book in hand, followed the reading with great interest, correcting here, encouraging there ; for the examinations, insignificant as they were, made even the Zambesi children nervous. Then came a general distribution of stuff, books, copy-books, and toys ; then games, played with great interest, inspired by our friend Waddell. He even tried to teach them cricket ! A sumptuous feast, and, in the evening, a magic-lantern exhibition, closed by firing a salute, wound up this happy day. Everything went off quietly and easily. After the distribution of presents, Lewanika, who is less of an orator than anything else, harangued the crowd, which pressed round our verandah, and, above all, reproved by name those chiefs who had not yet sent their children to school.

The queen, Mokwaë, only arrived the day after—also in great style, for she too is a great queen—and the feast was prolonged in her honour. We even had a second exhibition of the magic lantern, one of the best I have ever given. It was the first time I was able to interest my people in serious things ; and it was delightful, instead of the stolid demeanour of former times, to hear our children shouting, one above the other, " Oh ! there is Abraham, offering up Isaac ! You can see the cords, the knife, the angel, the ram ! . . . Look ! it is Joseph ; he is dreaming. . . . They are selling him. . . . He is in prison. . . . And this great lord, it is still Joseph." . . . The evening has done me good ; it has been an encouragement.

On the Sunday, our church was filled ; the audience was so packed that we estimated it at nearly five hundred persons. It was the first time I went up into my new pulpit. I have never occupied a more comfortable one, even in Europe. Mokwaë, together with many others, was much astonished that I did not at least share it with " the king, my brother and my friend." The king himself was troubled with other thoughts. He could not allow women to enter this house together with men. " Impossible," he said ; " they will sit outside, round the windows, with Mokwaë and my wives, and we men will fill the church." " No ! no !" I said ; " the house of God is for all, and the women will occupy the side reserved for them, as they always do." He argued, and clicked his tongue, but soon saw he had nothing to gain. I had often discussed the matter at his house without result, but here I was on my own ground.

The spectacle presented by the congregation was of a nature to impress the most stolid. Mokwaë, some of her sisters, the wives of the chief, and our fifteen or seventeen young girls, all arrayed in dresses of the most brilliant colours, formed an interesting group around Mme. Coillard ; while a good number of women, who could not or dared not yet dress in European style, had bound their heads with the handkerchiefs of which the men still claim the exclusive use.[1] The king seemed struck by it. When we entered, his old courtiers gave

[1] It is a singular fact, that in South Africa, according to M. Coillard's experience both in Basuto-land and Barotsi-land, the first indication on any heathen woman's part of a dawning inclination towards Christianity is that she begins to "cover her head"—not necessarily in church, but at home and out of doors.

the signal, and the whole assembly began to clap hands. I quickly mounted the steps of the pulpit, and imposed silence, reminding them that this was the house of God, where one recognised none but Him, and that once outside they could do honour to their king as much as they liked. I then made all the men uncover their heads. The cotton caps and handkerchiefs disappeared in the twinkling of an eye, and I had a serious and attentive audience.

We enjoyed Lewanika's visit, as we always do ; he himself seemed so pleased with it, that he begged me to allow him to make use of Aaron's dwelling till he could have another place built at Sefula. Mokwaë remained some days longer, " to see her dear Mother," in reality to make her cut out and sew dresses. My poor wife, so ill and weak as she is ! Mokwaë was well aware that she had only dragged herself out of bed to see her. But what right have we white people to be ill ?

SEFULA, February 26th, 1890.

My wife and I are happily together this time to celebrate the twenty-ninth anniversary of our marriage ; and in order to enjoy more of each other's society, we have given the school a holiday—so we are holding festival. Unhappily, my poor wife is ill, and has spent the whole day on her bed ; she is only well there. But duty, the great drill sergeant, is pitiless, and urges us on as harshly as a corporal making his men march. But these efforts daily repeated cost us daily more. In spite of that, would you believe we have had a picnic, about two hundred paces from the house, under a fine tree, in whose shadow we said we should like to repose till the Resurrection morn ? A little forest path leads to it. We are quite close to the house, and yet in the middle of the woods. My wife had had a mat carried out there, when a heavy shower came on. We let it pass, and had our tea all the same with M. Jalla and Waddell. In the evening, two of us out of four had fever. That is the Zambesi ! We sometimes wish we could live instead of vegetating.

April 8th, 1890.

The metamorphosis has really begun. Before long, our Zambesian solitudes may very well become a new centre of life and civilisation. Why not ? We are already dreaming of telegraphs, railroads, regular and frequent postal services, and transport without the nightmare of losing oxen ; and the dream is beginning to come true already. Only think, at the beginning of the month, we received the almanacs that do not generally come before the end of October ! It is because the country is opening up. And it will open up more and more, whether we wish it or not. Last year a concession was made to a mining company. This year it is another and a very powerful company, which, by a charter from the British Government, has received full power to acquire, conquer, and govern all the vast country stretching north of Khama's domains, from the Portuguese possessions on the east to the Portuguese possessions on the west, without limits. It has already assimilated all existing companies. It is a formidable tool in the hands of the English Government ; and its representatives, who have come to treat with Lewanika, do not conceal the fact that their aim is above all a political one. In this great European struggle for Central Africa, England is taking energetic measures to assure herself the lion's share. Should we blame her ? Ought we to be glad or sorry for it ? Who can read the future ? The great thing is to remember that, amid the surging of the nations, God reigns.

When we cast a look around us, we shudder with horror, so thick is the darkness, so fearful the corruption. A very dear friend has written to me : "Success is not only the good that you do, but also the evil that you hinder." The evil that we hinder we shall probably never know in its entirety. But we are permitted sometimes to know something of it. I have spoken of the village of sorcerers which the king has founded in our neighbourhood. Now, it is worth remarking, that since the atrocious murder of Moeya-nyana, one of the king's favourites, which I related to you three years ago, no one that I know of has been put to death for sorcery. The king is justly very proud of it. Having himself given up intoxicating drink, he wished to constrain all the chiefs to do the same. For a long time now, no beer has been drunk in the *lekhothla*, and Lewanika has formally forbidden its being made in the capital. They have grumbled a great deal, but submitted. I think the Barotsi take their revenge when they go to their own villages.

Another reform which has made progress is that of the

slave-trade.   The king himself is very kind to his slaves. This year, a caravan of black merchants came from Bihé.   The king learnt that, contrary to his express prohibition, these Mambari were secretly laying in a stock of "black ivory." When they were on the point of leaving, Lewanika freed all the slaves, and fined the Mambari heavily, or, rather, confiscated a part of their ivory.

M. Adolphe Jalla has been our guest for two months, and is a great help to me in the school.   Unhappily, this dear friend is only a temporary aid; for, in accordance with our decisions, he is going to found his own station at Kanyonyo, and we have no other reinforcement in view.   Since the beginning of the year, our school has passed through all sorts of turns and fluctuations of fortune.   For some time, it has been increasing, and we have now seventy pupils, of which the greater number desire nothing so much as to advance.   My wife is incapable of helping me.   I myself have not enjoyed my usual good health since the beginning of the year.   Whatever may happen, we will occupy the post and defend the fort till you send us help.

Our Sunday audiences keep up well, and gain, I think, in earnestness and attention.   But though we look, we do not see as yet the "little cloud, no bigger than a man's hand," appear. Do you, dear friends, continue to pray for us.   At the beginning of last month, we had a special week of prayer at Kazungula, Sesheke, and Sefula simultaneously.   We have felt the need of closing up our ranks and of mutually sustaining each other, and certainly God has blessed and fortified us.   But we are waiting for a shower to break up our clods and make our dusty furrows green.   A brother wrote to me lately : "If God would grant me the joy of seeing a single conversion here, it would be like a new baptism to me."   I can well believe it.

SEFULA.

Whit Sunday, May 25th, was a day of days for Sefula.   It was the baptismal day of Nguana-Ngombé.   The festival had been talked about for days.   I had duly informed Lewanika beforehand, and Mokwaë also, who happened to be in Lealuyi. Both promised to be with us on the occasion.   Lewanika, who has no notion of the secretaryship being a sinecure, nor of Seajika's pen rusting, sent me letters, asking for details and explanations of the ceremony. I believe that in his heart he did not much care to be present at the baptism of a Motoka— a serf. Circumstances came to his help : there were political disturbances, and then an army corps was coming back from an expedition to Lekhoa-khoa ; they were dying of hunger ; they must be disbanded ; but, first of all, exorcised and purified, which only the king can do. So, "to his great regret," he could not be present. We felt all the more keenly the absence of Karumba and Seajika, who servilely followed the king to these heathen ceremonies.

The same day, a woman died near us, who had a great many relatives in the neighbourhood. Consequently, nobody could come, not even our usual auditors ; so that the congregation that day was smaller than usual. But the Lord was with us, and it was a happy and blessed festival. In my preaching, I made a special appeal to the young men of our school and household. Nguana-Ngombé spoke under the influence of an ill-controlled emotion. He particularly addressed himself to his *thaka* (young men of his own age), after having once again told the tale of his conversion, and made a touching profession of faith. He ended by saying : "And you, my friends, why are you not converted ? You say that it is not fit for you to outrun your masters, that you wish to enjoy your youth and take several wives. You are afraid too, for the things of God are still an unknown abyss to you. And so you make a *njoko* of me " (a monkey). " You say, ' Wait ; let us see first where Nguana-Ngombé will fall—on a carpet of green grass, or among thorns.' That is what the baboons do. When they are hunting, and find a promising place, they throw one of their young ones into it, to see if there are no wasps or snares. If the monkey child is bitten or stung or attacked, if any misfortune happens to it, they leave it to its fate, and take to their heels. If, on the contrary, it finds peace and abundance, they swoop down, chase it, and seize its booty. I do not know how far I can answer for the future, but what I can say is this : ' I was a sinner, a great sinner, and Jesus has saved me. I am His.' " [1]

[1] *Author's Note.*—We asked Nguana-Ngombé for some explanations of this novel feature of natural history. He told us that he had been brought up in the woods, and that his parents had often made him observe this fact ; moreover, that it is so generally known among those that inhabit the forests that it has passed into a proverb : " They have made a *njoko* of that man."

M. Adolphe Jalla, in an address delivered in very correct Sesuto, welcomed him into the Church as a brother—an expression which sounded strangely in the ears of our Zambesians. He spoke from his heart, and was himself much moved. I then put, in a somewhat modified form, the questions which are used in Basuto-land. Nguana-Ngombé, standing up before the assembly, answered in a firm, distinct voice; then kneeling down, he received, with the name of Andreas, the seal of baptism.

At the second service, M. Adolphe Jalla also made an impressive appeal. In the afternoon, towards the evening, we had the Lord's Supper in the church for the first time. It was a public testimony which I thought necessary, but which cost us a great deal. Nevertheless, it was a solemn and blessed moment. I had taken the precaution of emptying the front seats; and in spite of our apprehensions, everything passed off in perfect order and complete silence. Oh, if you only knew what a cruel trial mockery is, and how difficult it is to face it! And the Zambesians are past-masters in this art. Mme. Gonin, the widow of one of my former fellow-students and friends, a pastor in Brighton, has just sent me the beautiful communion service which he used in his church, as a souvenir. To me personally, this circumstance added one more element of interest and emotion. As I said, Nguana-Ngombé took the name of Andreas (Andrew). He liked it, because, he said, "he was the first who followed Jesus." Of all our young men, Litia seemed the most impressed. "How happy you are," he said to his friend, coming out of the church—"how happy you are!" "And why should you not be so too?" asked Andreas.

While we were thus holding festival in the church, we were passing through times of great political agitation and anxiety. You have heard of the formation of the great South African Company. It has received from the British Government a charter, which will give it powers similar to that of the great East India Company. It has already extended its protectorate over the Matabele country. It has also sent an expedition to treat with Lewanika, which was going on to Msidi (Mosili) (where our brother Arnot is working), thence to reach Lake Nyassa and the mouth of the Zambesi. This expedition, for some reason or other, broke up when it reached the Zambesi, and only its chief, Mr. Lochner, with a servant, came to the

Valley, ill, and short of everything in the way of provisions. To offer him hospitality at Sefula was a manifest duty.

Mr. Lochner is, I believe, an officer of the Mounted Police, probably better adapted for camp life than for diplomacy. His arrival in the country was the signal, or the occasion, for inconceivable conspiracies and intrigues. Evilly disposed persons sent about a report in the Sesheke province that the missionaries—and that was aimed directly at me—had already induced Lewanika to sell a part of his country, and that they were preparing to sell the rest. This spread like a prairie fire. Suspicion is the weak point of the native character ; and these suspicions were stirred up to such a point, being fanned by the general discontent, especially that of the chiefs, that we were led to expect anything, even a revolution ; even to being maltreated ourselves and expelled from the country. The chiefs of Sesheke took a very high tone. Secret messengers—for nothing here is done openly—followed each other to Lealuyi without ceasing ; everything pointed to a violent opposition. Poor Lewanika seemed at times to be perfectly distracted amid all these intrigues. Mr. Lochner himself, ill-advised from the beginning, thought it would be good policy to scatter presents lavishly. The Barotsi accepted them all greedily, laughed in their sleeves, and mocked him behind his back, saying, " Poor innocent ! he fancies we don't see through him ; he is trying to cut a road through our jungle."

The king himself, excited and embittered, did not show himself in the best light, and more than once his negotiations with Mr. Lochner narrowly missed breaking off short in an angry broil. I in my turn had to speak out, and threaten the king to wash my hands of his affairs if he did not treat them with more dignity and uprightness. He offered the representative of the Company fourteen oxen for slaughter as a gift of welcome, and at the same time politely declined the rather considerable presents the latter pressed upon him, while business was still being transacted. This was wise on his part. At the same time, he came to Sefula, with Mokwaë and a good number of his principal chiefs, to spend several days, at Mr. Lochner's invitation, under the pretext of being present at a feast which the latter, as a loyal Briton, wished to give in honour of the Queen's birthday. The 24th of May was past ; we were at the beginning of June. No matter ; Mr. Lochner killed three or four oxen ; and in the evening, after my little magic-lantern exhibition, given in honour of this visit of the authorities of the country, he treated us to a display of fireworks. At the first rocket, there was a general commotion, and I began to fear a scuffle and accidents. But order was quickly restored ; and every rocket, every Roman candle, every Bengal fire, each more wonderful than the other, was greeted with suppressed exclamations of admiration and bewilderment.

You can understand that the real aim of the king's visit was a more serious one. Both he and his councillors wanted thoroughly to understand the burning question of the day, before the meeting of the Grand National Assembly which was about to be convoked. This I desired no less than they, and had therefore made a translation in writing of all the documents.

On June 20th, the country being submerged, the king's canoes came to fetch M. A. Jalla and me. Mr. Lochner, at my suggestion, preceded us by several days. It was important to avoid anything which in the eyes of the natives might identify us with his mission. The *pitso* or National Assembly, and the Council of the Chiefs, lasted five days—and five days well filled. M. Jalla and I were careful to bring out clearly the definite and perpetual character of the concession, which is equivalent to the complete abandonment of the country under certain conditions. In the National Assembly, as in the Chiefs' Council, I applied myself to a thorough definition of the difference between the concession of last year, which has passed into the hands of the Company, and the one now occupying our attention. Sharply and with all the authority I could command, I rebuked the Sesheke chiefs who were present, the king himself and his councillors, for lending an ear to the first-comer, when the affairs of the nation are in question. I had the right to do so. When I protested my nationality, and my disinterestedness in these transactions, they responded on all sides, "Yes, yes ! we know you are not English ; you are French ; you are our *Moruti*, our father, and you watch over our interests." I exhorted them neither to accept nor reject blindly the proposals made to them, but to ask Mr. Lochner and me all the questions which preoccupied them ; and they did so. Some were good and intelligent ones ; others ridiculous. But it was evident that general opinion was in favour of the Company's protectorate. If there is one man who perfectly understands the situation, it is certainly Lewanika himself, and it is on him and on his council that all the responsibility of these important transactions rests.

The treaty having been translated and explained, I do not know how many times, it was signed publicly in sight of the whole *pitso* on Friday, June 27th. It conceded the mining rights of the whole country to the Company exclusively, reserving over the whole Batoka territory 4 per cent. annually of the total output of the mines in favour of Lewanika and his successors. The country, which was opened to all the Company's employés, and to traders, was nevertheless to be closed to emigrants. The Company, extending its protectorate over it, engages to defend it from outside attacks ; it respects the rights of the king and chiefs over their subjects, and does not interfere between them. It recognises the king's exclusive right to hunt large game and elephants, and assures to him, and to his successors in perpetuity, an annuity of £2,000, besides the dividend above mentioned. The signing of this treaty was a curious spectacle. All, under some title or another, wished to subscribe their marks to it. Those who were sent away went off grumbling ; others, squatting in front of the little table, would not move till the pen had been put into their hands. I believe the good people imagined that they would thus secure their quota of *mali*—that is, *money* !

The treaty having been duly signed and witnessed, Mr. Lochner rose, and, in a neatly turned little speech, offered to the king the presents he had had arranged on the public place— guns, Martini rifles, muskets, a splendid saddle, bales of blankets, etc. The Gambella presented them to the nation, crouching, with the upper part of his body bared, and the assembly applauded with much clapping of hands. Then, in the name of the king, he offered Mr. Lochner, for the directors of the Company (the Dukes of Fife and Abercorn), the two most beautiful tusks I had yet seen. Each weighed nearly a hundred-weight ; and when held up by two men, they formed an arch

more than six feet high.[1]   This little ceremony was very
striking, and it dignified the conclusion of these important
assemblies.   The Barotsi themselves, Narubutu, the Gambella,
and all the chiefs at their head, assembled before the king, and
gave themselves up joyfully to shouts of *shoalela*.

This was the end.   At present, I must abstain from comments.   We have our fears ; we also have our hopes.   For my
part, I have no doubt that for the nation this will prove the one
plank of safety.   It was not in the power of these tribes, only
bound together by the chains of an abject and a disgraceful
servitude, to oppose a permanent barrier to the invading floods
of emigrants and gold-seekers.   To-day, they knock at the door
and ask for a treaty ; to-morrow, they would have broken it
down and invaded the country as masters.   The Barotsi are
incapable of governing, and, left to themselves, they would
before long have annihilated each other.   Treacherous plots
against Lewanika, which we thought extinguished, still smoul-
dered under the ashes.   To realise this, one had only to see
the attitude of Makoatsa, Khama's ambassador, the same one
who brought us hither, and to hear his message, a real menace.

" Barotsi," he said, " I have tasted a delicious food, and I
have shared it with you ! What have you done with it ? I have
sent you messengers like Makoatsa.   How have you received
them ? To-day, I hear sinister rumours ; you speak again of
revolution.   Take care ! Lewanika is my friend ; and if you
dare to make attempts against his life or power, I am Khama !
You will see me with your eyes and hear me." [2]

An interesting document, of which I possess a copy, is the
delimitation of the frontiers of the kingdom.   Fortunately, there

---

[1] They now flank the chimney-piece of the Company's Committee Room
in St. Swithin's Lane, E.C. ; but the king persists in protesting that it was for
the Queen, through her son-in-law (*i.e.* the Duke of Fife), that he gave the
tusks.—*Author's Note.*

[2] Khama's message related to the Chartered Company as well as to the
missionary, both of whom he had introduced to Lewanika by the same messenger, Makoatsa, his accredited and acknowledged ambassador to Lealuyi.
Lewanika desired British protection for a double reason—to guard himself
against internal revolutions, and against infractions of his territory from without.   Knowing that Lewanika had applied to be taken under the protectorate
of the Queen, Khama, in response to his request for advice, had sent this
well-known messenger, through whom (by letter and by verbal message) he

were chiefs at all the extremities of the country, which gives it great value. In a general way, the boundary, taking for its point of departure the confluence of the Kafué with the Zambesi, extends up the river to the junction of the Chobé (Linyanti or Quando). On the west, it extends up this river, the Linyanti, as far as the twentieth degree east longitude of Greenwich ; on the north, it follows the watershed of the Congo and Zambesi to the Kafué, whose course it follows on the east (across the country of the Mashukulumboe) to its junction with the Zambesi : a gross superficial area of two hundred thousand square miles. From twenty to twenty-five principal tribes are scattered through this vast territory ; but you must not conclude from this that the country is populated, or that the numerous tribes form a homogeneous nation—that would be a great mistake. It must be borne in mind, nevertheless, that all these tribes acknowledge the authority of Lewanika, and regularly pay tribute to him. Although he does not interfere in their internal administration, his representatives (his Residents) exercise a general supervision.

In the midst of all these preoccupations, the post from Europe has arrived. It announces numerous deaths. M. Jousse's was a heavy blow to us. For more than thirty years, he had been a faithful friend to me. It was he who initiated me into the practical details of missionary life, and to him is due the foundation of the Leribé station.[1] A Frenchman by birth, he remained pre-eminently French in the midst of foreign influences, which tend more or less to alter the character ; and this was another tie to bind us. He was at once a man of heart and a man of action. And when he had reason to reverse

strongly recommended Mr. Lochner and his mission. So also did the Administrator of Bechuana-land, Sir Sidney Sheppard, and the High Commissioner himself, giving Lewanika to understand that what the Chartered Company had to offer was what Lewanika really wanted.

Naturally, therefore, Lewanika treated with the Company as truly representing the British Government, whose protectorate he craved. Hence his anger and utter dismay when he awoke to the real fact, although it had been fully explained to him before, that the Chartered Company is not the British Government itself.—*Author's Note.*

[1] M. Théophile Jousse, well known in South Africa as a distinguished member of the S.M.E.P. in Basuto-land. He had retired from the foreign field, and died in France in the midst of active labours on behalf of missions.

a too severe or premature judgment, he was the first to acknowledge it, with admirable candour. His attitude on the subject of the Barotsi Mission was a striking example of this. He disapproved of it, and even fought against it. " Though I am no prophet," I wrote to him once, " to-day you fight against this mission, brother Jousse ; one day, you yourself will be pleading its cause." And only a little while ago, he wrote to me about it : " My ' History of the Barotsi Mission ' is just going through the press ; it is my last effort and my last labour, after which I shall await my Master's call. He will not delay." Now he has entered into rest.

With this post, we again received the saddest news from Sesheke. I therefore hastened my departure. In the midst of my preparations, we had an alarm, of which I must say a few words.

M. Adolphe Jalla had to return to Lealuyi after the *pitso* for important business. The next day, he came back late to Sefula. It was 11 p.m. when we all separated. Towards midnight, light taps on the walls of our bedroom (closed by a simple curtain), and the soft voice of our little Samocheta, snatched us from the depths of our first sleep. " My father, the roof of the kitchen is on fire ! " With one bound, I was at the spot, and my wife closely followed me. Andreas (Nguana-Ngombé) was on the roof with some others, pouring buckets of water on the flames. In an instant, all our girls and boys, directed by my dear wife and M. Jalla, were vying with each other in goodwill ; some ran to the river, others searched all over the house for the last drop of water, while Litia and the other boys passed the buckets. Andreas struggled bravely on the roof, in spite of the intolerable heat. The *tocsin* was sounded, according to the custom of the country, and the forest resounded with cries of alarm. Some of the school children, attracted by curiosity, came running to see the dreadful sight, wrapped up in rugs and skins, for the cold was intense ; but when they were sent for water, they fled to the village. The elder ones, with one or two exceptions, remained in bed, " overcome," they said next day, " by cold and sleepiness." As the smoke still increased, I ordered Andreas to tear the thatch off the roof. Then I went inside to see what I could do with a hand-pump. At this moment, Andreas made a hole. A bright

flame leaped out of the thatch and ascended to the roof ridge.
"It is all up," I said to Adolphe Jalla ; "the house and out-
buildings will all be burnt down ; let us save what we can."
I sought my wife to warn her.   Going into the dining-room, I
cast my eyes on our harmonium, for we shall yet live to sing.
My selection could only be limited, and my mind was quickly
made up.   My wife, self-possessed, as in all great emergencies,
calmly set to work.   Andreas, Litia, and the other boys did not
quit their post ; and it is their courage and coolness which in
God's hands have saved us.   By 3.30 a.m., we had completely
mastered the fire.   Is it not wonderful?   In Basuto-land, we
had galvanised iron over our heads.   Here we have thatch—and
thatch, too, dried by months of tropical sunshine without, and
within by the constant fire of the kitchen.   With our walls of
stakes and reeds, on this sandy hill, far from water and help,
what could have saved us, without a special intervention of
Providence?   The cause was a fire in the chimney, which the
sparks communicated to the roof.   The intervention of Providence was this.   At a particular moment—ten minutes afterwards would have been too late—one of our girls went out into
the court, saw the flame, and uttered a cry of alarm, which
roused Andreas.   The remarkable thing is, that the girl, Aaron's
former servant, was sleeping here *for the first time*.   She had
long been begging us to receive her.   We could not do so ; but
at last my wife took pity on her ; often allowed her to share
the work and food of our girls ; and at last, conquered by her
entreaties, we took her in for good.   It was her first night ; she
could not sleep—for joy no doubt—or else an angel woke her,
so that she might save our property and lives.   We shudder at
the thought that we might have been without clothes, food, roof,
or resources of any kind in so inhospitable a country.   It is no
use thinking of iron roofs here.   But we have something better.
"Behold, He that keepeth Israel shall neither slumber nor sleep.
The Lord is thy keeper" (Ps. cxxi. 4, 5).

CHAPTER XXIV

A Journey to Sesheke—Losses of Cattle and Waggons—M. Jeanmairet's Illness and Departure for Basuto-land—Arrival of Mlle. Kiener—Difficulty of Obtaining Canoes—Kazungula—Death of the Jallas' Second Child—Litia's Courage and Progress—The Absence of the Marriage Tie among the Barotsi—Infanticide—The Tyranny of Custom—A City of Refuge—Progress—An Ox to sell—Return to Sefula—Difficulties of Transport—Litia's Departure for Morija.

SENANGA, AT THE ENTRANCE OF THE VALLEY,
July 13*th,* 1890.

SITTING doubled up on my bedding, in the prow of my canoe, I shall try, as I have already done more than once, to make use of the long monotonous hours for my correspondence. Last year, I promised myself that, once home again, it would need the strongest reasons and the most unusual circumstances to tear me away. And yet, here I am again on the way, and my absence from Sefula will last two or three months. For the mission has come to a deadlock, and I can truly say I have rarely had so many dilemmas to face at once.

Must I sadden you again, by telling you of the insurmountable—yes, *up to the present insurmountable*—difficulties which meet our land transport from Sesheke to Sefula? It is a wound in the flanks of our mission, and I do not know how and when it will be healed. I am getting quite hopeless about it. At the beginning of March, I had sent Franz and Kamburu to Sesheke with two waggons and two extra teams of native cattle, eighteen oxen in each, which I had procured by barter. One was destined for Sesheke, and the other for Kazungula; they were to be kept there, and used for the transport service. Unfortunately, M. Jeanmairet, who had been planning for some time to come and see us with his family, and needed Franz's services as a driver, thought to hasten his return to

ON THE ZAMBESI, BELOW NGONYE FALLS.

[*To face page* 393.

Sesheke by handing over to him both the teams mentioned above.[1] Alas! at Loanja, at the entrance of the tse-tse haunted woods, only three days from Sesheke, our old transport waggon completely broke down. Franz had to ply to and fro between the place of the accident and the Njoko, carrying the packages of the two waggons in small loads. These packages were objects of barter, school and mission-station furniture. At the last trip, on the banks of this Njoko of infamous memory, the second waggon broke down in its turn. To complete the misfortunes, the oxen began dying off; and Franz, who, though much improved, has no more enterprise than he need have, waited there, on the banks of the Njoko, two hundred miles from Sefula, for the help which, without either waggons or oxen ourselves, it was not in our power to send him.

Meanwhile, besides the storms and political complications which rendered my presence at my post indispensable, the news which one express after another brought me about M. Jeanmairet's health became more and more alarming. I immediately sent to Franz, telling him to leave his loads on the veldt, and hasten with part of those bullocks still remaining, to bring help to the Jeanmairets. I wrote at the same time to my niece, trying to dissuade her from her project of travelling to Cape Colony alone, in winter-time, with her little child and her sick husband, and to come instead to Sefula. We thought that a change of air, even at the Zambesi, complete rest, and assiduous care, might, with God's blessing, make my nephew better. Unfortunately, my letter crossed an express, telling us that, as M. Jeanmairet's state was becoming more serious, and an English hunter had placed his waggon and oxen at my niece's service to leave the country immediately, she begged me earnestly to send Franz to her, the only driver we have in the mission. She thought he had returned long since to Sefula. Then it seemed to us imperative that I should go myself to Sesheke, judge *de visu*

---

[1] This requires a word of explanation. Franz was returning to Sefula with supplies. M. Jeanmairet thought he would travel faster, and come back to fetch the Jeanmairet family, if he had double teams, and consequently gave him the oxen (in addition to his own) which were intended to be kept at Sesheke, for transport between that place and Kazungula. The results were disastrous. The Jeanmairets were alone at Sesheke, the L. Jallas being at Kazungula.

of the situation, and bring back Mlle. Kiener,[1] whose departure
from Europe we have heard of only at the same time as her
arrival at the Zambesi.   Mr. Waddell, with my cart, guided by
Karumba, will go to set up our old waggons again, if possible,
and then pass on to meet me at Sesheke, while I go down the
river by canoe.   In default of oxen, some large calves will be
broken in on the way, as the cart is light.

The king has again behaved in a manner worthy of himself.
We had just left him.   Nevertheless, he insisted on coming to
spend some days at Sefula, *ho laeletsana*—a great institution
among the Barotsi, at which, spitting in each other's faces, they
make their farewell speeches and say good-bye.   Christians
" commend each other to God and to the Word of His grace."
Lewanika is not yet so far on.   But this consideration on his
part and these tokens of friendship are none the less precious.
He, as you know, has a monopoly of the large canoes ; and
whatever I may do, I cannot procure them myself.   He, poor
man ! cannot satisfy every one's demands.   He must have boats,
and not a few, for the service of his harem ; he must also have
some for hunting, particularly for fishing ; and he must have
others for public use, and for eventualities ; so that he himself
often runs short of them.   Lately, a trader has demanded
twenty ; Mr. Lochner took away twelve or thirteen.   So it is
not surprising that I could only get three from him.   But he
had reserved his own for me.   It is forty-three feet long, twenty-
eight inches at its greatest width, and twelve inches in depth.
It is very difficult nowadays to find tree-trunks big enough to
make canoes this size.   So I shall travel in state ; and Litia, too,
will accompany us, as indeed is necessary.[2]

KAZUNGULA, *August 1st*, 1890.

My stay at Sesheke has been a most melancholy one.   The
Jeanmairets were no longer there, and everything showed it.
Not a soul to bid us welcome ; not a dog, not even a fowl, to
give the station a little life.   On the shore were the fragments
of my old boat ; a little farther on, reed partitions thrown down,

[1] A young Swiss lady who was coming out to help Mme. Coillard, and
is still a valued member of the mission staff.

[2] Litia, the king's eldest son, was going to Basuto-land to school.

palisades pulled up, torn photographs, papers everywhere, broken pottery, and I know not what else, all bearing witness that something like death had passed there.[1]   I waited a long time before Franz, who had the key, came to open for me the door of this beautiful new house, which had cost my dear nephew so much trouble.   And once inside these rooms, empty as they were, or littered with household goods hastily thrown together, I felt such deep melancholy seize me, that I shut the door, and went to encamp two or three hundred yards away.   I still hoped to reach M. and Mme. Jeanmairet at Kazungula ; one of my old friends, whom I met returning thence (wishing no doubt to give me pleasure, and probably to receive a *setsiba* for his trouble), swore to me by all his gods that he had left them there, installed in their tent.   His description was so vivid I felt almost tempted to believe it.   The next morning, we arrived at Kazungula, only to learn that my nephew and his family had left eight days before, and were already too far for me to think of reaching them on foot, and giving them a farewell kiss.   Where will they go ?   God will guide them ; yet it needs a great effort to silence our own fears and anxieties.   Will they return ?   When ?   God knows.   Meanwhile, we suffer terrible distress on their account.

One compensation for my bitter disappointment is the arrival of Mlle. Kiener.   In reading the *Journal des Missions*, which I found here, and in speaking to her, I have been very much struck by the wonderful ways in which, unknown to us, God has brought her to the Zambesi.   She will certainly be a precious help to us.

An old friend, who is neither a Frenchman nor a Presbyterian like me, writes to us that God has abundantly blessed him in his business, and that he has made his fortune.   " This is a talent," he says, " which God has confided to me, and all my desire is to make use of it."   He wishes to maintain two evangelists under my care.   M. Mabille just had two who were disposed to come.[2]   What is most astonishing in all this is, that our friend, a lawyer by profession, has always been

---

[1]   M. Jeanmairet's state had suddenly become so alarming, that, to save his life, the family had been obliged to leave in their friend's waggon, without time for preparation or information to the others.

[2]   At the Morija Training School in Basuto-land.

a zealous evangelist himself, though without the title. His prosperity has not diminished his zeal for the evangelisation, not only of the whites, but of the blacks, in the great centres of the diamond fields and gold mines. Oh the power of the love of Jesus! It laughs at the barriers which often separate the children of God.

At Kazungula, I was very glad to see our dear friends the Louis Jallas again—*dear friends* in reality! The Sunday, the first we have spent together, was a sweet and blessed one. At our little private service in the afternoon, we consecrated their baby to God by baptism. On my arrival, I had thought the child very pale, and not at all well. Still, the parents were not seriously uneasy about her. The next day, about three in the afternoon, they called me in great haste, and I arrived in time to see the little one's life pass out of this poor world as her spirit went up to heaven. It was a sorrowful privilege to have to prepare the last cradle for the little body. The funeral took place the next day in the presence of two or three Europeans, and of fifty or sixty Zambesians. I spoke alternately in three languages.

The calmness and resignation of our poor friends are beautiful to see. But it is impossible to count all our little graves without saying the Zambesi climate is a cruel one.

As to things at Sefula, my last letter, I think, left you under the best impressions. Seeing our dear pupils so eager to buy books, you might have thought them quite near the kingdom of God, and imagined that we had nothing but success in our school. Far from it. Our pupils are still terribly wild; they cannot bear restraint for long. Most of them have their own slaves and villages. At home, they are masters. And it frequently happens that, on the slightest pretext or none at all, they go off *borotsi* as they say (that is, *to the Valley*), to enjoy the liberty of fishing and boating, and the servile adulations of their subordinates. When they return *mosito* (i.e. *to the woods*, where we live), others go away; and farewell to progress.

One day, Mokwaë's son, Kaïba, was not at morning prayers. Before we knew of it, messengers had run in the night to Nalolo to tell the queen that her son was unwell. They returned with the order to bring him immediately to her.

The next day, Mokwaë called Litia in great haste. "Kaïba is ill," she said to him, "and the divining bones say that you must go and sacrifice at the tombs of our ancestors." "Morena," replied Litia calmly, "I am no longer in that darkness, and I have forsaken those ways. I no longer pray to the dead." Mokwaë made many remonstrances, and argued a long time; but finding she gained nothing, she said, "Very well, you need not go in person. Some one will pray in your place, only you must take a handful of grass impregnated with 'medicine,' and sprinkle the offerings." "But, Morena," replied Litia respectfully, though firmly, "I cannot even do that, for it would be the same as if I went myself on a pilgrimage to the tombs." Mokwaë had to yield the point; but, deeply offended, she forbade him to sing hymns in the village.

None of our pupils share Litia's scruples. And when I tell you that this is not the first time the dear boy has taken up such a sturdy attitude towards his father and Mokwaë, you would expect, as we do, to see him soon declare himself for the Lord. In fact, I do not know what keeps him back, for we believe that the grace of God is certainly working in his heart. He has long since given up a number of heathen customs, and he has thrown away his heathen ornaments and charms. He has a pronounced taste for everything connected with civilisation. As his father can refuse him nothing, he is always dressed like a European, although clothes are difficult to procure in a country like this, without shops. He is clean in his person, intelligent, eager for instruction, and clever at using ordinary tools. He has built himself a little cottage— of course, under Mr. Waddell's direction—roofed it himself, and furnished it with a bed, seats, tables, and shelves, all rather primitive, but of his own making. This little room is always a model of order and cleanliness at whatever hour one may visit it. One valuable quality for the position he may one day occupy is a strength of will not at all common in a young man. It sometimes degenerates into obstinacy. He exercises great power over those around him; and while growing daily in popularity, he permits nobody to be familiar. Though now moral, truthful, and honest, he has not always been so; and when his conscience awakens, he will make us many confessions. But at present it is still asleep. Is it to be wondered at that, with these inclinations, and being almost the same age as Nguana-Ngombé (eighteen years), he has formed an intimate friendship with him ? They would have shared the same room, and taken all their meals together, if we had not imposed some restrictions out of prudence. I have said thus much about this young fellow, in order that his name may have a special place in your prayers.

Our young girls, at present ten in number, are very far from giving us as much pleasure. They are growing up ; and growing up unconverted, they are the more difficult to manage. The king's eldest daughter, always surrounded by slaves and flattered by everybody, thus preserves a little prestige which often contradicts our authority. The lack of straightforwardness, of truthfulness, and of common honesty in these children calls for much vigilance and great firmness ; and with Mme. Coillard's bad health, the task is overwhelming.

But God is good. We have to repeat it at every step. The arrival of M. Adolphe Jalla at Sefula is indeed a new proof of it. We very much appreciate the valuable acquisition which the mission has made in this young brother. The Waldensian Church has already large interests in the Barotsi Mission, and she has cause to rejoice in it. These are powerful ties, added to those which previously united us to her. M. Adolphe Jalla has come to us already possessed of a good vocabulary of Sesuto, and has never yet needed an interpreter. Without losing any time, and also, I think, without consulting his own tastes, he has buckled on his harness, and set to work with me to teach A B C (which is not exactly an attractive occupation) and the elements of arithmetic and geography—a task as ungrateful here as it was interesting in Basuto-land. You see, ours is a locksmith's trade ; and if we succeed in putting the key of knowledge into the hands of the generation confided to us, we shall not have laboured in vain.

The more we learn to know our Barotsi, the more difficult seems our task. I am not now speaking of the school, which after all is not the most important branch of it. I have already spoken to you about their marriage, this union of nothing but caprice, which ill-temper may break to-morrow. Is this really the ideal which theorists of both sexes, who consider themselves the great lights of the nineteenth century and the great

champions of humanity, dare to propose to our old ultra-civilised
and ultra-Christianised Europe? What progress!

When man's highest instincts are blunted, he ceases to be
a man, and becomes a brute of the worst kind. Infanticide
sufficiently proves it. The cases of it here are fearfully common.
The life of a little being, elsewhere cherished, is not of much
value—a trifling excuse is sufficient to sacrifice it. It cries,
worries its mother, annoys its father, is perhaps an obstacle
to a new marriage. It need not matter! Its mother or grand-
mother stuffs its mouth with ashes, digs her nails into its throat,
and at night the poor little corpse is thrown out on to the
dunghill, where the wild beasts, always prowling about, undertake its burial. The details are too disgusting to be described.
And what is most heartrending—for in Europe equally horrible
crimes are committed—is that all this is done publicly with
everybody's knowledge. Public opinion does not in the least
deter from these revolting atrocities. They are accepted, and
no one has anything to say against them. This crime must be
laid at the door of slavery, so brutalising and degrading is it,
petrifying the heart, and making of a man a mere chattel.

But nothing is more tyrannical than the customs. At their
least violation, everybody is up in arms. Each one believes
himself to be their accredited guardian. Certain Levitical laws
pertaining to woman and to her duties, from whatever source
they may be derived, are strictly observed among the Barotsi.
There are also others established by custom. For instance,
a child must never be born in its father's house. The husband
makes a sort of kennel for his wife in the fields, and there she
must stop till she is strong enough to crawl back to the
village with her infant. In case of an abortion, a woman is
also left in the fields under a miserable shelter, where she lives
in complete isolation, eating the meagre fare brought to her
every day. She is thus sequestrated till the new moon. For
the same reason, her husband is confined to the court of his
house; all communication with his neighbours is forbidden,
and all visits to his cattle-fold or fields. They fear he may
exercise some evil influence over men, cattle, and things.
Consequently, the whole community watches to see that the
custom is rigorously observed. At the new moon, he and his
wife will be made to pass through certain purifications, and

only after having cleansed themselves in the river will they return to their ordinary course of life. Karumba found himself in this predicament lately, and he and his friend Seajika conformed punctiliously to the rule of the country. During a whole month, Karumba remained a prisoner in his own house, without his friend, who passed his door twenty times a day, daring even to greet him.

Nevertheless, ideas of humanity, justice, and goodness are making their way. I have already told you of Lewanika's efforts to crush sorcery and the crimes it engenders. His sincerity was lately put to a severe test. While he was away hunting, one of his most faithful servants, busied with the near return of his master, thought of the thousand and one details which escaped the others. His companions, jealous of the favour he enjoyed, had sworn his destruction. An opportunity was found. What was the meaning of this preoccupied manner, these comings and goings, where no one else dared even to enter? They carried their accusations to old Narubutu, the preserver of ancient customs. After the fatal administration of poison to fowls, the old man declared himself to be perfectly convinced. "Hasten, my children," he said, "and execute justice on this sorcerer before the king's return,"—a recommendation very welcome to such people. Monare, the accused servant, was warned in time to flee, and took refuge with us. He related his story, we received him, thoroughly determined to save him.

It was not long before messenger after messenger came, ordering me to deliver up their victim. "I shall no more do it," I said, "than I shall deliver *you* up when your turn comes, if you seek refuge with me. We also are *Natamoyos*, ministers of mercy." I do not know how far my argument prevailed, but at least they respected my authority sufficiently not to lay their hands upon Monare, who stood beside me, explaining his conduct. Days passed, and the king returned from his hunting. More messages and commands ; more refusals. "You asked me one day," I said to the king, "what I should have done, if you had taken refuge with me, and if Mathaha had ordered me to deliver you up. You know my answer. Monare's case is the same."

At the end of eight days of parleying and protestations from the king, who swore that he would answer for Monare's life, I sent him under Litia's guard, with injunctions to let him escape again at the least sign of danger. But the king kept his word. He confronted Monare publicly with his accusers, unfolding and exposing without any difficulty the jealousy of those who had once more failed to deprive him of one of his best servants. He rebuked them sharply, publicly congratulating himself upon the fact that in the missionaries he had humane men who backed him up ; then addressing himself to Monare, he said, " You will go to your village, back to your children ; and I will see which of this rabble will do your work and take your place." And so ended this incident.

There is the same progress with regard to slavery. Recently a man led an ox to his chief. " I want a man," he said. " Will you get me one ? Here is the price." " Why, where do you come from," answered the chief, " that you think you can still buy slaves under Lewanika ? "

You will remember that already last year some Mambari (black traders from Benguella and Bihé) had bought a certain number of slaves in exchange for powder, beads, and stuff. Just when they seemed to be going, Lewanika had them stopped, took away their slaves, and confiscated part of their ivory. He even thought he had gone too far, and asked my opinion. You can easily guess it. It is a fact to be noted, now that British influence is going to penetrate the country.

Our poor Lewanika ! Why does he stop when he is on such a good road ? One day, when he was with us, while we were singing hymns, each choosing one in turn, I asked him to choose one also. " One ! " he said, " but all are full of Jesus. Let us have *Motsualle oa Morena*" (" The Lord's Friend "). This is the Sesuto title of the hymn beginning " *Litaba tse hu imelang*," a translation of " What a Friend we have in Jesus ! "

Sometimes people make rather a curious application of religious ideas. You can be present, if it interests you, at the purchase of an ox. A little time ago, a man brought one from a distance to sell me. The price, already fixed by custom, was soon decided, and the bargain was about to be concluded. " But," remarked one of our men incidentally, " your ox limps." " Yes, indeed it does," said the vendor ; " to tell the truth, it has limped ever since our expedition against the Mashukulumboe

It got better for a time, and then it began to limp again."
" Really ? " I said in my turn. " Yes, really." " But, my friend,
I cannot buy a lame ox."

The poor man saw that he had given himself away. However, not the least disconcerted, he replied, " But my ox is
not lame—look ! " " But have you not just said before us all
that it has been lame ever since your return from the Mashukulumboe country ? " " I ? Never ! You are mistaken. My ox
has never been lame." The animal was seized, and it was
proved to have a dislocated shoulder. No matter ; my man
stuck to his story in the face of everybody—his ox had never
been lame ! The poor fellow stayed three days to convince
me that it did not limp now.

This instance of audacity in lying is by no means an isolated
case. It would be laughable, if it were not so profoundly sad.
" Servant of God," said this individual, appealing to my feelings,
" do not break the bargain. Jesus would never do that ; He
would accept my ox. Jesus is good ; He would not send me
away empty. Servant of Jesus, be like your Master. Jesus
is kind."

Well, we must not refuse sound lessons, even from cheats
and flatterers !

SEFULA, *October 30th*, 1890.

I returned home on September 18th, after an absence of
two months and eight days. Though it was an unspeakable
joy to return to my own fireside, yet, alas ! causes of sorrow
were not lacking either. My journey, which was less well
organised than last year, was less successful also in the matter
of transporting our luggage and supplies. The canoes which
had transported Mr. Lochner, the Chartered Company's agent,
to Kazungula were to be passed on to my service for returning.
But all these canoes were of small capacity and overladen with
paddlers ; so that, while running into greater expense than last
year, I was able to accomplish much less.

Our conveyances are falling into an alarming state of decay.
Besides my old family waggon, which no longer exists, we had
two transport waggons, which were quite new. They have
been seven years at work, and now they are both in ruins.
And yet Mr. Waddell, with his wonderful skill, has often repaired

them, and set them up again.   Poor man! he thought he had
mended the one which had collapsed at Loanja, so that it could
go one last journey, at least as far as Sefula.   But at the very
first motion, even before stirring from its place, the wheels
fell to pieces.   The naves were completely rotten; they were
mere touchwood.

Besides this, there is also the matter of the oxen.   I told
you I had sent to Sesheke two teams of eighteen oxen each,
for the service between Sesheke and Kazungula, and *vice versa*,
and that nearly all these oxen have perished.   This new
disaster eclipses all the former ones, and involves me personally
more deeply than any one else.   So there is one route which we
must perforce consider closed for a long while to come.   There
remains the river way.   It is a last resort, which does not
by any means solve the difficulty, because, as I explained
to you, we are entirely dependent upon the king and his
caprices for canoes ; and as he himself confesses, it is in every
way to his interest to serve the traders first of all, who bring
him merchandise and ammunition.   And as waggons only
arrive at the Zambesi during one season of the year, we shall
always find this a great embarrassment.   I say nothing of the
expenses, of which you yourselves can judge by the accounts.
But I cannot keep silent about the dangers of the navigation.
Four of our canoes this year were capsized in the rapids.   The
canoes were saved, even the cases were fished out, some of
them fifteen days after the accident.   You cannot form any
idea of our losses.   Thus, a big bale of coloured materials—
our small cash for daily use—which my canoe-men had "put
in the sun to dry" (!) (without unpacking it, of course), I
found three weeks later, when I was able to open it, in such
a state of fermentation and decomposition as can be more easily
imagined than described.   The same with cotton blankets and
pieces of calico.   The same, alas! with nearly all our cases.
Out of fifteen which reached us, some of which we had been
expecting for two or three years, not three were intact.   All
the others, either opened at the custom-house or badly
soldered, contained heart-breaks over which we must draw a
veil, out of regard for our friends.   And yet it must be grasped
thoroughly that the transport is very heavy.   From the Cape
to Kazungula, it costs no less than £3 5s. per cwt.   And

to that must be added the costs of freight, custom-house, and bonding-house, of duties, and of agents (which last are no trifle), and then the cost of canoeing from Kazungula to the Valley.

One case did reach us safely. As it was too large for the canoes, I had it sent after us. It was one we had been expecting from friends in Holland for three years or more ; it took eight men to carry it, and the transport alone cost us £15. We opened it : nothing but blotting-paper and blank cheque-books down to the very bottom ! They had sent us by mistake a case of stationery intended for a Dutch bank in the Transvaal.[1]

M. Adolphe Jalla is starting for Kazungula. He has shown himself a most valuable helper, and has taken such an interest in the school that I ask myself if he would not perhaps be in his right place at Sefula, to occupy himself specially with the teaching. We must have a *boarding* school for the youths, and in our thoughts it will one day give birth to an Evangelists' College, for that is after all our principal object.

We have decided to send Litia to Morija. He will start with M. Jalla, accompanied by four other boys, all among our best scholars. Lewanika has already given me £50 towards his journey and maintenance. His own ambition for him is, that Litia should go to England and see civilised life. The immediate consequence of Litia's departure for Basuto-land is the disbanding of our school. We expected something of this, but the crisis seems more serious than we thought. This departure also creates difficulties for the future which we did expect, and which we can only avoid by founding an establishment for young men without delay.

Our political horizon is of the darkest, and I know not

---

[1] M. Coillard wrote to the bank whom it concerned to tell them of this mistake, and some months later received a letter of polite regret, requesting him to burn all the cheque-books in the presence of witnesses, after noting their numbers in a duly attested declaration that they had been destroyed ; and this was done. The blotting-paper he might keep, and it was the only compensation ever received for the £15 transport expenses. Similarly, a chest of the commonest and worst-made boots and shoes found its way to Sefula, having been redirected thither in error by some agent : scarcely two pairs fitted anybody on the station. As for Mme. Jeanmairet's wedding trousseau, which did not arrive till two or three years after her marriage, it was all utterly destroyed in the river.

what next year may be preparing for us. We are accused
of having deceived the king and sold his country, so that we are
quite in disgrace. I feel I have written you the saddest of all
my letters ; I am sorry for it, but I cannot help it.[1]

[1] In July 1890, M. Goy, who had hitherto been at Sefula, returned from
a visit to Basuto-land with his newly married wife, and was put in charge
of the Sesheke station, vacated by the Jeanmairets. About the same time,
Mr. Buckenham, of the Primitive Methodist Mission, brought a little band of
pioneers to Barotsi-land, hoping for permission to establish a work among the
vassal tribe of Mashukulumboe. They could not have arrived at a more unpro-
pitious moment for their own success. The Barotsi, angered by their king's
treaty with the B. S. A. Chartered Company, instantly identified the English
missionaries with the foreigners, whose policy they dreaded (without understanding it), and treated them with every indignity. The French missionaries,
hoping to shield them, took their part, thereby incurring the same hostility ;
and hence arose serious complications, related in the next chapter.

CHAPTER XXV

SEFULA, *April* 1891.

A MONG the lukewarm friends of missions, I have sometimes heard the remark that missionaries' letters are generally sunshiny pictures without shadows ; which, to say the least of it, would be very inartistic—very little in harmony with nature. Though I protest against this assertion, which is only based upon ignorance, or else upon a generalisation of isolated facts, yet it is a tendency I can very well understand, if it be not exaggerated. Just as we like to share all our hopes and joys with our friends, just so far do we shrink from saddening them with gloomy tales of anxieties, disappointments, and difficulties, incessantly renewed. But after all, our true friends, those who are associated heart and soul with our labours, need to know everything, to read between the lines, and thus be initiated into the web of our life—do they not ? For them, as for ourselves, the evangelisation of the heathen world, in the place where it is carried on, is certainly not a tissue of strange customs and adventures as thrilling as a romance ; it is a desperate struggle with the Prince of Darkness, and with everything that his rage can stir up in the shape of obstacles, vexations, opposition, and hatred, whether by circumstances or by the hand of man. It is a serious task. Oh, it should mean a life of consecration and faith !

Already you can guess—can you not ?—that we have passed

406

through some particularly trying times. Well, yes! When
the clouds pile themselves up, black and heavy with tempest,
it is idle to tell yourself that the sun is always shining radiantly
beyond, in the depth of the skies. You would like to *see* it ;
and when the mist thickens round you, and sends an icy shiver
into your very heart, would you not prefer to close your lips,
bury yourself in the folds of your mantle, and pursue your way
in silence until the sky clears again? But no ; I must overcome
that and speak.

To begin with, we have run the risk (and, for all I know,
may yet be running it) of embroiling all our relationships with
this man for whom I have conceived so great an affection, but
who, alas! as king is so deplorably incapable. He is a weathercock, changing with every wind, soft wax that receives every
impression, hopelessly at the mercy of the most contrary influences. Poor Lewanika! You know the concession he made
to the B. S. A. Chartered Company. Well, intriguing men,
some of them Europeans, animated by motives which I need
not qualify, left no stone unturned to excite the king's suspicious nature, and stir up his anger ; they have represented
his transactions with the Company in the falsest light, accusing
us ourselves of having designedly deceived him, and of having
sold our services and our influence to the Company—we, who
have not even received a single penny for all the provisions we
had to procure for its agent and his followers for their return
journey when they left. As for our hospitality during the
two months he was our guest, of course there could be no
question of payment for that. These calumnies and others
no less absurd have completely upset the king. In the old
days—six or seven years ago—they would have compromised
everything : our property, our lives, our mission.

Thus we have been scratched in the thorny field of politics,
which is certainly not ours. We have fallen into a hornets'
nest. We do not yet know the final turn affairs may take.
What we do know is, that " the Lord reigneth," and that He
can just as easily turn the malice of the wicked as the mistakes
of men, all events and all circumstances, to the accomplishment
of His eternal designs.

The season this year has been exceptionally rainy—a
dismal season for us in one sense. Everything is impregnated

with that warm moisture which is only known in the tropics. Our foot-gear, our books, even those we use daily, are all covered with mildew. As to the eatables, we won't speak of them. At no season will anything keep at the Zambesi, except in hermetically sealed canisters. And when necessity obliges one to open any of these canisters, if the contents are not to be lost, they must be finished up at once. Meat, which with us is so scarce and difficult to procure, will only keep two days; on the third it is already tainted, and disgusts one.

For two successive years now, Lewanika has chosen a site for his temporary capital, but for lack of water the canoes could not land there. This is the third time. Will it be the same? No one can understand it. The divining bones were earnestly consulted, and the oracle was heard. The gods, above all the formidable Katuramoa, were wroth at Lewanika's unheard-of innovation. What was he going after in the neighbourhood of these white men, when " the traditions of antiquity had devoted quite another part of the country to the king's residence "?

Thus were the gods made to speak by the conservative party, and it is influential: old Narubutu worthily represents it. Lewanika, who wanted to keep the thing secret, was surprised and mortified when I spoke to him about it. He had decided not to put himself in the wrong with the manes of his ancestors, but to conform to tradition: consequently, he was quietly making his preparations. But after a serious conversation I had with him in January, he let himself be shaken. He held a council; and, strange to say, the chiefs also yielded, and they resolved to make a last attempt this year, and install the temporary capital at Sana, in our neighbourhood. The work was vigorously pushed on, and two miles from us, as the crow flies, a village is now rising from an islet, an exact reproduction of Lealuyi, only on a more modest scale. The plan is the same, and so are the arrangements of the king's private establishment, his harem, his kitchens, his various offices, the *khothla*, and the various quarters of the town; there is the same labyrinth of concentric alleys and narrow passages. So there is an old desire accomplished, after ardent prayers which God has deigned to grant. Yes, but how about the flood? It is late; the prognosticators are already swearing that there will not be one. In vain messengers have been

"NALIKUANDA"—A ROYAL PROGRESS.

sent, one after another, to the upper country—no use! Decidedly, we are not popular in the spirit-world, and Katuramoa has a grudge against us!

But lo and behold! one fine day a note from the king announces, as great and good tidings, that the flood, which has come a little suddenly, is already sufficient to bear the monstrous royal barge, and that at last he is coming to Sana. Soon afterwards, a canoe arrives with a pleasant message to go and meet him at Sebembi.

Life at the Zambesi is monotonous—no recreation, or very little ; so this was too good an occasion not to unbend a little. We were soon in canoes—Mme. Coillard, Mlle. Kiener, Mr. Waddell, Andreas, the girls, the boys, all our pupils big and little ; and for the first time we had the joy of gliding on the waters of our canal. We were the first at the rendezvous. We could hear the low rumbling of the war-drums, but it was distant. And to keep ourselves from looking at the sun, which was going down, and the clouds, which were mounting up, the ladies visited the huts, and we talked to the men grouped about the public square ; then we all sang hymns together. That is our bell in the villages, but a very cracked bell, I can assure you. Then we spoke of the Lord Jesus to these poor creatures. During this time, the drums had drawn nearer. In a moment, we were on our feet, grouped upon the edge of the water, and gazing into the immensity of the submerged plain. "There they are! there they are!" and many voices took up the cry. In truth, a black mass was appearing on the horizon, growing visibly greater and broader, breaking up and taking on the appearance of a forest floating on a lake. The women, congregated on one side, uttered their customary piercing cries, while among the groups of men and youths remarks full of curiosity flew about like sparks. "What! two *Nalikuandas ?* Just look! When was the second one born?" And it was true.

The Barotsi had as usual patched up and restored the great official barge, but Lewanika took it into his head to do something better. Shutting himself up with some selected workmen in an enclosure forbidden to the public, he set to work. The bottom and sides of canoes, taken to pieces, furnished him with planks. Then dovetailing them together, and adjusting

them very skilfully, he caulked them with the caoutchouc
of the country, made a double bottom, put up a pavilion
decorated with red-and-white stuff, and amid the wondering
gaze of his people he launched his own *Nalikuanda*. You can
guess how they admired it. I should not be surprised if some
poet had already sung it. Being longer and narrower than
the official barge, it is also much lighter, and does Lewanika
credit. After tacking about for a long time in the open, the
two wonders of our Barotsi navy arrived, escorted by the canoes
of the princesses (distinguished by their tents of matting), by
those of the councillors, chiefs, and favourite attendants of the
king, and by a multitude of slaves—altogether several hundreds
of canoes, bristling with paddlers, and spread over the plain
like an immense army of ants on the war-path. It was a novel
and interesting sight to us.

But the sun had reached the horizon. We exchanged a
hand-clasp and a few words with Lewanika, who was surprised
and quite delighted to see the ladies ; we went a little bit of
the way together ; and then, while he was betaking himself to
his new quarters, we returned by our canal. As we approached
the station, the current became stronger and the water shallower ;
we advanced but slowly. The clouds, which had gathered black
and dark, burst over us ; it was a waterspout. All who could,
escaped on foot. We remained alone with our little crew.
Wrapped up in mackintoshes as stiff as cardboard, which had
split to rags before ever being used, we endured this deluge
with the best grace we could, while our men pulled and pushed
the canoe very good-temperedly. In spite of this adventure, we
did not regret the day, once we were safe at home.

A problem which propounds itself and causes me great
embarrassment is that of reconciling the demands of teaching
with the urgent need for evangelisation. We cannot perform
the one duty conscientiously except at the expense of the
other. It pains me to think that our sphere of activity is so
limited, when we have the whole nation before us as our
undisputed field. The shortest walk in these torrid climes in
the sands and the swamps exhausts me, and makes me dread
the exertion. Besides, these walks cannot radiate very far : so
how can the distant villages be reached? The temporary
removal of the capital to our neighbourhood, with the great

movement it necessarily creates, imposes on me new duties, which must not be neglected, for it offers us precious and unique opportunities, which we *must* turn to account. This was the lesson read me by the king the other day with a touch of ill-humour : " I shall take good care not to make the people go to Sefula. It is for all of you to reach them. I am tired of telling them to send their children to the school, and they are angry with me about it. I have brought thee the heart of the nation. Now the business is thine, not mine."

Is it not strange that just at this moment, when the work demands new efforts and we would need to multiply ourselves, I find myself alone to meet it ? And to crown these complications, I have just lost my horse, that faithful servant I owed to the generosity of a friend, whom I have often blessed without knowing him. So I have nothing left but my legs, which are not very young. But "no man goeth to war at his own charges." We have the right to count upon the Master Who has sent us.

Allow me to invite you to spend Easter Sunday with us, and you will get some idea of how far our experiences can be called encouraging. It was the first Sunday Lewanika spent at his new capital. We were counting on him and on a great influx : perhaps it would even be impossible for us to have the service in the church. The sky was grey, but there was no rain—a fairly good sign. At dawn, in accordance with our usual habits, the bell announced the Day of Rest. At half-past nine and at ten o'clock, it once more rang to assemble our audience. Except for our pupils, not a soul responded. Some men and two or three women came in late. But the Lord was with us, and the service was remarkably serious and interesting. Then I put on my thick boots, and we all set off for the capital, excepting of course the ladies. The king, friendly and chatty as he always is, pleaded a slight indisposition, and I found it impossible to persuade him to come to the service. I imagined that he had perhaps to go through certain purifications before he could show himself in the *khothla* of his new village. I put the question directly to him, and he laughed.

At his request, I pointed him out the portion of Scripture I was going to read and explain, and betook myself to the public

square. The handbell had gone the round of the village, and
had ceased ringing ; the public crier was heard no more, and
still I had only a handful of men before me. Of course there
were no women, since the king's were not there, and the latter
would not have dared to appear without his orders. On every
side work was going on ; they were building, dressing hides,
and repairing canoes. No one troubled about the meeting. We
had recourse to our last bell ; we set to work to *sing*, and sang
a long time. Some men sauntered slowly up, one by one : I
counted them ; and when I began to preach, I may have had an
audience of sixty. I reached home late, weary and discouraged.
But, in the evening, we had a blessed meditation together, and
took the Communion. For us, it was indeed the repast which
the Risen Saviour Himself prepared for the sad and worn-out
disciples who had " toiled all night and taken nothing."

Since then, we have been in a waggon with our ladies to
spend a day at the capital. This brought us in return a
succession of visits—long visits, lasting three-quarters of the
day. First of all, there were the king's wives ; then those of
the Gambella and the other chiefs. The king himself is entirely
taken up with antelope hunting ; but his messengers do not
let the grass grow on the path between Sana and Sefula. We
deeply feel our responsibility during the three months that lie
before us. For three years, this has been the subject of earnest
prayers. Many of our friends, too, have united with us in
asking the Lord for Lewanika's conversion : we are looking for
it ; we expect it. As he said to me himself the day before
yesterday, he knows the truth, he loves the things of God, but
Satan and the world are contesting him with us. It is difficult
for a *rich* man to enter into the kingdom of God.

The school ! It suffered a violent shock from Litia's departure for Basuto-land. This dear boy exerted a much greater
influence than I imagined. All those slaves who attended it
with him have now forsaken it. Our young men's village,
having now no recognised authority which can be exercised
out of school hours, has become once more what it was
formerly—a den of brigands. It is not so much the pupils
themselves as their slaves. There has been a tremendous
revival of thieving—a perfect eruption. I had taken a great
deal of trouble to sow a field ; we have had no crop—maize,

pumpkins, beans, sugarcanes, everything has been stolen, even a fence I had undertaken, of which the last post will soon have disappeared. My minimum and maximum thermometers have gone the way of my two aneroids, and are of no use to the thieves.

Even at school, there is always a leaven of insubordination. The scholars know we have no authority over them, and that, however ill they behave, no one, either the king or their parents, will have a rebuke for them. Moreover, discipline is a delicate and difficult matter. But, on the whole, our school is always the one bright spot in the work of Sefula. Our pupils are making progress, and the task of teaching them has been a serious one. Oh, if the Spirit of God would but work among them, and bring about true conversions, what a change there would be! Until the time of blessing, may God continue to give us grace and patience! We are ready for anything rather than to have no school,—ready, if needs be, to sow nothing more in our field, so often plundered; not to complain, if we are robbed. . . . We must suffer in silence, until better days. They will dawn at the Zambesi as in Basuto-land, and then our trials and vexations will be a subject of astonishment to our successors, and an irrefutable proof of the influence of the Gospel.

My pictures to-day are not lacking in shadows, alas! And yet another must be added, the darkest, the blackest of all. I do it with shame and sorrow; but do it I must, if I would be truthful, and give you even a glimpse into the nature of some of our difficulties. You will remember that, besides Lewanika's daughters, we had three other girls, on whom we had centred much affection and many hopes. Illusive and deceptive dreams! Of these three, two had to be summarily turned out of our house. They used to get over the enclosure of the court at night, and, in accordance with the morals of the country, gave themselves up to the disorder of the village, and, evading our vigilance, made appointments with their accomplices in the woods in broad daylight. You can guess the rest. It is quickly told; but what is not told, and cannot be, is the suffering, the moral torture, we have passed through, especially my poor wife. It was during my last journey to Sesheke that she began to make these overwhelming discoveries. Her distress, her bitter tears, added to the great weakness of her condition, almost killed her. We had often shuddered at the contact with the appalling corruption that reigns around us and poisons our atmosphere, but we did not as yet completely realise that we were living in the midst of Sodom. The notion of sin does not as yet exist. Young and old glory in their shame ; there is no sense of it. Should a young girl fall, she is no way disgraced ; public opinion fastens no stigma upon her ; and her masters, if she has any, have a slave the more. Forgive me for putting things so crudely. But it is well you should know that, when we speak in veiled words of corruption, it is an abyss that we are hiding out of deference to you and out of modesty. These are not commonplaces, a conventional way of speaking? No indeed, dear friends. They are appalling realities, which haunt us, so that the hours of darkness bring nothing but sleeplessness or nightmares. To work here without losing courage, and to keep alive the smoking flax of faith, one must believe, and believe firmly, that the Gospel of Christ is truly the power of God unto salvation upon all that believe. Whoever doubts it would lose his way, coming to the Zambesi, unless God had mercy on him and unsealed his eyes.

Our poor, poor children ! So much for the result of three years' toil ! We would fain believe that the tears of our poor Nyama were to some extent sincere ; and that though she had to leave our house in disgrace, the good seed so lovingly sown in her heart will some day spring up, and that she will one day become a steady, sober woman and an earnest Christian. The other, Namusi, pained us even more by her hardness, her insolence and duplicity, than by her fall. On her return to Lealuyi, the king wished to make an example. He put her in prison, took away all her European clothes (her wardrobe was well garnished, and she was very proud of it, poor girl !), and distributed them to the first-comers. Imagine the effect upon us the other day, when we went with the ladies to the capital, at seeing grown-up young men dressed up in the unfortunate girl's nightdresses, and in *setsibas* made out of her skirts. In the bitterness of my grief, I would myself have cleared the house of the last of our girls. But my wife was of another mind—one more in harmony with that of the

Friend of sinners. She received three fresh little girls from
Lewanika ; and—we are going to begin again.

It was in the midst of this terrible trouble that Mlle. Kiener
came to us like an angel sent by God. The shock was
terrible to her, and her vocation had to stand a severe test at
the beginning. A real daughter for us in the house, a tender
and devoted friend for my wife, an active and capable help in
the school, she has already been a great blessing ; and in our
hearts, as in our lives, she is making a larger place for herself
every day.

It was in these circumstances, too, that our friend Adolphe
Jalla left us for his long journey to the south, whither
he is going to meet his fiancée ; and the tempest had far
from subsided when our dear friends from Kazungula arrived,
M. and Mme. Louis Jalla. Our heavenly Father had prepared this balm for our sore hearts. This was the very
first visit from friends that we have received at Sefula. To
say that we enjoyed their visits sounds commonplace, and yet
it is true. They were indeed a blessing to us. We could
talk and pray together. M. Jalla was no idle visitor. As
a member of the Barotsi missionary family, he fully entered into
the work at Sefula, equally with his dear wife. He preached,
he taught and directed the school, as he would have done at
home, while a slight illness confined me to the house. I will
not enter into details. Their passage here has left a wake
of brightness, like the ships which in the tropics furrow the
phosphorescent waves. I am glad the people know them, and
I am sure they like them.[1] What a comfort it would be to
know that the great village of Mambova had at last been

---

[1] M. L. Jalla writes of this visit : " On December 18th, we arrived at Sefula.
The station had a festival air. We could scarcely recognise Mlle. Kiener,
the fever had so transformed her already. What beautiful trees there are at
Sefula ! We counted more than twenty in the inner court alone. The
station is quite a little world, where it seems to me the feeling of solitude, so
frequent with us, ought to be entirely unknown. We spent a whole month
of rest and intimate enjoyment at Sefula, installed in the pretty little house
Litia had once occupied. Sometimes we went out all together to make a
little tour in the wide garden of Sefula, admiring the immense avenue of
bananas planted by M. Coillard. Everything here is on a large scale,
except perhaps the crops. One traces everywhere the skilful hand of
Mr. Waddell. I specially admired the chapel, which is a masterpiece, given

transferred to Kazungula! We are counting on it. Lewanika
has been sending one order after another for two years ; but
he has not the power of making himself obeyed. And yet it
is a position of indisputable importance for the nation, seeing
it is the gate of the country. Besides this, great changes will
take place in this part of the country, if, as I believe, the
queen, Mokwaë, finally selects Sesheke for her residence.

I am sorry to close this letter without being able to point
to the slightest symptom of an awakening of conscience around
us. We are still breaking up the ground. And what a business!
We may plough and we may sow, but the seed remains buried
under the clods, and choked among the briers of a frightful
paganism. It would be enough to make us lose courage, if
we did not know that it is precisely under the ground in secret
and in silence that the seed sprouts.

What strikes us and distresses us in our dear Zambesians
is their incredible levity. They laugh and scoff at everything
and everybody. They have none of that decorum, that grave
and respectful politeness, which constitutes the charm of social
intercourse among the Bechuana in general and the Basuto
in particular. I consider those young people fortunate who
come out directly from Europe to the Barotsi, without having
made acquaintance with other tribes. They are spared many
bitter disappointments.

The Basuto, like the Athenians, are all, and always, on the
scent of anything new. " *Taba ke life ?* " (" What is the news ? ")
is the invariable salutation of two strangers meeting one another.
Here people flee and hide from one another, if they can ; the
stronger insults and robs the weaker. You may come from
the ends of the earth : what does it matter to them what is said

the conditions of the country. It is almost always filled. I was happy
to employ a good part of my time at the school. Mlle. Kiener is fighting her
first battles there, and I was sometimes surprised to see those great boys,
naturally so turbulent, obeying her words, uttered as they were in a quiet yet
firm little voice. After Mr. Waddell, Nguana-Ngombé is M. Coillard's
right hand. What an invaluable boy ! and at the same time so unselfish.
Above all, it is thanks to him that it has been possible to achieve the great
work of a canal joining the Sefula River to the Zambesi, and permitting
canoes to come within five minutes of the station. But what is specially
encouraging with Andreas is his earnestness, his faithfulness to the Lord,
in spite of the many snares laid for him on every side."

and done over there? Lewanika is, as far as I know, the only one—without exception—who puts such questions to you. Here, to live is literally to amuse oneself. All is frivolity; there is nothing serious in life—nothing. You enquire after somebody's health. People laugh in your face; they look at one another, and ask what you mean. You should go more directly to the point, and ask if this somebody is amusing himself, and they will instantly and emphatically answer you, "*O nts'a bapala hantle*" ("Yes, he is amusing himself thoroughly"). Should you meet some one from the capital, and ask what is the news, unless the king be laid up, the invariable reply is, "*Le roi s'amuse*"; "*Morena oa bapala merôpa e ntse e lela*" ("The king is amusing himself, and the drums are still beating").

Unhappily, the duties and responsibilities of life share this evil influence. The Zambesians have few sources of joy, and the trials which elsewhere stir the depths of the soul, here do scarcely more than brush over the surface of empty hearts. Theft, lying, murder, atrocities and corruptions under their most revolting forms, do not seem to astonish anybody. People are amusing themselves—that is their way of doing it. A father, whose daughter, placed in a missionary's house, is already destined for a young chief's harem, recommended our brother not to look after her too much, but to shut his eyes a little to the girl's relationships with the boys of the establishment. He said, in language which cannot be translated into plain English, "Let them amuse themselves." At our age, there is something absurd in being gravely greeted with, "*Salang! le bapale hantle!*" ("Rest in peace and amuse yourself well"). But sometimes the absurdity wrings tears from one's eyes, as when one day a man came from Sesheke, bringing us the news of little Marguérite's death, my niece's child. "And how did you leave M. and Mme. Jeanmairet?" enquired my wife. "Oh, very well; they were amusing themselves." "What! amusing themselves, when their child had just died?" Whereupon the man burst into a loud peal of laughter.

There is something profoundly sad in this, because I think it is the key to the Barotsi character. For them, nothing is serious. Everything degenerates into amusement or disgust: moreover, they are not capable of intellectual effort, and cannot bear the least restraint. One can easily understand the very slight hold the things of God have upon these frivolous natures.

"Son of Man, can these dry bones live?" "*Lord, Thou knowest.*"

SEFULA, *April 14th*, 1891.

I am at leisure to-day; for it has pleased all our pupils, without exception, to give us three or four weeks' holiday, in order to go with the king to Ruena to hunt antelopes; and naturally the king could not refuse. It is a monster hunt; the people betake themselves thither in battalions, and they have a *grande battue*. The antelopes, encircled on all sides, take refuge on an islet, the canoes draw together, the circle closes, grows smaller, and to the first spear flung by the king a general slaughter ensues. Every one goes frantic. They roast meat to repletion; they have the chance of picking up a skin or two for the winter. How can one blame our young Zambesians for throwing off the constraint and monotony of school, and giving themselves up to the delights of this savage life?

I followed them in a canoe ten or twelve days later, in order to spend the Sunday with them and preach the Gospel. Meanwhile, I continue to visit the capital, although I do not find much encouragement there for my meetings. The king is always friendly, and so are the people. But the women are quite horrified when I press them to come. "What! we to go on the public square, without being able to hide ourselves from the men's eyes, as we can at Lealuyi! Surely the *Moruti* is not serious?" And, in fact, they do not come, not one of them. So the work has to be done from house to house.

I was much touched, in reading last year's Report, to see there a sum of 225 f. (£9) anonymously given at Neuchâtel "for M. Coillard's horse." Now, how could this person know that in 1891 I should be in want of a horse? Is it not really remarkable? I have indeed lost my horse, that good old servant who knew me so well, and without whom I never went any excursion. Everybody else knew him too. From as far off as they could see his white coat, they would shout, "The missionary!" And everybody ran up, men and women too. "Ah! it is the Lord's Day to-morrow, is it not? We will come?" And the boys would make the excursion with me, merrily and noisily. It all reminded me of my life in

Basuto-land,—a somewhat faint reflection of it, to be sure ; but still it brought back pleasant memories.   Now it is my old legs which must carry me, a little less briskly, a little more painfully, and perhaps a little less far, through our sands and morasses. If the work is to be done on a more modest scale, still it will be done all the same.   And until I get some new legs, God will give strength and courage.

I was speaking the other day of the new outbreak of thieving. I had laid down my pen, and the ink was scarcely dry, when a thief, braving the rain, made a journey of four or five leagues, in order to enrich himself after the fashion of the housebreaking fraternity.   He had certainly taken his observations and timed his visit admirably, to judge by the care with which he had made his selection, whether in my study or my dark photographic chamber, of which he even carried off the serge *portière*. Only—he had forgotten that at the end of the rainy season running would leave traces on the sand.   At daybreak, as soon as I had given the alarm, all our boys were on the scent.   The thief made light of that.   Had he not a little magic horn, which he shook as he went along the road, firmly believing that those who pursued him would either drop down in sleep or be struck blind ?   Towards midday, he had halted in the shade, among the woods, in order to admire his booty, and enjoy an entirely new sensation, that of combing and brushing his hair—for he was in possession of a dressing-case.   Suddenly, he heard a rustling in the brushwood ;   he perceived a troop of armed youths, and with one desperate bound sought safety in flight. All in vain ; they seized him, throttled him, and brought him to the station.   The next day, I sent him to the king.

The unfortunate creature was so unlucky as to be a Mongeti, and not to have a Morotsi for his master.   The occasion was too tempting to parade their virtue.   After having left him all day tied up in the full sun, the chiefs condemned him to be bound hand and foot, with two big blocks of wood attached to his legs, and to be thrown into the river.   The king had prudently retired.   When he learnt the sentence, he thrice sent to ask the great chiefs if they were serious.   " Serious ?   Most certainly ! We must make an example ; it is quite time."   " Very well," said the king, " but let us at least wait for the missionary's opinion.   Meanwhile, throttle the rascal for me."   They under-

stood. Two stakes were driven into the ground, as far apart
as possible ; they stretched out his arms and legs, and bound
them to these stakes. His head and abdomen were tightly
fastened to two crosspieces—a regular crucifixion ; and there
the poor unfortunate was left in the most terrible situation,
devoured all night long by mosquitoes, the whole day by flies
and thirst, and scorched by a burning sun—a spectacle which
attracted and amused a curious crowd.

I need not tell you my indignation, and the nature of the
messages upon messages I sent the king. I was about to betake
myself to the village, when I received the assurance that the
poor wretch had been loosed. Indiscreet tongues have assured
me that, in spite of the king's orders, he was left thus crucified
for a day and two nights—thirty-six hours—while his cries and
groans excited the general mirth.

What made me so indignant was that, a short time ago, the
slave of a Barotsi chief had committed a much greater robbery, under greatly aggravated circumstances. Though he was
caught red-handed and conducted straight to the *lekhothla*, the
great chiefs had not even a reprimand for him. " He is the
child of a Morotsi," they said : "his fault is ours ; we will pay
his fine." And this individual strutted about, unashamed, after
as before. I did not want their fine ; but the kind people spared
me the embarrassment of either accepting or declining it.
Don't talk to me of Blind Justice at the Zambesi. She has
uncommonly good eyesight.

During my last visit to the king, the latter returned to his
favourite theme—an industrial school. He is so engrossed with
the idea of having boys whom we have polished up a little, that
he bribes mine away one after another—in a manner, moreover,
which does him little honour.

SEFULA, *June 16th*, 1891.

We are in the midst of a tempest : other letters will have
told you this already. We have never before been in such a
gale, so furious and persistent. It is still the affairs of the South
African Company that are upsetting people's minds. Without
being a St. Paul, I too have my " Alexander the coppersmith,"
who has done and still " does me much evil." I needed this bitter
sorrow and painful humiliation, and I pray daily that I may be

filled with the same spirit as David, who in the day of his adversity endured Shimei's insults, and replied to those who would have avenged him, " The Lord hath said unto him, Curse David."[1]

The last incidents that have arisen confirm me more and more in the conviction that the treaty made last year with the Company has been the lifebuoy as much for the nation as for Lewanika himself. But to-day we are quite alone in our opinion. Our adversaries, who have posed as the champions and saviours of the nation, have represented things very differently. Insinuations, calumnies, and the false light thrown on facts have found a fertile soil in the radically suspicious, excitable, and vindictive nature of our poor Barotsi, and have quickly borne their fruits of distrust, threats, and insults. The excitement of the Sesheke chiefs is at its height ; and the king himself, rightly or wrongly, says that it is partly to this that we must attribute the ill-treatment Mr. Baldwin (the Methodist missionary) has suffered, and that M. Goy has, in part at least, so nobly shared. Serious dangers are threatening us. Should a *pitso* take place on Mokwaë's return with the chiefs of Sesheke, or should a rumour spread that the Company wishes to avail itself of the treaty to enter the country forcibly, what will become of us—of me ?

The king himself understands me, and is incapable of doing us the least harm ; but he is still more incapable of protecting us. He is trembling for himself : hence his persistence in throwing on me alone all the responsibility. If the vengeance of the Barotsi demands a victim, he will deliver one up much sooner than expose himself. Alas ! he has just given us a sad proof of this.

The Methodist missionaries have been a year in the country, and, poor things ! have had all sorts of troubles ; besides which, they have not yet been able to learn the language, and this impairs their popularity. On the feeblest of pretexts, one of them has been shamefully and cruelly ill-treated, at Queen Mokwaë's, near Sesheke. This has naturally been bruited all through the country.[2] It was from Lewanika himself that I

---

[1] See 2 Sam. xvi. 10, 11.

[2] The story of these troubles was briefly as follows :—The queen, Mokwaë, had gone on a hunting expedition, leaving her "palace" under the

first heard of it : then came the letters of our brethren Louis
Jalla and Goy, full of an earnestness and elevation that would
have pleased you. I read them to the king. It was given
to me also to be faithful, both in private and in my Sunday

guardianship of one of her attendants. One of the English missionaries
entered the court to speak to the warder, not knowing it was contrary to
etiquette to do so in the queen's absence; and the next evening, while
taking a moonlight stroll with one of his colleagues, he brought the latter into
the palace court, to show him how it was built; and, to illustrate his explanations, he traced some lines on the sand with his foot. Instantly, the warder
accused them both of sorcery against the queen, who, directly she heard of
it, sent for both the missionaries. Only one of them, Mr. Baldwin, was able
to attend, the other being ill with fever. M. Goy went with him to act as
interpreter and advocate. Their reception augured ill. The queen refused
to see them. They found chiefs and men all assembled on the public place.
Mr. Baldwin was denied the usual courtesy granted to the missionaries of
sitting on his camp-stool, but was forced like an accused and already condemned man to squat bare-headed on the burning sand and under a broiling
sun. M. Goy, indignant, protested, but in vain, and then shared the humiliation
of his brother. The mock proceedings had hardly begun when a chief
suddenly threw himself upon Mr. Baldwin, crying out, "Seize him !" About
five hundred men instantly surrounded them, crying, "Strangle him ! Throw
him into the water !" M. Goy, thinking to save him, flung his arms round
him ; but the people were so infuriated, that, after a hand-to-hand struggle,
in which both the missionaries were cruelly ill-used, they succeeded in
tearing them apart. The chiefs of Sesheke held M. Goy fast, abusing him as
a "thief" and "arch-sorcerer," for espousing Mr. Baldwin's cause. Meanwhile, Mr. Baldwin was far more severely handled by the queen's followers,
who tortured him by twisting his arms and legs, and sent him back to his
defender, unrecognisably disfigured with blood and dust. In this state, he
was again forced to sit on the burning sand in the sun for an hour. At
last Mokwaë said, "I consent to pardon him, but he must pay a fine";
to which Mr. Baldwin agreed, in order to save his life. All night long,
M. Goy heard them repeating ferociously around him, "Yes, we will kill
that white man ; he wanted to bewitch our queen, and get possession of
the country." Next day, Mokwaë offered M. Goy canoes to return to the
station, but he was obliged to insist that Mr. Baldwin should be in the
same boat as himself, for fear she might have given orders to have him
abandoned on an islet or thrown into the river.

It was not till after two or three years of probation and sufferings such
as the foregoing, that, through M. Coillard's persistent endeavours on their
behalf, the Primitive Methodists were allowed to settle in Mashukulumboe-
land. Mr. Baldwin is now in charge of the station. Mr. Buckenham, the
leader of the band, died in 1896, after a long and painful illness, brought
on by the climate and the hardships and privations they had gone through.
M. Goy, their champion, died about the same time, and from similar causes.

preaching, at the *lekhothla* (2 Cor. v. 20 : " We are ambassadors
for Christ "), and to denounce the conduct of Mokwaë and the
chiefs of Sesheke as a grave offence against God, Whose servants
we are.   The king certainly shared my feelings.   He was very
much displeased by the affair, and he cast all the odium of
it upon the Sesheke chiefs.   Mokwaë, according to him, was
nothing but a tool in their hands.   He wanted to send them
a severe reprimand, but was grieved that he had nobody
courageous enough to convey his message to them.   It was in
vain that together we went over the principal personages of
the Valley.   The Seshekians are formidable, and everybody
dreads them.   Lewanika, while opposing our Methodist
brethren's going to the Mashukulumboe, or, as I earnestly
begged them, to the Batoka, left them free to stop in the
country or to go.   Scarcely had I reached home, when his mood
changed.   His messengers came one on the top of the other,
all contradictory, and each one more bitter than the last.   He
had requested me, by letter, to write to the English missionaries
in the sense above indicated, and then sent the letter back
to me full of indignation, telling me by the hand of Seajika
himself, that he had never asked me to write, that it was all
the lies and inventions of that liar Seajika, and that, as it was
I who had introduced these gentlemen, he owed it to me to
tell me the message he had already sent them.   And this
message is a very hard one for the Methodists.

The conclusion is, that the king refunds the fine Mokwaë
had made them pay, but orders them to quit his country
immediately.

My impression is that he is afraid of the Sesheke chiefs, and
that he has not the courage to take the part of the Methodist
missionaries.   He sacrifices them to get out of his difficulty,
which is not very reassuring for us.   But do not fear.   God is
watching over us ; He reigns.   For some time, a spirit of murmuring and discontent has increasingly prevailed, and bodes no good.
Lewanika is not ignorant of it, but that does not prevent him
from irritating instead of conciliating his people.   At his last
hunt, there were two strikes among the thousands of men who
followed him.   They had already accompanied him, much
against the grain ; and in spite of the very cold nights, he went
so far as to forbid them the camp, even though they had not

their blankets. This was because he had had some misunderstanding with the great chiefs. Just now, all our district is again agitated. Panic has seized everybody, and the villages are deserted. It is the *Lefunga*—the Terror of the king. Messengers swoop down on all the villages, carrying off the children, boys and girls, the prisoners of a certain age being knocked down with blows. Later on, it was the turn of the women, to be taken forcibly for disposal according to the king's caprice. At the *lekhothla*, the men were throttled wholesale.[1] And all because a few workmen took some of the materials of the temporary capital, which the king has now left in order to return to Lealuyi. It is whispered that these men are accused of aiming at the king's life, in order to put some one in his place.

One piece of news Mokwaë has sent the king by express messenger is, that the Matabele have crossed the river below Kazungula. Mokwaë has taken flight, and is returning to the Valley.

What complications in this unhappy country ! I do not believe this last news until it has been confirmed. They have cried " Wolf " so long. But one fine day, when people have ceased to believe in him, the wolf may very well make his appearance.

Just now, there is an alarming recrudescence of paganism ; it is boldly lifting its head again. One would say we had lost ground. Lewanika himself is not always very pleasant, either with his subjects or even with us. And we need much prudence and charity, if we are to maintain our mutual good relations.

I told you that the king had sent orders to our Methodist brethren to leave the country, and that all my efforts in their favour had failed. Since then, he has yielded to my importunities, and has given them permission to stay, " in order to learn the language and customs of the people here." I bless God for it. I knew that, with their losses of cattle, our friends *could* not leave ; and I feared that, if they remained in the face of the king's orders, they would be subjected to all sorts of annoyances. The king declares that he will not allow them to

---

[1] The torture of throttling, very frequently employed by the Barotsi, is generally practised in such a way as to cause, not death, but simply a prolonged fainting fit. Then the victim is brought back to his senses by blows.

go and found a mission either among the Mashukulumboe or
the Batoka. I can only hope that, when minds have calmed
down a little, and we can discuss matters reasonably, he will end
by yielding.

SEFULA, *July 28th*, 1891.

It needs to be known that the soldier of Christ does not
gather the laurels of his crown of life in a delightful garden,
where he can tread the primrose paths in velvet slippers.

We have already learnt much of the art of war since we
came to the Zambesi, but it has been learnt as one learns everything in practical life, at the expense of a personal experience
which is often hard and humiliating. And then, when we begin
to grow into good soldiers, our career will be run, we must pile
arms and yield our place to others. Our regrets cannot be at
having to lay down our arms, but at not having had all that
experience which would have made us good soldiers at the
beginning of the combat. It is a poor thing to be a conscript
all one's life.

What makes me speak like this is, that, with all our experience in Basuto-land, I fear that as yet we have not perfectly
understood our Zambesians. One would say we were laying
the foundations of our edifice in shifting sands. Our efforts have
had no result these six years that we have been in the country.
When we think we have laboriously raised a few stones, some
incident (apparently insignificant) occurs, and the whole thing
collapses.

This is what is happening with our school. Since Litia's
departure, there has been a stampede among our pupils. We
have brought them back one by one, thanks to perseverance ;
and out of the *débris* of our beautiful school of last year, we
have once more made something respectable. Mlle. Kiener is
entirely one with us in this work, which we constantly bear in
our hearts and prayers. But lately, our pupils go off, they disperse and complain of hunger. We often give them flour and
fish which we buy ourselves. But I think it is just an excuse.

Stealing has come into fashion again, just as it was three
or four years ago. This year, I had to give up cultivating anything, because they robbed us of everything, and we could save
nothing. They do not even respect the fences that enclose our

cattle, and yet there is no lack of fuel at our very doors. The other evening, two poor young slave-girls were caught pulling up the remainder of our sweet potatoes. What could be done to them? They said they were hungry. We detained them two days, and fed them well; then we sent them away with a little exhortation to themselves and to their young master, a youthful prince among our pupils. I don't think we shall be forgiven for having caught these thieves in the act. Thence dates the upset of our school, but they take good care not to tell us the reason. Am I not right in speaking of shifting sands? Still, deeper down than the sand we shall find a solid stratum, and we are seeking that. We may have to begin again, but we *will* succeed. If ever any one comes to help us who can give himself up to the teaching entirely, we shall increase the number of boys who live with us, and who are, among all our pupils, those who give us most satisfaction. What we need, until we can have converted fathers and mothers, is to have pupils in our own house, completely severed from the system of slavery prevailing in the country. Meanwhile, I ask myself whether the Lord has not wished thus to direct my attention more especially towards the work of evangelisation.

CHAPTER XXVI

The Death of Mme. Coillard—Her Last Visit to the Capital—Litia's Confession of Faith—Her Last Illness—" Do be in earnest, do !"—The Burial-place—Sympathy of the Barotsi—The Firstfruits of the Harvest— A Little Slave-boy—Nyondo—Queen Victoria confirms the Agreement of the Chartered Company—A Deficit.

" He hath done all things well."—MARK vii. 37.
(Moravian text for October 28th, 1891.)

SEFULA, *October 31st,* 1891.

I AM still quite stunned by the blow which has just struck me. My wife, my beloved wife, is no more! She left me for heaven on October 28th, at ten o'clock in the morning ; and the day before yesterday, in the afternoon, we accompanied her mortal remains and laid them in the tomb. She was only ill in bed for nine days ; but those days, so rich in hallowed memories, are worth a lifetime. It was more than a Pisgah ; it was the glory of Mount Tabor ; for she had a presentiment of her approaching departure which almost amounted to a revelation ; and except for short, momentary intervals, she had the full possession of her faculties.

Her bad health had long become chronic ; but when she had got through the hot season, especially the months of September and October, and reached mid-November, when the rains begin, she generally felt herself revive. This year, the season was particularly depressing. In vain we slept with doors and windows open ; we stifled within our cottage, where at night all the heat of the day seemed to concentrate, and sleep brought no refreshment. We sighed for the rain. Two evenings before her death, the sky for the second time became overcast ; and when in the middle of the night I replied to her pressing questions that there was a shower, I had to place her for a moment close to the window, so that she might hear " that delicious rain " falling.   At the hour at which I am writing, it is pouring ; it has been falling since yesterday, and promises to fall all day.   The soil is no longer red hot ; the air is fresh, and one can breathe : but she is in the grave !

When, at the beginning of the month, we gave holidays to the school, she entreated me to take her in the light waggon to Lealuyi with Mlle. Kiener.   I could have wished to put off this visit ; she seemed to me too poorly for it.   But she was so much in earnest about it that we started.   She did all she could to forget herself and make the journey pleasant : she was so happy to be able to go !. . . She felt that she had a mission to accomplish, and that the present only was hers, not the future, even the nearest. She was too weak to visit people in their homes ; but the women, the chiefs' wives especially, soon besieged her in her hut, and she gave herself entirely up to them.   The first days were well employed in cutting out and sewing dresses, all the time talking in friendly fashion about the things of God.   She was happy. We all were : we thought God would bless our visit.

The Sunday morning, accompanied by one of our girls, she had a long distance to walk through the fields.   Thereupon, a horrible bird of prey came up—not at all the ordinary secretary- bird, but something of the vulture kind—which is kept in the village because it kills and eats serpents.   This creature, excited no doubt by my wife's umbrella or the colour of her dress, pursued and attacked her so furiously that the men and women who ran up at her cries of distress had great difficulty in rescuing her.   They had scarcely left her when the serpent-eater returned to the charge, even more fiercely than before.   Some passers-by came up, rescued her once more, and she returned to the village in a fainting condition.   As she had no wounds on her person, we thought she would escape with her fright and the loss of her umbrella.   She recovered sufficiently to be present at both services.   The evening one, which moved us all deeply, filled her with unspeakable joy.   Our dear Litia, in a simple and touching speech, made a public profession of his conversion ; and while he was speaking, Mokamba, a young man of the royal family, was also weeping, and then broke into sobs !   " A Morotsi weeping !. . . and weeping about his sins !   I thought a Morotsi had no tears to shed.   Why, it is a sight I would have travelled three hundred miles to see; and yet," she said, "we have only had to come from Sefula." She repeated that it was the most beautiful meeting she had been present at on the Zambesi! I bless God for the ray of His glory with which He lit up the evening of her life.

On the Monday, she was laid up, and was no better on the Tuesday. "Take me back to Sefula," she said; "it is there that I would die: do not let me die here." The Wednesday, as she seemed a little better, we took advantage of it to return home. She bore the journey better than we expected, and alighted by herself from the cart. Entering the house, she turned to Mlle. Kiener, whom she dearly loved, and whom, contrary to her usual habit, she addressed as "thee." "Here I am; safely arrived at last, darling," she said; "I did not complain, it is true, but I suffered very much. Now let me get to my bed." She never left her room again but once. The next day, hearing me play on the harmonium and sing while the dinner was being served, she got up noiselessly, and in her dressing-gown dragged herself to the dining-room. "Let me play for you, dear," she said, gently, "and spare your precious voice as long as I can. Let us sing 'The Golden Gate.'" She played and I sang. A peculiar earnestness and solemnity invested the whole scene. Little did I think that it was our very last hymn together on earth, and that my beloved fellow-pilgrim was so very near "the Golden Gate." Indeed, *she* had sighted it. When the last notes had died away, we could not speak. She quietly left the harmonium, and went back to her bed, no more to rise. And shortly after she had left me behind and gone . . . through "*the Golden Gate.*" The fever made terrible progress, in spite of my efforts and our prayers. But I was blinded; I still hoped: I thought I had seen her more ill.

She had no such illusion; she said so to me, with an accent of tenderness, which it wrings my heart to remember. "My beloved," she said, after looking at me long and fixedly, tears filling her eyes, "you will soon have no Christina. . . . You will be alone—quite alone. . . . But God is good, and His mercy endureth for ever."

She had one day of great anguish. Her whole life passed before her. She wept as she poured out her heart, "I am

wretched !—oh, so wretched !—an unprofitable servant; the least,
the most unworthy, of the Lord's servants ! Oh for zeal, for
zeal ! *Do be in earnest, do !* [1] she exclaimed.

In the momentary wanderings of her thoughts, she passed
anew through all the trials and distresses that have made this
year exceptionally hard. That was very painful for me, but
thank God it did not last. Jesus was there. With the breath
of His love, He dissipated these dark clouds, and flooded
her soul with serenity and peace. " Oh ! *He is good*—yes,
He is good," she often repeated, " and His mercy endureth for
ever." And she spoke of the things above, as one who is
already on the threshold of heaven, and for whom faith is
gradually changing into sight.

She was very sensitive to physical suffering, and this aspect
of death had often troubled her. We talked of it very freely,
and often prayed together about it. On the eve of her death,
she said to me, " Dying is not as difficult as we thought, and
as I feared ; it is not painful ; and then it is such a short passage,
when '*underneath are the everlasting Arms.*'" This beautiful
passage (Deut. xxxiii. 27), so wonderfully sweet in her mother-
tongue, had often upheld us in our distresses. And that other,
too, in Ps. lxxiii. 23, 24, which she loved to repeat, and which like
a river of living water had refreshed her whole career : " Nevertheless, I am continually with Thee ; Thou hast holden me by
my right hand. Thou shalt guide me with Thy counsel, and
afterward receive me to glory."

Before returning for the last time to her bed, which had just
been made, she asked me to draw aside the curtain of the
open window. Gazing into the immensity of the sky, through
the foliage which the wind was lightly shaking, she remained
a moment in mute contemplation ; then she cried out with
a delight we shall never forget, " *Oh, que c'est beau, que c'est
donc beau ! Oh, how very beautiful!*" Had she then a vision
of the glory she was so soon to enter into? She reached her
bed with difficulty, " *Je suis enfin arrivée*," she said, laying her
head upon the pillow.

These were her last words. She had spent all these nights
without sleep. I myself was exhausted and much depressed by
a severe cold. But I felt so comforted, when at length I saw

---

[1] These last words in italics were uttered in English, her mother-tongue.

her close her eyelids, and sink peacefully to sleep, that I could not leave her. I was full of hope. Alas! this sleep ended by making me anxious. Towards the morning, a change took place which alarmed me. I could no longer deceive myself: it was indeed the sleep of death. In my anguish, I would have had one more last word, one last look of farewell. But no, I had not that comfort. Mlle. Kiener entered, then Waddell, then Andreas—a little group of desolate mourners; we wept in silence, we cried to God, we watched. The Lord was there. Soon the breathing became more feeble and irregular, and then ceased altogether. God in His mercy had spared her the sufferings of a long and painful death-agony.

How sweet to her must be the eternal rest of the saints! How weary she was—she who had always been so strong, so active, and so full of energy! You will not be astonished that the question of a voyage for her health had once presented itself to my mind, and that I spoke to her seriously of it. Travel for her health! Far from her to condemn those who do it, but to travel for herself seemed to her selfishness and lack of confidence in God. " No, life is too short, and the work is too great; let us be faithful to our post until the end. The Master *knows* that I need health, and He can, if He will, give it me here, without my going elsewhere to seek it." And we spoke no more of it. When we were married, rather more than thirty years ago, she spoke these words to me: " I have come to Africa to do the work of God with you, *whatever* it may be and *wherever* it may be; and remember this—*Wherever God may call you, you shall never find me crossing your path of duty.*" It was more than a beautiful saying; it was the principle of her whole life. If she had one passion, it was for the intimate and sedentary life of the domestic hearth. She had always sighed for a house which should be her *home.* And for more than fifteen years we lived together, building and rebuilding ruins, living in temporary structures and in the midst of wars, travelling far away in the deserts or living in exile. Then there was a lull in our tempestuous life: we returned to Leribé; we built the church, our Ebenezer; there was life around us. Those were bright days. The house too was built—I thought it was our nest; and for her sake I did my best to line it softly. Two years had not gone by before we started for Banyaï-land. " We have weighed anchor," she said ; " we are sailing into the Unknown ; but God knows where we shall land."

Who would then have said it was to be at the Zambesi ? The Zambesi was to her the post of duty ; it became the post of suffering.   There she suffered morally even more than physically. Never, during the thirty years of our life together, had we had such bitter disappointments, nor such painful and burning trials. Our work needed to be consecrated by sufferings.   But God has not forgotten us.   Our friends in Europe, known and unknown, have surrounded us with their sympathy and prayers. Andreas, Mr. Waddell, and Mlle. Kiener, each in their place and in the full measure of their strength, have shown towards us, towards her especially, an affection and devotion which have been a blessing to us, and which our adorable Master will remember, since He has said, " I was sick, and ye visited Me."

November 12th (?).

Her mortal remains rest under the shade of that great forest tree where we used to have picnics, and where we liked to go sometimes, when she was able, to sit, talk, read, or meditate.   I had had a space cleared all round, and a little path made leading to it.   " What a delicious spot !—how calm ! how restful !   Let me rest here when I die, will you not ? " she said to me one day. And it is there that she reposes.

God upheld me for that terrible burial-day that I so dreaded. I was able to see to all the details of the funeral ceremony, thanks to the affectionate help of Waddell, Andreas, and Mlle. Kiener, each in their own department.   I was able to read, pray, exhort, and even sing beside that grave which was taking from me the most precious thing I had on earth.

Yes, I was able to sing the song of triumph and hope, " Jesus is risen from the dead," the thirty-fourth in our Sesuto collection. My appeals were listened to with gloomy attention.   I must have seemed very strange to these poor people.   We were all in our best clothes ; the children of the house had scarves of white calico, in sign of mourning ; the coffin, covered with white, had been decorated with a cross and wreaths of foliage by the affectionate hands of Mlle. Kiener ; and we sang !

Lewanika had sent the principal chiefs of the nation who were about him just then ; Litia and some of our other young

GRAVE OF MADAME COILLARD, SEFULA.

[*To face page* 432.

men were there, and so were those women of the neighbourhood who had sufficient courage to conquer their fears and prejudices. Lewanika, being too unwell to come himself, sent me an ox. "Those were his tears." It seems that it is the habit to send some present, when one cannot go oneself to the burial of a member of *one's own* family. I did not accept it till I had fully assured myself it was nothing but a pure and simple expression of sympathy. Mokwaë, too, sent her principal personages ; and others keep coming one after another ! Poor people ! they cannot give what they have not got themselves. I was much touched yesterday to see a poor man, unknown to me, come to present me with a pair of fowls, together with a little speech of real sympathy ! I shall not lose sight of this good Matondo.

It is already fifteen days, fifteen long days, that I have been alone—days that have seemed like months. She has entered into that repose she so longed for ; she gazes on the King of glory in His beauty, that Jesus whom she loved and served. I would not, even if I could, call her back to this life of sufferings and of sin. But when I had followed her to the threshold of eternity, when I had seen her already radiant with the glory of heaven, when the portals of the City of God closed upon her, and I found myself alone, quite alone in darkness and in tears, my heart was broken.

She lived, she laboured and suffered, as few missionaries' wives have done. The Lord took her, and He did it tenderly. For more than thirty years—mingling her life with mine—she was, after my Saviour and God, everything to me. She was at the centre of all my projects, bearing her heavy share of labours and fatigues through evil report and good report with unparalleled devotion. In her, I lose a true *wife* in all the force of the term—one whom I had received as "a favour from the Lord." I could always count on her judgment and the wisdom of her counsels. If God had clearly called me to the ends of the earth, she would joyfully have followed me thither, without consulting |either her tastes or her ease. It was a terrible blow to her to leave Leribé, the work of our youth. But she made the sacrifice without a murmur, telling me that she should no longer have a *home* down here, and that she would be henceforward a stranger and a pilgrim on the earth.

These dark days have had their rainbow too, and I have cause to bless in the midst of my tears. I, who travel so much, was at home. It was such a delight for her. My birthday, the 17th of July, had so often found us separated, that this year it was a pleasure to see her so happy. When I think that at the moment of her departure I might have been travelling, that Mlle. Kiener might not have been with us, my heart overflows with gratitude towards God. Mlle. Kiener has been a real daughter to us. My wife, among ourselves, took pleasure in calling her "*Dieu-donnée*"; she loved her tenderly. There was a strong current of sympathy between them. During the whole of this year that our dear sister has spent at Sefula, a year exceptionally full of trials and sufferings, she has been a joy and blessing to us. Again, we have that faithful Waddell, so affectionate and devoted, and our dear Andreas. That is all our little world; it is soon reckoned up; but it was complete.

And then she had the joy of seeing the firstfruits of the harvest. What will these firstfruits yield? I know not. But at any rate, for the moment, there they are. Besides Andreas, *four* of our young men profess to have found Jesus. Could she have desired a finer sunset?

The year had been a hard one. Never, during our thirty years together, had we passed through so many sufferings and distresses. She often said, "What a year! I wonder how it will all end." Everything seemed against us—everything! A bad spirit of hostility, aroused by a man who once possessed all my confidence and affection—my " Alexander the coppersmith " —everywhere prevailed, possessed the king, and upset our school. We were losing ground: we felt it. Litia, whom we rejoiced (with some trembling, it is true) to see going to Basuto-land, almost from the first had misunderstandings with our friend Jalla; and after having made the journey difficult for him, left him at Mangwato, and came back to the country alone with his companions. We dreaded the effect of this rash act; and we had good cause to; for when the news came, our pupils left us in a body the next day: as for the king, he no longer deigned to reply to my messages. We went on just the same with the children of the house, and the few pupils we could recruit in the neighbouring villages. At the end of a fortnight's sulking, our pupils came back, somewhat crestfallen to find that we could have a school without them.[1]

But all the same, the spirit was not good. We were tired of the struggle. Well, the last week before the holidays, a little boy, one of the slaves of the queen's son, who followed his young master to school, declared himself for the Saviour. When he came into my room to speak to me, I could not believe my ears. "Moruti, I come with great news: *I have found Jesus!*" He had been serious and exercised in his soul for a year; he had even worked with his hands, in order to procure books which others received from their masters or bought with young bullocks. When I had heard him, and he had prayed with me, I ran to my wife and said, "Think, darling, what news! Mpututu has just been speaking to me; he says he has found Jesus!" I leave you to imagine the joy there was in our little family circle. Poor Mpututu! I do not know why we were so surprised at his conversion. Alas! it is that, while praying earnestly, we have after all very little faith, and we say very naturally to "Rhoda," when beside herself with joy she announces the granting of our prayers, "Thou art mad!" We are not much better than the Christians at Jerusalem—if only we were as good! This poor boy, who toiled for two months to procure himself the books which no one would have thought of giving him, had not even some bits of skin or a mat to sleep on. I knew nothing of this. It was winter: he accompanied Mr. Waddell far into the forest to cut wood for carpentering. The weather was cold; and all night he was heard shivering and crying, "*Mawe! mawe!*"—the Barotsi cry of suffering. Mr. Waddell did everything he could for this slave, whom they treat worse than a dog. But this recollection touches and confounds me. Why did he not rather work for a blanket? One does not grow accustomed to suffering. Mpututu does not sleep under cover; he is one of those who sleep outside at his young master's door. Will this really be our Onesimus?

[1] This behaviour on Litia's part, unfortunate as it seemed at the time, turned out to be the best thing that could have happened. During his stay at Mangwato, Litia fell entirely under Khama's Christian influence, conceived a boyish devotion to him, and returned home determined to be henceforth a Christian, and, when he should be a chief, to govern like Khama.

As for Litia, whose return, as I have said, troubled and disturbed us, we had long been expecting him to come to the Saviour's feet. From the first interview I had with him, all our fears vanished. " My father," he said, beaming with joy, " I am no longer the Litia of former days : I am converted ; I have found Jesus ! " I do not know up to what point he has the sense of sin, and I cannot tell whether, in the position he occupies, he will be a consistent Christian. For that, the work of God's grace in his heart will need to be real and deep. But, to judge by the conversations I have had with him, and by his prayers, I cannot help believing in the sincerity of his conversion. You know that a long time ago we believed that the grace of God had begun its work in him. But it seems that it was the prayers and exhortations of a young man at Mangwato that caused the scales to fall from his eyes. And at the last service at which my wife was present on earth, when the sun was touching the horizon, the dear, dear boy, standing in the midst of the assembled people in the public square, made a simple but touching confession of faith. During this time, his travelling companion wept and sobbed. We were all moved. " Oh that Thou wouldest rend the heavens ! " my dear wife often repeated in earnest prayer during her illness. Well, that is what she saw and heard—the first drops of the showers that we expect, the first notes of the song of victory before leaving the field of battle.

I was just finishing this letter, when some one knocked at my door. It was Nyondo, an interesting Mashukulumboe boy, a slave of the king's. I have already mentioned him to you. He had conceived such a desire to learn to read that Lewanika allowed him to come to us. He is indeed the best of all our scholars in every respect, and before long he will excel all those who have been at school before him. His conduct, in the house as at school, is almost irreproachable. He is serious, obedient, above all truthful, which is so unusual here, and respectful. We often asked ourselves what kept him back, and we prayed much for him. We had seen him at my appeals with his head in his hands, trying to hide his tears. All in vain : he says his conscience was so ploughed up, that often he went at night, more than once in the same night, to Andreas, to ask from him the help of his

exhortations and prayers. " I do not sleep," he said to me ;
" I watch and weep all night: my heart is sick ; I cannot even
eat. I have told my comrades I am ill. What can I do ? " I
spoke and prayed with him. Bless the Lord, O my soul!

Shortly after the death of Mme. Coillard, I received one after
another, after nine or ten months passed without news, two
voluminous mails, bringing, amid many tokens of sympathy, the
news of the definite establishment of the British Protectorate
over the Barotsi country, and the recognition by Queen Victoria
of the contract entered into between Lewanika and the B. S. A.
Chartered Company.   This news reduced to nothing the
calumnies representing this contract as simply delivering up
the country to the exploitation of a commercial society, without
any of the advantages which result to a native tribe from the
superior control exercised by a civilised government. While
making known this news to Lewanika, the Governor of the Cape,
Sir H. Loch, announced to him that the Queen had named as
her representative to him the explorer Mr. Johnston,[1] and that
the latter would come to the Valley as soon as he could.

This was all that was needed to dissipate our political clouds.
Lewanika says he rejoices in it.   Already he had received
serious remonstrances from Khama, sent by Litia, on the
subject of his change of front.   These despatches arrive at an
opportune moment, for a great *pitso* of the chiefs of the country
is being assembled.

This is not to say we are entering upon the golden age.
The golden age only exists in the past of old men, and in the
imagination of poets.   There will ever be some evil, much evil,
side by side with a little good.   But if this little good be the
salvation of these tribes by the establishment of a firm and
equitable government, it is much, it is everything.   For more
than three months, all the people of the Valley and its neighbourhood have been working unremittingly at canals, feeding
themselves as best they can.   As usual, the king's emissaries are
scouring the villages, maltreating some, seizing the cattle of
others.   The poor people are driven to extremity.   All that
is to avenge an insult sustained by a messenger of Queen

---

[1] Now Sir Harry Johnston. However, he went to Nyassa-land instead ;
and it is only this year (1897) that an Imperial representative, Mr. Coryndon,
has been appointed to Lealuyi.

Mokwaë's, while she was at Sesheke. And the affair is not over. Everybody suffers and groans : the people find it hard to suppress their murmurs and discontent. It is said (and I believe it) that but for us a revolution would have broken out.

But why must it be *now* that we receive the distressing news of a terrible deficit, which will paralyse us just at the moment, perhaps the only one, when we still have so many open doors, and when we *must* give a new impulse to our mission ?

So Faith will ever be a conflict. At times, I feel it is very weak, very timid, my poor little faith ! Pray for us that it may not be " according to our faith," but " according to the riches of *His grace.*"

CHAPTER XXVII

De Profundis—A Visit to Lealuyi—The Yellow Heart of the Barotsi—Painful Defections—Dr. Johnston—Arrival of Paulus—The Methodist Mission— A Thunderstorm—Plan for a Station at the Capital—An Appeal.

LEALUYI, *November 23rd,* 1891.

I HAVE come to the capital to spend Sunday. I ought to have come here sooner, but I could not ; and last Thursday, on the eve of my departure, I was still so unwell that I feared for a little while that I should have to break my word a second time. What a poor nature is ours to be at the service of so great a cause and so unfaltering a Master ! Why did God not choose angels and archangels for this most sublime of ministries ? Through what an abyss of condescension does the Almighty cast His eyes upon the most unworthy of His creatures, to associate them with the greatest of His works—the work of Redemption ! Ah ! it is because it needs one who has himself been lost, without hope, and then saved, to speak to others of the Saviour ! One must oneself have heard that sweet word, " Son, be of good cheer ; thy sins be forgiven thee," if one would beseech his fellow-creatures to be reconciled to God.

It is a month to the very day since we were here with *her,* in this same dwelling. The temporary arrangements we had made are still there intact—even to the little enclosure of mats in the corridor where I slept. It was thither that she would slip away twenty times a day, and then come back smilingly to take her place again among those chattering, giggling women who overran the house. Poor things ! how little they guessed her weak, suffering state, when she applied herself thus to cutting out and putting together their dresses ! I can still hear her conversation, full of sweetness, the fresh and impressive exhortations that she addressed to them while telling

them the parable of the Prodigal Son. Poor creatures! they
pretended to know nothing about the Holy Scriptures, absolutely
nothing but the scandalous history of Ham, which they never
tired of commenting on, and out of which they got great
amusement. I live again through those days of ineffaceable
memory. Everything speaks to me of *her*, everything reminds
me of her, even to that horrible serpent-eater, which, perched
on the top of a house, has been watching me since daybreak,
to pursue and attack me like her. Horrible brute! it is tenacious
of life; the blows of my walking-stick made it retreat, but still
they did not *vanquish* it.

Lewanika, who is absorbed in the construction of a new
Nalikuanda, hastened to pay me a visit of condolence. He
was really sad, and I felt grateful to him for saying so little.
I had a message for him. Afterwards there was his mother,
whose age and position give her especial claims on my affection;
then his sister, the Princess Katoka, an empty-headed creature,
but kind-hearted enough at bottom; then his wives, who came
in groups, chattering, giggling, and teasing one another—mere
will-o'-the-wisps—they got on my nerves. Squatting down on
their mats, they sat and worried me to their hearts' content—
one wanted thread, another begged for soap, a third wanted
a handkerchief and what not. They looked fixedly at me, no
doubt thinking me more silent than usual, and became serious
in their turn. "See, my sisters, how sad he is!" And then they
all mourned with me. I then reminded them of *her* last visit,
her last exhortations. I spoke to them of her last days. I told
them with what determination and what joy she had sacrificed
her life for the Barotsi, by giving it unreservedly to her Master....
Then there was an explosion, a lugubrious chorus of lamentations.

These women gone, others came. Then it was the turn of
the chiefs, the great attendants of the king, of my acquaintances
and my *friends* of every degree. God strengthened me. I felt
it was one of those unique opportunities that He gives us in
a lifetime to "adorn the Gospel" and glorify Him. Weary of
this funeral levée, exhausted by the journey and the stress of
feeling, I nevertheless went to visit the king's principal wife,
Ma-Moramboa, perhaps the only person here in whom my wife
had any confidence. She was a *friend* for her, and they often
exchanged presents. She was secluded in a hut by a custom

which recalls one of the Levitical laws ; and being unable to come to me, she had sent message upon message, asking me to visit her, which is quite permissible. I found her seated on her mat, surrounded by her companions, and robed in beautiful material, the last present she had received from *her*. The intention was good. I sat down upon a mat before her ; but I felt at once that I had gone to the wrong place to get any real comfort for myself. I let her talk of anything and every-thing, cross-examine me as she pleased, and ply me with those indiscreet questions which the Barotsi alone possess the secret and the audacity of asking. She managed wonderfully, just like a heartless woman. I only answered her by mono-syllables or by silence. My gravity seemed to puzzle and amuse her. She evidently did not believe in the sincerity of a man who suffers. To her, it was merely a matter of con-ventionality. And when I attempted to speak seriously to her, she began to wink and make signs to her companions, and ended by bursting out laughing. She made many apologies to me ; but I had received a wound in the tenderest part of my being, and I went to seek comfort in a solitary walk and communion with my God. It was twilight ; darkness fell ; everything within and without toned down into harmony, and calm succeeded storm.

SEFULA, *January 30th*, 1892.

These three months have been like lead. I thought this January would never end. The days, with their occupations, go by indeed ; but the nights !

Since the departure of my dear wife, my trials and chagrins have only gone on accumulating. These are the dregs of the bitter cup of affliction. I should resist it, if I did not receive it from my Father's own hands. Everything has been against me : men, circumstances, friendship, reason—yes, everything, *faith excepted*. At a distance, it is impossible for you to realise how thorny are all the details of my present life. It is possible, too, that to me in my isolation, without anything to take my thoughts off them, they assume exaggerated proportions. Some of my troubles date back to a long day ; others arise from sources whence I could never have expected them. The crisis is lasting a long while ; the future is dark and threatening,

But she, who suffered so much in the evening of her life, she at least is in port, she is safe, in peace and in the glory—already she enjoys the saints' everlasting rest.

Let me to-day open an entirely new chapter of our difficulties. It will not be useless, in spite of the somewhat humdrum and personal character they may have in your eyes.

You know what the Barotsi call *the yellow heart*. It is that incurable disease the contact with which made us suffer so acutely. I knew very well that they coveted everything, from the shoes on your feet to the hat on your head ; that they could, without the slightest remorse, cut a man's throat for the sake of seizing his coat ; that they are past-masters in the arts of ruse and dissimulation. But I still had something to learn.

Ever since he had seen my waggon, Lewanika ardently wished to possess one too. I procured one for him at the cost of infinite worries and personal losses. Anybody else would have felt he owed me a fraction of gratitude. Not he ! He was seized with *yellowness of heart* ; and in order to provide a conductor for this waggon, which, but for me, he would never have possessed, he simply carried off Kamburu from my service. It was playing me a very cruel trick, after Franz's departure for Mangwato. He knew I had no one else who could wield the whip, that I found myself in the greatest embarrassment ; indeed, my material works were paralysed by the blow. No matter. This was not the first of our servants whom he has taken from us ; he has several others, who in various capacities have been trained and polished in my service.

A few days after the departure of my dear wife, Litia too had *the yellow heart*. I did not think him capable of the astute machinations by which he took from me, for his personal service, a charming boy we had had more than two years in our house. He knew him to be active, obedient, diligent, and extremely anxious to learn. He also knew that I had a great affection for him, and that, alas ! I was already founding hopes upon him for the development of the work. But Litia is Lewanika's own son ; nothing else matters—everything must give way to his rights and caprices.

Now it is again Lewanika's turn to have *the yellow heart*. And it is my Andreas he is carrying off. He has long known the value of this boy. And as he has an absolute monopoly of everything good in the country, he could not resign himself to seeing him in the service of the missionary instead of in his own. Consequently, he set Seajika and his associates on his track, for he would never have had the courage to snatch him openly from me by an act of authority, although I could more easily have pardoned that. Andreas used to hide nothing from me; for long he resisted every temptation and every intrigue. But Lewanika and his agent would never believe themselves beaten. Either bribed or intimidated, Andreas gave way little by little to the king's prestige; the flattery and friendship of Litia did the rest. Poor boy! We could not understand why he had lost his spirit, nor why his reserve had become quite embarrassing. He too was serving an apprenticeship to the art of dissimulation. Certain slight incidents did indeed cause us some uneasiness now and then; and it certainly happened occasionally that we felt the force of an under-current. But we sought the cause elsewhere, and a long way from its true source. Besides, our relationships with the king had so far improved, our confidence in Andreas was so great, that I did not guess the blow he was secretly preparing for me. Every one around me knew, it seems, and wondered under their breath at the king's knavery and heartlessness; but they took good care not to whisper a word of it to me.

Then Litia's marriage took place with the girl whom we had brought up.[1] We spared no pains to make it a brilliant and happy festival. And brilliant and happy it was, as much as heart could wish, thank God! and I am sure it will long be talked about. But it left a sting in my heart. Will it be believed, that not only did the queen, abruptly and without warning me, carry off our young cattle-herd one evening, a trusted servant, who had been placed in my service by the king's consent (a proceeding which suddenly threw me into great perplexity), but Lewanika himself profited by his visit to have a private talk with Andreas, and finally make sure of his prey.

Eight days later, while he was overwhelming me with attentions at Lealuyi, whither I had gone to spend some days, he sent to Andreas (but still *secretly*, for nothing is done openly

---

[1] Komoïo, daughter of a headman. Dr. Johnston, who was present on the occasion, gives a vivid description of it in his book "Romance and Reality in Central Africa."

here) the order to hold himself ready, and two days after my
return to Sefula a canoe came to fetch him. This thunderbolt
stunned us all. Andreas, much ashamed, declared himself that
he had no reason for leaving me. He did not even avail
himself of the sole pretext of which he might at a pinch
have made use—my refusal, which I had reasons for making
peremptory, to give him Litia's room. No ; but leave he
must, notwithstanding. And all we could say simply broke
against that rock. By the next morning, his packages were
done up, and before midday he had really and finally left us.

Every one around us is astonished ; for even though they long
knew of the king's intrigues, and are used to his ways of acting
towards his own subjects, they still thought up to the last
moment that he would hesitate before depriving me of a boy
who was looked upon as if he had been my own child. For
me it is a bereavement, and one difficult to bow to, because
of the duplicity of which I have been the victim. Farewell
now to the dream of making a good evangelist of our first
convert ! Alas ! he is going to make a rapid ascent of the
social ladder. The king, who honours him with his confidence,
immediately gave him an independent establishment, a house
and slaves, and full liberty to provide himself out of his
private kitchen, whenever he does not feed him at his own
hands.[1] Cattle and a village are in the near future ; and,
above all, the thing by which he had long but hitherto *in vain*
tempted him, a *wife*. Who will this wife be ? A mere slave,
or a girl of royal blood ? We shall soon know. He will
neglect nothing to rivet the chain, that is certain.

To understand my sorrow, you must know what Andreas
had been for seven years in our house to my wife and me. I
may be reproached with having made too much of him. The
reproach would be just, if he had not shown himself worthy of
all our confidence and all our affection.[2] Although to-day he
is caught in the toils, he is still my son in the faith, whom my
love and prayers will pursue in all his wanderings until he
returns to the paths of truth.

[1] *I.e.* by handing him what is left in the royal dishes, after the king's own
meals—a privilege reserved for the most favoured attendants.

[2] See former letters and also M. Louis Jalla's remarks about Andreas,
page 416.

But I do not hide the fact that this history of Andreas has an aspect which makes me anxious. What will be the type of our Christians in a country where a blind and tyrannous autocracy absorbs everything, and where physical and moral slavery kills all individuality? But I do not despair. The Gospel of Christ and the power of the Holy Spirit have already in all ages worked as great miracles and brought about equally great transformations in the world.

One ray of sunshine has, by God's grace, shone in the midst of all these clouds—the visit of Dr. Johnston of Jamaica. It will probably not be news to you that for fifteen years he has carried on an admirable work among the blacks there. The idea came into his mind of bringing these children of emancipated slaves to do something for the evangelisation of their fathers' country. If they are not equal to founding and maintaining a mission themselves, they can at least furnish helpers to those which already exist, and be a comfort to European missionaries in their manual and evangelical labours, whatever nation or denomination they may belong to. The idea was greeted with enthusiasm, and Dr. Johnston set out with six of his best men. Being very well known in Canada, England, and Scotland, he has found no lack of sympathy among Christians, and the religious papers have brought to our notice his great meetings in Exeter Hall and elsewhere. It was by Benguella that he penetrated into the Dark Continent. At Bihé, he left four of his companions with the American brothers. Certain considerations led the Doctor to change his itinerary; and instead of directing his way to Msiri's capital (Msidi or Mosili), he decided to pass by the Barotsi. He proposes to follow the course of the Zambesi, and remount the Shiré.

Dr. Johnston passed six weeks between Lealuyi and Sefula, but most of the time we were together, either here or at the capital. He is a clever and passionate photographer; consequently, we did a good deal of photography together. His visit was a time of enjoyment and refreshment to us all, especially to me. We had a great deal of talk, but few *discussions*. I acted several times as interpreter for him and his companions, both here and at Lealuyi. With himself, I was struck by that freshness and power which point to an earnest study of the Word of God, and a burning zeal for the salvation of souls : I was not less struck by the seriousness and elevation displayed in the addresses of his two companions. What a difference from our Christians in South Africa! At the risk of terrifying you and seeming heterodox, I believe that slavery has had a great deal to do with it. The Gospel is for all, but especially for the poor and wretched. One feels, in contact with these former slaves of Jamaica, that for them the Gospel is a power and life which has taken possession of their hearts and their whole being. Our friend—let us say our *friends*—left us on January 17th.

You know already that we have an evangelist come from Massitissi—Paulus Kanedi. He has been here six weeks. Alas! he too is a widower, and always ill. In these circumstances, and taking into account the manners of the country, it is out of the question to assign him an isolated post. For the moment, therefore, his place is with me, and he forms part of my family. He knows little, and hence he is almost useless for the school. But as a man and as a Christian, I learn more and more every day to love and esteem him. In all the business of Andreas, he behaved towards us, as towards Lewanika himself, with a faithfulness and firmness that surprised me. His prayers always do me good. I feared at first he would be a burden to me : I am beginning to hope better things. The worst of it is, that he is alone. What will he do later on ? I cannot tell. Meanwhile, with the work of founding the new station of Lealuyi on my hands, I shall have the opportunity of making use of him, and learning what stuff he is made of.

SEFULA, *February* 10*th*, 1892.

Andreas has come to spend a whole week with us, which has given me the opportunity of having some serious talks with him. These talks have not resulted in bringing him back to my house—I no longer counted on that—but they have confirmed me in the conviction that he too, poor boy! has been the unconscious victim of plots, woven and carried out with as much skill as determination. His lack of vigilance is no less blameworthy than his want of frankness, once he found himself caught in the net. He arrived like a prodigal son. A few moments later, he went and installed himself in his room and soon found himself quite naturally *at home*. He made a general inspection of the out-buildings, cast a glance over the kitchen, and presided as in old days over the general distribution of food. Next day, he employed himself with the buying of our flour, maize, etc., which he does much better than I. His modesty, his eagerness in making himself useful, all reminded me of his best days. He went away again this afternoon, with the intention of returning in a fortnight for two weeks—if Lewanika, that is, will allow him. For, unhappily, he is no longer free, and now God alone can break his bonds and restore him to liberty. The object of his visit was, in the first place, to see me, because he had heard of my sleeplessness, but it was also to obtain from me the authorisation to do the work of an evangelist at Lealuyi. There can be no question of giving him an official status. But his good mood reassures us a little and gives us pleasure.

February 27th, 1892.

I have just come back from Lealuyi, where I have made a longer stay than usual. Mr. Buckenham, of the Primitive Methodist Expedition, had preceded me, in order to give Lewanika the satisfaction of a private interview. But our friend, not knowing a word of Sesuto, and only finding a rather unsympathetic interpreter there, resolved to await my arrival before leaving the capital. You know there is a man there, a European, who was once one of ours, one in whom I had reposed great confidence. Unhappily, he was only wearing a mask, and he wore it admirably. When he cast it off—after having left us apparently on the best of terms—he took up the position of an inveterate adversary towards the mission in general and towards me in particular, both as regards politics and religion. He declared himself an infidel and an atheist, and set to work to preach his propaganda with a zeal worthy of a better cause. The king has already been a long while under his influence. It is natural enough that this man should have used every artifice, so as, if possible, to cause all my plans of installation at Lealuyi to miscarry. These few words of explanation were necessary, in order to make you understand what follows.

Lewanika received me coldly, and, contrary to his habits, kept himself aloof. The next day, Mr. Buckenham begged for a fresh interview, which took place at my house; the king shuffled, put all sorts of trifling questions to our brother, and only replied to his by monosyllables. Finally, gathering up all his courage, he said, " You shall not go, either to the Mashuku-lumboe or to the Batoka, nor to any tributary clan; but you may come and fix yourselves at Lealuyi and Nalolo. That is my last word." Our brother explained to him the reasons which opposed such an arrangement, seeing that there were already missionaries, and that I myself was making preparations to fix myself at Lealuyi, that others were expected to occupy Nalolo and other important places, and that, moreover, it was the rule, for the sake of harmony among the Churches, not to encroach upon a field of work which another had already occupied. " I won't have that sort of monopoly,"[1] replied the king. " Besides, the French missionaries have given me all they have to give, and that is nothing. What have I to do with their Gospel and their God? Had we not gods before their arrival? Have they seen their God of Whom they talk so much? What do we want with all that rubbish heap of fables that you call the Bible? Are they any better than ours? What does your school do for us? For you, it is the trade you live by; for us, it is a purposeless and unprofitable folly. What *I* want is missionaries of all kinds, working side by side here, at Lealuyi and Nalolo, especially missionaries who build big workshops and teach us all the trades of the white men. What can *I* do with Christians who only know how to read and write and pray to the God of the white men? What *I* want is carpenters, blacksmiths, armourers, masons, and so on. That's what *I* want, industrial missionaries; that is what all the chiefs want: we laugh at all the rest." Lewanika had laid aside all reserve, and thought himself very valiant. So it was no longer only the cause of our Methodist brethren that was at stake, but ours also; and he knew I had come to make definite arrangements for my installation at Lealuyi! I answered him calmly; but as he had made up his mind beforehand, my arguments seemed to produce very little impression. He left us abruptly, and appeared no more.

[1] As a missionary has pointed out, the native chiefs quickly learn the lesson that competition cheapens everything, and encourage missionaries of different hostile denominations to settle near them, hoping thereby to obtain salvation on easier terms.

The Sunday morning, next day, I sent him a message for the service, to which, if I understood it rightly, he replied ironically. Without letting this discourage me, I rang the bell, and we went with our young men to the *lekhothla*. Not a soul! We began to sing, and some men came up one by one, so that when I began to preach I had about fifty auditors. I introduced the evangelist Paulus to them, who spoke warmly and modestly; then Mr. Buckenham delivered an address full of point and good sense. I was pleased to see the Gambella present, with his wives and some of the principal chiefs. It was a good service, and we felt God's presence there. The men stayed long after us at the *lekhothla*, to talk with Andreas and our other young men about the great question of the day. The afternoon service was more numerously attended, and not less helpful. Lewanika did not leave his house all day.

What was not my astonishment in the evening to see one of his attendants, who brought me a message from him: "The king enquires after your health, and asks if he can come and dine with you."

"Tell him I am not well, but that there is nothing much the matter with me; and as to the dinner, I have only a cup of tea and a bit of dry bread. If Lewanika wishes to share them with me, he is welcome, as he always is."

Soon after, a succession of noisy hand-clappings from the king's house to my own announced the procession of servants, carrying the food and the royal dishes. He himself did not keep us long waiting; he arrived quite beaming, all honey, making laudable efforts to enliven the conversation. The meal finished, the dishes were handed to Paulus and Andreas, which is not at all customary, and from them the remains passed to our other boys. The king shouted to them from within the house, "It is not I who am feeding you; it is your father the *Moruti*; it is his own food, you understand." The table was scarcely cleared when a tremendous clap of thunder resounded, which almost threw us to the ground. This first clap was followed by a second one, then by a torrent of rain. I was telling Lewanika some features of Nero's history, when suddenly the reed door opened, and a mass of people pressed in. Litia, the Gambella, and the principal chiefs at their head, unceremoniously made an irruption into our midst, obliging us to retire to the back of the hut, and filling the house, the wide concentric corridor, the external verandah, and I believe the courtyard itself, all packed like herrings. "Ah! ah!" cried the king, "there they are—there are our people; I knew it—there they are!" My astonishment evidently amused him. I understood absolutely nothing of all this. Silence having been obtained once more, he explained to me that this was one of the Barotsi customs. When there is a storm, and it thunders, all the men related to him, and all the chiefs who are at the capital, run to him, into the very room, wherever he may be, so as to die with him, if the lightning should kill him. This evening, they knew he was with me.

This brought back to me a recollection of my childhood. How many times in the middle of the night have I not seen our neighbours, Catholic and Protestant, rushing in to my mother? "*Mon petit*," my mother would say, "read us a psalm and a prayer!" Then, when the storm had passed over, each one would thank my dear mother and "*le petit*," and return home with the sense of a great deliverance. This recollection inspired me. We sang hymn after hymn, Lewanika and our other *habitués* choosing; then came the reading of two or three verses, a few short words, a prayer, which was heard in profoundest silence; and this singular audience, which had fled the day, and which God brought me at night, dispersed quite astonished, with clacking of tongues.

Lewanika himself having made advances to me, our relations resumed their ordinary course. We had all our meals together, and we spent long hours in each other's company. However, it was in vain I pleaded the cause of our Methodist brethren and the Mashukulumboe Mission; he would not hear of it. So they have no other alternative but to settle down beside us, and enter into competition with us—which they will never do—or else to cross Lewanika's frontiers, and seek a field of labour beyond. I strongly advise this, and I think they would not be losing their time if they went to explore the region which extends north of the Zambesi between the Kafué and Zumbo. If I were at the head of this expedition, and knew Lewanika as I do know him, I could not resign myself to give up the project of a mission to the Mashukulumboe. Lewanika will end by yielding. But that is not a sufficient basis for others to build upon it, especially after so many reverses. It is difficult to make others share one's own faith, especially those who are supporting you and expecting success. Mr. Buckenham consequently left me to my own affairs at Lealuyi, and returned thence to Sefula.

In our subsequent interviews, Lewanika quite recognised that, in the scene to which I allude, he had insulted me, and he excused himself as best he could. He said he was harassed with anxieties, which was natural enough ; he protested his old and warm friendship for me, and assured me that my transfer to the capital was in no way questioned by him, but that the chiefs were animated by quite other feelings. They had heard so much of missionaries who, instead of preaching the Gospel, taught all sorts of trades, that they said openly those were the missionaries they wanted here. " You shall hear them yourself," he added ; " I will call them all to the *pitso* to-morrow to discuss these affairs."

He kept his word, and the *pitso* took place. I greatly feared it was a preconcerted affair ; and I was not reassured— far from it. Beforehand I assembled my young men, and we made it a subject of earnest prayer. The *pitso* lasted two hours. It was, as usual, a running fire of little speeches, of which I took careful notes. I expected keen opposition ; but, to my great surprise, all without exception spoke of me and my plans in the most favourable and sympathetic terms. " Gambella, you bring us good tidings, when you tell us that the *Moruti*, our father, will at last come to live near us. We have long desired it. It is difficult for us to send our children to Sefula—it is too far—and they often want for food. Here we can send them to school regularly, and go ourselves to the preaching on Sundays. His life is dreary out in the woods : he is a Morotsi, he loves the plain " (*borotsi*), " and he seeks the society of other Barotsi. If we did not love him, should we have built him a house here, one of the finest in the town ? Let him come : this is his home. We shall rejoice in it and say, *Thank you.*" " We have seen strange things," cried a great chief : " foreigners closeted with our king, overrunning our *malapa* " (courts), " taking our wives and children into their confidence. We heard them speaking of mines, of trades, and of presents, without our being told what it was all about. And we asked ourselves, 'Whither are we drifting? Are we at the mercy of foreigners?' To-day our father comes amongst us; all these plots will end. He is a Morotsi, and his home is here." This was the gist of all the speeches. Lewanika had not dared to be present. In his absence, Litia spoke last, representing a new element in the nation. He spoke well and to the point, and even with an authority and boldness which astonished me. He reproached the Barotsi with their want of sincerity, and even with their servility. He dared to say to them, "You come to worship when the king comes; but when he does not come, why do you keep away? Is it to him you pray? Is *he* your god?"

Lewanika, being officially informed of the result of this *pitso*, expressed his great satisfaction thereat, and seemed to rejoice in it. He promised me canoes for the transport of the materials which we are preparing at Sefula, and undertook, if I needed it, to procure workmen for me, and wood for the constructions, at wages to be settled between us.

And now, dear friends, we are in the presence of grave questions, and questions which are difficult for us to solve. The Jeanmairets' growing conviction is that they will not come back to Barotsi-land. There is Sefula, too, which my departure will leave vacant, and which must at all costs be filled up without delay. We ourselves have but one lifetime; we cannot give more. It is for you in Europe to act promptly and energetically, if you would save the mission. Remember we are no longer living in the old days, when everything went at the slow and measured pace of the oxen. We live in times of upheaval, of sudden transformations, and of crisis. Oh, let us rise to our responsibilities while the helm is yet in our hands!

SEFULA—MR. WADDELL AND THE BOYS AT WORK.

[*To face page* 453.]

CHAPTER XXVIII

SEFULA, *April 24th*, 1892.

I HAVE been deeply touched by all the expressions of sympathy I have received in such large numbers. Let these dear friends know that they have done me much real good. I feel myself less alone in this solitude, to which I cannot get used. And then, you know, a fresh crop of griefs and trials has come upon me, which has filled up the measure of my bitterness. Sometimes it seemed that I could bear no more of these sufferings and distresses: and yet the cup was not full; it must needs run over. But Jesus does not forget His own: " In all their affliction He is afflicted." He remembers His promise, and His presence becomes so much the more precious a reality when darkness thickens and sorrow deepens.

Our life here is pursuing its usual tenor. Mlle. Kiener and Mr. Waddell surround me with care and affection. But you can understand the great, great place is always empty. The number of boys living with us has increased, and a spirit prevails among them which makes us hope for some real conversions. Our audiences, too, are increasing. Two or three women are, I believe, very near the kingdom of God. But I only speak of it tremblingly, so great and bitter have our disappointments been already. In a few days, we shall celebrate the marriage of our girl Sebane with Franz, our conductor, who has returned from Mangwato. What a joy it would have been for my wife, after the tears she shed over the others!

It has lately pleased God to strengthen our faith by answering

our prayers in a very remarkable way.   A visit I had to make
to the capital was particularly weighing on me.   I expected fresh
battles with the king, and sometimes I confess I feel tired of
the struggle.   We had asked God in special prayer meetings
to restore to us the king's confidence and affection, smooth
over all the continually recurring difficulties of my establishment at Lealuyi, and to "deliver us from these unreasonable
and wicked men" (2 Thess. iii. 2) who hinder His work so
seriously.   Well, without my knowing it, the most inveterate
enemy of our mission had quarrelled with the king; he
reproached him with his ingratitude, and with the neglect and
privation in which he had for some time left him.   Especially
he could not forgive him for despising and refusing to follow
his advice and drive us out of the country—that is, M. L. Jalla
and me, whom he represented as men who had sold themselves to the gold-seekers, on account of the part I took in
the transactions between Lewanika and the B. S. A. Chartered
Company, and also because of the fact that M. Jalla had
wished to accompany Dr. Johnston across the Batoka country.
Lewanika, weary of all these calumnies, ended by thinking that,
after all, we who kept silent might very likely be his best
friends; and he made advances to his missionary, whom he
ound just the same as before.   The trader was so incensed,
that one day while I was there he left Lealuyi after the stormiest
of scenes, having with great difficulty obtained a canoe from the
king to descend the river and clear out of the country.

Lewanika presented me with a canoe, which he had promised
me for two years; he changed it three times for me, so as to
be sure of giving me something which should really please me.
Yesterday, telling me that illness prevented his coming to visit
me at Sefula, he let me know that the little hillock which we
had chosen to construct our future station upon was now completely submerged.   But he proposes another larger one for me,
two or three feet higher, which has been used as a cemetery for
the petty chiefs of Lealuyi.   These are the floating straws we
catch at.   What can we do?   We are dwarfs in faith, and little
suffices to encourage us from the moment we can see God's
hand in it.   Moreover, it is only lately that the king, of his own
accord, has sent back his sons and daughters to school.   All
the big ones have followed Andreas and Litia, and have left.

That is an advantage.   However, the number of pupils, which
tends to augment, already stands at forty.

At my last visit to Lealuyi, I found the whole village upset
on account of one man and woman.   According to the Barotsi
custom, the woman, in consequence of an abortion, should have
been secluded outside the village in a wretched little hut, while
her husband should have been confined to his courtyard without
seeing anybody, without even daring to go and see his own cattle
or visit his field until the appearance of a new moon, for fear
he should spread the scourge of which he had himself been the
victim.   As it was in the first quarter of the new moon, the
woman and her husband did not take kindly to the idea of
such a lengthy quarantine, and they concealed the occurrence.
Twenty-four hours had not elapsed before the report went round.
And this man was one of the principal officers of the king's
establishment, a *sekomboa*—a man of some forty-five or fifty
years of age, a favourite with his master, and universally
respected.   But it availed him nothing.   His peers, the other
likomboa, fell upon him, carried him off, tightly bound, to the
river, tore out his hair with their formidable nails ; then seizing
him, they throttled him under water until he was nearly dead,
beat him with rods to bring him back to his senses, and left him
on the bank in torrents of rain.   It was not difficult to show
Lewanika the cruelty of such proceedings, and the next day the
poor unfortunate returned home under cover of the night.   I
went to see him, but I could scarcely persuade him to come out
of his hut into the court, he felt so deeply humiliated.   The
paganism of the Barotsi is coarse and cruel.   It tramples on all
rank, all dignity, all respect ; nothing awes it.

We have the mission party of the Primitive Methodists here,
and we enjoy their neighbourhood.   We see each other every
day, either at our meetings for prayer and edification, or at our
singing evenings.   The king has flatly refused to let them
establish themselves either with the Mashukulumboe or with
the Batoka, or elsewhere in his country.   But the influences to
which he was then subject have had their day ; and if our friends
have faith in their vocation, and have patience, I still think God
will open to them the door of Mashukulumboe-land.

My saw-mill is in full activity.   Mr. Waddell is preparing
materials for the construction of our tabernacle at Lealuyi.   It

will be a copy of the one here, but a little larger.   And as soon as the waters have subsided—the flood is a whole month late this year—we shall begin the transport of all this material, and build. But it is easier said than done.   We are in extreme perplexity. Under actual circumstances, there is no one but M. Louis Jalla who can take my place here.   When I leave Sefula, the greater part of the school will follow me to Lealuyi?   Who will conduct that school at Lealuyi?   Paulus, a widower like me, will certainly second me as far as he can.   He is an earnest Christian and a zealous evangelist, but nothing at all as a schoolmaster.   And as for myself, I no longer feel equal to the sole charge of so heavy a task.   I have no longer the spirit and spring necessary for that ; and if I am to do the work of a good evangelist at the capital, I shall not have the time either.   And the other posts, who will occupy them?   The Jeanmairets have finally announced that they are no longer with us.   And over all that—the pall of a deficit.   May God help us !   And you, too, dear friends, help us while it is yet time.   Do not wait till it is too late.

I must stop, but not without telling you again how touched I have been by the prompt way in which friends have supplied me with a new mount.   It is not a mere luxury, I assure you. My worthy friend Khama has sent me word that he is making it his business to look out a good one for me, though good horses, *salted ones* (that is, those whom the horse sickness has already inoculated) are rare and dear.   But He Who has furnished the means to buy one will also find us the beast.

(To Mme. Boegner, at the Maison des Missions, Paris.)

May 12th, 1892.

In spite of the effort it costs me to write, I must thank you for your kind and affectionate lines.   We lived more at the Maison des Missions than you might think. . . . And when I say *we*, it is of *her* I speak.   We were only *one* in everything. You judge rightly of our union, when you say it was one of the most perfect it can be given to enjoy on earth.   Oh, how I look back on those thirty years of pilgrimage with her ! . . . No one will ever know what she was to the work of God, and what she was to me as a *missionary*.   You know her tastes.

She loved society, and she loved her home. She enjoyed her visit to Europe immensely. Like the bee, she took her honey from every flower. In her extraordinary memory, nothing was forgotten, nothing was obliterated. And friends with whom we had made but a very short stay would be very much astonished to learn what a large place they occupied in her remembrances. She was my index. And the home life ! Not any more than I, indeed far less than I, had she roving tastes. But when the call of God made itself clearly heard, immediately, without hesitation, without consulting with flesh and blood, she sacrificed everything, left everything, even her dear Leribé, and did it cheerfully.

In the midst of all the storms which raged during the last two years of her life, she always said, with feeling, that God had given her a great blessing and a great joy. The great blessing was Mlle. Kiener, the great joy was my presence at home. I did not make a long absence last year. I was at home for the first time for several years on my birthday. And what a festival she prepared ! She felt it was the last time she would be with me for that occasion. It reminds me of one of the first anniversaries of our wedding at Leribé. We had had to be separated for some weeks previously—she to go to Harrysmith in a waggon, to fetch wood for building purposes, and myself to ride round among the Churches on a special mission. But we had appointed to meet each other at Leribé on February 26th. All the rivers were swelled. In spite of many difficulties and adventures, I was faithful to the tryst. She would have been there too. But the Caledon was in full flood. The waggon was there on the banks, and the clouds continually gathering. I took a great resolve. The chief Molapo chose six or eight persons, well known to be good swimmers ; and with a troop of young men, under the direction of Nathanael Makotoko, I went to the Caledon. The parleying did not take long. She put on a woollen dress, descended to the overflowing river, and calmly yielded herself to two vigorous Zulus, who held her up under the armpits. Zulus were swimming before and behind her, all the young men of the village, up and down the river, in the most perfect order, and the whole procession struggled in deepest silence against the rapid current. One could only see her shoulders above the stream. To say what I went through during this crossing would

be impossible. I thought of Christiana crossing the Jordan. . . .
Once arrived at the bank, I received her : all our men and our
people disappeared. She put on her riding habit, and a few
seconds later the joyous and noisy cavalcade arrived at our
little hut, seven feet square, and built of turfs.

Now she has crossed the Great Jordan. I accompanied her
to the shore : I could go no farther. The palace of glory has
opened its doors to her, and I had a glimpse of the splendour
that shone out. But they have closed again. Soon they will
reopen, and I shall rejoin her. No more separations then—
no more bereavement. " He will wipe away all tears from our
eyes."

SEFULA, *June 30th*, 1892.

All your letters are here before me. They come from
almost everywhere, echoing a universal sympathy. During ten
days, every evening after supper and family worship, you might
have seen me in my study, alone with you, and up to a late hour,
drinking deep of the overflowing cup of your consolations.
Which of us would dare to doubt the communion of saints and
the real unity of the Body of Christ ? I would not have been
without one of your letters, for each has its own drop to sweeten
the bitterness of my cup. Each, too, brings its own jewel, which
I in turn lay at the feet of my blessed Master, as a tribute
worthy of Himself alone.

You have understood that I am a poor suffering human
being, who may be depressed and discouraged. On the field
of battle, in the midst of the conflict, surely it is not unworthy
of a soldier to give a thought and a tear to that comrade who
falls at his side ! Jesus wept. But the warrior must not falter ;
the fight must not relax.

You appreciated her whom I mourn. She was not demonstrative ; she had a horror of everything that approached the
theatrical and aimed at effect. But once she had opened her
heart and given her confidence, it was for ever. " You are a
rich man," wrote one friend. Rich ?—when, in losing her, I have
lost my all ? And yet it is true. " He became poor, that I through
His poverty might become rich "—even in this world. In Jesus,
I have found everything. With His kingdom, He has given
me everything. Because He has taken it to adorn His palaces,

He has not therefore bereft me for ever of the treasure that came to me from Him. No! But her departure has revealed in the hearts of God's children, in almost every country of Europe, an inexhaustible mine of prayer, faith, love, sacrifices, and blessings, which are an inestimable security for our dear Barotsi Mission. "It is impossible," writes a friend, "that you should not have your part in the joy of Easter. Here below, Tabor cannot last for ever. But Jesus has said, 'Ye shall rejoice, and your joy no man taketh from you.' The joy of Pentecost has always lasted. Has not the Lord been faithful?" Yes indeed: the joy of Easter and the joy of Pentecost. Let us not live absorbed in the past, nor yet bemoaning ourselves in the present; but let us rather work while it is day, in view of eternity. David said, and he had excellent reasons for saying, "It is good for me to have been afflicted." There are blessings which we can only receive through that channel; there are great lessons we can learn only in the school of the Man of Sorrows.

I am told that our bereavement has been blessed to some souls in Europe. I believe it has been so even here. She often repeated, "Il a compté mes allées et mes venues—*my wanderings*"[1]; and I would add, "Her tears are in His book," and her prayers. The little movement which rejoiced her last looks on earth has not, it is true, produced all that we expected from it. Still, there is a small number of persons who seek the Lord, and some who even profess to have found Him. I have gathered up those who inspire me with most confidence into a class of *enquirers*, as the English would say—not yet a class of catechumens—and to these I give special instruction. At the outside, they number ten or eleven, counting Litia and his wife. Besides some young men who live with us as pupils or as workmen, there are among them three women from a neighbouring village, for whom we have prayed for more than two years. They are a joy to us. Besides our private prayer meetings, where we do indeed feel that our Methodist brethren are a strength to us, we have had to begin a meeting of this kind on Wednesday mornings. Very few come to it each time outside our little group of regular attendants; but it is a means of drawing intimately together, and a great interest to us.

[1] Ps. lvi. 8.

But we wish to accomplish a *real* work : on the One
Foundation we would not build wood and straw, but silver,
gold, and, if possible, precious stones. And these conversions,
while encouraging me, because I cannot entirely fail to recognise
the action of the Holy Spirit therein, do not give me full satisfaction. The leaves of repentance are certainly there, so the
tree must have life ; but I would like to find more fruit. The
notion of sin is feeble among our Zambesians. I should like
to see sinners stricken down like Paul on the road to Damascus,
and agonised souls who cannot contain the cry, " What must I
do to be saved ? " It seems to me that these poor heathen
must necessarily pass by Sinai before coming to Calvary. God
forbid that I should "limit the Almighty" ! He can open the
heart of Lydia as well as strike down the Philippian gaoler.
Such examples are not rare in Europe, especially among those
who have grown up in a Christian atmosphere. But I am
speaking of poor pagans who have been sitting in the darkness
of superstition and in the mire of sin. I have a dread of those
professions in which the joy of salvation shines at the same
moment as the sorrow of repentance—of those Israelites who
have certainly fled from Egypt, and even passed the Red Sea,
but who die in the desert, without reaching the Promised Land—
of those believers who have never known what the Holy Spirit is.
And the number of them is great, elsewhere besides in Africa.
The example of my dear Andreas prevents me from rejoicing
without fear. While preserving his profession, he has not
prospered spiritually since he left us, and the world is beguiling
him. I ask you most earnestly to join your prayers with ours
that the Lord may bring him victoriously through the crisis,
which will decide his whole life, and deliver him from the terrible
snares set for him. There is indeed a question of giving him
to the king's eldest daughter as an official husband.

Finally, you know that for two years especially we have
had dark days and times of great difficulty. These burdens
you cannot share, nor help us to carry them, except by sympathy
and prayer ; and that you have done. We have felt it. The
situation has considerably improved in every respect : passions
have cooled down ; the king is undeceived, he has recognised
his best friends, and has drawn towards us again. Little by
little our relationships are returning to their former footing ; it

is again the era of " *Ntate ea rategang* " (" Beloved father)," as
we say here, because it is the term Lewanika uses in the notes
he addresses to me, when he is in a good humour. With the
chiefs of the Valley, we always have excellent relations ; for
the king, in all these affairs, has a party of his own. It is
with the chiefs of Sesheke more especially that we have lost
ground. For a moment, we believed that our dear mission was
within an ace of ruin. God has mercifully saved us and
delivered us, in answer to your prayers and ours.

But workers are lacking. Shall we content ourselves with
the glory of seizing and occupying a field which others envy us,
and which we have neither the strength nor the faith to cultivate ? No, no ; I am insulting the zeal that upholds us, and
which is about to attack the regions of the French Congo. I
appeal to France, to Switzerland, to Italy ; I appeal also to that
very interesting Church of Belgium, because it is said to be a
missionary Church. Beloved brethren, send us reinforcements !
Christian young men, come to our help ! Fathers, mothers,
who pray every day, " Thy kingdom come," place, oh ! place
your Isaacs on His altar, consecrate your Samuels to Him.
Give us *ten* choice men—*ten men* chosen and called by God—*ten
men* whose faith does not rest upon the shifting sand of modern
criticism, but upon the Rock of Ages—*Jesus*, delivered for our
offences, and raised again for our justification. It is a real
warfare—let us be under no illusions as to that ; but its object
is glorious, and the victory is certain. Rather die than desert
the post, one of the outposts of the conquering army of the
King of kings. We are mounting to assault the fortress ;
we shall hold out at the breach ; there we shall plant the
standard of the Cross. A handful of soldiers—*ten men* of
Stephen's type—and the day is ours !

With men, funds are needed. The men will come, since
one is already announced. Thank God ! help is at hand. The
funds ! One voice cries to me from beyond the sea, " You
have burdens enough which we cannot bear with you ; *leave
that one to us—it is ours*." That is a good word. It is more
than a word. Already you are bringing your coppers, your
silver, and your gold. You have understood, " The Lord hath
need of it."

Ps. ciii. 1.

CHAPTER XXIX

Distresses and Deliverances—In a Canoe to Lealuyi—Good Reception—
Military Ceremonies—A Camp Meeting—Sunday at the Capital—A
Slave Market—How long?

SEFULA, *May 26th—30th*, 1892.

ANOTHER storm! . . . How do the storms arise on the
Zambesi? They are so frequent, so unexpected, and so
threatening! . . . Scarcely has one passed over our heads than
another has already arisen and is muttering on the horizon.
What an atmosphere this is, where one's nerves never have
time to relax! Oh that we too could possess in great measure
that wisdom that cometh from above, that we might "walk in
wisdom toward them that are without"! And yet, it seemed
to us that the wind had swept away the clouds, and that for
the first time for a long while our sky had once more become
blue and clear. Indeed, in the middle of April, I had returned
from Lealuyi, recognising with gratitude the answer (*remarkable
for us*) of our ardent and special prayers. Almost without
expecting it, we were delivered from these "unreasonable and
wicked men" (2 Thess. iii. 2), who had so seriously hindered
the free course of the Word of the Lord. The king had
approached us again, and he had smoothed over all the difficulties which he had previously opposed to our installation at
the capital. Three times, he had changed the canoe he had
presented to me, and each time for a better one. He even
furnished me with canoes to fetch our supplies from Kazungula,
and this "out of friendship," and of course without there being
any question of payment. So all was going on for the best,
as in the best of all worlds.

Unfortunately, our brother Buckenham, the chief of the
Primitive Methodist Expedition, had to go to Kazungula on

his own affairs, and thought the occasion of my going too good
to be missed.   On my advice, he asked Lewanika for a canoe ;
and as I foresaw a refusal, I warned the latter that in the last
resort Mr. Buckenham could go down in my own canoe, if
it were not possible for him to procure one.   The king replied
evasively, and Mr. Buckenham left with my people.   As soon
as he heard this, Lewanika could not contain himself with rage.
We had done him out of a good sum of money, on which he
was already counting.   " What right had the *Moruti* to hire
people out to this stranger ?   Are they not his " (*i.e.* the king's)
" own slaves ? "   And then he raised the great question, " What
will their wages be ? "   For Lewanika desires nothing but *money* ;
he dreams only of that.   In vain I assured him that my
canoe, like those he had lent me, was going to fetch our
supplies, and was under the orders of the petty chief whom
he had himself placed at the head of this expedition ; that Mr.
Buckenham had only taken advantage of this opportunity—as,
moreover, I had told him beforehand he would do.   Nothing
was of any use.   Bitter little notes and unpleasant echoes
brought to my ears the insults the poor man was raining on
my head, surrounded by his *likomboa*, flatterers and courtiers
of the vilest sort.   I even sent the evangelist Paulus to spend
some days with him, so as better to explain this voyage of our
Methodist brother in my boat.

I thought for a moment that he had succeeded.   What was
not our astonishment to learn a few days later that Lewanika
had secretly sent a young man who attends school, and who
is the guardian of his daughters here, an order to strangle all
the workmen who are working here for me, all without exception !
This young man, whom, moreover, I believe to be not far from
the kingdom of heaven, dared not do it ; he contented himself,
out of respect for me, with snatching his piece of calico from
the first workman I paid.   This was the signal for all sorts
of vexations.   The petty chiefs who attend our school, the boys
and young men in their suites, rubbed their hands gleefully.
Then they began once more, as in former days, to strip the
passers-by, and to lay violent hands on the produce brought
us for sale.   There was a new panic.   All our workmen—and we
had a good many, for we are preparing all the materials here
for our new station at Lealuyi—all our workmen, I say, with

the exception of two, who exhibited really admirable courage, fled by night, and for three weeks no one dared to bring us anything whatever to sell. If some one ventured to come and see us, he hid first in the bushes, watched his opportunity when no one could see him, and only spoke in whispers.

Although ill, and scarcely able to stand on my legs, I started for Lealuyi, where, according to my custom, I stayed several days. Was the king touched by my weak and emaciated condition? Probably, for he exerted himself to surround me with attentions and amiability. In my long conversations with him, I made it a duty to remind him of the great lessons of the revolution which had driven him away into exile. I had no difficulty in convincing him that this clique of *likomboa* did not respect him any the more because he plagued the servants of God without cause, strangers in his country and utterly at his mercy. He wished to raise the wages of the workmen to an absurd extent, and impose on us terms which were far too onerous and humiliating. I held out ; and he ended by giving in. He even pretended to be indignant, because people had exceeded his orders to annoy us. He sent for the young man whom he had made his policeman and spy.

" The *Moruti*," said he, " has conquered me. I was vexed, and scolded him. Now, it is done with. Let the young men who wish to do so work as usual, and see to it that nobody annoys the people any more who come to him to sell their millet."

Here we have a manifest answer to our prayers, and we bless God for it.

These are details which may seem very slight to you, but life, even the greatest life, is made up of them. And when detail is added to detail, when one petition after another is granted, then the Christian who observes and forgets not finds he is indeed " compassed about with songs of deliverance " (Ps. xxxii. 7). We have just had a fresh illustration of this. Nevertheless, the people's confidence is not yet restored ; we are without workmen, and famine is threatening us.

The work does not stand still, notwithstanding, thanks to the staff of our establishment. But the day before yesterday, we had measured out our last portion of flour. At our family worship, it was not a " vain repetition " to recite aloud together, " Give us *this day* our daily bread." All day, I was on the

watch to see from what direction the help would come.
Nothing! We were astonished, and in the evening we said so
to the Lord. "O men of little faith!" That very evening,
while we were on our knees, a messenger from the king arrived
at the village. He brought us two wild geese ready cooked,
and a great package of dried hippopotamus flesh, from the king,
"my friend and brother." How could we help thinking of the
prophet's ravens, and being penetrated by the sense of God's
faithfulness? The same messenger brought me also from
another of my "friends" a hundred and twenty tiny little
potatoes—just a hundred and twenty—which had been offered
me a few weeks before for the modest sum of £2 10s. in kind!

The next morning, two men lurking in a byway asked
me in a whisper if they could bring the flour and corn which
they had to sell, and which they had hidden in the bushes.
"Unquestionably," I answered aloud, before everybody present,
"and at once; you have nothing to fear." Consequently, the
market is about to reopen. The Lord carries on His children's
education by His own methods; but how often we have to come
back to the A B C of faith and unreserved confidence!

One anxiety—for anxieties here are an ill-weed, the nettle
of life—was the thatch, the long grass I needed to cover the
church, the cottage, and the huts of the new station. It was
said that Lewanika and his son Litia, who are also building, had
gathered all the little that has grown this year. The fact is,
I suppose, that they were afraid of the king. Then I announced
that I would begin to buy on a certain day. Before the day
appointed, I refused what they began to bring me from hither
and thither. But on that day, from dawn, there was an un-
accustomed stir on the station : men, women, and even children
came in long files from every direction with their trusses, like
red ants on the march. And every day, except Saturday, which
I had reserved for myself, it was the same thing ; so that in two
weeks I had what I needed—more than two thousand trusses!
To the great discontent of my Zambesians, I then had to close
the market.

I hope that this building and the others of the new station
will cost the mission nothing, and will not turn aside a centime
of its funds. I reckon to devote to it the remainder of a sum
which a revered friend in England (Mrs. H——) had specially

given for the construction of a dwelling-house. We are in the midst of full preparations. I no longer need a house: a little cottage like this will suffice for me. The eternal "mansions" are not far off.

July 1st—9th.

I am getting really better, thank God, and I feel myself less of a burden to my friends and myself. The yearly inundation is over; the plain is drying up: the low-lying parts, however, are still impracticable pools and quagmires. So, to go to Lealuyi, I have to make up my mind to descend my canal, and follow the interminable windings of the river, which triple or quadruple the distance. The journey is one of deadly monotony! For want of rowers, I had taken my small boat; but it was so loaded with my four boys, myself, and my few packages, that at the slightest movement it took in water and threatened to sink. I sat shivering with my feet in the water and my clothes soaked, for the cold was intense. It was my poor boys I pitied. It is true that they were not, like me, condemned to almost absolute inaction. They could give themselves exercise with their paddles, but the water that streamed from their oars was sprinkled over their bodies by the icy wind. At every shower bath, one heard an ill-suppressed "*Mawe!*" while the others would try to joke a little to keep up their spirits.

The sun had disappeared on the horizon, and we were still a long way from the capital. The moon, in its first quarter, shed a misty light, that only made the cold more piercing and our situation more doleful. It seemed to me we ought long before to have found the entrance of Lewanika's canal which leads to Lealuyi. Could we have missed it? No landmark either between these banks, which rise like two walls, nor, when they sink, in this immense plain, dreary and silent. And with these interminable and inextricable zigzags, it is impossible to find one's bearings. Now we were looking towards the crescent moon, now we were turning our backs and retracing our steps, only to face about once more until a neighbouring promontory sent us off in a new direction. I began to be uneasy, and my boys too. Supposing we had already passed the canal? . . . The moon had long set, and we were still rowing on. . . . At last, here is the canal! . . . No mistake about it this time.

The canoes have made a way through the reeds that choke it up. We venture in. No sign of a village—not a living soul to give us a word of information. At long intervals, a tiny intermittent fire indicated a solitary bivouac, but only at an unknown distance. All talk is hushed, and in this lonely silence nothing is heard but the monotonous cadence of the oars, and the hoarse plaintive cry and flapping wings of an occasional water-fowl who flies off alarmed at our approach.

Suddenly, a flaring torch lights up the night; dark forms loom forth like silhouettes on a screen. Then a voice, " Holla! who are you? Are you the *Moruti*?" " Yes, the *Moruti*," joyfully answers one of my boys. A few more vigorous strokes bring us to a troop of young men, who glide their canoes alongside of ours. They are excited and very talkative. According to the etiquette of the royal service, which does not permit one attendant to carry two things at a time, however small, they come to me bringing, one a cup, another a pot of milk, a third is furnished with a kettle, while the man following him bears a chafing-dish full of live coals. All is forgotten now; faces brighten up; tongues are unloosed.

While my boys spring to the shore, and brood over a fire of reeds, there am I with my feet on the generous chafing-dish, swallowing a strong decoction of something they tell me is tea. All I know is that it is something *hot*. We won't say Lewanika has nothing good in him after this.

He had learnt I was benighted; and fearing I should lose my way and spend the night without shelter, he had sent these young men with two canoes to look for me, and had had the delicate thought of sending me a kettle of tea with the precious chafing-dish. Soon afterwards, we were in port. Ten minutes' walk on dry ground, and I reached my court, where—a luxury indeed here—a bright fire was burning. After having shaken hands warmly with the king, who was waiting for me, and exchanged a few friendly words with him, we bade each other good-night. I drew the mat over my door, and went to seek in my damp blankets a little warmth and sleep. It was near midnight.

I should not like to say that my visit was inopportune. No. But I had more occasion to observe than to evangelise directly. The queen, Mokwaë, of Nalolo, was still there on a visit. She is my neighbour, for our courts touch one another. The very next morning, she did me the honour of coming to share my breakfast, attended by her sort of husband, who scarcely quits her more than her shadow. She should have started the same day for Nalolo. " But," she said flatteringly, " now that *our father* has arrived, there can be no question of that. I shall not start till Monday." I was much obliged to her for this, on account of Sunday.

I also learn that an army corps of about three thousand men has just arrived ; but, according to the custom of the country, it is still camped at a distance in the plain. Lewanika had sent it in April to " chastise " the Balubale, who by their incessant attacks on their neighbours were compromising the public safety.

The return of this expeditionary army is quite an event. In order to receive it, the king has had a pavilion of mats erected outside the town. About ten o'clock, the drums announced that it was near. A black mass that one could descry in the distance then began to move, slowly advanced, and halted some way off, to do homage to the sovereign by going through all the phases of the usual royal salutation. Then this compact mass broke up and formed different detachments, who made it their business to represent the war they had just been engaged in, which had covered them with glory ! Here—less, though, than in Basuto-land—each one sings his own exploits. The sight is certainly picturesque. Each is bedizened in his own fashion ; plumes of every sort abound—leopard skins and pieces of stuff, which have been carefully preserved for the occasion. And these gaudy, variegated colours, with their agitated movements, their infinite combinations through whimsical evolutions and contortions, dances and feigned attacks, produce the effect of a gigantic kaleidoscope. Thus passes the greater part of the day.

Then the chiefs in a body, whom the messengers brought up by short stages with much clapping of hands, approach and await like statues the order to make their report. These are admirably laconic. Their microscopic speeches, which according to etiquette, had to pass through several mouths before reaching the royal ear, did not last a quarter of an hour. And yet these braves told us everything : their various mishaps ; the fright of the Balubale, who at their approach fled into the woods ; the death of twenty-six or twenty-eight Barotsi chiefs of all grades (they take no count of the slaves) ; the rich booty they are carrying or leading away—a unique herd of cattle, arms, a number of women and children, and then, and above all, alas ! the *small-pox*, which has already claimed numerous victims, and is still raging in the camp. . . . Lewanika was equally sparing of words to express his approbation ; but he gave what they valued far more than speeches and praises—he gave them fifteen oxen to kill. Soon night came ; the camp-fires sparkled out like a little town illuminated, and the uproar all night long told us that Mr. Gaster, so powerful on the Zambesi (and *elsewhere*) was satisfied.

That happened on Saturday. What sort of Sunday should we have ? The day promised to be fine. To be sure, the wind was blowing a little, and I feared that Lewanika, on the pretext of neuralgia in the face, from which he suffers, would absent himself from the service. I paid him an early call, and found him most favourably inclined. He had already given orders to have a shelter prepared for him. I was walking about, meditating, until the hour of meeting, when, to my consternation, I saw a party of warriors, who have their home here, advancing and entering the town. They halted long, massed on the public place. It was the signal for a general excitement, which rose and attained its maximum when, after kneeling and clapping their hands, they dispersed each to his own house. The women, who were grouped in the alley-ways, jostled against the men in every direction, uttering piercing yells that made one long to stop one's ears. They went and besieged the court of each important personage in turn—and every Barotsi personage is important—and gratified him with a serenade ; while the latter, enthroned upon a mat or a stool, received the congratulations, the hand-kissings, and the delicate spittings of his near relatives. These sharp cries, these sing-song salutations, these minor chants, all this excited coming and going, this noise and racket, ended by getting on our nerves, and making us feel melancholy.

As to the meeting, no question of that. Wait ? We might wait in vain. Even when calm had been somewhat restored, and the king ordered his drums to be beaten, we only had a miniature audience. Their minds were otherwise engaged. And then, what must Lewanika do but take possession of the shed in the *lekhothla* where his wives the princesses generally sit to screen themselves from the vulgar eye. Consequently, Mokwaë could not show herself, although she had put on her fine robe of crimson velvet for the occasion, nor could any of the princesses, nor yet any other women. It was a disappointment for me. The congregation of the evening would be better : it is generally the case.

Between the two meetings, I betook myself to the camp. But to whom should I address myself to call the men together, since all the chiefs were at the village ? God would direct me. I went straight before me. Behold, the men sprang up to meet me, seized my hands, and saluted me as an old friend ! It was a cross-fire of salutations. " *Lumela, Moruti ! Lumela, Ntate oa Rôna !* " (" How do you do, teacher ? How do you do, father ? "). You have guessed that these are my neighbours from Sefula. This was a capital method of bell-ringing ; it succeeded brilliantly.

While we were exchanging the bulk of the news, an assembly had already collected. Then I started a hymn, which powerful voices rang out to the far distance. This was my second and loudest bell. People ran from the extreme limits of the camp, and I had the joy of preaching to a numerous and attentive audience. When I had finished, they still kept on arriving : the crowd had doubled. So we had a second singing and a second sermon ; then the Lord's Prayer, repeated on their knees by hundreds of men, closed this interesting meeting. I noticed that the prisoners of war, the Balubale women and children, had grouped themselves near me. Probably, they had never seen a white face before. I addressed some words to these poor creatures through an interpreter, which they received with many hand-clappings ; then I took my leave in the midst of the thanks and salutations of all these people.

Thence, let us go in another direction to visit fifty Mashu-kulumboe. This was an embassy that Nashintu, the chiefess of whom I have already spoken to you,[1] had sent to Lewanika. Samoïnda, the son of this influential woman, had in his youth been carried off by the Makololo. To-day, he is a man in the prime of life, and possesses a certain social position among

the Barotsi. Lewanika had the happy idea of sending him to
visit his mother, who is still living, and who had never seen
him again. Nashintu recognised her son, and, touched by this
delicate attention, sent him back with this embassy and a
present of cattle for the king. So I had a conversation, the
nature of which will be easily understood, with these Mashukulumboe, who interest me so much. Poor people! "We had
indeed heard of the *Moruti*" (I am known only by this name);
"but now our eyes have seen him." Shall I ever have the joy,
before leaving this world, of seeing the Gospel penetrate to
them? We work, we pray, always hoping it will please the
Lord to open this door for our Methodist brethren. Oh! if
we were but stronger!—if we were but *richer*!—if . . .

At Lewanika's entreaty, I decided to prolong my stay at
Lealuyi to the end of the week. He said, truly, that he had
not time to see me during the day. He made up for it by
coming after sunset, to share his dinner and pass the evening
with me. It was a return to old times—those times of which
the memory is so sweet to me. During four consecutive days,
from morning till evening, he was entirely absorbed by the
division of the booty—the unfortunate prisoners, henceforth
reduced to slavery. I had the curiosity to see how he proceeded with it. I took care not to go, as usual, and sit down
beside him. I even avoided sitting down at all, so that they
should not misunderstand my presence. It was nothing more
nor less than a sharing of human cattle, which it made one's
heart ache to witness. I had never yet been so close to a
slave-market.

Picture to yourselves thousands of Barotsi crouching in a
circle before the king and the principal chiefs of the country.
In the midst, heaped up close together, are *hundreds* of these
unfortunate prisoners. Not a single man among them; no
young men. And for a good reason. A man is never made
prisoner; he is killed and disembowelled. There are not even
any old women. What could they do with them? These are
young women, the greater number with little children on their
backs; or they are young girls, and a multitude of children
of all ages from one to twelve, and of both sexes. See one
band after another, six or seven at a time, who are made to
rise and approach, and who are subjected to a minute inspection,

while thousands of eyes are fixed upon them with unabashed cupidity. The women, emaciated, frightened, and to our eyes revoltingly filthy, generally hang down their heads. According to their national custom, they are in a state of nudity, which provokes the mirth and the obscene remarks of the multitude. There is a great consultation under the pavilion ; then a chief advances towards the poor wretches to execute the king's good pleasure. The unweaned babe, fortunate little creature, is left for some time at least at its mother's breast. But all the others who can walk already are so many domestic animals, which are distributed right and left. Poor children ! no more mother or father for them ! But they will get used to it ; and one day they too, like these men of to-day, will find their pleasure and their glory in making orphans.

Here is a little child scarcely three years old, who is being snatched from a young woman's arms. He shrieks and kicks about, wrenches himself free, and runs into the midst of the crowd, quite lost, and crying for his mother, who has already been carried off. This unrehearsed effect is a capital joke for everybody. "Knock him down !" they shouted laughingly to his master. He understood his own interests better than that and soon got the better of the refractory little creature. And now it is the turn of another young mother. "Take that baby away !" (apparently her firstborn). But she, heedless of her situation, seizes it and clutches it convulsively in her arms. Fire darts from her eyes, and from her lips a torrent of words, highly mirth-provoking to all around me. One could see that she was ready to perish rather than part with her own flesh and blood. They were already proceeding to violence, when Lewanika let himself be moved, and ordered them to leave her child to her. Fortunate warrior ; he is a lucky fellow ! Two domestic animals instead of one ! I could stand it no longer : I fled from these sickening scenes, which succeeded one another during several days. O my God ! how long ?

Keep the frame for a few days, and change the picture. The distribution of slaves is concluded. Behold a phalanx of more than two hundred and fifty men advancing. The circle opens ; it enters silently, and deploys. Each man carries a broken bow, with a quiver full of arrows, a bundle of spears, or else a gun, which he carries reversed. These warriors are

those who have distinguished themselves, and the arms they
carry are those of the enemies they have killed or disembowelled.
Each has killed his man ; some have killed several. And all
of them are not there. Some are ill ; some are gone home ;
others, finally, are dead in their turn. In this choice company,
there are several young men from my school. One or two hang
their heads on seeing me. While praises are being dealt out
to these braves, I yield myself to all sorts of reflections, I make
a calculation, and find they must have captured more than six
hundred women and children, without counting those who have
died of small-pox or of ill-treatment, and that they have killed
more than three hundred and fifty men, without counting the
wounded and those who crawled away into the woods to die
of their wounds. Must we carry this calculation further into
the moral domain ? No! War is horrible ; it is the great engine
of the great murderer of the human race ; and he does his best
to bring it to perfection in every country. Enough ! We who
are always vaunting our light and our civilisation, shall we be
the first to cast a stone at these poor Barotsi ?

SEFULA, *September 26th*, 1892.

I hope that, in the course of next month, I shall at last be
able to begin the preliminaries of my installation at Lealuyi.
But workmen are scarce, owing to the small-pox, which is still
raging. I have succeeded very well in obtaining vaccine from
cows. Hundreds of people have been vaccinated ; and even
though nearly all have had the small-pox, it has taken a
very mild form, and only one to my knowledge has died.
But the difficulties we have to battle with ! The king wished
the vaccine to be used exclusively for himself, his sons, his
children, and his nephews ; later on, he consented to have it
for his village as well. As for the natives, either they had no
confidence in their own people, or else, once vaccinated, they
did not come back again. So long as they were vaccinated
themselves, what did it matter about the rest of the nation ?
In order to get the lymph, therefore, I was obliged to renew
my experiments, inoculate cows, and, with the virus thus
obtained, vaccinate the people. One cannot always be successful
All the boys and nearly all the girls in the house have been
ill, and it was interesting to see the close connexion between

the good vaccine and the small-pox. Just now we have a poor girl covered with pustules. I have vaccinated her three or four times unsuccessfully. The poor child is unrecognisable. This is the eleventh day—the crisis. On seeing her body, and especially her arms, covered with these frightful spots, she has done nothing but sob all the morning. She thinks she is going to die, and is afraid of being buried in the " Christian fashion." [1] Poor little thing!

Everything around us is in a sad state : whole villages are entirely deserted ; the fields are left fallow, and we are expecting a frightful famine.

M. L. Jalla is starting on his return journey to-morrow. His visit, like the arrival of M. and Mme. Adolphe Jalla, has done me good.

How long can I remain at Lealuyi? I am anxious not to tie myself down to it. I will make as much of the responsibility as possible rest upon Jacob, the evangelist whom the Jallas have just brought with them—so that I shall be able to withdraw without being missed. It is not that I wish to retire or leave the mission. No! Wherever I am, or whatever I may be doing, the Barotsi Mission has my heart. I shall die in its service, if the Lord grant my prayer. But I am not good for much, and it may well be that the Master will soon lay me aside.

---

[1] The Barotsi always bury in a sitting posture, facing eastwards, " with their eyes towards the first ray of morning." They believe that if they are buried " Christian fashion" (*i.e.* flat on their backs), they will rise again as serpents.

A SACRED PLACE—A ROYAL TOMB AT LIRUNDU, NEAR LEALUYI.

[*To face page* 475.

PART IV

L E A L U Y I

1892—1896

MARTIN LUTHER'S HYMN.

THROUGH our own force we nothing can,
  Straight were we lost for ever ;
But for us fights the proper Man,
  By God sent to deliver.
    Ask ye who this may be ?
    Christ Jesus named is He,
    Of Sabaoth the Lord,
    Sole God to be adored :
  Tis He must win the battle.

From " Lyra Germanica."

LEALUYI

CHRONICLE

Oct. 28th, 1892 ...	...	Station established at Lealuyi.
July 9th, 1893 ..	...	Church opened at Kazungula.
March 11th, 1894	...	Church opened at Lealuyi.
June 24th, 1894	...	Arrival of M. and Mme. Béguin from Switzerland, and of the evangelists John and Willy from Basuto-land—Mlle. Kiener leaves Sefula for Kazungula.
July 1894 ...	...	Third Conference (at Kazungula)—Beginning of the first general awakening on the different stations.
Oct. 14th, 1894...	...	Station established at Nalolo under M. and Mme. Béguin.
Oct. 1894...	...	Litia established as Prefect of Sefula with his wife.
Nov. 1894...	...	M. and Mme. Adolphe Jalla leave Sefula and settle at Lealuyi—Foundation of a school for native evangelists—Mr. Waddell leaves for Europe on account of his health.
May 6th—June 15th, 1895		M. Coillard's voyage of Evangelisation to the Balubale and Balunda, on the Upper Zambesi, from Lealuyi to Kakenge.
July 26th, 1895 ...	...	Arrival of M. and Mme. Boiteux from Switzerland, and M. Davit from the Waldensian Valleys, and of the evangelists Aaron Ndjelepa and Theodore from Basuto-land.
Sept. 1895 ...	...	Fourth Conference (Lealuyi).
Oct. 30th, 1895...	...	M. Coillard leaves Lealuyi ill.
Dec. 18th, 1895...	...	M. Coillard and the Louis Jallas (on furlough) leave Kazungula.
Feb. 15th, 1896...	...	Arrival at Bulawayo.
June 18th, 1896...	...	Arrival of M. Coillard in Paris.

CHAPTER XXX

Lealuyi at last—A Double Anniversary—The Fourth Station founded—
The Small-pox—The Kingdom of Darkness—The Plagues of Egypt
—The Fighting-ants—Lewanika's Vacillations—The Stations boycotted
—The Blockade raised—Warriors decorated.

LEALUYI, *October* 31*st,* 1892.

SO here I am at last, at Lealuyi—that hornets' nest, so
dreadful and so dreaded. I know very well that I shall
not be alone here. You will be with me in your thoughts and
in your prayers. And Jesus Himself will be here too, as
He has always been with His servants, in the lions' den, in the
fiery furnace, in the darkness of a stormy night, in the prison—
everywhere. He has promised it, and we know by experience
what His promises are. It needs nothing less than this assurance to enable me to face all that awaits me, which I already
foresee with some misgivings. But God "has given us, on behalf
of Christ, not only to believe on Him, but also to suffer for His
sake." St. Paul said, before going to Jerusalem, where the last
persecutions awaited him, "But none of these things move me,
neither count I my life dear unto myself, so that I might finish
my course with joy, and the ministry which I have received of
the Lord Jesus, to testify the Gospel of the grace of God."

The foundation of this new station is the realisation of many
wishes. May it be a real taking possession! May this new
lighthouse cast its rays far into the heart of this thick darkness!
And, above all, may the Master Whom I serve, He Who is *our
wisdom*, and in Whom are hid all the *treasures of wisdom*, give
me the *wisdom* which this post, difficult above all others, requires,
and the zeal which knows how to redeem the time!

It was the evening of October 27th that I left Sefula. The
next day was a double anniversary—that of the Adolphe Jallas

marriage, and of the day on which she who has left me entered into everlasting glory. Joy is not incompatible with grief. Never did the Lord speak more of joy than in His last conversations with His disciples, on the eve of His death. A Christian's sorrow is never without its rainbow, and my sorrow also had one. The sun shines, but it is in a sky full of clouds and rain. And whilst rejoicing heartily with my young friends, I would not—I felt I must not—let my presence cast a shadow on their festival. Moreover, I had need to be alone with God. And I departed.

On the 28th then, the very day, at the very hour even, on which the previous year I had closed the eyes of my beloved wife, I arrived alone, outspanned my waggon, and pitched my tent on this isolated and barren hillock, at the entrance to the capital. The mound, which is some six or eight feet above the level of the plain, and measures one hundred and seventy-five yards by sixty-five or seventy, is the sorcerers' hillock, the Calvary of paganism, and is locally called Loatilé. It is there that sorcerers are executed, being first poisoned, and then burnt alive.[1] No one has ever yet lived here; no one passes by it. The brushwood and thorn bushes which cover it are the haunt of stinging flies and every imaginable venomous insect, of mice, serpents, and other reptiles from the surrounding plain, especially at the time of the floods; it is infested by innumerable armies of fighting ants; and, finally, it is the citadel of the termites, who have, in fact, constructed it, and whose voracity surpasses anything I have yet seen. Under these thorns and briers, among creeping and crawling beasts, lie broken bows and assegaï shafts, the decaying fragments of wooden stools and bowls, calcined human bones, bleached by the sun, discoloured by the damp. All round and everywhere stretches the plain—that barren, melancholy plain so dear to the Barotsi. The eye loses itself in the vast expanse. The horizon is bordered on the left by a pale blue line, and on the right by a similar though more accentuated one. These are the thinly wooded sandhills which

---

[1] It must be borne in mind that the Barotsi, in calling people *sorcerers*, do not mean the same as we do. A sorcerer is a person who secretly compasses the death or misfortune of another. The magicians, or priests of the occult art, whom *we* should call sorcerers, are Ma-Mbunda, *witch-finders*, detectives or secret police, and are of course regarded as public benefactors.

once formed the banks of a vast lake. Near me in front is the big village, the capital of an immense but sparsely populated country. This capital presents nothing very imposing—a confused mass of round huts with pointed roofs like beehives, from which in the evening there arises a dull murmur, the stir of human life, and the roll of drums, which frighten the evil spirits away all night long while the king slumbers.

From the midst of these huts arises the thatched roof of the king's house, a veritable palace in the eyes of these poor people. This house dominates everything. It is the centre of the harem, as the harem is of the town, and the town of the kingdom. And the royalty reigning in this palace of wattle and thatch is the centre of all. Everything exists for it, everythings hangs on it, everything is absorbed by it. It is an autocracy which permits no one any liberty. It is the misfortune of the country ; one of the most formidable obstacles which civilisation—by which I mean progress and Christianity—has to encounter. This town is my Jericho, this power is my Goliath, inasmuch as it personifies paganism and its sovereign pontiff. Ah! had I but the faith of Joshua and David !

The last days spent at Sefula were necessarily painful, very busy, and very tiring. Ever since their arrival, the Adolphe Jallas have surrounded me with an affection that goes to my heart. There was nothing new in that, as regards my young brother. I know him of old ; but he has enriched us by bringing us a helpmeet like himself, of very loveable character, and of an eminently practical turn of mind. She has adapted herself to the Zambesian mode of living without any apparent effort, and with a cheerfulness which charms us. We must form an industrial and educational centre for our mission, and I still think that Sefula is the right place, and M. Adolphe Jalla the right man for it. These kind friends wanted to take upon themselves all the trouble of preparing my residence here, whilst I was to remain taking my ease at Sefula ! I am grateful to them for it ; but when one gives oneself, it must not be by halves. I am prepared for anything, except to impose knowingly upon the goodwill or unselfishness of my friends.

We have now worked at Sefula during six years. You can understand that it is impossible for me to look back on the past without deep emotion, and still deeper gratitude. God is love—yes, He is love. And He is the Lord God of hosts, the God of battles. Not only has the Angel of the Lord encamped round about us to protect us, not only has He often " compassed us about with songs of deliverance," but He has fought for us. He is my strength and my song, and He will be so until the moment when He Himself shall finally beat down Satan under our feet.

Do you ask what are the results of these six years of labour ? Where are our sheaves ? Alas ! I could speak of our toil, our illusions and disillusions, of our best-founded hopes and our most bitter and poignant disappointments. Even that is something. We have cleared the ground, ploughed, sown, watered. That was the task which the Master had set us : perhaps we were not fit for anything else. It is for others to reap the harvest. And we shall rejoice together.

One of the great hindrances to the work at Sefula is the instability of the population around. Like all their congeners, they are naturally of a roving nature ; but in addition to this, their state of serfdom frequently imposes tasks upon them, which force them to leave their homes for days and even weeks together. Hence the irregularity of our congregations and the lack of progress. But at any rate our young colleagues will find Sefula one of the most interesting corners of our field ; and with their resilient youth, and the irresistible power of a love for souls, they will certainly make it flourish.

I am leaving Mlle. Kiener at Sefula, as also my friend Waddell for a time. Now, completely severed from all this tender, watchful, and loving care, my loneliness grows even drearier, and my life harder. But One still remains : He is enough for me. " In His presence is fulness of joy, and at His right hand are pleasures for evermore."

My arrival here has not made any great sensation, for I am not a stranger ; then, too, the site of the station is on the hither side of the village coming from Sefula. The king had been sulking with us for several days, because neither M. Jalla nor Mr. Baldwin would buy an ox, which he sent to me to sell, at *his* price. Nevertheless, he showed himself affable, and seemed pleased to see me arrive—so pleased, indeed, that he could not believe it was an accomplished fact, and more than once during the conversation asked me, laughing, when I was going back to Sefula. I announced that from the first Sunday all services would be held on the site of the new station. It was like a flash of lightning to Lewanika : he perceived, perhaps for the first time, that something was to take place close to his person, and yet independent of him ; that the immediate control of our congregation, our school, our services, our hours, our acts and movements in short, would, in part at any rate, escape him. He thereupon exhausted all his arguments to induce me to change this resolve, and continue to hold all the services at the *lekhothla*. It was in vain. We have groaned too much under that iron yoke to submit any longer ; and cost what it might, I was determined to free our work, and to open the way to our meetings for all, women and slaves, who would not dare to appear in the *lekhothla*.

On Sunday, therefore, October 30th, after eight o'clock, I sent Nyondo[1] to a little mound near the village, where he rang a handbell for twenty minutes. About fifty men had already assembled one by one at our camp ; and we asked ourselves if these, perhaps, might not be our whole congregation. Soon we saw the road sprinkled with little groups coming towards us ; then another larger group—Litia and his suite ; then another still larger, a black mass, which moved slowly. The beating of drums and wailing of the *serimbas* told us from afar that it was the king. He took us by surprise, and for ten minutes everything round us was in a commotion. It was a splendid audience of men and young fellows, the best that I have had here for a long time, from one hundred and fifty to two hundred persons ; but not a single woman, unless we count our two converts from Sefula, Ma-Moendarubi and Ma-Moendabaï, who are working here. For a long time past, I have not been able to have a single woman at our services. The king's wives excuse themselves on the ground that the lack of shelter exposes them to the eyes of the public, which is not permissible, and the others that they would never dare to go and sit in the *lekhothla*, where the princesses themselves fear to go, and that they are only *dogs*, and cannot show themselves before the king. As to the slaves, they do not yet comprehend that the Gospel is for them ; it is forbidden fruit, which they think is only for their masters.

---

[1] A Mashukulumboe boy previously mentioned.

I revolved all this in my mind, and reflected on the transformation which the Gospel might produce in a few years
amongst this people, while I was trying to make clear to their
understanding these words of St. Paul to the Romans : "*I am
not ashamed of the Gospel of Christ: for it is the power of God
unto salvation, to every one that believeth.*" But the clouds
were gathering up, and for the first time this year the rain
began to fall. I had to cut my address short. In the twinkling
of an eye, our two tents, which were already full enough, were
stormed and carried by the court party, who packed themselves
into them like herrings. The common people did not stir.
Those who had any kind of skin on their shoulders, or any
cotton garment, even if in rags, held it over their heads, for
the benefit of themselves and of their neighbours, and all who
were enjoying such improvised shelter imagined themselves to
be under cover. In the presence of the king, they did not
betray the least discontent or impatience. Lewanika and his
suite took possession of my own tent. He said triumphantly,
"Did I not tell you, Moruti? I have some wisdom too."
"Yes, only you forget that the public place" (*lekhothla*) "has
no shelter either. We will build one."

This *contretemps* troubled me. I asked God to direct me
as to what I could do to save the situation. As soon as the
rain stopped, and my audience were preparing to go away, I
sat down outside in the midst of them, and with all the spirit
I could muster began to teach them that beautiful Sesuto hymn
by M. Casalis—

> They who know not Jesu
> In their sins are dead ;

and when I had got them well interested, and was sure of their
attention, I took up the subject which the rain had interrupted
without any further formality, but as familiarly as possible.
They listened to me ; every eye was fixed on me ; and I could
thus speak for a long time. Oh, may I myself ever believe
more deeply that the Gospel of Christ, the good news of
salvation, is indeed the power of God Himself, and *not mine*!
Why do I not see it with my own eyes among the Barotsi, as
it has been seen in the South Sea islands, in Corea, among the

Telegus, and elsewhere? " Behold, I am the Lord, the God of all flesh : is there anything too hard for Me? "

The king then took leave, to the sound of his drums ; and his retinue swept away all our congregation—not a soul would have dared to remain behind. Do you understand that the hostility of this man can hinder our work and do us harm ? But he will be converted, truly, radically ! Very well, my friends ; then do you join with us in making his conversion the subject of earnest and persevering prayers. " If thou wouldest believe, thou shouldest see the glory of God." At 4 p.m., in spite of the threatening weather and our apprehensions, we again had a congregation of from sixty to seventy men. The king was not there, but the Gambella and some of the principal chiefs came. The evangelist Paulus gave us an address on the same subject as that of the morning, full of force and originality, which riveted their attention, and did me good too. Then Litia, like his father in the morning, took every one away in his suite, and we remained alone with our boys.

We talked over our impressions with our friend Paulus. *He* is decidedly optimistic, and augurs well from the day. Then, Lewanika is evidently determined to be agreeable. He noticed that I had left my cows at Sefula, and sent a message telling me to send to his chief herdsman every day for a pot of milk—a rare thing here. The Gambella also sends me some, as well as one of my friends, who is under obligations to me, so that Paulus and I live in plenty. This morning, it was a large joint of hippopotamus which one of the king's cooks brought me, and which I hastened to send on to Sefula. That and other gracious little attentions of the same kind—visits and conversations—are trifles, it is true, but they show which way the wind blows, and serve to raise one's courage. What is most evident is that we have a work before us—an immense work, difficult in the highest degree ; and to accomplish it, we must not be content with our old methods. Oh for a more complete self-surrender !

The small-pox continues to make terrible havoc. Mild cases are now rare. It rages everywhere in its most virulent form, and cuts down many victims in a few days. Even those who have been vaccinated do not all escape. It must be said that the heat is unusual. Every day the king announces some fresh deaths. (To-day is the 4th of November.)

The unfortunate Ma-Mbunda (witch-doctors), who, in their inveterate opposition to vaccination, had been making a very good thing out of their medicines and charms, are dying off like flies.   All our staff at Sefula, with one or two exceptions, have escaped.   One of my boys had the disease so badly that for three days we despaired of his life.   Now he is rapidly recovering, but alas! we fear he has lost his sight.   Poor Sachono! blind at seventeen years of age, and for life!   Another, Seonyi, is seriously ill in his turn, although he has been vaccinated.   It is a trial to us in the middle of all our work, for he had taken a fancy to wielding the driver's whip, and for want of a better we were satisfied with him.   Thus it is quite a hospital that I have left at Sefula.   Mr. Baldwin, of the Primitive Methodist Mission, has already passed through this trial ; but, thank God, he had it, like myself, in a mild form.[1]

LEALUYI, *November 18th*, 1892.

My little hillock, a mountain in our mimic Holland, bears the name of Loatilé.   I am not surprised that our Zambesi people are afraid of it.   We have a good share of some of the Egyptian plagues here.   The brushwood which covered it, and still partly does so, like a thick rough head of hair, was the haunt of innumerable swarms of every kind of insect, and of legions of reptiles—a perfect paradise for collectors.   I am not one, and for the time being would gladly resign the place to some enthusiast in that line.   The lizards are bad enough ; but the snakes !   I counted no less than five species of these ophidians, for which I have anything but a weakness.   I find nothing to admire in a serpent, its markings no more than its subtlety. The *mamba*, viper, cobra, and all their tribe are bedfellows not at all to my taste, and I feel I have done a good action when I bruise the head of one of these reptiles which symbolise Satan.   Neither have I any greater tenderness for the infinity of centipedes, and beetles of every kind, which creep out of the ground, and crawl everywhere ; nor for the swarms of mosquitoes, flies, and nameless insects, which sting or bite mercilessly, and the sight of which alone is enough to makes one's flesh creep.

Some of these insects sleep during the day ; the light and

[1] Besides M. Coillard and Mr. Baldwin, Mme. Louis Jalla and her little boy Waldo had small-pox during this epidemic, but mildly.

heat drive me from the tent, which becomes unbearable ; and whether I will or no, I breathe the open air, the burning air of our latitudes, but still the *open* air.   But in the evening my canvas shelter becomes both an antheap and a beehive stirred up.   I am no longer master in my own house.   It is impossible to keep a candle alight.   One must surround the eating of one's supper with as much precaution as if one had stolen it, then blow out the candle, and choose between the alternatives of going to bed or philosophising in one's chair, or else of sitting down at the bivouac fire with the boys—all excellent things in their way, if they were not a necessity.   On a beautiful moonlight night, or even when the darkness of a starless sky inclines you to meditation, you would like to stroll up and down the camp, absorbed in thought ; but that is impossible.

But there is another little enemy, far more formidable than those I have just mentioned, the presence of which gives me much trouble.   It is the fighting-ant, the terror of man and beast, of which every one relates the most incredible stories, travellers, hunters, and all.   Our little hillock, like all the mounds which are scattered over the plain, is nothing but an anthill, which these indomitable warriors dispute with their rightful owners, the termites, making it at once their fortress and their refuge.   The first scouts have scarcely made their appearance when the body of the army has already invaded the place.   Distance is nothing to them ; they go far afield for their prey. Their sense of smell or sight (for scientists dispute about the two senses) is keener than that of vultures.   One sees them setting out in innumerable battalions, in serried well-disciplined ranks, winding about like an immense living ribbon of black watered silk, two or three inches across.   Where do they come from ? Whither are they going ?   Nothing stops them.   Some object perhaps blocks their way : if it be anything inanimate, they skirt it and pass on ; if it be alive, they vie with each other in attacking it, they swarm over it in heaps, while the armies continue their way, silently and busily.   Should it be a ditch or brook, they at once form into a compact mass at the edge. Is it an assembly to discuss the matter ?   Probably, for soon the mass stirs, sways, passes over the ditch or stream, and pursues the course of its incessant and mysterious march.   A multitude of these soldiers have sacrificed themselves or been sacrificed for the public benefit, and these legions, whose only science is to conquer or die, have passed over the corpses of their victims.

Woe betide the man who steps on this black ribbon! Before he has even perceived it, hundreds of these angry warriors cover him from head to foot, and dig their pincers furiously into his flesh. It is enough to drive one mad. Large deer, and even the most formidable carnivora, can do nothing against these tiny enemies. They low, bellow, or roar, and run away. As to the lord of creation, who destroys and exterminates the most savage of cetaceans and mammals both on sea and land, he is quite as helpless before this insect. Alas for his dignity! he is compelled instantly to strip off all his clothes, and rub himself down the best way he can, perhaps even to singe himself. At night, the acme of torture is reached. I do not like to dwell on the thought of a missionary or his wife ill with fever in a room and in a bed which these ants have invaded. Can one picture to oneself the agony of a man coated with grease, bound hand and foot, and thrown as a prey to these implacable, flesh-eating insects? Nero, and later on the Inquisitors, were ignorant of it. Our Barotsi bear the palm in this particular; such a refined torture could not escape them.

The neighbourhood of the capital is an anthill of another kind—a hornets' nest, as I told you. Will it ever become a bed of roses? It certainly is not one now. Lewanika is a man for whom I feel a real affection, in spite of all his faults and caprices; and he knows it. As head of the nation, however incapable one may think him of reigning, he has the right to respect and consideration. "Honour to whom honour is due." It is Scripture: "Fear God; honour the king." But he has whims. He is cunning, arbitrary, and thoroughly selfish. He has a sense of justice, noble ambitions, moments of generosity, and fine ideas; but all are paralysed by a distressing weakness of character, which makes him the tool of the first-comer. Thus, when he commits unjustifiable public actions, when he allows his subordinates to perpetrate those crying iniquities in his name which revolt even the Barotsi, when he meddles with things not within his province, and demands from us not only what is outside of ours, but what is, moreover, incompatible with our ministry and our principles, my duty is, first of all, to be faithful. So it is not astonishing that I should be above all a

Micaiah[1] to this autocrat, who is incessantly befooled by the servile adulations surrounding him. For this reason, there will always be ebbs and flows in his relationships with me, answering to the caprices of his personal attendants. They were at low tide when I arrived, and I felt it in more ways than one. I see too much and at too close quarters.

Famine is endemic at the capital. Three little caravans of Bihéans, which arrived one on the top of the other, absorbed all the available provisions at exorbitant prices, and the exactions of which these traders were the victims are becoming the rule. And then, though we are in Africa, how far removed we are from liberty! Not one man would dare to sell one of those bundles of rushes which he had cut, not one of those women, much as they long for white beads, would dare to do a day's work for me, without express permission from the king. We might starve to death at the gates of this large village without any one knowing it; for not only is the market closed until the king chooses to open it, but no one would venture to visit us as long as his Majesty did not do so publicly. Everything must proceed from or towards him. That is what prevented my vaccination from becoming popular, that is what stifles all innovation and all individuality, and is one of the most formidable obstacles to our Sunday congregations. At Sefula, we had more elbow room. At Sesheke and Kazungula, our brethren's liberty is in proportion to their distance from the capital. The Gospel will remedy all that, and will work great transformations. The other day, Lewanika was struck by that sublime prophecy of Isaiah's, which our Saviour applied to Himself, and which I had chosen as the subject for meditation: "The Spirit of the Lord God is upon Me; because the Lord hath anointed Me to preach good tidings unto the meek" (Fr. Ver., *the poor*).

I have just had a week's visit from all the Sefula friends— M. and Mme. Adolphe Jalla, Mlle. Kiener, our friend Waddell, who is still working at the saw-mill,[1] and our little girls,—quite a festivity for me. It was so kind of them to bring their

---

[1] 1 Kings xxii.

[2] A sawmill sent out by some friends in Glasgow, worked by oxen. Waddell was getting the planks and beams ready at Sefula to build the new station at Lealuyi.

overflow of life and spirits to the hermit's cell at Loatilé! They shared my eminently rustic life—one prolonged picnic. They had to put up with all kinds of misadventures which it was not in my power to spare them : rain while the cooking was being done in the open air ; the sun and the heat—that unbearable and unavoidable heat which the white canvas of the tents reflects ; the invasions of insects, nocturnal attacks of the fighting ants, which drive every one from their tents and beds,— misfortunes which, alas ! were crowned by the loss of Mme. Jalla's horse. This animal was not a mere luxury for her. I had lent her husband the horse he had brought me, as he had unfortunately lost his own, so that she could accompany him on his Saturday journeys. Poor creature ! it began to cough in the evening, and we gave it some medicine, but the next morning it sank down on the edge of the road to Sefula and died.

I cannot tell you the good this visit did me. It is delightful only to look at happy young people full of activity and energy, and it makes me feel quite young again myself. Everything was transformed as soon as they arrived. No one was idle except myself, and they would not allow me to work. *La maréchale* and *la colonel*, in Salvationist phraseology, looked after everything. Mlle. Kiener saw to the housekeeping, as in old days, and privately gave my boys—what, alas ! they have the greatest want of—lessons in order and cleanliness. For my part, I feel how much I need the grace of God to keep me sweet-tempered and patient while serving this new apprenticeship.

Mr. Waddell, like the good friend he is, set to work at once on the erection of a very rudimentary shelter, which is needed until we can build our church. He had prepared the modest roof at Sefula, and Mlle. Kiener had sewn the canvas for it, so that the work was soon finished. But that canvas ! Just see how God provides for our needs. I had ordered some a good while ago for another purpose. The trader long forgot to send it ; and when he did, to make up for his neglect perhaps, he doubled the quantity. It was no use remonstrating—the canvas was there ; and as it turned out, we should not have had our shelter but for his mistake. When completed, this tent will measure thirty-three feet by twenty-one. Quite close to it, suspended from two strong posts firmly set up, hangs the bell, which was to begin its work next day. That day—Saturday—

we paid a pleasant visit to the king, hunted up the people
in the village, had a specially earnest prayer meeting in the
evening, and all was ready. On Sunday morning, the sky
looked grey, but there was no rain. We were still at breakfast,
and had not yet begun to ring the bell, when the beating of
drums announced the king.

There he was, approaching with a large suite, a mass of men,
but of course not a single woman. It was not an easy thing
to seat all these people. The king is the only deity they
recognise ; once he is settled, his atrocious band of musicians
installs itself in front of him, the common herd fill up the space,
not only around his Majesty, but also round the principal chiefs,
each according to his rank. But I am master here ; and, in
spite of a little hesitation, contemptuous smiles, and clicking
of tongues, my authority was recognised, and they submitted.
Order once established, and the rows formed, the service began,
and our brother Jalla made an urgent appeal, taking for his
text the words of Philip to Nathanael : " *Come and see.*" Then,
after we had had a few moments' conversation with Lewanika,
the whole congregation departed in procession, to the sound
of drums and *serimbas*.

Unfortunately, both M. and Mme. Jalla had bad attacks of
fever. To be ill here, in a baking hot tent, is not very cheerful ;
so our friends were obliged to cut their visit short and return to
Sefula. But since then, messengers constantly pass between
here and there. Who knows if we may not one day have
a telephone. Why not ? Africa is the home of surprises and
amazing transformations.

November 21st, 1892.

To-day, our audience was smaller, in spite of our visits to
the huts, and all the promises they made us. The people do
not dare to come yet, even those men who are not chiefs, nor
yet the king's personal attendants. The Gospel—the *Thuto*, as
they say—belongs exclusively to the king : forbidden fruit for
the people. The king himself came without his insufferable
band of music. He made a demonstration of another sort.
As he has five or six horses, he put them all in requisition for
himself and his young men. Ten minutes' walk is too much
for the heavy dignity he carries, and he took care to tell me

so. I no longer dispute the question with him. I have asked him several times, if the ten minutes is too much for him, to show me some other site, *no matter where*, that the station can occupy ; and as he confirms what we all know, that there is no other, and that it is here and here alone that we can build, we do so. The preaching was followed by an informal meeting, in which our friend Paulus catechised the congregation with surprising authority. To set a good example, the king replied with much spirit and intelligence. We sang a great deal ; but it may be said in passing that I have not yet succeeded in making our hymns popular. The Zambesians sing like crows, and it is difficult enough to get them to do even that.

Lewanika remarked that there was no hymn like his favourite " *Litaba tse gu imelang.*" [1] " But," said Paulus respectfully to him, " I do not understand why the king likes this hymn so much, since he does not know Jesus ? "

Lewanika, somewhat embarrassed by so direct a question, replied, " You mean to say that I do not believe. It is true. But all the same, it is good to know that there is somebody on whom one can unburden all that perplexes and saddens one. To be *the friend of the King*" (*Motsualle oa Morena*)— " that is no small thing."

At nightfall, I received the post. Among others was quite a packet of old letters, dated from the first months of 1891, some of which were discovered by a friend in some forgotten corner of the post-office at Palapye,[2] whilst others returned from a long journey to Fort Salisbury, and a still longer quarantine there. Who knows how many other letters and papers may not have strayed in the same way, and been definitely lost, besides those eaten by the white ants ? You see that our postal service still leaves something to be desired. But don't grow discouraged about writing, dear friends. Remember that your letters are one of the greatest blessings we have in this country, where, always called upon to give out,

---

[1] Known in Sesuto by the title of " *Motsualle oa Morena* " (" The Lord's friend "); a translation of—
> " What a friend we have in Jesus,
> All our cares and griefs to bear ! "
See page 401.

[2] Properly spelt and pronounced *Palapchwe*.

without ever receiving anything, we soon become empty and exhaust ourselves. Your correspondence takes the place of all the intellectual and religious life from which we are cut off. If you only knew how delightful the moments are which you thus spend with us! We forget our little miseries, and even the great ones appear less hard. Our loneliness and our gloom are lightened, when we hear that the sun is shining with you! In speaking thus, I think more of my dear young colleagues than of myself. They have their careers before them ; and believe me, it is an arduous and unthankful task. Thus they need to be powerfully upheld by every possible means ; and correspondence, remember, is one of the most powerful of these.

November 30th.

The work advances but slowly. The clearing away of the larger bushes is finished. We are now demolishing and trying to dig out and level our anthills. We have destroyed a great quantity of nests and queens. The anthills are formed of a labyrinth of chimneys into which a man's body could enter, and of innumerable passages which communicate with each other and lead to the nests. These sponge-like nests are made of such soft substance that they fall to powder at a touch. As for the queen, it is nothing but a bag of living matter, a grub with an ant's head, without legs or means of locomotion. We have also waged desperate war against the fighting ants, destroying their fortresses with fire and boiling water. Perhaps this will procure us a temporary respite ; but doubtless the floods will be the signal for fresh invasions.

I do not know why I can never speak of this ant plague without thinking of Lewanika and his followers. They have so thoroughly succeeded in poisoning Lewanika's mind that he cannot yet believe in the disinterestedness and purity of our motives. He suspects everything, even our kindnesses and attentions to him. Thus he is always on the defensive, and he is as jealous of his power as if he thought me seriously capable of usurping it. And then, my absolute refusal to take orders from him, like his purveyor or trader, does not fail to irritate him at times. He cannot understand that there can be a man near him who *dares* refuse to barter with him his own clothes, his personal provisions, building materials, or anything which excites the desire of his Majesty or Mokwaë or Litia. I force myself, with God's help, to maintain my relations with Lewanika on a higher level, without complaining or losing my temper.

One morning, I had gone to sit beside him in the *lekhothla*. After a few minutes, what was my astonishment to hear the principal chiefs make the following proclamation : " Listen, O Barotsi ! It is the king's word. The *Moruti* has come to dwell among us. The king rejoices greatly, and so do we. It is not that he is going to found another village, but he has much work to do. Here then is a fountain of beads and stuffs. Work for him, men and women, young men and maidens. He has garments and ornaments for you. To-day we open the gate to you. Go ! "

Before I could return, there was already a good quantity of reeds and millet awaiting me. Thank God, the blockade is raised !

CHAPTER XXXI

The first days of December 1892.

WE are no longer isolated. What a change already since Lewanika withdrew the interdict he had laid on us, in order to show his authority! People visit us, and, above all, they bring us reeds. Food is scarce and very dear. Of course, I had great difficulty in fixing the price of reeds. They knew I needed them ; therefore (the principle is the same everywhere) advantage must be taken of their neighbour's necessity. For example, here is a big-wig of the country, one Mokuamboyo, one of the principal chiefs, who comes strutting along in a voluminous shirt reaching to his ankles. He is followed by half-a-dozen slaves, each carrying a handful of these precious reeds. He wants four yards of cloth ; and rather than break off the transaction I give him half—that is to say, ten times the right value. This transaction takes me a good part of the morning. A very few such clients would fritter away the whole of my time, and tax my patience to its utmost limits. Sometimes it happens that, after an interminable palaver, the poor people go away grumbling and threatening to close the market. I have now given up this business to the catechists, and with advantage. They have more tact and patience ; they can sit down and talk and make the acquaintance of the men ; and, far from closing, the sale gets more lively, and we shall soon have all we want, if it goes on like that.

Every day the sun is like fire. In the afternoon, the sky gets well covered with clouds, but generally a wind springs up which sweeps them away, and covers us with dust. Nothing escapes this dust, especially in a tent. A nice seasoning for the evening meal! I was saying this to myself one day, when a message came from the king, which disturbed me not a little. "Know," said he, "that the Ma-Mbunda, the initiated, the Masters of the Secret Art, have been consulting the divining bones. This morning, the principal chiefs, with the Gambella at their head, came to tell me the result. Well, it is I myself whom the bones have seized upon and denounced. They accuse me of having brought the curse of small-pox on the nation, and of preventing the rain from falling. So, if I am cruel, do not be surprised."

The first thing in the morning, I went to the king, accompanied by Paulus and Jacob.[1] I found him in the *lekhothla*, and sat down beside him. He was nominating new chiefs to replace those that the small-pox had carried off—and they were many! On ordinary occasions, it would have been an interesting ceremony. But Lewanika was anxious and irritable. He had fits of absent-mindedness, and cast furtive looks around him. As soon as he could, he rose and asked me to accompany him.

But in the large rectangular shed of the *lekhothla*, an unusually loud clamour was going on all the time. "They are still at it," said the king to me as we parted. I wanted to see what was going on there, and forced my way through the dense crowd which surrounded the hut. Inside, six or seven old Ma-Mbunda, squatting on some skins, were convulsively shaking baskets filled with every imaginable object—bits of human skeletons, bones of strange animals, spines and scales of fish, rare shells, curious seeds, the hair of wild beasts, indescribable charms, and so on, *ad infinitum*. These wizards were absorbed in the study of each combination, muttering cabalistic formulas; whilst their acolytes, ranged in a circle round them, made a frightful clatter with their rattles (formed of gourds and the fruit of the baobab tree), wooden harmonicas, bells, and tom-toms. The people, packed like herrings, looked on with craning necks, staring eyes, and mouths agape. And all this by the express orders of the headmen in full *lekhothla*, under the very eyes of the king, whom they thus publicly accuse of the

---

[1] Both catechists newly arrived from Basuto-land.

nation's misfortunes! I was watching this weird scene, absorbed in gloomy reflections, when a messenger came to call me.

Lewanika, intensely agitated, was issuing orders to one of his favourites. Shortly afterwards, a great tumult of confused voices made itself heard on the public place. The king's messenger had assembled the crowd, given his message, and finished by crying, " Seize them!" Hundreds of voices replied, each louder than the other, " Seize them! Seize them!"

Every one threw themselves on the wretched Ma-Mbunda, and fought for the pleasure of throttling them. They had already been seized, one by the legs, another by the arms, others by the neck, when a second messenger arrived, who ordered the release of the miserable men, and warned them to have more respect for the Throne in future. The excitement calmed down; the Ma-Mbunda had already profited by the moment's confusion to escape. In former days, and that not so very long ago, they would have been put to death relentlessly. Lewanika lost no time in asserting his authority, and it is well; but I asked myself anxiously whether he had really put an end to the danger which threatened him, and about which he certainly was not mistaken. God grant it!

December 7th, 1892.

Lewanika has sent word to me to be present at the grand ceremony of decorating, as we should say, the warriors who distinguished themselves in the last campaign against the Balubale—that is to say, those who had, no matter how, killed one or more of their enemies.[1] There were several hundreds, and amongst them I noticed some quite young boys, who were not among the least proud. They were arranged in rows, their faces painted with white clay—one, two, or more circles round their eyes, according to the number of their respective victims, giving them a wild and horrible appearance. In front of the king and his councillors were little piles of cloth of every hue, to which each helped himself in turn, according to the number of his marks. He immediately tied the stuff round his neck, letting it float behind, which gave a little colour to the ceremony, otherwise very dull. There was not the smallest attempt at

---

[1] This had not been a marauding raid, like that against the Mashukulumboe, but a legitimate expedition to put down a rebellion.

applause or any other demonstration. To shed blood is such an every-day thing here! What a contrast to certain Basuto *pitsos* that I have seen! Nevertheless, the poor Barotsi display these bits of calico and printed cotton with the same pride that our soldiers bear a metal cross and red ribbon.

The building of our huts advances slowly. The walls consist of a circle of sixteen stakes in all, driven in, and the interstices filled with reeds. A roof of rough wicker-work the shape of an inverted funnel, a few bundles of fine grass which cover it more or less incompletely, three coats of mud and cow-dung, and the house is complete. Only, it is some time before it is dry and habitable. Coming from the tent, the hut will be like a palace for solidity, shelter, and coolness. Still, it is nothing compared with those which were built four months since for the royal harem. *They* are worth seeing, and Lewanika and the Barotsi are very proud of them. Made in the same manner as the huts, with all the proportions kept, I confess that there is something fine and imposing about them. I doubt if one could find anything to approach them among the tribes of the South. It is the same old plan as that which the Makololo copied from the Bechuana, but greatly elaborated and improved upon—two concentric walls, covered with a single immense roof. Everything is admirably finished off, from a native point of view at least.

These Barotsi astonish me: they are certainly the most industrial of any blacks I have known. They do everything necessary with only a few implements, and those of the most primitive kind. The smiths form a clan apart. Not only do they make all the arms for the country, the hoes, nose-picks,[1] etc., but give them a model, and they will make nails of the desired size, hatchets, spades, etc. They will not be of steel, but a good imitation of it. There are also armourers—a very small number, I must say. True, they cannot make the barrel of a gun, but they can fashion the butt-end and mount it for you with as much finish as a European. Those who work in wood and basket-work are more numerous.

Lewanika likes work. Under the shadow of a thick grove,

---

[1] The Barotsi substitute for a pocket-handkerchief a curved steel instrument, something between a palette-knife and a small spoon, very supple and prettily engraved.

[To face page 497.

HOME OF A MAKUENGO FAMILY (A BUSHMAN TRIBE).

which serves him as a sanctuary for his heathen rites, he has had a workshop built, into which none but handicraftsmen may enter. You will find him there in his leisure hours, working with his own hands, with about ten workmen under his orders. What does he do there? Or, rather, what does he not do? Sometimes it is a little fancy canoe, or the portable framework of an immense tent which is to serve for his annual hunts, an ingenious camp-bed or a vehicle of his own invention to transport the white men's canoes to the Ngonye Falls and bring him back plenty of money! Sometimes it is a musical instrument, a harmonica, which he is making; or else it is a flat surface on which he enjoys carving some wild animal, fish, or birds; or else it is an ivory bracelet or hairpin which he chisels very delicately.

Every year, he invents a new model for his royal barge. Last year's *Nalikuanda* was a monstrous thing, a hundred and twenty feet long, in which he tried to carry out the vague ideas he had gleaned here and there of the way in which white people build their boats. It was not a success. It gives one a feeling of regret to see so much labour thrown away in the service of such noble ambitions. The gondola which he made for his sister, the queen, is less pretentious; it is built according to the traditions of the country, and is in its way a little masterpiece. Poor Lewanika! He is in advance of his times; he leaves his people far behind him. He is incessantly teasing me to establish my saw-mill here. He spends half his time in it; he would like it to work for himself alone in the first place. What is the use of a saw-mill at Sefula, or of a forge and such a beautiful stock of tools! It is not *Moréneng* (the king's residence)! How happy he would be if he had a Mackay near him! You can understand that he turns out good workmen, but unfortunately they and all their talents are for his own exclusive use.

For us white people, whom they do not as yet rank very high in the social scale, they work badly and unconscientiously: it is not obligatory. For themselves, they do not work at all: not only is it not a necessity, but it is a wish they are forbidden to indulge in. Let me give you an example in passing. A clever workman, trained under Mr. Waddell, a good honest fellow (he certainly made a big hole in a herd of goats we once had, but

still honest according to the notions of the country), had conceived the idea of constructing a little hut like ours for himself.
The stakes had already been driven in and the framework
of the roof made, European fashion; but when he wanted to
put it up, the Barotsi, who had spied on him, fell upon him,
pulled up the stakes, destroyed the framework, and only
granted him the privilege of bowing down and rendering royal
homage, because they had saved his life and spared his throat.
How can one hope for progress under such a system? But
you may be sure the system will die out, and the people will
find scope for the development of their industrial talents.

January 2nd, 1893.

My huts, of which I have six, have given me much trouble.
I get on pretty well with the men, but it is beyond me to
make the women work for a whole day—and, unluckily, I
think they know it. All the same, I must employ them, for
plastering is exclusively their work. Happily, the wife of
Jacob, the evangelist, is there, and I give up this department
to her. She is a woman herself, a native, and made of good
stuff, and she manages wonderfully. Thus you see I have
valuable helpers in the Basuto catechists. Paulus is only
lent to me. His place is at Sefula. If affection were the
only consideration in the placing of the workers, he would
always remain with me. I like his uprightness; I admire his
courage and faithfulness; and I feel myself attracted by his
inner life—a rare thing in a native, but this is what gives him his
power. I have said that school-teaching is not his strong point,
but as an evangelist I have never found his equal. He is an
original and magnetic preacher—a priceless gift to Barotsi-land
from the Church of Massitissi. Jacob and his wife are both from
Morija, and are valuable helpers and friends; they call themselves our " children." They are calm, undemonstrative people,
but clean, tidy, always pleasant, and always ready to do a service
without being officious.

The most serious of my difficulties is—*cow-dung*, our mortar
here as in Basuto-land. I have no cattle on the place, and the
few which the natives keep are not enough to supply the hundreds
of households in which the floors and walls have to be renewed,
or in which work has simply to be found for the slaves. The

superstition of these poor people forbids women, at any rate at certain times, to enter the cow-sheds : only men have that prerogative. Moreover, the precious article must be collected before the cattle come out of the enclosure to go to pasture, or else it will bring ill-luck. This results in my being obliged to buy the good graces of the two men who have charge of the cow-herds. But every one courts their favour, and, in spite of my liberality, I am often not the first to be considered. Then there are also several bits of machinery which have to be greased— several little holes which let the beads drop through and the calico melt away ! That is why these wretched huts, which are so easily erected, keep us waiting such a time before they are habitable.

Then, whilst the wind and sun are doing their share of the work, it is my turn to take my flight. There is only one place where I can go—only one which attracts me like a magnet. It is there that I spend Christmas and New Year's Day. Sefula is my Bethel. We took the Communion together. Two places were empty : one resplendent with the glory of life, like the Lord's empty tomb ; the other, alas ! dark and sad, like that of the disciple who betrayed our Saviour.

We closed one year and inaugurated another by one of those meetings for edification and prayer which true brotherly communion and the presence of God make so sweet. Our Methodist brethren were with us—a few more glowing coals in our little fire. We know what 1892 was like : what will 1893 be ? God knows.

Lewanika seemed impatient for my return, and sent messages to enquire after my health and the cause of my delay. And as soon as I arrived, he hastened to come and see me. Poor man ! he wanted to ask advice from some one ; for he too has his anxieties.

During my absence, rain had fallen, and the gales had been raging with such violence that my camp was unrecognisable. In ten days, the grass and even the brushwood had reasserted their rights, as if in revenge ; and when we penetrated to the tents, the smell of mouldiness choked us. The whole place was a mass of mud, alive with frogs and millipedes. A hurricane had upset everything and broken my crockery. That good fellow Paulus had pushed his scrupulous fidelity to the point of even keeping the fragments of my cups and plates ! It was too much of a good thing. I fled from the ruins, and installed myself in one of my huts, which is scarcely any better. The termites, centipedes, *seuruyi*, warrior-ants, had taken possession of everything before my arrival ; but it was the frogs more especially who had made it their rendezvous. They were every-where—on the ground, on the walls, in the roof. They fall on one's head in bed, into the dishes on the table ; they are not afraid of a bath in a cup of coffee, and have the impudence to croak in my face from the edge of my inkstand, now whilst I am writing. This is a prelude to the nocturnal concert which awaits me. It is quite regal. Lewanika has drums, and I have frogs : both are noises ; and one gets equally used to either.

January 23rd, 1893.

The rains have come at last—those rains which have set the world of deities and diviners to work. It rains every day, and between the showers the heat is suffocating. One would think that the sun takes its revenge for the rain by drawing up the moisture with a fierceness calculated to burst one's lungs. We live in a vapour bath, and, as a result, colds and fevers are very prevalent. I am not very strong, but still I am up and about. I splash about through the mud, for there is mud everywhere. We found it difficult to reconcile ourselves to the sand at Sefula which slips about under one's feet, but we had forgotten what mud is. Give us sand when it rains, and clay when it is fine ! I have tried to combine the two. Every day, on payment of glass beads, women and girls bring me sand from the plain to fill up the depressions in our little hill. It is a work of patience, but it will transform the place, and my successors will profit by it. The young men are digging a deep ditch, and are making a mound, which will be a protection against *honest* thieves.[1] It will make a rectangle of the place, two hundred and twenty yards by about a hundred and sixty-five. An entrance is to be made for the public and for vehicles ; and a broad causeway describing a large bend, crossing the canal by means of a modest wooden bridge, will unite us to the capital, and will enable us to come and go dryshod even in the flood time. All this work, together with our buildings, is not done in a day. But it

---

[1] *I.e.* thieves who shrink from daring much.

has been begun ; and if Goα preserves my health and strength, all these plans ought to be realised this year. With taste and energy, a young missionary coming later on will be able to make a habitable place—an oasis in the midst of this desolate plain—out of this Golgotha of paganism.

In spite of all our difficulties, we have been able little by little to obtain all our building materials, thatching, reeds, etc., and to bring over all the grass, timber, stakes, and planks that we had got together at Sefula. To-day, the hollows in the plain are full of water, the roads are covered, and transport is becoming impossible ; but they are bringing us the last load   Soon we shall be hemmed in and imprisoned in our islet, and every one will leave the capital for the high land which borders the plain. We shall not ; but if our health holds out we shall devote ourselves to our building, and get on with the works. We shall also be free to make evangelising journeys and visits by canoe.

During this time, my hermit's cell has been greatly honoured. First, I am no longer alone. My friend Waddell has finished the preparatory work which kept him at Sefula, and has rejoined me. How proud I was to install him in one of my huts, when he only expected a tent ! For the dear man, though he undergoes the miseries of gipsy life very willingly, does not do it with impunity, and he works hard. He is simple in his faith, but firm as a rock ; and displays admirable fidelity towards every one, especially Lewanika. Without him, I should never have been able to undertake the establishment of this new station. Our friends ought to know this. In the mission field, artisans have often proved a deception and a cross. Our friend is one of the rare examples who glorify God by being an honour to their work.

He arrived with our Methodist brethren, Mr. and Mrs. Buckenham and Mr. Baldwin, who came to spend the first week of January with me. Their special object was to see the king, and form definite plans for the establishment of their mission among the Mashukulumboe. I had obtained his consent some time ago to the foundation of this new work, in spite of the opposition I had had to suffer on my own account. However vacillating he may be, Lewanika has not broken the promise he gave me ; on the contrary, he has confirmed it. Only, he does not wish our brothers to go till the winter. He is sending there

himself to found a large Barotsi village ; and besides, the missionaries are *white* ; and for those who understand the suspicious mind
of these races, these are both very strong reasons, among others,
for recommending patience and prudence. He has, moreover,
resolved to prepare the roads, he says ; to make every enquiry
on the route ; and even to send for some Mashukulumboe, who
will themselves conduct the missionaries to their country.

In announcing this piece of news to you, I am thrilled with
gratitude and joy. What good and great news it will be for
all true friends of Africa, and especially for those English
Christians who for three years have associated themselves with
all the trials of this enterprise ! For us, it means the planting
of a new outpost for the Grand Army. We feel ourselves
reinforced. Another effort, and we shall join hands with our
brethren at Garenganze, and then with those on the Congo !
I have only been able to offer my friends a very meagre
hospitality. I fill very badly the place in the household of the
one who has departed. And then it rained, and my guests
were in the mud. We were invaded by the fighting-ants, who
more than once forced one or other of us to flee from his bed,
and huddle himself (or herself) on the table till daylight. But
in spite of all, Mrs. Buckenham, who suffers in one leg, told
me she was rested. And then we were able to gather together
every day, and join in prayer.

After them, came *our* party—the Zambesi family, the
A. Jallas and Mlle. Kiener. Another delightful ten days of rest
and enjoyment. The ladies undertook the household work, and
our brother Jalla the preaching. Their stay had its inevitable
accompaniment of torrents of rain and invasions of ants ; but
they were able to return to Sefula without having been ill, and
before the plain was submerged. It was beautiful to see the
women from the village coming to visit these ladies. The
hermit's cell was quite sunny and animated, and the good these
dear, kind friends have done us still remains.

January 25th.

In my last letter, I confided to you the anxieties which our
converts had already given. That state of things, alas ! has
grown much worse since then. Lewanika has never been more
pleasant than since he ceased to boycott the station. He comes

pretty often to spend an afternoon with me, and complains that I do not visit him oftener. Sometimes, if I am passing through the place, he leaves the *lekhothla* and invites me in to see him ; and he treated our visitors from Sefula with the greatest deference and cordiality. But, all the same, I fear that, in spite of all these professions of friendship, he secretly has a hostile feeling towards us. He is a full-blooded Morotsi ! I notice that all the members of his household keep their distance, and generally here the courtiers flatter those whom their master honours with his favour. Few of our former pupils attend the meetings. Seajika is still, alas ! what he always has been—a chameleon. Mokamba (the one who wept publicly) has received a wife, and has been promoted : on becoming one of the great chiefs of the country, he discovered that his profession no longer held good, and was incompatible with the heathen practices which he has not the courage to resist. Litia has openly returned to heathenism and taken a second wife. As for Andreas, my poor boy, he has decidedly made shipwreck. Thanks to a journey which he has just made to Mangwato, and to Lewanika's weakness, the prospect of becoming the king's first son-in-law has for the moment escaped him. He has taken a wife in the heathen fashion and without telling us, and has not come near us since. He enjoys the king's favour : it is his misfortune. Of those who still remain to us, I dare not say anything : we expect other defections. Has the wind then, which blew last year, raised nothing but chaff? We can but cling tremblingly to the hope of keeping two or three grains of wheat.

" All that is very sad," said Lewanika the other day, assuming a confidential and sympathetic manner. " We shall be looked upon as children, as idiots and objects of contempt, in the eyes of the nations. I am certainly to blame in the matter, since it was I who gave wives to these young men. But who can command them to become true believers, or forbid them to forsake their faith ? But," he added, shaking my hand warmly, " do not give way to sorrow, my father ; they will return ! They are your children. And others will come who will be the sort of believers you seek." Even he, poor man, has made many steps backward. He knows the truth ; he has even a leaning towards the things of God, which evidently attract him.

But the venom of scepticism[1] poisons his better inclinations, and, as he himself says, the chains he is bound by render him helpless.   He bought dresses for all his wives, mantles and fashionable hats for the principal ones, in view of Sunday.   The poor women dressed themselves up to show me them, but to come to the service to-day would be an unheard-of infraction of its dignity on the part of the royal harem.

I am not more valiant than I need be.   There are hours, known to God, when in the melancholy silence which surrounds me I review these nine years of ministry on the Zambesi.   I see those labours, I still feel those burning tears, and a horrible oppression seizes on my heart.   " Have I laboured in vain? Have I spent my strength for nought, and in vain ? "   If my confidences grieve you, remember that the reality is cruel ; it defies us shamelessly, pursues us, fixes itself on us like a vampire—nothing makes us forget it, not even sleep.   Ah ! I understand the sufferings of St. Paul, which he compares to those of childbirth.

But shall we question the mission which God has entrusted to us?   Shall we doubt that the Gospel is still the *power of God* —for the Barotsi as well as for all the nations of the earth? Away with such a thought !   In spite of all our disasters, I have the profound conviction that we have already forced the wedge of the Gospel into the social system of this nation.   It is for others to drive it home with redoubled blows, and this mighty paganism, solid and formidable as it appears, will break up, as it has done at all times and in all countries.   There is already more than one breach which tells us so.   So do not lose courage.   The prodigal son may go far and fall very low ; but his return to his Father's house is still possible.   These experiences, hard and humiliating as they are, are not peculiar to us.   Our adorable Master has passed through them ; St. Paul knew them, like all the soldiers of the Cross whom God has sent out as pioneers in all centuries.   Only, when we admire a tree laden with ripe, juicy fruit, we forget how many flowers have perished.

I have read Mackay's life, that splendid hero of Uganda.

[1] Injected by "Alexander the coppersmith," who diligently persuaded Lewanika that the Bible was merely a collection of legends, like those of the Barotsi themselves.

The book itself is not satisfactory ; it only intensifies one's desire
to know personally the man "whose praise is in all the Churches."
But there are pages and passages in his letters which I should
like to underline and copy for our friends.   In describing
Uganda and Mtesa, he unconsciously paints the Barotsi people,
and draws Lewanika's portrait with a master-hand : the same
duplicity, the same degradation, the same inexpressible corruption, the same tyranny and cowardice, the same contradictory
mixture of good and evil, the same contempt of human life,
and I would add and emphasise the words, the same *insecurity
of property and person*.   Barotsi-land is Uganda on a smaller
scale.   Our experiences pale beside those of its heroes.   We have
not yet been judged worthy of a martyr's crown.   Nevertheless,
we have suffered.   The very existence of the mission hung only
by a thread.   But this thread was in God's hand.   So, courage !
The most humiliating reverses often precede the most glorious
successes.   The battle may appear beyond our strength, but let
us beware of laying down our arms.   The victory is none the
less certain for being delayed.   Do we not know the voice which
rules the tumult of battle, and cries to us, "Be of good courage !
Lo, I have overcome the world !"

    "Wherefore lift up the hands which hang down, and the
feeble knees."   "Quit you like men."   If the ground gives way
like quicksands beneath our feet, let us cling to the immutable
promises of God, and the Lord Himself will show us His glory,
even in this stronghold of Satan.

CHAPTER XXXII

February 28th, 1893.

I AM again far from well, though not exactly ill. Difficulties
and confusions are constantly recurring, and I confess that
I feel my courage almost exhausted. The struggle frightens me.

My establishment, which is reduced to the strictest simplicity,
is not going on well. In all sorts of details, I am at the mercy
of three boys, of whose continued service I am not at all sure,
and to whom everything must be taught—the elements of
cooking, order, cleanliness, and everything else. Formerly, I
used not to feel such thorns, for then they bore roses as
well. Now, only the briers remain, on which I am caught a
hundred times a day, especially when I am ill. Never mind ; I
shall hold out as long as I can : but till when ? If only I could
finish the establishment of this station, and then—*see the glory
of God* in this miserable country where Satan reigns !

To tell you the truth, I had not thought it possible for me
to grow seriously interested in anything on this earth again,
except in the preaching of the Gospel ; and to my great astonishment, I find myself absorbed by work which leaves me little
leisure, even when I am well. My little hill has already under-
gone such a transformation that the Methodist brethren did
not recognise it the last time they came to see me. There are.
no longer any bogs or brushwood ; the whole building site even
is cleared and covered with sand. The foundations are far from
being finished, but we are vigorously digging away at them

506

Every morning at daybreak, troops of women, girls, and even
boys, jump into the water like ducks (for the plain is already
submerged, and our Loatilé has become an island), and come with
hoes and wooden dishes to apply for work in return for a few
strings of beads. We take forty, fifty, even as many as eighty,
and send back the others. But they go away grumbling, and
return the next day, nothing daunted. We take advantage of
this crowd to have a short service with them ; they attend
willingly, for it gives them a few moments' rest. But *on Sunday*
the water is too deep and cold for them to come to the services !

Mr. Waddell is putting the last touches to my thatched
cottage. The care which this kind friend puts into this work
troubles me ; it seems to me almost a profanation. But I shall
go, and the house will remain for some one else. It will be the
first dwelling-place in Africa that I shall have occupied alone.
Happily, it will not be for long. The last chapter ought to be
the shortest.

As for the king, he is still a weathercock. Our relations
with each other have again become very nearly what they were
in our best days—except, I must add, as regards the confidence
I used to have in him. The character of the Zambesians is like
the cataracts of Musi oa Tunya : one cannot sound them, nor
yet even see the bottom. Lewanika often visits me, and seems
interested in all that goes on here. He knows how to put on
an appearance of great friendliness, which deceives strangers,
who only see him in his official garb, all smiles. I have had
to battle for several years, in order to uphold and protect the
character of the Gospel ministry, which Lewanika persists in
putting on a level with that of such traders as the floods of
immigration cast up in this country like scum. He thinks us
obliged to furnish him with everything he needs or covets, and
that at *his own* exorbitant prices. Thus he insists we should
exchange our own provisions and barter-goods, valued at the
current prices of Kimberley, *minus* damages and cost of transport, for canoes which he reckons at £5 or £10 in gold, and
bullocks at £12 or £15, whether we want them or not ; and
would force us to sell him a sack of coffee for £1 which cost us
£15 and more. Woe betide the one who allows himself to be
drawn in ! He has *eaten* his Majesty ; he has abused his
confidence and by means of insults the king ends by forcing

his hand. And woe betide the man who will not buy! Insults
are rained upon us all then; especially on me, as I am the
oldest and the nearest to him. "What good are you all?
What benefits do you bring us?" he exclaims in his fits of
anger. "What do I want with a Gospel which gives neither
guns, nor powder, nor coffee, nor tea, nor sugar, nor workmen to work for me, nor any of the advantages I hoped
for?" And the consequence is the boycott which he immediately establishes round us, after having disparaged us in
his little circle of courtiers. They threaten to strangle any
who serve us, or dare to sell us a dish of millet or a pot
of flour.

I had just written these words, when I saw an express
messenger arriving from Sefula. He brought bad news. The
thefts which have been committed for some time since upon
the A. Jallas have been repeated so often and so impudently,
and have assumed such proportions, that they suggest an
organised pillage. All negotiations with the missionaries are
forbidden by order of the king. "All day long," says M. Jalla,
"the station is overrun by people, who are not content with preventing all buying and selling, but seem to cherish evil designs
against ourselves as well." And poor Mme. Jalla adds naïvely,
"It is no good for me to say that we are in God's hands: that
does not prevent me from feeling frightened." The other day,
some poor men, who had come from a long way off with their
little merchandise, and had not yet heard the king's orders, had
scarcely put their baskets down before the mission-house, when
a band of men fell upon them, seized their flour, and drove
them away with insults and threats. With our Methodist
brethren close by, things are going on still worse. Their serving-
boys, egged on in a very transparent manner by the king's
emissaries, picked a quarrel with them for no reason whatever,
and demanded immediate payment. Mr. Buckenham refused.
Upon this a great uproar arose, and one of these young men,
armed with a thick stick, sprang at Mr. Buckenham, and dealt
him such a violent blow on the head that the wound bled
profusely, whilst another took the skin off his hands. "And
when I left," added the messenger, "the excitement was at the
highest pitch."

I had believed myself to be outside all these questions of

bargaining. I flattered myself I had at any rate won *that* battle. Not at all. The hostility has been growing for some time : one would need to be blind not to see it. Lewanika's very demonstrations of friendship warn us that it is so. Last Sunday, in spite of the fine weather, he did not come to the service. I had scarcely rung my bell, when he rang his. He was going to the *lekhothla* with his drums and all his band of music. No one, therefore, dared come to the service, except those who were already there—the big chiefs, who looked as if they were sitting on thorns. The next morning, I sent Paulus and his colleague Jacob to him, to ask why, even if he could not or would not come to the preaching, he should have done a thing he never does—go and preside at the *lekhothla* with his drums, and thus prevent the people from coming. For it is compulsory for all the men to run to the *lekhothla* as soon as they hear his Majesty's drums. He replied in no measured terms that he had done it on purpose, because Mr. Buckenham had just refused to buy at his own price the oxen which he had sent to him. " What is the use of missionaries who will not trade with me? What have I to do with such people? Tell them that *I will starve them*—him " (*i.e.* myself) " as well as the others." And he had already taken his measures and sent his orders.

I was in consternation ; for, having kept clear of these transactions with Mr. Buckenham, I only had a vague knowledge of the questions at issue. I answered nothing.

To-day, when he knew everything I have been relating, he sent me one of his confidential servants. " I have been waiting since yesterday," said he, " when I sent you my words. Why have you nothing to reply? Answer me." " Tell him that I have nothing to reply ! " Then I withdrew, in order to rest. I am expecting him to come himself to-morrow or the day after. And if he does not succeed in entangling me in a dispute—from which may God preserve me !—he will treat the matter lightly, after the manner of the Barotsi : " Oh, I was only grumbling ! You white people always take offence when any one snaps out at you. I have snapped out ; it is done with ! "

Lewanika is a great baby—and a spoilt baby too. But he is also a mischievous one—a child who plays with fire. He is not the only one to bite ; he lets loose all his dogs, and sets them on

us.   Once released, it is vain for him to try and hold them back ;
they bite too, and that without mercy.   Everything seems to
predict that we still have a hard time before us.

Lewanika has judged me charitably ; and he has done me
much honour in identifying me with my friends at Sefula,
and with our Methodist brethren.   He has made me share the
disgrace and the pricks he has inflicted on them.   It is because
he thinks we are so entirely one, and he is right.   Therefore,
we are strong.   Together we will combat on our knees.   Perhaps
he himself will soon see " they that be with us are stronger than
that they that be with them."   Ah! but when I see the clouds
have so long been gathering around us, I cannot keep from
crying to the Sentinel Who watches, Who neither slumbers nor
sleeps, " O Watchman, what of the night ? "   A voice replies
through the darkness, " The day cometh."   O my God ! may
it be without the return of night !

My correspondence, which I only look upon as a more or
less instantaneous photograph of what goes on here, is with me
a subject of much solicitude before God.   But I often reproach
myself with taking you too much into my confidence.   It is all
very well when it is a question of our encouragements and joy ;
but this is nothing but sorrows and mortifications—mortifications
unparalleled in South Africa.   Yet such is our life.   Why
should our friends refuse to share it because it is hard ?   Is it
not rather the moment, now or never, to rally our ranks, to
conquer or die ?   And though Satan may seem to triumph now,
to mock at us and baffle us, I have confidence in that *league of
prayer* with which our European friends encircle us, much more
than in the little we do here.   I tell myself over and over again
that *if we believe* we shall see the glory of God.

March 1st, 1893.

The news from Sefula is no better.   Lewanika has renewed
his order and threats in order to stop provisions on all sides for
our friends and myself (for they do all my marketing, as I can
procure nothing), and to have every one maltreated who dares
infringe this law.   Thus famine stares us in the face, and my
friends are already taking precautionary measures by sending
away all superfluous mouths.   Shall I also be obliged to send
away my workmen and stop my works ?   It is not the first

time that Lewanika has tried this barbarous method. But God will not allow His servants to die of hunger. There is always water in the fountains of Jehovah, and ravens will never be lacking to feed us.

Our Sefula friends pay every attention to their elder brother. It is from them that I receive supplies of butter, curds, eggs, etc. ; it is there that they knead my bread, do my washing, and smooth the ruggedness of my life, as far as is possible at sixteen or seventeen miles' distance. Messengers, too, often run between Sefula and Loatilé, and never without bringing some kind message or affectionate word. We almost live a common life. Every one is so good to me, and I bless the Lord for it.

October 13*th*, 1893.

We had some very stormy interviews with Lewanika. That of March 10th, at which our Methodist friends Mr. Buckenham and Mr. Baldwin were present, was the most terrible : it was also the last. He ended by understanding that our refusal to trade at his bidding and on his terms was a matter neither of obstinacy nor ill-will on our part, but of principle. Soon afterwards, he recognised that he was wrong, and gave in. Since then, our relations have become more and more agreeable. I visit him of course, but he often likes to come and spend part of the day with me to have " a quiet chat," which is not possible at his place.[1] But his heart is not touched ; his conscience is not awakened.

Still, I had not yet succeeded in getting the women to hear the preaching of the Gospel, and this greatly distressed me. As soon as the princesses cease coming, no other woman would dare to do so. We enlarged our tent for their benefit ; I set myself to visit them ; and in order that they should not shelter themselves behind the king, I pleaded with them before him, to such good purpose that they ended by yielding. One day, I saw them coming, got up in the most extraordinary costumes ; but their courage failed them at the sight of the king and congregation, and they fled to the catechists' courtyard. They came another day, but hid themselves behind the reed partition

---

[1] One day, as he was reluctantly taking leave, Lewanika looked round the missionary's room and said, " This is my home ; I have no other. I have twenty-one wives, but no home ! "

of our "tabernacle." Another time the evangelist and Mr. Waddell succeeded in making them sit half facing the assembly at some distance off. The following Sunday they arrived late as usual, whilst we were singing, and the slaves unrolled their mats in the same spot with a great deal of noise and ostentation. I left my place—or descended from the pulpit, if you prefer to put it that way—went up to them, took the mats, and spread them out near me on my left. The poor ladies looked at each with stupefaction, then at me entreatingly, while the king roared with laughter, and the petrified congregation stopped singing and preserved a stolid silence, with staring eyes and gaping mouths. I remained unmoved, and without another word signed to them to sit down. At last they did so, and the service continued. The victory was won. Since then, those who come always sit *there*, and I have no more attentive listeners.

Each of these ladies and each child of royal blood must have a mat with a good margin all round. But patience! The days of mats too are numbered ; they will disappear in their turn, and princes and princesses will learn to sit down like every one else in God's house.

Besides the women, I should have liked to reach the children. But how ? One day, taking advantage of the king's favourable mood, I spoke to him of the great wish I had to start a school. "Very well," he said ; "fix a day." "To-morrow." "Good ; it shall be to-morrow."

The next day, a Monday, turned out a wretched winter day. I looked sadly at the sheet of water and the marsh between us and the village, and I asked myself if I had not been a little rash. All the same, I rang the bell, and soon troops of children, big boys and girls, ran from the village, and some in canoes, others wading through the water and splashing through the mud, arrived breathless, and planted themselves in front of us. "*Ke rôna !*" (Here we are !") they cried, as if they had been awaiting the signal for a long time. A man, who was more sedate, presented them to us in the king's name. They were mostly his servants and children, with their numerous followers. I took down more than seventy names, and a few days later the number had exceeded a hundred and seventy ! I expected a great diminution when the novelty should have worn off, and a diminution there was; but till just lately we have had an average of from a hundred and ten to a hundred and twelve pupils. From necessity as much as from principle, I left the responsibility of this school to our good Jacob and his excellent wife. My dear brother Adolphe Jalla lent me the services of the evangelist Paulus Kanedi, who has developed gifts for teaching which I did not know he possessed; and with myself assisting as far as possible, the school has become full of life and interest, in spite of many still unfavourable circumstances.

The basis of instruction is necessarily Bible history, reading, writing, and a little arithmetic. But I attach great importance to singing, and in my eyes it is second only to the Bible. Experience has shown me more than once that the simplest hymns, saturated with the Gospel, are like certain kinds of seed in this country, to which God has given wings. When they are ripe the pods burst, and they are carried about by the wind, no one knows whither. Some, the greater number probably, are lost; but who knows?—one, a single one, may fall in some favourable spot, unknown, and there germinate, become a great tree, and bear seed in its turn—seed with wings! Thus, even though the Barotsi sing like crows, and are very little in earnest about it, we sing, and sing a great deal.

I have also been led to take up evangelisation in the homes— a very difficult work, but all the more interesting on that account; and the good that can be done in this way has greatly impressed me. Unfortunately, my efforts have been limited by our numerous material labours, of which I must say a few words. Waddell prepared a little cottage with a single room for me. That done, we concentrated our efforts on the building of the church, of which the framework and part of the materials had been prepared at Sefula. It is sixty feet long by thirty-three broad, lighted by thirteen windows. The roof is supported by eight strong pillars, and a porch with two doors completes it. The walls, made of enormous logs of a certain hard wood which resists the ants' mandibles, rest on sockets of the same wood; the interstices are filled in with reeds, and the whole is whitewashed and plastered, which gives it an appearance of solidity. We have taken every precaution possible to secure its lasting. The whole piece of ground which it occupies was dug out first to a depth of two or three feet, and then filled with fine sand brought from the plain ; each piece of wood which the ground covers has been carefully tarred.   This building, which ought to be furnished with benches, will be the marvel of the country, be it said to the honour of our friend Waddell, who has put all his heart and strength into the work.   May it soon be too small !   And above all, may we have the joy of being able to say of many of our dear Barotsi one day, " This and that man was born in her " ! [1]

Another piece of work, much greater than I had at first supposed, is the causeway, which, forming half of an elongated ellipse, will allow us to communicate with the town dryshod in bad weather.   Strange ! women and children can even in winter splash through mud and water for the sake of selling a little flour or getting a few beads, and the men do not hesitate to do the same thing in order to come and lounge about—a thing I do not encourage ; but on Sunday it is cold, they are afraid of the water, they have no canoes, and how can they come to the preaching ?   And it is just to do away with all such pretexts that I have begun my causeway.

Our Barotsi, though they have plenty of bad qualities, are clever with their hands and industrious.   When they saw us building at Sefula with the materials of the country, they said that they could do as well themselves ; and, in fact, Lewanika has now a larger and finer house than that at Sefula.   The queen's envy was excited, and her house in its turn is larger and finer than her brother's.   And then Litia and Katoka must each have one, and Mpololoa is going to have her own built.   Of course, they applied to me for all the nails and ironwork.   What should Mokwaë do one day but send me by some of her highest dignitaries a gold sovereign !   How it ever came into her possession I don't know.   She thought the sight of this piece of gold would have a magic effect on me, and induce me to give her in exchange not only all the nails necessary for her building, but also locks, door, windows, even furniture into the bargain, not forgetting the looking-glass !   Lewanika was more reasonable.   He knew I had no more nails.   I gave him one as a pattern, and since then his blacksmiths have made them for him in all sizes, and the same with spades.

It is the same thing with the canal.   When they saw me

[1] Ps. lxxxvii. 5.

making mine with a handful of workmen, they said to themselves, " We can do something better." And they did. Thanks to the thousands of hands which they can command, not only does the canal at the present time put the capital in communication with the river, but it is continued through the hills and woods to the lakes and a little river, which will make it a perpetual watercourse, while at the same time it drains the marshes, and has changed them into fertile fields. Even to-day, at the height of the dry season, it is flowing, and the canoes pass proudly up and down it.

And it is the same thing with my causeway. Stirred up by emulation, Lewanika wished to share the work with me. He will bring his part of it as far as the canal, to which mine leads from the station, and we shall there construct a little foot-bridge. You should see the enthusiasm with which these young men, from a hundred to a hundred and fifty, divided into shifts, work all the afternoon, digging, carrying turfs in their hands, and working to the time of their wild songs. I make a very poor show with my handful of hired men, one or two pickaxes, and six or seven spades, notched and broken. What would I not give to have some spades ! They will come--but when I have no longer any use for them. Never mind ! the work advances little by little, and I buoy myself up with the hope that it will be done before the floods. No one who has not seen it can have any idea of the work accomplished, and we should never have been able to undertake it without the saw-bench given by our Scottish friends.

Besides the preparatory work done at Sefula, in the forest, and at the saw-bench during a whole year, without counting the thatch and the reeds which I was able to buy on the station itself, without counting either the hundreds of women and children who for months at a time have done a good share of the work, we have during this time employed more than two hundred and fifty workmen, each for a month, costing on an average from 10s. to 13s. per month, including food and wages.

The sum of £300, which a friend in London (Mrs. H——) had specially devoted to the construction of a dwelling-house, had already been partly used for the purchase of materials and fittings—nails, screws, paint, window-panes, etc. The rest will defray the cost of the church. Other gifts, and my personal provision of cloth, will cover all expenses, including Mr. Waddell's wages. This is a great satisfaction to me.

Mr. Waddell is going to Scotland. He has well earned this rest. Devoted as he was personally to my dear wife and myself, it is for the mission that he has toiled and exhausted his strength.[1] Mr. Waddell is not an ordinary workman. When I think of his capacities as a cabinet-maker, of the wages which he was earning, of all the efforts which were made to secure his services, I say that this man, in giving himself as he did to our mission, which was still only a project, has given us a splendid example of self-sacrifice. Far be it from me to sound his praises! The work of his hands does that—a colossal work (let me use the word; it is not too strong), an incessant labour for nearly ten years. We *have* had missionary helpers of that stamp, such as Gosselin and Maeder, but they are rare. It is because it needs a more than ordinary measure of grace cheerfully to occupy this humble place in the mission field, and to glorify God in it. It is a living illustration of that beautiful word, " Mind not high things ! "

So now you know our present situation. There is nothing brilliant to record, alas !—no conversions, and no return as yet of the wanderers I am still sorrowing over. But the sky has cleared, at any rate for a time.

One word more in closing. You know of my illness, and all the affectionate care with which my friends at Sefula have surrounded me. I will say with Daniel, " And I fainted and was sick certain days : afterwards I rose up and did the King's business." Nevertheless, the thought has firmly possessed me that *the time is short.* I suffer in thinking of the little that I do, the little that we have done, and the much that still remains. When I review the missionary field, and hear from all sides the joyful songs of the reapers, I ask myself sadly why we, after nine years' labour, have still to be painfully ploughing and sowing our seed with tears ! I do not speak of Japan, nor Corea, nor the South Seas, nor of Telegu, where Christians are baptised by thousands. I pass over no less interesting corners of the field, and halt at the Congo, where the climate has made so many

---

[1] Sad to say, since his return to Scotland, Mr. Waddell's health has completely given way, and it is doubtful if he will ever be able to return to Africa, much as he himself desires it.

victims, and where the Gospel has saved so many souls! There are missionaries who have only been four years among the Balolo, and already there are some Balolo Christians. Explain me this phenomenon! The facts are there. Are we not preaching the same Gospel? Are we not dealing with the same race?

We are longing to travel throughout the country, to publish the good news of salvation everywhere. But we are nailed to our respective stations : impossible to move. I grieve over our small numbers. What are they among so many?

CHAPTER XXXIII

The Mail lost—The Primitive Methodist Missionaries—Absence of Skilled or Unskilled Labour—Procuring Thatch—Construction of the Causeway —The Bridge—Termites again—An Important Question of Fashion in Beads—The Rainy Season—The Water-supply—The Abyssinian Well —A Terrible Disappointment—The Matabele Invasion—Faint-hearted Patriots.

May (? 2nd) 1894.

I T was 9 p.m. on Saturday evening. We had just left our little prayer meeting, when a messenger was announced to me from Sefula. "Ah! that is good ; the post at last!" I opened the packet, which was not large. *Nothing* from Europe! I tore open the envelopes from Kazungula, Sesheke, and Sefula. My breath was taken away! The whole of our March budget sunk in the Mambova Rapids, and lost for ever! The Adolphe Jallas' correspondence, Mlle. Kiener's and mine, my business letters and cheques, a banknote for £10, my long letter to you, my friends—the whole lost, hopelessly lost! What consternation! Why does God allow these misfortunes to happen to a correspondence which is the object of so much solicitude and prayer on both sides ?

It often happens that our letters from Europe make excursions to Mashona-land, and even to Mozambique and Quilimane ! And then, after lying forgotten and mildewed in some corner, and after having been sent from pillar to post all over the continent, they reach us, like flotsam, with torn envelopes and addresses covered with obliterated stamps—fortunate if they arrive at all. But their precious messages have lost nothing of their freshness or perfume.

Our friends the Primitive Methodists have experienced the same vicissitudes of correspondence as ourselves. Our poor friends have had far greater difficulties than we. They left us at the end of June (1893), and only reached the Mashukulumboe country at the end of December. While I admire our brother Buckenham for his energy, perseverance, and manual skill, which altogether have been the salvation of his expedition, and our young brother Baldwin for his gentleness, his deep and intelligent piety, and his modesty, I must say Mrs. Buckenham's patience edifies me profoundly. The title of *hero* must not be lightly bestowed ; all are not heroes who appear so. There are heroes in the shade who suffer and struggle in silence. We know nothing about them, but God does ; and I think our sister is one of them.[1] I am in full sympathy with our brothers in their great enterprise. As you know, I was one with them from the beginning in heart and prayers, and I follow them with all the affection of which I am capable. The Master's work is everywhere ours ; the battle waged with the common foe is His, whatever may be the colours of the flag under which our brethren are fighting.

Let us return to the point where my last report left off.

What so greatly complicates missionary life, on the Zambesi more than anywhere else, is the manual labour. Not only are we without the help of artisans—with the exception of Waddell —but it is impossible for us to obtain, as elsewhere, the aid of workmen, trained or untrained, or even of European vagabonds. There are none in the country. It is vain to aim at simplicity, and to be content with little ; in a country like this, where everything has to be created, this labour forces itself upon one, and forms one of the important factors of civilised education for the people committed to us. For myself, I have had one of the rarest blessings which a missionary can enjoy in Mr. Waddell's help. But I cannot bear to see my young colleagues, for want of help, using up the best years of their life, to the detriment of evangelisation, in rough work which they have never before attempted, under a weakening and deadly climate. Among our mission workers, no name is engraved with deeper affection and esteem than that of Gosselin, a simple mason, in the early days of the Basuto Mission. But his mantle has not fallen on any earnest young artisan or technical expert in

---

[1] Mrs. Buckenham returned to England in 1896, having lost her health, her husband, and her only child in Africa.

France. Yet Mackay of Uganda is an example well calculated
to stimulate self-devotion, and I am jealous for my country.

We count here by season and years as you in Europe do
by weeks and months. All outdoor work has to be finished
in a given time—that is, during the dry season. The rainy
season, followed by the flood, makes it almost impossible for
several months. So we are obliged to make the very most of
the last days of the dry weather. And I had set my heart
on building the mission-house at Lealuyi. One day I accidentally
made the sad discovery that nearly all the thatching I had
secured at Sefula and laid by, was rotten. It was rather late :
the plain was on fire ; and, in our jungles, nothing stops these
fearful conflagrations, and nothing escapes them. Lewanika,
in order to help me, hastened to find out whether the *Moruti*
was in want of grass. They soon brought me some from
different places ; but these people, born traders and hagglers,
never fail to take advantage of one's distress. If I remember
rightly, the practice is not peculiar to Barotsi-land ! A bundle,
or rather a large handful, for a *setsiba*, two and a half yards of
cloth ! It was Hobson's choice : take it or leave it. I left it,
without hesitation. Our Barotsi need lessons in commercial
morality. So I mounted Grisette, and went to Sefula. I
announced my prices, which varied according to circumstances.
There was a general emulation, and all set to work vying with
each other.

Here and there, on the outskirts of the forest, along the
ditches, they gathered, handful by handful, blade by blade, the
precious grass which, as if by a miracle, had escaped the flames.
In three weeks, the supply was complete. Of course, I could
not remain away from Lealuyi all that time, and Mme. A. Jalla
very kindly charged herself with all the worry and vexation
of the negotiation. This service, which is pleasant only when
performed for others, is certainly not the sole one for which I
am under obligations to her. We had such a scarcity of provisions that our friends at Sefula were forced to reduce their
staff. I myself could not do this without completely stopping
all the building. When my provisions were exhausted, Mme.
Jalla was once more my providence. Many a time I had been
asking myself what I should give to my troop of workmen
in the evening, when a little manioc flour arrived just in time

from Sefula. And these friends sent me everything, keeping nothing in reserve for themselves. They lived from hand to mouth; after the morning meal, they trusted to God for the evening one. Well, be it said to the glory of our heavenly Father, neither they nor I, nor of course our people, ever lacked a single meal.

Do you remember the projected causeway which was to join the station to the village? We were to share the work with the king. He, like a true African, never in a hurry, took the matter very calmly. "If it is not finished this year, it will be done next." That is not my principle. I was determined to have done with it this year. But with my seven or eight notched, broken, and mended spades, the work did not advance quickly. Happily, my little band of workmen made up for this by a fit of somewhat rare willingness; so much so, that we were able to bring the work to a close well before the heavy rains.

The king, also, took the matter seriously in hand. Under the guidance of one of his principal servants, Mokanoa, an intelligent and active man, he set all his young men to work. You should see them, as soon as dawn breaks, running at the sound of Mokanoa's bell, and, without other tools than a few roughly made wooden spades with which to break up the clods, and their own arms to carry them, come and go in parties, singing. It is just like an ants' nest. Do you notice that sudden commotion interrupting the work? Do you hear that uproar, that confused sound of voices, that deafening applause? One of the number has arrived too late, and the young men are amusing themselves by throttling him on the spot. It is an every-day diversion. The one who is throttled to-day will be on the *qui-vive* to revenge himself upon one of his friends who in his turn may be too late to-morrow. It is thus that the causeway on the side of the village rises and advances. They claim to work better than we do; and I do not dispute that at all.

The causeway finished on either side of the canal, we require a bridge. A bridge? Let us be more modest—a little foot-bridge (*passerelle*). Waddell, with his assistants, worked at it for a fortnight. To look at it, you would never believe that; it looks so simple. Four enormous posts of a very hard wood, which they were certain would not rot, were firmly driven in on the

two banks of the canal (fifteen feet broad at that place), and
joined by a well-made scaffolding with strong bolts. These
support a planking raised like a look-out, ten feet above the
level of the plain. It is four feet wide, with a balustrade and
parapets, simplified as much as possible ; four steps on either
side ; and there you have our bridge. You should have seen
the interest with which great and small, chiefs and slaves,
assembled every day to examine the details, and ascertain the
progress made. For the Barotsi themselves construct bridges
too. What do they not do ? I have seen the remains of some
on the Motondo : a few forked stakes stuck in at intervals over
the breadth of a swamp or river, some poles thrown across
them without a nail or even a rope, and that is a Barotsi bridge.
And over this queer erection, which totters at the slightest touch,
a whole troop—a whole army even—will creep in Indian file,
and, clinging like monkeys, will crawl, clamber, and reach the
other side. I don't answer for accidents. Nevertheless, they
admit that ours is better—indeed, monumental. Without wishing
to boast, we share their opinion to some extent, and think it
looks very well in the landscape.

But the old wiseacres of the nation had to be reckoned with ;
they could not bestow their praises unstinted. They swore
that the Barotsi would never dare to venture over it. The very
thought of it hurt the soles of their feet, and made them feel
giddy ! All the same, some valiant spirits came forward to risk
the attempt. One solemnly seized the rail with both hands,
and mounted step after step very cautiously ; while another, for
better security, climbed up on all fours. But once aloft, how
marvellous to see the canoes pass to and fro unhindered beneath
their feet, while the eye lost itself in the illimitable expanse
around ! Their delight tempted others. However, the big-wigs
of the country still pretended to prefer crossing by canoe rather
than compromise their dignity, until they should have a chance
of trying it one day on the sly. As for the boys, they are
the same all the world over. They made fun of this timidity
swarmed all over the bridge before it was finished, and soon,
I fear, they will be using it as a diving-board. But the
education of the public was soon accomplished, and the bridge
became the fashion ; so much so that the king took fright, and,
if I had not intervened just in time, he would have forbidden

the slaves to use it—indeed, he had already done so. When he found I would not allow that, he would never cross the bridge again. He pretended it made him giddy, and likewise his chief wife !

The animation which reigned there from morning till night formed an agreeable contrast to the vast plain, barren, silent, and dead. It was a reflection ; and though doubtless a very pale one, still a pleasant reflection of the tide of European life. How many times have I not stood before my door, my eyes following those little bands of people wending over the causeway, and climbing the bridge, in order to hear the Gospel ; and the happy noisy troops of children, jumping and romping along the road on their way to school ! If it were not for that causeway and bridge, how many should we have, now that the plain is submerged ?

Goaded on by the flood, which gained ground every day, and rose, rose, rose, imperceptibly, I began the preparatory works necessary for the construction of the dwelling-house, at the same time actively pushing on that of the church, into which also Waddell threw all his heart and soul, as he does into everything he touches. We had to excavate the site to a depth of three feet, and fill it in with fine sand—not, indeed, to stop the depredations of the ants, but to hinder them to some extent. For what is there that can really stop these invincible destroyers ? During one single night, they gnawed up a pair of shoes. One's clothes, portraits, and texts hanging on the walls, precious books on the shelves of the modest library, all suffer the same fate. Cases of provisions too ! Omit the smallest precaution, and when you go to open them the chances are that you will find nothing but a little damp earth, a whole colony of ants, and some pellicules of wood, as light as feathers, instead of the strong boards of which the cases were made. Thieves can do nothing here ; but these formidable insects always work secretly and get the better of you. There is no precaution which we have not taken to protect our temporary buildings. We char the stakes ; we use tar when we have any ; and on an anthill like this, which is entirely their work, we raise our buildings upon a strong foundation of sand, several feet in depth, which the ants have more difficulty in getting through than earth. It is a great labour, but we have no other means less expensive and more efficacious at hand.

The work is done by women, whom we pay by the day with white beads, the current money of the country. With a string or two of these beads at the most, one can get everything—a pickaxe, a skin, or a fish ; it pays a doctor or storyteller, or propitiates the gods.[1] As long as I had any, I had a crowd of female workers ; but my supply ran out. I offered blue ones, which even I certainly thought pretty, though I detest that kind of thing. My Barotsi ladies turned up their noses and scoffed at the idea. Besides their colour, which is not fashionable, they are accursed, and are only known by the sinister name of *sa ku fa marena* (" the death of the kings "). They assert that the great Sepopa had on a necklet of them when his subjects revolted and attacked him, and that in his flight he went to die of his wounds on the bank of the river. How can one reason with such people ? They would not take my *sa ku fa marena* at a gift. Meanwhile, the flood was steadily rising. Can you picture my dilemma ? A caravan of Mambari from Bihé arrived in the nick of time. With much difficulty, and as a great favour, I was able to obtain two pounds of these precious beads for the sum of £1 ! As soon as they were sold to me, the women hastened up. I spoke conciliatingly to them. I showed them my little store, which did not fill a plate, and declared to them that that was all, and that in consequence I should be obliged to give them half white and half blue. Marvellous to relate, they trusted me, and began working energetically. When the white were finished, I offered them the blue rather timidly. " The blue ones are also beads," they replied, to my great astonishment. And so the work could go on. In the eyes of God, nothing that concerns His children is insignificant.

Unfortunately, we were in the midst of the rainy season ; the flood was every day diminishing the circle round my ant-

---

[1] The native doctors are not all impostors ; some of them possess a real though empirical acquaintance with indigenous specifics, and even some surgical skill. M. Goy, who was suffering from a tumour in the knee, allowed one of these medicine-men to operate upon him in the presence of M. and Mme. L. Jalla. The man set to work with little wooden knives, and, almost before they could look round, had excised it with remarkable neatness and dexterity. Thereupon he jumped up, and spat in all their faces—a necessary part of the operation, it appeared, to ensure healing of the wound. However, the missionaries, as a rule, never seek native medical attendance, because it is indissolubly mixed up with pagan practices.

hill, and the now excavated site of the house became a pond.
Lewanika was moved at the sight, and of his own accord stopped
the similar work which he had begun for himself, so as to let
the women and girls all come and work for me. Every day
I had an average of one hundred. I divided them into parties,
putting my own workmen at the head of each. All these
parties went, returned, and crossed each other, beating with
reeds on their wooden bowls to the cadence of their songs.
But the water still rose, and rose quickly. It spurted up at
every spadeful, and we disputed the sand and earth with it inch
by inch. At last, one fine morning it had flowed in and
covered everything, and our anthill was nothing but a little
island. I was forced to dismiss my crowd of workers. They
were sorry, and so was I ; but not only had I completed the
foundations of my house, I had even made an ample provision of earth to daub and plaster it. In a photograph I took
you can distinguish the heaps, which hide all but the roofs of
my huts.

One of our great difficulties here at Lealuyi, and a very
serious one, is the entire absence of drinkable water. When
the plain is dried up, the depressions and holes in the ground
form pools and ponds, which for a longer or shorter time resist
the action of our fiery sun. The thick muddy water, greenish
and stagnant, is alive with frogs, which croak all night, and
at certain stages of their existence invade us everywhere—a
veritable Egyptian plague ; and infinite numbers of animalculæ
multiply therein, only too visible to the naked eye without the
help of a microscope. There also men, women, and children
repair to bathe, quite promiscuously and unashamed. Many
a time I have seen them washing their patients covered with
small-pox before my very eyes. And it is there, incredible as
it may seem, that the slaves draw water for themselves and
for their masters. You are horrified at all this ; you try to
argue and point out to them one of the causes of the horrible
diseases which prevail here, but are unknown in the South.
They listen to you with a stupid and scoffing air ; and, pitcher
on head and body dripping from their ablutions, they run off
to tell the story in the village, and laugh at your absurdity.

We are rather more particular. The water for the king and
ourselves is obtained from a lake of fresh water. But the said

lake is a long way from here: it takes nearly two hours for a good walker, which every Zambesian is, to fetch two pails, and even then they arrive half empty. And our water-carriers are boys who only take service with us for a few weeks at a time. Who can be certain that they take the trouble to go so far at all, instead of getting the water at the first pool they come to? Alas! the nauseous smell of the coffee, the subsequent sickness and colic, leave little room for doubt about it. You scold him well one day, and the boy makes fun of it, finishes his time, and leaves you; his successor does the same; and you have to begin again, until, for the sake of peace, you end by keeping silent. My establishment is necessarily reduced to the most modest scale, and my own inconvenience has only a relative importance. But if a family were established here, who can say what enormous difficulties would be created by the needs of the best-regulated household!

These considerations more than sufficed for me, and I determined to procure one of those *tube wells* so well known in England and the Colonies, since they proved so serviceable in the Abyssinian Expedition. A gift from some generous friends made the purchase possible. Like the saw-mill and the brick-making machine, it reached here without the loss of even a screw—a surprising fact, I assure you. Our friend Waddell could not contain himself for joy on seeing it. "Two hours," said he, "and I shall have set it going!" I gave him two days. As a matter of fact, we have both worked at it unremittingly from morning till night for two weeks! One pipe cracked, and another broke under the repeated blows of the hammer; it was necessary to saw, and in several places to screw, the portions together again. In the end, after all these hopes and fears and great exertions, we have not succeeded! I am neither a practical geologist nor a mechanic, and in my ignorance I foolishly supposed that I should find abundance of pure water at a depth of fifteen or twenty feet. The most superficial examination should have made me foresee a different result. For it is just at this depth that a bed of dense clay is generally found, and unless it can be got through it is impossible to find water. You can guess with what a beating heart I sounded my pipes as they were sunk, and finally saw the last one go down. I sounded again. Five feet of sand! Such a business

as it was to pump that sand out! By dint of perseverance
we succeeded at last, and you will enter into our delight at
finding we had five feet of water in the tube. It was short-
lived, though ; for this water once drawn (and it was only half
a bucketful), the well remained dry till the next day. It was
impossible to go deeper—I had no more pipes. The inundation
has brought no change ; the water has not risen an inch. If
only we could dig a well, a real well, like Mr. Paton of Tanna,
in the South Sea Islands! *If!* But for *ifs*, what might not
be done ? However, I do not admit that my well is a complete
fiasco. With additional tubes, I still hope that one day pure
fresh water may spring up.

From the month of July till the end of December we lived
under constant alarms. At first vague and always contradictory
rumours came to us from the South, from which the indubitable
fact stood out that the Matabele had invaded the Batoka
country. Eye-witnesses related—and it proved but too true—
that they had plundered the fields, burnt the villages, mutilated
and massacred the men, impaled the women, hung up little
children by the feet and roasted them, satiated their thirst
for carnage, and committed nameless atrocities, which the
pen refuses to describe. They added that, seized with terror,
all the people from the South, the chiefs foremost, had fled
to the woods and islets—the fortresses of this country ; that
the Matabele had sacked Kazungula and Sesheke, and were
advancing by forced marches on the capital. What had become
of our colleagues in the midst of this upheaval ? No one
told me a word. I succeeded with great difficulty in obtaining
a messenger from the king ; but he had hardly arrived at
Sesheke when he threw away our letters, and I have not seen
him since.

It was one Saturday night that the king, having just left
me, received the news, and hastened to tell me. The war-
drums began to beat, and the men to utter cries and fearful
howls. What a night! The next day, all who could took
flight. The chiefs conferred, and decided to go out and meet
the enemy. All the week, the king was besieged for powder,
and certainly his supply was not inexhaustible. Assegaïs were
furbished up, shields were made, and iron bullets cast ; while
men came running from all sides in small bands, chanting their

valour on the public square, and performing mock combats.
At the last moment, the chiefs—doughty warriors !—thought
better of it, and discovered that it would be wiser to retire to
the islets. " And then ! let the Matabele come ; they will see
that we are Barotsi ! " A stormy council was held. The king,
angered, declared he would take the field himself. The chiefs
gave way, and went to camp at Mongu, five or six miles from
here. However, at the end of a few days, not being able to
get together a sufficient number of soldiers, they returned to
their homes. Lewanika, once more angry, managed by dint
of threats to reassemble a good number of men, and, without
listening to the protestations of his councillors, began operations
in his own way.

His plan was to defend the fords of the Njoko, Lumbé,
and Ruyi by strategic works, redoubts with loopholes, of which
he made me a copy in miniature on the banks of the canal on
his return. Where did he get this idea from ? I do not know.[1]
To execute it, he divided his army into three corps. The works
finished, the want of food and the absence of fresh rumours,
made him return home. We did not long enjoy this relative
quietness.

Khama sent word to Lewanika that war was imminent
between the Whites and the Matabele, and advised him to guard
the fords of the Zambesi. There could be no doubt as to the

---

[1] Colonel Baden-Powell, in his "Matabele Campaign" (Methuen 1896),
pp. 480-482 makes some observations which may help to explain this, when we
remember that all the Barotsi traditions point to the tribe having come from
Mashona-land : "Near Fort Haynes (Mashona-land), one hundred and five
miles from Fort Salisbury, were said to be some ancient ruins ; so we rode
over to see them. They were the remains of an old kraal, strongly fortified
with a circular stone wall, a wide ditch, and a triple row of trees, which are
now very big. It was certainly an ancient ruin, but not of the class of the
Zimbabye ruins, near Victoria. . . . Taberer, Chief Native Commissioner,
attributes the fortified kraals to the Vorosi people, who inhabited the country
before the Mashona, and have now disappeared northwards. They are a far
cleverer race than most South African natives. The rock drawings in
Mashona-land, generally attributed to Bushmen, he says are by them, and
are superior to the usual Bushmen's drawings."

The Rev. A. Merensky, writing in 1871, says : "A guide of the Banyaï
tribe told us much about this mysterious spot (Zimbabye) . . . and that a
populous black tribe had formerly dwelt there, but about fifty years before
had gone northward."

RAPIDS OF SAPUMA.

[*To face page* 529.

issue of this war, and they knew that Lobengula's intention was to invade the Barotsi country. Great then was the danger, and no one could ignore it any longer. Again the war-drums began to roar, and again panic seized everybody. The men held a mockery of a *pitso*, in which each tried to outdo the other in vaunting his own prowess ; they wasted a great deal of powder, intoxicated themselves with noise, and bedizened themselves with feathers and wild-beast skins, which they really believed invested them with the courage and ferocity, as well as with the appearance, of their original owners. The excitement having worked itself off, they again took the field. Lewanika was to stay behind ; but as his son Litia left with all the great chiefs, one was justified in believing it to be serious this time. Moreover, all the gods of the country had been consulted, all had given their assent, and the assegaïs that had been laid on their tombs were carried solemnly at the head of the army as a symbol of their favour. I refused to be present at their last parade, but the chiefs all came to salute me before starting. I recommended them above all to refrain from pillage ; for, in the absence of a commissariat, it is by brigandage that such an army subsists.

War despatches are unknown here. Custom dictates that an expedition once on its way sends no direct message to the king until it has reached its destination, and accomplished its mission. He knows nothing of its movements except what rumours and passers-by bring him. We thought it far away in the country of the Batoka, when a messenger came mysteriously to announce its return.

And, in fact, the next day we saw the long Indian file deploying and winding silently over the plain till it re-entered the town. What had happened ? You might go on guessing for ever. This was the secret. They had seen all sorts of bad omens—that is to say, extraordinary and inexplicable things ; here they found a dead rabbit, there a land tortoise, farther on a serpent—no more was needed. Those braves who could not contrive to flee in the night were simultaneously taken ill, it would seem, and the whole army began to melt away. The chiefs alone, upheld I believe by Litia, were trying to resist the contagion of cowardice, when one night a tempest broke ; lightning struck

a shelter under which were about forty men, who all "died"!
Thirty-eight returned to life, but two remained "dead." [1] This
time, it was all up; there could no longer be any doubt; and
all the chiefs with one accord raised the camp to return to
their homes—this time for good. So much the worse for their
country, if it is in danger! And the saddest part of it is, that
there was not one voice raised in disapproval—quite the contrary.
Lewanika was the sole exception: and was he in earnest? And
if the Matabele had actually invaded the country, what would
have become of this people and of us? But God reigns! He
is full of compassion. In spite of all the depravity of our poor,
benighted, yet beloved Barotsi, for them the hour of judgment
has not yet struck. It is still the time of grace; and we praise
Him for it.[2]

[1] The Barotsi use the word "dead" for almost any condition of helplessness or inaction—as, for instance, the attitude of prayer. Lewanika, who
takes a lively interest in European politics, and when the mail comes in
always asks how the Franco-Russian alliance is progressing, remarked to
M. Coillard one day, "I think the French are very like the Barotsi; they
are very fond of *killing their king* "—by which he merely meant " overthrowing
their government."

[2] As to this Matabele raid, M. L. Jalla wrote from Kazungula: "I
decided [in September 1893] to make acquaintance with the Batoka, and see
with my own eyes the havoc wrought by the enemy. I found the chief
Siakasippa camped under a shelter of branches at half-an-hour's distance
from his village (which had been burnt), and surrounded by about fifty men
and women who had escaped from the massacre. I only saw two *old* men
and two or three children : all the rest had perished miserably at the hand
of the Matabele. The chief did all he could to welcome me, and even forced
me to accept a lamb, though all his cattle had been carried off except eight
sheep. To crown his misfortunes, the small-pox was raging among them.
Siakasippa is a fine-looking man, a true warrior—very unlike our poor Barotsi.
The Matabele were going to raid the Mashukulumboe ; but during Siakasippa's
absence to visit Lewanika on business, a petty chief, who had a grudge
against him, secretly told the Matabele they would find much more cattle
among the Batoka. An impi detached itself from the main band, reached
the Batoka by forced marches, and taking their victims quite by surprise,
surrounded them before they suspected anything. The people fled into the
woods, but the Matabele stationed themselves on every path, even making
new ones to be certain of letting no one escape. Then one morning they
swooped down from all parts—more than fifty directions at once—upon these
poor creatures, and made an appalling slaughter, over which they spent the
whole day ; they also took an enormous number of prisoners, whom they
throttled immediately. Then they camped for the night on the banks of the

Nguesi. There took place another horrible butchery. All the prisoners were murdered without exception, and the details given by some eye-witnesses who were left for dead, but revived by the fresh night air, make one shudder. Some men were hung by the feet to trees, and left thus with assegaïs in the body ; others bound to a tree trunk and burnt by slow fires, to judge by their shrivelled and blackened hands. Numbers of little children were strung by the feet to a long perch, under which the enemy lighted fires, the better to enjoy the cries of these little victims. And so on. I wished to go there. When we reached [the spot] the camp was just as the enemy had left it. On all sides bones were lying about, scattered by the hyænas or vultures, who had been enjoying the carcasses for the last month. Judging by the remains lying among the skeletons, the majority of the prisoners had been women, especially young girls."

CHAPTER XXXIV

Fall of the Matabele Kingdom—Levity of the Barotsi—A Royal Weathercock — House-to-House Visitations — Prisoners — A Sad Story — Queen Mokwaë's Visit—A Lesson in Good Manners—*Il faut souffrir pour être belle*—Dedication of the Church—A Festival—Lewanika's Oratory—The King as a School Inspector—A School Treat—Drastic Discipline—The Chief Sindé—The Great Flood—*Matindis*—Flight of the Natives—Their Return—The Goliath of Paganism.

May—June 1894.

IN my last letter I spoke to you of the Matabele, and the alarms and panics they were causing us. Our brother Louis Jalla will have told you what can be told of the atrocities perpetrated on the Batoka, the traces of which he has seen himself with his own eyes. Alas! they have long been the scourge of the nations, and not without reason has their name alone been the terror of these parts. What a mystery is this long-suffering of the Lord! But these human tigers had filled up the cup of their iniquity, and it overflowed: the innocent blood of women and little children cried to God—judgment has come at last! As a nation, the Matabele have ceased to exist.[1]

For ourselves—I mean for the Barotsi—the end of the Matabele means peace and security, in so far as external affairs

---

[1] Six months later, M. L. Jalla paid a second visit to the Batoka, and heard full details of Lobengula's death, from the consequences of a wound received in the engagement with Major Wilson's force at the Shangani River.

"The ball having lodged in the large intestine, a native doctor tried in vain to extract it. Led by Ndosa, a younger brother (the same who had conducted the expedition to the Batoka last July), Lobengula sought a last refuge in the Kodje Mountain, a little distance from Sinamane's Mountain, on the right bank. There he died. His body, after being exhibited during several days to the gaze of his little band of followers, was placed in a lions' den, seated on the royal throne, with two guns on either side. He was covered up with blankets and numerous things belonging to him; then a great cairn of stones and are concerned. Probably Lewanika will now be able to carry out the plans he had formed for establishing villages on the river-bank as far as its confluence with the Kafué. Several chiefs have already been designated for these various posts ; only, as we have already seen, the Barotsi have no more courage and patriotism than need be. This much is certain, and it will directly affect our beloved mission, that Litia, the king's son, is soon to be installed at Kazungula itself, as chief of the whole province of Kazungula. Once invested with such great power, what will this young man become ? Will he be a helper to our brother Louis Jalla, or a thorn in his side ? I have some hope that he will return to the Lord, and then all will be well. He could not be under better influences than at Kazungula.

You will naturally ask what became of the mission in the midst of all this confusion and material work. Ah ! how I should like to be able to rejoice your hearts by telling you we are no longer clearing the ground ! But we shall long have to go on doing that among the Barotsi. Still, there is no reason to be discouraged. The longer and more laborious the time of sowing, the richer will be the harvest. " Let us not be weary in well-doing ; for in due season we shall reap, if we faint not."

Our services, which have been fairly well attended, have often been of a solemn character. What troubles me, and would make me despair if it were not for the power of God's grace, is the incorrigible levity of our Barotsi. When we believe that a serious and deep impression has been made, and we watch it full of hope, we find, alas ! that it has " passed away like morning dew." Nothing is more heart-rending than the contrast between the audience which I thought captivated by the preaching of God's Word, and the noisy mocking laughter of the groups which form after the service. One would not believe they

rocks was erected over him, and the cavern surrounded by a strong palisade of tree trunks. While this was being made, the lions came back to their lair, and killed two Matabele chiefs—to the survivors an evident sign of the chief's satisfaction, since he had thus himself chosen his attendants for the other world. A number of bullocks were then slaughtered in honour of the dead, and the flesh which could not be eaten on the spot was left to the vultures and hyænas. Thus perished this bloodthirsty chief, the Attila of South Africa. Let who will bewail the disappearance of this power. We, the nearest neighbours of the Matabele, can only thank God for having at last put a stop to their massacres."

were the same individuals. And do not think that I speak of the young people only, who in all countries are accused of fickleness ; but it is the men and women whose position and age ought to have sobered them. It is Satan's turn then ; he takes away the good seed and sows tares. I have tried to start a sort of Sunday school at that hour (after the service, I mean), but without much success.

As for Lewanika, he is always changing. His mind is convinced, but he lacks the courage to break away from customs which he condemns. He likes the things of God, and he never misses a single service unless he is unwell. Certain addresses and certain hymns have by his own confession moved him almost to tears. He has even been on the verge of sending away all his wives—" sweeping out his harem," as he says ; but he thus ran counter to a social and political institution, and roused the opposition of all the chiefs ; so he recoiled from it. He does not hesitate to deplore his wrong-doing towards us ; he recognises it, and respects all who have the courage to tell him the truth. But for all that, he has not yet got *conviction of sin*. He admits his crimes and faults, but he explains them away and palliates them ; he has not yet learned to tremble before God. And then, I must add, he always has before him the spectre of the revolution of 1884, which drove him into exile. " How is he to be converted *by himself* ? If only he could count on a single one of his chiefs, a single one of his household officers, a single one of his wives ! " The man is unhappy ; he wins one's heart, and makes one pity him. You should have seen with what eagerness, I ought to say with what joy, he did his best to popularise the evening services which I held in his court at the beginning of the flood-time. His wives, and their servants, the village women ; his own servants and slaves, and even other men who are not free to enter the precincts as they please, were all there : the court was almost always full. And in the middle, sitting by my lantern on the royal mat, which the common herd are not allowed to approach, he urged all the young men who could sing to squat down on it beside him—his own children and slaves like Nyondo, without distinction. These meetings were ostensibly for hymn-singing ; but there was always a message as well—all the more direct, because it was so familiar. And with all that, he has those backslidings, those contradictions,

those relapses even, which I understand, but which grieve me.
Poor Lewanika! How difficult it is for a rich man to enter into
the kingdom of God!

Evangelisation from house to house has often encouraged
me. I have been able to convince myself that the preaching of
the Gospel is sometimes understood where I had least expected
it. But it also initiates me into much of the darkness and
moral misery.

Here is a young woman, who hastily picks up a piece of
charcoal as I pass, breaks it in half, and begs me to hit her with
it. Poor thing! seeing my pale face, which she does not admire,
and my white suit, " she is afraid of bringing a monster like
me into the world."

Here is another young woman, lying on a mat in her courtyard. She is ill. In a corner, quite close to her, I notice on
a heap of sand from the river, where two young plants of maize
are growing, a little altar of reeds. There every morning at
sunrise, she offers to *Nyambe*, the Supreme God, an oblation
in the shape of a dish of water, hoping thus to obtain his favour
and secure her recovery. How is it possible not to be moved in
the presence of these gropings in the dark?[1]

Here is the prison, or rather here are the prisoners, who are
also toiling at earth-works. There are not many of them—five
or six in all, and even that is too many. Their gaoler, " the man
with the sack and rope," has to ration them as best he can : that
is to say, to starve them. And to prevent their running away,
he boasts that he ties them every night to a post and gags them.
Each of these wretched creatures has his own history. The men

---

[1] As to these altars, M. L. Jalla writes as follows (September 1889) :
" One Sunday at 8 a.m., I found Mahaha " (a worthy chief at Sesheke, several
times mentioned by M. Coillard) "in the midst of about fifty of his people,
especially women. ' We have come together to pray.' ' Really. To pray
to whom ? ' ' Why, to Molimo.' ' But where is your god whom you pray
to ? ' ' There he is,' replied Mahaha, showing me a fine *mozungula* tree, in
front of which they had made a little shed with grass and stakes. Beside it,
they had built a little altar with some pieces of wood, and on it, as an offering
from the chief, a skin cloak, and a wooden dish full of water : this latter is
the indispensable offering when they are asking for rain. ' Who told you
that this tree was Molimo ? ' ' Why,' he answered, surprised, ' Molimo has
told us all from all time that he descended into this tree, and that we must
pray to him there.' "

are all incorrigible thieves, and have only got what they deserve. Among the women, there is one who interests me. She is young, bright, and intelligent. She has told me her story. A man of remarkably gentle character, one whom I like very much, had married her. One day, the king's sister, Katoka, who had just got rid of I know not what number on the list of her husbands, cast her eyes on this man, and took him. He had to forsake his young wife : quite an easy matter here. Unfortunately, a little later on, a mouse was found in the princess's house—a dead mouse ! There was a great commotion, and the cry of witchcraft was raised. The bones did not fail to designate the young woman, and she was made a convict. A few years ago, she would have been burnt alive. Ah, my friends, paganism is an odious and a cruel thing !

I must say a word about the queen, Mokwaë, who has just visited us. She had been expected for a long time, and her arrival was a great event in our little world, and, as usual, the occasion for great demonstrations. Her tricoloured sunshade, her startling European costumes, and those of the king's wives, formed a striking contrast to the grease and yellow ochre of the crowd of other women. In this I suppose one must recognise the progress of civilisation, and it is for that reason I mention it.[1]

She made a stay of six weeks, and the king showed her the greatest deference. Although she did not sit in the *khothla*, as at Nalolo, all the matters treated of there were submitted to her as her right. She also busied herself about

---

[1] The Barotsi are passionately fond of clothes, and despise such tribes as the Mashukulumboe, who wear none. The wearing of them was not introduced by the missionaries, nor is it in any way a question of Christianity *v.* Paganism. When Major Serpa Pinto passed through Lealuyi before M. Coillard's first visit, he found the chiefs all decked out in faded Portuguese uniforms, one of which he identified by means of a note in the pocket as having once belonged to a friend of his own, a high Government official. The favourite costume of the Barotsi consists of a pair of trousers ; a shirt, worn *outside* it, rather long ; and a waistcoat, but no coat. But if they cannot have all three, the waistcoat is the object of their desires, because, they say— alas for the Rational Dress Association !—it pulls them together and supports the figure ! Nevertheless, with all their industrial talent, they seen to have but a very elementary idea of spinning or weaving. All their clothes are bought. They have a rooted idea that woven fabrics are produced by water-sprites in the sand at the bottom of the sea or of deep rivers.

certain troubles in her brother's harem. Not that she made matters any better herself; for Mokwaë, who is not more considerate than need be, often wounds people to the quick, especially when it is a question of other women. She considers herself, as the *katoka*, charged with the education of the king's wives. And all this is mingled with a certain kindliness, which makes her remarkably maternal with the children of royal blood. I have seen her assemble the women and girls of the harem, covered as they are with the most fantastic ornaments, and, in spite of her inconvenient stoutness, stand the whole day under a burning sun, teaching them songs and dances of olden times, which are now forgotten, and are of doubtful taste, to say the least.

Her Majesty had fallen out with me, and not altogether without reason. She is persuaded that it is in my power to give her a missionary, and that if she has not got one, it is from ill-will and obstinacy on my part. More than once already the reinforcement has failed at the last moment, just when we thought we had got it.[1] But how should *she* know that? Her principal chiefs share her ill-humour, and sometimes give proofs of it to me in a manner not altogether agreeable. I was therefore obliged solemnly to renew the promise that this year she should not be disappointed, and that a missionary should certainly go and establish himself at Nalolo. After our past experiences, it was certainly compromising myself very much; but the mission itself will be compromised, and that much more gravely, if we cannot occupy Nalolo next year. In the meantime, I am re-established in her good graces and those of her people, and they do not fail to remind me of my engagement every time we meet to discuss the site of the station, and to excel themselves in fine promises. You understand, do you not, dear friends? Do not imagine that it is the cry of the Macedonian, or think that the inhabitants of Nalolo, especially their chiefs, are yearning for the Gospel. No; it is only a question of dignity. Lewanika has his missionary, a European missionary; and why not Mokwaë? In their estimation, a white missionary is a good milch cow! However that may be, Nalolo is the second capital of the

---

[1] MM. Vollet and Edgar Kruger, who had both started for the Barotsi Valley, had to give it up, and stay in Basuto-land.

kingdom. Thus it is a post of great importance, which must be occupied without further delay.

Mokwaë has a high conception of her dignity. You know she is almost as much *morena* (supreme chief) as Lewanika himself. She has her court like him, and the same dignitaries ; she surrounds herself with the same ceremonial ; she receives the same honours, and she knows how to exact them, if need be. Thus it is natural enough that she should insist on being upon the same footing with regard to the missionaries, and even on occupying the same place at their table whenever she pleases, without further ceremony. Unfortunately, she is far from having her brother's good manners, his habits of scrupulous personal cleanliness, and above all his great discretion. I therefore permitted myself one day to give her a lesson on the subject, and some paternal advice, which she happily took in good part, and she has since then endeavoured to follow it. Mokwaë has one good quality—she never sulks.[1]

Whilst our friends from Sefula were here, we invited her to come and spend a day with us. She was delighted with the idea : she made a grand toilette for the occasion, and arrived when the sun was blazing. At her desire, I conducted her to the church, which she had not yet seen—a marvel of architecture

---

[1] The lesson was this : Mokwaë had come to the station one morning at 8 a.m. to call on Mme. A. Jalla, who also happened to be there on a visit. She stopped on till tea-time with her dirty retinue (Lewanika takes his daily bath as regularly as an Englishman, but his example is not followed by his relatives), and she would not take the broadest hints. When tea was ready, the missionaries sent her out a cup, and afterwards went inside and sat down without inviting her. Mokwaë, furious, passed her cup to an attendant, and went away, which was, in fact, what they all wanted her to do. Some days after, M. Coillard *invited* her to tea, and told her everybody was *morena* in his own house, and that it was inappropriate to her own dignity to *beg* for invitations.

Lewanika understands good manners thoroughly, though when he is in a bad temper he does not always practise them. His intercourse with Europeans, too, has tended to improve him in this respect, for in the main he has been very fortunate in his experience of them. One of his earliest visitors, who did not come up to the chief's standard, would have been very much astonished to hear his remarks about him. "Has Satory" (Queen Victoria) "not got any nice men about her person ? " "Certainly ; she has plenty." "Then I hope, when she sends *me* one, he will be a *gentleman*. That one was not even a man ; he was a wild beast."

for the country, and a very good piece of carpentering even for
Europe. I did my best to explain to her all the secrets known
to me about the sawing and joinery. We stood talking for
a long time; and from the interest she exhibited, I supposed
she was taking mental notes for her future constructions.
Thence, I took her round my little garden, where, to her great
joy, I made her a present of a box of young eucalyptus plants.
After that, it was the turn of my huts, my mysterious studio with
the red panes, and my bedroom, to which Lewanika alone has
access. Like a true lady, she politely thanked me, and told me
that everything had interested her—"immensely," I suppose.
Then the poor woman, whom I thought looked tired, dropped
into a chair on the verandah, and with a characteristic grimace
abruptly tore her shoes off her feet, and flung them on the
ground.

"My father," she said, "give me some medicine for my feet;
they are hurting me dreadfully!"

Poor creature! if she had not got boots on—real boots! New
ones too, and so small for her that I cannot understand by what
exercise of ingenuity she could ever have squeezed her feet into
them. And I had kept her standing about for more than an
hour! What martyrdom for the poor woman!

"Medicine for the feet! Come, Mokwaë, put these boots
aside; they are much too small for you."

"Then my father will give me his shoes?"

I smiled.

"Mine would not fit you either, Mokwaë."

"Ah," she remarked, casting her eyes on our friend Waddell's,
"there are some that will do."

"I have no others, *Morena*, nor has the *Moruti* either,"
replied Waddell, in alarm.

"And you wish the Morena Mokwaë to go barefoot?"

Indeed, there was nothing else for her to do, for there is no
shoemaker as yet either at Lealuyi or Nalolo. We were highly
amused by this little incident. My friends even went so far as
to accuse me of a little spark of malice, but of course I don't
admit that!

On the whole, Mokwaë's visit gave us pleasure. I saw her
often, both at her house and mine. Except when she was
unwell, she did not miss a single one of our services either. At

her place, too, I had good meetings : her large court was always full.   Mokwaë is intelligent and open to good influences—also, alas ! to bad ones, as we well know.   I was astonished to see how she understood the preachings, and how much she was interested in the school.   Hence I rejoice very sincerely to think that she will at last have a missionary with her this year.   It is quite time for it.   But, in order to occupy Nalolo, we shall be obliged to abandon our dear Sefula, and leave it in the hands of a native evangelist.   We have no one else to place there. And when somebody comes to Sefula, I fear he will find hardly anything but ruins !

In spite of the length of my letter, I must let you witness the dedication of our church.   It was a festival which had filled our thoughts and prayers for many weeks beforehand.   Well, it was heralded by a great disappointment.   We had been counting on our dear friends from Kazungula and Sesheke ; we had made splendid plans, for it is not often that the Zambesi family is seen complete.   The people rejoiced with us, the king especially ; and already our pupils were enthusiastically practising some little songs of welcome, when the news arrived, like a slap in the face, that the whooping-cough had unexpectedly caused all our dreams to melt away !   Our friends could not come.   Africa, always capricious, is the land of disappointments.

What was the use now of hurrying till we were breathless ? I postponed the festival, and it took place in March instead of at Christmas.   All the household from Sefula arrived ten days beforehand—in canoes of course, for the plain is inundated. What a transformation for the hermitage of Loatilé !   What exuberance of life and activity everywhere ! and what a magnet for my parishioners at Lealuyi !   While brother Adolphe, as we call him among ourselves, is ready to help me with eye and hand in everything, the ladies immediately took up all the cares of the household.   They also took my poor boys in hand, who certainly do their best, such as that is ; they reminded them of their lessons—quite forgotten, alas !—in order and cleanliness, and tried to extend their culinary accomplishments a little. That will not go far.   All the same, I am grateful to them, and so are my boys ; for, left to themselves, the latter have done a great deal, according to Serotsi standards, when they have merely shown their goodwill.   One cannot ask more.

The days were well filled with the occupations that had accumulated. But there was room also for the heart, if only in the evenings on my little verandah : a space for confidential chats and singing of our French hymns—echoes from our own land with their moving associations, lifting our hearts towards our heavenly country, our Father's house, where God Himself shall wipe away all tears from our eyes.

The services of Sunday, March 3rd, were of a very solemn character. It was the last time that we assembled under the tent. That good old tent, now all in rags, has its own story. It was together with these same friends that we put it up, under great difficulties. It has sheltered us for sixteen months from rain and sun. To me, its very threshold is sacred. M. A. Jalla preached on the *miraculous draught of fishes.* I, in the second service, would have liked to *draw up the net.* Can you wonder that, in scanning the many familiar faces of this fine congregation, the ten years of this Barotsi Mission passed before my mind? In spirit I travelled to Leshoma, then to Sesheke, thence to Sefula. I halted at Lealuyi. I thought of my preachings, of my shattered hopes, of those conflicts known to God alone ; and my heart filled with sadness, I repeated with the Apostles, " Toiled all the night . . . and taken nothing." This night has indeed been long and dark and stormy ; the work has been hard and unremitting. Nevertheless—*nothing !* Should we lose heart? should we doubt the power of the Gospel which we preach? the grace of God which has yet triumphed over the hardness and depravity of my own heart? Nay, Lord—*at Thy word* I will once more " let down the net."

The 11th of March arrived. The humble edifice which we were about to consecrate to God's service is the exact copy of that at Sefula, only larger and better built. The saw-bench given by our Glasgow friends has made a work easy for us which without its help would have been impossible. It is not completely finished ; there are no windows and no doors—calico will supply the place of the former, and reeds of the latter. There are only a few benches and a platform with a little table instead of a pulpit. Above the platform, against the wall, stand out the words, " Glory to God !—*Khanya e be go Molimo !* " echoing the sentiment that fills our hearts, " Hallelujah ! "

The day opened favourably, although the sky was cloudy.

Though it was the rainy season, it did not rain that day ; and we thanked God for that. As early as half-past eight, a little group made itself visible outside the village, and quickly climbed the bridge. Another appeared ; then a third, the princesses, dressed in brilliant colours ; and, finally, the mass of the people, " the black populace," *bontsu bô* as they say here, just as though the aristocracy were white. Soon the station was filled by a noisy, chattering crowd. Lewanika, contrary to his usual custom, arrived the last.

Without losing any time, Adolphe Jalla and I prepared the groups, and gave them minute directions how to enter, so as to avoid too great a confusion. The bell rang, and everybody, in the prescribed order, assembled once more on the site of our tent, which had disappeared. After singing came prayers, and an address, in which, after alluding to the appeals of the preceding Sunday, I renewed the many injunctions regarding order and respect.

Lewanika also made an attempt at a little speech. The poor man is anything but an orator, monarch though he be ; and he made a mess of it altogether. He began by calling to account the great chief of Katuramoa, who, being tipsy, proceeded to unfold a long discourse, which he perhaps understood himself, but which we had to cut short. He then turned to the Gambella, as representative of the chiefs, and asked him why he prevented his people from coming to church. The Gambella, who, by this time, ought to have grown hardened to this sort of compliment, took or pretended to take it as a personal affront ; and not deserving it, he respectfully but firmly read his royal master a lecture. The king, nonplussed by these two unexpected rejoinders, made some general remarks, recommending the people to go and hear the preaching of the Gospel and to send their children to school. Then summing up : " What other white man," he cried warmly, " has ever taken the trouble, like this one, to put up a building, not for his own exclusive use, but for ours ? Do you not see that there is something within the breast of these men—these missionaries? What advantage do they reap by wearying themselves thus for us ? Say ! And you, Barotsi, who despise their instruction, and refuse to send your children to school, are you so very wise and intelligent? Perish

our customs and superstitions! They keep us chained in darkness, and carry us on to ruin! I see it! Yes, I see it!"

We struck up a hymn, and entered, myself at the head of
the so-called procession, in order to preside at the installation
of our uncivilised congregation, while Waddell acted policeman
at the door, and our brother Jalla outside. Good-bye to our
precautions and directions! The chiefs and queens had hardly
entered before there was an indescribable scrimmage at the
entrance. I had foreseen this. Happily, our singing drowned
the uproar; and when quietness had been restored, the sight of
the audience congregated in this vast building had something
very striking in it. We began by singing a national orison,
composed for the occasion. Then after a prayer of dedication,
I endeavoured in a short address to make our Barotsi clearly
understand the character of this building, which was consecrated
to God's service; and the basis of our teaching—*the Word of
God*, true and eternal, a very different thing from the puerile
legends of paganism. Adolphe Jalla in his turn gave us a
fervent address from 1 Cor. ii. 2. I say *us*, for we took to
ourselves a good share of this "sincere milk,"[1] meant for people
who are still nothing but babes in knowledge.

To know nothing but Jesus Christ—that was just the keynote
needed; and it is, above all else, the keynote of the whole
missionary life. I will not speak of our hymns, which you do not
know. One day, we shall all sing the New Song together, the
Song of the Lamb, in the language of heaven: something far, far
beyond even that chorus of thirty thousand children, and I know
not how many thousand of adults, which I heard once in the
Crystal Palace Gardens, and which has ever remained one of the
most glorious souvenirs I have carried away from Europe. I need
not tell you with what emotion I took part in the singing of the
hymn (No. 214) which I had written for the dedication of the
church at Leribé. The comparison and contrast between these
two ceremonies, twenty-three years apart, were too painful for me.

We came away from this service with pleasant impressions.
It had lasted two hours, but attention and seriousness had been
maintained to the end. That is much for heathen, and above
all much for Barotsi.

---

[1] 1 Pet. ii. 2.

In the afternoon, after the great heat, during which all nature seems to sleep here, the road was again fringed with knots of men and women ; and when the bell rang at four o'clock, the church was filled, though less crowded than in the morning. I spoke on "living stones" (1 Pet. ii.).   As the Lord's labourers, we also seek these *living stones* among our dear Zambesians. Our ambition is to be able to offer some to the Master, that He may be able to find a place for them in the building of His spiritual edifice.   While others can cut, carve, and polish, we are still occupied in clearing the quarry.   But however rough the work may be, it is necessary, and we still have hope.

The sun was setting when we came out of the church, and it was as much as we could do, under the last glimmer of twilight, to distinguish the long ribbon of living beings disappearing into the village.

In the evening, we, tiny band as we were, assembled once more in the now empty church, to receive a message from the Lord Himself (Zech. ii. 5),[1] and commemorate His death together.   All was calm and silent, without as within.   Jesus was there, and spoke to our souls.   After this day, so happy, yet so laborious, we felt that He invited us also, like His wearied disciples, to follow Him "apart," and renew our strength in the intimacy of His Communion.   Blessed moments !   "It is good to be here."

The next day was the examination and school treat.   Ever since midnight, it had been pouring with rain, and the water was rising quickly.   If that continued, the causeway would also be covered in two days' time.   In spite of the rain, the children ran over ; they had no garments to get wet, and they did not want to be cheated out of their treat—quite right, too.   Happily, the rain stopped towards noon, and the sun shone.   At the sound of the bell, every one was there : not all the same people as the previous day, of course ; but the full number of pupils, and the king, the queen, and all the aristocracy.   One very dark cloud was the fact that our friend Jacob, the head of the school, was ill—indeed, very ill—but his wife took his place with a self-possession we all admired.   Norea is a thoroughly nice woman.   Our little ones sang us a song, composed for the

---

[1] "For I, saith the Lord, will be unto her a wall of fire round about, and will be the glory in the midst of her."

occasion, in which they claimed to be our children, and asked us to be "lenient towards them, and not ask them puzzling questions!" Dear children, they have fairly won our hearts; it is a delight to us to see them running, jumping, and making merry; so we tried rather to hurry over the examinations. But that did not suit the king at all, nor Litia either, both of whom have passed through this ordeal; and they would not let us off without our also questioning the big girls, and the young men with sprouting beards, who stumble at the first line of the alphabet. They were the attendants of the king's children; and they think, if they put in an appearance at school, that is all that is necessary.

The examination over, we had to listen to the chiefs, who, assuming a threatening tone, as usual on public occasions, censured the people who were not there. The king himself was more sensible: he gave each his due—thanked the missionaries, taxed the men with lying, and put his own wives in the same boat. "It is you who are the hindrance to the school, and entice the children away. But as for me," he added, "understand, that if a child does not attend school, do not say he is mine. I will not own him."

At last, we went out, to the relief and delight of the children! You should have seen them sitting in groups, impatient to begin. The king had had an ox killed for their sole benefit. We added to that coffee, sugar, and maize cakes. Nyondo, standing up, said grace; then all fell to, as hard as they could, and everything was soon polished off! But the dessert was still to come! Mokanoa, the king's attendant, arrived, the upper part of his body bared [1]: he knelt down; they formed a circle round him, and clapped hands. Then they listened in dead silence. "The king says: 'With him, as with the *Baruti*, the school is a serious matter. Know then, all ye his children and slaves, that whichever of you plays truant without cause will be throttled, Serotsi fashion" ("applause," *i.e.* hand-clapping), "and whichever attends school and makes no progress will also be throttled, Serotsi fashion. Remember, he tells you this once for all. So beware!" They clapped hands again, and then

[1] Indicating a message from the king—a very solemn and ceremonious occasion.

dispersed, but not for long.   They had seen the preparations
for the magic lantern.   The show succeeded wonderfully well.
There were even chiefs of the Balunda present.   When finally
Waddell let off one or two rockets as a sign of dismissal, they
were almost seized with panic.   They will not soon forget this day.

Among the auditors from a distance who were present at
the dedication, the most distinguished was Sindé, an important
chief of the Balunda tribe, who has fled before the Portuguese,
and put himself under the protection of Lewanika, whose
suzerainty he recognises.   Being an intelligent man, he was so
struck with what he saw and heard that he instantly begged
to have a missionary placed with him ; he even went so far as
to confide his sons to Lewanika, so that they should attend the
school ; but these boys, terrified at the prospect of being left
alone among the Barotsi, who do not enjoy a good reputation,
took flight.   Judging by the information I have received, and
by the ceremonial with which Sindé is surrounded, he must be
a powerful chief : he alone, of all I have seen here, made his
entry into the capital almost as Lewanika's equal, with drums,
serimbas, and a numerous procession ; his musicians played
every day before Lewanika, and a place of honour was reserved
for him at the *lekhothla*.   So there is an important field opening
before us ; and it is by no means the only one.

Our friends had returned to Sefula.   The inundation was
rising all the time, and we were beginning to ask ourselves how
many more days we should be able to remain on our island.
The king knew of my intentions.   He declared that he would
not leave either ; and that if he were forced to it, he would
only do it in the last extremity.   He knew that it was quite
out of the question for me to accompany him to his village
of refuge.

In spite of Jacob's illness, I reopened the school immediately,
with one hundred and eighty pupils.   There *was* chaff, and a
great deal of it, in this heap.   Still, we are confronted with an
enormous task, for which our forces are far from sufficient.
Litia and Mokamba, as I think I have already told you, are also
making up to us again ; and at their request, I had begun a
special class for them.   It is not that I believe they have any
serious desire to learn, and still less, alas ! to return to the
Lord ; but I should like, if I could, to remove all the stumbling-

stones out of the road to salvation, as they used to do for the cities of refuge.[1] The services of the two Sundays following the dedication were particularly solemn.

Unfortunately, the flood was still rising; the causeway had completely disappeared, and a large part of the village was inundated. And this was only the beginning. From Kabombo and the northern region, it was announced that there had not been such a flood within the memory of man. Islands which generally keep their heads far above water were completely submerged. Fields were devastated, and trees even on the borders of the woods were uprooted and carried away. Every year the Barotsi complain that the inundation is too slight, and regret bitterly the good old times, when they could organise their annual national hunt—that is, the wholesale slaughter of large antelopes, which they hemmed in upon the islets of the submerged plain. This year, they were fully compensated, and now they grumble that the flood is too great. It is curious to see the roofs emerging from the waters, canoes drifting before the wind in the midst of the village, and a herd of cattle gravely sitting in the *lekhothla*! I wonder if Lewanika's tame gnu presides at this strange parliament. Poor creatures! they have had enough of the inundation; and so have the people too, in spite of its charms and benefits. These Barotsi are quite amphibious; they are only happy in the water and in the mud. They live in it, and sleep in it, even when they might avoid it. .A few handfuls of grass for a carpet, a few branches for a mattress, and there they are, perfectly set up. Tastes differ like the sense of beauty; each one has a right to his own. One day, when I brought Lewanika into my little garden to show him some young eucalyptus trees of which I am very proud, he stopped before the church, and looking over the vast watery plain, he exclaimed after a long silence, "How beautiful! Not a tree! not one!" What would he say to-day?

As for me, I feel depressed by this panorama, smitten as it is with sterility and death. Ten years ago, when I visited the capital after the revolution, and Mathaha led me to the hill Mongou, which Livingstone had chosen as the site of the station

---

[1] Deut. xix. 3: "Thou shalt prepare a way . . . that every slayer may flee thither."

he was never to found, I deeply offended my guide by telling him that I did not at all share his enthusiasm for this inundated plain.   I wanted to return there the other day, while making an evangelising tour by canoe.[1]   What a desolation!   But I forgot that while sitting under a solitary tree, and preaching Jesus to a few poor natives I met there.   Formerly, there was nothing more melancholy than the sandy plain of Kimberley, burnt up by the sun.   To-day, diamonds are found there!

From thence, passing Kanyonyo, I wanted to visit the great village of Mokoko.   What was my astonishment to find myself paddling in a large and deep canal!   Lewanika had spoken of it certainly, but as if it were a thing of small importance.   And yet, when it is finished—and it is almost finished now—it will drain all the valley-side of Mangoko, the temporary capital, as far as Sefula, more than twelve and a half miles, and will bring its waters to our canal.   And what is best of all, is the immense quantity of arable land thus reclaimed by drainage.   So there is our canal number three!   Don't tell me nothing can be done with such industrious and imitative people!

At the entrance to a pool, we wished to turn the canoe; and in order to take their place behind, three of my boys leapt out on to a little island.   A cry of distress was heard, and they sank up to the neck; a moment more and they would have disappeared.   We were too near for the danger to be serious.   But it was curious to see the islet rise again to the surface of the water.   It was an example of those terrible *matindis*, as they are called here; rafts of grass so strongly interlaced that you can walk on them; but it must always be very cautiously; for if there is a tear in the tissue, and you make a false step, it is all up with you, just as if you fell through a hole in the ice on a pond.   Ah, if these *matindis* could speak, what lamentable stories of secret drownings they could tell us!

In consequence of these said *matindis*, the journey became more laborious.   My white sunshade misled the people, who took me for the king; and as soon as they saw us, the women began to utter piercing cries, the men to put themselves in position to give the royal salute, and all to rush towards us in troops.   I sent Nyondo to undeceive them.   What discomfiture

[1] See page 176.

for the poor creatures! Some ran off to the village; others threw themselves flat on the grass. One old man, rallying, cried out, "It is the Moruti, *Ntate oa Rôna*" ("our father"); and when I reached the village, I already had round me an audience of about a hundred persons, big and little, whose number was soon augmented by other little bands. I tried to teach them a simple hymn, and to engrave on their memory a verse which the Spirit of God may engrave on their hearts, and spoke to them familiarly of the Lord Jesus, who came to seek and to save that which was lost. This was a day employed as I wish they all were.

The Barotsi, who complain every year that the inundation is too slight, grumbled now that it was too great!

It was on the evening of Easter Sunday that Lewanika told me he had to go away the next day, in spite of the people's wish. The water had invaded the market-place, and come up to his own door. Accordingly, next day, he arrived before breakfast in a great hurry, to take leave of me. All those who could had already left. They did not even wait to set the *Nalikuanda* afloat, the back of which had been broken in coming out of the ship-building yard. They even forgot the drums. It was a flight! I accompanied him some little way by canoe. My anthill, which was a little higher than that of the capital, still held its head above water, but it grew smaller every day. The flood had invaded the workmen's huts, and the foot of some of our buildings; the garden was sinking and disappearing perceptibly, and of my "study" beside the church scarcely enough remained for the regulation prisoner's walk. Were the water to rise only a foot higher, we should be obliged to do like everybody else, though reluctantly, for I had cut out plenty of work for myself, and it was easier for me to go about evangelising by canoe from here than from Sefula. Meanwhile, we had a bad time of it with the rats and snakes which had taken refuge on our hillock, as well as with the infuriated ants, both black and red, which never left it. And how melancholy it was to look at the watery plain, which extended on all sides as far as eye could reach! Not a sound! not a soul! not a sign of life!

Nyondo tried to keep on school for about ten boys who remained in the village, and did very well. Helped by Jacob, we shared the Sunday duties. I generally went to Mangoko, the king's temporary village—a journey of three hours each way, which the wind made somewhat disagreeable and dangerous, for it often happens that a gust of wind upsets the canoes and wrecks them like nutshells.   But in spite of the sun and wind, it is a great compensation to preach the Gospel to this audience of men and women, who are generally so serious and attentive.

At Lealuyi, in the deserted village, we could always assemble from one hundred to one hundred and fifty slaves of both sexes, who came together eagerly enough when we went there (though they could not all come to us for want of canoes), and who were very much astonished, poor things! that we should trouble ourselves about them, so firmly rooted in their minds is the notion that the Gospel is only for their masters.   Happily, the inundation, which at its full height very nearly reached my house, but respected it, went down rapidly ; and by the time I returned from Sefula, where I had only been to spend Whitsuntide, the king announced to me the good news of his approaching return.   Last Saturday, the 19th, I accepted with pleasure an invitation to go and meet him, and spent part of the day with him in the *Nalikuanda* (now repaired), of which they are so proud.   It was a day of rejoicing for everybody.

I am pretty well accustomed to the noise and racket of grand occasions.   But the sight of these crowds of men and women throwing the water over their heads and bodies, uttering wild cries as salutations to the king, has a strange effect upon me.   If I had not known the cause, I should have taken it all as an emblem of sadness and mourning ; so true is it, alas ! that even the joys of our poor Africans are sad.

The school is about to be reopened, and the work will resume its regular course.   What a pity it is that we shall have to give it up in a fortnight to go to Kazungula, and leave Jacob and his wife all alone !   Please God, we shall be there for Litia's installation.[1]   The " lords of Sesheke," who are coming to escort him, are daily expected.   The canoes which will conduct our young princes Litia and Kaïba will bring the supplies we are all looking forward to.   It is the happy solution of a difficulty ; it simplifies the question of canoes for the king, and

---

[1] As chief of the new village, removed from Mambova to the official ford of Kazungula.

half compensates us for the food of eighty or a hundred men during more than two months.

But the great changes and dilemmas of the situation never cease to occupy our minds. We have to fight against a Goliath which defies us at our very hearths—namely, the appalling corruption, which seems to be at once the scourge and sceptre of this country. It cannot possibly be told, still less can it be exaggerated. Social institutions; the absence in matrimonial affairs of any contract, even the most elementary; polygamy; above all, slavery, that perennial source of so many ills,—all help to promote it, and to kill conscience. Public opinion is silent, and never denounces the atrocities that are committed in broad daylight. I knew plenty about it, alas! and thought I had nothing more to learn on the subject, but more frequent and more intimate contact with the capital revealed undreamt-of abysses. There is no such thing as youth in this country; childhood itself is scarcely known. One unhappy word excuses everything. " *Ba bapala !* " say the grown-up people, even their own parents. " They are amusing themselves." Who should reprove them? All have played with sin, all have *amused themselves* in their time, do it still, and glory in it; they are only following in the footsteps of their parents, as their own children are now treading in theirs. As the king himself said with some sense of shame, " We have grown up wallowing in the mire: how should we save our children from it?" Our experiences here have been hard and humiliating: the neighbourhood of the capital is pestiferous, and now I understand all the mortifications we tasted in our beautiful school at Sefula, and the apparent non-success of the Gospel-preaching. But that is not to say we should be discouraged. If the evil is great, we are bringing the sovereign remedy. And if a "sanctified" people could arise in the midst of so corrupt a city as Corinth, we may believe that here too, in the dregs of Zambesian paganism, God will glorify Himself. Ah! if we could but have an awakening!

CHAPTER XXXV

Arrival of M. and Mme. Béguin—Conference at Kazungula—Hopeful Prospects—Journey from the Capital to Kazungula—Projected Journey to Basuto-land—An Appeal for Medical Missionaries—Sixtieth Birthday —The Victoria Falls—The Plain on Fire—Sefula forsaken—An Awakening of Consciences at last—Lewanika and his Converted Wife— Hindrances in starting for Basuto-land—Inauguration of the Station at Nalolo—The Waggon breaks down—Renunciation of the Journey—A Work of God—Litia's Prefecture at Kazungula—His Repentance.

KAZUNGULA, July 25th, 1894.

BEHOLD one of our beautiful Zambesian dreams realised : the meeting at Kazungula of all the European members of the Zambesi missionary family ! It is a rare thing for us to see the perfect success of plans formed a long time beforehand with all our hearts set on them. We had fixed our eyes on this meeting as one does on an express train which one sees appearing in the distance. One has scarce caught sight of it, before it whistles, passes, and vanishes. Our meeting has already come to an end—already our party is broken up ; our friends the Goys left yesterday, and to-morrow it will be the turn of ourselves from the Valley. We can sit down together for a moment to talk, but only in the midst of packing provisions, loading canoes, and all the anxieties of departure.

Strangers and pilgrims, shall we ever find ourselves all together again ?

It is hardly possible ! But something will remain—the sunny memory of these delightful days. In these distant regions, where moral and spiritual solitude surrounds our steps, the present is so monotonous and prosaic, that we cannot help living much in the past, and dwelling on those Elims where we have rested and been blessed.

It was with a sinking heart that I left Lealuyi ; and I was

KAZUNGULA—THE MISSION STATION.

[*To face page* 552.

not the only one.   I made my farewells with the presentiment
that my ministry was accomplished.   Never before had my
audiences been so numerous and regular, nor so attentive ;
never yet had the interest in the things of God appeared so
great.   For a long time our voices had been lost in the desert
with no echo, but already we seemed to see the dry bones move,
and we only awaited the breath of the Spirit of God to revive
them.   And why leave now ?   What shall I find on my return.
The people, too, were sad.   Formerly, it was very different.
" What shall we do without you ? " said Lewanika.   " We will
take care that they come to church, but——"

It was at the bad season.   The inundation had abated too
much for the canoes, and not enough for travelling on foot ;
so that communications were difficult.   It was not without
trouble that the king managed to collect the fifty good canoes
we needed.   But he worked with a will.   And on the day of my
departure, he was there from seven in the morning, seeing to
the loading of the canoes, distributing and organising each crew.
He accompanied me part of the way, to assure himself that
all was well.   And then, with a hearty shake of the hand, he
turned his canoe, to re-enter the town, while we plunged into
the long grass and reeds to continue our route.   Poor Lewanika !
Three days running he despatched a courier to get news of us
and wish us a good journey.

Mokwaë, too, received us amicably.   She counted it an
honour to show us over her neat establishment—her house, her
outbuildings, and her young trees ; but, happily, my shoes were
neither too tight nor too new, as hers were at Lealuyi !   She
loaded us with provisions for our journey, and would have
detained us at least a day, in order to offer us the tangible
"expression of her high esteem "—namely, the customary ox.
We were too much pressed for time : it will graze till our
return.

Our voyage was a ten days' picnic, without shadows and
almost without adventures, though we certainly shivered with
cold in our tents (only three degrees above freezing-point in the
morning) ; and there was some excitement in passing the rapids,
where accidents are so frequent.   On July 7th, the firing of
guns announced our arrival at Sesheke, and brought to the
bank our friends the Goys, and all who remained of the

population, since the chiefs had gone to the Valley. How Sesheke has changed! One can scarcely recognise it now. To begin with, the bay, that beautiful bay, is filled with sand and detritus, and is now nothing but a marsh covered with grass and reeds. Everything that we built there has disappeared. But the Sesheke of to-day, with its mission-house built by Jeanmairet, its church, its magnificent bell, its outhouses, its reed palings, its clusters of passion-flowers, its well-kept paths, creates a pleasant impression, and shows what a man of taste can make of an arid desert. The attitude of the people also has greatly changed. It is now one of respect, and perhaps even of affection and confidence. If there had been other Christians at Sesheke besides M. Keck's daughters, I could have believed I was inhaling a breeze from the Maloutis.[1]

And at Kazungula, one day's journey from Sesheke, what a warm reception awaited us! Flags floated above the trees, and a motto of welcome displayed itself in front of the house. Our friends were there on the bank, awaiting us. I hardly know how we disembarked at the gap in the reeds, wading and leaping upon the canoes which served as a bridge for crossing a pool of water. Scarcely had we exchanged greetings when a circle was formed, and a hymn of welcome arose, very well sung in parts by the girls and boys. Everywhere, all was neat as a new pin. The station was keeping holiday. One glance at the little garden, which gives an air of civilisation to this wild spot, and at these buildings constructed without any external aid, proclaims that our friends the Jallas are hard workers. They have toiled indeed. Ten years ago, we crossed the river with our waggons for the first time, and camped a couple of paces from here, near a shadeless tree, and under a poor shelter of straw, open to all the winds. Ten years! How much has happened since then!

If union makes strength, it also makes joy; and if, while extending itself, our family circle is not weakened, we shall perpetually renew the experience that one can be happy even at the Zambesi, and that we are neither exiles nor martyrs. A real spirit of mutual love and esteem, and the determination to

---

[1] The Drakenburg Mountains. Mme. Goy and her sister are the daughters of a Basuto-land missionary, M. Keck.

place the interests of the work far above all personal considerations, have characterised our meetings and discussions. The presence of the Lord made itself felt in our prayer-meetings, and in the Gospel-preachings we had every evening. One in particular was on the plaintive cry of the prophet, "Who hath believed our report?" and nothing could be more touching than to see twenty young girls rise spontaneously, and declare themselves for the Lord. Most of them belonged to Kazungula itself, and some others to Sesheke and the Valley : many of them had already felt the need of making an open profession of having found the Saviour. Others, even among our boatmen, are under serious impressions. We do not know what the result of this movement will be. We even tremble, recollecting our past griefs. But even if the wind that is now blowing raises much chaff, will there not be a single grain of good corn?

You know that when I left the Valley I had proposed making an evangelising tour in the Batoka and Mashukulumboe countries. M. Louis Jalla had offered to accompany me. But in the course of our discussions, it became evident that it would be desirable for one of us to go to Palapye,[1] and thence on to Kimberley ; partly to prepare for bringing forward the reinforcements the Committee promise us for next year, and partly on account of the post, the agents, and other matters which we cannot arrange by letter. As none of my colleagues could leave their families or stations for so long a time, I put myself at their disposal. From Kimberley to Basuto-land by rail, it is only a step. So it was decided that I should go so far, and knit up the family ties which unite us to our brethren in Basuto-land, and to plead the cause of the Barotsi Mission among the Churches. To me, it is another fatherland : we lived and laboured there for twenty-six years. The bare thought of returning thither in my present circumstances, and after all the changes which have taken place there, made me tremble. But I am convinced of the expediency of this voyage, so I must not hesitate. Hence, I am renouncing my journey to the Mashukulumboe, and am returning to the Valley, to set my house in order, and take leave of Lewanika and my dear Barotsi, before starting.

---

[1] Pronounced Palapchwe.

On July 17th, my colleagues and their wives wished to celebrate my sixtieth birthday. They assembled in a neighbouring room at 4.30 a.m. and sang to me, " *Oui, je bénirai Dieu tout le temps de ma vie.*" Yes, *praise* : that must indeed be our theme. They thought to awaken me with these sweet tones ; and I was deeply touched. I found it difficult to believe I was really sixty years old. Our brother Jousse said that, after sixty years, a missionary is no longer good for anything. Yet I still feel young in heart. But, all the same, there is some truth in this assertion, and I too am travelling little by little towards the waste-paper basket.

I hope you will not lose sight of the appeal we are making for two medical missionaries. How is it, that among the young Christian men who have chosen this profession, not a single one has yet offered himself for the Zambesi ? Is it because the climate is so unhealthy ? is it because we are so often ill, that not a single doctor has yet heard the call of God ? Remember, too, that we must have some one for Sefula, a special man who understands machinery and can direct the labour. Waddell must leave to consult a doctor and to see his mother. For more than six months the poor man has been a martyr to rheumatism. He will go down the river with me, and we shall (D.V.) start as soon as he has finished the necessary repairs to the cart.

August 6th, 1894.

While our friends Béguin and Adolphe Jalla were directing their steps to Sesheke on the way to the Valley, I had to await Litia's arrival as chief of Kazungula, in order to have his canoes for the return journey. Meanwhile, M. Louis Jalla and I left—he, my kind-hearted brother, with the sole object of bearing me company—to visit the Victoria Falls. I had not seen them for sixteen years. It was a delightful little ten days' trip, without hindrances or serious adventures. It is true that, being badly shod, and a little less lively than my sturdy travelling companion, I returned helpless in both feet, part of the way dragging myself along, the other part carried in a chair on the vigorous shoulders of four Zambesians. But this incident can have no serious consequences, and only the bright memories of our excursion will remain. One gains a great deal in making more intimate acquaintance with such a friend as Louis Jalla, in whom a loveable nature and inexhaustible patience are united with indomitable energy.

And what shall I say of this sublime and terrifying spectacle? this maddened river plunging into dark, unfathomable gulfs? If man, poor worm! feels crushed by the majesty of his Creator's infinite power, the Christian is moved by the inward witness of the Spirit to remember that this Creator is his Father, and that this infinite Power is at the service of His mighty and no less infinite Love. He erects himself from the dust as a citizen of the Kingdom of God, a prince of heaven, with a crown of joy upon his head. What should he fear? what can man do to him? His Father is the Almighty, and loves him with illimitable love. "Who shall separate us from the love of Christ? . . . I am persuaded, that neither death, nor life, nor angels, nor principalities, nor powers, nor things present, nor things to come, nor height, nor depth, *nor any other creature*, shall be able to separate us from the love of God, which is in Christ Jesus our Lord."

SEFULA, *October 4th*, 1894.

Here we are, still in the midst of this cruel season of burning winds, where, under a scorching sun and upon a scorching soil, everything is languishing for the first drops of rain. The plain is on fire. Night after night, the gigantic illuminations transport the imagination into other worlds— entrancing, grandiose, phantasmagoric! Something thrills you in the darting flames and terrible crackling. You feel your impotence in the face of this element, which like a serpent entwines and swallows up all before it, whose advance none can arrest. What a vivid illustration of those words of the prophet, "For, behold, the day cometh, that shall burn as an oven; and all the proud, yea, and all that do wickedly, shall be stubble: and the day that cometh shall burn them up, saith the Lord of hosts, that it shall leave them neither root nor branch."

The wind dies down; we are in a furnace. Masses of thick black smoke, reflecting a livid light from the flames that devour the jungles, roll over the earth and heap themselves one above the other. You suffocate beneath them; respiration is agony.

By day, the winds sweep pitilessly over the immensity of

the plain, overhung by a gloomy pall, flecked and fringed with pale clouds of smoke. They give themselves free career! Far and near, from every point of the compass and towards the horizon, nothing but tornadoes. These cyclones arise one knows not where ; they mount up, and whirl round and round, piling up black formidable columns in colossal and fantastic shapes, which, ever mounting and whirling, scatter themselves into the air, race one another furiously, and then, as if to escape the caprice of the game, vanish, only to resume their vagabond course elsewhere. And woe to him who crosses their path! Nothing can shelter him from this wind of the plain. It pursues him everywhere, scourges his face relentlessly, and follows on his heels into his very house, where it seems to spit powder upon everything. Like an impish child on the watch for a chance of mischief, it sweeps up cinders, sand, and gravel, and scatters them, only to sweep up and scatter them again. We count the days of this terrible month. It must be one of those ill-omened moons, which the Barotsi never celebrate with festivals. At the appearance of a few flakes of cloud, hope revives. Alas! a gust of wind—a clap of thunder—and they melt away. Nothing remains but the fiery sun, and the insatiable fury of the gale.

The date of my letter is not an error ; I am at Sefula. I am writing to you in this old room, riddled by white ants, but to me a Bethel full of sacred memories. My dear Sefula! It has changed very much. The buildings are beginning to look dreary and dilapidated. As for the forest, the natives everywhere destroy the trees ; we have the greatest trouble to make them respect any, and they leave nothing but brushwood. Mlle. Kiener is no longer there,[1] nor Mr. Waddell either. The workshop is closed ; so is the forge : the saw-mill is mute and melancholy. The Adolphe Jallas in their turn are leaving it to go to Lealuyi, and the Béguins to Nalolo, and only the evangelist Paulus Kanedi and his wife will remain in a corner of the court : dear people they are, who make little stir, and love a quiet retreat. One's heart swells in thinking of days gone by, and especially of all we should have liked to do at Sefula. We found there nothing but impracticable marshes

---

[1] Her residence had been transferred to Kazungula.

and jungles, the haunts of panthers and hyænas. We wanted to make it a centre of industry and education, a fruitful source of elevation, progress, and prosperity for the country. And here is Sefula without a missionary, and almost abandoned ![1]

And yet, why should not Sefula have its day, and fulfil its beneficent mission ? Why should we not have, besides a school of evangelists, an industrial school, which should sap the foundations of slavery? For we have materials enough and to spare for a beginning. Our dear Barotsi, of whom I have had so much evil to say, have their good side too—their industry, in which they leave far behind every other South African tribe I have known. At this moment, they are building a European house like ours at Lealuyi—of course, for Queen Mokwaë— and another much larger, which is to serve as a *khothla*, or court of justice ; and all this will be done with native products and industry—*all*, including the nails and the metal of which they are made. Canals are in fashion : Lewanika is making them, and Mokwaë also, in four or five parts of the Valley at once.

Now that I am leaving for Basuto-land, I could, if I would, take with me a whole legion of young men, all vying with one another to be respectful and pleasant. The ambition of some is to go and work with the Basuto, and return each with a gun on his shoulder ; of others, to join the Bible school of our blessed Mabille, whose renown has reached even here. It is useless to argue, and try to show them the insufficiency of our resources ; they are deaf to all reason ; and to cut short their importunities, one must just harden oneself, and say, not " I *cannot* take you " —they do not believe that—but " I *will* not." But we must confess that it is hard for the dear boys, when they profess so

[1] Sefula had originally been selected as a mission station because it was the only healthy spot available near the capital. As long as it was the headquarters of the mission (especially on its industrial side), it acted as a magnet to the semi-nomadic population. But when M. Coillard left for Lealuyi, and Waddell's health obliged him to go to England, the people dropped off or moved away. M. Coillard's projected journey to Basuto-land, and afterwards his long illness, made it imperative for him to have a colleague at Lealuyi, and the staff was so limited that there was no choice but for the A. Jallas to move to the capital. Mr. Mercier started nearly two years ago to establish an industrial school at Sefula, but the disturbed state of South Africa made it impossible for him to get there till July 1897.

great a desire to learn, and become *evangelist-schoolmasters* (for we pile up the functions in Barotsi-land). Mind, I would not venture to guarantee the purity and disinterestedness of each one's motives. But still, we cannot be indifferent to it, any more than to the needs of the work.

You know how we appreciate the evangelists who come to us from Basuto-land ; for the most part these men are among the very elect. But the distances, the difficulties of travelling, and the expense will always and perforce limit their number. It would be no more advantageous to send our Zambesians to Basuto-land, than it would be wise and economical to send our Basuto to France to make French pastors and missionaries of them. Their pretensions and requirements would threaten to be in inverse proportion to their good sense and efficiency. M. Louis Jalla has three of his pupils at Morija, and I have consented to take one of mine there. But I do it against the grain, and simply because I cannot help it. It is a great risk. In speaking thus, it must not be imagined that I throw a shadow of discredit on a school which of all the Basuto schools commands my fullest and deepest sympathy. Oh no ! Only what we need, and what is imperative, is *our own Bible school*, here at the Zambesi, and *without delay*. We must from the beginning inculcate a missionary spirit in our Christians, an aggressive activity, the need of giving what they themselves have received.

In these days, much is said in the religious world about what they call *self-supporting* missions. For my own part, I should prefer a *self-propagating one*. It would be more genuine ; it would be unassailable, because it is the very essence of Christianity, and the sap of the spiritual life in each disciple of the Saviour.

I came to Sefula to despatch Kamburu with my Cape cart, which I shall rejoin at Kazungula, proceeding thither by canoe. But I have been here four days, and no Kamburu has appeared. I came also to perform the marriage ceremony for Seonyi and Nosiku, who have both grown up with us. The girls had remained with Mme. A. Jalla when I left Lealuyi ; both profess to be converted, and certainly a transformation has been worked in them, which we can only attribute to the grace of God.

The rest you will have heard already : in each of our

stations a movement has taken place of which we would only speak with the greatest reserve, though we cannot be absolutely silent on the subject. It first manifested itself at Kazungula among the children living in the mission-house, and was greatly accentuated during our stay there at the time of the conference. But it was at Sefula that it took the greatest proportions. In a few weeks, the number of those who publicly declared their wish to serve God rose above sixty. Quite a third of the number are school-children, M. Jalla tells me ; others are men and women, who have nothing as yet to recommend them to our confidence beyond this public profession, which, after all, among these poor volatile Zambesians, compromises them very little. But there are others whose faces are very familiar to us.

At Lealuyi, I was struck, on my return from Kazungula, by the audience ; our church, big as it is, overflows. On the first Sunday after my arrival, it was as full as on the day of the dedication ; the benches, the aisles, even the steps of the platform which serves as our pulpit, all were filled, not an inch to spare. Even then, more than fifty people, who could find no room inside, pressed around the doors to listen ; and this, in spite of the fact that public works and local causes have for the moment dispersed the floating population, always considerable at Lealuyi. And I must say there is something solemnly joyful in the attention and seriousness of this splendid audience in the midst of such heathen surroundings. Here, also, we have had spontaneous professions, some of which have moved our hearts ; but I do not encourage them.

If we were not working among people with whose desperately frivolous character we are well acquainted, and if we had not had, or had at least been able to forget, the hard and humiliating lessons of the past, perhaps our joy would be less mingled, and our hopes more vivid. We hardly know what to think in the presence of such a new movement. We wonder anxiously if it be really the beginning of an awakening of consciences, the first drops of those showers for which we have prayed and waited for so long. God knows our ardent and sincere desire is not to make a brilliant show in the eyes of men, building wood and stubble on the Rock of Ages (those materials abound everywhere), but to build thereon precious stones, gold, and even silver, however little, so long as it is sound metal.

To speak candidly, I am not without apprehensions. I fear lest this movement, which seems so widespread, may yet be without depth. I fear that the king's favourable inclinations, which are known to every one, and the spirit of imitation and excitement, may have a good deal to do with it. This pessimistic view is probably peculiar to myself, and is perhaps not shared by my brethren, and I am sometimes vexed with myself for it. How often does it happen that our souls agonise in supplications; and yet when these are granted, we are so astonished that we cannot believe it. We are always saying, " Rhoda, thou art mad." Yet we believe. " Lord, help Thou our unbelief."

LEALUYI, *October 1st.*

Yesterday was the day of farewells, one of those days one prefers to leave behind. M. and Mme. Adolphe Jalla came for the occasion, as they were to replace me. Jacob Moshabesha also bade good-bye. He will go to second M. Béguin at Nalolo, where their installation is to take place next Sunday. Each of us four spoke, and there is no need to add that this service had that character of solemnity which makes one realise the presence of God. It was the same in the afternoon meeting, which prolonged itself till dusk. All seemed to leave regretfully.

It was a sight to draw tears from the angels of heaven to see, amongst others, children—yes, *children !*—rise up to confess their thefts and unveil their immorality. We were probably the only persons present to be astonished at it, and to feel shame covering our countenances. Who can fathom the abyss of corruption in which they all grovel, since even these children, little ones scarcely twelve years of age, are already familiar with vice ? One trembles only to think of it. Nevertheless, to judge by their serious air, one must believe in the sincerity of these testimonies. Pressing appeals, driven home by hymns, also of *appeal,* sung as solos and choruses by us four only, missionaries and evangelists, held the assembly spell-bound. In the midst of a great silence, Lewanika suddenly apostrophised one of his wives, who occupied a seat in another part of the church, a charming young woman, gentle and timid as a dove.

" Nolianga," he cried, " why are you silent ? You who

love the things of God so much, and whose conscience has
so long been exercised, why do you remain silent? Say, why
do you not declare yourself for Jesus? What do you fear?
Of whom are you afraid? I hinder no one from becoming
converted and serving God. Speak therefore!"

During a profound silence, in which everybody seemed to
hold their breath, their eyes fixed on her, one heard nothing
but stifled sobs. Nolianga did not speak, any more than she
who watered the Saviour's feet with her tears, and wiped them
with the hairs of her head.

But the incident is of great moment in the eyes of the public,
and it is the topic of all conversations. No one is mistaken
as to the significance and purpose of the king's words; but they
wonder why he does not go further, and take the decisive step.
In the harem, they had been already pointing at poor Nolianga.
Her rivals were treating her as an ambitious hypocrite. "She
is only pretending to be converted," they said, "so as to please
the king, and become his sole wife when he declares himself
a Christian." What will it be now?

This Nolianga, who is still young, good-looking, and amiable,
is a daughter of the famous king Sepopa, and is, therefore, a
second cousin of Lewanika's. She has long been attracted to
the Gospel. Being a great friend of Norea, Jacob's excellent
wife, she has taken advantage of the latter's friendship to study
the things of God, and also to learn to read. The work of
grace has operated visibly in this beautiful soul. Some time
ago—*without our knowledge, mark!*—she confessed to the king
that she could no longer resist the call of God. In becoming
a Christian, she knew she must leave his seraglio. But she
entreated him not to dispose of her at his pleasure, and give
her to anybody as a wife, according to the custom, but to
leave her entirely free to marry or not, and to build her house
where she wished. Lewanika granted her petition. In fact,
I think the dear man is very pleased at it. It is what he has
long been wishing and expecting. He wished to leave to God
the task of dispersing his wives, whom he has not the courage
to send away. And then, if only some of his *likomboa* (household
officers) and principal chiefs were converted first, how easy
it would be for him to follow them, instead of his having to
tread all alone—he who is never alone—the narrow path that

leads to life. Tell me, do you not pity him ? Let those friends who make his conversion a subject of prayer on no account grow weary.[1]

SEFULA, *October 16th.*

The 14th having been fixed for M. Béguin's installation at Nalolo, I was forced to hasten the completion of my preparations for the journey, as I was not returning to Lealuyi. The evening before my departure, Thursday, the 11th, the church filled without even a stroke of the bell, and I was able once more to address a few serious words to my dear people. I confess it was a relief to me when this meeting was over. The Adolphe Jallas returned to Sefula the following day early, while the king remained with me the whole morning, and wished to accompany me alone part of the way on foot, to rejoin my canoes.

A singular concurrence of circumstances forced me to modify my plans a good deal, in order not to abandon them altogether. I was not able to send my Cape cart from Sefula : some of the boys had given me the slip ; Kamburu himself had not turned up, and he informed me at the last moment that he had fallen ill at the village where he had been stopping. Again ; another man failed me—my good Semonja, a second Nathanael (though a less intelligent one than he of Leribé), who usually accompanies me on my journeys, and was to have done so on this. It was the more curious, as he had a great desire to make the journey with me, and had entreated me not to leave him behind. As he is a man of remarkably serious character, and an important chief—one, too, who professed to have given himself to the Lord—I had consented, thinking that a visit to Khama and to the Churches of Basuto-land might do him good, and strengthen him in the faith. The jealousy of the other chiefs, it seems, made him draw back, added to the importunities of his wife (who is a woman of high rank, a daughter of Sepopa ; and she knows it !) ; so I did not insist. It was in vain for Lewanika to try other plans for me ; they

---

[1] Nolianga still remains true to her profession, and is quite unmolested. But in leaving the king's harem, she had to abandon her royal rank, and work for her living—practically the servant of those women whose equal, if not superior, she had hitherto been.

AT NALOLO—THE QUEEN'S BARGE, AND SITE OF MISSION STATION.

[*To face page* 565.

did not succeed—at least, not in sufficiently good time. So I renounced the water-way, which I had only chosen to diminish the fatigue of the long journey, and to gain a little time.

The canoes only brought me to Nalolo. I arrived there the Saturday morning, a few hours before my friends Adolphe Jalla and E. Béguin from Sefula. The village was almost deserted. But soon after my arrival, the war-drums, the *maoma*, the noisy salutations, and general excitement announced the queen. She was returning from a visit of inspection to a canal, which she also has had dug, to unite the temporary capital she will occupy during the inundations with the river. Mokwaë won't be behind anybody else ; and they say at Nalolo that her canal, like her house, will be the largest and finest in the country.

The next day, we had our service in the *lekhothla*. It was not so well attended as I had expected. To be sure, the women were hidden behind a partition of reeds, and we, placed under a shed, could not even see all the men, who were crouching down anywhere in the shade. There was no lack of speeches : in the space of an hour and a half, we had no less than nine or ten, with a few hymns in between. I say nothing about our own addresses, of which the aim was to present the servants of Jesus Christ as ambassadors to the people of Nalolo, so that no one should be mistaken as to their character or their mission. The address of the Gambella from Lealuyi, who represented the king and spoke in his name, was marked by sound sense. Those of the queen, of her husband, and of the principal chiefs, while expressing their joy in at last possessing the missionary they had so long been begging for, betrayed some natural apprehensions on the thorny subject of slavery. In the afternoon, I once more addressed to these people the appeals and warnings suggested by the prospect of my departure.

I afterwards learnt that the Gambella had strongly, but *secretly*, recommended the queen and her councillors to exercise a strict surveillance as much over M. Béguin's workmen as over his purchases of food. Poor Barotsi, they cannot conceal their weakness ! But all the same, our friends the Béguins have a fine work before them, and a great one. Our brother young, full of enthusiasm and energy : it is pleasant to see, and it fills us with hope for the future, not only of the station he is founding, but also for our beloved Barotsi Mission.

He has already built two rather primitive little huts, by way of taking possession. Apart from the fact that the country is in nowise beautiful, the situation of the station is second only to that of Kazungula. It will be raised on a little mound, commanding the river at the place where it makes a fine bend, constituting the port of this second capital of the kingdom. On all sides, the view extending over the vast plain which we call the Valley is limited only by the horizon. A solitary palm tree, at some little distance, serves as the sole landmark. But wait a little, and the church will arise like a blessed beacon in the land of darkness, and "the wilderness shall blossom like a rose."

SEFULA, *October* 20*th*.

Incredible as it may seem, after my having left Sefula on the day appointed, the 11th, here I am back again! In fact, our last meeting had taken place, we had bidden each other farewell, at the signal of departure the waggon had moved away, and little by little the station was lost to sight among the trees. Scarcely half an hour later, a cracking sound roused me from my thoughts, and the waggon stopped. A spoke in one of the large wheels had broken, and we found that it was quite rotten. The paint had concealed it all from me. What should I have done if such an accident had happened a few days later in the marshes of the Motondo? Happily, we were still close to the station. We brought back my poor mutilated cart, not without difficulty; for in the clearing where we were, my boys, so-called leaders, managed to run it up against a tree and to break the pole.

While M. Adolphe Jalla had gone in haste to Lealuyi to receive the provisions brought by the canoes, M. Béguin, who is very clever with his hands and full of goodwill, threw off his coat, and set to work to mend it. He did so, as quickly and as well as any man not in the trade could have done under the circumstances. A piece of wood was stuck into the place of the broken spoke, and another, green and roughly squared, in that of the pole. The waggon, thus patched up, *grosso modo*, could now proceed; but how far? A more thorough examination proved that it was in a far worse condition than

I had at first imagined. I have neither the taste nor the talent for wheelwright's work, and among the Zambesian boys I had with me not one knows how to handle a tool. It would have been folly—tempting God—to try to undertake such a journey at all risks, with a worm-eaten, rotten, dislocated waggon. After two days of struggles and reflections, I had to recognise the finger of God in all these hindrances, and to renounce my expedition. Much as it had cost me to consent to a journey to Basuto-land, and to maintain my resolution after the news of the departure of my best friend,[1] it cost me no less now to give it up. It was such a sudden and complete upsetting of all my thoughts and plans, that if there had been the slightest possibility of going on I should not have hesitated to do so.

For an old traveller like myself, the fault—and an *inexcusable, unpardonable* one—was that of not having satisfied myself as to the condition of my cart. As I have said, the paint, that cloak of misery—and there are many such in this poor world—and the fact that I had carefully preserved these wheels under cover, had deceived me. Our climate, the wind, the sun, and the sand deteriorate everything : it is heart-breaking. A friend, moved to pity at the thought of our losses and difficulties, had indeed counselled me to get iron wheels ; but the wheels alone are not enough, and then they would have to be constructed with a view to our sands. Others have advised camels ! Where should we procure them ?

With a little common sense and foresight at the right time, how much work, how much fatigue and trouble, I should have saved myself. Nevertheless, I cannot help thinking there must be a purpose in it, both for the people and for myself. God forbid that I should hesitate when He sends me, or run when He holds me back ! A soldier does not dispute the orders of his chief, however strange and contradictory they may appear. So I shall calmly return to Lealuyi, and put myself into harness again. Adolphe Jalla would have been overwhelmed by the work and the manual labour both at once, and Willie Mokalapa[2] by the increasing school, which numbers already more than one hundred and ninety-five pupils ! " How glad I am," wrote dear Adolphe, " of the decision you have made to remain, and

[1] M. Mabille, who had just died, May 20th, 1894. See Introduction.
[2] A Basuto catechist newly arrived.

not to venture into the desert with this miserable waggon!
For, in view of the present spiritual awakening, it is important,
to say the least, that you should not be absent, and I firmly
believe that God has stopped you to bring you back here."

This awakening I have already spoken about. It continues.
I had just retraced my steps with my invalided carriage, when
letters reached me from Kazungula. What refreshing news!
Our brother Louis Jalla tells me that, among others, one of
my former boys, Likulela, whom Litia had taken away from
our house,[1] has also publicly declared himself for the Saviour;
and he has given them satisfaction and pleasure during several
months, just as he did to us.

And then Litia himself wrote to me, expressing his repentance, and his ardent desire to return to his God. I guessed
the rest when I received from our evangelist Willie Mokalapa
the following note :—

"According to the desire and at the request of the king,
I am letting you know, my father, that Litia has written to
him, humbling himself for his wanderings, and informing him
of his return to God. He asks the king's authority for sending
away his second wife, and exhorts him to hesitate no longer,
but to give himself to Jesus, and accept him as his Saviour.
He quotes John iii. 16, and adds, underlining the words, that
he that believes is not condemned. The king has answered: 'I
am very glad to hear that you are taking your place again
among the children of God. But I rejoice with trembling.
Is your profession to-day any more sincere than that of yesterday? What proof have I? Be a man to-day, be true, and do
not again deceive God, the missionaries, and the nation. Yes,
send away Mokena. You have been a stumbling-block to every
one. I myself felt ashamed and sorry when the missionaries
spoke of you as a renegade. My councillors, believing me to
be on the point of becoming converted, said, "How can you
think of it! Here is your son, who has been brought up
by the missionaries, and taught by them—he had even believed
these things, and now he denies them! Is it not a proof that
there is nothing good or true in them?" Perhaps one day
I too shall enter into them.'"

[1] See page 442.

However pessimistic my views of the present movement may be, it is undeniable that it is sufficiently pronounced to turn the thoughts of the people towards the things of God. "Now, faith cometh by hearing, and hearing by the Word of God." So why should we not dare to expect great things? What is there impossible to our God? Is His arm shortened, that He cannot save? Has His ear grown heavy, that He should not hear?[1]

[1] With regard to Litia's return, M. L. Jalla wrote: "He arrived [at Kazungula to be installed as official chief], and was received with immense enthusiasm, especially as this year his father had given him the right to the royal salutation, the *shoalela*. With Litia, a new era seemed to be beginning. A few days after his arrival, he banished the native beer from the village, and officially declared that he had renounced the invocation of his ancestors and consultation of sorcerers; and he urged all his subordinates to attend the services and send their children to school, saying the missionaries had come not only for the chiefs, but for everybody, men and women alike. All that of his own accord. . . . Instead of inaugurating his village by a heathen ceremony, he requested me to consecrate its founding by prayer to God. Of course, I acceded; and on the day of the ceremony, Litia publicly repeated all these declarations. Having united with us one Monday evening for the meeting of converts, he made us a frank and humble declaration of breaking with the world and giving himself to God. 'Henceforth,' said he to these young men and women (the converts), ' I am one of you. I look on you as my brothers, for I too desire to be a child of God, and ask of Him the strength to be faithful to Him this time.'

"The next Sunday (October 7th, 1894), Litia rose once more before a numerous audience, and said to the crowd, 'Henceforth, do not look on me as one of you any more, for I have broken with the bonds of Satan in order to become a child of God. If I have sent away my second wife, it was not because I did not love her, nor yet because there was anything between us. I did it solely to obey God, and serve Him. Make haste and be converted to Him, now that He gives you the chance, and removes all hindrances. You shall not say any more that it is your masters that hinder you.'"

Africa has been the grave of so many Christian professions, both native and European, that one dares not build too much upon Litia's present promise. But since the foregoing events, his conduct has been exemplary, both as a chief and as a convert. As to the marriage question, *the* crux of African chiefs, he is not only a monogamist, but he (alone among his countrymen) accords to his wife the position in which Christian marriage places her: every day she and their child sit down to table together, European fashion. This may seem a trifling matter in our eyes, but nothing could proclaim more loudly to his people that he had forsaken a heathen harem for a Christian home.

CHAPTER XXXVI

A Parish Visitation—The King's Mother—Two Staunch Conservatives—The
Resurrection—Wina and the Question of Polygamy—Hugging their
Chains—A Royal Baby—A Little Prisoner—Photography under Diffi-
culties—Nyondo's Wedding—Christian *v.* Heathen Marriage—Paulus's
Zeal outruns Discretion—Before Governors and Kings—The Christians
acquitted—Sickness—The Water Supply—The Bible School begun—
The New Year.

LEALUYI, *November 24th,* 1894.

WORK on the great canal of the capital is at an end, at
least for this year : the canal, dry only the other day,
is now flowing on a level with its banks, and canoes go to
and fro, drifting and crossing one another incessantly. The
Barotsi are proud of it, and so are we. The capital is overflowing with people who are returning home—the Makoma,
Mayéyé, and others. It is a good opportunity for evangelisation,
so I take my book and stick, and start.

My first visit is to the king's old mother, Inonge. She is
ill ; she gives me a lengthy diagnosis of her case. Her heart, it
seems, is no longer in its place ; it is suspended above her lungs ;
it throbs and throbs, comes up into her throat, and then——I
spare you the rest.

I touch on the things of God. She hates them. Poor old
woman ! she is eminently conservative. She has never once set
foot inside the church. *She* in church, indeed !

" All my children, grandchildren, sons-in-law, and daughters-
in-law are there," she says. " How could I see myself with them ?
It could not be. And then, I have no legs."

This is a hyperbole which does not prevent her from going
about, and even travelling. But I seized the opportunity to
tell her the story of the man sick of the palsy, which surprised
her very much. She laughed heartily at the idea of being

570

brought to the church by four of her men. For anything else, it would only be quite natural. To turn the conversation, which had become slightly embarrassing to her, she began to beg. Upon this, I rose and left. She kept back my boy to pour out her full heart to him. I am such a miser, it seems ; " formerly, yes, formerly, I knew she was the mother of my brother (the king), and I did not forget her. Now I give her nothing, not even a woollen blanket."

Stage by stage, house by house, at last I reach the dwelling of Narubutu, another conservative, like old Inonge, also old and blind : he retains all his faculties, and possesses them in a marked degree. No one has had so great an influence as he, as much in public affairs as over Lewanika himself. I always enjoy a talk with him ; we are great friends. This time, it is he who begins upon me.

" I am dying of dulness," he says ; " I have no one to talk to. You have told me to pray to God, your God ; but if this God of yours were true and good as you say, He would have cured me long ago. And you, have you any affection for me ? I don't believe you have, although you tell me so. If you had, you would have persuaded God to restore my sight long ago, since you are His servant, and stand well with Him."

" You are old, Narubutu."

" What do you say, Moruti ? Blind because I am old ? My brother is older than I am, and he is not blind. Why should *I* be ? "

" God permits such things that we may seek Him. He does to us what wise parents do to their children ; it is His rod, and He only uses it to make us *good*. Ah, my friend, if you too were to change, everything within you would be light, peace, and joy."

" Light ? Nonsense ! Do you mean to say that I should see God ? Who has seen Him. Have you ? "

" Tell me, Narubutu, have you a soul ? "

" Of course I have one : who doubts it ? "

" But have you seen it ? "

" Of course not : can anybody see his soul ? I only know I have one. But," continued the old man, as if to elude my conclusion, and as if a new idea had come into his head, " where does one go to when one is dead ? We Barotsi say that the soul goes to the gods (*melimo*) somewhere, but I do not know where."

I read him several passages of the Word of God on this subject. John v. 28, 29,[1] struck him, and he interrupted me with,—

" What ! you say that the dead, *the dead*, will rise again, and see God ? Rubbish ! Lies ! "

He burst into a loud fit of laughter. By this time, the courts of his harem were full of men, who laughed too, and applauded by clapping their hands.

" Don't laugh so much, my friends ; this is not nonsense. It is a certain truth that the dead will rise again : all those will rise who die, whether hunting, travelling, on the river, or in the deserts,—those whom you have burnt as sorcerers, those you have killed ; children, old people, slaves, masters—*all !* "

Fresh bursts of laughter, but short-lived ones.

" You say," said old Narubutu, " that all will live again, even sorcerers, and my children, my grandchildren, myself ! It is not possible ; it is not true. What is dead, is dead, and does not live again."

" Really ! You are evidently not aware that the thing has already happened. A Man was put to death ; His hands and feet were nailed to two pieces of wood crossed. He was so completely dead, that, when they pierced His side, congealed blood came out—blood and water. He was put into a tomb ; but on the third day, He came out alive. It is an incontestable fact. This Man was God's own Son, the same Who spoke the words which have so surprised you." And then I read Rev. vii. 9 :—

" I beheld, and lo, a great multitude, which no man could number, of all nations, and kindreds, and people, and tongues, stood before the throne, and before the Lamb, clothed with white robes, and palms in their hands."

" What do you say to that ? "

" I say," said the old man pensively, " that if it is true, it is very astounding."

Then leaving him to his reflections, I took up my seat, and went to sit in the great court, filled with people who had come

---

[1] "The hour is coming in the which all that are in the graves shall hear His voice, and shall come forth ; they that have done good, unto the resurrection of life ; and they that have done evil, unto the resurrection of damnation."

to greet Narubutu before returning home. Their faces lighted
up. I had first to renew acquaintance (for I have a bad memory
for names, alas! and they know it) with each chief of a little
village,—here one to whom I gave some medicine I know not
when; there another who had met me I know not where. And
then, when I resumed the subject of the Resurrection of the dead
and of the Last Judgment, you should have seen all the craning
necks, fixed eyes, motionless heads. If only I could visit them
at home!

Soon afterwards I found myself at Wina's. He is a *sekomboa*,
an important personal servant of the king—a true Zacchæus
among these gigantic Barotsi. He is remarkably gentle and
amiable, and comes regularly to the services, always dressed
up in a soldier's tunic, of what origin I know not. His eyes,
rather dull, like those of most of our blacks, nevertheless denote
much intelligence. His court, too, was full of strangers. His
wife is there, a pleasant young woman, caressing a baby. I
caress it too, which sets every one at their ease and smiling.
So there I am one of them at once.

Wina began by asking me questions about conversion, and the
most intelligent among his visitors did the same. I encouraged
this, and answered every one and everything. The conversation
became very animated; everybody was interested.

At last, before getting up, "Tell me, Wina, my friend," I
said, "tell me why you are not converted—you who know the
truth so well?"

"But I *am* going to be converted. Certainly we shall
become Christians in time. Do you not see how Lewanika is
opening the way for us? Only wait a little; have patience.
We are coming."

"Don't talk to me about others; speak about yourself. You
are going to be converted: you are coming—but *when*? Have
you fixed the day? Tell me. Why not to-day—now?"

He hung his head.

"Because I am afraid," he said; "the law of God is hard,
difficult."

I made him read Matt. xi. 28-30, word by word: "My yoke
is easy."

"I understand," he said, with a long sigh. "But—but, you
see——"

" Now, my friend, tell me frankly what your difficulty is."

" My difficulty is that of all the Barotsi ; it is the *women*. How is it possible for a *Moruti* to live with only one wife, and be satisfied and happy ? "

" Ah, yes ! the women," repeated all the men, who filled the court.

His wife added, " Neither do *we* want a Gospel which forbids several women to belong to one man, to help each other, and keep each other company."

I looked very straight at her.

" Are you speaking the truth, woman ?   Then what is that malady which consumes you all, what you call *lefoufa* (harem jealousy) ? "

They all clapped their hands.   " That is well said ! "

" Oh," said the poor woman, with some confusion, " I was not speaking seriously.   I just wanted to see what you would say."

" Ah ! very possibly.   But *I* am quite serious."   Then turning to Wina, I said to him, " I quite understand you, my friend ; of course, it must cost you a great deal to give up your wives and all your carnal pleasures.   But suppose you are eating dry bread " (a great privation for the blacks, and a hard necessity), " and I am eating mine with honey " (which the Barotsi chiefs consider a great delicacy, and try to keep for their own exclusive use), " tell me, would you not envy me ? And if you saw me sharing these delights with other friends, and left you on one side, what would you say ?   If, on the contrary, I were to say, ' Wina, leave your dry bread, and come and share my honey ' ? "

" Oh, I should clap my hands ! " (laughter).

" Well, that is just what I am doing.   You are still gnawing the stale, old bread of polygamy and all your old customs.   I have found in the things of God a honey which is my daily delight.   I invite you, I press you, to come and eat out of the same dish with me.   You hesitate, and laugh disdainfully, and say to me, ' I cannot forsake the dry, old crust that I am gnawing.'   If you would only taste my honey, how you would laugh with joy !   You would say, ' How stupid I was to stick so obstinately to that dry, stale bread, like a poor slave, when I could be eating honey to my heart's content, like a great lord ! ' "

The lesson was understood, and I left them all to repeat it

and comment on it at their leisure.   Ah, how I wish I could pass it on to *all* those who are hesitating between the deceitful joys of the world and the service of the Lord Jesus !

December 7th.

Litia, when he left for Kazungula, had asked me to send him the photograph of his child, whom Lewanika is keeping here to bring up.   He is now a little fellow of two.   But, would you believe it? no one has yet seen his face beyond the circle of his near relatives and the slaves attached to his service. Nobody is *supposed* to know his name, nor yet whether he is a boy or a girl.   For two years, none but those in his service have entered the court where he is growing up ; and if he himself has been obliged to go out, it is only wrapped up in furs to the point of suffocation.   If he has to travel in a canoe, he is carried thither, hidden in this way.   And then, once he is deposited in his tent of mats, they are careful to close it at both ends.   This is the lot of all children of the blood royal.   At length, one day it happens that the little captive, carried away by impatience, upsets the reed door, and darts jubilantly out into the open air, followed by his stupefied slaves !   Then there is nothing for it but to present him to the king in the evening, and to grant him that liberty which makes the happiness of the poor.   You understand ; it is the *evil eye* that they fear, although the poor little prisoner is covered with amulets.   There is probably another reason—namely, the mystery which generally imposes on the vulgar.   The Barotsi kings pretend to a divine origin ; and, to put it mildly, they certainly like to remind the people of it.

So this is the dear little visitor brought me with Lewanika's express authority by Maondo, one of the king's wives, an intelligent and amiable person, who has charge of him.   Poor little fellow ! she showed him to me, a big bundle very carefully wrapped up, carried on the back of a slave.   " Would I not, at the king's request, consent to take the little prince's likeness ? " " Certainly—but I cannot take it, hidden as he is in that bundle. She must unpack him."

Great was her trouble—long and earnestly she pleaded. Making one concession after another, she would have consented to unpack him (I had enjoyed the privilege of seeing him a long time ago, so apparently *I* have not the evil eye), but it must be in my room, with the windows carefully closed ; she would even have consented to my doing it in the court, on condition that I ordered all our boys and girls and all our workmen to hide. It was no use arguing—all my eloquence was so much waste of breath ; she would not yield, nor I either ; and, astounded at my obstinacy, she returned home sadly with her great bundle, without having unpacked it.[1]

This incident, apparently insignificant, would alone suffice to show how the Barotsi cling to their customs, while themselves recognising that they are unreasonable and bad. For a long while yet, these will be hidden shoals to our poor Barotsi Christians.

December 29th.

We have had our festivals, and an extra one thrown in, nothing less than Nyondo's marriage. Do you know who Nyondo is ? He was a poor Moshukulumboe, a slave of the king, who obtained leave to come to us, so as to attend the school. He has been converted, and is a real joy to us. His gravity is imperturbable ; if he laughs, it is only by accident, especially in presence of his superiors ; he is very reserved, a man of few words, but truthful and honest—it was not always so. In my house, he has almost taken the place of Nguana-Ngombé. The good qualities he has developed since becoming a Christian have won for him the king's esteem ; and, I need not say, my own affection. He is not very intelligent, but he has a heart, and I discovered it when I least expected it. His greatest desire is to become an evangelist-schoolmaster. The king is aware of this, and gives him full liberty.

He engaged himself to a young girl whom he had obtained from the king (although the latter much appreciated her services) and had placed with Mme. A. Jalla, where she developed in every way, and was eventually converted.

This was the marriage which took place on December 21st, the first to be celebrated in Lealuyi. We expected to see a crowd. But no ! The church was not full, the benches only

---

[1] Eventually, but not till weeks later, she consented to unroll the royal infant, and he was photographed in the mission-court before children and slaves.

KABAKO RIVER – RAPIDS ABOVE THE FALLS (EXPLORED BY F. COILLARD).

[*To face page* 577.

moderately occupied. The king was there with some of his *likomboa*; but none of the great chiefs, except Semonja, who is a Christian. The ceremony was none the less very impressive. In my address, I necessarily made a point of bringing out the Divine institution of Christian marriage, in contrast with the sores and rottenness of polygamy; and the position of a Christian wife with that of heathen women.

I wondered whether they had really understood me. Understand? They understood so well, that my whole discourse was carried from door to door and commented on, till the whole village was in a ferment. The men were furious; the women wondered "what they had done to make God angry."

December 31st.

That was Friday. We were celebrating Christmas on Sunday. The execution of our well-prepared hymns and choruses was as good as we dared to hope from the materials we had to work with. The evangelists were there,—Paulus Kanedi, from Sefula; Jacob Moshabesha, from Nalolo; and our Willie: so it was a good opportunity for Gospel-preaching. Adolphe Jalla opened the service with a splendid address: "The Subject of Joy" [*i.e.* the Birth of Christ]. The others followed. But Paulus, our Boanerges, launched thunderbolts: he spoke like one inspired, addressing all classes of his audience by turns—the queens, the slaves, the chiefs, the king, each one had his account to settle. Oh why were these powerful, these most solemn appeals accompanied by an unfortunate gesture—*the* most unfortunate imaginable? Paulus pointed with his finger at his hearers! That was bad enough for the general public; but when he addressed himself directly to the king, there was almost an explosion. We ourselves knew nothing of this; we never even suspected it. But when we were outside, it burst all bounds; every group was expressing itself without reserve. Anywhere, the forefinger of an orator shaken in a person's face is in doubtful taste; but here, and among all black people, it is the gravest insult that a man can offer to another! Only, our worthy Paulus thought that everything was permitted to a preacher, even this unfortunate gesture, without its giving offence. He made a mistake. In the afternoon, none of the *likomboa* and none of the chiefs were at the second service, not even the king.

This was a bad sign. The very next day, two men came, in the name of the chiefs, to summon the evangelists and some of our boys to the *lekhothla*. Being too unwell to drag myself thither,[1] I was compelled to ask M. Adolphe Jalla to go, hoping that his presence would act as a restraint on the Barotsi, and insisted that the king should himself preside over the court. From 10 a.m. till 5 p.m., we were the prey of terrible anxieties. I was, above all, concerned about my boys, and could only confide them to the Lord, Whom they were called upon to confess. For themselves, they had neither shame nor fear. They were at once put in the place of the accused—that is to say, of the *condemned* ; they also knew, that in all probability they would not leave the place without being cruelly garotted, and—who knows what more beside ?

M. Adolphe Jalla will tell you of the courage and grace God gave to our young men ; the outrageous insults which the excited chiefs rained upon their heads, and upon those of the evangelists. He will tell you of the terrible moment of suspense which elapsed between the defence our brothers made for themselves and the king's speech, and the astonishment of hearing him frankly and without the least ambiguity take the part of our boys, our evangelists, and ourselves, and partially unveil the intrigues of the chiefs, who clung to futile pretexts, in order to vent the hatred with which the Gospel inspires them. God be praised ! It is a deliverance ; I scarcely dare to say a victory. For these old limbs of paganism will not allow themselves to be beaten, and will be sure to hatch other plots. But the final issue is not doubtful, and that gives us courage and joy. It will strengthen our young Christians.[2]

What has saddened us in this affair is the conduct of my friend Semonja, the influential chief who generally accompanies me on my journeys. He is converted, and is both amiable and earnest ; but he was afraid to take our part. He came to-day

---

[1] M. Coillard was seriously ill at this time.

[2] Paulus frankly apologised for his unintentional discourtesy, and protested the respect he felt and had always shown for the king. "But," he concluded, "that will not prevent me from speaking the truth and warning you about your sins."

It was after this speech that Lewanika astonished every one by taking the evangelists' part.

(the 31st) to humble himself for his behaviour. But such cowardice makes one anxious.

The Adolphe Jallas left on Saturday for Nalolo. So I was alone with the evangelist, to whom I gave the whole of the first part of the service, reserving the preaching for myself. At the door, I was warned that the chiefs had driven away all the young men from the bench in front of them. Coming in, followed by Lewanika, I made them sit down in the place I had indicated, and in a short speech I quietly explained to them that the House of God is not their *lekhothla*, where every one has his assigned place. At home, a chief is everything : at court, he is only a servant. In the same way, when we come to church, we leave all our dignities and grandeurs at the door : here, God alone is Master, He alone is great. Then I preached on Luke xix. 14 : "We will not have this man to reign over us." In the afternoon, the Gambella sent me as a present two beautiful paddles. Why ? There was no message.

I think I have discovered the clue to all this excitement. They fear that the king will become a Christian ; and that when he has dispersed his whole harem, he will abolish polygamy, and force his chiefs and every one else to content themselves each with one wife.[1]

I have had a bad attack of hæmaturia ; for more than a fortnight, I have only been able to drag myself about ; but I am better, though not very grand yet. I do not want to complain ; but it is only right you should know that I am not good for much. My heart is still young—I feel it ; but the old tent is wearing out.

I hope to reopen my Bible school the day after to-morrow, after the Christmas holidays. A Bible school on the Zambesi ! This title is pretentious. I have only four pupils, whom I clothe and feed, and who manage my domestic work, such as it is. They are my children, as well as my pupils. They are housed in two huts, one with a big hole and a little hole, which serve as door and window ; it is the schoolroom ; four posts stuck in the ground and a couple of boards form the table.

---

[1] And so it was. Old Narubutu and the Gambella went one night secretly to see the king, expostulated with him, and, getting angry, declared that they would not have a Christian for king. Lewanika foresaw a revolution, and forthwith drew back from conversion.—*Author's Note.*

The other hut is the dormitory, which they keep fairly clean. The number of these pupils might be doubled or tripled; but, for the time being, I keep to these four. The scarcity of food is one reason; another is that the character of our young Zambesians requires to be tested, and their vocation no less.

Moreover, it is only a trial—a little beginning here. My inclinations certainly do not lead me to shut myself up for three or four hours with a class: far from it. I should like to have wings, in order to travel about the country and publish the Gospel—the Good News. I chafe at our being thus penned up at home. We see many crowds of strangers here, and we do our best to send them away with at any rate some spark of truth. But preaching to them here is not reaching them at home. I have been forced by circumstances thus to busy myself with these young men, whom, as you know, I was reluctant to send to Basuto-land. It is certainly not that I have anything against the Bible school at Morija, for you know how I love it. But we must not make Basuto of our Zambesians. We need a Bible school *here*.

You will be sorry to hear that my predictions about Sefula have been only too fully realised. The winds which precede the rainy season have been extraordinarily violent this year, and they have broken a large tree, which has fallen on the saw-mill, seriously damaging the roof and almost bringing the walls down. It is very sad to think of all that splendid machinery left there to get ruined, when a man of Waddell's stamp could save so much of it, and be such a help to us.

Our church here is not finished. Will it ever be? We have fifteen large holes in the walls instead of windows and doors. The windows we have covered with calico, which had to be renewed more than once, though we certainly have none to spare. But no calico, however strong, could withstand these gales; it is torn to shreds like paper; indeed, the whole building is a perfect Cave of the Winds. You can have no conception of their violence; I trembled for the church itself. So all those windows you see in the photograph, and several others, I had perforce to fill in with reeds. I only left just enough open for us to have light inside to see by.

According to our latest news, Waddell was still at Kazungula, eating his heart out. How I do regret that he did not return

with me! He would have been able to repair the waggon a
little, and by this time we should both of us have been well
on our way southwards. For myself, a medical examination
is almost as necessary as for him.[1] But how travel without
a vehicle?

I think one of the principal causes of our illnesses here
is the water we are obliged to use. The first rains sweep, or
rather wash, down the country, and thus the lake from which
we draw our water becomes the common sewer. Bad at all
times, it does not keep twelve hours then, and acquires a smell
and taste which make one feel sick. It is impossible to swallow
the morning cup of coffee. I have two filters, but they don't
work well, either of them.

While scribbling all this, here I find myself using my pen
for the first time on January 1st, 1895. My good wishes for the
New Year will reach you late, but I send them all the same.
Ah, those good wishes, how easy they are to utter, and how
every one will be offering them in all parts to-day! And after
a few days, who will think of them? That is not the case
with us. Members of the same missionary family, knowing
and loving one another, sharing the anxieties, responsibilities,
and joys of the same work, we do not need the New Year to
remind us of each other, do we? Only, the year is gone, and
the new one which comes to us with all its store of blessings
and trials, unknown and unthought of, sets on our mutual
intercessions a seal of special solemnity. What should we ask?
Do we know? Let us simply lay our friends, our beloved
ones, together with the work of our hearts and lives, at the
Lord's feet; and let us say in faith: "Lord, they are Thine
—bless them! Yes, bless them! 'O satisfy us early [Fr. Ver.
each morning] with Thy mercy; that we may rejoice and be
glad all our days. *Make us glad according to the days wherein
Thou hast afflicted us. . . . Let Thy work appear unto Thy servants,
and Thy glory unto their children. And let the beauty of the
Lord our God be upon us ; . . . yea, the work of our hands establish Thou it.'*"

---

[1] The Committee had already urged M. Coillard some time before to
return to Europe on furlough; but he declined, feeling that the staff was too
small, and that his young colleagues would be overwhelmed with the work.
Since then, reinforcements had come out.

CHAPTER XXXVII

The Drought—Medical Missions—M. and Mme. Béguin at Nalolo—A Visit to Sefula—Locusts—The Return of a Prodigal (Mokamba)—A Bible-woman—A Real Awakening—Average Rainfall—Royal Pretensions.

SEFULA, *April 1st*, 1895.

IF I fall into the conventionalities of those idle people in civilised life who can only talk about the weather, so much the worse for my correspondents ; but it is a fact that the past season has been an extraordinary one. The rains, which begin regularly towards November 20th, were two months late ; and, instead of the heavy downpours which flood everything, we have had suffocating heat, a fiery sun, and burning winds which swept the clouds away as soon as they formed on the horizon. At the end of February, by which date the plain has usually been under water for eight weeks, one could easily cross it on foot. Our Barotsi were miserable ; they had not seen such a thing for twenty years, and they had already given this phenomenal year the name of "walk on foot," "walk dry-shod" (*oka enda banje*). For, to them, no inundation means no hunting, no furs for the winter, no change of residence, and that does not suit their roving disposition. But there is another side to it, which affects us all—namely, illnesses, such as influenza, ague, and above all fevers, which rage as much among the natives as among the Europeans, and spare few.

Consultations without appointment, and the dispensing of medicines, are by no means recreations. The *Moruti's* post is no sinecure at such a time. Not a day passes without our regretting the absence of a professional doctor amongst us.

Is our urgent appeal from Kazungula really to remain without an echo ? Has no man of that profession yet felt himself called of God to this vocation, the grandest that exists ? To go from village to village, doing good, healing the sick, and preach-

582

ing the Gospel of the Kingdom of God after the example of
Jesus Himself, and walking in His footsteps! Is there upon
earth, I wonder, a calling more worthy of a young Christian's
holy ambition?

Oh, if I could but grow young again, how ardently I would
apply myself to the study of medicine! And, thus furnished
with the fullest possible equipment, medical and theological,
with what joy I would go forth to relieve the physical and
moral miseries of these poor heathen! They do not understand how it is that the messengers of Jesus "who healed all
manner of disease" cannot cure those of the body as well as
those of the soul. A cure is in their eyes a proof of our
apostleship. And can we blame them?

Every member of the mission party has had fever, and here
is Mlle. Louise Keck, who, in despair of ever acclimatising
herself, is returning South. And we had hailed her arrival with
such joy and hope!

Above all, our poor friends the Béguins have suffered. The
reports we heard about them startled us, and I went to Nalolo
to see them a few weeks ago. They were then comparatively
better, and thus my visit resolved itself into a mere friendly call.
I found them in a wretched hut, dark and stuffy, quite blocked
up with their boxes. They had reserved a little corner, which
they used as a bedroom, and another still smaller one, which
they called their dining-hall, though you have almost to eat
off your thumb for want of space; there is even a third, which
they dignify by the name of drawing-room, on the strength of
two chairs which are crowded into it. I felt quite grieved for
them, for this young lady especially, so recently severed from
the comforts of civilised life.[1] But the activity of our young
brother, from whom energy seems to issue at every pore; the
courage and unflagging spirits of his young wife, in this rude

[1] Mme. Béguin (the only daughter of a professor at the University
of Lausanne) had left a luxurious home less than two years before. Though
she was a mere girl, and had occupied herself with nothing but music and
painting since leaving school, she accommodated herself to the uncivilised
life without the slightest difficulty or discontent. Speaking generally, the
testimony of the Zambesi missionaries is that the most highly cultivated
adapt themselves the most quickly and easily to the new conditions, and the
women better than the men. As regards health, that of the former has been
incomparably better than that of the latter.

apprenticeship, through which we all have to pass; the smiles of their flourishing baby,—all combined to form a happy contrast, and did me real good.   Soon these dear young friends will install themselves in the large temporary house which M. Béguin has already reared.   It will be a palace to them.

Their work is still in those difficult *first stages*, when missionaries and natives are seeking to know and educate each other.   Mokwaë and her councillors never lose sight of their dignity; and they are nowise modest in their pretensions. They take it very ill, when one seeks to bind them down to anything like a rule, even for the Sunday services.   Nevertheless, little by little our friends are establishing their position. Here, too, a little "tabernacle" has been erected, which can shelter half the audience.   The services are well attended; and the school, under the devoted care of Jacob and his wife Norea, is flourishing splendidly.   Here, too, they speak of earnest souls who will declare themselves some day.   One can scarcely believe that this station has been founded so recently, and we praise God for it.

But I am forgetting—it was about Sefula that I wanted to speak.   For some time, I had been thinking of paying a visit there—a visit I dreaded as much as I desired it.   Circumstances made it an imperative duty to do so.   Besides the work, which is developing admirably, and requires our superintendence, our evangelist Paulus and his wife are always ill, especially the latter.   The dear man wrote very gloomily; and he had reason to.   He was thinking about his death, and was asking his friends what his young widow would do.   Both are terribly emaciated, though the serenity of their inner life is reflected on their wan faces.

I therefore left Lealuyi last Tuesday with my five boys—my whole household.   From the flooded plain, we entered our own canal, full to the brim.   Alas! about three-quarters of a mile from the station, we found it so blocked with sand and tangled grass—those invincible *matindi*—that the stream overflows on every side, forming pools and marshes into which one sinks up to the knees.   It is a work to be done all over again; but it would have cost very little to keep it up, if there had been a missionary at Sefula.   My boys, who knew I was not well, seized a little canoe they found there, and cheerfully carried

it from pool to pool, determined I should make the journey
dry-shod ; and at last landed me on *terra firma*.   I did the rest
of the road on foot.

We forced our way through clouds of locusts, the scourge
of the country. We have them at Lealuyi, but nothing to
compare with what we find hereabouts. They have hatched
themselves, and grown up here on the borders of the plain,
and in the brushwood. Their wings are too weak for them
to fly high and far, for they have only just cast their skin ;
you raise swarms of them at every step you take, while passing
over masses which remain piled up on the ground. They have
devoured the fields of maize, manioc, and sorgho—they spare
absolutely nothing. The people are making desperate efforts
to dispute with them anything edible that remains. When
they fly, the shrill and incessant cries of men and women,
accompanied by violent gestures, make them rise, and the wind
carries them off ; but when they are in the first stage, that
of a wingless cricket, they go straight on, and nothing stops
them : they cross water by swimming, and we are told that
their serried battalions even extinguish the grass fires, by
which the fields are surrounded. Every one is fearing famine,
and already provisions are scarce and dear. Yet we are told
this is only the beginning. But a very curious thing is the
mortality among the locusts. They are found everywhere in
great numbers on the ground, heaped together, clinging to
shrubs and blades of grass ; you think they are alive—you look
closely at them, and they are all dried up. And, from what
I hear, it is the same in the provinces of Sesheke and Kazungula.
Some unknown *nyaka* (witch-doctor) will not lose the opportunity of claiming it as the result of his " medicines " and
cabalistic incantations. Intelligent men say that they are
poisoned by eating certain noxious plants. It is possible ; but
we believe that God has heard the prayers of His children,
and has had compassion on this people.

In spite of the desolate aspect of the station, and the
recollections which every corner and every object call up, one
breathes here an atmosphere of calm which is unknown at the
capital. It is good to be here again under the shade, to
meditate in the solemn silences of these woods. And there, at
a stone's throw, under that ancient tree, how near one feels to

heaven! Involuntarily my thoughts go out to those many friends who are also in bereavement. *Sursum corda.* It is not at the place of parting that we should halt; no, nor yet at that turn of the road where we bade those supreme farewells that wrung our hearts and darkened our lives. Our beloved ones are no longer there. It is to the place and the hour of reunion that our hopes and desires look on—to the Father's house, where our beloved ones have gone before us, where Jesus awaits us, whither each footstep bears us on, and where God Himself will wipe away all tears from our eyes. God is not the God of the dead, but of the living. Let us seek Him not among the dead, but amid that cloud of witnesses who compass us about.

But, among the ruins of Sefula, I would like to gather you one or two flowers at least.

The movement of which you have heard already, and which arose simultaneously in all our stations, though perhaps in a less degree than at Kazungula, where it began, was very marked at Sefula. The number of those who have made a profession is already over eighty. No doubt all that is not pure gold, but some of it certainly is. The numerous meetings we have had during the last eight or ten days have thoroughly convinced me of it. Besides my own young men, who took an active part in it, two Christians from Lealuyi had followed me. One was Semonja, or Sebeho—the Barotsi always have several names—a man in the prime of life, who is under the king's orders always to accompany me on my journeys. He says himself that a long while ago, under the influence of the Gospel teaching, he sent away two of his three wives, before having made the least profession. I knew nothing of it, and indeed thought he had only been married once. But besides his remarkable evenness of temper, his considerateness, and his thoughtful and respectful conduct, there was an indefinable something about him which won my heart, and imparted to my journeys a charm of which I have never spoken. And when his heart was touched by grace, I felt more joy than surprise. There has been no stumbling in his case. On one occasion,[1] he troubled us by his lack of courage, but he repented of that.

[1] See page 578.

The other is Mokamba, the same young man who wept over
his sins, during the last meeting my dear wife attended, and
impressed her so deeply.   Since then, he had wandered from
the right way.   Having become a great chief, young as he was
he took several wives to maintain his dignity, and later on
he became the king's son-in-law, instead of our poor Nguana-
Ngombé.   But his conscience gave him no rest, and during a
long journey he made, it awoke irresistibly.   On his return, he
found his first wife converted, and then he hesitated no longer.
He had already sent away his inferior wives ; he dismissed one
last one to whom he had clung, and declared himself frankly
for the Saviour whom he had forsaken.   He unites unusual
gentleness with great force of character.   The presence of these
two Christian chiefs has made a deep impression here.

Yesterday, apart from the prayer meeting with which it
began and ended, was divided between two great meetings,
each lasting about three hours.   The first was a general meeting.
The heathen, in spite of the locusts, against whom the poor
things were desperately defending their fields, came hurrying
in from every side.   The church was full.   After I had introduced the subject of Lot fleeing from Sodom, I left my young
men and these two Christian chiefs to speak.   A tone of great
respect and seriousness characterised the addresses of my boys,
and they enforced attention.

Semonja, a typical Morotsi, spoke with conviction, calmness,
and authority.   I was surprised to see how he captivated
the audience by his address—a long one for a Morotsi.   But
Mokamba did not merely captivate them ; he carried them
along with him.   " They ask me," he said, " why I have
abandoned these *mekhoa ea lefeela*" (these vain customs)
" we have learnt from our fathers.   It is because Christ has
delivered us from them at the cost of His Blood.   They ask
me why, four years ago, I wept and sobbed in that great
assembly at the *lekhothla*.   Why ?   Ah ! it was because the
destruction of Sodom was not a mere threat to me.   My own
house was on fire.   And when I awoke from my sleep of death,
it was not by the door that I flung myself out.   No, I forced
a hole through the wall, I know not how, at the risk of being
scratched by the broken reeds.   But once I was outside, prostrate
on the earth, and stripped of everything, realising the danger I

had been in, I began to tremble, to weep with joy and emotion. I was saved. You tell me that I shall return to the world. Yes, if I forsake Jesus. But do you know, at one time the current had already carried me away? I should have been swept into the abyss, and have perished" (an allusion to the Musi oa Tunya, the Victoria Falls). "Jesus came with His canoe; He seized me and placed me on the bank. And shall I throw myself into the waves again? God forbid!" Urgent appeals followed, something quite new to me at the Zambesi.

The second meeting was still more characteristic. It was exclusively a meeting for professing Christians, who, as at Lealuyi, are divided into three classes, according to their age, their degree of knowledge, and the satisfaction they give us. All were not present, yet there were nearly seventy, amongst whom were ten children, a few young girls and youths, men and women, former workmen, our old acquaintances, who were once so hardened and insensible.

After a few words of introduction, I allowed any one to speak who chose. Men and women availed themselves of the permission, and with surprising liberty.

One woman, a true Bible-woman, for she knows how to read, related her evangelising tours.

"Come, come," said some heathen to her, "what you are telling us is all nonsense. You who say you believe, have you ever seen the God that the white men speak of? You pray: does your bread fall out of the sky?"

"No one has ever seen God," she replied, "but He has made Himself known to us by His Son Jesus. And is it not really from the sky that we get our bread? Whence comes the dew? Whence the rain that makes our corn grow? And where, I ask you, shines the sun which makes it ripen?" Then, fixing her eyes on Mokamba, she addressed herself to him, and asked for an account of his return to the world. "Your fall made us the laughing-stock of the heathen. How are we to know that you are sincere now?"

"My mother," answered Mokamba humbly, "I thank you for the question you have put to me. Ah! I know that it is not by anything I may say to-day that you will be convinced: it can only be by life in the future. It is only by its fruits that the tree is known. That is all I can say. But God is my

witness that I am true. Here is the sad story of my return
to the world : it will be a lesson to everybody. When you saw
me weeping in the midst of the *lekhothla*, I was sincere. The
sword of the Word of God had pierced through me ; and afterwards, I had found peace. It was a joy to me to go with Litia
to the meetings at Sefula. But when I was promoted to the
dignity of Liomba " (the third chief of the country), " I allowed
myself little by little to grow absorbed in business. I soon
found it irksome to go to Sefula every week : it was too far. I
let myself go. Our father said to me indeed, ' Mokamba, take
care ; you are backsliding.' I tried to reassure him, and to
make a fresh effort, but I ended by getting quite tired of the
whole thing. And when our father came to install himself at
Lealuyi, I had fallen, and I had nothing but the skin of a
Christian. He said to me, ' Mokamba, go on reading the Bible
every day, just the same.' That is what saved me. Every day
I read my Bible. But I could not read it long without its
condemning me. And then I shut it sorrowfully. The
preachings, too, condemned me, and I dared not look the
servant of God in the face. I was unhappy. But in the midst
of my wanderings, I prayed constantly. God had pity on me,
and now I am happy. Let my history be a warning to you,
believers."

Many fine things were said in this meeting, where everybody
spoke freely : the principal theme being *Lot's wife*. A poor
woman told us that she came from the farthest part of the
Valley of Sefula. On the way, she found people working in
their fields. She accosted them, and invited them to come and
hear the Word of God. They answered contemptuously, " It
is no longer the *Baruti*, it seems, who come to remind us of
the Lord's Day ; it is these chits of women. Be off ! Go and
pretend to be a believer, if you imagine the missionaries will
give you beads and stuff."

" Oh, my masters," answered the poor thing, " I am only a
slave : I am nothing, but I feel the need of learning the things
of God. Oh no ! it is not stuffs I am seeking. What should
I do with them ? I have never worn anything but this apron
of skin. But I am a great sinner, and what I am seeking is
the pardon of my sins."

The sun set : whether we would or no, we were obliged to

close this beautiful meeting, in which my faith was strengthened and my soul was blessed.

I have already written about this awakening. Perhaps you thought me too wise and prudent. I dreaded excitement; I was afraid that this movement, favoured by the friendly disposition of the king and chiefs, would be superficial, and that our European friends, anxious, like ourselves, to see God's work prospering at last, might give it proportions which here it does not possess. I repeat, that what we wish above all is to build upon the One Foundation gold, silver, and precious stones, not wood, hay, and stubble. It would have been a sin to deny the work of God's Holy Spirit in thus beginning to awaken consciences. At Kazungula, and even at Sesheke, where the circumstances are very different from ours, I believe the movement has more reality than here, according to the accounts of our brother Louis Jalla; and my estimates apply chiefly to what passes under my own eyes. In any case, the Lord has visited us. It is in the consciences that work is being silently accomplished—we feel it; one day, it will burst forth. The Lord will still do great things.

Here is one very encouraging fact for us. You remember our beautiful school at Sefula in former days, which has been scattered throughout the country, even as far as Kazungula. How many times I have thought of the time and strength we sacrificed to it! Well, at the present moment, nearly forty of our former pupils have to my knowledge made a profession of faith, and all, with few exceptions, know how to read. Our teachings, all those books which were bought with such enthusiasm, and then remained as if buried in the earth—nothing has been lost. "He that observeth the wind shall not sow: and he that regardeth the clouds shall not reap."

LEALUYI, *April 29th*, 1895.

In Africa, everything is surprise and caprice; one day a famine, the next abundance, even superabundance. Drought distresses us; and then again, it never rains but it pours. The post is the toy of the same caprice. More than once, we have been nine long months without receiving a single letter. We are only at the end of April, and we have already had four

posts from Europe, dated from the first fortnight in January.
Will it last?

Besides the vagaries of the post, there are those of the
weather. The rains—those rains so ardently desired—have at
last fallen, at long intervals, and in thunderstorms, modifying
our burning atmosphere, but very slightly. On the whole,
this season, which people were already anathematising, has
reached the minimum of rainy seasons. Perhaps a comparative
table of these would interest you. Here it is :—

						Inches.
1885-86	...	...	Nov. 25 to March 4	...	...	28·46.
1886-87	...	...	Travelling.			
1887-88	...	...	Nov. 21 to March 7	...	...	35·12.
1888-89	...	...	Nov. 14 to May 12	...	...	28·58.
1889-90	...	...	Nov. 7 to May 7	...	...	36·92.
1890-91	...	...	Nov. 20 to April 5	...	...	42·95.
1891-92	...	...	Oct. 16 to April 24	...	...	33·35.
1892-93						
1893-94	...	...	Nov. 20 to April 6	...	...	35·98.
1894-95	...	...	Nov. 24 to April 29	...	...	28·88.

This gives for the above years an average of 33·78 inches.
The annual flood does not depend solely upon the rainfall we
have here, but also upon that of the Upper Zambesi basin.
We have had an inundation, tardy and slight, but still we have
had one.

Lewanika has had two great hunting expeditions, and is
preparing a third. Unfortunately, he reserved for himself
exclusively the pleasure of piercing with his own hand the
antelopes which crowds of men, in tiny canoes, or up to their
chests in water, had chased and then surrounded on the anthill
where the king awaited them. Alas! alas! the pretensions
of royalty multiply in an alarming manner; ceremonials are
becoming more and more complicated, and if it goes on much
longer, there will soon be no place under the sun for subjects
and slaves. The progress in civilisation is entirely for the
king and his family—nothing for the people. Lately, they were
three days discussing at the *lekhothla* the question of stools
and certain ornaments of ivory and beads which the people
had taken the liberty of making since the death of Sepopa,
sixteen or seventeen years ago. Lewanika confiscated and
forbade them, as being the exclusive appanage of the royal

family. This is certainly not the path of humility and conversion. It is not even that of good policy. And I thought
it my duty, in a *tête-à-tête* with my poor friend, to show him
the danger and folly of such blindness. He pleaded that in
ancient times it was the distinctive and exclusive privilege of
kings : why should it disappear to-day? I asked him if he
himself were a king of ancient times, he who dressed like a
European, built himself a European house, drank coffee, tea, etc.

" These old customs are miserable ruins which the poor
have taken possession of, as they have of certain old palaces
in Europe. Why dispute them when you have better things ? "
Did I convince him ? He said so, but I have not yet perceived
it. This is a mournful page. I pity Lewanika very much ;
they make a deity of him, and that by his own choice. How,
in the midst of such servile adulation, can he still believe
himself an ordinary mortal, and feel himself a poor sinner
before God ?

Lewanika treated us gentlemen to the honour of a beautiful
excursion in *Nalikuanda*. He took us from the other side
of the Valley to Thapa, where Mpololo lived, the last chief
of the Makololo, not far from Kama, where the celebrated
Sepopa at first established his residence. We were surprised
at the congeries of villages. It is, like Sefula, a centre of
population, and the king assures us that it is the same all
round the Valley. We ought to found some stations with
numerous outposts. But—where are the men ?

[*To face page* 593.]

KABAKO FALLS.—TRIBUTARY OF THE ZAMBESI, RIGHT BANK.

(Explored by F. Coillard.)

CHAPTER XXXVIII

June 1895.

I HAD long cherished a desire to visit Katuramoa and Libonda. Alone at a station, caught in the toils of daily duty, always taken up with the most pressing one, I had so far found it impossible to carry out this wish. But now that the Adolphe Jallas are here, I am a little less tied. The rains are over ; winter will not be here for some time ; the plain, though drying up, will still bear canoes : so this seems a favourable moment. Once at Libonda, why should I not go on to "regions beyond"? I communicated my project to Lewanika, who scolded me in friendly fashion for not having done it before ; but this did not prevent his doing all he possibly could to facilitate my journey. He insisted, first of all, on my taking three canoes instead of two ; and I must acknowledge that, for all my belongings, our provisions, my boys' little bundles, and their mats, there was not one too many. Mine having been destroyed by the breaking down of a bank, the king procured me another for my personal use. But this canoe deceived us by its fine proportions. Badly shaped, badly ballasted, it would only move lying over on its side, so that the paddlers had great difficulty in preserving their equilibrium, and I, feeling the force of every wave, rocked to sleep in the full blaze of the sun, several

593

times narrowly missed rolling overboard.   The rowers were only found with difficulty, as is always the case at this season.

Liomba (Mokamba) and my good Semonja contended for the charge of my little expedition.   Liomba prevailed, and obtained the king's permission without difficulty.   But I soon saw that this *little* expedition would become a rolling snowball. Liomba, being the king's son-in-law, must have at least two canoes ; his friend Taü-ira (the lion roars), who never leaves him, has his own too ; then two of our scholars of the blood royal were burning to accompany me, and the king can never refuse them anything.   Then, at Lewanika's order, Liomba will take up three guides on the way, each of course with his dug-out and his little retinue.   So that, instead of two or three canoes, here is a flotilla of ten, and forty men !   It almost alarms me : it is not at all what I want.   I shall not have to pay all these people, it is true ; but I shall have to feed them.   It is a comfort to me that among them we have a little band of ten who profess to be converted.   They can all read and sing—two elements which, with God's help, I hope to turn to account.

Lewanika had profited by our delays to send messengers to certain chiefs of the Balunda and Balubale, to announce my visit. He came himself to preside at our parting with the Jallas ; and after committing each other to God, we left.   It was at midday on May 6th.   Lewanika soon perceived the defects of my canoe ; and before we had gone a mile, he asked me to return and change it ; but once gone, I *was* gone.

The plain at this season is a floating prairie, enamelled with flowers ; rosetted water-lilies, with their delicate tints of blue, pink, and white ; and a kind of convolvulus, which proudly erects her great magenta trumpets, only dipping them reluctantly as our canoes go by.   But it is also diversified by tall grass and reeds, through which we have to force our way.   If we catch sight of a canoe in the distance, we hail it eagerly.   Here and there are villages, or rather hamlets, thinly scattered, and almost lost in the expanse.   We do not pass one of them by : we take time to have a little talk with the people, who are glad to see us ; and to sing a hymn to them.

The first evening we reached Katuramoa.   It is a wretched straggling village, the huts congregated on two parallel slopes of sand separated by a marsh which is drying up.   But, as you know, it is one of the sacred spots of the country, and one of the principal shrines to which the Barotsi make pilgrimages. The very soil must be trodden with veneration, and strangers there may not speak above their breath.

Katuramoa was formerly the capital of *Mboho*, the first king of the Barotsi ; but being situated on the river-bank, it was ruined and carried away by the stream. It disappeared long ago. He himself is not buried on the spot where his tomb is shown. The legend relates that the real grave, the site of which is no longer known, was found one day open and empty. The divining bones certified, without any contradiction, that Mboho, when in the other world, took it into his head to move elsewhere ; they indicated the spot he had chosen and since then, it is thither that people resort to consult the manes, close to a village which has inherited the name of the ancient capital.

Mboho enjoys great authority in the country. He presides at all the national councils, and at the foundation of each new capital. Nothing is done without him. It is to him that the *Nalikuanda* owes its first visit every year. Hence, when, this year, Lewanika, instead of conforming to the established usage, invited the missionaries to make an excursion with him in the royal boat in a different direction,[1] it was in his mind and in the eyes of the people a significant sign of the times, an indication that the old national customs were falling one by one into desuetude, to give rights of citizenship to Christianity.

Had it been necessary, I could have convinced myself of this by questioning the guardians of this tomb : " You profess to interpret the oracles issuing from the tomb. Explain to me how you hear them."

"We hear nothing," they said, with apparent frankness; "but it is our duty to make the national traditions and customs respected, and submit to the desires of the national chief."

Liomba (Mokamba) went a great deal further in a speech he addressed to them. With a boldness that astonished me, he said, " And you think I am still going to pray at Mboho's tomb ? Why did you not run after me, the Liomba, to seize me the moment I set my foot on the ground ? It was

---

[1] See end of last chapter.

because, to us, to the one who addresses you, these customs
are, as you very well know, the ruins of an old deserted
village, and nothing more.   What ! you of the common
people throw your dead into the fields, you hide your graves,
and say that to approach them is to attract the greatest of
misfortunes ; and then, your kings, who are men like any
others, you bury in the middle of a village ! Of those who
prayed to other gods, you make gods in their turn, whether
they have been good or bad ! Well, know henceforth that
these were men like any others, like you, like me.   They are
dead ; their bodies are decayed, eaten by worms, like those of
their slaves ; but their souls are gone to their Creator and their
Judge."

It was at a meeting in the evening that he spoke like this—
one to which our hymns had attracted a hundred and fifty or
a hundred and sixty persons.

The next day, after a journey of three hours *across country*,
we arrived at Libonda.   This village has its traditions like
Katuramoa ; for it was founded by the daughter of Mboho,
Boanjikana, who bore the title of queen, *Khosi ea Mosali*.

The king is expected in these parts for one of his great
hunts.   As soon as our canoes and my white umbrella were
seen in the distance, the villagers thought it was he, and at
once began to shout the royal salutation with all the force of
their lungs, while our men screamed themselves hoarse in their
efforts to undeceive them.   So we had to submit to this desecra-
tion of royal honours, and had a good laugh afterwards at the
expense of these poor people and their mystification.   However,
they could not help laughing just as much themselves.   Katoka,
the king's sister, is chieftainess of Libonda.   She does not live
there, and only goes there very seldom ; nevertheless, she has
an establishment there worthy of herself, and well kept up.
When we had installed ourselves in her vast court, we visited
the village from house to house, as at Katuramoa.   We arrived
thus at the house of a venerable man, nearly blind, who talked
to us about the good old times.   He had known Livingstone, and
pointed out the spot where he had camped, which still retains
his name.   When we spoke to him of the Saviour, he listened
attentively, grew pensive, and then said, " It is just what Nyaka[1]

---

[1] The Doctor.

said to the Makololo ; but the chiefs would not hear of it.
And now, *where are they ?* "

Most of the men were out and away, performing various
forced labours. This did not prevent our having a fine meeting
in the evening, chiefly of women and children. I remarked
with astonishment the spirit with which they sang the very
hymn I had intended teaching them, " *Bonang, sôna, o fihile* "
(adapted from the English " The great Physician now is here ").

" But you know it already ! Who taught it to you ? "

" It was Bangueta," cried several voices at once ; " and we
know others too."

This Bangueta is a child of about thirteen, whose father had
brought him to school at Lealuyi. He was one of the first
to declare himself for the Lord, but not one of those who
inspired us with most confidence. During the holidays, he
fell ill at his parents' house ; he obstinately refused to let them
pray to the gods or practise heathen rites for his recovery.
" Send for the missionary's medicine, pray to the God Who is
the only living and true one, and I shall get well." And, as
a matter of fact, he did recover. I had the details from his
father. This dear child has succeeded in teaching some hymns
to the women and young people of Libonda, and this was one
of them. How heartily the refrain was taken up !—

> Sweetest Name on mortal tongue,
> Sweetest carol ever sung:
>   Jesus ! blessed Jesus !

How sweet it will be to sing that Name above in the home
of holiness and glory, when we shall see His glorified Person,
and understand the length and breadth and depth and height—
yes, all the immensity of His love !

Several of my young men spoke earnestly, but with tact.
The next day at six o'clock, all hastened together again to
hear us singing, in spite of the cold. Libonda is surrounded by
villages ; it is a centre almost made for our sixth station—when
we get the man.

On Wednesday, May 9th, we set out for Lepakaë. The
journey was a laborious one, the canoes having to force their
way through tall grass. We passed several little villages, each
of which has its story ; for this is the cradle of the nation.

We stopped at the *Mafulo*—that is, the hunting-box they are preparing for the king. There were a great many men there at work, and I met several of my "friends," amongst others a man of the king's household, who has been forced to return to his home in the neighbourhood for some time in consequence of a dreadful disease. He is a very intelligent and trustworthy man. We had to gratify them by inspecting their work, and sitting down awhile to chat. As this good servant of the king, a *sekomboa*, is over the tribute in the districts I wish to visit, he gave me a great deal of information, and ended with a big sigh of regret that he could not come with me himself. At this moment, a canoe approached which we had all been watching for some time. When we saw these men bending to the oars, and straining every muscle, some one remarked, " Those are king's messengers ; when he sends us, that is how we row." What a good object lesson for our Christians ! These men were, in fact, hurrying after us, to bring us a change of oars. Good Lewanika ! This is not the only civility he has paid us on this voyage. At Kapakaë, where we arrived in the evening, worn out, we found a great ox, which he had sent orders should be given to us. We were obliged to stay there a day to cut it up, and we took advantage of this to make acquaintance with the people of the village. I ought to say to *renew* their acquaintance ; for the men, and even the women, who are often summoned to the capital to perform forced labour for the king, are familiar with the preaching of the Gospel. So we do not find ourselves among strangers after all.

This great village of Kapakaë was that of Lewanika (then known as Robosi) before he was elected to the throne. In the middle of heaps of heads and horns of every kind of animal, they showed me a shrub loaded with vertebræ—all the trophies of his chase.[1] Lewanika was not only passionately fond of hunting ; he was also a warrior. He specially distinguished himself in the campaigns against the Makololo, and in the

---

[1] A kind of altar which a hunter never fails to erect to the manes of his ancestors, and where he dedicates the first-fruits of his hunting and some of the vertebræ or horns of the animals. A picture of this hunting-box appears in Cassell's "Story of Africa," vol. ii., p. 208. Vols. ii. and iii. of that publication contain many views of Barotsi-land from M. Coillard's photographs.

terrible massacres which exterminated that unhappy tribe.
The oracle—some oracle or other—interpreted by the bones,
ordered a black cow without horns to be given to this "Son
of the Nation," now a warrior of renown. Sepopa (then king)
added thereto a number like it, all black and without horns.
This is the *kapakaë*, whence the village derives its name. We
had been so astonished to see this great herd of hornless cows
and oxen ; and this was the explanation.

We found there an old woman named Mobuka, grand-
daughter of Moramboa, and great-granddaughter of Mboho [1]
(you see the lineage is not a very ancient one !), an interesting
person, who was quite proud to remind me of a certain occasion
when she had heard the Gospel preached at Lealuyi. It was
not the same with some young women, who, seized with terror
at seeing everybody kneel and close their eyes for prayer, fled,
saying, "They are going to die ; they are dying !" In connexion with this, they tell me that, on my arrival in the country,
when I was preaching in the *lekhothla*, old Narubutu reproved
the people. "Why be so credulous and confiding?" said he.
"Do you know what these people are capable of doing, when
they keep us prostrate with our eyes shut? Do like me ; be
prudent ; put your hands over your eyes ; and if you see the
white man speaking also on his knees with his eyes shut, do
not trust to that !—shut *one* eye, *one eye only ;* take great care
not to close both, and look through your fingers."

On May 11th, a Saturday, we took leave of our friends at
Kapakaë. After an hour and a half of labouring through
jungles, we at last emerged upon the river, an old friend whom
we had lost, and were very glad to find once more. What a
relief to us all! We definitely forsook the inundated lands,
the plain so dear to the Barotsi, at about fifty-six miles above
Lealuyi. How beautiful, how majestic, this Liambaë is! Its
gigantic windings meander between the north-east and the
north-west ; it flows in a deep bed without a single islet,
between banks which at this season are still bare, but which
will soon be fringed with the verdure of the trees. Palms
increase in number ; they are scattered over the plain either
isolated or in groups, and give a peculiar character to the

---

[1] The first Barotsi king, whose tomb is the shrine of Katuramoa. See
page 595.

landscape. But, alas! the locusts have not respected them;
they have so shorn their heads, that, at a distance, one would
take them for so many cabbages stuck on the tops of long
poles. Not very poetical, certainly; but—there they are!
The arborescent vegetation which begins to show itself here,
and which, for the Barotsi, marks the limit of their plain, is
absolutely devoid of any tropical character. The plain does
not terminate so abruptly as at Senanga, its southern extremity,
where the river flows confined, or rather framed, between wooded
hills. Still, it is not long before we perceive, on the right and
left, low hills running parallel to the river, and converging at
the Rapids of Sapuma; but they do not narrow in the bed—its
width is not diminished. We still find some Barotsi villages on
the banks; but these are the last. We are entering the district
peopled by the Mamboë.

This tribe, which speaks a dialect of the same tongue as the
Barotsi, is a link between these latter and the Balunda and
Balubale, who live still farther away. Their villages are
scattered along the river, generally hidden in the woods at a
little distance. The Mamboë say that they emigrated to this
country at the same time as the Barotsi; they come from the
north-east, from the banks of the Kafué, in the neighbourhood
of the Mankoya and the Mashukulumboe, where the greater
part of the tribe is still to be found.

They are intrepid hippopotamus hunters, and have a passion
for this adventurous life. Their little canoes, two or three yards
long, and just wide enough to squat in, are to them almost what
the horse is for the Arab of the desert. You should hear their
wonderful tales in the evening in camp, when all the young
men, eyes fixed and mouths gaping, are hanging on their lips.

We went to spend our first Sunday in one of their villages
at Noyo's. We met some travelling Barotsi there, and people
also came from the neighbourhood, so that we had a good
congregation. I made our young men speak; and one of them,
a Moshukulumboe, who promises to become a "son of thunder,"
closed with these words, uttered in passionate accents: " I tremble
for you; you are lost, *lost*, as I myself was. Be converted to
God, or you will perish hopelessly. I fear for you, my brothers
and my sisters in bondage, for Satan deceives you in making
you believe that the good news of salvation is only for our

masters. I tremble for you too, my lords—I who am, as you say, nothing but a dog of a slave, a *nothing*. As for you, you puff yourselves up, you imagine that you will enter Heaven because you are great. Know then that slaves—yes, your slaves —have already outstripped you ; and if you do not take care, you will find the door shut. Oh ! let me beseech you ; make yourselves little, quite little, before God ; throw yourselves on the ground, in the dust ! You will say contemptuously, 'Why does this *moshimane* [slave boy] speak to us like this—to us, his masters ? Has he lost his head ?' Oh, my lords ! it is that I was lost, and Jesus has saved me ! "

I spent the afternoon at the village—a collection of miserable grass huts which have never been plastered, without floors of trodden earth, without courtyards, lost in the midst of brush-wood and filth. The women and children fled at my approach. It grieved me to the heart. I sat down in the middle of a group of men.

" Do you know that the king has made a great canal which crosses the whole plain, from Nangoko to the river ? "

" Yes, we were there, at it."

" Really ! And what to do ? You were no doubt watching and admiring the king, who was digging out his canal all by himself, and who will one day be one of your gods ! "

They laughed. " The king had summoned the whole nation. Thousands of men worked at it for months and months. It was the same the following year, and yet it is not finished. We have not reached the two lakes which are to supply it, and it dries up during part of the year."

" Well, look at this great river. Do you know whither it goes ? "

" No."

" Have you ever seen it dry ? "

" Never."

" Well, it is the work of God, the true God, Whom we preach. No one helped Him. He spoke, and the river began to flow ; and it will go on flowing until God Himself says, ' It is enough ! ' "

This gave rise to questions and comments. The time flew rapidly by.

The next stage brings us to Njonjoro's, who, with another

little Momboë- chief, was to serve as our guide and interpreter. Before arriving there, we saw the confluence with the Zambesi of the Loeti, a little river which comes from the west, winding about a great deal (so they tell me) ; then, a little farther on, that of the Kabombo, on the left bank. This is the principal tributary of the Zambesi, formed by two currents of water, which rise in the environs of the late Sekufele's capital. They flow first from north to south, then unite in one wide and deep stream, the Kabombo, which flows directly west, to rejoin the great river. All this I learnt from information which seems to me trustworthy. The panorama has something grand about it, but it is too vast to be photographed.

Our people pointed out two little canoes which were rapidly approaching the Kabombo, and disappearing under the trees which fringed the shore. " They are running away, the rascals ! " they cried, and instantly gave chase to them, though with no unfriendly intentions. Not long ago, the people fled everywhere, and the villages were deserted at the first glimpse of a Morotsi, and not without reason. It is no longer the case, even in these secluded spots. We found the rowers, with a dozen other fishermen, peacefully squatting in the wood, drying and roasting some fish. On seeing us, their faces lit up. " *Lumela, Moruti ! Lumela, Moruti !* " There was quite a chorus of "*Lumela, Moruti !*" for each wanted to make his own greeting heard. " When you told us, that Sunday coming out of the House of Prayer, that you would come and visit us, we doubted it ourselves. And yet you have come ! *Lumela, Moruti !* " They eagerly offered us their broiled fish. Formerly, my people would have seized it for themselves. We spoke to them of the Lord, we sang a hymn to them, and parted from them like old friends. Everywhere we find men who have heard the Gospel at Lealuyi. I feel more and more anxious to see how far the echoes of our preaching have gone. We frequently see strangers at the church, and I often ask myself how much of the Gospel they carry away. I make it my duty always to address some friendly word to them on coming out. We also visit them as regularly as possible. What darkness ! Never mind ; the bread cast upon the waters will return to us when we least expect it. Only let us be faithful : the promise is positive and sure.

The country is now thickly wooded but little or not at

all broken. The majesty of the river becomes unbearably
monotonous. It is a lifeless landscape. The wild animals,
where they exist, flee before you have seen them, except for
here and there a hippopotamus disporting itself, or a crocodile
asleep on the sand : elsewhere, perhaps, a king-fisher rising
the flutter of whose wings somewhat recalls our own skylarks.
After ten o'clock in the morning, all is silent ; everything sleeps.
It is the silence of death. Here, however, is the chirp of a bird
I have never heard before. It has only two notes, remarkably
pure and powerful : *sol do ! sol do !* But they suffice it to praise
its Creator.

The country is inhabited by the Balubale on the right
bank of the Zambesi, and by the Balunda on the left. To
judge by the troops of men and women, who run up everywhere
along the banks to see the *Moruti*—a great curiosity in these
parts !—these regions ought to be fairly thickly populated.
But the villages are hidden at some distance in the woods,
and the river-banks are deserted. The Balubale and Balunda,
according to themselves, have a common origin, and the sources
of the Zambesi are their cradle. They have similar customs,
although they speak different dialects. Their mode of building
is the same ; the hut, which is only quite a small *square*, six
feet each way, has nothing by way of wall but short stakes,
scarcely three feet high, driven into the ground, filled in with
grass or lined with a mat, and supporting a *round*, pointed
roof.[1] No plastering ; no floors of trodden earth ; no enclosure
of reeds, which gives the most humble dwelling some degree of
privacy. Even in these dens, the poor people still find means
to light a fire, and keep themselves warm during the night.
Here, as among the Banyaï, this is the blanket of the rich as
well as of the poor.

The men, in order to cover their nakedness, wrap themselves
carelessly in some deer-skin, which they allow to trail between
their legs ; while, as for the women, they, poor creatures, have
scarcely the traditional fig-leaf. Both, but especially the men,

---

[1] Among the African natives of the *South*, the huts are always round ; a
right angle or straight line are things they scarcely comprehend. This is
natural enough, for everything they see is round—the sky, the sun, the moon,
the horizon and so on. The square shape increasingly prevails, as one goes
farther north.

expend all their vanity on their head-dress. Each gives free
scope to his or her imagination and fancy : one carries a fringed
mane, which he has constantly to shake back in order to let
his face appear ; another adorns himself with a chignon ; a
third with a multitude of little plaits. One has his hair all
shaggy, as if in imitation of a forest ; whilst another wears his
covered with great lumps, which remind one of ant-hills. They all
cover these marvellous coiffures with a superabundance of grease,
mixed with ochre or other colouring matter. I can understand their pride in them ; it takes several days' hard work to
complete them. They are inordinately fond of *mpote*—a very
intoxicating beer made from honey. And, to secure this precious
honey, they make hives of bark, which they place in the trees.

Human life has little value with them ; they barter their
slaves as elsewhere they do domestic animals. I am assured
that it is a common thing for a boy, a girl, or a baby to be
stolen. They throttle it, cover its head with a gourd, and go
and sell it in a distant village for cloth, beads, or some such
trifle. These are the most superstitious people I have ever
seen. Everywhere the eye meets " medicines," charms, and
amulets, on the confines of the village, in the market-place, and
in the huts, as well as on their persons. On every hand one
finds little altars made of reeds, and here and there a miniature
thatched roof, which shelters some object sacred in their eyes.
Nothing is done without consulting the bones. It is thus that
these poor creatures, suspicious of everything and everybody,
pass their existence in the bondage of fear.

With them, the power which was formerly concentrated in
the hands of a single chief, tends to become ever more and more
diffused. A curious thing about it is, that it is not transmitted
from father to son in direct descent, but through the son of
the reigning chief's sister. Finally, these Balubale and Balunda
are now in great measure tributary to the Barotsi.

Our object was first to visit *Sindé*, the great chief of the
Balunda, whose actual place of residence is about forty-four
miles from the confluence of the Kabombo.[1] He had fled from
a territory claimed by the Portuguese to Lewanika's country,
and under his protection to shelter himself from Portuguese
slave-hunters—blacks and mulattoes.

See page 546.

Temple.　　　　　Hut.　　　　Domestic Temple.　　　　Granary.

VILLAGE OF BALUNDA TRIBE, SHOWING HUTS AND GRANARIES.

[To face page 604.

The news of our visit, which had been first announced by Lewanika's messengers, had been noised abroad. A small Barotsi chief placed here—a prefect, as we should say in Europe—one Siyonda, stopped us as we passed. " Do not go on," he said ; " farther on you will find famine. Stay here for a day, so that we can give you some provisions." From the evening on, the neighbouring villagers brought us abundance of them ; and the next morning, the chief Kapele, Sindé's brother, was seen, arriving at the head of a long Indian file : it was manioc, sorgho, maize, pumpkins, and our provisions for the journey. Our canoes were filled till they were ready to sink. We passed some hours talking with these worthy people, and explaining the good news of salvation to them ; and then bade each other *au revoir* till our return. We did not then foresee under what circumstances that return journey would be made.

We arrived at Sindé's on the 17th. A marsh separated us from his village. The same day, he paid us a visit of welcome, and brought us an immense calabash of *mpote*. His face fell when I thanked him, but refused it ; and all my people did the same, some because they were Christians, others simply in submission to the king, who has forbidden it. Sindé possessed a herd of barely twenty head of cattle, which he had received from Lewanika. No matter ! hospitality before all things. He sent us *two*, one for myself, the other for Liomba (Mokamba). We accepted one, and sent back the other. " The *Moruti* is my father," said Liomba ; " we will eat together ; a single animal will be plenty for both of us." Sindé insisted, not understanding the delicacy of this refusal. We insisted too. The chief then sent a little boy, a slave, as a present to Liomba. " You will not have my ox ; at any rate accept this slave." " Thank you," replied Liomba, " I have enough men to serve me. We believers have learnt that we ought not to treat the creatures of God as beasts of burden. Restore this child to his mother ; and if you are determined I should accept something from you, a piece of cloth will suffice, and I shall be grateful." Sindé immediately sent him the printed calico which he himself was wearing. It was certainly a little soiled— it had done its duty ; but one could not take it amiss, for it was the pledge of a warm and generous heart.

The morass did not prevent me from going with all my people to spend Sunday at the capital of the Balunda. This capital does not amount to much ! On the edge of the forest is a large square enclosure, made of grass tastefully interwoven, which contains the chief's harem : outside are about fifteen huts, scattered about ; and that is all. But if there were a missionary residing with him in a suitable place, this would be altered.

We sat down under the shade of a tree, the only one in the village, and a very stunted one. They hastily constructed a shelter of mats in front of us for the chief: the village women and the men from the neighbourhood, whom he had assembled, grouped themselves round us, and I began. I explained the Commandments, laying special stress upon some of them. Sindé could not restrain himself from making remarks, some of which were quaint enough. He asserted his rights of life and death over his subjects, and protested against what I said of slavery. He became serious, however, and listened with deference to the testimony of Liomba (Mokamba) and of Taü-ira, forcible as it was, and full of good sense.

On the 21st, we moored our canoes as near as possible to the village belonging to Mosoandunga, a chief of the Balubale, and Nyakametsi, an intelligent chieftainess of the same tribe. Mosoandunga is the principal chief against whom the Barotsi waged that disastrous war four years ago.[1] He had made his submission since then ; and in accordance with the orders of Lewanika, his suzerain, he had recently come to establish himself where he now is. I walked eight hours to visit him at his own home (there and back, of course). I had made up my mind to do so, and I think it gratified him. He did not make me dance attendance on him for more than the half-hour necessary to preserve his dignity. To pass the time, I was amusing myself by counting his huts, of which there were in all half a dozen, with their smoky roofs showing above the brushwood, when I heard the deafening noise of a large drum, carried by two men. It was Mosoandunga, who was advancing towards us, escorted by a troop of young men. He is pretty stout ; and as he sat down, his folding-chair collapsed under him. We kept our countenances all the same. When

[1] See page 468.

once the ice was broken by the salutations, we conversed for
some time ; and then he collected the people, whom he had had
summoned from the neighbouring villages, and whom curiosity
had attracted in great numbers, and we spoke to them of God
and of the Lord Jesus.   When I told them to kneel down for
the prayer, there was a certain amount of hesitation among
the women, who were seized with fear.   " Never mind," cried
Mosoandunga, " we shall only die for a minute ; *we* know very
well what it is ; *we* have seen how they do at Lealuyi."   It
was dark when we regained our camp.

During the morning of the next day, wild cries, and a noise
of little bells, accompanied with the sound of the drum, resounded
through the woods, and announced from afar the chief Mosoandunga.   He soon appeared, carried in a hammock at a swinging
trot.   He came to return our visit, arrange with us to send an
express messenger to the great chief Kakenge, to warn him of
our arrival, and to send a letter by him for the Brethren,[1] who
are with his mother, Nyakatoro, with a message for her.   The
chief's own brother took charge of this important mission, and
promised to perform the journey in three days, while we should
occupy at least eight.

Our measures thus taken, we went to spend our second
Sunday at Sapuma.   Sapuma !   Should one give it the name of
Rapids or *Fall*?   There, as at Seoma (Ngonye), and on a formidable scale at Musi oa Tunya, an upheaval has blocked the
bed of the river with a strong dam of igneous rocks.   But, in the
middle, for a distance of about forty-five feet, the concentrated
force of the river has undermined and broken through the dam,
and it is through this breach that it rushes in a furious torrent.
Fifteen miles higher up, there is a repetition of Sapuma, but
on a smaller scale—another barrier of rocks, through which
also the river has made a breach in two or three places : this
is Yorose.   Between these two barriers is an uninterrupted
rapid, where navigation is of the most difficult and dangerous
kind.   In themselves, the walls of rock give a character of
grandeur to Sapuma ; but the coast, the river scenery, in short
the setting of the landscape, is insignificant.

We spent a blessed Sunday at Sapuma—one of those days

[1] Dr. Fisher and Mr. Cyril Bird, of the Garenganze Mission, known as
Mr. Arnot's.

which count in life, and which will also count in eternity. Our
meetings were such as one leaves reluctantly. " It is good to be
here ! " The Lord was there amongst us ; we felt it. Towards
evening, the bands of Balubale, who had heard us spoken of,
came out of various parts of the forests, and thus gave us an
opportunity of preaching Jesus to them.

We were reduced to short commons. The people promised
to bring us some food for sale early next morning. We waited
for them till midday, whilst carrying our canoes above Sapuma.
They came at last, but only with a few handfuls of cereals,
which we bought at famine prices.

We hoped for better things from the chief Senyama, whose
place we reached at 2.30 p.m. ; and simply in order to give
them time to prepare their goods, we yielded to their importunity, and encamped for the night. I profited by this halt to
make a little excursion with Liomba and my boys. The chief
lives on the banks of the Kabako, one of the tributaries on the
right of the Zambesi. To judge by the broad and deep junction,
like that of the Kabombo, one would think it was a large river.
Wishing to see a cataract, which we were told was close by, we
set out in canoes. It was a curious excursion, which certainly
did not lack charm or novelty. We had not gone a mile and
a quarter before the river-bed had considerably narrowed.
Soon, it became nothing more than a labyrinth of pools, bogs,
and streamlets, covered by an impenetrable thicket of mangrove.
The paddles were useless. We could only advance by means
of grasping the branches and roots which barred our passage,
stooping or lying down in the canoe, as occasion arose, to save
our heads ; lucky when we did not miss the main stream. A
little higher up, the channel deepened, and the stream emerged
from the tangle ; but, soon finding it obstructed again, we
moored the boat, and made the rest of the journey on foot.

The villages were numerous, and we lost ourselves in the
fields of manioc. The men and women who saw us took to
flight ; but as they were soon reassured, our escort rolled on
like a snowball ; and when we arrived at the cataract, we had
quite a hundred people following us. Unfortunately, the sun
had reached the horizon, and we were obliged to hurry.

The stream coming from the west, flows over a rocky bed,
which slopes suddenly. There is a boiling torrent there, which

leaps noisily over the rocks obstructing its passage ; then, at the edge of a gigantic horseshoe wall, it rushes in a pretty cascade, thirty feet high, into a vast and deep basin, where it again grows tranquil. The country is slightly accidented. The lines of the wooded hills, breaking in the far distance, seem to open up glimpses into infinity. Needless to add that it was night before we got back.

The next day, all that I could buy was half a bag of sorghs, and that took up all my time till midday. I will not mention what it cost me in beads, calico, and, above all, patience !

We were thus obliged to push on to the Lumbala, another tributary on the right bank. We had been told that it was a thickly populated centre, and that was true. We arrived there on May 29th. I sent to the nearest villages. The people there were all either drunk or drinking, so there was nothing to be had ; and our poor men were still forced to be on rations. It was a very astonishing thing ; for, ever since we left Sapuma, we had been escorted by troops of men and women, flocking together to see the *Moruti*. We stopped from time to time to tell them the Good News which we have come to preach. They listened, their eyes fixed, necks craned, and mouths gaping. Here, there was a chief preparing his *liyumbu*—that is to say, " the food of hospitality " ; there, a tardy chieftainess, who kept us waiting for nearly an hour, promising us abundance ! They both arrived with empty hands ; there was no longer any question of food even. It was only a ruse, a wicked device, because they knew that we were famishing. They wanted to see the great curiosity of the day, this double phenomenon, a *Moruti* who was also a white man. A monster they had never yet seen—two persons in one. Should we repay them with ill-temper ? Poor people ! they themselves are in want. The black clouds of locusts, which have not left us since we quitted Katuramoa, tell us enough. No. It is better, while their great ivory eyes are fixed upon my person, to speak to them of God, of His justice and His love.

Happily, a right spirit prevails among our people. The prospect of soon arriving at Kakenge's revives their courage. " He is a great chief : at his place we are sure to be well received : we shall forget all about our hunger." Alas ! how little they thought what awaited us !

We made forced stages: we passed over to the right bank of the Ruena—a little river which curves round from the west. It was somewhere about here that, once upon a time, stood the capital of Kakenge, the great chief of the Balubale.[1] To-day, the inheritor of this name has removed; but not far away, for hamlets are scattered or sometimes thickly grouped on the bank; one sees foot-passengers crossing one another's path, miniature canoes ascending or descending the current; all is life and movement. Everything tells us we are near it.

We did, in fact, arrive on May 30th, in the middle of the day, and in suffocating heat. We had been told, "A long way off you will see a great, grand house, very high; there is not such another in the country. It is the Kakenge's capital." Sure enough, we did see on the top of the hill a pointed roof of thatch, dominating the little huts which scarcely rose above the surrounding brushwood. It was certainly there.

We anchored the canoes in the midst of a curious crowd, especially of children. After having announced ourselves, we waited long for the chief's answer. That did not disturb us; we know that kind. At last it came, and it was brought by some middle-aged men. "They know the right way of doing things at Kakenge's," thought I.

But without even saluting us, disregarding the most elementary courtesy, these men, in Kakenge's name, and in rough, haughty tones, delivered us the order to cross the river and camp on the opposite shore. What a blow! For the shade and the fuel-wood, it might have been better for us; but it cost me much to put the river between ourselves and the people we had come to visit, and that was what I replied. Liomba himself, and our Barotsi, took the thing as an insult. Kakenge is a vassal whom Lewanika has just invested with his authority. There was bitterness in our first interview, and it left us under a painful impression.

Half an hour afterwards, the same messengers returned, this time with a mob of young men all armed with guns! "The chief Kakenge says that, since you wish it, you may stop and

---

[1] Many of the African chiefs have territorial names, which each adopts as he succeeds to the sovereignty. The title is attached to the dignity, not to the family, and the dignity is elective.

camp here."—" All right ; but what sort of way is this to receive us ?—with *guns !* " After a somewhat heated altercation, which happily I was able to moderate, we obtained the concession that all the guns, which were increasing with every fresh arrival, should be returned to the village.

This first danger warded off, it was impossible for me to accept the situation, strained as it already was, and so entirely without cause. So I sent one of these men to tell the chief I earnestly requested to see him, and that without delay. He replied that the dignity of a great chief like himself did not permit him to receive a stranger thus ; that he would see, and would send me word in some days if he saw fit. This was crude enough ; and during this time bands of armed men kept coming up from various directions. Night fell ; the drums began to beat ; they fired one gunshot after another ; they shouted and yelled ; it was an appalling hubbub ; the dances had begun, and dances of a character we could not mistake. No one slept that night. However, we were not attacked.

The next morning, I once more sent the same message to Kakenge, emphasising the fact that it was of all importance I should see him. He replied that he, on his part, wanted to know what I meant by coming into his country with a band of Barotsi without his permission, and without even warning him ; that, before seeing his face, he required Liomba, as much as myself, to pay him the *mosapo*—that is, the homage, or rather the tax, he exacts from black Portuguese traders who enter his country.

I referred to the messengers I had sent him, to the letter I had asked him to forward with my message to his mother Nyakatoro. I told him I was not a merchant, nor even a traveller, but a *Moruti*, and that I had only come into his country to teach the things of God. I added that I would not refuse to make him a present when I should see what manner of reception he accorded me, but that I would never consent to pay him the *mosapo* of the Mambari, so he could look on that as settled once for all. Thus the whole morning passed in parleying. Kakenge ended by appearing to yield ; and without making any further attempt to exact the famous *mosapo*, he bade us to the *lekhothla*. He was there, throned on a stool, draped in a thick blanket of coloured wool, under the shade of an enormous blue cotton umbrella, held by a slave. The place was full of men, decked out in their war-paint, and surrounded by bundles of guns. The circle opened before us, only to close again behind, and they made us sit down in the blazing sun, opposite to, but at a distance from, the chief. I saluted him, and so did my people ; he responded only to me, and we studied each other for some minutes.

I tried to explain clearly the object of my voyage, insisting on the fact of the messengers I had sent him. Unfortunately, my Mamboë interpreters were paralysed with fright, and my words had to pass by six mouths—six new editions—before they reached him. Kakenge was not in a mood to listen to my explanations, which he treated as lies. He roughly inter-rupted me, and himself broke into a passionate speech which no one could interpret to me. " What does he say ? " I asked of Liomba. " Oh, he is full of anger ; he is insulting and threatening us." His face and gestures, as well as the anything but soothing attitude of his people, said it sufficiently ; and I took full cognisance of it.

He kept us there more than an hour, roasting in the sun ; and when he had worked off his effervescence, he suddenly rose, and disappeared hastily into the court of his harem. Thus ended this interview on which I had so counted.

My people, who for the most part understood the language, were terrified. All were gloomy and silent ; each was entirely wrapped up in his own thoughts. Sinister rumours, moreover, were flying from mouth to mouth. Two of my men had contracted blood-brotherhood with some Balubale[1] ; and these new brothers, faithful to inviolable obligations, had confided to them that Kakenge, out of pure hatred for the Barotsi, had sworn our perdition ; and that if we escaped his hands, he had given orders up the river to have us arrested and massacred. There is a certain chief up that way, named Kalipa, whom Lewanika had deposed in favour of the present Kakenge, and he had undertaken the affair. Liomba was the only one who kept calm. As for Taü-ira, he tried to console his friends in

---

[1] This ceremony consists in extracting blood from each other's arm, and mixing it up with some porridge, which both parties eat together out of the same dish. Henceforth they are one, and have no more secrets between them. Such an alliance is never known to be broken.—*Author's Note.*

misfortune by repeating philosophically that "after all one can only die once." Others, I learnt later on, had secretly laded their canoes, and planned to fly in the night. I had caught several others loading their guns. Moreover, seeing the youths of the village—the men did not show themselves—coming and going in our encampment, sitting on our mats, touching everything, and behaving impudently, my dread was that our young men would yield to these provocations, and thus fire the magazine. All this time we had had no food.

Our evening meeting was what it could only be in these circumstances. Not one was absent. I exhorted my poor people to put their trust in God. I told them of our adventures with Masonda among the Banyaï, and set forth the wonderful deliverance the Lord had granted us. "Well, my friends," I said, "mark my words; it will be just the same here. God says in His Word that the heart of the king is in His hand, and that as the rivers of water, so He turneth it.[1] I have always proved that true in my experience, even when we came into your own country, where we met with more difficulties than you imagine. The heart of Kakenge is as much in the hand of God as that of Lewanika and that of Masonda. To-morrow, you will see, Kakenge will not only send us food, but he will also give us words of peace, and not a hair of our heads will fall to the ground."

My words may seem audacious and rash; they were the words of absolute *conviction*. These men heard them with astonishment. After that, no one thought of running away. No one slept, of course; all were crying to God, and the heathen more than the others. As for myself, I was calm and confident, because I felt that the glory of my God was at stake. The morning broke; we had not been attacked. But where was the promised deliverance?

I sent to Kakenge to say I was going to see him, myself alone. "Wait," he answered me; "I cannot talk with a hungry man."

Was this the first gleam of our granted prayer? Not to my people, at any rate—quite the contrary. The whole morning passed thus—waiting. *Nothing!* The afternoon wore on.

Prov. xxi. 1. See page 28.

Nothing! At last, towards three o'clock, a procession which I saw coming out of the village advanced slowly towards us. *It was the promised food from Kakenge!* Baskets of manioc, millet, sweet-potatoes, fowls, and what not! Every one assembled.

"*Moruti*," said an old man, "here are the *liyumbu* of Kakenge. Now make him a present, worthy of himself and yourself. The other day, you gave him stuff—it was blood-stained" (*i.e.* red); "and he passed it on to his slaves: you added white, and he offered it to the gods; beads too, and he distributed them to his wives. He himself has had nothing from you as yet: you have beautiful things; give!"

These were delicate matters, and took a long time to adjust. It was not easy for me to please them, for the good reason that I had not provided myself for such an eventuality. At last, I put my hand on a piece of stuff which caught the eyes of my Balubale; and not to embroil matters anew, I said to my people, "Come, I will carry it myself to Kakenge; let us go and thank him for his food." Finding I was determined, the baffled messengers of the chief reluctantly placed themselves at the head of the file.

Seeing us break into the *lekhothla* without further ceremony, Kakenge fled into his court. I sent him the stuff, and said to my people, "Now for the royal salutation." Taken aback, they instantly stood in position, and their mighty "*Yo-sho*" and hand-clappings produced such an effect, that, while the messenger sent to thank me for the stuff was still speaking, Kakenge himself, in despite of his dignity, hurried up, took his stool, and came and planted himself right in front of me. His face was beaming. "Now," he said, "I believe in your good intentions. Forget my ill-temper in these past days. I had sent orders up the river to have you arrested; I am going to countermand them, and announce you to Nyakatoro. My own people shall conduct you. Only," he added, "do not take the Balubale for women."

Suddenly, he threw himself backwards, stiffened himself, kicked about, tore himself with his nails, and made frightful contortions, rolled his eyes, ground his teeth, and uttered horrible cries. Then, calming himself with equal suddenness, he rose, and darted into his court. We remained stupefied! I had thought at first that the man had a fit, and I wanted to fetch some

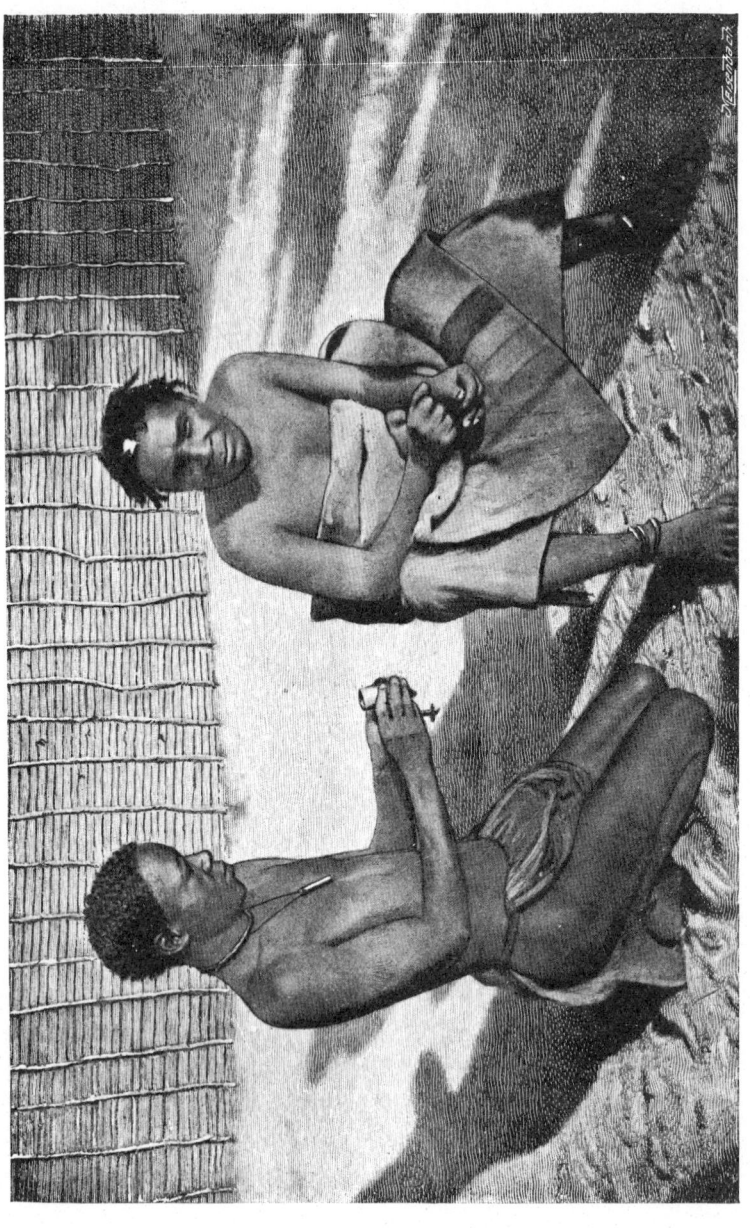

THE CHIEF KAKENGE—SLAVE PRESENTING SNUFF-BOX.

[To face page 615.

water; but all his people had risen, and were uttering savage cries to applaud him. Then I realised that Kakenge was vaunting his courage by imitating a ferocious beast struggling with his prey and devouring it. If I had only had my camera!

This last tragi-comic scene would somewhat have tarnished the bright impressions of my companions, if Kakenge had not hastened to send us a friendly messenger with a little food, inviting us to go the next day and "sing at his place." That would be Whit Sunday. God had glorified Himself. I felt moved that evening, when I saw my people round their fires cooking their food. Some were talking, commenting with animation on the occurrences; the youngest ones were reproducing the savage scene they had just witnessed; others were thoughtful and said nothing.

Prudence made me renounce pursuing my voyage as far as Nyakatoro's, and that will be understood without further explanation.

The next day, the Day of Pentecost (Whit Sunday), we went to the *lekhothla*, no longer in disgrace this time. The guns had disappeared; Kakenge and his men grouped themselves around us; our singing attracted the women and children of the village; and there, too, we published the good tidings of salvation. Liomba greatly astonished Kakenge when he told him that he was himself a believer—he, the king's son-in-law, Liomba (*i.e.* second minister of state). He doubtless thought —and he is not alone in that—the Gospel was for the poor and little ones of the earth; and not for the great ones, whom God would honour in a special way, or who, perhaps, would honour God by entering His heaven.

I surprised him in my turn by announcing my decision to turn back. "They will say it is Kakenge who turned you back," he said. But seeing I was quite decided, and that none of his promises could shake me, he absolutely would not have us take leave of him till the next morning. "But we want to start early!" "No matter, they will wake me!" And sure enough, very early on Monday, while the tent was being struck and the canoes laded, we ran to his place, and found him waiting for us. I was even able to take a bad photograph of him, in spite of his objections. He gave us another basket of flour. "Come back next year," he said to me ; " you will find no more obstacles on your road, and you shall take two of my children to teach. I would give them to you to-day, but the road to Lealuyi is still untrodden." I was quite of his mind. Once in our boats, I leave you to guess if our boatmen rowed or not ! The dark spot was— famine.

As we descended, we learnt that a chief named Kenya, in the hope that we should call at his place, had in fact intercepted our messengers, and even the letter he was to have sent on to Kakenge. His village was too far from the river, and we had put off our visit to him till the return voyage. Out of spite, he would send nothing on. That partly explains the attitude of Kakenge, and exonerates him in my eyes. I confess that, when he said he had received nothing from us, I did not believe him. However that may be, I think the foregoing incident contributed not a little to kill inter-tribal animosities and confirm peace. One thing is very certain, and that is that, if I could make this same voyage again later on, even with a band of Barotsi, we should not have the same dangers to risk a second time.

The unlucky Kenya, learning of our adventures, was beside himself, and raced after us. We could not wait for him ; famine was driving us on, and that prevented us from taking his child (from Mosongo's), to bring him to school, as had been agreed upon. While condemning him, we did all we could, by means of his brother Mosoandunga, to calm and reassure him.

On our return, our worthy friend Sindé received us with the same hearty warmth as when we went. Unfortunately, a violent ophthalmia, which confined him to his house, prevented our seeing him. From the same cause his own son and two of his nephews could not start with us either to come to school.

From the beginning of the voyage, I had felt a keen anxiety about our boatmen : their conversion was the subject of my prayers ; individual exhortations and pressing appeals had been often addressed to them. Especially had our morning and evening worship always been solemn, and became still more so after our adventures with Kakenge.

One evening (it was at Sindé's, on June 9th), we were camping in a bushy wood, feebly lighted up by the pale rays of the moon. You might have seen me with all my people squatting round the central fire of our bivouac. A feeling of deep solemnity had taken hold of us. I had once again addressed serious words to these men, who for six weeks had shared my life in this adventurous voyage. I had ceased speaking, and silence had followed my words. At last a boy burst forth.

"I am Mosesanyane of Lepakaë," he said in a quivering voice. "Last year, I worked at our father the *Moruti's*; when my time was up, I ran away with an arrow in my heart. I said to myself, 'Pooh! that will pass off; it is only a stray shaft'; and I thought my wound was healed. But at Sapuma a new arrow pierced through me. When I thought of the great day, when even the kings, the great ones, and the rich, would call upon the rocks and mountains to fall upon them, I asked myself how I, poor and little as I am, could possibly escape. Since then, I have never ceased to call upon the Lord Jesus to have pity upon me. I believe He has heard me, and I am His."

Another, a grown man, declared that it was our adventures with Kakenge that had opened his eyes, and decided him. "When our father asserted that the heart of even Kakenge was in the hand of God, I said to myself, 'We shall see: is the *Moruti* a seer?' That seemed to us just as strange as the word of Jesus to His disciples, 'He sleeps, and I go to awake him out of sleep'; and yet the man was certainly dead. Well, yes! God has worked a miracle. When we were expecting to be massacred, He changed Kakenge's heart towards us. God hears prayers: that is true indeed. After having been driven by terror to prayer, I have begun to pray for the pardon of my sins."

A third (a terrible character this one, and well known; the last person from whom we should have expected such language) said, "When in Sapuma I saw my brother-in-bondage, Molonda, declare himself for the Lord, it had such an effect upon me that I fled into the forest, and there I wept and cried like a child. 'Matengenya is very bad,' I said to myself: 'it is true; he is an adulterer, a thief, a liar; everybody despises him.' Is he therefore too bad for Jesus to save him? No. *He* came to seek and to save the lost. They told me so. I laughed at it; now I believe it."

Then there was another; then yet another,—ten altogether;

eleven, counting one of our Mamboë guides, a man whose hair is turning grey. This mighty hunter of hippopotami, astonished us at first by the eagerness with which he listened to what we were saying about the Lord Jesus, and the fire with which he transmitted to others what he had grasped. " It cannot be," we thought, " that he is nothing but a speaking-trumpet, giving out all and keeping nothing. What a powerful evangelist the grace of God might make of him in these dark regions !" He, too, declared himself for the Lord. In the night, the current carried off his canoe ; he left us to seek it, and we saw no more of him. But if he holds on, we shall often see him at Lealuyi, in spite of the distance.[1]

Finally, there was a twelfth. Yes, indeed ! a dear, interesting young man for whom we had intensely wrestled in prayer. He was there beside me, trembling in every limb and ill-controlling his emotion, his head hidden in his hands. I waited for him, but he said nothing. After the meeting, he sent word to me that he " could hold out no longer," and that he must declare himself *to-morrow*. He did not do so ; courage failed him : the next day it was still *to-morrow*. He has not yet done it, alas ! and to-day, for him, it is still *to-morrow*.

It was on Saturday, June 15th, that we joyfully re-entered Lealuyi, happy to find ourselves once more with the dear Adolphes ; and once more to see Lewanika, our young men, and everybody else ; and filled with gratitude to God, Whose good hand had visibly been upon us during the whole of this six weeks' voyage.

The next day, at morning service, the church was full. Mokwaë of Nalolo was on a visit. Those who profess to have found the Lord Jesus during the voyage rose, and once again individually declared they desired to follow and serve Him. But of these ten, two were not there ; they had turned back, and one, I fear, for ever. May the others persevere !

" Whoso is wise, and will observe these things, even they shall understand the loving-kindness of the Lord " (Ps. cvii. 43).

June 1895.

---

[1] By *river* 373 miles.

CHAPTER XXXIX

Serious Illness—A Journey South—Lewanika's Farewell—Death of Seonyi—
MM. Gibbons, Reid, and Bertrand—A Retrospect—A Grave in the
Wilderness—Bulawayo—A Contrast—A Forecast—The Matabele
Rising—The Rinderpest—Mafeking—Kimberley—Cape Colony—The
Dutch Mission—*The Drummond Castle*—Farewell to Africa.

KAZUNGULA, *December 12th*, 1895.

I MUST send you a few lines, or you will be thinking me
much worse than I am. But I am ill: I have told you
of it. I have long been fighting against it, but the complaint
increases, and imposes on me the duty of leaving the country,
so as not to be a burden to my friends.

When I started on my journey towards the Sources of the
Zambesi, I was even then suffering very much, but I did not
wish to confess, even to myself, the gravity of my condition, and
hoped that the rest and change of air would bring about an
improvement. But no! On my return, the trouble got worse,
to such a point that the question of a journey to Europe forcibly
imposed itself. It had long haunted me ; but I always regarded
it unwillingly, and with a feeling akin to terror.

It was under these circumstances that we held our Conference
at Lealuyi in September. I greatly rejoiced at being able to
accommodate all my colleagues at my table. Not only did they
all attend with their wives (except M. and Mme. Boiteux, who
had but recently arrived, and remained at Kazungula), but we
also enjoyed the rare privilege of a visitor's society—Captain
Alfred Bertrand, of Geneva (so well known in Switzerland for
his travels round the world), who brought us a breath from his
own mountains, and a spark of that ardent life which glows in
his own city. Rarely have I ever seen a Christian visitor take
such an interest as he did in our work. He so initiated himself
into every detail of station life—the schools, the *lekhothla*, public

worship, house-to-house visiting—that we came to consider him absolutely as one of ourselves, and he took part in our discussions and our home life, just as he felt inclined. And when, on his departure, I asked him not to forget either our Barotsi or our work, I felt that this man had given us a part of himself. Others will speak of his achievements : of himself we can never say too much.

But I was scarcely ever able to appear at meals with my friends—at those love-feasts, so long looked forward to ; and it was only nailed to my bed that I was able to preside over our sessions and take part in our deliberations. Moreover, my colleagues themselves insisted that I should start for Europe, as soon as ever it was possible. Hence, I could no longer hesitate, and arranged to leave as soon as possible with the Louis Jallas, who were returning home on furlough.

I earnestly wished to visit the village at least for one last time : this desire of my heart was not granted—a disappointment so much the more bitter as I could not receive visitors except very rarely. I had the sad satisfaction of an interview with Andreas, my poor prodigal son. He will return, I am confident, and his confessions strengthen this confidence ; but for the moment he is still feeding the swine and envying their husks. The king, who came to see me pretty often, said to me one day, " Ah ! if I am not converted yet, it is not your fault. You have given yourself no rest, but you did not give me any either." And later on, as we were about to cross the river, he sent to let me know that he had dismissed two of his wives, giving me to understand that this was to be the prelude to dispersing his whole harem. He was just " flying a kite," I suppose, to see which way the wind blew—what sort of sensation a radical measure would produce among the chiefs and the nation generally. In my reply, I conjured him not to bargain with God any longer, but to give himself frankly and fully. Pray for him !

On October 30th, three years after my arrival, almost to the day, I left Lealuyi, the anthill of Loatilé, which has grown so dear to me, and, borne on a litter, I started, quite alone, for Sefula. The Adolphe Jallas, who wished to accompany me part of the way, were to leave the day after, and wait for me at Nalolo. The journey was a dreary and painful one.

It was for the first time in my life that I found myself slung like this on a mattress, which the porters jolted at every step. And then the litter broke and had to be mended several times; night fell, and with it a violent thunderstorm; the waggon, which had gone on ahead of us, had stuck in the sand some way off. It was midnight when we reached the station: there were no lights in the windows—no one was expecting us—and who was there to expect us, I should like to know? What a desolation! Let us not speak of it. I threw myself on my bed, and writhed in agony till morning. I spent two days at Sefula. Apart from my own purely personal experiences, the farewell meetings, very interesting and numerously attended, were a ray of sunshine for me.

On the Saturday morning, I set out again in my litter for Nalolo. But before my doleful procession started, an express messenger reached me from Adolphe. His body was streaming with perspiration; his eyes were haggard, his voice hoarse, his lips trembled. I opened the note he held out. What stunning news! My boy Seonyi had just shot himself dead! Wishing to shoot some ducks for me, he pulled his gun out of the baggage pile by the muzzle, and of course, according to the incorrigible custom of all the South African natives, it was loaded and cocked. A jerk fired it off, and the unhappy lad received the whole charge in the temple. What a cloud over the beginning of this journey, which everything had already conspired to make so sad!

The dear Adolphe Jallas first, and then the Goys and Louis Jallas, lavished every care upon me that affection could prompt. Still, to be ill, alone and without enlightened medical treatment in a country like this, is very painful. God is merciful to His children, and He was to me; for, besides the friends I have named, He let me discover among my boys, not merely an affection I was already well aware of, but also a devotion I had never imagined could exist, but which has never faltered. Semonji especially proved himself an admirable nurse, foreseeing or guessing my wants, devising all sorts of means to tempt my appetite and cheer my sick-room, and doing it all eagerly, cheerfully, yet noiselessly. He never left me, night or day. What should I ever have done without him? What should I ever have done if he had wearied of my service? He implored

me not to leave him behind me ; and if I go to Europe, he shall
go too.   I know it is a great risk, but I seem to see God's hand
in it so clearly that I have no fears.   As to my poor Nyondo,
he is married, so there can be no question of taking him.   And
besides, we are counting upon him for evangelisation.   Poor
boy ! every time my departure was talked about, he laid his
head on his knees, and burst into tears.[1]

I have been three weeks at Kazungula, waiting for the
waggon which was bringing my baggage from the Valley.   Here,
I met Captain Gibbons, a member of an interesting expedition
about which I must say a word or two.   It was composed of
Mr. Reid from London, Captain Alfred Bertrand of Geneva, and
himself, an officer of the British army.   This was Mr. Reid's
third or fourth journey in our Zambesi regions.   We had met
him in 1885, at the moment when our expedition had just
crossed the river.   He was then hunting hippopotami.   A
typical English gentleman, full of good humour and good spirits,
it was an immense pleasure to have him at our modest table
and under our straw roof.   Singular to say, he was accompanied
by some Batoka boys who had been in our service, and during
the meal he called us to admire the melodies they were singing
in their camp, which we had ourselves taught them at Leshoma
years before.   He of course had no idea where they had learnt
them.   So the seed was not quite lost after all.

It was at the capital that we met him again with Captain
Bertrand, of whom I have already spoken.   Since then, they had
been exploring the course of the Machile, a little tributary of
the Zambesi, and accomplished work which they will doubtless
bring before the public and the Geographical Societies of London
and Paris.   I did not see them again at Kazungula ; they had
already started for Europe.   Captain Gibbons had remained.
He had set himself the task, for which no one could be better

---

[1] Semonji, one of the school-pupils, must not be confounded with Semonja,
an important chief, already mentioned several times. Semonji, after Mme.
Coillard's death, was one of the first to show that the Gospel had really
touched his heart; and when M. Coillard's illness became serious and chronic,
this boy, aged about sixteen, constituted himself his nurse, and accompanied
him to Europe.   He was placed at Dr. Grattan Guinness's Training College
(Harley House, Bow), where he is now being trained for an evangelist-schoolmaster—a career which his character and conduct fully justify his friends
in choosing for him.

qualified, of mapping out the whole course of the Zambesi. Accustomed to camp life and military discipline, he made but little—too little perhaps—of the comforts of civilised life. Unfortunately, he was ill, and so was I. If he could not come to meals, I dragged myself as far as his tent, and exchanged good-morning with him. I felt very sorry for him, for the weather was rainy, and his tent was in the mud. If he were better, we would converse, as far as I was able, upon the history and customs of the country, and criticise together the beautiful charts he had already begun. What would I not have given to be in better health, and better able to take advantage of this few days' intercourse! He has great plans and noble ambitions; he is capable of enduring much and accomplishing much, if God grant him health; and that is what I desire for him.

My waggon has arrived at last, and in a few days we shall cross the river. What a difference between the passage to-day and that of 1884! Then, not a soul in that immense region knew even the Name of the Lord, not one prayed to Him. Divided into two bands during the transport of our goods, we used to answer each other from one bank to the other, at the evening bivouac, by singing "*Tlong ho Yesu*" ("Come to Jesus"), and our voices lost themselves in the desert without an echo.

To-day, let us acknowledge it to His glory, "the Lord hath done great things." This very station of Kazungula, with its great village, where everything is so prosperous, testifies to that. We reckon five flourishing stations, and on each of them a greater or lesser number of Zambesians who profess to have found the Lord. To-day, they are praying here and singing the praises of God.

BULAWAYO, *January* 1896.

Our journey to Kazungula had been exceptionally easy; but once we had left it, our track was nothing but one frightful quagmire, where our oxen sank to their bellies, often without foothold to give them the slightest purchase on the waggons; and the latter were continually collapsing, all four wheels at once. Twenty-one days after leaving Kazungula, a distance of only three days' march had been accomplished. So, suffering exhaustion, eating little and sleeping less, I often wondered if

I should live to the end of this journey, so extraordinarily adventurous and laborious as it was.

But who can weary of repeating that the Lord is good and faithful? How His presence lightens our darkness! It is then that He teaches us "songs in the night," so that even the slime-pits and solitudes of the desert are changed into so many Bethels.

Between Pata-matenga and Bulawayo, the journey was much less difficult. When we quitted the Palapye road, we left the deep sands behind, and travelled over firm ground. The country is wooded, with clearings here and there. But it is always the *bush*, whose thorny thickets obstruct the path, and wage war upon our waggon-tilts. There is nothing, absolutely nothing, in the arborescence to remind us that we are in the tropics.

From Pata-matenga (a heap of hovels, turned into a farm) as far as Bulawayo, a distance of about three hundred miles, we did not meet a living soul, except for a few Masaroa (Bushmen), who wander in these woods. What is the future of this country? Will it ever be inhabited, colonised?

At present, the deathlike silence, unbroken save by the creaking of our waggons and the crack of our whips, brooding over these immensities of space, seems to breathe an indefinable spell. One feels a mere atom, impotent and lost.

One day, as we were going along through a little green valley between low wooded hills, we all halted as if involuntarily before an isolated tree, at the foot of which a thorn hedge encircled a tomb. On the trunk, some friendly hand had removed a square of bark, and roughly traced this epitaph :—

STUART

5 JAN. 1895

He was, it seems, a captain in the English army, full of energy and love of adventure, who, after having been quartered at Natal, was going back to his native land. But before leaving Africa, he wanted to see the Victoria Falls. He set off quite alone, with one or two native porters, and reached his goal. On the way back, he was attacked by fever. Tortured with thirst and forsaken by his boys, he lay down under this tree and died there. A passer-by, or some one who had heard of his fate, came and buried him. And do not think that is an isolated case. Far from it. Many sad stories are told about English officers, young men of good family, all full of life and impetuosity, dreaming of nothing but adventures in this land of liberty, but utterly devoid of prudence: they start off hunting, quite alone, lose themselves in the woods, and end by dying of thirst. There they sleep, their names and resting-places alike unknown, until the Resurrection Day.

As the deer breaks—as the steer breaks—from the herd where they graze,
In the faith of little children we went on our ways.
Then the wood failed—then the food failed—then the last water dried—
In the faith of little children we lay down and died.
On the sand-drift—on the veldt-side—in the fern-scrub we lay,
That our sons might follow after, by the bones on the way.

It was on the 15th [February 1896] that we at last reached Bulawayo.[1] I cannot describe the attentions and kindnesses with which I was surrounded. The authorities of the town came to visit me, and arranged with the doctor to urge my staying two or three months at the hospital as their guest, until the latter thought me well enough to continue my painful journey. Every one, to the Sisters of Mercy who have the direction of the hospital, lavished care upon me with a devotion which touched me deeply, and did me real good. And among the little number of personal friends I found there, was young Howard Moffat, who seemed as though he could not do enough for me. He spared neither his time nor his trouble nor his money to provide comforts for his father's friend, and the disciple, not to say the admirer, of his grandfather, Dr. Moffat of venerable memory.

This was the spot, you remember, where, eighteen years ago, Lobengula held us prisoners. What changes since then! Here is a town laid out on an immense scale, which promises to become another Johannesburg. You would be astonished at the price of land, and that of provisions generally. And the life one leads there, little as you would believe it, is as agitated,

---

[1] The proper phonetic spelling of Bulawayo and Matabele is *Bolawayo* and *Matebele*. They have been left unchanged in the text, so as not to confuse the English reader.

as busy, as in London. There is no time to see or talk quietly with anybody. It is an incessant whirl. The site of the town covers a vast flat space, surrounded by lightly wooded rising ground, and already sprinkled with villas. What will Bulawayo be in twenty years ?

   *   *   *   *   *   *

But before we left, dark clouds were mounting on the horizon, sullen rumblings of thunder were heard, and soon a violent storm burst. It was that second Matabele war which during so many months held England in suspense.

The Chartered Company's Government, sure of having finally crushed the Matabele as a nation, and of having for ever destroyed their military power and prestige, had irritated them by confiscating their remaining cattle to pay the expenses of the war. (For alas ! we know too well that it is the vanquished who have to pay the cost of their own disasters and humiliation !) And among the African natives, to take away the cattle of one's enemies is always a provocation, and a declaration of war in itself. Then came the adventurous undertaking of Dr. Jameson, followed by his check and captivity, which was sounded far and wide among them. No more was needed to turn the heads of these exasperated savages. They held secret palavers to hatch rebellion. But rumours of them reached the Europeans ; they were even discussed when I was in Bulawayo ; the authorities themselves were not in ignorance ; only, no one believed it was serious. We all know the rest ; it is contemporary history.

The country, too, like all those in these intertropical latitudes, had been visited by several scourges, from which it was still suffering. A few years ago, it was the small-pox which had decimated the population. Now, it was the locusts, who disputed with the inhabitants the scanty harvest which had survived the great drought.

But a far more general plague than the small-pox, and a much more terrible one than the locusts, suddenly made its appearance, and dogged our steps. This was the *rinderpest*.

No one who has not lived in Africa can form the least idea of this awful calamity. It mowed down the whole bovine race in its passage. Hundreds of carcasses lay here and there, on the roadside, or piled up in the fields. In vain did the natives gorge themselves, careless of the consequences. In vain did

legions of vultures and beasts of prey gather to devour them.
They could not overtake the quantity, and the carrion lay there,
putrefying everywhere.   More than nine hundred waggons,
loaded with merchandise, without teams or drivers, stood
abandoned along the Bulawayo road.   In a few weeks—a few
months, let us say—I am assured that eight hundred thousand
head of cattle—some say nine hundred thousand—perished in
Khama's tribe alone.

Never within the memory of man had such a thing been
seen.   The Government grasped the situation from the beginning.
But in spite of all the sanitary cordons, and the severest pre-
ventive measures, the scourge pursued its course relentlessly.
After sweeping over the Zambesi countries and those of the
Matabele and Bechuana, the Transvaal and the Orange Free
State, it has penetrated into Basuto-land and Cape Colony, and
still goes on, spreading consternation and ruin.

Wars, drought, famine, pestilence, locusts, cattle-plague !
Why so many calamities in succession ?   Why ?   Ah ! without
prying into the secret designs of Providence, may we not ask
ourselves if by these solemn warnings the Almighty is recalling
Himself to a generation that is forgetting Him ?   Let us draw
nigh to God, and He will draw nigh to us.   Let us cleanse our
hands and purify our hearts.   Let us humble ourselves in the
sight of God, and He shall lift us up.   He will bring good out
of evil and light out of darkness.

Even from the economic point of view, the dark cloud will
have its silver lining.   The black race, and the great majority of
farmers, all those whose chief wealth consisted in horned cattle,
are ruined.   May we not reasonably believe that honest and
honoured work, agriculture and industry, will receive a fresh
impulse, and will thus open up new sources of wealth ?   Railways are now a necessity.   Already the one which starts from
Cape Town is rapidly advancing towards the interior.   By the
end of 1897 it will have reached Bulawayo, while that of Beira
will come as far as Salisbury.   And then ?

As for the Louis Jallas and myself, we can only bless God
and adore His ways.   A fortnight's delay on our journey, and
we should have found ourselves, even before reaching Bulawayo,
in the midst of the rinderpest, and in the midst of the war—
stopped short, no matter where, finding it impossible to move

and at the mercy of these terrible Matabele, for whom brigandage and massacre are pleasure trips.

" The good hand of our God was upon us." Everywhere along our way, we found friends, who overwhelmed us with kindness. There was the noble chief Khama, whose friendship (now of twenty years' standing) has always been so precious to me, and whom I found totally unchanged and unspoilt by his visit to England. How delighted he was to tell me about all the wonders he had seen and the kindness he had received ! But next to his audience of the Queen, his most vivid and agreeable recollection was of the evening he spent at Mr. Chamberlain's house, witnessing conjuring tricks.

Then, too, there were the Rev. and Mrs. Willoughby (L.M.S.) and Mr. and Mrs. Williams, and also the magistrate of Gaberones, Mr. Surmon, an old Basuto-land acquaintance, who in this time of difficulty and distress, and for him of heavy work, placed his carriage and mule team at my service for several days, in order to convey me to Mafeking, then the terminus of the railway.[1] Neither can I forget the kindness I received from Mr. and Mrs. Speight.

My young Zambesians opened their eyes indeed, when they entered a real railway carriage for the first time. And when the train moved off, they gasped with astonishment. " But, my father, they haven't even inspanned the oxen yet ! " It was a night journey, and lasted till morning ; but the boys never closed an eye.

At Kimberley, I was soon installed at the hospital, on the

---

[1] At Palapye the travellers disposed of their teams and conveyances. M. L. Jalla hired two waggons for the rest of the journey, and taking M. Coillard's baggage, followed the main transport road. A few miles north of Mafeking, however, the travellers were stopped at the quarantine station, and their ox-teams shot down on the road, for fear of the rinderpest. Their waggons, of course, had to remain *in situ*, along with hundreds of others ; and the contents, embracing all M. Coillard's property, were put in charge of a trader at one of the wayside " stores," but during the Matabele war the cases went astray. Through the energy and kindness of Mr. Whiteley, the merchant whose name has so often been mentioned in these pages, three have been recovered ; but the rest, it is to be feared, have been hopelessly lost, with their contents : photographic negatives, journals, notes of native history, traditions, and customs, philological studies, specimens of native art and industry—in a word, the accumulations of forty years' labour among various South African tribes.

same terms as at Bulawayo, thanks to and under the care of
Dr. Mackenzie. He is the son of the venerable missionary of
that name, whom I had long known. A serious operation and
kind nursing set me on my feet again. It was performed so
skilfully as to astonish one of our most famous specialists in
Paris, and laid me under a debt of profound gratitude to
Dr. Mackenzie.

I must mention one of my hospital souvenirs. One day,
the matron entered my room, bringing me *a potato on a plate and
a rose in her hand.* Yes, a rose ! the only one in her garden ; a
potato ! the most common—not to say vulgar—of vegetables :
two things I had not seen for twelve years ! How good that
potato was ; and, still more, how lovely was that rose, and how
sweet it smelt ! One needs to have been shut up oneself for
weeks together, between the four white walls of a hospital ward,
to enter into it. And when I saw the bouquet sent me every
day by a lady I scarcely knew, this message of affection went
straight to my heart. Now I can appreciate the " Flower
Mission " for the hospitals, which I always admired. God bless
the Flower Mission !

Being too weak to bear the fatigue of a visit to Basuto-land,
I had to give it up, to my great regret. Thirty-seven hours
by rail brought me to the Cape. At Wellington, I was present
at what is called the " South African Keswick," and spent, in the
home of Mr. Andrew Murray, and that of his brother-in-law,
the venerable Dutch pastor Mr. Neethling, at Stellenbosch, some
of those days one can never forget. There I met Mr. Dudley
Kidd, of the South Africa General Mission, and my venerable
friend Mr. R. C. Morgan, of the *Christian.* It was Mr. Neethling
who started among his colleagues, the pastors of the Dutch
Church, a subscription of £1 a piece to procure a carriage for
me, and they responded so cordially that he was able to remit
the sum of £115 to me for this purpose.

A souvenir and a contrast ! Forty years ago, I landed at
the Cape. The Synod of the South African Dutch Church was
in session there at the time. What prejudices then against
the natives, against missions and missionaries ! And yet even
then, one saw the first gleams of a new dawn. In this Synod
there was one small group of men who possessed the sacred fire,
and who were urging the Church in the direction of missions.

Mr. Andrew Murray was one. From the different congregations, they had obtained money, but not men. Dr. Robertson, pastor of Swellendam, was sent to Scotland. To his powerful appeals, two young men responded,—a Scotchman, Mr. MacKidd, who died shortly after ; and a young Swiss, M. Gonin, who was completing his studies in Edinburgh at the time. They were accepted ; and a third joined them in Africa—a young Boer, Mr. Hofmeyr, full of zeal and devotion as they were. They founded their first mission to the north of the Transvaal. Later on, a second was planted among those very Banyaï whose needs we had made known ; and, finally, a third, side by side and in perfect harmony with that of the Free Church of Scotland, at Lake Nyassa.

The Murray family, which is in South Africa what that of the Monods is in France, has already given five or six of its members to these different missions. One of them I must mention, Willie Neethling, whose bright career, already richly blessed, was so soon to be interrupted by his tragic death. He was the son of Mr. Neethling, of Stellenbosch, whose wife is the Rev. Andrew Murray's sister. I had met him near Mafeking. He was then newly ordained, and on his way to occupy his first mission station, at Mochuli (Linchwe's place), accompanied by his sister ; and was, like myself, stopped by the rinderpest. He, full of ardent life—myself, apparently, upon a dying-bed. In the following February [1897], during a furious hurricane, part of the roof of his church had fallen upon him, and he only survived a few hours.

We who are left behind stand painfully perplexed at seeing these young lives, so full of promise, cut short at the beginning. Do we question God's wisdom ? Not so did he. " God makes *no* mistakes," he kept repeating with his dying breath. " He is good—*so* good. Never doubt His love."

His mother wrote to me, " I received the news on Saturday. The next day was the first anniversary of his ordination. I was going to church, not for that ceremony, but to celebrate his *coronation* ; for well I know his Lord will crown him with eternal joy."

We feel humbled and stimulated by the spectacle of this ardent youth, so absolutely, so joyfully surrendered ; and of this mother, whose serene faith, shining through her tears, counts it an honour to give a beloved son to his Saviour, to the heathen, and to death. Be it far from us, the faithless whisper of a Judas, " To what purpose is this waste ? " Nothing is lost which is offered to God, and which God accepts—not even the perfume of this short but beautiful life, poured out to Him.

To us, all this is a sign of the breaking down of former prejudices : we are looking forward to a time of blessing for the South African Dutch Church, the sister of our own, and through it to the dawn of a new day for heathen Africa.

Feeling now so much better—indeed, quite well—a terrible temptation seized me to go back to the Zambesi. But how ? The rinderpest and the Matabele war together made it impossible ! So I embarked.

At that season, all the steamboats plying between London and the Cape are always full, the places having been retained for months beforehand. My friends hastened to secure a place for me on an intermediate steamer, the *Warwick Castle*. But when Mr. Cartwright discovered that I should have to occupy a second-class cabin with five other passengers, he did everything he could to persuade me to wait a week longer and start in the *Drummond Castle*, and even went to the office to change my place ; but *every* berth on the *Drummond Castle* was taken.

As it turned out, I had a cabin all to myself; there were but few passengers, and among them there were a good many Afrikander Christians from the Paarl, with whom we had daily worship and happy intercourse. The weather was superb, the sea calm, and the voyage as enjoyable as heart could wish.

But we had only been a few days on shore, when we heard the appalling news of the wreck of the *Drummond Castle* at midnight off the coast of Ushant. Only three lives were saved !

Sympathy can scarcely find expression in the presence of so awful a calamity and so many tears. May these sorrowing ones find in Jesus—Himself the Man of Sorrows—the rest and comfort of their hearts !

As for myself, how should I not pause to consider and try to comprehend the voice of my God ! After a career of forty years, so chequered, and so full of adventures, dangers, and trials, but also of deliverances and blessings, brought back so recently from the brink of the grave, escaped from the ravages of the rinderpest and the massacres of the Matabele, rescued as it were from shipwreck, and given back as by a miracle to the health which I no longer even hoped for, I ask myself if it be not that my Master still has something for me to do, whether in Europe or in Africa.

CONCLUSION

AFRICA has had her valiant missionary pioneers, English and American, German and French—men whose names we, their successors, can only pronounce with profound veneration. "There were giants in those days." One of them, M. Arbousset, when he first set foot on African soil, beheld the mighty ramparts of Table Mountain towering above him. To his eyes it symbolised the power of that paganism he had come to attack in the name of his God ; and he exclaimed, " Who art thou, O great mountain ? before Zerubbabel thou shalt become *a plain.*" [1]

And as, leaving this land of the negro, where I have so long laboured and suffered, I contemplated that same formidable pile, melting in the distance and sinking from my sight, I seemed to hear the voice of my God above the tumult of my thoughts and recollections, recalling His promise, " The mountains shall depart, and the hills be removed ; but My kindness shall not depart from thee."

Yes, the promise has been made good, " All the promises of God in Him are Yea, and in Him Amen." [2]

Pioneer work necessarily bristles with difficulties. Never yet has the Gospel made a triumphal entry into any country with flying colours and by a royal road. By the door and the dungeon of a prison it entered our old Europe ; by the manger of Bethlehem, by the agony of Gethsemane, by the shame of Calvary and the death of the Cross, it was manifested to the world. The Lord Himself, in sending out His disciples, did not promise them anything else. " Behold, I send you forth as

[1] See Zech. iv. 6, 7, R.V., "This is the word of the Lord unto Zerubbabel" (= the scattered in Babylon), and the parallel passage in Jer. li. 24-26.

[2] 2 Cor. i. 20.

633

lambs among wolves." "They shall deliver you up to be
afflicted . . . and persecuted." "Ye shall be hated of all
men." "Ye shall be beaten, and ye shall be brought before
governors and kings, for My sake." "The disciple is not above
his Master." "In the world ye shall have tribulation : but be
of good cheer ; I have overcome the world."

Such have been our own experiences. Difficulties have
often risen before us, many and menacing : all, one by one,
never all at once, have been smoothed away and overcome.
Often they have sprung up where we least expected them.
But to find ourselves first borne forward on a wave of popular
sympathy, and then misunderstood and forsaken at the very
moment for action by those whom we esteemed and on whose
co-operation we were relying, has not been the least among
them.

Moreover—will it be believed ?—the eclectic character of our
mission has not opened to us the doors of as many hearts as one
would have supposed, and it has closed many, both at home
and abroad. In foreign countries, in England especially, where
works of every kind have so greatly multiplied, it is increasingly
difficult to obtain a hearing. On the one hand, we are regarded
as respectable beggars ; on the other, as wandering children,
supported, loved even, but not quite approved of. Among
certain circles in France to-day, as then, it is precisely the purely
evangelistic nature of our work with which we are reproached.
"What national interests," people ask, "have we in Basuto-
land, in Barotsi-land especially ? Why do you not speak to
us about our own colonies—about Maré, Tahiti, the French
Congo, and Senegal ? " To-day, it is Madagascar which, like a
burning house, absorbs the attention of our religious public.
I well understand it. How could it be otherwise, when one
sees such a great and noble work, one with such a glorious
past, threatened by the intrigues of men whom France has
expelled from her own borders, and for whom the end justifies
the means ? But people go further, and with regard to Basuto-
land some even have not hesitated to pronounce the words
abandon, exchange. As if one would so lightly abandon prosperous gold or diamond mines for the sake of exploiting others
whose rightful owners have been expropriated by the caprice
of politics !—as if one could barter Churches like chattels ; souls

brought forth in such travail, reared at the cost of so many sacrifices, families which are bidden by the sacred bonds of spiritual kinship to cling to us, as we to them! And yet we, *we* who are still bearing the bitter loss of 1871, are asked to create in the realm of missions a parallel to that mournful anomaly Alsace-Lorraine!

Ought we not rather to believe that God never confronts us with *an absolute impossibility*, and that with new duties and new responsibilities He opens up to us new treasures of His grace? The greater the share He gives us in His work, the greater is the honour for us. On our fathers, He bestowed the privilege of confessing Him upon the scaffold and the rack. For us, their children, it is no less a privilege from Himself to glorify Him by sacrifices of men and money in the mission field. Madagascar will yet prove the *Ecole Militaire* of our Huguenot Churches.

But let us hasten to add that in many, many quarters storehouses of prayer and faith have been thrown open to us. And if the Lord should ask us, as He once asked His disciples, "Lacked ye anything?" we could but answer gratefully, "Nothing, Lord."

The Barotsi kingdom lies between latitudes 12·30° and 18° south; 20° and 27·30° longitude east of Greenwich. It embraces the whole basin of the Upper Zambesi west of and including the Kafué River. It stretches from the outskirts of the Kalahari Desert on the south, to the watershed between the Congo and Zambesi systems on the north. Thus it is not a mere province, but an empire, as the old Portuguese themselves called it—one of those native empires now very rare, which have still contrived to maintain their independence. Lewanika is no petty chieftain, but a potentate who possesses the right of life and death over thousands of subjects, and whose authority is recognised by more than twenty-five tribes. Besides being very intelligent, with ideas of justice which are somewhat uncommon among his congeners, he is nobly ambitious of seeing education, industry, and civilisation, as far as he understands them, develop among his people. Like most of the South African chiefs, he too has been influenced by the prestige of "Satory"—of Queen Victoria. Having emancipated himself from many of the customs, superstitions, and prejudices of his surroundings, he of his own initiative, and not without much opposition, applied for the protectorate of Her Britannic Majesty and of her Government. But harassed as he was, and is, by the civil wars which have devastated his country, and by the encroachments of the Congo Free State, the Portuguese, and the Germans, and also by the sanguinary raids of the Matabele, it was the *direct Protectorate* of the Imperial Government that he desired.   In response to his overtures, the Administrator of Bechuana-land, and Her Majesty's High Commissioner at the Cape, both recommended him to accept the advances of the British South Africa Chartered Company. Believing then that he had found in the latter the direct representatives of the Queen and her Government, he confided to them at once his own interests and those of his people, by making a treaty with them, and conceding mining rights.   He did it in good faith.

It is earnestly to be hoped that the authorities will prove scrupulously faithful to the pledges made in their name, the more so as they represent strength, civilisation, and Christianity ; and will show that for them it is not a mere matter of getting all possible profit out of a country, but of elevating and pro-tecting a people.

It must, however, be confessed that the contempt with which Lewanika considers himself (and not without some reason) to have been treated up till now, the promises that have been made to him and never kept, the grave errors committed which have more than once compromised the peace of the country, have already sown a deep distrust in the minds of a race which is at once conscious of its weakness and of the danger threatening it—a distrust which should be dispelled at all costs and without delay.

The future of the country must of necessity depend entirely upon the selection of the administrative staff.   May the Imperial Government exercise a wise choice, and may the magistrates show themselves worthy of the Power they represent, and win the confidence of this interesting people in these critical times !

The line of mission stations at the present moment slants westward from latitude 15° south beyond latitude 14°, and may extend itself indefinitely to the north and the east.   The climatic conditions are such that we might say as the spies

Slave saluting.   Ma-Moramboa.   Lewanika.   Nyondo.

LEWANIKA AND HIS CHIEF WIFE.

[*To face page* 636.

said about Canaan : " It is a land that eateth up the inhabitants thereof." It is a true White Man's Grave. What
we, following Livingstone's nomenclature, very improperly call
the Valley, is nothing but the bed of a dried-up lake, about
twenty-five miles wide : its length is ill-defined, but it certainly
extends more than one hundred and fifty miles. It is a
denuded plain, traversed by the river, scattered over with
anthills and a few clumps of trees which overshadow the
tombs of the ancient kings. Submerged for about three
months every year, it becomes a lake again ; sudden squalls
of wind render its navigation dangerous for the native canoes.
The anthills and groves stand out like tiny islets, which
become the refuge of rodents and reptiles of all sorts.

The rainy season generally begins at the end of November,
and lasts until March or April. The annual rainfall is about
thirty-four inches. The rainiest months are December and
January ; the hottest are October and November, which immediately precede the rainy season. The thermometer often rises
to 113° F. (45° C.)—rarely, but occasionally, higher ; and falls to
46° F. (8° C.), sometimes to 37·05 F. (3° C.), rarely lower. The
difference of day and night temperature varies in different
localities, from 18° to 27°, or even 45° F. (10°, 15°, or 25° C.),
taking maxima and minima. The altitude is 3,300 feet, and,
except for the Batoka country and the region of the rapids,
is mostly flat and sandy. The line of low hills which runs
parallel to the river, and the dunes which surround the
Valley, are covered with forest, or rather scrub, which in no way
reminds one of the luxuriant vegetation found elsewhere in the
same latitudes, but which nevertheless is very rich in timber-wood,
as well as in various secretions. Doubtless industry will turn
them to account some day.

It also abounds in honey and in wild fruits,[1] which are a real
godsend to our Zambesians in time of famine, while the river
itself is an inexhaustible resource, on account of the fish which
swarm in its waters. Fish, indeed, is one of the most important
elements in the food of the Zambesians. They go wild over it.
Never yet have I seen them disgusted with any fragment of
it they could snatch from a bird of prey, no matter how stale,

[1] In a former note, it was stated that there is no fruit in Barotsi-land
—*e.g.* no cultivated fruits.

to use no stronger word. Their fishing tackle is extremely various. They make bow-nets (*nasses*), and large nets of every size, and weirs of reeds, which are private and hereditary property. What they do not eat, they dry ; and I have not the slightest doubt that it is to the abuse of this diet that they owe many of their hideous and fearful diseases.

It is no part of my purpose, and space would fail me, to speak of the wild animals of these regions. Mr. Selous has already done so, with his unapproached knowledge of the subject. Livingstone, when he reached the banks of the great river for the first time, was struck with astonishment at the incredible quantity of big game. Scarcely twenty-five years later, although it had already diminished considerably, I felt the same astonishment on the same spot. But this hunter's paradise threatens soon to disappear ! Among these innumerable flocks, the rinderpest—if one may believe the elephant hunters—has already made terrible havoc, and has thus propagated itself. But it is the native hunters themselves, who, totally destitute of conscience in this respect, are hastening the extermination of certain species. It is high time that strict and intelligent laws should protect what survives ; and one cannot too highly applaud the project Captain Gibbons is promoting—namely, to convert the neighbourhood of the Victoria Falls into an immense park for the African fauna.

It is not uninteresting to know that the tse-tse fly is ever tending to recede from the parts it formerly haunted, following the buffalo in its migrations. Beasts and birds of prey, lions, leopards, hyænas, crocodiles, etc., are, unfortunately, still as common as ever.

To return to the climate after this digression, for which I ask pardon. What I have said of the country sufficiently explains how malarial fevers are endemic there. The natives themselves are subject to them. Europeans vegetate rather than live ; they get used to it without acclimatising themselves thoroughly. In this connexion, the statistics of the mission have an eloquence of their own. From 1884 to the present day, the staff has numbered 43 persons, 24 Europeans and 19 Basuto. 6 have died in the country (3 Europeans and 3 Basuto), and 10 have had to leave, all but one or two on account of health. Add to these 12 children (6 those of

Europeans, and 6 of Basuto catechists) and 4 men (all Basuto) belonging to the first expedition, and the number amounts to 22.

Quite recently M. Goy's death took place at Sesheke, closely followed by that of Mr. Buckenham, of the Primitive Methodist Mission—two strong and valiant men. To us, the survivors, these last losses have been a great shock. More than ever we feel that the time is short. And, alas! we have not a single medical man. Young Dr. Dardier, of Geneva, scarcely lived six months : no one has taken his place, and up to the present our appeals have fallen unheeded.

And now, if we make up the account of these twelve years, what have we to show for it ?

We cannot take a census of the work of the Holy Spirit. The arithmetic, like the geography, of the kingdom of heaven is not that of this world. If we count every stroke of the axe in the field we are clearing so laboriously, it seems to us that the work makes no progress, and we are tempted to cry with the prophet, " *C'est pour le vide et le néant que j'ai travaillé.*" [1] And it is the task still before us which is so overwhelming.

However, if, after these twelve years of labour, we cast a backward glance, there *has* been a certain progress, which we must take note of, to the glory of God.

Unquestionably, a great change is already operating in the country, which will become more marked as time goes on : the interdiction of spirituous drinks, of the slave-trade, and of the barbarous practice of " smelling out sorcerers " ; increasing security of property ; and respect for human life,—tokens of civilisation, of a real need felt by the Barotsi themselves for developing their industrial tastes and talents : there, in various domains, are victories which the Gospel has won over paganism. " And it is not only the good we may have done," as a friend wrote to me ; " it is the evil—and who could fathom it ?—that the presence of the Gospel *has* hindered."

In spite of the departures and defections, which have so often distressed us, we have, at the present moment, eight European missionaries (including myself), seven ladies, six native evangelists and their wives, all devoted to our dear mission, all united in the intimate bonds of a family.

But what especially fills me with joy and gratitude towards

[1] Isa. xlix. 4.

the Lord is *that school of evangelists* which we have confided
to our dear brother Adolphe Jalla, with ten pupils.   My poor
Seonyi was the eleventh, and Semonji would have been the
twelfth: all young men of the country, and the fruit of our
schools.

And then there are M. and Mme. Mercier, who are about to
restore the ruins of Sefula, and there open at last our *industrial
school.*   Are not these the first streaks of light which herald
the dawn of that day when God's glory will shine through this
land ?

These five stations, scattered along the river, over a course
of more than three hundred miles, form each a centre of
education and evangelisation.   Although the awakening of two
years ago has by no means produced all we hoped for, and
although we cannot even yet " bring our sheaves with rejoicing,"
yet we can at least show a few ears, the first-fruits of the future
harvest.   With our industrial school, which, by honouring honest
work, will break the bands of slavery, and with our young school
of evangelists, with the co-operation of our friends and the
blessing of God, we look for great things.

Our annual budget stands actually at from £2,000 to £2,800 ;
and if up to the present time our resources have responded to
our needs, we can without misgivings still count upon God and
upon our supporters, even though our expenses necessarily go
on multiplying.

I cannot refrain from cherishing the hope that my departure
from the Zambesi is not final.   God can renew my youth,
and permit me to return one day to this great field of work.
And when the harvest has come, those who sowed and those
who reap shall rejoice together.

But still we are only *On the Threshold of Central Africa.*
Each of these pages reminds you of it !   Gaze if you can into
the thick darkness of the country itself, and of the regions
beyond.   What are our five stations?   What is that of the
Primitive Methodists among the Mashukulumboe, or that of our
friends the Brethren on the banks of Lake Bangweolo, where
Livingstone fell ?   Just enough to enable us to feel and show
the darkness which surrounds us !   Sometimes we feel like
sentinels lost in these advance posts.

For myself, after living there and returning, I am haunted

as by an awful nightmare. Have you never, my dear reader, been struck by the strange curse which from time immemorial has hung over Africa? What is its origin? It is a mystery. I see it everywhere: on her coasts, without bays or inlets, swampy and pestilential; in her rivers, rendered useless for navigation by their sandbanks, their rapids, and their cataracts; in her limitless deserts; in her forests, with their impenetrable thorn thickets; and in her barbarous inhabitants, crushed by slavery and superstition. Her very soil is cursed.[1]

Plagues, incessantly renewed, devastate her richest regions. Her own children, in their huts of straw and reeds, only live like birds of passage; they are not at home. Their very festivals inspire you with melancholy; their songs are dirges whose minor tones draw tears from your eyes. They are far from thinking that we Europeans possess the monopoly of beauty, and yet it is from our own white colour that they borrow the symbol of happiness and joy: "their hearts are *white*." But when they suffer and are sad, "their hearts are *black*"; yes, black as their skin. And thus it is that all through their lives, from their birth-kennel to the vulture-haunted Aceldama where their bones decay, they personify, they bear the very stain of misery and suffering.

Is not this malediction engraved in characters of blood and fire upon her whole history? Even before knowing Africa, Europe robbed her of her children, and sold them over-seas like cattle in the market. Then, when explorers had brought to light the riches of the country, these *Christian* nations rushed upon the spoil, divided the continent up between them, and, unknown to the legitimate owners of the soil, disputed for the fragments of this unhappy Africa.

And yet what claims she has upon our interest! Even the Psalmist in his vision beheld "Ethiopia stretching out her hands towards Jehovah." She has her part in the promise of salvation and blessing to all nations: her tribes, too, will have their place

---

[1] It is worthy of remark that the natives themselves recognise this. Lewanika one day asked M. Coillard who were the descendants of the three sons of Noah. M. Coillard replied that it was generally believed the descendants of Japheth had peopled Europe. "And of Shem?" "Asia." "You need not tell me that Ham was the father of Africa. I knew it long ago." "Why so, Lewanika?" "Ah, my father—the curse!"

in the glorious multitude out of every people, and tongue, and kindred, and nation, whom the Apostle saw before the Throne of God and the Lamb.

Will not Africa, too, have her day? When will it dawn? What will it be? Amid the confusion of European greed and injustice, what is to become of these black races? We feel the dignity of manhood outraged, and our Christian sentiment revolts, when we hear people callously speculating on their extinction, like that of the North American Indians. Their extinction! Yes, perhaps, if these *Christian* nations, unmindful of their pledges, trample down the rights of the weak with impunity, and flood them with their *eau-de-mort*.

But there is an unconquerable vitality in the black race which gives us hope. In Natal, within twenty years, the Zulu have doubled their number; in thirty years the Basuto have quintupled themselves, and have overflowed into the Orange Free State and Cape Colony. In this race, we find skill, intelligence, the sense of duty, fidelity, love of work, desire for progress: in a word, the essential qualities of mind and heart—and examples of such are by no means rare—which make *men*, which inspire great movements and noble deeds. Ah! if they could only look forward to the centuries of Christian education which have made us what we pride ourselves on being, who can say what might not be their future?

In presence of the immigration, a tide which nothing can stem, and which will soon invade the very heart of this ill-fated continent; in presence of the mines that are being opened up, and of these European towns now springing forth in the solitudes as if by magic, these railways advancing always farther and farther inland : in the midst of this upheaval, which announces the birth of a new world—upon us, Christians, this noble task devolves, the work of rescue. If we cannot save nations, at least let us save men, let us save souls! Far be it from us to shirk our responsibility, and repeat Cain's hard speech: "Am I my brother's keeper?" The good old time has gone by when everything in Africa moved at the measured pace of oxen. To-day the age of steam and electricity has invaded us. The time is short; let us redeem it. It is high time for the Church to bestir herself; we have played at missions long enough. What we need is to cast aside the mask of all mere religiosity, all that is simply form and tradition, and *to live at the height of our profession.* Long enough we have patronised the work of God, and have interested ourselves in it as amateurs : what we need to-day is to make it *our* work, to feel each of us his or her personal responsibility, to spend and be spent for it—not what we possess or can spare, but our very selves. Those who pray upon the mountain must feel their oneness with those who fight in the plain ; and the victory will be certain.

When we see missionary festivals so run after—when we hear these stirring hymns, these sublime and moving protestations of our compassion for the perishing heathen, and of our entire devotion to Him Whom we acknowledge as *King*—should we not expect to see a whole crusade on the march for the conquest of the world, singing, " Onward, Christian soldiers " ? One might suppose that all we have and all we hope for had been laid on the altar, waiting for nothing but the fire from heaven.

And in reality what have we done ? What have we given ? What have we sacrificed ? Where does this spirit of renunciation show itself in the details of daily life ? What discipline are we willing to submit to ? What ease, what luxuries, have we denied ourselves ?

Have we not indeed often grudged to God's service even what we could spare ? And, alas ! even this half-hearted zeal soon evaporates. The fit of spasmodic devotion once over, we take back from God what we had professed to give Him ; we return to the idols of our hearts—refuse His claims, and leave the heathen to perish without compunction.

One could understand this in those who have only tasted the stagnant waters of merely traditional piety. But how explain it in those who really have " with joy drawn water out of the wells of salvation " ? How can they help echoing the invitation, " Ho, every one that thirsteth, come ye to the waters " ?

" He that drinketh of the water that I shall give him," said the Saviour, " shall never thirst, but it shall be in him *a well of water springing up* unto everlasting life."

They have drunk of this spring ; they know the " unsearchable riches of Christ " ; they are persuaded that " all things are theirs, even the deep things of God." I speak to those to whom these expressions signify *realities*. They feel and acknowledge that they have entered upon a great inheritance. Yes; but these "springing wells" flow, alas! like some of the watercourses in our African deserts—only to lose themselves in the barren sands of their own lives. They only live for themselves, and, while knowing the love of Him Who gave Himself for us, are altogether indisposed to pay in their own person, and give their own lives for their brethren.

But besides the misery of the heathen, and the desire to impart blessings we have ourselves received, we have a third incentive—the greatest of all : the Second Advent of our Lord.

In our day, is not the painful scene of the Prætorium renewed ? We see Jesus coming forth, wearing the crown of thorns and the purple robe ; and while the people press round, some to mock at His kingly crown, and to tear in pieces, if they could, the seamless robe of His Godhead, others are ready even to crucify Him—the Son of God.

To this scene succeeds another. The crucified Christ, triumphing over death as He had triumphed over sin and the world, is set down at the right hand of God, alive for evermore. But He has promised to return, and we are expecting Him. Yes, "all power is given to Him in heaven and upon earth, and a Name that is above every name" ; "every knee must bow to Him, and every tongue confess that He is Lord."

He must reign ! The times are rapidly fulfilling themselves. " Yet a little while, and He that shall come will come, and will not tarry." It is His own last word : " Surely I come quickly " ; and our hearts respond in ardent prayer, " Even so, come, Lord Jesus."

But we cannot rest in idle contemplation, and content ourselves with hastening His return by the barren ardour of our longings. He desires, He deigns to associate us with His work of redemption—we whom He loves and has redeemed. It is His will that *we*, and not the angels of heaven, should publish the Good News to all nations, and that we should be His witnesses to the uttermost parts of the earth. And it is His will, moreover, that we should do it in the spirit that animated Himself. "Who, *for the joy* that was set before Him endured the Cross, despising the shame."

And if it be a privilege to *work* with Him, by Him and for Him, and a privilege to *believe* in Him, is it not one still greater if He counts us worthy to *suffer* for His sake? True discipleship brings its own reward, *a present and actual one*;—let us say it most reverently—intimate acquaintance with the personal and living Saviour. St. Paul desired to know nothing but Jesus Christ and Him crucified. "Yea, doubtless I count all things but loss for the excellency of *the knowledge of Christ Jesus my Lord*."

To know Him—is not that enough to kindle within us that holy passion which sets Him above everything and at the centre of everything, so that we can say with the Apostle, "The love of Christ *constraineth* us," and to sum it up in one word, "To *live* is Christ"?

Are any who have heard the call of God hesitating, dreading to obey it? Do you remember Abraham, "the father of all them that believe"? The Lord said to him, "Get thee out of thy country, and from thy kindred, and from thy father's house, unto a land that I will show thee . . . and I will bless thee . . . and thou shalt be a blessing." "He obeyed, and went out, not knowing whither he went"; and his only inheritance was a grave for his wife. Ah! but there was a promise too: "Fear not; *I* am thy shield, and thy exceeding great reward." And was it not fulfilled? Will any who have followed, however remotely, in his footsteps deny that it has been made good to them? No indeed! It was God Himself who uttered it, and He keeps His word.

The climate of Africa is dry—the spiritual atmosphere still more so. It is one in which mere sentiment and enthusiasm rapidly evaporate. After these forty years, nothing but realities, *proved realities*, can remain; and this is one of them. It is the same Almighty God whose unchanging faithfulness upholds us now.

"And the Scripture, foreseeing that God would justify the heathen through faith, preached before the Gospel unto Abraham, saying, 'In thee shall all nations be blessed.' So then they which be of faith are blessed with faithful Abraham."[1]

*   *   *   *   *

Gal. iii. 8, 9.

To the beggar who knocks at our door, we give a mite out of pity, or to appease our consciences : from the Sovereign we humbly ask the favour of being permitted to offer him a gift worthy of himself. Let us not treat as a beggar One Who is the Prince of the kings of the earth. May we rather crave the honour of offering Him our wealth, our strength, our talents, our future, yes, our whole life—like an alabaster box full of precious ointment, that we would break at His feet! He alone is worthy of it.

And after serving Him gladly on earth, we shall serve Him still in glory ; and with overflowing hearts we shall sing amid the great multitude that no man can number around the Throne, " Worthy is the Lamb that was slain to receive power, and riches, and wisdom, and strength, and honour, and glory, and blessing."

The following verses appeared in THE CHRISTIAN *of February 25th, 1892, and are here reproduced by the kind permission of the Editor.*

ON THE DEATH OF MADAME COILLARD, ZAMBESIA, SOUTH AFRICA.

" There came a woman having an alabaster box of ointment of spikenard very precious ; and she brake the box, and poured it on His head . . . and anointed the feet of Jesus . . . and the house was filled with the odour of the ointment."—MARK xiv. 3 ; JOHN xii. 3.

FAR in the land where Afric's sun is burning
   She lies at rest,
The clay to earth, the soul to God returning.
Vain are our tears, and vain our hearts' sad yearning :
   He knoweth best.

Long years of toil, endurance, high endeavour,
   Lost souls to save ;
Long years of weeping, hoping, praying ever—
Till Death's cold clasp her strongest tie should sever—
   And then the grave.

No marble slab, her lofty virtues telling,
   Marks her release ;
But one, whose heart with anguish deep is swelling,
Prepares with loving hands her humble dwelling,
   And all is peace.

They laid her near the tree, whose branches weeping
   Shadow the mound ;
And there, in faith, though eyes be dimmed with weeping,
Her life's work done, they leave her calmly sleeping,
   In holy ground.

And o'er the tomb, in fondest recollection,
   They sing and pray ;
And to the heathen preach Christ's resurrection,
How she will be restored to their affection
   At His bright day.

Oh, lonely missionary, comfort taking
   Beneath the rod !
The heathen shall be Christ's ! The day is breaking ;
A little while, and then the glad awaking,
   At Home, with God.

           M. A. P.

GLOSSARY

THE limits of this work do not permit me to make more than one or two remarks on the Sesuto or rather se-Suto tongue, one of the Bantu group, as it is called.

This language, in its different dialects, is spoken by the whole vast Bechuana family, which occupies the interior of South Africa from the Orange River northwards. The Zulu family lies parallel to it on the East coast, and the Namaqua, Korana, and Ovambo on the West. Thus it is spoken throughout the Orange Free State, the Transvaal, and Bechuana-land itself. On the Upper Zambesi it is the *lingua franca* of most of the twenty-five tribes which compose the Barotsi Empire, having been imposed upon them by the Basuto themselves, who, under the name of Makololo, led by the valiant chief Sebetoane, subjugated them in a former generation. And although the Makololo have been completely exterminated, their language has survived them.

It is now generally known among English readers that these languages are inflected by means of prefixes : *e.g.*—

> *mo-Suto,* sing., a Basuto native.
> *ba-Suto,* pl., more than one Basuto native.
> *bo-Suto,* the Basuto kind.
> *se-Suto,*   ,,   language.
> *le-Suto,*   ,,   country.

It is worth remarking that, among autocratic tribes, where men are considered the property of the chief, the plural is formed in *ma* : *e.g.* ma-Tabele, ma-Tolela, ma-Subia, ma-Mbunda. But *mo* is invariably the singular prefix. It would be well if English writers could agree to adopt the same method as the French, which is strictly grammatical, and write mo-Rotsi, ba-Rotsi, se-Rotsi, etc., treating the prefix simply as an article, which it is. In the following vocabulary, I am doing this.

The se-Suto already possesses a considerable elementary literature. The New Testament, and a collection of hymns, one of the richest known to me in South African missions, have both passed through several editions, and the Old Testament is in its third, besides a good number of educational religious works. The output of these is very considerable and always increasing. The central depôt is at Morija.

Lastly, there is a monthly magazine, edited in se-Suto, *Leseli Nyana la le-Suto* (Little Light of Lesuto), which was started by M. Mabille twenty-seven or twenty-eight years ago, and which is widely read wherever the language is spoken.

ba, noun prefix, indicating plural.
ba-ketu or *ba-kwetu*, compatriots.
bana-ba-marena, children of the royal family.
ba-ruti (pl.), teachers, hence missionaries.
ba-shimane (pl.), slaves (of lower degree than *ba-tlanka*).
ba-tlanka (pl.), inferiors, servants, serfs.
Ba nyanda, = " I don't want to," " I would rather not " (allied to *ho nyanda*, to have secret forebodings, to murmur secretly).
bapala (*ho bapala*), to amuse oneself, to play.
bô, noun prefix, indicating either (1) *the kind*, or (2) an extension of meaning, whereby a singular substantive is formed into a collective one : *e.g. Bô-Arone* means " Aaron and the people with him."
bontsu boo, " that black thing," *i.e.* the common people, the proletariat.
bo-rena, the chiefs, the governing body.
bo-Rotsi, the Valley or low country.

É, é, "Yes."

fatse, (1) country, (2) world.

Gam'ella, title borne by the Prime Minister.

kamarie, a young girl.
ka metla, all the time, always.
ka môso, "And to-morrow "=" Thank you " : a very characteristic expression, contracted from " *Ka môso le ka' ma maobane*," and implying " I am delighted with what you have given ; evidently you are rich ; please continue your favours."
kandelela, a greeting (kneeling and clapping of hands).
ka-ngombio, a small musical instrument on the principle of the piano. A dozen tongues of metal (more or less) are arranged on a board five or six inches long ; it is placed over a gourd to make it sonorous, and played with the thumbs.
kaofela, all, everything.
kashandi, the king's private office near the *kuandu*.
Ke khotse, " I am satisfied " (*i.e.* with food).
khosi, chief, one of the nobility (less than *morena*).
khothla, same as *lekhothla*.
Ke lerumo, "It is the spear " (*i.e.* civil war).
Ke teng, "It is well."
koloï, waggon.
kuandu, the king's private dwelling in the midst of his harem.

lekhothla, public place or forum where the king dispenses justice; forbidden to women except during a case in which they are implicated.

Lengolo (Sesuto)
Lengoalo (Sechuana) } (1) writing, (2) the Holy Scriptures, (3) all instruction.

lefoufa, harem jealousy.

li-komboa (plural ot *se-komboa*), the king's personal attendants, the officers of his household, who form a court party always in rivalry with the heads of the government departments (se-Rotsi).

Liomba, Second Minister of State.

litaola, divining bones, auguries.

liyumbu, food of hospitality; a ceremonious gift in kind to a guest.

lochu (Sechuana), death.

Lumela! = "Good day": the universal greeting, meaning "Believe me" (your friend, etc.).

ma, noun prefix, forming plural.

ma, mother or matron.

mabele, native corn, sorgho seed.

ma-chaba-chaba, numerous tribes.

ma-lapa (pl.), courts fenced with reeds.

mali, money.

ma-Luti, chain ot mountains.

ma-Mbari, half-civilised negroes of Portuguese colonies.

ma-Mbunda, a powerful tribe which claims as a speciality a great knowledge of medicines and divining, and possesses the monopoly of the ordeal poison, the *moati.* They are not *slaves,* but *subjects* to the Barotsi kings. Hence the mistake of travellers, who believed them to be a ruling tribe on a level with their rulers, the Barotsi, and have erroneously spoken of "the Marotsi-Mambunda Empire."

mandé, a valuable shell used as an amulet.

maori, title borne by the king's wives (se-Rotsi).

Ma rôna, "Our mother."

ma-sole, soldiers (from English).

ma-tindi, floating islands and bridges ot strong matted rushes (se-Rotsi).

matsa, desert pools (Dutch *vleys*).

Mawe! a cry of suffering or astonishment (se-Rotsi).

mo, noun prefix, indicating singular.

moati, a violent poison, used for trial by ordeal (se-Rotsi).

moïfo, a picked regiment of braves.

molatlehi, lost (in foregoing text wrongly spelt *moatlegi*).

mo-Limo (plural *me-limo*), God: this title is applied by the natives to tribal deities, *e.g.* their own deceased kings.

mo-Loki, Redeemer.

monere, father: a title of respect given by the Basuto to missionaries (from the Dutch *mynheer*).

mo-Nyaï, a ba-Nyaï native.

mo-rena (pl. *ma-rena*), supreme chief or king (in Scripture = Lord).

mo-réneng, the king's residence, the capital.

mo-Rotsi, a ba-Rotsi native.

mo-ruti, a teacher : title given to missionaries by the Barotsi.

mo-sali, a woman.

mosapo, formal present exacted by chiefs from traders.

mo-shimane, a slave.

mo-sito, a forest.

mo-thlanka, a serf (in contrast with the aristocracy).

mothata, india-rubber tree.

mo-tsualle, a friend.

mpote, intoxicating honey-beer or mead.

Munda, the flood.

Nalikuanda, title of the king's state barge.

Natamoyo, the Minister of Mercy, protector of accused persons, whose privilege it is to control the punishments inflicted by the chiefs, and even the king. He can liberate any one at his discretion and without trial. To flee to his house or touch his person is enough to save one. He is chosen by the king, but must always belong to the royal family.

njoko, monkey, baboon (se-Rotsi).

nkoli, gourd.

Ntate, father, " The one who loves me " : a term of affection.

Ntate oa rôna, " Our father."

ntho, a thing.

nyaka, doctor, medicine-man.

Nyambé, the Supreme God, symbolised by the Sun, and worshipped on certain occasions by all. *Nyambé* conveys a more exalted and definite idea of the Deity than *Molimo*, to which dignity the Basuto and Barotsi raise their ancestors. The deceased kings are *melimo*, tribal gods, and still rule the nation, but do not bear the title of *Nyambé*, which is reserved for the supreme, mysterious, unknown God (se-Rotsi).

Pumenoko, " I am satisfied" (*i.e.* content, pleased).

Salang ! "Rest in peace !"

se, prefix, indicating the language.

se-komboa, see *li-komboa*.

sekukurume, medicine horn (se-Rotsi).

se-Nyaï, language of the ba-Nyaï.

serimba, drum or tom-tom, a sort of harmonica, formed by a series of wooden notes placed over gourds (se-Rotsi).

se-Rotsi, language of the ba-Rotsi.

se-tlaping, (1) tongue, (2) lie.

setsiba, a piece of cloth or calico two and a half yards long (the usual garment, and practically current coin).

Shangwe, Sir, Master—an expression of courtesy (se-Rotsi).

Shoalela, the royal salute (se-Rotsi).

Taba ke lifé? "What is the news?"
Taü-ira, "The lion roars."
Taü-tona, male lion.
thaka, equals-in-age.
Thuto, the Gospel.
tlobolo ea Molimo, God's guns, *i.e.* sky rockets.
tsipi, (1) bell, (2) Sunday service.

KINGS OF BAROTSI-LAND.

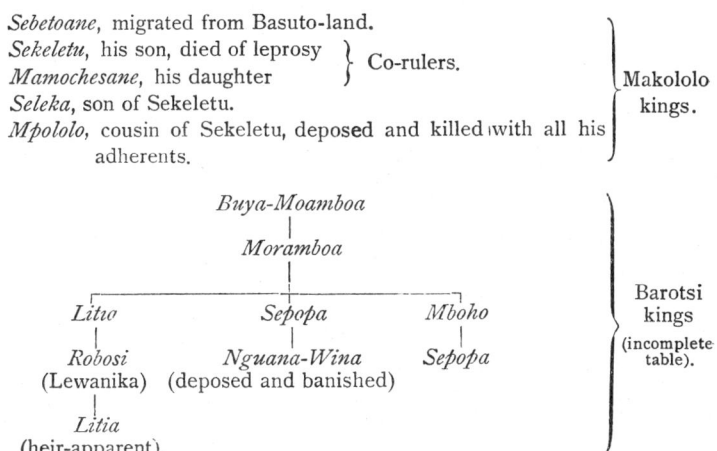

Sebetoane, migrated from Basuto-land.
Sekeletu, his son, died of leprosy ⎫
Mamochesane, his daughter ⎬ Co-rulers. ⎪ Makololo
Seleka, son of Sekeletu. ⎭ ⎪ kings.
Mpololo, cousin of Sekeletu, deposed and killed with all his
 adherents.

Buya-Moamboa
|
Moramboa
|

Litio   *Sepopa*   *Mboho*
| | |
Robosi   *Nguana-Wina*   *Sepopa*
(Lewanika)   (deposed and banished)
|
Litia
(heir-apparent).

Barotsi
kings
(incomplete
table).

INDEX